D1825102

Berlitz®

Intermediate **French**

Course Book

Berlitz Publishing/APA Publications GmbH & Co. Verlag KG
Singapore Branch, Singapore

INTERMEDIATE FRENCH

Contacting the Editors
Every effort has been made to provide accurate information in this publication, but changes are inevitable. The publisher cannot be responsible for any resulting loss, inconvenience or injury. We would appreciate it if readers would call our attention to any errors or outdated information by contacting Berlitz Publishing,
95 Progress Street, Union, NJ 07083, USA. Fax: 1-908-206-1103,
email: comments@berlitzbooks.com

Printed in China
Reprinted in August 2005
ISBN 800302-88-AMC

Text: Rosi McNab
Editorial: Christine Frohly, Sheryl Olinsky Borg, Juergen Lorenz, Lorraine Sova, Dominique Wenzel, Piotr Brynczka, Diane Gigantino
Production: Steve Maher, Wee Design Group, Molly Pike Riccardi, Kent Wilkinson
Audio Producer: RPL, Paul Ruben Productions
Interior Design: Max Crandall
Illustrations: Max Crandall, Mona Daly, Elise Dodeles, Andy Levine, Chris Reed, Isabelle Verret, Guy Ruggiero
Maps: MAGELLAN Geographix, Parrot Graphics
Cover Photo: © Getty Images/EyeWire Collection
Inset Photo: © Royalty-Free/CORBIS

Contents

Unit 1 is about everyday life. You will become familiar with the language you need to know in order to:

- talk about your home life
- say what you usually do during the weekend
- say what you have done, using the past tense

La vie quotidienne

1

Word Bank

le beurre	*butter*
les céréales *f.pl.*	*breakfast cereal*
la confiture	*jam, jelly*
le lait	*milk*
la margarine	*margarine*
le miel	*honey*
l'œuf *m.*	*egg*
le pain	*bread*
la tartine	*slice of bread with butter or jam*
la tasse	*cup*
le yaourt	*yogurt*
le week-end	*weekend*
jusqu'à	*until*
mais	*but*
normalement	*usually*
quelquefois	*sometimes*
toujours	*always*
vers	*about (of time)*
se réveiller	*to wake up*
réveiller	*to wake someone else*
se lever	*to get up*
lever	*to lift/raise*
se laver	*to get washed*
laver	*to wash something/ someone else*
s'habiller	*to get dressed*
habiller	*to dress someone else*
se raser	*to shave (oneself)*
raser	*to shave someone else*
*boire	*to drink*
faire la grasse matinée	*to sleep in (lit: do a "fat" morning)*
faire du jogging	*to go jogging*
prendre une douche	*to take a shower*
prendre un bain	*to take a bath*
prendre le petit déjeuner	*to have breakfast*
manger	*to eat*
rentrer	*to go home*
sécher	*to dry*

Que faites-vous le samedi matin?

What are you doing on Saturday morning?

RECORDING

1. ***Listen to these people saying when they get up on a Saturday. Then match the number of the interview with the right clock. Remember, children in France usually go to school on Saturday morning so families often have to get up early, as usual.***

RECORDING

2. ***Listen to Lucien describing what he normally does on a Saturday. Number the pictures in the right order.***

RECORDING
3.

Que fait Aurélie? *Listen and match the pictures with the phrases that describe what she is doing.*

a.

b.

c.

d.

e.

Elle prend une douche.

Elle prend son petit déjeuner.

Elle se lève.

Elle se réveille.

Elle se sèche les cheveux.

RECORDING
4.

Listen to Thomas describing what he usually does and what he sometimes does in the morning. Fill in the missing words.

a. ________________ je me lève à sept heures, mais ________________ je me lève à six heures.

b. ________________ je prends une douche, mais ________________ je fais du jogging.

c. ________________ je ne prends pas de petit déjeuner, mais ________________ je mange une tartine.

d. ________________ je pars à huit heures, mais ________________ je pars à sept heures.

normalement *usually*
quelquefois *sometimes*

RECORDING

5.

What do these people eat for breakfast? Listen and put the right number beside each picture.

Je mange du/de la/des ...	*I eat (some) ...*
Je ne mange rien.	*I don't eat anything.*
Je bois du/de la ...	*I drink (some) ...*
Je ne bois rien.	*I don't drink anything.*
Je ne prends pas de petit déjeuner.	*I don't have breakfast.*

6.

A vous! *How would you tell Sylvie what you do on Saturday morning? Complete these sentences about your usual routine.*

a. Normalement je me lève à ________________.

b. Quelquefois je ________________.

c. Normalement je prends/je ne prends pas de ________________.

d. Quelquefois je prends/je ne prends pas de ________________.

Pronunciation

RECORDING

Listen to Sylvie saying the parts of **s'appeler** *and* **se lever**. *Notice the different sound in the* **nous** *and* **vous** *forms of the verb. Repeat them after her, then practice repeating the question forms.*

Comment t'appelles-tu? *or* **Comment tu t'appelles?**

Comment vous appelez-vous? *or* **Comment vous vous appelez?**

A quelle heure te lèves-tu? *or* **A quelle heure tu te lèves?**

A quelle heure vous levez-vous? *or* **A quelle heure vous vous levez?**

Close-up

Reflexive verbs

You have already met one reflexive verb: **s'appeler**—*to be called (lit: to call oneself).*

The verb **lever** *means to lift, but* **se lever** *is to lift yourself, in other words, to get up.*

Laver *means to wash, but* **se laver** *means to wash yourself or get washed, and so on.*

s'appeler

je m'appelle	nous nous appelons
tu t'appelles	vous vous appelez
il s'appelle	ils s'appellent
elle s'appelle	elles s'appellent

se lever

je me lève	nous nous levons
tu te lèves	vous vous levez
il se lève	ils se lèvent
elle se lève	elles se lèvent

Note that **appeler** *doubles the* **l** *and* **lever** *takes a grave accent over the* **e** *in all except the* **nous** *and* **vous** *forms.*

The other reflexive verbs follow the regular **-er** *verb endings.*

Le week-end

The weekend

Word Bank

l'après-midi *m.*	*afternoon*
le déjeuner	*lunch*
le matin	*morning*
le repas de midi	*midday meal*
le soir	*evening*
à la campagne	*in the country*
en été	*in summer*
en hiver	*in winter*
alors	*then*
ou	*or*
puis	*then/next*
si	*if/whether*

se faire bronzer	*to sunbathe*
faire les courses	*to do errands*
faire une balade en vélo	*to go for a bike ride*
faire un pique-nique	*to go for a picnic*
faire de la planche (à voile)	*to go windsurfing*
faire une randonnée	*to go for a hike/long walk*
faire du sport	*to play sports*
jouer au football	*to play soccer*
jouer au tennis	*to play tennis*
rester	*to stay*
se reposer	*to rest*

RECORDING

1. ***Listen to these people talking about how they spend the weekend. Decide who is speaking and put the right number from the recording by each picture.***

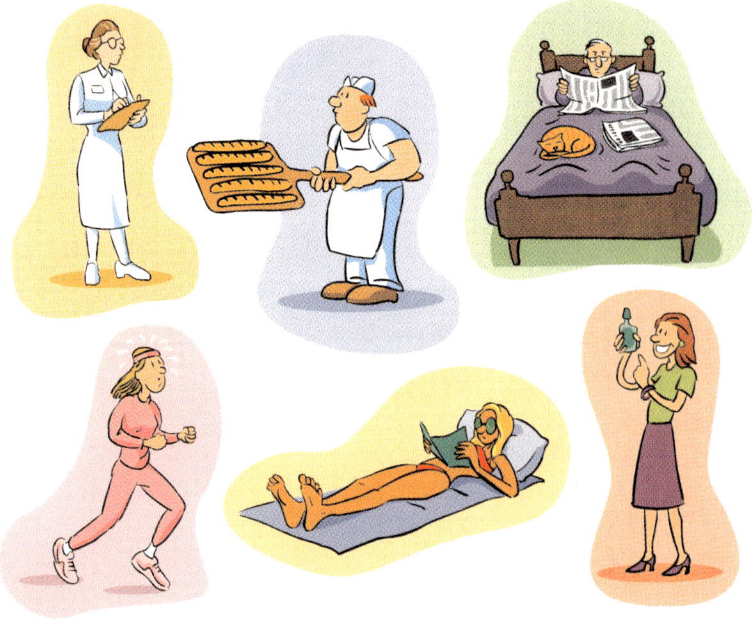

infirmière
professeur
secrétaire
boulanger
vendeuse
homme d'affaires

Vous savez ...
You know ...

C'est le jour le plus important.
It's the most important day.

avant d'aller au collège
before going to school

RECORDING

2.

What do these people do on Sunday? Listen and find out.

S'il fait beau ...
If it's nice ...

S'il ne fait pas beau ...
If it's not nice ...

RECORDING

3.

What are you being invited to do? Put the right number beside the pictures.

a.

b.

c.

d.

e.

f.

g.

h.

Voulez-vous vous joindre à nous?
Would you like to join us?

Quel beau temps!
What lovely weather!

Il y a juste le bon vent.
The wind is just right.

Did You Know?

The **pique-nique** *is a part of French life. Many picnic areas can be found at the roadside and at regular distances along the highway. The ones on highways also have restrooms and are called* **Aire**.

RECORDING

4.

Listen to these people saying what they would like to do. Write down the letter of the picture on the previous page that corresponds to the activity.

a. Je voudrais aller au restaurant. J'ai faim.

b. Je voudrais faire de la planche.

c. Une randonnée, quelle bonne idée!

d. Je veux aller à la plage pour me faire bronzer un peu.

e. Qui veut jouer au tennis avec moi?

f. Je voudrais visiter le château.

J'ai faim. *I'm hungry. (lit: I have hunger)*

Did You Know?

There are many beautiful **châteaux** *(castles) and stately homes to visit in France, and nearly every old town has at least one château. Many are well preserved, and some are still private homes. The* **Châteaux de la Loire** *(along the river Loire) are among some of the most famous.*

5.

A vous! *Now choose five activities and practice telling Sylvie that you would like to do them.*

Example: Je voudrais faire un pique-nique.

6.

Now it's your turn to invite a French friend. How would you suggest these activities? Practice saying your suggestion aloud!

Example: Voulez-vous aller à la plage?

S'il fait beau on pourrait aller/jouer/faire ...

S'il ne fait pas beau on pourrait rester/visiter ...

Pronunciation

RECORDING

Now practice saying these sentences, first as statements and then as questions. Listen carefully and try to imitate the rising intonation for questions and the falling intonation for statements.

Statement	Question
Le matin on va en ville.	**Le matin on va en ville?**
L'après-midi on va à la plage.	**L'après-midi on va à la plage?**
Le soir on va au restaurant.	**Le soir on va au restaurant?**

Close-up

Rappel! <u>On</u> *with the* **il/elle** *form of the verb can be used in conversation to mean "one" or "we."*

Times of day

In French you do not need to use a word for "in" with times of day:

le matin	*(in) the morning*
Le matin on va en ville.	*In the morning we go to town.*
l'après-midi	*(in) the afternoon*
L'après-midi on va à la plage.	*In the afternoon we go to the beach.*
le soir	*(in) the evening*
Le soir on va au restaurant.	*In the evening we go to the restaurant.*

Qu'est-ce qu'on a fait hier?

What did we do yesterday?

Word Bank

l'anniversaire *m.*	*birthday*	pendant	*for, during*
le fast-food	*fast food restaurant*	faire les magasins	*to go shopping (lit: to "do" the shops)*
ensemble	*together*	rencontrer	*to meet*
hier	*yesterday*		

RECORDING

1. ***Listen to these people describe what they did yesterday. Put the right numbers from the recording beside the pictures.***

C'était mon anniversaire. *It was my birthday.*

RECORDING

2. ***Listen to Thierry describing what he did this morning. Fill in the clocks.***

Qu'est-ce que Thierry a fait ce matin?

What did Thierry do this morning?

RECORDING

3. *Listen to Sylvie talking about what she did yesterday morning, afternoon, and evening.*

Put "A.M.," "P.M.," or "evening" by each picture.

4. **A vous!** *Now choose five sentences and complete them to say what you did yesterday morning.*

a. Je me suis réveillé(e) à ________________.

b. Je me suis levé(e) à ________________.

c. Je suis resté(e) au lit jusqu'à ________________.

d. Pour le petit déjeuner j'ai mangé du/de la ________________.

e. Pour le petit déjeuner je n'ai rien mangé mais j'ai bu ________________.

f. J'ai quitté la maison à ________________.

Pronunciation

RECORDING

Now let's practice saying what you have done using the perfect tense. Listen and repeat these phrases after Sylvie and think about what they mean.

je me suis réveillé(e)

je me suis levé(e)

je me suis lavé(e)

j'ai pris une douche

je me suis habillé(e)

je suis allé(e) en ville

j'ai mangé un croissant

j'ai bu un café

j'ai quitté la maison

Close-up

To say what you have done you use the perfect tense of the verb.

In most cases the perfect tense is formed by using the present tense of **avoir**, *to have + the past participle (as in English):*

J'ai mangé mon déjeuner. — *I have eaten my lunch.*

Some verbs form the present tense using **être**, *to be + the past participle:*

Je suis allé(e) en ville. — *I have been to town. (lit: I am gone to town)*

With verbs that take **être**, *the past participle agrees with the subject. So, for the feminine you add* **e** *and for the plural you add* **s**:

Mon père est allé en ville. — *My father has gone to town.*
Ma mère est allée au bureau. — *My mother has gone to the office.*
Mes frères sont allés au match de foot. — *My brothers have gone to the soccer game.*
Mes sœurs sont allées au cinéma. — *My sisters have gone to the movies.*

Close-up

Note that all the reflexive verbs take **être** *and the past participle:*

Je me suis levé(e).	*I got up.*	Elle s'est habillée.	*She got dressed.*
Il s'est rasé.	*He shaved.*	Vous vous êtes réveillés.	*You woke up.*

Forming the past participle:

a. **-er** *verbs—always take off the final* **er** *and add* **é***:*
manger ⟶ mangé

b. **-re** *verbs—usually take off the final* **re** *and add* **u***:*
répondre ⟶ répondu

c. **-ir** *verbs—usually take off the final* **r***:*
finir ⟶ fini

Just as in English there are many irregular past participles and these do need to be learned.

The most common ones are:

avoir—*to have*	eu
J'ai eu la visite de ...	*I (have) had a visit from ...*
être—*to be*	été
J'ai été à Marseille.	*I have been to Marseilles.*
boire—*to drink*	bu
J'ai bu du vin rouge.	*I have drunk/I drank some red wine.*
faire—*to do*	fait
J'ai fait la vaisselle.	*I have done/I did the dishes.*
lire—*to read*	lu
J'ai lu le journal.	*I (have) read the newspaper.*
mettre—*to put*	mis
J'ai mis le bol sur la table.	*I (have) put the bowl on the table.*
ouvrir—*to open*	ouvert
J'ai ouvert le paquet.	*I (have) opened the packet.*
prendre—*to take*	pris
J'ai pris un bain.	*I have taken/I took a bath.*
recevoir—*to receive*	reçu
J'ai reçu une lettre.	*I (have) received a letter.*

Some **-ir** *verbs take* **u** *in the past participle:*

venir—*to come*	venu
Il est venu en retard.	*He has come/He came late.*
voir—*to see*	vu
Il a déjà vu le film.	*He's already seen the movie.*
vouloir—*to want*	voulu
J'ai voulu ...	*I wanted ...*

If this all seems very complicated, don't worry. The parts you need most will all be explained again each time you need to use the perfect tense.

Checkpoints

Use the check list to test what you've learned in this unit and review anything you're not sure of.

Can you ... ?	*Yes*	*No*
• *say what time you normally wake up* Normalement je me réveille à ... heures.	❑	❑
• *say what you eat for breakfast* Je mange du/de la/des ...	❑	❑
• *say you don't eat anything* Je ne mange rien.	❑	❑
• *say what you drink* Je bois du/de la ...	❑	❑
• *say you don't eat breakfast* Je ne prends pas de petit déjeuner.	❑	❑
• *say in the morning* le matin	❑	❑
• *say in the afternoon* l'après-midi	❑	❑
• *say in the evening* le soir	❑	❑
• *say you would like to play tennis* Je voudrais jouer au tennis.	❑	❑
• *say you would like to go to the beach* Je voudrais aller à la plage.	❑	❑
• *suggest what you could do if it is nice* S'il fait beau on pourrait ...	❑	❑
• *suggest what you could do if it isn't nice* S'il ne fait pas beau on pourrait ...	❑	❑
• *say you could go to the movies* On pourrait aller au cinéma.	❑	❑
• *say you could go to a restaurant* On pourrait aller au restaurant.	❑	❑
• *use the perfect tense to say when you woke up* Je me suis réveillé(e) à ... heures.	❑	❑
• *use the perfect tense to say when you got up* Je me suis levé(e) à ... heures.	❑	❑

Can you … ?	***Yes***	***No***
• *say what you ate for breakfast* Pour le petit déjeuner j'ai mangé du/de la/des …	❑	❑
• *say what you drank* J'ai bu …	❑	❑
• *say when you left home* J'ai quitté la maison à … heures.	❑	❑

Learning tips

Where you see an accent circonflexe try adding an "s" after the vowel to see if it will help you to find related words in English:

château	*castle*
pâté	*paste*
arrêt	*arrest (stop)*

Do you want to learn more?

Look through the sports section of a French-language newspaper. See how many of the sports have similar names in English and in French.

For more practice, see Extra! on page A1.

Unit 2 is about food and meals and also about not feeling well. After completing this unit you will be able to:

- talk about food and meals at home
- say what you like and dislike
- order meals in a restaurant
- say how something is made
- tell someone that you don't feel well

Boire et manger

2

Word Bank

les légumes *m.*	*vegetables*
l'ail *m.*	*garlic*
les carottes *f.pl.*	*carrots*
le céleri	*celery*
les champignons *m.*	*mushrooms*
le chou	*cabbage*
le chou-fleur	*cauliflower*
les haricots *m.*	*beans*
les oignons *m.*	*onions*
les petits pois *m.*	*peas*
les pommes de terre *f.*	*potatoes*
les radis *m.*	*radishes*
la salade	*lettuce*
les tomates *f.*	*tomatoes*
les produits laitiers *m.*	*dairy products*
la crème fraîche	*cream*
le beurre	*butter*
le fromage	*cheese*
le lait	*milk*
les œufs *m.*	*eggs*
le yaourt	*yogurt*
la viande	*meat*
l'agneau *m.*	*lamb*
le bœuf	*beef*
la dinde	*turkey*
le gibier	*game meat*
le jambon	*ham*
le porc	*pork*
le poulet	*chicken*
le ragoût	*stew/casserole*
le veau	*veal*
la volaille	*poultry*
les cuisses de grenouille *f.*	*frogs' legs*
le dessert	*dessert*
les escargots *m.*	*snails*
les noix *f.*	*nuts*
le poisson	*fish*

Qu'est-ce que vous aimez manger?

What do you like to eat?

RECORDING

1. ***Listen to these customers at a market stall. Which vegetables are they buying and in what quantities? What do you think they are going to make?***

choucroute

soupe aux champignons

salade mixte

Now you choose some vegetables and practice asking for them in various quantities.

un kilo	*1kg*
un demi-kilo, une livre	*½kg*
deux cents grammes	*200g*
deux cent cinquante grammes	*250g*
cinq cents grammes	*500g*

RECORDING

2. ***Listen and write down what meat each person likes to eat. Choose a suitable dish for each!***

steak frites

blanquette de veau

salade niçoise

poulet rôti frites

DidYouKnow?

Fresh fruit and vegetables are plentiful in France and in larger towns are usually bought fresh at the market every day. Even smaller towns have fresh fruit and vegetable stalls most days of the week.

Et vous, qu'est-ce que vous aimez comme viande?

Qu'est-ce que vous aimez comme viande?	*What sort of meat do you like?*
Je n'aime pas tellement ...	*I don't really like ...*
Je suis végétarien(ne).	*I'm a vegetarian.*
Ça manque de goût.	*It lacks taste/flavor.*
Je suis très steak frites.	*I am a great "steak and fries" person.*
le poulet rôti	*roast chicken*

RECORDING **3.** *Listen and find out which speaker chooses which dessert.*

tarte au citron
crème brûlée
gâteau au chocolat
glace aux fraises

Je suis allergique aux cacahuètes.
I am allergic to peanuts.

Je fais un régime.
I'm on a diet.

Ça me donne mal au cœur.
That gives me indigestion/That makes me sick to my stomach.

Je ne mange pas de choses sucrées.
I don't eat anything sweet.

Ça me fait grossir.
It makes me fat.

Je ne peux jamais résister à ...
I can never resist ...

RECORDING 4.

A vous! *You have been invited to dinner and your hosts want to know what you like and don't like to eat. Tell them.*

J'aime …

Je n'aime pas tellement …

Je ne mange pas de …

Je suis très …

Je suis allergique à la/à l'/au/aux …

RECORDING 5.

Sylvie is asking some people what they think of snails. Listen and check what they say.

Comment trouvez-vous les escargots?
What do you think of snails?

délicieux
delicious

curieux
strange

un goût particulier
a special taste

insipide
tasteless

bof!
not a lot (usually accompanied by a shrug of the shoulders)

beurk!
yuk!

dégoûtant!
disgusting!

Did You Know?

If you are invited to a formal meal in a French restaurant or home you will probably be offered an apéritif first to prepare the palate, e.g., a Pernod or other aniseed-based drink or even a glass of champagne. The meal then traditionally consists of five courses:

Hors-d'œuvre: *a small starter of perhaps salad, paté, snails, or soup.*

Entrée: *usually a fish, cheese or egg dish.*

Le plat principal: *meat and vegetables.*

Le fromage: *cheese and bread.*

Le dessert *or* **un fruit**.

Note that the dessert is served after the cheese, with usually a strong black coffee to finish it off. Do you know how to ask for a decaffeinated coffee?
Un déca, s'il vous plaît.

RECORDING 6.

A vous! *Practice asking a visitor what he or she likes.*

Aimez-vous … ?

Mangez-vous … ?

Préférez-vous … ?

Comment trouvez-vous … ?

Voulez-vous du/de la/des … ?

Pronunciation

RECORDING

Practice saying these phrases after Sylvie and Jacques, paying particular attention to the pronunciation.

Le bœuf est délicieux.	**La tarte est délicieuse.**
Les escargots sont délicieux.	**Les fraises sont délicieuses.**
Le goût est curieux.	**La glace est curieuse.**
Les fromages sont curieux.	**Les cuisses de grenouille sont curieuses.**

Close-up

Toujours la politesse! *(Being polite at the table.)*

Rappel! *If you are offered something and want it, say* **"Oui"** *or* **"S'il vous plaît." "Merci"** *on its own means "No thank you."*

If you are full and don't want any more, you can say **"J'ai assez mangé,"** *I have eaten enough, or even* **"J'ai déjà trop mangé,"** *I have already eaten too much.* **"Je suis plein(e),"** *I am "full" is a slang way of saying you have had too much to drink (lit: I am tanked up) and should be avoided.*

Adjective agreement

	m.	*f.*
sing.	Le bœuf est bon.	La tarte est bonne.
pl.	Les escargots sont bons.	Les fraises sont bonnes.

Adjectives ending in **x** *don't change for the masculine plural:*

	m.	*f.*
sing.	Le bœuf est délicieux.	La tarte est délicieuse.
pl.	Les escargots sont délicieux.	Les fraises sont délicieuses.

Au restaurant

At the restaurant

Word Bank

les asperges *f.*	*asparagus*	la galette	*savory pancake*
l'assiette *f.*	*plate*	le pain	*bread*
la demi-bouteille	*half-bottle*	le poivre	*pepper*
le cendrier	*ashtray*	le repas	*meal*
le couteau	*knife*	le sel	*salt*
la crêpe	*pancake*	le sucre	*sugar*
la cuillère	*spoon*	là	*there*
la farine	*flour*	formidable	*super/fantastic*
de blé noir	*buckwheat*	rempli(e)	*filled*
complète	*whole wheat*	salé(e)	*salty/savory*
la fourchette	*fork*		

Le Bistro de la Gare

Menu à 12 euros

ENTRÉES
AU CHOIX:
La Bouillabaisse froide en gelée
La Salade veriée aux pignons de pin
Soupe du jour

VIANDES ET POISSONS
AU CHOIX:
La Suggestion du jour (avec supplément):
Suprême de volaille
Filet de poisson frais du Bistro
Le Coeur d'aloyau "sauce beouf"
Le steak au poivre

ACCOMPAGNEMENT DE LÉGUMES
AU CHOIX:
Les Pommes allumettes fraîches
Le Chou-fleur au gratin

FROMAGE OU DESSERT

RECORDING

1. *Listen to the clerk at your hotel advising these tourists where to eat. Check the places she recommends.*

J'ai faim.	*I'm hungry.*
Vous êtes pressés.	*You are in a hurry.*
à toute heure	*all the time*
pas grand-chose	*nothing much*
en quittant	*leaving*
un petit quelque chose	*a little something*
pas loin du tout	*not far at all*
à cette heure-ci	*at this time (lit: at this hour here)*

RECORDING

2. *Listen to find out what these people order. Put the speaker's number beside the appropriate dish on the menu opposite.*

3. **A vous!** *Choose a meal for yourself and a friend and practice saying your order aloud.*

Je voudrais …	*I would like …*
pour moi	*for me*
pour lui/elle	*for him/her*

RECORDING

4. *Listen to find out what each customer is asking for or complaining about.*

Je n'ai pas de ...	*I don't have a ...*
Avez-vous ... ?	*Do you have ... ?*
encore	*more*
Il n'y a pas de ...	*There isn't a ...*

RECORDING

5. *More practice in understanding spoken prices! Listen to find out what each check comes to, then put the number of the speaker by the appropriate total. Practice saying the numbers aloud.*

Pronunciation

RECORDING

More practice with numbers. Repeat these numbers after Sylvie:

9 18 27 36 45 54 63 72 81 90 99

Now repeat these numbers after Jacques:

5 10 15 20 25 30 35 40 45 50
55 60 65 70 75 80 85 90 95 100

Close-up

In French the verb **avoir**, *to have, is used in certain expressions where in English the verb to be is used:*

J'ai faim.
I am hungry.

Avez-vous faim?
Are you hungry?

J'ai soif.
I am thirsty.

Avez-vous soif?
Are you thirsty?

J'ai chaud.
I am hot.

Avez-vous chaud?
Are you hot?

J'ai froid.
I am cold.

Avez-vous froid?
Are you cold?

The **ne** *is often omitted in spoken French:*

J'ai pas de ...	*I don't have a ...* (je n'ai pas de)
J'sais pas.	*I don't know.* (je ne sais pas)
J'ai rien vu.	*I haven't seen anything.* (je n'ai rien vu)
C'est pas grave.	*It doesn't matter.* (ce n'est pas grave; *lit: it isn't serious*)

J'ai mal au cœur

I feel sick

Word Bank

le bras	*arm*
le cœur	*heart*
le corps	*body*
les dents *f.*	*teeth*
le dos	*back*
le genou	*knee*
la gorge	*throat*
la jambe	*leg*
la main	*hand*
l'oreille *f.*	*ear*
l'œil *m.* (les yeux *pl.*)	*eye*
le pied	*foot*
le talon	*heel*
la tête	*head*
le ventre	*stomach*
le dentiste	*dentist*
le médecin	*doctor*
le service des urgences	*emergency service*
les médicaments	*medicine*
l'ampoule *f.*	*blister*
les analgésiques	*painkillers*
la crème antiseptique	*antiseptic cream*
la cuillère à soupe	*tablespoon*
la cuillerée à soupe	*a spoonful*
le sirop	*syrup*
le pansement	*bandage*
les suppositoires *m.*	*suppositories*
emmener	*to take (someone)*
prendre un rendez-vous	*to make an appointment*
tousser	*to cough*

RECORDING

1. *Listen to these people and write down what is wrong with them.*

Qu'est-ce qui vous arrive?	*What's wrong with you?*
J'ai mal à la/à l'/au/aux ...	*My ... hurt(s).*
J'ai mal aux dents.	*I have a toothache.*
J'ai de la fièvre.	*I have a temperature. (lit: fever)*
J'ai trop mangé.	*I've eaten too much.*
Je me suis fait mal à la/à l'/au/aux ...	*I've hurt my ...*

RECORDING

2. **A vous!** *Listen and practice saying what's wrong with you!*

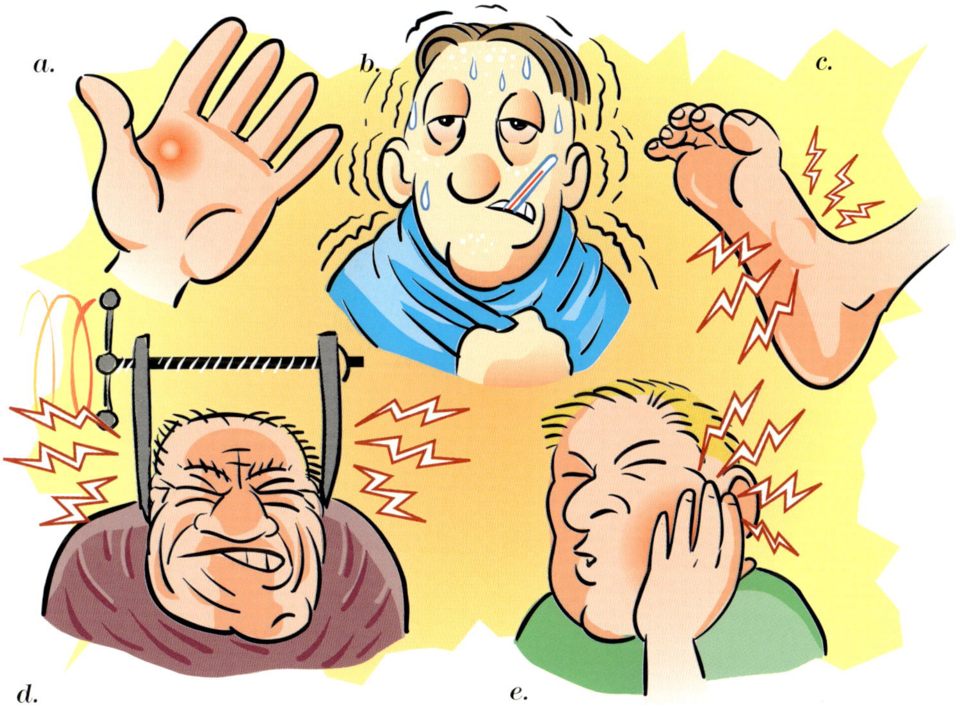

RECORDING

3. *Listen and write down when these people have an appointment. Listen again to check your answers.*

a.

b.

c.

d.

e.

Faites le numéro 15. *Dial 15.*

RECORDING

4.

Listen to this conversation in the doctor's waiting room. Write down what is wrong with each patient.

chez le médecin	*at the doctor's*
J'ai une grippe.	*I have the flu.*
J'ai de la toux/Je tousse.	*I have a cough.*
Je suis enrhumé(e).	*I have a cold.*
J'ai pris un coup de soleil.	*I have a sunburn.*
Je me suis coupé le doigt.	*I cut my finger.*
à cause du temps	*because of the weather*

RECORDING

5.

A vous! *Now you ask for an appointment and say what is wrong with you.*

Je veux un rendez-vous avec le médecin/le dentiste.
I want an appointment with the doctor/dentist.

Je me suis cassé une dent.
I have broken a tooth.

J'ai perdu un plombage.
I have lost a filling.

RECORDING

6.

Listen to the pharmacist at the drugstore. What remedy is she giving her customers and what instructions does she give? What do you think might be wrong with them?

Je vais vous donner des comprimés.
I'll give you some tablets.

Je vous propose ...
I suggest (to you) ...

Avez-vous quelque chose pour une grippe/un mal de gorge/un mal de tête?
Do you have something for the flu/a sore throat/a headache?

Did You Know?

To buy any medicines in France you have to go to a ***pharmacie****. Medicines are not allowed to be sold elsewhere. The pharmacist is also fully qualified to prescribe medicines for most straightforward ailments, and will tell you if he or she thinks you need to see a doctor.*

Pronunciation

RECORDING

Listen and repeat these phrases after Sylvie and Jacques.

J'ai mal au cœur.

Tu as mal au dos.

Il a mal à la tête.

Elle a mal aux oreilles.

Nous avons mal à la gorge.

Vous avez mal aux dents.

Ils ont mal aux pieds.

Elles ont mal aux yeux.

Et vous, qu'est-ce que vous avez?

Moi? Je n'ai rien, moi!

Close-up

Rappel!

à + le/la/les

m.	*f.*	*pl.*
à + le = au	à la	à+ les = aux
J'ai mal au cœur.	J'ai mal à la gorge.	J'ai mal aux dents.

Perfect tense

Most verbs take **avoir** *in the perfect tense:*

J'ai perdu un plombage. *I have lost a filling.*

These verbs take **être**:

aller—*to go*
arriver—*to arrive*
entrer—*to enter*
monter—*to go up*
rester—*to stay*
venir—*to come*
partir—*to leave*
sortir—*to go out*
descendre—*to come down*
tomber—*to fall down*

All reflexive verbs take **être**:

Je me suis levé(e). *I got up.*
Il s'est coupé le doigt. *He cut his finger.*
Nous nous sommes habillés. *We got dressed.*
Ils se sont couchés. *They went to bed.*

en—of it/of them

Vous en prenez deux. *You take two (of them).*

Checkpoints

Use the check list to test what you've learned in this unit and review anything you're not sure of.

Can you ... ?	*Yes*	*No*
• *ask for 1kg of potatoes* un kilo de pommes de terre	❑	❑
• *ask for 500g of cheese* cinq cents grammes de fromage	❑	❑
• *say what sort of meat you like* J'aime le porc/le bœuf/le poulet.	❑	❑
• *say you are vegetarian* Je suis végétarien(ne).	❑	❑
• *say you don't like something very much* Je n'aime pas tellement ...	❑	❑
• *say you are full* J'ai assez mangé.	❑	❑
• *say if you are on a diet* Je fais un régime.	❑	❑
• *say you are allergic to peanuts.* Je suis allergique aux cacahuètes.	❑	❑
• *say it's delicious* C'est délicieux!	❑	❑
• *ask if someone prefers chicken* Préférez-vous le poulet?	❑	❑
• *say you are hungry and thirsty* J'ai faim. J'ai soif.	❑	❑
• *order steak and fries* Un steak frites.	❑	❑
• *ask for some more bread* encore du pain	❑	❑
• *say you don't have a knife* Je n'ai pas de couteau.	❑	❑
• *say you don't want a dessert* pas de dessert	❑	❑
• *say you feel sick* J'ai mal au cœur. Je suis enrhumé(e). J'ai de la fièvre.	❑	❑

Can you ... ?

	Yes	*No*
• *say you would like to make an appointment* Je voudrais prendre un rendez-vous.	❑	❑

Learning tips

Listen to a family soap opera on television and notice how many "filler noises" are added. Listen again to the dialogs, or to a French film, and build up a list of useful "noises" to fill any gaps in a conversation or to give you time to think of what to say next. Here are a few to remember:

euh	*er*
hum	*um*
et alors	*and then/but*
mais voilà/et voilà	*(but/and) there you are*
et puis	*and then*
vous savez	*you know*
dis donc!	*well I never! (to express surprise)*
peut-être	*perhaps*
normalement/d'habitude	*usually*
ben	*well, er*
ouais	*yeah*
tiens!	*well!*

Do you want to learn more?

Many French-language housekeeping magazines have cooking recipes. If you can get hold of one, see how many of the ingredients you can identify. Also, some products you buy may have instructions or contents listed in French as well as in English on the packaging. The next time you're buying wine, keep a look out for French wines and study the labels to see how much information you can understand.

For more practice, see Extra! on page A2.

Unit 3 is about going on vacation. You will become familiar with the language you need to know in order to:

- say where you like to go on vacation
- and where you have been (using the past tense)
- say what you like to do
- and what you have done on your last vacation (using the past tense)
- find a place to stay and make a reservation

En vacances 3

Word Bank

le bord de la mer	*seaside*
la campagne	*the country*
le camping	*camping/campsite*
les grandes vacances	*the summer vacation*
le groupe touristique	*tour group*
les lieux historiques	*historic sites*
la mer	*the sea*
la montagne	*the mountain(s)*
la plage	*the beach*
le soleil	*the sun*
l'est	*east*
le nord	*north*
l'ouest	*west*
le sud	*south*
les Antilles	*the Caribbean islands*
l'Orient	*the East*
faire du tourisme	*to go sightseeing*

Où allez-vous en vacances?

Where do you go on vacation?

RECORDING

1. ***Where do these people like to spend their vacation? Write down the letter of the place each speaker prefers and say where you like to go.***

a.

b.

c.

d.

J'aime aller ...
I like to go ...

DidYouKnow?

Les grandes vacances. *The summer vacation is also referred to as* **la grande évasion***—the great escape. In August in France almost everyone goes on vacation and Paris virtually closes down, except for foreign tourists. The majority of French people spend their holidays in France as the country has something to offer everyone and the weather can usually be relied on in summer to be hot and sunny. The vast majority still go to the seaside, where they stay on well-equipped campsites or in apartments or hotels. The next most popular vacation is* **le tourisme vert***—holidays in the country.*

RECORDING

2.

Listen to these people saying where they are going to go this year. Write down the letter of the region they are going to.

cette année	*this year*

RECORDING

3.

These people are going further afield. This exercise is to help you become familiar with words that you would recognize if they were written down, but which are not always as easy to understand when spoken by a French person. Listen for these words and check them when you hear them.

les Antilles	Australie	la Martinique	New York
Londres	Los Angeles	Stratford	Sydney
l'Outback	Oxford	Washington	Japon
Las Vegas	walkabout	l'Orient	Tahiti
les Etats-Unis	le Grand Canyon		

RECORDING

4.

Who are these people going with? Listen to find out.

ma famille

mes copains

mon petit ami/
mon copain

ma petite amie/
ma copine

mes enfants

Nous sommes quatre.	*There are four of us.*
mes copains	*my buddies*
mon copain/ma copine	*my boyfriend/my girlfriend*
tout(e) seul(e)	*alone*

RECORDING

5.

Listen to Sylvie asking where these people went last year.

Où êtes-vous allé(e) l'année dernière?	*Where did you go last year?*
Je suis resté(e) à la maison.	*I stayed at home.*
comme toujours	*as usual*
On y va chaque année.	*We go there every year.*
vous savez ...	*you know ...*
les flirts	*flirts*
le fric	*dough/cash (slang word for money)*
le surf des neiges	*snowboarding*

6. **A vous!** *Answer the following questions.*

Où allez-vous cette année et avec qui?

Cette année je vais __________________ avec __________________.

Où êtes-vous allé(e) l'année dernière et avec qui?

L'année dernière je suis allé(e) __________________ avec __________________.

Pronunciation

RECORDING

The past participles usually sound the same in the masculine, feminine, singular, and plural. Listen to Sylvie and Jacques and repeat each phrase after them.

m.	*f.*
Je suis allé aux Etats-Unis.	**Je suis allée à Miami.**
Je suis resté en France.	**Je suis restée à Paris.**
Nous sommes allés en Angleterre.	**Nous sommes allées à Londres.**
Ils sont restés à la maison.	**Elles sont restées en ville.**

And now practice the letter "l" by repeating these phrases:

J'aime visiter les lieux historiques.

J'adore le soleil.

Je voudrais aller aux Antilles.

Je suis allé(e) en ville.

Il est tout seul.

Elle est toute seule.

Close-up

Rappel!

The word for "in"

a. *With feminine countries use* **en**: **en France**, **en Amérique**

b. *With the names of towns and cities use* **à**: **à Washington**, **à Tokyo**

c. *With masculine and plural countries use* **au**/**aux**:

à + le = au	J'habite au Canada.
à + les = aux	J'habite aux Etats-Unis.

The word for "my" also changes to agree with the word it precedes.

m.	*f.*	*pl.*
mon mari	ma femme	mes enfants
my husband	*my wife*	*my children*

Before feminine nouns that begin with a vowel, you use **mon**:

mon ami—*my (male) friend*   mon amie—*my (female) friend*

BUT

mon petit ami—*my boyfriend*   ma petite amie—*my girlfriend*

In conversation **on** *(one/we) is often used instead of* **nous** *(we). It is followed by the third person singular (***il/elle** *form) of the verb:*

on va/nous allons	*we are going*
on est allé/nous sommes allé(e)s	*we went*
on fait du camping/nous faisons du camping	*we go camping*
on a fait du camping/ nous avons fait du camping	*we went/have been camping*

Être *+ past participle agreement*

With verbs that take **être** *in the perfect tense, the past participle agrees with the subject. So, for the feminine you add* **e** *and for the plural you add* **s**:

m.	*f.*
Je suis allé en France.	Je suis allée en France.
Nous sommes allés en France.	Nous sommes allées en France.

BUT

On est allé en France.	On est allé en France.

Qu'est-ce que vous aimez faire?

What do you like doing?

Word Bank

le canoë-kayak	*canoeing*
le chalet	*chalet*
le cheval	*horse*
le cyclisme	*cycling*
l'équitation *f.*	*horse-back riding*
l'escalade *f.*	*rock climbing*
le foot	*soccer*
le golf	*golf*
le hockey sur glace	*ice hockey*
le jogging	*jogging*
la luge	*sledding*
la natation	*swimming*
la neige	*snow*
le parapente	*paragliding*
le patin à glace	*ice skating*
la pêche (au brochet)	*(pike) fishing*
la planche à voile	*windsurfing*
la plongée	*diving*
le rafting	*rafting*
la randonnée	*hiking*
le repos	*rest*
le ski	*skiing*
le ski nautique	*waterskiing*
le ski alpin	*downhill skiing*
le ski de fond	*cross-country skiing*
la tranquillité	*peace and quiet*
les vacances de neige	*winter vacation*
la voile	*sailing*
le volley	*volleyball*
le VTT (vélo tout terrain)	*mountain biking*
adorer	*to love*
aimer	*to like*
détester	*to hate*
s'imaginer (galoper)	*to imagine oneself (galloping)*
préférer	*to prefer*
répondre (aux questions)	*to answer (questions)*
alors	*well/then*
même	*even*
pendant	*during*
quand	*when*
vraiment	*really*
actif/active	*active*
affreux/affreuse	*awful*
fantastique	*fantastic*
génial(e)	*great*
reposant	*relaxing*
stupide	*stupid*
superbe	*superb*

RECORDING
1.

What do these people like doing? Listen and write down the activities they enjoy.

pendant les vacances	*during the vacation*
fana de (sport)	*(sport) fanatic/fan*
un peu	*a bit*
Vous le connaissez?	*Do you know it/him?*

RECORDING
2.

And what do they dislike? Listen and find out.

Je suis paresseux/paresseuse.
I am lazy.

et tout ça
and all that

allongé(e) sur la plage
stretched out on the beach

C'est dangereux.
It's dangerous.

On risque de mourir d'un cancer.
You risk dying of cancer.

Did You Know?

More and more people are choosing to combine sport and relaxation by going on activity vacations. The most popular sports in France are **la pêche** *and* **le cyclisme**. *The famous "Tour de France" is a 4,000 km cycle race which lasts three weeks and includes very difficult mountain sections in the Alps or Pyrenees. Other sports that are fast gaining popularity are* **la planche à voile**, **la plongée**, **l'escalade**, **le VTT,** *and* **le ski**. *A more sedate but by no means less popular sport is* **la pétanque**, *a form of bowling played outside, often in the town square.*

RECORDING

3. *Listen to Sylvie asking these people if they have ever tried paragliding. What do they think of it? Write down what they say.*

Avez-vous jamais essayé de faire du parapente?	*Have you ever tried paragliding?*
une fois	*once*
deux fois	*twice*
plusieurs fois	*several times*
jamais	*never*
C'était …	*It was …*
quelque chose d'extra	*something great*

RECORDING

4. *Now listen to find out what they would like to do.*

Qu'est-ce que vous aimeriez faire?
What would you like to do?

J'aimerais (essayer)
I would like (to try)

Je voudrais bien (apprendre)
I would really like (to learn)

J'ai peur.
I'm afraid. (lit: I have fear)

RECORDING

5. *Listen to find out what these people do on their winter vacation. Match the speaker with the appropriate picture.*

RECORDING

6. **A vous!** *Prepare your own answers to the same questions.*

Qu'est-ce que vous aimez faire?

J'aime ____.

Et qu'est-ce que vous n'aimez pas faire?

Je n'aime pas ____.

Avez-vous jamais essayé de faire du parapente?

J'ai essayé ____ fois.

Avez-vous jamais fait du rafting?

Jamais.

Pronunciation

RECORDING

Practice asking the questions after Sylvie:

Qu'est-ce que vous aimez faire?

Et qu'est-ce que vous n'aimez pas faire?

Avez-vous jamais essayé de faire du parapente?

Now practice saying the parts of the verb **aimer**, *first in the affirmative, then in the negative. Notice how most parts of the verb just sound like the letter "M"!*

j'aime	**nous aimons**
tu aimes	**vous aimez**
il aime	**ils aiment**
elle aime	**elles aiment**

je n'aime pas	**nous n'aimons pas**
tu n'aimes pas	**vous n'aimez pas**
il n'aime pas	**ils n'aiment pas**
elle n'aime pas	**elles n'aiment pas**

And finally, practice saying:

j'aimerais	**Aimeriez-vous?**

Close-up

Say what you like and don't like and ask someone what he/she likes to do:

J'aime	*I like*
J'adore	*I love*
Je préfère	*I prefer*
Je n'aime pas	*I don't like*
Je déteste	*I hate*
Aimez-vous ... ?	*Do you like ... ?*
Préférez-vous ... ?	*Do you prefer ... ?*

Say what you would like to try and ask what someone would like to try:

J'aimerais essayer (de faire du parapente).

I'd like to try (paragliding).

Aimeriez-vous essayer (la luge)?

Would you like to try (sledding)?

Quel hôtel?

Which hotel?

Word Bank

l'auberge *f.*	*inn*	les insectes	*insects*
l'auberge de jeunesse *f.*	*youth hostel*	le lac	*lake*
la chambre d'hôte	*bed and breakfast*	la nuit	*night*
l'étoile	*star*	décider	*to decide*
la ferme	*farm*	louer	*to rent*
le gîte	*full-service rental cottage*	passer	*to spend (time)*

RECORDING

1. ***Listen to these two couples deciding where they are going to spend the night.***

un hôtel quatre étoiles	*a four-star hotel*
Ça te convient?	*Does that suit you?*
donnant sur (la mer/la rue)	*overlooking (the sea/the street)*
Que tu es exigeant(e)!	*How demanding you are!*
On pourrait louer ...	*We could rent ...*
Moi non plus.	*Me neither.*

RECORDING

2. *Listen to the details of these hotels and check their facilities.*

	Hôtel de la Poste	Hôtel Superbe	Hôtel Bellevue	Grand Hôtel	Hôtel des Pêcheurs
Family suites					
Twin beds					
Single bed					
Bath					
Shower					
TV					
Phone					
Pool					
Fitness/ Gym					
Garage/ Parking					

Quel hôtel préférez-vous?
Which hotel do you prefer?

Lequel préférez-vous?
Which one do you prefer?

le salon
living room

hors de la ville
outside of town

Did You Know?

Most French hotels are controlled by the **Office du Tourisme** *and are awarded stars according to their standards; the more stars, the better (and the more expensive) the hotel. There are many hotel chains, e.g.,* **Formule 1**, **Campanile**, **Ibis**, **Mercure**.

Logis de France *are family-owned hotels known for their more personal and regional flavor.*

Les gîtes ruraux *are full-service country cottages or apartments for rent.*

Chambres d'hôte *are rooms in private homes offering breakfast. Most towns have an official campsite, as well as many private campsites, which will be well equipped and managed. In the peak season, especially in August, it's essential to make reservations early, as many places are booked from year to year.*

3. **A vous!** *Find two things to say about each hotel.*

L'hôtel de la Poste	est/n'est pas ________________.
	a/n'a pas de ________________.
L'hôtel Superbe	est/n'est pas ________________.
	a/n'a pas de ________________.
L'hôtel Bellevue	est/n'est pas ________________.
	a/n'a pas de ________________.
Le Grand Hôtel	est/n'est pas ________________.
	a/n'a pas de ________________.
L'hôtel des Pêcheurs	est/n'est pas ________________.
	a/n'a pas de ________________.

RECORDING

4. *Listen to find out which hotel this couple prefers. What reason do they give? Match each hotel with the phrase used to describe it.*

a. trop petit	Hôtel de la Poste
b. idéal	Hôtel Superbe
c. trop bruyant	Hôtel Bellevue
d. trop cher	Grand Hôtel
e. trop grand	Hôtel des Pêcheurs

Il n'y a qu'une étoile. *There's only one star.*

RECORDING

5. **A vous!** *Now you practice saying which hotel you prefer and why. Listen and repeat each phrase.*

Quel hôtel préférez-vous? Pourquoi?

Je préfère l'hôtel ________________ parce qu'il est/a ________________.

RECORDING

6.

Listen to these people at the hotel reception asking if there are any rooms available. What are they asking for?

Avez-vous une chambre libre?	*Do you have a vacancy?*
une chambre pour deux personnes	*a double room*

RECORDING

7.

A vous! *The clerk is asking you some questions. How would you answer them? Listen and complete the dialog.*

Receptionist: Bonsoir monsieur, madame.

You: *(Ask if they have a room free tonight.)*

Receptionist: Oui. Pour deux personnes?

You: ______________________________.

Receptionist: Vous restez combien de jours?

You: ______________________________.

Receptionist: Votre nom, s'il vous plaît?

You: ______________________________.

Receptionist: Pouvez-vous épeler?

You: ______________________________.

Receptionist: Signez ici. Vous avez une voiture?

You: ______________________________.

Receptionist: Le garage est au sous-sol. Le code du parking est 34 77. Votre numéro d'immatriculation, s'il vous plaît?

You: ______________________________.

Receptionist: Chambre numéro 243, au deuxième étage, l'ascenseur est là-bas. Voilà la clé.

Pronunciation

RECORDING

Listen and repeat the names of these hotels after Jacques:

l'hôtel de la Poste

l'hôtel Superbe

l'hôtel Bellevue

le Grand Hôtel

l'hôtel des Pêcheurs

Now ask where they are:

Pour aller à l'hôtel de la Poste, s'il vous plaît?

Où se trouve l'hôtel Superbe?

L'hôtel Bellevue est au bord du lac?

Le Grand Hôtel est loin d'ici?

Il faut combien de temps pour aller à l'hôtel des Pêcheurs?

Close-up

Rappel! *To make a negative in French you add* **ne** *(or* **n'** *before a vowel) in front of the verb and* **pas** *after the verb:*

Vous êtes suisse?

Non, je ne suis pas suisse.

Il est japonais?

Non, il n'est pas japonais.

When you say there isn't something in French you add **de** *(of/any) after the negative and leave out the word for "the" or "a":*

Il n'y a pas de piscine.

There isn't (a) swimming pool.

Je n'ai pas de femme.

I don't have (a) wife.

Yes and no

Avez-vous une voiture?

Do you have a car?

Oui, j'en ai une.

Yes, I have one (of them).

Non, je n'en ai pas.

No, I don't have one (of them).

Vous n'avez pas de voiture?

You don't have a car?

Oui, c'est vrai. Je n'ai pas de voiture.

Yes, that's right. I don't have a car.

Si, j'en ai une!

Yes (indeed), I do have one!

Vous voulez un hôtel de luxe?

Do you want a luxury hotel?

Pas du tout!

Not at all!

Checkpoints

Use the check list to test what you've learned in this unit and review anything you're not sure of.

Can you ... ?	***Yes***	***No***
• *say where you like to go* J'aime aller au bord de la mer. J'aime aller à la campagne.	❑	❑
• *say where you are going on vacation this year* Cette année je vais à/en ...	❑	❑
• *say who you are going with* J'y vais avec mon mari/ma femme. J'y vais avec mon copain/ma copine. J'y vais avec mon petit ami/ma petite amie.	❑	❑
• *say where you went last year* Je suis allé(e) à/en ... On est allé ...	❑	❑
• *say you stayed at home* Je suis resté(e) à la maison. On est resté à la maison.	❑	❑
• *say what you like doing* J'aime faire de la planche à voile. J'aime jouer au tennis.	❑	❑
• *say you don't like sunbathing* Je n'aime pas me faire bronzer.	❑	❑
• *say you would like to go rafting* J'aimerais faire du rafting.	❑	❑
• *say you have never been paragliding* Je n'ai jamais fait de parapente.	❑	❑
• *say you have tried once/twice* J'ai essayé une fois/deux fois.	❑	❑
• *say you prefer the hotel with a pool* Je préfère l'hôtel avec piscine.	❑	❑
• *say the hotel is too big/small/expensive* L'hôtel est trop grand/petit/cher.	❑	❑

Can you ... ? | *Yes* | *No*

- *say what kind of room you want* ❑ ❑
  une chambre pour une personne
  une chambre pour deux personnes avec douche
  avec un grand lit
  à deux lits
  pour deux nuits
- *reserve a room* ❑ ❑
  Je voudrais une chambre pour ...

Learning tips

Remember, always try to read aloud. Put your hands over your ears so that you can hear yourself even if you speak very quietly. Try it!

Do you want to learn more?

If you have access to the Internet, you should be able to find tourist information in French as well as in English. Otherwise, French or Canadian tourist offices may be able to give you some brochures in French. See how much you can understand and how many of your favorite vacation pursuits you can name in French.

For more practice, see Extra! on page A4.

Unit 4 is about where you work. You are going to learn some formal language in order to:

- arrange a meeting and use the phone
- recognize and describe people
- talk about the weather
- talk about money

Au travail

4

Word Bank

l'adjoint(e)	*assistant*
l'agenda *m.*	*diary*
le chef	*head (of department)*
le client	*customer*
la comptabilité	*accounts (department)*
la conférence	*conference*
les coordonnées	*telephone number*
le dîner	*dinner*
le discours	*talk*
l'entreprise *f.*	*firm/company*
l'usine	*(small) factory*
le PDG (le président directeur général)	*the CEO*
le personnel	*staff*
le poste (de téléphone)	*(telephone) extension*
la présentation	*presentation*
le rendez-vous	*appointment*
la réunion	*meeting*
le service	*department*
la société anonyme (SA)	*incorporated company*
la standardiste	*switchboard operator*
l'usine *f.*	*(big) factory*
la visite	*visit*
le vol	*flight*
le voyage d'affaires	*business trip*
assister à	*to attend*
proposer	*to suggest*
rentrer	*to return*

Le personnel

Staff

é accent aigu **è** accent grave **ê** accent circonflexe

ç cédille **-** trait d'union

RECORDING

1\. *Who's who at the Société Bonchoix? Listen and fill in the names of some of the members of the staff.*

Le chef du service technique

____

Le chef comptable

____

Le PDG

____

L'adjointe du PDG

____

Le chef du service marketing

____

RECORDING

2.

Listen to these telephone conversations. Some of the people to whom the caller wants to speak can't come to the phone. What reasons are given, and when can the caller telephone again? Listen again and check your answers.

Pourrais-je parler à ... ?	*Could I speak to ... ?*
n'est-ce pas?	*isn't it?*
Ne quittez pas.	*Hold on.*
C'est de la part de qui?	*Who is speaking?*
Je regrette.	*I'm sorry.*
Il/elle n'est pas là.	*He/she isn't there.*
Il/elle est en réunion.	*He/she's in a meeting.*
avec un client	*with a client*
en communication	*on the other line*
en voyage d'affaires	*on a business trip*
parti(e) déjeuner	*at lunch*
pris(e), occupé(e)	*busy (lit: taken)*
Voulez-vous patienter?	*Would you like to hold?*
Je vous le/la passe.	*I'm putting you through to him/her.*

3.

Tell Sylvie the names of the people at **Imprimat**, *and choose five to practice spelling. (Tip: Replace the names with names of people you know and practice spelling them.)*

le PDG	M. Vincent
l'adjointe du PDG	Mme Daniaud
le chef du service marketing	M. Thibault
le chef du service technique	M. Chaudron
le chef du personnel	Mlle Martineau
la standardise	Mlle Carriou

RECORDING

4. *Who has a meeting with whom and when? Listen and draw a line to join the right people and times.*

Mr. Haydn-Jones	Mr. Weston	Mr. Bradshaw	Ms. Walker
M. Leclerc	Mme Sibbille	M. Varin	Mme Yon
mardi	mercredi	jeudi	vendredi
10h30	11h20	14h30	15h

Complete the text and then read it back aloud.

a. ________________ a rendez-vous avec ________________ à ________________ heures.

b. ________________ a rendez-vous avec ________________ à ________________ heures.

c. ________________ a rendez-vous avec ________________ à ________________ heures.

d. ________________ a rendez-vous avec ________________ à ________________ heures.

RECORDING

5. *You're trying to make an appointment to meet M. Dubarry. His secretary reads you what is in his diary for this week. Listen and fill it in.*

Lundi
MATIN
APRÈS-MIDI

Mardi
MATIN
APRÈS-MIDI

Mercredi
MATIN
APRÈS-MIDI

Jeudi
MATIN
APRÈS-MIDI

Vendredi
MATIN
APRÈS-MIDI

RECORDING

6. **A vous!** *This is your diary. Tell M. Dubarry's secretary what is on your schedule and when you are free to meet him.*

Mon.		arrive at Ch. de Gaulle 14:55. Transfer to Hotel Bellevue
Tues.	A.M.	free
	P.M.	visit to Electofans, factory tour
Wed.	A.M.	meeting with technical services of Electofans
	P.M.	free
Thurs.	A.M.	presentation at Pub SA
	P.M.	free
Fri.	A.M.	appointment with MD Electofans
	P.M.	depart Ch. de Gaulle 15:45

Pronunciation

RECORDING

Now practice saying names, job titles, and some other useful telephone phrases after Sylvie and Jacques.

Pourrais-je parler au PDG, M. Gaston?

Pourrais-je parler à l'adjoint du PDG, Mme Hivet?

Vous pouvez me passer le chef du service marketing, M. Guinard?

Vous pouvez me passer le chef du service technique, M. Pinchon?

Je voudrais parler avec M. Lecuyer, le chef de la publicité.

Je voudrais parler avec le chef comptable, Mme Catillon.

Ne quittez pas.

Voulez-vous patienter?

Ma femme? Je vous la passe.

Mon mari? Je vous le passe.

Close-up

Direct object pronouns

me—*me*	nous—*us*
te—*you*	vous—*you*
le/la—*him/her*	les—*them*

Je vous le passe. *I am putting him through.*

Word order

You already know that reflexive pronouns come in front of the verb:

Je me lave.	*I wash myself.*
Vous vous levez.	*You get (yourself) up.*

Direct object pronouns also come in front of the verb:

me	Il m'entend.	*He can hear me.*
te	Je te comprends.	*I understand you.*
le/l'	Jean? Je le vois.	*Jean? I (can) see him.*
la/l'	La pomme? Tu l'as mangée?	*The apple? Did you eat it?*
nous	Il nous a invités.	*He invited us.*
vous	Il ne vous a pas invités.	*He didn't invite you.*
les	Les enfants? Ils les ont laissés à la maison.	*The kids? They left them at home.*

Notice that in the perfect tense, with avoir, the past participle agrees with the object pronoun. So you add **e** *if the pronoun is feminine,* **s** *if it is masculine plural, and* **es** *for the feminine plural. As the ending is not normally sounded in conversation you do not need to worry about it.*

M. Dubarry arrive

Mr. Dubarry is coming

Word Bank

les affaires	*belongings, "things"*
l'anorak *m.*	*anorak*
les baskets	*sneakers*
le chemisier	*blouse*
la casquette de base-ball	*baseball cap*
la chemise	*shirt*
le costume	*suit (for men)*
en costume cravate	*in a shirt and tie*
les gants	*gloves*
l'imperméable *m.*	*raincoat*
le manteau	*coat*
le motif	*pattern*
l'ordinateur portatif *m.*	*laptop*
le pantalon	*pants*
le parapluie	*umbrella*
le téléphone portable	*cell/mobile phone*
le porte-documents	*briefcase*
le sac	*bag*
le grand sac de sport	*carryall*
le tailleur	*suit (for women)*
environ	*about*
toujours	*always*
frisé(e)	*curly*
mince	*thin*
ondulé(e)	*wavy*
permanenté(e)	*permed*
raide	*straight*
organiser	*to organize*

RECORDING

1.

Listen to these descriptions and decide who you are meeting.

a. b. c. d.

Que puis-je dire?	*What can (should) I say?*
les couleurs vives	*bright colors*
sûr de soi	*sure of himself/self-confident*
à peu près	*about*
Il/elle sourit beaucoup.	*He/she smiles a lot.*
C'est facile de le/ la reconnaître.	*It is easy to recognize him/her.*
parce que	*because*
si grand(e)	*so tall*

RECORDING

2. **A vous!** *Sylvie is meeting these people. Describe them to her so that she can recognize them.*

Gordon Brown

Lucy Stockwell

RECORDING

3. *M. Dubarry has lost his things. Which are his? Listen and find out.*

lequel/laquelle/lesquels/lesquelles?
which one(s)?

celui-ci/celle-ci/ceux-ci/celles-ci
this one here/these ones here

celui-là/celle-là/ceux-là/celles-là
that one there/those ones there

Vous avez vraiment eu de la chance, monsieur!
You're in luck, sir! (lit: you have really had luck)

RECORDING

4. *Jacques is reading out the weather forecast for the day. Listen and draw a line to join each region to its appropriate weather conditions.*

Dans . . .		
le nord	il pleut et il y a du vent	*it's raining and windy*
le sud	il fait beau	*it's nice*
l'ouest	il y a du soleil/il fait chaud	*it's sunny/it's hot*
l'est	il fait froid	*it's cold*
les Alpes	il y a du brouillard	*it's foggy*
les Pyrénées	il neige	*it's snowing*
le Pas-de-Calais	il y a des orages	*there are storms*

Quel temps fait-il?

What's the weather like?

RECORDING

5. **A vous!** *Now you say what the weather is like in the States.*

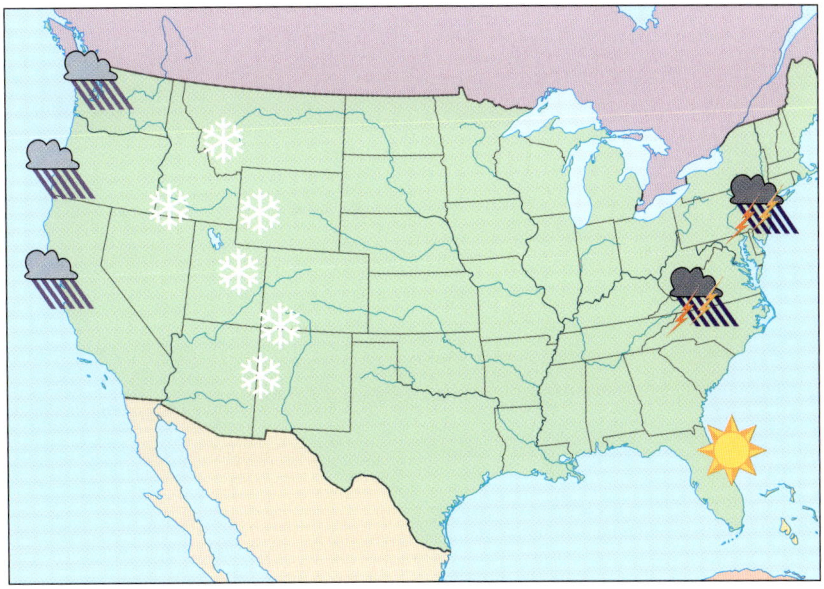

a. Dans le sud ________________________________.

b. Dans l'ouest ________________________________.

c. Dans l'est ________________________________.

d. Dans les Rocheuses ________________________________.

6. *Look at these pictures and decide what the weather is going to be like.*

a. *b.* *c.* *d.*

Quel temps fera-t-il?	*What is the weather going to be like?*
Il va faire ...	*It is going to be ...*
Il va pleuvoir/neiger.	*It is going to rain/snow.*
Il y aura ...	*There will be ...*

Pronunciation

RECORDING

Listen to Sylvie and Jacques talking about the weather and really try to copy their accents and intonation. Remember that **t** *and* **d** *at the end of the word are not pronounced.*

Quel temps fait-il?

il pleut

il y a du vent

il fait beau

il y a du soleil

il fait chaud

il fait froid

il y a du brouillard

il neige

il y a des orages

Quel temps fera-t-il?

il va pleuvoir

il y aura du vent

il va faire beau

il y aura du soleil

il va faire chaud

il va faire froid

il y aura du brouillard

il va neiger

il y aura des orages

Close-up

Describing people

Il est grand/petit/de taille moyenne.

He is tall/small/average.

Elle est grande/petite/de taille moyenne.

She is tall/short/average.

Il/elle a les cheveux longs/courts/mi-longs.

He/she has long/short/shoulder-length hair.

Il/elle a les cheveux raides/frisés/ondulés/permanentés/teints.

He/she has straight/curly/wavy/permed/colored hair.

Il/elle a les cheveux blonds/châtain/roux/bruns.

He/she has blonde/chestnut/red/dark brown hair.

Il/elle a les yeux bleus/marron/gris/bleu-gris.

He/she has blue/brown/grey/blue-grey eyes.

Il/elle porte ...

He/she is wearing/wears ...

Which one? This one/that one

These pronouns change to agree in number and gender with the nouns they replace.

	singular		*plural*	
	m.	*f.*	*m.*	*f.*
Which one?	Lequel?	Laquelle?	Lesquels?	Lesquelles?
This one/these	Celui-ci	Celle-ci	Ceux-ci	Celles-ci
That one/those	Celui-là	Celle-là	Ceux-là	Celles-là

L'argent

Money

Word Bank

la banque	*bank*
le billet (de cinq euros)	*(€5) bill*
le Chronopost	*express mail*
la commission	*commission, charge*
la devise	*currency*
le distributeur automatique	*ATM*
l'horodateur *m.*	*parking meter*
la monnaie	*change*
la pièce (d'un euro)	*(€1) coin*
la pièce d'identité	*identity card*
la carte bancaire	*banker's card*
la note	*hotel bill*
le taux de change	*exchange rate*
le traveller/le chèque de voyage	*traveler's check*
régler	*to settle (a bill)*

RECORDING

1. ***Listen to this conversation at the bank and number these sentences in the order in which you hear them.***

Deux cents dollars.

Bonjour madame. Je voudrais changer des chèques de voyage.

Dollars.

Il y a une commission à payer?

Pas pour les chèques de voyage.

RECORDING

2. **A vous!** *Now you try exchanging 500 dollars into euros. Complete the dialog and practice reading it aloud, then listen and answer the bank clerk's questions.*

Bank clerk: Bonjour monsieur/madame. Vous désirez?

You: (Say good morning, I'd like to change some traveler's checks.)

Bank clerk: Quelle devise?

You: (Dollars.)

Bank clerk: Combien?

You: (500.)

Bank clerk: Vous avez une pièce d'identité?

You: (Say yes, here it is.)

Bank clerk: Un instant. Bon, signez ici.

You: (Ask if there is a fee to pay.)

Bank clerk: Pas pour les chèques de voyage.
Au revoir monsieur/madame.

RECORDING

3. *Listen to these exchanges. Then, after each letter, tell how much money is needed.*

a. Pour une chambre?

b. Pour l'horodateur?

c. Pour une télécarte?

d. Pour acheter des timbres?

RECORDING

4. *Listen to these customers at the post office. What do they want? Put the number of the speaker beside each item.*

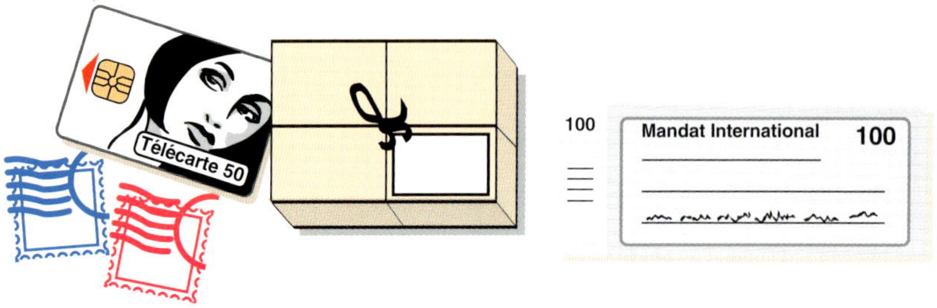

5. *For most French public telephones you need to have a* **Télécarte**, *which you can buy at a post office or newsstand. These are some of the instructions you may see. Match the phrases.*

a. Décrochez.	1. *Insert the card.*
b. Introduisez la carte.	2. *Lift receiver.*
c. Fermez le volet.	3. *Dial the number.*
d. Patientez SVP.	4. *Number dialed.*
e. Numérotez.	5. *Close the shutter.*
f. Numéro appelé.	6. *Wait, please.*

Pronunciation

RECORDING

Let's have more practice at pronouncing some useful words and phrases. Listen and repeat after Jacques and Sylvie.

une carte bancaire	**J'ai perdu ma carte bancaire.**
un chèque de voyage	**Je veux changer un chèque de voyage.**
un chèque bancaire	**Vous prenez les chèques bancaires?**

Here's a useful phrase:

Où est-ceque je peux changer de l'argent? *Where can I change some money?*

Now you are all set for your visit to France. **Au revoir et bon voyage!**

Close-up

Here are some more useful words and phrases you might see on machines.

Distributeur de billets

ATM

Faites l'appoint.

Put in the exact change.

L'appareil ne rend pas la monnaie.

No change given.

Appuyez sur le bouton.

Press the button.

Attendez.

Wait.

Tapez le code (du parking).

Key in the code (for the car park).

Poussez.

Push.

Tirez.

Pull.

Checkpoints

Use the check list to test what you've learned in this unit and review anything you're not sure of.

Can you ... ?	***Yes***	***No***
• *ask to speak to the CEO M. Dumas* Pourrais-je parler au PDG, M. Dumas?	❑	❑
• *ask to speak to his assistant* ou à son adjoint(e)	❑	❑
• *ask for extension number 27* poste 27	❑	❑
• *say who you are and spell your name* C'est de la part de ...	❑	❑
• *ask if you can leave a message* Je peux laisser un message?	❑	❑
• *suggest a meeting for Tuesday at 11:00* Je vous propose un rendez-vous mardi à onze heures.	❑	❑
• *say you are busy/free* Je suis pris(e)/libre.	❑	❑
• *say you will be in a meeting Tuesday morning* Mardi matin, je suis en réunion.	❑	❑
• *describe someone so they can be recognized* Il est grand/elle est petite. Il a les cheveux longs et blonds et porte un jean et des baskets. Elle a les cheveux marron courts et porte un tailleur rouge.	❑	❑
• *say you have lost your umbrella* J'ai perdu mon parapluie.	❑	❑
• *ask what the weather is like* Quel temps fait-il?	❑	❑
• *describe the weather* Il fait beau mais il va pleuvoir et il y aura des orages.	❑	❑

Can you ... ?	*Yes*	*No*
• *talk about money*	❑	❑

Je voudrais changer un traveller.
Je voudrais changer des dollars.
Je voudrais régler ma note.
Excusez-moi. Avez-vous de la monnaie?
une pièce de deux euros
un billet de dix euros

Learning tips

Think of all the things you have said in your own language in the last few hours. How many of them were questions? Probably most of them! Now think of yourself arriving in France or another French-speaking country. What are you going to want to say? Where is the ...? Do you have a ...? How do I get to ...? How do you do? Have you been waiting long? Would you like a drink? What time is it? When ...? Imagine that you have just arrived and decide whether you are there as a tourist, on business, or to visit a friend or colleague. Make a list of ten questions you are going to need and practice them until you are really fluent.

Do you want to learn more?

Look up the French names of the items around your home or office in a dictionary. Then write out name tags in French and attach them to the items. Self-adhesive notes are ideal for this, as they are easy to peel off.

For more practice, see Extra! on page A5.

Unit 5 is about your home. You will become familiar with the language you need to know in order to:

- say where it is
- say what it is like and how long you have lived there
- and what rooms there are

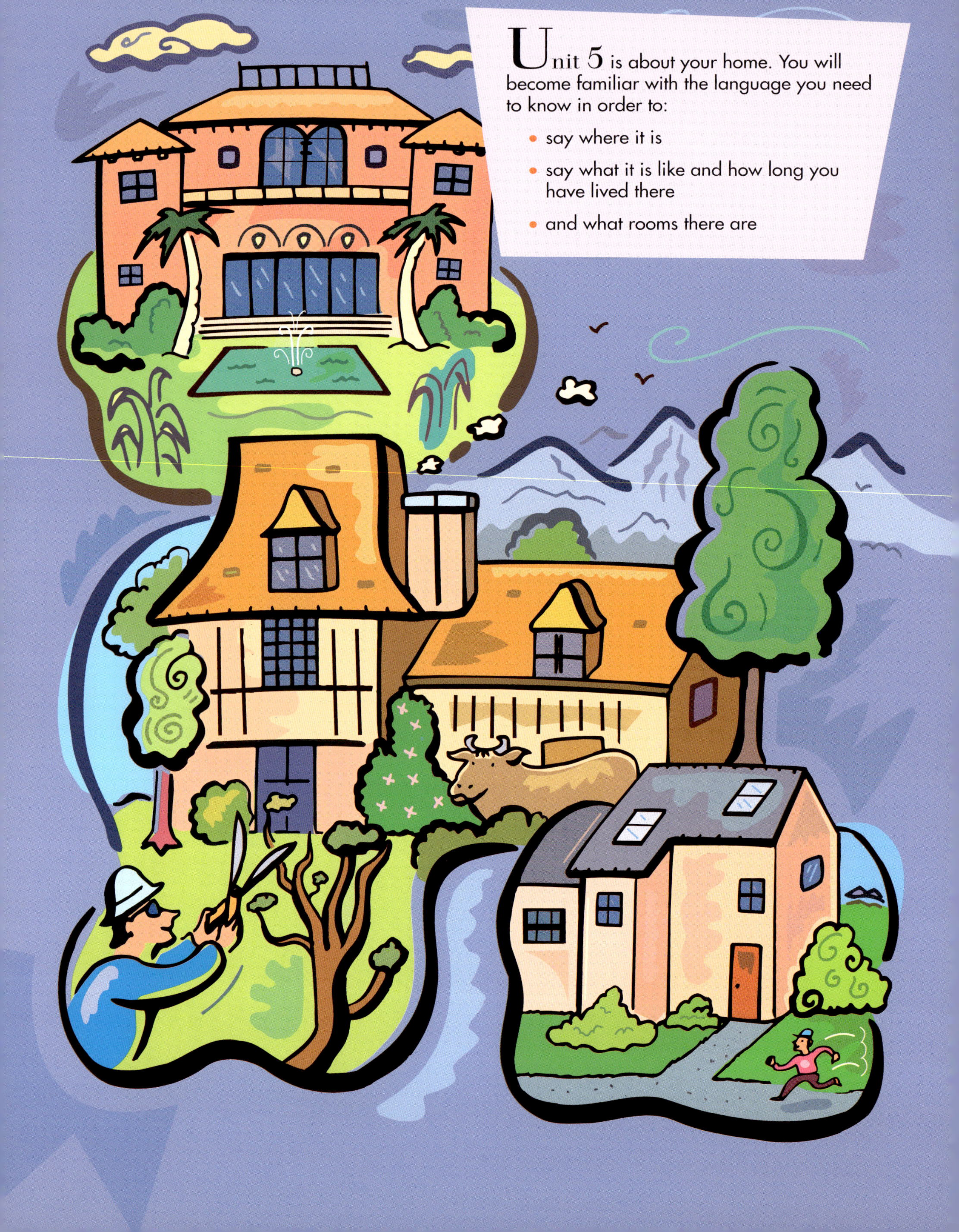

Chez moi

5

Word Bank

la banlieue	*suburbs*	beau/belle	*nice, beautiful*
le centre	*center*	près de	*near (to)*
la grande surface	*large store*	loin de	*far (from)*
l'hypermarché *m.*	*large supermarket*	à côté de	*beside*
le marché	*market*	en face de	*opposite*
le quartier	*neighborhood*	entre	*between*
la ville	*town*	à deux minutes de	*two minutes from*
le supermarché	*supermarket*	écouter	*to listen*
ancien/ne	*very old*		

Chez moi

My home

RECORDING

1. *Listen to these people talking about where they live.*

Où habitez-vous?	*Where do you live?*
chez moi	*at my house*
au centre-ville	*in town*
en banlieue	*in the suburbs*
près du centre-ville	*near the center of town*
à la campagne	*in the country*
dans un village	*in a village*

RECORDING

2. *Listen to these young men saying where their houses are and choose the phrase that is most appropriate for each.*

C'est en face de l'église.	*It's opposite the church.*
C'est près de la poste.	*It's near the post office.*
C'est à côté de la pharmacie.	*It's next to the drugstore.*
C'est à deux minutes du supermarché.	*It's two minutes from the supermarket.*
C'est entre la banque et la boulangerie.	*It's between the bank and the bakery.*
C'est où exactement?	*Where exactly is it?*

3. **A vous!** *Now can you say where these houses are?*

a.

b.

c.

RECORDING

4. *Now listen to find out whether these men like living where they do and what reasons they give. Match the speaker with the appropriate phrase.*

C'est comment?
What is it like?

a. C'est un quartier très calme.	*It's a very quiet neighborhood.*
b. Il y a du monde.	*There are a lot of people.*
c. C'est bruyant. Il y a beaucoup de circulation.	*It's noisy. There's a lot of traffic.*
d. C'est un petit hameau ancien.	*It's a little old hamlet.*
e. Il y a de belles propriétés.	*There are some beautiful houses.*

RECORDING

5. *Listen to find out how they get to the shops. Match the speaker with the appropriate method of transportation.*

a. On prend le bus.

b. On y va à pied.

c. J'y vais en voiture.

d. J'y vais à bicyclette.

Pronunciation

RECORDING

Listen and repeat the phrases after Jacques. Would you recognize the places or neighborhoods if someone said them to you in those phrases? Listen again and check.

Now repeat these questions.

Où habitez-vous?

C'est où exactement?

C'est comment?

Pour aller en ville?

Close-up

Notice how these words and expressions are followed by **de** *(of):*

près de	*near to*
loin de	*far from*
à côté de	*beside*
en face de	*opposite*
à deux minutes de	*two minutes from*

Rappel!

	m.	*f.*	*pl.*
(de + le) =	du	de la	(de + les) = des
	de l'	de l'	

Some place names which include **le**, **la**, *or* **les** *also follow this rule:*

J'habite près du Havre. *I live near Le Havre.*
C'est loin du Mans. *It's far from Le Mans.*

Val-Thorens est à côté des Menuires.
Val-Thorens is next to Les Menuires.

C'est près de La Haye. *It's near the Hague.*

C'est à deux minutes des Halles.
It's two minutes from Les Halles.

C'est en face du Mont-Blanc. *It's opposite Mont Blanc.*

Ma maison

My house

Word Bank

l'appartement *m.*	*apartment*	le jour	*day*
l'immeuble *m.*	*apartment building*	le mois	*month*
le jardin	*garden/yard*	la semaine	*week*
le lotissement	*housing development*	joli/e	*pretty*
la maison	*house*	moderne	*modern*
le pavillon	*detached house*	vieux/vieille	*old*
l'an *m.*	*year*		

RECORDING

1. ***Listen and find out who lives in which house. Match the picture with the number of the speaker.***

a.

b.

c.

d.

e.

RECORDING 2.

What are the houses like? Listen to find out.

Rappel!

assez *quite* très *very*

RECORDING 3.

Listen to find out which floor these people live on.
Draw a line from each person to the appropriate floor.

M. and Mme Dubois
Mlle Fourrier
M. Simon
La famille Bourjeout
Jacqueline
La famille Bertrand
Nicolas
le lapin de Nicolas

au rez-de-chaussée	*on the ground floor*
au premier étage*	*on the 1st floor*
au deuxième étage	*on the 2nd floor*
au troisième	*on the 3rd*
au quatrième	*on the 4th*
au cinquième	*on the 5th*
au sixième	*on the 6th*
au septième	*on the 7th*
au huitième	*on the 8th*
dernier/dernière	*last*
dans le grenier	*in the attic*
au sous-sol	*in the basement (lit: below ground)*

*Unlike the United States, in France, the first floor is the level above the ground floor.

RECORDING

4. *How long have they been living there? Listen and find out.*

Vous habitez ici depuis combien de temps?
How long have you lived here?

Vous y habitez depuis combien de temps?
How long have you lived there?

depuis	*since/for*
depuis un mois	*for a month*
depuis deux ans	*for two years*

RECORDING

5. **A vous!** *Now it's your turn to say where you live. First answer Sylvie's questions, then practice asking them yourself.*

Où habitez-vous?	J'habite ...
C'est quelle sorte de maison?	C'est ...

Vous y habitez depuis combien de temps?
J'y habite depuis ...

Pronunciation

RECORDING

The letter "h" at the beginning of a word is not pronounced. Listen and repeat these words and phrases after Sylvie.

l'hôtel

Pour aller à l'hôtel, s'il vous plaît?

l'hôpital

L'hôpital est tout près.

J'habite à Tokyo et j'y habite depuis deux ans.

Mon frère habite à La Haye, en Hollande.

Ma sœur habite au Havre, en France.

Close-up

Rappel! *All nouns are masculine or feminine. Adjectives used with feminine nouns mostly add* **e**:

m.	*f.*
grand	grande
joli	jolie
petit	petite

Irregular adjectives

Some adjectives have different endings for the feminine:

m.	*f.*
ancien	ancienne
beau	belle
blanc	blanche
vieux	vieille

L'appartement est grand/petit/vieux/ancien/beau/joli

La maison est grande/petite/vieille/ancienne/belle/jolie

Depuis

In French when you are talking about how long you have been doing something you use **depuis** *(since/for) and the PRESENT tense:*

J'habite ici depuis cinq ans
I have been living here for five years.

J'apprends le français depuis deux mois.
I have been learning French for two months.

Je sors avec lui depuis l'année dernière.
I have been going out with him since last year.

À la maison

At home

Word Bank

l'armoire *f.*	*wardrobe*
l'ascenseur *m.*	*elevator*
la baignoire	*bathtub*
le balcon	*balcony*
le canapé	*sofa*
la chambre	*bedroom*
la commode	*chest of drawers*
la cuisine	*kitchen*
la cuisinière	*stove*
la douche	*shower*
l'emplacement *m.*	*space, spot*
l'entrée *f.*	*entrance*
l'escalier *m.*	*stairs*
le fauteuil	*armchair*
la fenêtre	*window*
le frigidaire/frigo	*fridge*
le garage	*garage*
le lave-vaisselle	*dishwasher*
le lit	*bed*
la machine à laver	*washing machine*
les meubles	*furniture*
le miroir	*mirror*
les petites annonces	*classifieds*
la pièce	*room*
la porte	*door*
la rivière	*stream*
la salle	*room*
la salle de bains	*bathroom*
le salon	*sitting room*
la salle de séjour	*living room*
la salle à manger	*dining room*
les toilettes	*toilet/bathroom*
la vue	*view*
chaque	*each*
acheter	*to buy*
donner	*to give*
donner sur	*to look on to*
faire une liste	*to make a list*

RECORDING

1.

Listen to find out who lives where. Put the right number by each floorplan.

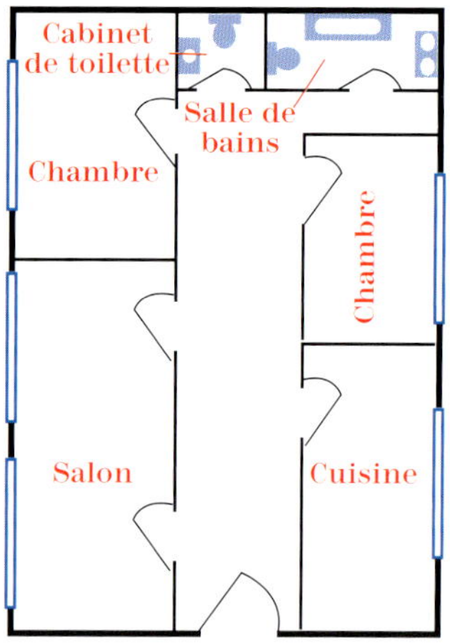

a.

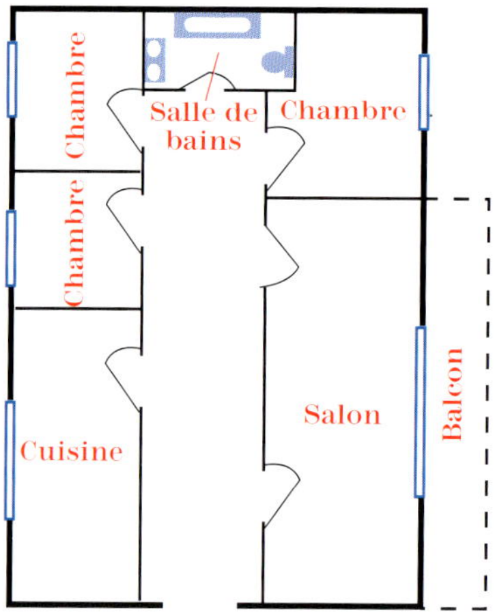

b.

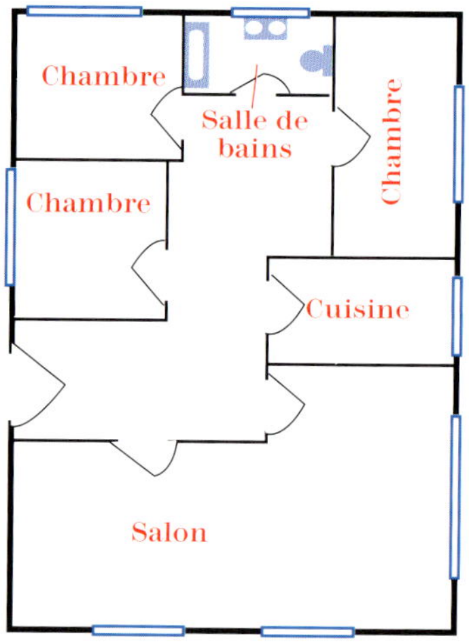

c.

RECORDING

2.

Jacques and Sylvie are apartment-hunting together. Listen and check the things they say they need, then write in the number of bedrooms they want.

à louer	*for rent*
Qu'est-ce qu'il leur faut?	*What do they need?*
Ça suffit.	*That's enough.*
C'est trop cher.	*It's too expensive.*
Moi aussi.	*Me too.*
Ah non, ça alors!	*Certainly not!*

Did You Know?

When talking about their houses the French often say how many rooms they have (excluding the bathroom and kitchen), so **un trois pièces** would have two bedrooms and a living room, **un quatre pièces** would have three bedrooms and a sitting room, and so on.

3. *Read these ads and see how many words you know.*

L'ISLE ADAM
Maison 4 chbres, s. à manger, salon avec cheminée, cuis. et salle de bains équipées, gar., 1.700m2 clos, €380.000
Part. tél

Appartements
Maisons
ventes, province

VILLA A HYERES

33 Bord estuaire Gironde
Girondine restaurée
150m2, jard., gar., ponton
16/57.46.16.00

Offres vides 3e

St MARTIN
PRES BEAUBOURG
A LOUER
4P. s/cour, 90m2, refait neuf, 2e ét. asc., cave.
€1650 + €40 ch part.
(1)45.27.50.34 répondeur

2PIÈCES 45 M^2
PROX M° BALARD
44.19.62.62

-METRO CRIMEE-
4P. 74 M2 - €212.000

TOULON
Quartier résidentiel, bord de mer. Part. vend magnifique F4, gd séjour/s. à manger, 2 chbres, co-ppté gd stand. avec parc arboré et piscine, €280.000

RECORDING

4. *Now you are being shown around the apartment. Listen and write down which room you are being shown by the real estate agent.*

Il y a de la place pour ...
There is room for ...

RECORDING

5. *Listen and check the items of furniture that Jacques and Sylvie still need to buy.*

Il y avait ...	*There was ...*
Il n'y avait pas de ...	*There wasn't a ...*
Tu es sûr(e)?	*Are you sure?*
J'en suis sûr(e).	*I am sure (of it).*
Il y en avait un(e).	*There was one (of them).*
Ça suffit pour le moment.	*That's enough for the moment.*

Pronunciation

RECORDING

The accent circonflexe is often used over a vowel which would be followed by an "s" in related words in English. Listen and repeat these phrases.

août *(August)*

Les vacances sont au mois d'août.

arrêt *(stop)*

Où est l'arrêt d'autobus?

château *(castle)*

Le château de Versailles est très beau.

fête *(feast/festival)*

Bonne fête!

île *(isle)*

On fait une excursion aux îles d'Hyères.

Close-up

Il faut

We have already come across the expression **il faut**, *meaning it is necessary:*

Il faut aller en ville pour trouver un hôtel.

Il faut *can also be used to say you need something:*

Il me faut un stylo à bille.	*I need a ballpoint pen. (lit: it is necessary to me)*
Il te faut un fauteuil.	*You need an armchair. (lit: to you)*
Il lui faut un plan de la ville.	*He/she needs a town map. (lit: to him/her)*
Il nous faut un frigidaire.	*We need a fridge. (lit: to us)*
Il vous faut un billet.	*You need a ticket. (lit: to you)*
Il leur faut un horaire des trains.	*They need a train schedule. (lit: to them)*

En

When you say "I have one" in French you must add **en** *(of it, of them) in front of the verb:*

Avez-vous des crayons?	Oui, j'en ai un.
Do you have any pencils?	*Yes, I have one (of them).*
Est-ce qu'il y a une table?	Oui, il y en a une.
Is there a table?	*Yes, there is one (of them).*

Different ways of saying "yes"

oui	*yes*
oui, d'accord	*yes, I agree (lit: agreed)*
si*	*yes, I do*

***Si** *is used after negative questions:*

Vous ne voulez pas le frigo?	Si.
You don't want the fridge?	*Yes, I do.*

Rappel! De *after the negative:*

Il y a ...	*There is/are ...*
Il n'y a pas de ...	*There isn't/aren't (a/any) ...*

Checkpoints

Use the check list to test what you've learned in this unit and review anything you're not sure of.

Can you ... ?	***Yes***	***No***
• *say where you live*	❑	❑
• *say where something is*	❑	❑
• *say you live in a house/apartment*	❑	❑
• *say on which floor someone lives*	❑	❑
• *say you have lived there (two) years*	❑	❑
• *say the house is nice*	❑	❑
• *say there is*	❑	❑

- *say where you live* . . . . ❑ . . . . . . ❑

  J'habite en ville.

  J'habite à la campagne.

- *say where something is* . . . . ❑ . . . . . . ❑

  C'est en face de l'église.

  C'est près de la poste.

  C'est à côté de la pharmacie.

  C'est à deux minutes du supermarché.

  C'est entre la banque et la boulangerie.

- *say you live in a house/apartment* . . . . ❑ . . . . . . ❑

  J'habite dans une maison/un appartement.

- *say on which floor someone lives* . . . . ❑ . . . . . . ❑

  Il/elle habite au rez-de-chaussée.

  Il/elle habite au premier étage.

- *say you have lived there (two) years* . . . . ❑ . . . . . . ❑

  J'y habite depuis (deux) ans.

- *say the house is nice* . . . . ❑ . . . . . . ❑

  La maison est belle.

- *say there is* . . . . ❑ . . . . . . ❑

  Il y a une cuisine et une salle de bains.

  Il y a un salon/une salle de séjour.

  Il y a trois chambres.

  Mais il n'y a pas de salle à manger.

  Il y a un frigo.

  Mais il n'y a pas de lit.

Learning tips

Creating "associations" often helps you to remember new words:

chambre	*chamber*
jour	*journal (daily paper)*
an/année	*annual*
lit	*litter (a "carrying bed" or a lot of puppies asleep!)*
maison	*mansion*

Can you think of some more to help with these words?

dormir	*to sleep*
premier	*first*
ville	*town*
fille	*girl*

Do you want to learn more?

When you look up a word in a French-English dictionary, make sure to read all the meanings. A single word, depending on its context, will have several different meanings. So when you want to say something in French, think of how you're going to use the word you need to look up, then check the various usages listed.

For more practice, see Extra! on page A8.

Unit 6 is about long-distance travel using public and private transportation. After completing this unit you will be able to:

- talk about a trip you have taken and arrange to rent a car
- make arrangements to travel by train
- get around with your own or a rental car

En voyage

6

Word Bank

l'arrivée *f.*	*arrival*	le réseau	*network*
l'assurance *f.*	*insurance*	la route	*the road*
l'avion *m.*	*plane*	le supplément	*supplement*
le billet	*ticket*	le train	*train*
le car	*long-distance bus*	compris(e)	*included*
le départ	*departure*	de bonne heure	*early*
la durée	*length of time*	en retard	*late*
le guichet	*ticket office*	avec une demi-heure de retard	*half an hour late*
les heures de pointe	*peak times (rush hour)*	souvent	*often*
le permis de conduire	*driver's license*	conduire	*to drive*
la pièce d'identité	*identity card*	*venir	*to come*

Arrivée en France

Arriving in France

RECORDING

1. *Some people you met on vacation in Cannes are telling you how they got there. Listen to find out what method of transport they used, then write down the time taken for each trip. Notice the use of the perfect tense to say when they arrived.*

	en train	en car	en moto	en voiture	en avion
Durée	______ heures	______ heures	______ heures	______ jours	______ jours

Il y a (une heure/deux jours).
(An hour/two days) ago.

RECORDING

2. *Listen to find out when they left and when they arrived in Cannes.*

	Départ	Arrivée
mercredi	______ heures	______ heures
jeudi	______ heures	______ heures
vendredi	______ heures	______ heures
samedi	______ heures	______ heures
aujourd'hui	______ heures	______ heures

DidYouKnow?

Beaune *is a historic town in the Bourgogne region famous for its red wine.* **Avignon** *is a medieval town in Provence which was once the seat of the Pope.* **Grenoble** *is a historic town centrally situated in the Alps.* **La route Napoléon** *is the route across the southern Alps used by Napoleon on his return from exile. The* **TGV (train à grande vitesse)** *is a very fast express train, for which seats have to be reserved in advance.*

RECORDING 3.

A vous! *Now it's your turn to tell your French friends about your trip. Prepare what you would say using the perfect tense, then practice saying it aloud. Listen to check your answers.*

a. Je suis venu(e) ...

b. Je suis parti(e) ...

c. Je suis arrivé(e) ...

New York	dép.	mardi 18.00
Paris Roissy	arr.	mercredi 7.00
Paris Gare de Lyon	dép.	vendredi 14.45
Lyon Perrache	arr.	vendredi 17.15
Lyon Perrache	dép.	dimanche 11.15
Cannes	arr.	dimanche 14.15

RECORDING 4.

Simon has just flown in from New York to Paris Charles-de-Gaulle. At the information desk, what methods of transport is he advised to take to get to downtown Paris? What are the advantages and disadvantages of each? Listen to find out.

Métro RER Roissy bus Taxi

DidYouKnow?

Most overseas flights to Paris arrive at **Charles-de-Gaulle** *airport at Roissy, situated to the north of the city and named after the leader of the French resistance who became the first French President at the end of the second world war. Other Paris airports include* **Orly** *and* **Le Bourget**.

*Before boarding a bus or train, you have to buy your ticket from the ticket office—***le guichet***—or from an automatic dispenser and stamp it in one of the validating machines. If you plan to do a lot of traveling by public transport, inquire about special reductions or tourist passes.*

RECORDING 5.

This person wants to rent a car. Listen and answer the questions.

a. What sort of car does she want?

b. For how many people?

c. For how long?

d. What does the agent ask for?

e. What does she have to pay extra for?

f. How does she pay?

g. Where is the car?

RECORDING

6. **A vous!** *Now you practice renting a car. Listen and be prepared to answer the questions!*

You: *(Say you want to rent a car.)*

Clerk: Quelle sorte de voiture?

You: *(You want a big one for four people.)*

Clerk: Pour combien de jours?

You: *(A week.)*

Clerk: Vous avez votre pièce d'identité et votre permis de conduire?

You: *(Say yes, here they are.)*

Clerk: Vous payez comment?

You: *(Ask if he takes Master Card.)*

Clerk: Oui, bien sûr.

You: *(Ask him if he has a map of the town.)*

Clerk: Oui, les voilà.

You: *(He's forgotten to tell you where the car is. Better ask.)*

Clerk: Oh, excusez-moi, c'est dans le parking là-bas, emplacement A5.

Pronunciation

RECORDING

Repeat the parts of the verb **venir** *in the present tense.*

Now practice the perfect tense.

Je suis venu(e) en train.

Tu es venu(e) en avion.

Il est venu en moto.

Elle est venue à pied.

Nous sommes venu(e)s à deux.

Vous êtes venu(e)(s) mercredi?

Ils sont venus en voiture.

Elles sont venues en car.

Close-up

Venir

Present tense

*venir—*to come*

je viens	nous venons
tu viens	vous venez
il vient	ils viennent
elle vient	elles viennent

Perfect tense

je suis venu(e)	nous sommes venu(e)s
tu es venu(e)	vous êtes venu(e)(s)
il est venu	ils sont venus
elle est venue	elles sont venues

on est venu(e) *we came*

On prend le train

We're taking the train

Word Bank

la gare	*station*
le quai	*platform*
un aller-retour	*a round-trip ticket*
un aller simple	*a one-way ticket*
après-demain	*the day after tomorrow*
prochain(e)	*next*
composter	*to validate a ticket*
rater	*to miss*

RECORDING

1. ***Listen to this woman giving information about train times and write them in.***

	train 1	*train 2*	*train 3*
a. Lyon			
b. Caen			
c. Nice			
d. Lille			
e. Nantes			

Le train part à quelle heure?	*What time does the train leave?*
Il faut changer.	*You have to change.*
Il y en a un autre.	*There is another (train).*
trop tôt	*too early*
attendez	*just a moment (lit: wait)*

RECORDING
2.

Listen to these conversations to find out: a. which train these people choose; b. which platform it leaves from; c. when it gets in; and d. whether they have to change. Fill in the table.

Destination	départ	quai	changement à	arrivée
Lyon				
Caen				
Nice				
Lille				
Nantes				

Le train pour Caen part de quel quai?	*Which platform does the Caen train leave from?*
Vous savez?	*Do you know?*
Je regrette.	*I'm sorry.*
Vous l'avez raté.	*You've missed it.*
Vous pouvez ...	*You can ...*

RECORDING
3.

A vous! *How much does each passenger pay and where are they going?*

Ticket Price	Destination
1. € ________	________________
2. € ________	________________
3. € ________	________________

DidYouKnow?

To book a ticket in France you can use **Minitel**, a public service database that is accessed through the home telephone. Alternatively you can use **Socrate**, a program available on automatic ticket machines at most mainline stations.

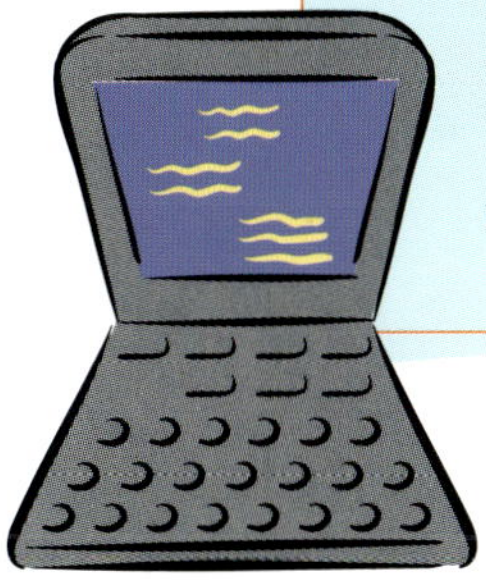

RECORDING

4.

Which tickets are these people buying? Listen and put the right number by each ticket.

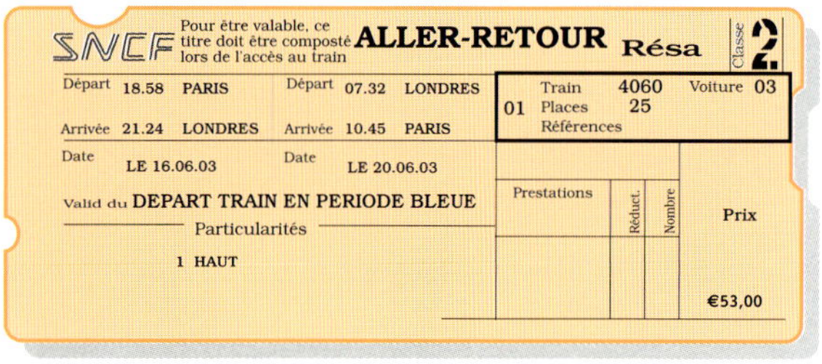
SNCF Pour être valable, ce titre doit être composté lors de l'accès au train ALLER-RETOUR Résa Classe 2
Départ 18.58 PARIS Départ 07.32 LONDRES
Arrivée 21.24 LONDRES Arrivée 10.45 PARIS
Train 4060 Voiture 03
01 Places 25
Références
Date LE 16.06.03 Date LE 20.06.03
Valid du DEPART TRAIN EN PERIODE BLEUE
Particularités
1 HAUT
Prestations Réduct. Nombre Prix
€53,00

a.

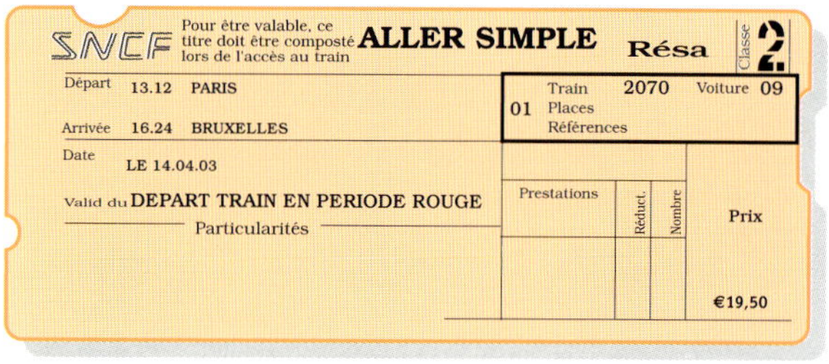
SNCF Pour être valable, ce titre doit être composté lors de l'accès au train ALLER SIMPLE Résa Classe 2
Départ 13.12 PARIS
Arrivée 16.24 BRUXELLES
Train 2070 Voiture 09
01 Places
Références
Date LE 14.04.03
Valid du DEPART TRAIN EN PERIODE ROUGE
Particularités
Prestations Réduct. Nombre Prix
€19,50

b.

SNCF Pour être valable, ce titre doit être composté lors de l'accès au train ALLER-RETOUR Résa Classe 1
Départ 20.30 PARIS Départ 10.23 CANNES
Arrivée 07.41 CANNES Arrivée 23.39 PARIS
Train 5061 Voiture 07
01 Places 65
Références
Date LE 10.04.03 Date LE 24.04.03
Valid du DEPART TRAIN EN PERIODE BLANCHE
Particularités
1 HAUT
Prestations Réduct. Nombre Prix
COUCHETTE 00 01
ENFANT 02 01
€89,60

c.

SNCF Pour être valable, ce titre doit être composté lors de l'accès au train ALLER-RETOUR Résa Classe 1
Départ 20.30 PARIS Départ 10.23 CANNES
Arrivée 07.41 CANNES Arrivée 23.39 PARIS
Train 5061 Voiture 07
01 Places 65
Références
Date LE 10.04.03 Date LE 24.04.03
Valid du DEPART TRAIN EN PERIODE BLANCHE
Particularités
1 HAUT
Prestations Réduct. Nombre Prix
COUCHETTE 00 01
ADULTE 00 01
€179,00

d.

RECORDING

5.

A vous! *Practice what you would say to buy a round-trip ticket to London. Listen and answer the ticket officer's questions.*

Ticket officer: Bonjour monsieur/madame.

You: *(Say good morning.)*

Ticket officer: Vous désirez?

You: *(Say you want to go to London, a round-trip ticket.)*

Ticket officer: Vous devez réserver. Vous voulez en première ou deuxième classe?

You: *(First class.)*

Ticket officer: Fumeur ou non fumeur?

You: *(Non-smoking.)*

Ticket officer: Vous voulez partir quand?

You: *(Tomorrow evening.)*

Ticket officer: Demain soir.

RECORDING

6.

There's been a delay. Listen and check how late the trains are.

ARRIVEE Paris–Gare de Lyon

En provenance de

Lyon	19.45	________
Marseille	20.32	________
Dijon	20.56	________

Le train a du retard.	*The train is late.*
en provenance de	*from*
être retardé	*to be delayed*

RECORDING

7.

You're going to be late arriving from Dijon. You'd better phone the hotel to let them know when you are due to get in—fortunately there is a phone on the train. Make sure you have your **carte de téléphone***!*

Mme Ribault à l'appareil.	*Mme Ribault speaking.*
de	*from*
A ce soir!	*See you this evening.*

Pronunciation

RECORDING

First practice repeating the future tense of **arriver** *and* **aller** *after Sylvie, then repeat these phrases after Jacques.*

J'arriverai lundi.
Tu arriveras à quelle heure?

Il arrivera après moi.
Elle arrivera en retard.

Nous arriverons à la gare du Nord.
Vous arriverez à la place de la République.

Ils arriveront après-demain.
Elles arriveront de bonne heure.

Now make up your own phrases to use with the future tense of **aller** *and practice saying them aloud.*

J'irai	**Nous irons**
Tu iras	**Vous irez**
Il ira	**Ils iront**
Elle ira	**Elles iront**

Close-up

To say at what time you use **à**:

Le train part à onze heures dix et arrive à quatorze heures vingt.
The train leaves at 11:10 and arrives at 14:20.

À quelle heure? *At what time?*

The future tense

Sylvie uses the future tense to say when she will arrive:

J'ai du retard. J'arriverai à midi. *I am late. I will arrive at noon.*

Sylvie a du retard. Elle arrivera vers huit heures.
Sylvie is late. She will arrive about eight.

Le train a du retard. Il arrivera avec une demi-heure de retard.
The train is late. It will arrive about half an hour late.

In the future tense the endings are regular for all verbs. To form the future you add the endings to the infinitive of the verb.

arriver—*to arrive*

j'arriverai	nous arriverons
tu arriveras	vous arriverez
il arrivera	ils arriveront
elle arrivera	elles arriveront

Some irregular verbs have a stem change.

aller—*to go (stem changes to* ir*)*

j'irai	nous irons
tu iras	vous irez
il ira	ils iront
elle ira	elles iront

*You are unlikely to need to use the future tense as much as the near future. The near future (*futur proche*) is used more in conversation to talk about future events. However, you should be able to recognize it.*

The other most common irregular verbs are:

avoir—*to have*	j'aurai
faire—*to do/make*	je ferai
venir—*to come*	je viendrai
être—*to be*	je serai
pouvoir—*to be able*	je pourrai
voir—*to see*	je verrai

En voiture

Traveling by car

Word Bank

l'agglomération *f.*	*built-up area*	le rond-point	*rotary, traffic circle*
l'aire de repos *f.*	*unsupervised rest area (usually with toilets and picnic tables)*	la route nationale	*main road*
l'autoroute *f.*	*highway*	la route départementale	*minor road*
le bouchon	*traffic jam (lit: cork)*	la station-service	*gas station (with shop and refreshments or restaurant)*
le carrefour	*intersection*	la voie	*(traffic) lane*
les clignotants	*blinkers (turn signals)*	arrêter	*to stop*
les embouteillages	*traffic jam (lit: bottlenecks)*	céder (le passage)	*to yield*
les feux	*traffic lights*	doubler	*to pass*
la limite de vitesse	*speed limit*	mettre (les clignotants)	*to switch on (the turn signals)*
le panneau	*road sign*	payer	*to pay*
le péage	*toll*	ralentir	*to slow down*
la place	*square*	rouler	*to drive (lit: to roll)*
le pont	*bridge*	suivre	*to follow*

RECORDING

1. *Listen to the advice these people are being given and trace their routes on the highways.*

RECORDING

2. *These visitors want to know the way to the local supermarket. Listen and choose the right sketch.*

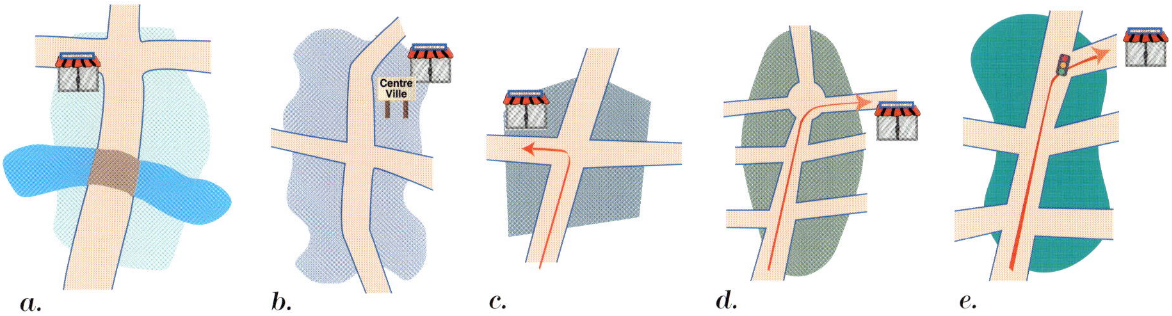

a. b. c. d. e.

RECORDING
3.

A vous! *Now it's your turn to give Sylvie the same directions.*

Allez ...	*Go ...*
Continuez ...	*Continue ...*
Prenez ...	*Take ...*
Suivez ...	*Follow ...*
Tournez ...	*Turn ...*

RECORDING
4.

Listen and write down what the speed limits are.

a. Sur les autoroutes, c'est ________________ kilomètres à l'heure.

b. Sur les routes à 4 voies, c'est ________________ kilomètres à l'heure.

c. Sur les autres routes, les routes nationales et les départementales, c'est ________________ kilomètres à l'heure.

d. En ville et en agglomération, c'est ________________ kilomètres à l'heure.

RECORDING
5.

Anne-Laure is learning to drive. What is her instructor telling her to do?

Mais non!	*No!*
Dis donc!	*Look (here)! Hey!*
Ah, voilà!	*Ah, there you are/that's it.*
Zut alors!	*Damn!*
Allez-y.	*Go on.*
Ça va déjà mieux.	*That's (already) better.*

Did You Know?

Highways in France are called **autoroutes** *and drivers have to pay to use most of them. A warning sign,* **Péage,** *indicates when you are entering the paying part of the system. You are normally instructed to take a ticket (***prenez un billet***) on entering and to pay at the* **Péage** *on leaving the highway.*

*Highway numbers are preceded by A (***Autoroute***) and highway signs are blue. The numbers of main roads are preceded by N (***Nationale***) and minor road numbers by D (***Départementale***). You may see a route marked by a green* **Itinéraire: Bis** *or* **Itinéraire du Bison Futé** *sign. This indicates an alternative route avoiding highways and built-up areas. The signs are often accompanied by a picture of a bison (***bison futé** *means the cunning bison).*

RECORDING

6. **A vous!** *Now you tell Sylvie to do the same things, without the expletives!*

7. *What do you think these signs mean? Pair up the words with the appropriate sign.*

a.

b.

c.

d.

e.

f.

g.

Cédez le passage *(Yield)*
Virages dangereux *(Dangerous curves)*
Passage piétons *(Pedestrian crossing)*
Passage à niveau *(Railroad crossing)*
Chanssée glissante *(Slippery)*
Rétrécissement *(Road narrows)*
Travaux *(Work zone)*

Pronunciation

RECORDING

Listen and practice giving the commands in the Close-up.

Close-up

Giving orders

Infinitive	**Vouvoyer** *(using the* **vous** *form)*
arrêter	Arrêtez au feu rouge.
céder	Cédez le passage.
continuer	Continuez tout droit.
doubler	Doublez.
prendre	Prenez la deuxième rue à gauche.
ralentir	Ralentissez.
rouler	Roulez moins vite.
tourner	Tournez à droite.

Checkpoints

Use the check list to test what you've learned in this unit and review anything you're not sure of.

Can you ... ?	*Yes*	*No*
• *say how you traveled* Je suis venu(e) en avion. Je suis venu(e) en train. Je suis venu(e) en voiture.	❑	❑
• *say you left (15:00 Tuesday)* Je suis parti(e) (mardi à 15 heures)	❑	❑
• *say you arrived (19:00 Wednesday)* Je suis arrivé(e) (mercredi à 19 heures)	❑	❑
• *say you want to rent a car* Je veux louer une voiture.	❑	❑
• *say for two people* Pour deux personnes.	❑	❑
• *ask if you can pay by credit card* Je peux payer avec une carte de crédit?	❑	❑
• *ask when the train to Paris leaves* Le train pour Paris part à quelle heure?	❑	❑
• *say the train arrives at 12:00* Le train arrive à Boston à midi.	❑	❑
• *tell someone they have to transfer* Il faut changer.	❑	❑
• *ask for a round-trip ticket to Lyon* Un aller-retour pour Lyon.	❑	❑
• *say smoking/non-smoking* Fumeur/non fumeur.	❑	❑
• *tell the hotel you have a room reserved* J'ai réservé une chambre.	❑	❑
• *say that your train is late* Le train a du retard.	❑	❑
• *say that you will arrive at 11 P.M.* J'arriverai à vingt-trois heures.	❑	❑

Can you ... ?

	Yes	*No*
• *give directions*	❑	❑

Allez tout droit.
Tournez à gauche au carrefour.
Tournez à droite aux feux.
Suivez les panneaux.

• *give instructions*	❑	❑

Arrêtez.
Ralentissez.
Doublez.
Cédez le passage.

Learning tips

Build up your own list of useful phrases to help you out of any difficulties and spend some time practicing them. Here is a starter kit:

Comment?	*Pardon?*
Encore!	*More!*
Pouvez-vous répéter cela?	*Could you repeat that?*
Parlez plus lentement, s'il vous plaît.	*Please speak more slowly.*
Je ne comprends pas.	*I don't understand.*
Je n'ai pas compris.	*I didn't understand.*
Je n'ai rien compris.	*I didn't understand a thing.*
Parlez-vous anglais?	*Do you speak English?*
Excusez-moi.	*Excuse me.*

Do you want to learn more?

Read as much French as you can find—newspapers, advertising brochures, whatever. Read a little at a time, and don't worry about bits you don't understand. Concentrate on getting the gist. Once you know what the subject is, you'll be able to guess the meanings of many new words from their context. Keep a note of words that are the same or similar in French and English, but look in your dictionary to check that the meaning is the same.

For more practice, see Extra! on page A8.

1 Extra!

le chat	*cat*
la chevelure	*head of hair*
le choix	*choice*
l'essence *f.*	*gas*
le goût	*taste*
la soie	*silk*
le savon	*soap*
sans	*without*
tant (de)	*so many*
chauve	*bald*
doux/douce	*soft*
impeccable	*perfect*
meilleur(e)	*best*
brûler	*to burn*
choisir	*to choose*
faire pénétrer	*to rub in*
grossir	*to get fat*
laisser	*to leave*
rouler	*to go (by vehicle)*

RECORDING

1. *Listen to the recording and identify what products are being sold in the television advertisements.*

RECORDING

2. *Listen to the recording and determine how long each of these promotions will last.*

Vous aurez une belle chevelure.	*You'll have a fine head of hair.*
Votre choix sera impeccable.	*Your choice will be perfect.*

2 Extra!

le contenu	*contents*
la moutarde	*mustard*
le persil	*parsley*
le plat à four	*baking dish*
le poivre	*pepper*
le sachet de levure	*packet of baking powder*
le saladier	*mixing bowl*
le sel	*salt*
à four chaud	*in a hot oven*
dedans	*inside*
haché	*chopped*
ramolli	*softened*
râpé	*grated*
ajouter	*to add*
beurrer	*to butter/grease*
cuire	*to cook*
mélanger	*to mix*
verser	*to pour*

RECORDING

1. *Listen to the recording and fill in the missing quantities on the list of ingredients.*

Un gâteau au jambon

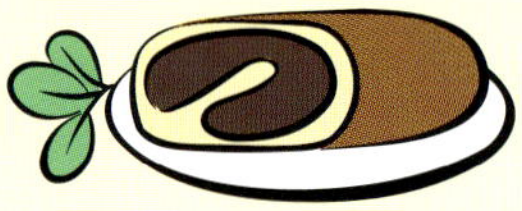

Il faut:

_____ oeufs
_____ cuillerées à soupe bien pleines de farine
_____ de jambon
_____ de beurre ramolli
_____ de gruyère râpé
_____ cuillerées à soupe de moutarde
_____ persil haché
_____ sachet de levure
_____ sel et du poivre

RECORDING

2.

Listen to the recording for activity 1 again and put the instructions listed below in the correct order.

a. Cuire à four chaud pendant environ trois quarts d'heure (thermostat 6–7).

b. Beurrer un plat à four et verser le tout dedans.

c. Verser le contenu du petit saladier dans le grand. Ajouter le jambon et mélanger le tout.

d. Dans un grand saladier, mélanger la farine, la levure et le gruyère.

e. Dans un petit saladier, mélanger les œufs, le persil, la moutarde, le beurre, le sel et le poivre.

3 Extra!

RECORDING

1. *Listen to find out what these people are packing. Where do you think they're going on vacation?*

RECORDING

2. *Where do these people want to go on vacation?*

4 Extra!

Une lettre ou télécopie pour réserver une chambre.
A letter or fax to reserve a room.

L'Hôtel Les Deux Sapins
Bois Vert

Monsieur,

Je voudrais réserver une chambre pour deux personnes avec salle de bains et donnant sur le lac, du 14 au 21 juin.

Je vous serais reconnaissant(e) de bien vouloir m'indiquer vos prix.

En vous remerciant d'avance, je vous prie de croire, Monsieur, à l'expression de mes sentiments distingués.

J. Clouseau

1. *Write a letter of your own; reserve two rooms with twin beds, bath, and television for four people from July 16 to 25.*

donnant sur …	*overlooking (lit: giving on to)*
Je vous serais reconnaissant(e) de bien vouloir m'indiquer vos prix.	*I would be most grateful if you could let me know what your prices are.*
En vous remerciant d'avance …	*Thanking you in advance …*
Je vous prie de croire, Monsieur, à l'assurance de mes sentiments distingués./Veuillez agréer, Monsieur/Madame, l'assurance de mes sentiments distingués.	*Yours faithfully*

A shorter form often used when sending a fax is:

Meilleures salutations	*Best wishes*

2. *Read the reply from the hotel.*

Cher M. Dixon,

Suite à votre lettre du 12 avril, le peux vous offrir une chambre pour deux personnes avec salle de bains et balcon donnant sur le lac au premier étage, et une chambre avec douche et WC donnant sur le lac mais sans balcon, au troisième étage. Toutes nos chambres sont équipées d'une télévision et du téléphone. J'attends votre confirmation avant de faire vos réservations.

Ci-joint des brochures avec nos prix et des informations sur la région.

En attendant votre réponse, je vous prie d'agréer, monsieur, mes salutations distinguées.

suite à	*following*
Toutes nos chambres sont équipées de ...	*All our rooms are equipped with*
ci-joint	*enclosed*

3. *Send a fax or letter confirming the reservation.*

Je voudrais confirmer la réservation ...

4. *Monique has been staying with you. Read and translate the letter she has written.*

Cher Jon, chère Amanda,

Je vous remercie de nouveau de votre gentille hospitalité. Les vacances aux Etats-Unis étaient vraiment magnifiques. En vous quittant, on a passé encore une semaine à New York pour voir les gratte-ciel, les musées, les théâtres et bien sûr les magasins. C'était vraiment impressionnant. Nous voulons revenir dans deux ans pour faire un tour des parcs nationaux. Vous voulez faire un tour avec nous?

Quand on est arrivé chez nous, il pleuvait et il faisait un froid terrible. J'étais très fatiguée, avec le long voyage et le décalage horaire, et j'ai dormi pendant 18 heures. La prochaine fois que vous venez en France, il faut absolument nous rendre visite.

Je vous envoie des photos que j'ai prises pendant le séjour chez vous.

Amicalement

Monique

cher/chère	*dear*
de nouveau	*again*
gentil(le)	*kind*
l'hospitalité	*hospitality*
magnifique	*magnificent*
En vous quittant ...	*When we left you ... (lit: on leaving you)*
encore un(e) ...	*another*
la semaine	*week*
le gratte-ciel	*skyscraper*
vraiment	*really*
impressionnant	*impressive*
le parc national	*national park*
fatigué(e)	*tired*
le décalage horaire	*time change*
pendant	*for, during*
La prochaine fois que vous venez ...	*Next time you come ...*
le séjour	*stay*
Amicalement	*With friendly greetings*
envoyer	*to send*
passer	*to spend*
remercier	*to thank*
rendre visite	*to visit*
revenir	*to return*
voir	*to see*
J'étais	*I was*
il faisait froid	*it was cold*
il pleuvait	*it was raining*

5 *Extra!*

RECORDING 1.

Listen to find out which chest of drawers is bought.

a. b. c.

RECORDING 2.

Make a list of the furniture the couple decides to buy for a new apartment.

6 *Extra!*

RECORDING 1.

Listen to the recording and choose the appropriate highway sign for each situation.

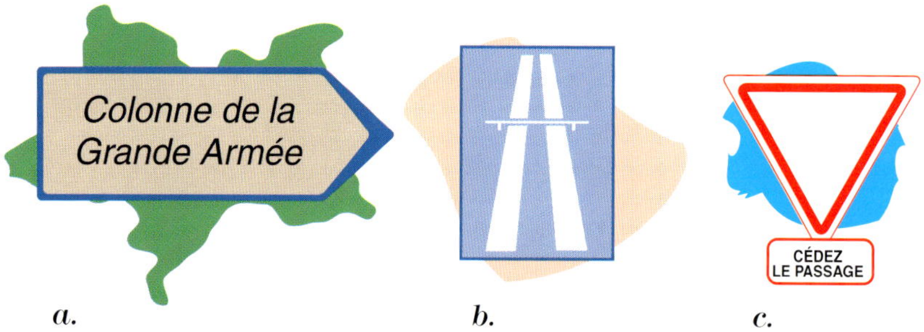

a. b. c.

Test 1

Review of Units 1–2

1. *Reflexive verbs. Put in the correct form of the reflexive pronoun.*

1. Je ______________________________ lève
2. Ils ______________________________ lavent
3. Elle ______________________________ réveille
4. Nous ______________________________ habillons
5. Comment tu ______________________________ appelles?
6. Vous ______________________________ levez à quelle heure?

2. *Fill in the missing verb.*

1. Je me ______________________ à six heures et demie.
2. Je me ______________________ à sept heures.
3. Je ______________________ une douche.
4. Je me ______________________ les cheveux.
5. Je m' ______________________.
6. Je ______________________ mon petit déjeuner.
7. Je ______________________ du thé au citron.
8. Je ______________________ de l'exercise.
9. Je ______________________ de la maison à sept heures et demie.
10. J' ______________________ au travail à huit heures.

arriver
boire
faire
habiller
se lever
manger
prendre
se réveiller
sècher
partir

3. *Complete the verbs.*

avoir		être	
J'ai	nous ________	Je suis	nous ________
tu ________	vous ________	tu ________	vous ________
il ________	ils ________	il ________	ils ________

4. *Make the past participle.*

Regular verbs:

1. aller
2. manger
3. répondre
4. rendre
5. finir
6. sortir

Irregular verbs:

7. boire
8. prendre
9. faire
10. ouvrir

5. *Find these people a suitable snack.*

1. J'ai faim.	*a.* Voilà du chocolat bien chaud!
2. J'ai soif.	*b.* Voulez-vous une glace?
3. J'ai chaud.	*c.* Voici une pression.
4. J'ai froid.	*d.* Nos glaces sont faites avec de l'édulcorant.
5. Je fais un régime.	*e.* Voici un steak frites.
6. Je suis diabétique.	*f.* Je vous propose une salade niçoise.

6. **Du, de la, de l', *or* des?** *Fill in the correct form.*

1. La poste est près __________ banque.
2. Le château est loin __________ centre.
3. L'hôtel est à côté __________ magasins.
4. Le restaurant est en face __________ hôtel.
5. La station de métro est à deux minutes __________ supermarché.

7. *What does the pharmacist suggest?*

1. J'ai une grippe.
2. J'ai mal à la tête.
3. Je suis enrhumé(e).
4. J'ai mal à la gorge.
5. Je me suis coupé un doigt.

a. de la crème antiseptique et un pansement

b. des pastilles et des mouchoirs en papier

c. des suppositoires

d. un sirop et des comprimés

e. des analgésiques

8. **Cherchez l'intrus.** *Find the odd one out.*

1. l'armoire; la commode; le frigidaire
2. le jardin; la cuisine; le salon
3. le canapé; le lit; le fauteuil
4. le pavillon; la fenêtre; la porte
5. la douche; la salle de bains; l'entrée
6. l'immeuble; la salle; la maison

9. *Describing people. Choose the right endings for talking about a woman.*

1. a. grand, b. grande
2. a. petite, b. petit
3. a. paresseux, b. paresseuse
4. a. active, b. actif
5. a. beau, b. belle
6. a. vieux, b. vieille

10. *Complete the dialog.*

1. Bonsoir monsieur/madame.
2. Oui. Pour combien de personnes?
3. A deux lits ou un grand lit?
4. Vous restez combien de temps?
5. Oui, bien sûr.
6. Le garage est au sous-sol. Vous avez la chambre numéro 56.

a. Avez-vous un parking?

b. Deux personnes

c. Bonsoir. Avez-vous une chambre de libre?

d. Un grand lit

e. Trois nuits

f. Avez-vous une chambre avec salle de bains?

Test 2

Review of Units 3–6

1. *More verbs ... Regular verbs, present tense. Put the right endings on the verbs:*

-er		-re		-ir	
J'arriv___	nous arriv___	Je répond___	nous répond___	je fini___	nous fini___
tu arriv___	vous arriv___	tu répond___	vous répond___	tu fini___	vous fini___
il arriv___	ils arriv___	il répond___	ils répond___	il fini___	ils fini___

2. *Which verb do they go with in the past tense?* **Avoir** *or* **être***?*

1. aller
2. avoir
3. faire
4. jouer
5. manger
6. partir
7. répondre
8. venir

3. *Complete the dialog.*

1. Bonjour monsieur/madame.	*a.* Demain soir.
2. Vous désirez?	*b.* Bonjour madame.
3. En première ou seconde?	*c.* Non fumeur.
4. Fumeur ou non fumeur?	*d.* Première.
5. Vous voulez partir quand?	*e.* Un aller-retour pour Paris.

4. *Give the imperative form of these verbs.*

1. aller—*to go*
2. continuer—*to continue*
3. prendre—*to take*
4. suivre—*to follow*
5. tournez—*to turn*

5. **Cherchez l'intrus.** *Find the odd one out.*

1. l'ail, le beurre, le fromage
2. le bœuf, l'agneau, les oignons
3. les tomates, la salade, les fraises
4. le lait, les radis, le yaourt,
5. la dinde, le poulet, les œufs
6. le veau, le porc, le jambon

6. *Put in the right form of* **avoir** *or* **être.**

1. Elle __________________ allée en ville.
2. Il __________________ eu une grande surprise.
3. J'__________________ fait de la planche.
4. Nous __________________ joué au basket.
5. On __________________ mangé des escargots.
6. Elle __________________ partie en retard.
7. Il n'__________________ pas répondu.
8. Ils __________________ venus en voiture.

7. **Grand ou grande?** *Adjective agreement. Choose the correct form.*

1. Mon appartement est grand/grande.
2. Le jardin est très joli/jolie.
3. La maison est dans une ville ancien/ancienne.
4. Les propriétés *(f)* sont beaux/belles.
5. Les rues *(f)* sont petits/petites.
6. Le pont est vieux/vieille.

8. *What is your excuse? You are answering the phone for Mr. Eastwood. How would you say:*

1.	He isn't there.	*a.*	Il est avec un client.
2.	He's in a meeting.	*b.*	Il est occupé.
3.	He's with a client.	*c.*	Il n'est pas là.
4.	He's on the other line.	*d.*	Je vous le passe.
5.	He's on a business trip.	*e.*	Il est parti déjeuner.
6.	Hold on.	*f.*	Il est en voyage d'affaires.
7.	He's at lunch.	*g.*	Il est en réunion.
8.	He's busy.	*h.*	Il est en communication.
9.	I am putting you through.	*i.*	Ne quittez pas.

9. **On va en vacances avec qui?** *Who are you going on vacation with? Fill in the correct form:* **mon**, **ma**, *or* **mes**.

1. avec __________ famille
2. avec __________ amis
3. avec __________ ami
4. avec __________ amie
5. avec __________ petite amie
6. avec __________ mari

10. *Choose the right question.*

1. Qu'est-ce que vous aimez faire?
2. Qu'est-ce que vous n'aimez pas faire?
3. Qu'est-ce que vous préférez?
4. Avez-vous jamais essayé de faire du parapente?
5. Qu'est-ce que vous aimeriez essayer?

a. Non, jamais.

b. Je voudrais essayer de faire du parapente.

c. J'adore l'équitation.

d. Je déteste le foot.

e. Je préfère les vacances à la montagne.

11. **Quel temps fait-il?** *Choose the right symbol.*

1. il pleut

a.

2. il y a du vent

b.

3. il y a du soleil

c.

4. il fait chaud

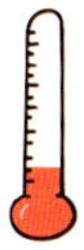

d.

5. il fait froid

e.

6. il y a du brouillard

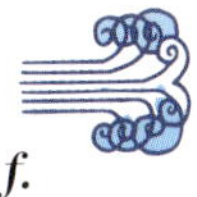

f.

7. il neige

g.

8. il y a des orages

h.

12. *At the bank. Complete the dialog.*

1. Bonjour monsieur/madame. Vous désirez?
2. Quelle devise?
3. Combien?
4. Vous avez une pièce d'identité?
5. Un instant. Oui, signez ici.

Pas pour les chèques de voyage. Voilà vos euros. Au revoir monsieur/madame.

a. Oui, la voilà.

b. Il y a une commission à payer?

c. Dollars.

d. Deux cents dollars.

e. Bonjour madame. Je voudrais changer des chèques de voyage.

Answer Key

Unit 1

Pages 1–4

1. 1. 6:45; 2. 9:00; 3. 8:15; 4. 4:00; 5. 10:30
2. shaving—3; getting up—1; eating breakfast with family—8; getting dressed—4; shower—2; buying bread—7; drinking orange juice—5; walking the dog—6
3. a. Elle prend une douche; b. Elle prend son petit déjeuner; c. Elle se lève; d. Elle se réveille; e. Elle se sèche les cheveux
4. a. <u>Quelquefois</u> je me lève à sept heures mais <u>normalement</u> je me lève à six heures.; b. <u>Normalement</u> je prends une douche, mais <u>quelquefois</u> je fais du jogging.; c. <u>Normalement</u> je ne prends pas de petit déjeuner, mais <u>quelquefois</u> je mange une tartine.; d. <u>Normalement</u> je sors à huit heures mais <u>quelquefois</u> je sors à sept heures.
5. a. nothing, coffee with milk—1; b. croissant, coffee—2; c. bread, butter, honey, or jam, coffee—3; d. cereal, margarine, and jam on bread, tea—4; e. egg, bread, yogurt, milk—5.
6. Answers will vary.

Pages 6–8

1. 1—nurse; 2—baker; 3—businessman; 4—teacher; 5—store assistant; 6—secretary
2. 1. bed until 11 o'clock and then goes to his mother's for lunch; 2. sport, soccer in winter and tennis in summer; 3. bike rides; 4. windsurfing/long walks; 5. restaurant
3. 1.b—a picnic; 2.c—château; 3.d—beach; 4.a—tennis; 5.e—windsurfing; 6.h—a bike ride
4. 1a. g; 2b. e; 3c. f; 4d. d; 5e. a; 6f. c
5. Answers will vary.
6. On pourrait jouer au tennis; aller à la plage; aller à Disneyland/au parc d'attractions; aller au jardin public; faire du shopping; aller à la piscine; aller au cinéma.

Pages 10–12

1. beach—3; theater—5; town—1; restaurant—4; tennis—2
2. woke up, 6:00; got up at 6:30; drank orange juice and read paper, 6:00–6:30; shower, 6:30; leave for work, 7:30; arrive at office, 7:55
3. A.M.—got up at eight o'clock and went to town; She did her shopping and met her boyfriend Jacques; they went shopping together.

   P.M.—fast food outlet and the cinema; then they went back to her house. She made a chocolate cake and they drank a cup of tea.

   evening—meal in a restaurant with friends
4. Answers will vary.

Unit 2

Pages 18–20

1. 1. 250g of garlic 500g of onions, a kilo of potatoes, and 200 grams of mushrooms; Soupe aux champignons
   2. Lettuce, 500g of tomatoes, celery, radishes; salade mixte
   3. a cabbage, 500g of carrots, and 50g of onions; choucroute
2. 1. beef, steak, pork—steak frites
   2. beef, steak, Burgundian beef, pork sausages, game meat—blanquette de veau
   3. no meat, vegetarian—salade niçoise
   4. steak, poultry, pork, everything—steak frites, poulet rôti, frites
   5. hamburgers, chicken, steak, fast food—Poulet rôti frites
3. 1. crème brûlée; 2. on a diet; 3. lemon pie, allergic to peanuts; 4. strawberry ice cream; 5. chocolate cake
4. J'aime la soupe aux champignons; Je n'aime pas tellement le poisson; Je ne mange pas de tomates; Je suis très chocolat; Je suis allergique à l'ail.

5. 1—Bof!; 2—délicieux; 3—délicieux; 4—dégoûtant; 5—insipide
6. Answers will vary.

Pages 22–24

1. 1.La brasserie, Salon de Thé, La Créperie
2. 1. soupe du jour
   2. filet de poisson frais du Bistro
   3. pas de dessert pour moi
   4. la salade variée aux pignons de pin
   5. le steak au poivre
3. Answers will vary.
4. 1. knife; 2. salt; 3. more bread; 4. ash-tray; 5. spoon and sugar
5. 1—€37,80; 2—€59,20; 3—€48,60; 4—€31,45; 5—€35

Pages 26–28

1. 1. eaten too much, feels sick; 2. bad back; 3. headache; 4. fallen and hurt knee; 5. cough, sore throat and temperature; 6. toothache
2. a. J'ai mal à la main. J'ai une ampoule.; b. J'ai de la fièvre.; c. J'ai mal au pied.; d. J'ai mal à la tête.; e. J'ai mal aux dents.
3. a. today at 16:20; b. tomorrow at 9:35; c. today at 17:10; d. Friday 10:45; e. call the ambulance: dial 15
4. cough and flu; cough and cold; cut finger
6. 1. tablets to take with water, three times a day before meals; 2. syrup—three tablespoons a day after meals; 3. suppositories to insert one in the evening and one in the morning; 4. antiseptic cream and some bandages; 5. pain killers—take two, four times a day.

Unit 3

Pages 34–37

1. 1. d; 2. a; 3. b; 4. a; 5. c
2. 1. g—Les Ardennes; 2. d—La Côte d'Azur; 3. a—Les Alpes; 4. e—La Bretagne
4. 1. mes copains—my buddies; 2. mon mari—my husband; 3. tout seul—alone; 4. Mon petit ami et mes deux enfants—my boyfriend and my two children; 5. un groupe touristique—a group of tourists
6. Answers will vary.

Pages 40–42

1. 1. hiking, cycling; 2. lying on the beach, getting tan, dancing; 3. windsurfing, cycling, mountain biking, tennis, skiing; 4. swimming, sailing; 5. fishing
2. 1. jogging; 2. tennis, volleyball, group sports, and soccer; 3. lying on the beach and sunbathing; 4. hiking
3. 1. never, it's awful; 2. several times, it's super; 3. once, fantastic; 4. twice, it's great; 5. several times, it's super
4. 1. paragliding, but afraid and it's expensive; 2. diving, tried it once and would like to learn; 3. horseback riding; 4. kayaking and rafting; 5. sailing; 6. paragliding
5. 1. skiing, cross-country skiing; 2. skiing, cross-country skiing, and ice skating; 3. snowboarding; 4. ice hockey and sledding; 5. snowboarding, skiing, cross-country skiing, ice skating, sledding, everything
6. Answers will vary.

Pages 44–48

2.

	Hôtel de la Poste	Hôtel Superbe	Hôtel Bellevue	Grand Hôtel	Hôtel des Pêcheurs
Family suites			✔	✔	
Twin beds					
Single bed					
Bath	✔	✔			
Shower	✔		✔	✔	✔
TV		✔		✔	
Phone					
Pool		✔	✔	✔	
Fitness/ Gym					
Garage/ Parking		✔	✔	✔	

3. Answers will vary.
4. a. Hôtel des Pêcheurs; b. Hôtel Bellevue; c. Hôtel de la Poste; d. Hôtel Superbe; e. Grand Hôtel
5. a. Je préfère l'Hôtel des Pêcheurs parce qu'il est petit.; b. Je préfère l'Hôtel Bellevue parce qu'il est en dehors de la ville.; c. Je préfère l'Hôtel de la Poste parce qu'il est au centre-ville.
6. two double rooms for tonight; a room with a double bed for two nights from 9–11 May;

One double room with a double bed and one with two singles from 12–15 May; A single room for tonight; For the week 14–21 August, one double room and a room with 3 beds; And a room with a shower and a bathroom for tonight and with a crib

7. a. Avez-vous une chambre libre pour ce soir?; b. Oui, une chambre à deux lits, avec douche et poste de télévision.; c. Pour deux nuits.; d. Answers will vary.; e. Answers will vary.; f. Oui. Vous avez un parking?; g. Answers will vary.

Unit 4

Pages 54–57

1. Le PDG, M. Gaston; l'adjointe du PDG, Mme Hivet; Le chef du service marketing, M. Guinard; le chef du Service technique, M. Pinchon; le chef comptable, Mme Catillon

2. 1. M. Gaston in a meeting, after 2 P.M.;
2. Mme Hivet, on the phone, ten minutes;
3. M. Guinard, with a client, half an hour;
4. M. Lecuyer, putting you through;
5. Mme Catillon in a meeting, she will call back if you leave your number.

4. Mr. Haydn-Jones—Mme Yon—vendredi 11:20

Mr. Weston—M. Varin—jeudi 15:00

Mr. Bradshaw—M. Leclerc—mardi 14:30

Ms. Walker—Mme Sibbille—mercredi 10:30

5. Lundi—10 A.M. meeting with chef du service marketing, 2:00 conference

Mardi—A.M. factory visit, P.M. free

Mercredi—A.M. with client, P.M. free

Jeudi—A.M. presentation, P.M. dental appointment

Vendredi—A.M. free, P.M. vacation

Next week—on vacation

6. J'arriverai lundi, Paris-Charles-de-Gaulle à 14h55 et je vais rester à l'hôtel Bellevue.

Mardi matin je suis libre et l'après-midi je fais la visite de l'usine Electofans.

Mercredi matin, j'ai une réunion avec le service technique d'Electofans et l'après-midi est libre.

Jeudi matin j'assiste à une présentation chez Pub S.A. et l'après-midi je suis libre.

Vendredi matin j'ai un rendez-vous avec le PDG de Electofans et l'après-midi je prends l'avion à l'aéroport Charles-de-Gaulle à 15h45 pour rentrer.

Alors je vous propose un rendez-vous mercredi après-midi

Pages 60–63

1. a. M. Proudhon; b. Mme Chaumont; c. Mme Hérault; d. M. Dubarry

2. Gordon Brown, le PDG, a soixante-cinq ans, et il est très grand, à peu près un mètre quatre-vingt-dix. Il a les cheveux gris, et quand il voyage il porte toujours un pantalon beige, un chemise à carreaux, un pull bleu foncé et une casquette de baseball.
Lucy Stockwell porte un polo, un jean, des baskets et un pull.

3. the briefcase; navy blue raincoat; large umbrella with bank logo; leather gloves (not wool)

4. le nord—il pleut; le sud—il y a des orages; l'ouest—il fait beau; l'est—il fait froid; les Alpes—il neige; les Pyrénées—il y a du soleil; le Pas-de-Calais—il y a du brouillard

5. a. Dans le sud il fait du soleil et il fait très chaud; b. Dans l'ouest il pleut; c. Dans l'est il y a des orages; d. Dans les Rocheuses il neige et il fait très froid.

6. a. il va faire beau/il y aura du soleil; b. il va faire froid; c. il va pleuvoir; d. il y aura du vent

Pages 66–68

1. Deux cents dollars (3); Bonjour madame. Je voudrais changer des chèques de voyage. (1); Dollars (2); Il y a une commission à payer? (4); Pas pour les chèques de voyage. (5)

2. Bonjour monsieur/madame. Je voudrais changer des chèques de voyage.

Dollars.

Cinq cents dollars.

Oui, la voilà.

Il y a une commission à payer?

3. a. €84; b. €1; c. €7,40; €14,75; d. €2

4. a. phone card—1; b. two stamps—2; c. send money form—3; d. small parcel—4

5. a. 2; b. 1; c. 5; d. 6; e. 3; f. 4

Unit 5

Pages 74–75

2. 1. two minutes from the supermarket; 2. it's opposite the church; 3. between the bank and the bakery; 4. next to the drugstore; 5. near the post office

3. a. C'est entre la banque et la boulangerie; b. C'est à côté de la pharmacie; c. C'est en face de l'église

4. 1. b; 2. a; 3. d; 4. c; 5. e

5. 1. bus—a; 2. car—c; 3. walk—b; 4. bike—d; 5. car—c

Pages 77–79

1. 1. a—large apartment building in town; 2. b—large house in town; 3. c—apartments in suburbs; 4. d—small house in country; 5. e—small development in suburbs

2. 1. large, modern, nice; 2. big, old; 3. small, old; 4. really old, small, pretty; 5. quite small, very new

3. M. Simon, ground floor; Jacqueline, first floor; La famille Bourjeout, second floor; La famille Bertrand, third floor; M. et Mme Dubois, fifth floor; Mlle Fourrier, eighth floor; Nicolas in the attic; his rabbit in the basement

4. a. M. Dubois—5 years; b. Mlle Fourrier—1 month; c. M. Simm—2 years; d. Mme Bourjeout—9 years; e. Jacqueline—10 months; f. M. Bertrand—3 years; g. Nicolas—2 days

5. Answers will vary.

Pages 82–83

1. a. 2; b. 3; c. 1

2. kitchen, shower, living room, garage, and balcony should be checked; 2 bedrooms

3. L'ISLE-ADAM
4 bedroom house, dining room, living room with fireplace, fully-equipped kitchen and bathroom, garage, fenced 1,700 m2 lot, €380,000. Sale by owner. Call.

APARTMENTS, HOUSES, SALES OUTSIDE PARIS

VILLA IN HYERES
33 (an area of France close to Bordeaux) by the estuary of the Gironde River, traditional restored house, 150 m2 lot, garage, dock tel: 16/57 46 16 00

UNFURNISHED 3RD (a borough of Paris)
St Martin close to Beaubourg
4 rooms on courtyard, 90 m2, completely remodeled, 2nd floor, elevator, basement storage, €1650 + €40 utilities, private landlord 01 45 27 50 34 answering machine

2 rooms 45 m2 close Balard Metro
01 44 19 62 62

Crimee Metro 4 rooms 74 m2 €212,000

TOULON
residential area by the shore. Sale by owner, beautiful four-room apartment, large living room/dining room, 2 bedrooms, luxury condo in wooded park, swimming pool, €380,000

4. 1. kitchen; 2. bedroom; 3. bathroom; 4. living room with balcony; 5. bedroom; 6. basement garage

5. a refrigerator; table for the kitchen; a sofa and armchair; a bed, a wardrobe and a mirror; a chest of drawers

Unit 6

Pages 90–92

1. 1. train, 5 hours; 2. coach, 3 days; 3. motorbike, 7 days a week; 4. car, 10 hours; 5. plane, 1 hour

2. 1. Jeudi, dép 15.30 arr 20.18; 2. Mercredi 8.00, Vendredi 17.00; 3. Samedi, 10.00, yesterday, 16.00; 4. Vendredi 22.00, Samedi, 8.00; 5. ce matin, 11.00, 12.05

3. Answers will vary.

4. the metro or the RER, which is quicker, but it is often very crowded; taxi is fastest but at rush hour there is a lot of traffic and it is expensive; Roissy bus to center of town every twenty minutes and takes about forty minutes.

5. a. not too big (Renault Mégane); b. 1 person; c. 3 days; d. identity card and driver's license; e. insurance; f. American Express; g. in the parking lot (space B7)

6. a. Je veux louer une voiture.
b. Une grande voiture pour quatre personnes.
c. Une semaine.
d. Oui, les voilà.
e. Vous prenez la Master Card?
f. Avez-vous un plan de la ville?
g. Où est la voiture?

Pages 94–97

1.

	train 1	train 2	train 3
a. Lyon	10:35	14:18	18:05
b. Caen	9:12	10:43	11:27
c. Nice	8:19	10:56	11:56
d. Lille	10:39	13:28	17:18
e. Nantes	7:22	11:09	13:47

2.

Destination	dép	quai	change à	arr
a. Lyon	10:35	5	Dijon	13:05
b. Caen	10:43	11		11:57
c. Nice	10:56	7		13:26
d. Lille	13:28	2		12:18
e. Nantes	11:09	1	Paris	14:26

3. €26.53 Calais; €92.60 Paris-Cannes; €11 Paris

4. a. 2; b. 1; c. 3; d. 4

5. a. Bonjour.; b. Londres, un aller-retour; c. Première.; d. Non fumer.; e. Demain soir.

6.

Lyon	19:45	2 hours late
Marseille	20:32	1 hour late
Dijon	20:56	due to arrive at 22:14

Pages 101–103

1. 1. A13 to Rouen then A15; 2. A6 to Lyon then A7; 3. A6 towards Beaune and A38; 4. A10; 5. A4; 6. A1 then A26, then tunnel

2. a. 2; b. 4; c. 1; d. 5; e. 3

3. 1. Allez tout droit et tournez à gauche au carrefour.; 2. Allez tout droit, traversez le pont et le voilà sur votre gauche.; 3. Continuez jusqu`au feu et puis et oui, tournez à droite.; 4. Suivez les panneaux centre-ville.; 5. Allez tout droit jusqu`au rond-point et prenez le première sortie.

4. a. 130km/h; b. 110km/h; c. 90km/h; d. 50km/h

5. yield; stop; turn right; pass; slow down; put signals on; stop

6. il faut céder le passage, arrêtez, tournez à droite, doublez, ralentissez, mettez les clignotants, arrêtez

7. a. Cédez le passage; b. Virages dangereux; c. Passage piétons; d. Passage à niveau; e. Chaussée glissante; f. Rétrécissement; g. Travaux

Extra 1

Page A1

1. 1. Rosée du matin (soap); 2. FINO (gasoline); 3. Votre Génération (magazine)

2. 1. one day; 2. two weeks; 3. one week

Extra 2

Pages A2–A3

1. <u>cinq</u> oeufs
<u>cinq</u> cuillerées à soupe bien pleines de farine
<u>200g</u> de jambon
<u>125g</u> de beurre ramolli
<u>100g</u> de gruyère râpé
<u>deux</u> cuillerées à soupe de moutarde
<u>du</u> persil haché
<u>un</u> sachet de levure
<u>du</u> sel et du poivre

2. 1. Dans un petit saladier, mélanger les œufs, le persil, la moutarde, le beurre, le sel, et le poivre.; 2. Dans un grand saladier, mélanger la farine, la levure, et le gruyère.; 3. Verser le contenu du petit saladier dans le grand. Ajouter le jambon et mélanger le tout.; 4. Beurrer un plat à four et verser le tout dedans.; 5. Cuire à four chaud pendant environ trois quarts d'heure (thermostat 6–7).

Extra 3

Page A4

1. Spain

2. 1. United States; 2. Northern Spain; 3. Mexico; 4. Italy

Extra 4

Pages A5–A7

1. Sample answer:

Monsieur,
Je voudrais réserver deux chambres donnant sur le lac avec deux lits chacune, salle de bain et télévision pour quatre personnes du 16 au 25 juillet.

Je vous serais reconnaissant de bien vouloir m'indiquer vos prix.

En vous remerciant d'avance, je vous prie de croire, Monsieur, à l'assurance de mes sentiments distingués.

David Dixon

3. Suite à votre lettre du..., je voudrais confirmer la réservation pour deux chambres du 16 au 25 juillet pour quattre personnes.

   Meilleures salutations,

   David Dixon

4. Dear John, Dear Amanda,

   I want to thank you again for your kind hospitality. Our vacation in the US was really magnificent. When we left you, we spent another week in NYC to see the skyscrapers, museums, the theaters, and, of course, the shops. It was really impressive. We want to return in two years to go for a tour of the national parks. Do you want to go on a tour with us?

   When we arrived home, it was raining and terribly cold. I was very tired by the long journey and the time change, and I slept for 18 hours. Next time you come to France, you absolutely have to visit us. I am sending you some pictures I took.

   With friendly greetings,

   (your name)

Extra 5

Page A8

1. black dresser
2. bedside table; chairs; mirror; lamps; sofa

Extra 6

Page A8

1. 1—a (yield sign); 2—a (historic site sign); 3—b (highway sign)

Test 1

Pages B1–B4

1. 1. me; 2. se; 3. se; 4. nous; 5. t'; 6. vous
2. 1. réveille; 2. lève; 3. prends; 4. sèche; 5. habille; 6. mange; 7. bois; 8. fais; 9. pars; 10. arrive
3. tu as; il a; nous avons; vous avez; ils ont; tu es; il est; nous sommes; vous êtes; ils sont
4. 1. allé; 2. mangé; 3. répondu; 4. rendu; 5. fini; 6. sorti; 7. bu; 8. pris; 9. fait; 10. ouvert
5. 1. e; 2. c; 3. b; 4. a; 5. f; 6. d.
6. 1. de la; 2. du; 3. des; 4. de l'; 5. du
7. 1. c; 2. e; 3. b; 4. d; 5. a
8. 1. le frigidaire; 2. le jardin; 3. le lit; 4. le pavillon; 5. l'entrée; 6. la salle
9. 1. b; 2. a; 3. b; 4. a; 5. b; 6. b.
10. 1. c; 2. b; 3. d; 4. e; 5. f; 6. a

Test 2

Pages B5–B10

1. -er

J'arrive	nous arrivons
tu arrives	vous arrivez
il arrive	ils arrivent

-re

Je réponds	nous répondons
tu réponds	vous répondez
il répond	ils répondent

-ir

je finis	nous finissons
tu finis	vous finissez
il finit	ils finissent

2. 1. être; 2. avoir; 3. avoir; 4. avoir; 5. avoir; 6. être; 7. avoir; 8. être
3. 1. b; 2. e; 3. d; 4. c; 5. a
4. 1. Allez!; 2. Continuez; 3. Prenez!; 4. Suivez!; 5. Tournez!
5. 1. l'ail; 2. les oignons; 3. les fraises; 4. les radis; 5. les œufs; 6. le veau
6. 1. est; 2. a; 3. ai; 4. avons; 5. a; 6. est; 7. a; 8. sont
7. 1. grand; 2. joli; 3. ancienne; 4. belles; 5. petites; 6. vieux
8. 1. c; 2. g; 3. a; 4. h; 5. f; 6. i; 7. e; 8. b; 9. d
9. 1. ma; 2. mes; 3. mon; 4. mon; 5. ma; 6. mon
10. 1. c; 2. d; 3. e; 4. a; 5. b
11. 1. c; 2. f; 3. a; 4. e; 5. d; 6. h; 7. b; 8.g
12. 1. e; 2. c; 3. d; 4. a; 5. b

Berlitz®

Dictionary

French – English
English – French

Dictionnaire

Français – Anglais
Anglais – Français

Berlitz Publishing
Union, NJ · Munich · Singapore

Contacting the Editors
Every effort has been made to provide accurate information in this publication, but changes are inevitable. The publisher cannot be responsible for any resulting loss, inconvenience or injury. We would appreciate it if readers would call our attention to any errors or outdated information by contacting Berlitz Publishing, 95 Progress Street, Union, NJ 07083, USA. Fax: 1-908-206-1103.
email: comments@berlitzbooks.com

Printed in Singapore by Insight Print Services (Pte) Ltd. April 2005

Contents

Table des matières

Preface

In selecting the vocabulary and phrases for this dictionary, the editors have had the traveller's needs foremost in mind. This book will prove a useful companion to casual tourists and business travellers alike who appreciate the reassurance a small and practical dictionary can provide. It offers them—as well as beginners and students—all the basic vocabulary they will encounter and have to use, giving the key words and expressions to allow them to cope in everyday situations.

Like our successful phrase books and travel guides, these dictionaries—created with the help of a computer data bank— are designed to slip into your pocket or purse, and thus have a role as handy companions at all times.

Besides just about everything you normally find in dictionaries, there are these Berlitz bonuses:

- simplified pronunciation after each foreign-word entry, making it easy to read and enunciate words whose spelling may look forbidding
- a unique, practical glossary to simplify reading a foreign restaurant menu and to take the mystery out of complicated dishes and indecipherable names on bills of fare
- useful information on how to tell the time and how to count, on conjugating irregular verbs, commonly seen abbreviations and converting to the metric system, in addition to basic phrases.

While no dictionary of this size can pretend to completeness, we are confident this dictionary will help you get most out of your trip abroad.

Berlitz Publishing

Préface

En choisissant les mots et expressions de ce dictionnaire, nos rédacteurs se sont souciés des besoins essentiels de l'étudiant et du voyageur. Cet ouvrage s'avérera indispensable aux touristes, globe-trotters, hommes ou femmes d'affaires qui apprécient l'appoint qu'apporte un dictionnaire pratique et de format réduit. Il leur offre le vocabulaire qu'ils seront amenés à rencontrer et à utiliser; il leur propose des mots-clés et des expressions leur permettant de faire face aux situations de tous les jours.

A l'instar de nos manuels de conversation et de nos guides de voyage déjà fort appréciés, nos dictionnaires – réalisés grâce à une banque de données sur ordinateur – sont conçus pour se glisser dans une poche ou dans un sac, assumant ainsi leur rôle de compagnons à tout moment.

Ce dictionnaire présente:

- une transcription phonétique facilitant la prononciation de chaque entrée
- un lexique pratique visant à faciliter la lecture du menu dans un restaurant et révélant les mystères de plats jusqu'alors inconnus
- des informations précieuses sur la façon d'exprimer le temps, de compter, sur les verbes irréguliers, sur les abréviations courantes, en plus des expressions usuelles.

Aucun dictionnaire de ce format ne peut prétendre être exhaustif, mais le but principal de cet ouvrage est de permettre à son utilisateur d'affronter avec confiance un voyage à l'étranger.

Berlitz Publishing

French-English

Français-Anglais

Introduction

The dictionary has been designed to take account of your practical needs. Unnecessary linguistic information has been avoided. The entries are listed in alphabetical order, regardless of whether the entry word is printed in a single word, contains an apostrophe, or is in two or more separate words. When an entry is followed by sub-entries such as expressions and locutions, these, too, have been listed in alphabetical order.

Each main-entry word is followed by a phonetic transcription (see Guide to Pronunciation). Following the transcription is the part of speech of the entry word whenever applicable. When an entry word may be used as more than one part of speech, the translations are grouped together after the respective part of speech.

French feminine headwords are shown as follows:

campeur … *m*, **-euse** *f* camper
descendant… *m*, **-e** *f* descendant
électeur … *m*, **-trice** *f* voter
citoyen … *m*, **-ne** *f*

The feminine forms of these headwords are: **campeuse** (pl ~s), **descendante** (pl ~s), **électrice** (pl ~s), **citoyenne** (pl ~s).

The feminine or plural forms of French adjectives have been supplied whenever they diverge from the standard rule for the word-ending in question. Similarly, the plural forms of nouns are given when not in accordance with the rules for the particular word-ending.

Whenever an entry word is repeated in irregular forms, or in subentries, a tilde (~) is used to represent the full entry word.

In irregular feminine and plural forms, a hyphen is used to represent the part of the main-entry word that precedes the relevant word-ending.

An asterisk (*) in front of a verb indicates that the verb is irregular. For details, refer to the lists of irregular verbs.

Abbreviations

adj	adjective	*num*	numeral
adv	adverb	*p*	past tense
Am	American	*pl*	plural
art	article	*plAm*	plural (American)
conj	conjunction	*pp*	past participle
f	feminine	*pr*	present tense
fpl	feminine plural	*pref*	prefix
m	masculine	*prep*	preposition
mpl	masculine plural	*pron*	pronoun
n	noun	*v*	verb
nAm	noun (American)	*vAm*	verb (American)

Guide to Pronunciation

Each main entry in this part of the dictionary is followed by a phonetic transcription which shows you how to pronounce the words. This transcription should be read as if it were English. It is based on Standard British pronunciation, though we have tried to take account of General American pronunciation also. Below, only those letters and symbols are explained which we consider likely to be ambiguous or not immediately understood.
The syllables are separated by hyphens, and stressed syllables are printed in *italics*.
Of course, the sounds of any two languages are never exactly the same, but if you follow carefully our indications, you should be able to pronounce the foreign words in such a way that you'll be understood. To make your task easier, our transcriptions occasionally simplify slightly the sound system of the language while still reflecting the essential sound differences.

Consonants

g	always hard, as in **g**o
ñ	as in Spanish se**ñ**or, or like **ni** in o**ni**on
r	pronounced in the back of the mouth
s	always hard, as in **s**o
zh	a soft, voiced **sh**, like **s** in plea**s**ure

The sign (') indicates a so-called aspirate h. It means that no liaison (*les huttes*—lay 'ewt) nor elision (*la hutte*—lah 'ewt) should be made.

Vowels and Diphthongs

aa	long **a**, as in c**ar**
ah	a short version of **aa**; between **a** in c**a**t and **u** in c**u**t
ai	like **air**, without any **r**-sound
eh	like **e** in g**e**t
er	as in oth**er**, without any **r**-sound

ew a "rounded **ee**-sound". Say the vowel sound **ee** (as in s**ee**), and while saying it, round your lips as for **oo** (as in s**oo**n), without moving your tongue; when your lips are in the **oo** position, but your tongue in the **ee** position, you should be pronouncing the correct sound

igh as in s**igh**

o always as in h**o**t (British pronunciation)

ur as in f**ur**, but with rounded lips and no **r**-sound

1) A bar over a vowel symbol (e.g. $\overline{\mathbf{ew}}$) shows that this sound is long.
2) Raised letters (e.g. $\mathbf{oo^{ee}}$, $\mathbf{^{y}ur}$) should be pronounced only fleetingly.
3) French contains nasal vowels, which we transcribe with a vowel symbol plus **~~ng~~** (e.g. **ah~~ng~~**). This **~~ng~~** should *not* be pronounced, and serves solely to indicate nasal quality of the preceding vowel. A nasal vowel is pronounced simultaneously through the mouth and the nose.
4) French vowels (i.e. not diphthongs) are relatively short and pure. Therefore, you should try to read a transcription like **oa** without moving tongue or lips while pronouncing the sound.

A

à (ah) *prep* to; at, on
abandonner (ah-bah$\overline{ng}$-do-*nay*) *v* desert
abat-jour (ah-bah-*zh$\overline{oo}$r*) *m* lampshade
***abattre** (ah-*bahtr*) *v* knock down; kill; dishearten
abbaye (ah-bay-*ee*) *f* abbey
abcès (ah-*psay*) *m* abscess
abeille (ah-*bay*) *f* bee
abîme (ah-*beem*) *m* abyss
abîmer (ah-bee-*may*) *v* *spoil
abolir (ah-bo-*leer*) *v* abolish
abondance (ah-baw$\overline{ng}$-*dah$\overline{ng}$ss*) *f* abundance; plenty
abondant (ah-baw$\overline{ng}$-*dah$\overline{ng}$*) *adj* abundant; plentiful
abonné (ah-bo-*nay*) *m* subscriber
abonnement (ah-bon-*mah$\overline{ng}$*) *m* subscription
abord: d'abord (dah-*bawr*) at first
abordage (ah-bor-*daazh*) *m* collision
aboutir à (ah-boo-*teer*) end at; result in
aboyer (ah-bwah-^{y}*ay*) *v* bark, bay
abréviation (ah-bray-v^{y}ah-*s^{y}aw$\overline{ng}$*) *f* abbreviation
abri (ah-*bree*) *m* shelter; cover
abricot (ah-bree-*koa*) *m* apricot
abriter (ah-bree-*tay*) *v* shelter
abrupt (ah-*brewpt*) *adj* steep
absence (ah-*psah$\overline{ng}$ss*) *f* absence
absent (ah-*psah$\overline{ng}$*) *adj* absent
absolu (ah-pso-*lew*) *adj* total, sheer
absolument (ah-pso-lew-*mah$\overline{ng}$*) *adv* absolutely
absorber (ah-psor-*bay*) *v* absorb
***abstenir** (ahp-ster-*neer*): **s'~ de** abstain from
abstraction faite de (ahp-strahk-*s^{y}aw$\overline{ng}$* feht der) apart from
abstrait (ahp-*stray*) *adj* abstract
absurde (ah-*psewrd*) *adj* absurd; foolish
abus (ah-*bew*) *m* abuse, misuse
académie (ah-kah-day-*mee*) *f* academy; **~ des beaux-arts** art school
accélérateur (ahk-say-lay-rah-*t$\overline{ur}$r*) *m* accelerator
accélérer (ahk-say-lay-*ray*) *v* accelerate
accent (ahk-*sah$\overline{ng}$*) *m* accent, stress
accepter (ahk-sehp-*tay*) *v* accept
accès (ahk-*say*) *m* access; approach, entrance, admittance
accessible (ahk-say-*seebl*) *adj* accessible; attainable
accessoire (ahk-say-*swaar*) *adj* additional
accessoires (ahk-say-*swaar*) *mpl* accessories *pl*
accident (ahk-see-*dah$\overline{ng}$*) *m* accident; **~ d'avion** plane crash
accidenté (ahk-see-dah$\overline{ng}$-*tay*) *adj* hilly; uneven
accidentel (ahk-see-dah$\overline{ng}$-*tehl*) *adj* accidental
acclamer (ah-klah-*may*) *v* cheer
accommodation (ah-ko-mo-dah-*s^{y}aw$\overline{ng}$*) *f* accommodation
accompagner (ah-kaw$\overline{ng}$-pah-*ñay*) *v* accompany
accomplir (ah-kaw$\overline{ng}$-*pleer*) *v* accomplish; perform, achieve
accomplissement (ah-kaw$\overline{ng}$-plee-*smah$\overline{ng}$*) *m* fulfilment, accomplishment
accord (ah-*kawr*) *m* settlement, agreement; approval; **d'accord!** all right!; okay!; ***être d'accord** agree; ***être d'accord avec** approve of
accorder (ah-kor-*day*) *v* grant; tune; **s'accorder avec** match
accoster (ah-ko-*stay*) *v* dock
accoucher (ah-koo-*shay*) *v* have a

baby, be delivered (of, **de**)
accouchement (ah-koosh-*mah*$\overline{ng}$) *m* childbirth, delivery
accoutumé (ah-koo-tew-*may*) *adj* accustomed
accrocher (ah-kro-*shay*): **s'~** *hold on
accueil (ah-*kur*^{ee}) *m* reception; welcome
***accueillir** (ah-kur-^{y}*eer*) *v* welcome
accumulateur (ah-kew-mew-lah-*t*$\overline{ur}$*r*) *m* battery
accumuler (ah-kew-mew-*lay*): **s'~** increase
accusation (ah-kew-zah-*s*^{y}*aw*$\overline{ng}$) *f* charge
accuser (ah-kew-*zay*) *v* accuse; charge
achat (ah-*shah*) *m* purchase; **~ à tempérament** hire purchase; ***faire des achats** shop
acheter (ahsh-*tay*) *v* *buy, purchase
acheteur (ahsh-*t*$\overline{ur}$*r*) *m*, **-euse** *f* buyer, purchaser
achever (ahsh-*vay*) *v* finish; complete, accomplish
acide (ah-*seed*) *m* acid
acier (ah-*s*^{y}*ay*) *m* steel; **~ inoxydable** stainless steel
acné (ahk-*nay*) *f* acne
acompte (ah-*kaw*$\overline{ngt}$) *m* down payment; instal(l)ment
à-coup (ah-*koo*) *m* tug
***acquérir** (ah-kay-*reer*) *v* acquire; *buy
acquisition (ah-kee-zee-*s*^{y}*aw*$\overline{ng}$) *f* acquisition, purchase
acquittement (ah-keet-*mah*$\overline{ng}$) *m* acquittal
acte (ahkt) *m* act, deed
acteur (ahk-*t*$\overline{ur}$*r*) *m* actor
actif (ahk-*teef*) *adj* active
action (ahk-*s*^{y}*aw*$\overline{ng}$) *f* action, deed; share; **actions** stocks and shares
activité (ahk-tee-vee-*tay*) *f* activity; work
actrice (ahk-*treess*) *f* actress
actualité (ahk-twah-lee-*tay*) *f* current events; **actualités** news; newsreel
actuel (ahk-*twehl*) *adj* present; topical
actuellement (ahk-twehl-*mah*$\overline{ng}$) *adv* nowadays
adapter (ah-dahp-*tay*) *v* adapt; **~ à** suit
addition (ah-dee-*s*^{y}*aw*$\overline{ng}$) *f* addition; bill
additionner (ah-dee-s^{y}o-*nay*) *v* add
adéquat (ah-day-*kwah*) *adj* adequate; appropriate, proper; sufficient
adhérer à (ah-day-*ray*) join
adieu (ah-*d*^{y}*ur*) *m* parting
adjectif (ah-jehk-*teef*) *m* adjective
***admettre** (ahd-*mehtr*) *v* acknowledge, admit; **en admettant que** supposing that
administratif (ahd-mee-nee-strah-*teef*) *adj* administrative
administration (ahd-mee-nee-strah-*s*^{y}*aw*$\overline{ng}$) *f* administration
administrer (ahd-mee-nee-*stray*) *v* run; administer
admiration (ahd-mee-rah-*s*^{y}*aw*$\overline{ng}$) *f* admiration
admirer (ahd-mee-*ray*) *v* admire
admission (ahd-mee-*s*^{y}*aw*$\overline{ng}$) *f* admission; entry
adolescent (ah-do-leh-*sah*$\overline{ng}$) *m* teenager
adopter (ah-dop-*tay*) *v* adopt
adorable (ah-do-*rahbl*) *adj* adorable
adorer (ah-do-*ray*) *v* worship
adoucir (ah-doo-*seer*) *v* soften
adoucisseur d'eau (ah-doo-see-*s*$\overline{ur}$*r* doa) water softener
adresse (ah-*drehss*) *f* address
adresser (ah-dray-*say*) *v* address; **s'adresser à** address
adroit (ah-*drwah*) *adj* skil(l)ful; smart
adulte (ah-*dewlt*) *m/f* adult, grown-up; *adj* adult, grown-up
adversaire (ahd-vehr-*sair*) *m/f* opponent

aération (ah-ay-rah-*s^{y}awng*) *f* ventilation
aérer (ah-ay-*ray*) *v* ventilate, air; **aéré** airy
aéroport (ah-ay-ro-*pawr*) *m* airport
affaire (ah-*fair*) *f* business, matter, case; affair, concern; deal; **~ de cœur** affair
affairé (ah-fay-*ray*) *adj* busy
affaires (ah-*fair*) *fpl* business; belongings *pl*; **chiffre d'affaires** turnover; ***faire des ~ avec** *deal with
affamé (ah-fah-*may*) *adj* hungry
affecter (ah-fehk-*tay*) *v* affect
affection (ah-fehk-*s^{y}awng*) *f* affection; ailment
affectueux (ah-fehk-*twur*) *adj* affectionate
affiche (ah-*feesh*) *f* placard, poster
affiler (ah-fee-*lay*) *v* sharpen
affilier (ah-fee-*l^{y}ay*): **s'~ à** join
affirmatif (ah-feer-mah-*teef*) *adj* affirmative
affirmer (ah-feer-*may*) *v* affirm; state
affliction (ah-fleek-*s^{y}awng*) *f* grief
affligé (ah-flee-*zhay*) *adj* sad
affluent (ah-flew-*ahng*) *m* tributary
affranchir (ah-frahng-*sheer*) *v* stamp
affreux (ah-*frur*) *adj* dreadful, frightful
affronter (ah-frawng-*tay*) *v* face
afin de (ah-*fang* der) to, in order to; **afin que** so that
Africain (ah-free-*kang*) *m* African
africain (ah-free-*kang*) *adj* African
Afrique (ah-*freek*) *f* Africa; **~ du Sud** South Africa
after-shave (ahf-terr-*shehv*) *m* aftershave lotion
agacer (ah-gah-*say*) *v* irritate, annoy
âge (aazh) *m* age
âgé (ah-*zhay*) *adj* aged, elderly; **le plus ~** eldest; **plus ~** elder
agence (ah-*zhahngss*) *f* agency
agenda (ah-zhang-*dah*) *m* diary
agenouiller: (ahzh-noo-*^{y}ay*): **s'~** *kneel
agent (ah-*zhahng*) *m* agent; **~ de police** policeman; **~ de voyages** travel agent; **~ immobilier** house agent
agir (ah-*zheer*) *v* act
agitation (ah-zhee-tah-*s^{y}awng*) *f* excitement, fuss; disturbance, unrest
agiter (ah-zhee-*tay*) *v* agitate; stir; **agité** restless
agneau (ah-*ñoa*) *m* lamb
agrafe (ah-*grahf*) *f* staple
agrandir (ah-grahng-*deer*) *v* extend; enlarge
agrandissement (ah-grahng-dee-*smahng*) *m* enlargement; extension
agréable (ah-gray-*ahbl*) *adj* pleasing, pleasant, agreeable; enjoyable
agréer (ah-gray-*ay*) *v* accept
agrément (ah-gray-*mahng*) *m* pleasure
agressif (ah-gray-*seef*) *adj* aggressive
agricole (ah-gree-*kol*) *adj* agricultural
agriculteur (ah-gree-kewl-*turr*) *m* farmer
agriculture (ah-gree-kewl-*tewr*) *f* agriculture
aide (ehd) *f* help, assistance, aid; *m/f* helper
aider (ay-*day*) *v* help, aid
aigle (aigl) *m* eagle
aiglefin (ehgl-*fang*) *m* haddock
aigre (aigr) *adj* sour
aigu (ay-*gew*) *adj* (f -guë) acute; sharp; keen
aiguille (ay-*gwee^y*) *f* needle; spire; **travail à l'aiguille** needlework
aiguiser (ay-gee-*zay*) *v* sharpen
ail (igh) *m* (pl ails, aulx) garlic
aile (ehl) *f* wing
ailleurs (ah-*^{y}urr*) *adv* elsewhere; **d'ailleurs** moreover, besides
aimable (ay-*mahbl*) *adj* kind
aimer (ay-*may*) *v* like, *be fond of,

love; fancy; **aimé** beloved; **~ mieux** prefer
aine (ehn) *f* groin
aîné (ay-*nay*) *adj* elder
ainsi (ang-*see*) *adv* so, thus
air (air) *m* air; tune; ***avoir l'air** look
airbag (air-*bahg*) *m* airbag
airelle (ay-*rehl*) *f* blueberry
aisance (eh-*zahngss*) *f* ease
aise (aiz) *f* leisure, ease
aisé (ay-*zay*) *adj* well-to-do
ajournement (ah-zhoor-ner-*mahng*) *m* delay
ajourner (ah-zhoor-*nay*) *v* adjourn, *put off, postpone
ajouter (ah-zhoo-*tay*) *v* add
ajuster (ah-zhew-*stay*) *v* adjust
alarmer (ah-lahr-*may*) *v* alarm
album (ahl-*bom*) *m* album; **~ de collage** scrapbook
alcool (ahl-*kol*) *m* alcohol; **réchaud à ~** spirit stove
alcoolique (ahl-ko-*leek*) *adj* alcoholic
alentours (ah-lahng-*toor*) *mpl* surroundings *pl*; vicinity
alerte (ah-*lehrt*) *f* alarm; *adj* smart
Algérie (ahl-zhay-*ree*) *f* Algeria
Algérien (ahl-zhay-r^y*ang*) *m* Algerian
algérien (ahl-zhay-r^y*ang*) *adj* Algerian
algue (ahlg) *f* alga; seaweed
alimentation (ah-lee-mahng-tah-*s^{y}awng*) *f* nourishment
alimenter (ah-lee-mahng-*tay*) *v* *feed
aliments (ah-lee-*mahng*) *mpl* foodstuffs *pl*; **~ surgelés** frozen food
allaiter (ah-lay-*tay*) *v* nurse
allée (ah-*lay*) *f* avenue
Allemagne (ahl-*mahñ*) *f* Germany
Allemand (ahl-*mahng*) *m*, **-e** *f* German
allemand (ahl-*mahng*) *adj* German
***aller** (ah-*lay*) *v* *go; **~ chercher** collect, pick up; **aller et retour** round trip *Am*; **~ prendre** *get; **bien ~** suit; **s'en ~** *go away; depart
allergie (ah-lehr-*zhee*) *f* allergy
alliance (ah-*l^{y}ahngss*) *f* alliance; wedding ring
allié (ah-*l^{y}ay*) *m* associate; **Alliés** Allies *pl*
allier (ah-*l^{y}ay*): **s'~** ally
allocation (ah-lo-kah-*s^{y}awng*) *f* allowance
allocution (ah-lo-kew-*s^{y}awng*) *f* speech
allonger (ah-lawng-*zhay*) *v* lengthen; dilute
allumage (ah-lew-*maazh*) *m* ignition
allumer (ah-lew-*may*) *v* *light; switch on, turn on
allumette (ah-lew-*meht*) *f* match
allure (ah-*lewr*) *f* pace
alors (ah-*lawr*) *adv* then
alouette (ah-*lweht*) *f* lark
alphabet (ahl-fah-*bay*) *m* alphabet
alpinisme (ahl-pee-*neezm*) *m* mountaineering
alternatif (ahl-tehr-nah-*teef*) *adj* alternate
alternative (ahl-tehr-nah-*teev*) *f* alternative
altitude (ahl-tee-*tewd*) *f* altitude
aluminium (ah-lew-mee-*n^{y}om*) *m* aluminium
amande (ah-*mahngd*) *f* almond
amant (ah-*mahng*) *m*, **-e** *f* lover
amateur (ah-mah-*turr*) *m* amateur
ambassade (ahng-bah-*sahd*) *f* embassy
ambassadeur (ahng-bah-sah-*durr*) *m*, **-drice** *f* ambassador
ambiance (ahng-*b^{y}ahngss*) *f* atmosphere
ambigu (ahng-bee-*gew*) *adj* (f -guë) ambiguous
ambitieux (ahng-bee-*s^{y}ur*) *adj* ambitious
ambre (ahngbr) *m* amber
ambulance (ahng-bew-*lahngss*) *f*

ambulance
âme (aam) *f* soul
amélioration (ah-may-l^{y}o-rah-*s^{y}awn̅g̅*) *f* improvement
améliorer (ah-may-l^{y}o-*ray*) *v* improve
amende (ah-*mahn̅g̅d*) *f* fine, penalty
amener (ahm-*nay*) *v* *bring; lower, *strike
amer (ah-*mair*) *adj* bitter
Américain (ah-may-ree-*kan̅g̅*) *m* American
américain (ah-may-ree-*kan̅g̅*) *adj* American
Amérique (ah-may-*reek*) *f* America; **~ latine** Latin America
ami (ah-*mee*) *m* friend
amiante (ah-*m^{y}ahn̅g̅t*) *m* asbestos
amical (ah-mee-*kahl*) *adj* friendly
amie (ah-*mee*) *f* friend
amitié (ah-mee-*t^{y}ay*) *f* friendship
ammoniaque (ah-mo-*n^{y}ahk*) *f* ammonia
amnistie (ahm-nee-*stee*) *f* amnesty
amoncellement (ah-mawn̅g̅-sehl-*mahn̅g̅*) *m* heap
amont: en ~ (ahn̅g̅-nah-*mawn̅g̅*) upstream
amorce (ah-*mors*) *f* bait
amortir (ah-mor-*teer*) *v* *pay off
amortisseur (ah-mor-tee-*sūrr*) *m* shock absorber
amour (ah-*mōōr*) *m* love; **mon ~** sweetheart
amoureux (ah-moo-*rur*) *adj* in love
ample (ahn̅g̅pl) *adj* detailed; full
ampoule (ahn̅g̅-*pool*) *f* blister; light bulb; **~ de flash** flash bulb
amulette (ah-mew-*leht*) *f* charm
amusant (ah-mew-*zahn̅g̅*) *adj* funny, entertaining
amuse-gueule (ah-mewz-*gurl*) *m* appetizer
amusement (ah-mewz-*mahn̅g̅*) *m* entertainment, amusement
amuser (ah-mew-*zay*) *v* entertain, amuse
amygdales (ah-mee-*dahl*) *fpl* tonsils *pl*
amygdalite (ah-mee-dah-*leet*) *f* tonsillitis
an (ahn̅g̅) *m* year; **par ~** per annum
analogue (ah-nah-*log*) *adj* similar
analyse (ah-nah-*leez*) *f* analysis
analyser (ah-nah-lee-*zay*) *v* analyse; *break down
analyste (ah-nah-*leest*) *m* analyst
ananas (ah-nah-*nah*) *m* pineapple
anarchie (ah-nahr-*shee*) *f* anarchy
anatomie (ah-nah-to-*mee*) *f* anatomy
ancêtre (ahn̅g̅-*saitr*) *m* ancestor
anchois (ahn̅g̅-*shwah*) *m* anchovy
ancien (ahn̅g̅-*s^{y}an̅g̅*) *adj* ancient; former
ancre (ahn̅g̅kr) *f* anchor
âne (aan) *m* donkey
anéantissement (ah-nay-ahn̅g̅-tee-*smahn̅g̅*) *m* destruction
anémie (ah-nay-*mee*) *f* anaemia
anesthésie (ah-neh-stay-*zee*) *f* anaesthesia
anesthésique (ah-neh-stay-*zeek*) *m* anaesthetic
ange (ahn̅g̅zh) *m* angel
Anglais (ahn̅g̅-*glay*) *m* Englishman; **les ~** the English
anglais (ahn̅g̅-*glay*) *adj* English
Anglaise (ahn̅g̅-*glays*) *f* Englishwoman
angle (ahn̅g̅gl) *m* angle
Angleterre (ahn̅g̅-gler-*tair*) *f* England; Britain
angoisse (ahn̅g̅-*gwahss*) *f* anguish
anguille (ahn̅g̅-*geey*) *f* eel
animal (ah-nee-*mahl*) *m* animal; **~ familier** pet
animateur (ah-nee-mah-*tūrr*) *m*, **-trice** *f* entertainer
animer (ah-nee-*may*) *v* enliven; **animé** busy, active, crowded

anneau (ah-*noa*) *m* ring
année (ah-*nay*) *f* year; ~ **bissextile** leap year
annexe (ah-*nehks*) *f* annex
annexer (ah-nehk-*say*) *v* annex
anniversaire (ah-nee-vehr-*sair*) *m* anniversary, birthday; jubilee
annonce (ah-*nawn̅g̅ss*) *f* announcement; advertisement; ~ **publicitaire** commercial
annoncer (ah-nawn̅g̅-*say*) *v* announce
annuaire (ah-*nwair*) *m* annual; ~ **téléphonique** telephone directory; telephone book *Am*
annuel (ah-*nwehl*) *adj* yearly, annual
annulation (ah-new-lah-*s^{y}awn̅g̅*) *f* cancellation
annuler (ah-new-*lay*) *v* cancel
anonyme (ah-no-*neem*) *adj* anonymous
anorak (ah-no-*rahk*) *m* anorak
antenne (ahn̅g̅-*tehn*) *f* aerial
antérieur (ahn̅g̅-tay-*r^{y}u̅r̅r̅*) *adj* prior, previous
antérieurement (ahn̅g̅-tay-r^{y}urr-*mahn̅g̅*) *adv* formerly
antialcoolique (ahn̅g̅-tee-ahl-ko-*leek*) *m* teetotaller
antibiotique (ahn̅g̅-tee-b^{y}o-*teek*) *m* antibiotic
anticiper (ahn̅g̅-tee-see-*pay*) *v* anticipate
antigel (ahn̅g̅-tee-*zhehl*) *m* antifreeze
antipathie (ahn̅g̅-tee-pah-*tee*) *f* dislike, antipathy
antipathique (ahn̅g̅-tee-pah-*teek*) *adj* nasty; unpleasant
antiquaire (ahn̅g̅-tee-*kair*) *m/f* antique dealer
antique (ahn̅g̅-*teek*) *adj* antique, ancient
antiquité (ahn̅g̅-tee-kee-*tay*) *f* antique; **Antiquité** antiquity; **antiquités** antiquities *pl*
anxiété (ahn̅g̅-ks^{y}ay-*tay*) *f* anxiety
août (oo) August
***apercevoir** (ah-pehr-ser-*vwaar*) *v* perceive
aperçu (ah-pehr-*sew*) *m* glimpse
apéritif (ah-pay-ree-*teef*) *m* drink, aperitif
apeuré (ah-pur-*ray*) *adj* afraid
apogée (ah-po-*zhay*) *m* height, zenith; peak
***apparaître** (ah-pah-*raitr*) *v* appear
appareil (ah-pah-*ray*) *m* appliance, apparatus, machine; aircraft; ~ **à jetons** slot machine; ~ **de chauffage** heater; ~ **photographique** camera
apparemment (ah-pah-rah-*mahn̅g̅*) *adv* apparently
apparence (ah-pah-*rahn̅g̅ss*) *f* appearance; semblance, look
apparent (ah-pah-*rahn̅g̅*) *adj* apparent
apparenté (ah-pah-rahn̅g̅-*tay*) *adj* related
appartement (ah-pahr-ter-*mahn̅g̅*) *m* flat; apartment *Am*, suite
***appartenir** (ah-pahr-ter-*neer*) *v* belong
appel (ah-*pehl*) *m* call, cry; appeal; ~ **interurbain** trunk-call; ~ **téléphonique** telephone call
appeler (ah-*play*) *v* call, cry; **s'appeler** *be called
appendice (ah-pan̅g̅-*deess*) *m* appendix
appendicite (ah-pan̅g̅-dee-*seet*) *f* appendicitis
appétissant (ah-pay-tee-*sahn̅g̅*) *adj* appetizing
appétit (ah-pay-*tee*) *m* appetite
applaudir (ah-ploa-*deer*) *v* clap
applaudissements (ah-ploa-dee-*smahn̅g̅*) *mpl* applause
application (ah-plee-kah-*s^{y}awn̅g̅*) *f* application; diligence
appliquer (ah-plee-*kay*) *v* apply;

s'appliquer à apply
apporter (ah-por-*tay*) *v* *bring; fetch
appréciation (ah-pray-s^{y}ah-*s^{y}awng*) *f* appreciation
apprécier (ah-pray-*s^{y}ay*) *v* appreciate; judge
***apprendre** (ah-*prahngdr*) *v* *learn; *teach; ~ **par cœur** memorize
apprenti (ah-prahn-*tee*) *m*, **-e** *f* apprentice
apprivoiser (ah-pree-vwah-*zay*) *v* tame; **apprivoisé** tame
approbation (ah-pro-bah-*s^{y}awng*) *f* approval
approche (ah-*prosh*) *f* approach
approcher (ah-pro-*shay*) *v* approach
approprié (ah-pro-pree-*ay*) *adj* appropriate, adequate, convenient; proper, suitable
approuver (ah-proo-*vay*) *v* approve; consent
approvisionner en (ah-pro-vee-z^{y}o-*nay*) furnish with
approximatif (ah-prok-see-mah-*teef*) *adj* approximate
approximativement (ah-prok-see-mah-teev-*mahng*) *adv* approximately
appuyer (ah-pwee-*^{y}ay*) *v* press; **s'appuyer** *lean
âpre (aapr) *adj* harsh
après (ah-*pray*) *adv* afterwards; *prep* after; ~ **que** after; **d'après** according to
après-demain (ah-pray-der-*mang*) *adv* the day after tomorrow
après-midi (ah-pray-mee-*dee*) *m/f* afternoon
apte (ahpt) *adj* apt
aptitude (ahp-tee-*tewd*) *f* faculty
aquarelle (ah-kwah-*rehl*) *f* watercolo(u)r
Arabe (ah-*rahb*) *m* Arab
arabe (ah-*rahb*) *adj* Arab
Arabie Séoudite (ah-rah-bee say-oo-*deet*) Saudi Arabia
araignée (ah-ray-*ñay*) *f* spider; **toile d'araignée** spider's web
arbitraire (ahr-bee-*trair*) *adj* arbitrary
arbitre (ahr-*beetr*) *m* umpire
arbre (ahrbr) *m* tree
arbuste (ahr-*bewst*) *m* shrub
arc (ahrk) *m* bow
arcade (ahr-*kahd*) *f* arcade
arc-en-ciel (ahr-kahng-*s^{y}ehl*) *m* rainbow
arche (ahrsh) *f* arch
archéologie (ahr-kay-o-lo-*zhee*) *f* arch(a)eology
archéologue (ahr-kay-o-*log*) *m/f* arch(a)eologist
archevêque (ahr-sher-*vehk*) *m* archbishop
architecte (ahr-shee-*tehkt*) *m* architect
architecture (ahr-shee-tehk-*tewr*) *f* architecture
archives (ahr-*sheev*) *fpl* archives *pl*
ardoise (ahr-*dwaaz*) *f* slate
arène (ah-*rehn*) *f* bullring
arête (ah-*reht*) *f* ridge; fishbone, bone
argent (ahr-*zhahng*) *m* silver; money; ~ **comptant** cash; ~ **liquide** cash; **en** ~ silver
argenterie (ahr-zhahng-*tree*) *f* silverware
argentin (ahr-zhahng-*tang*) *adj* Argentinian
Argentine (ahr-zhahng-*teen*) *f* Argentina
argile (ahr-*zheel*) *f* clay
argument (ahr-gew-*mahng*) *m* argument
argumenter (ahr-gew-mahng-*tay*) *v* argue
armateur (ahr-mah-*turr*) *m* shipowner
arme (ahrm) *f* weapon, arm
armée (ahr-*may*) *f* army
armer (ahr-*may*) *v* arm
armoire (ahr-*mwaar*) *f* cupboard

armure (ahr-*mewr*) *f* arm(o)ur
arôme (ah-*roam*) *m* aroma
arqué (ahr-*kay*) *adj* arched
arracher (ah-rah-*shay*) *v* extract
arrangement (ah-rahngzh-*mahng*) *m* settlement
arranger (ah-rahng-*zhay*) *v* arrange; settle
arrestation (ah-reh-stah-*s^{y}awng*) *f* arrest
arrêt (ah-*reh*) *m* stop
arrêter (ah-ray-*tay*) *v* stop; arrest; **s'arrêter** halt; pull up
arriéré (ah-r^{y}ay-*ray*) *adj* overdue
arrière (ah-*r^{y}air*) *m* rear; **en ~** backwards, back; behind
arrivée (ah-ree-*vay*) *f* coming, arrival
arriver (ah-ree-*vay*) *v* arrive; happen
arrondi (ah-rawng-*dee*) *adj* rounded
arrondissement (ah-rawng-dee-*smahng*) *m* district
art (aar) *m* art; **arts et métiers** arts and crafts
artère (ahr-*tair*) *f* artery; thoroughfare
artichaut (ahr-tee-*shoa*) *m* artichoke
article (ahr-*teekl*) *m* article; item; **articles d'épicerie** groceries *pl*; **articles de toilette** toiletry
articulation (ahr-tee-kew-lah-*s^{y}awng*) *f* joint
artificiel (ahr-tee-fee-*s^{y}ehl*) *adj* artificial
artisan (ahr-tee-*zahng*) *m* craftsman
artisanat (ahr-tee-zah-*nah*) *m* handicraft
artiste (ahr-*teest*) *m/f* artist
artistique (ahr-tee-*steek*) *adj* artistic
ascenseur (ah-sahng-*surr*) *m* lift; elevator *Am*
ascension (ah-sahng-*s^{y}awng*) *f* climb; ***faire l'ascension de** ascend
Asiatique (ah-z^{y}ah-*teek*) *m* Asian
asiatique (ah-z^{y}ah-*teek*) *adj* Asian
Asie (ah-*zee*) *f* Asia
asile (ah-*zeel*) *m* asylum
aspect (ah-*spay*) *m* aspect; appearance, look
asperge (ah-*spehrzh*) *f* asparagus
asphalte (ah-*sfahlt*) *m* asphalt
aspirateur (ah-spee-rah-*turr*) *m* vacuum cleaner; **passer l'aspirateur** hoover; vacuum *Am*
aspirer (ah-spee-*ray*) *v* aspire; **~ à** pursue, aim at
aspirine (ah-spee-*reen*) *f* aspirin
assaisonner (ah-say-zo-*nay*) *v* flavour
assassinat (ah-sah-see-*nah*) *m* assassination, murder
assassiner (ah-sah-see-*nay*) *v* murder
assécher (ah-say-*shay*) *v* drain
assemblée (ah-sahng-*blay*) *f* assembly, meeting
assembler (ah-sahng-*blay*) *v* assemble; join
assentiment (ah-sahng-tee-*mahng*) *m* consent
***asseoir** (ah-*swaar*): **s'~** *sit down
assez (ah-*say*) *adv* enough; fairly, pretty, rather, quite
assidu (ah-see-*dew*) *adj* diligent
assiette (ah-*s^{y}eht*) *f* plate, dish
assigner (ah-see-*ñay*) *v* allot; **~ à** assign to
assistance (ah-see-*stahngss*) *f* assistance; attendance
assistant (ah-see-*stahng*) *m* assistant
assister (ah-see-*stay*) *v* assist, aid; **~ à** attend, assist at
association (ah-so-s^{y}ah-*s^{y}awng*) *f* society, club, association
associé (ah-so-*s^{y}ay*) *m*, **-e** *f* associate, partner
associer (ah-so-*s^{y}ay*) *v* associate
assoiffé (ah-swah-*fay*) *adj* thirsty
assortiment (ah-sor-tee-*mahng*) *m* assortment
assurance (ah-sew-*rahngss*) *f* insurance; **assurance-vie** *f* life

insurance; **assurance-voyages** *f* travel insurance

assurer (ah-sew-*ray*) *v* insure, assure; **s'assurer de** ascertain; secure

asthme (ahsm) *m* asthma

astronomie (ah-stro-no-*mee*) *f* astronomy

astucieux (ah-stew-*s^{y}ur*) *adj* clever

atelier (ah-ter-*l^{y}ay*) *m* workshop

athlète (ah-*tleht*) *m/f* athlete

athlétisme (ah-tlay-*teezm*) *m* athletics *pl*

Atlantique (aht-lahng-*teek*) *adj*, *n* Atlantic

atmosphère (aht-mo-*sfair*) *f* atmosphere

atomique (ah-to-*meek*) *adj* atomic

atroce (ah-*tross*) *adj* horrible

attacher (ah-tah-*shay*) *v* fasten, attach; tie; **attaché à** attached to

attaque (ah-*tahk*) *f* fit, attack; hold-up; stroke

attaquer (ah-tah-*kay*) *v* attack, assault

***atteindre** (ah-*tangdr*) *v* attain, reach

attendre (ah-*tahngdr*) *v* wait; expect, await; **en attendant** in the meantime

attente (ah-*tahngt*) *f* waiting; expectation

attentif (ah-tahng-*teef*) *adj* attentive, careful

attention (ah-tahng-*s^{y}awng*) *f* attention, consideration; notice; ***faire ~** *pay attention, look out; beware; ***faire ~ à** attend to, mind; **prêter ~ à** mind

atterrir (ah-tay-*reer*) *v* land

attestation (ah-teh-stah-*s^{y}awng*) *f* certificate

attirer (ah-tee-*ray*) *v* attract

attitude (ah-tee-*tewd*) *f* attitude; position

attouchement (ah-toosh-*mahng*) *m* touch

attraction (ah-trahk-*s^{y}awng*) *f* attraction

attrait (ah-*tray*) *m* attraction; **attraits** charm

attraper (ah-trah-*pay*) *v* *catch; contract

attribuer à (ah-tree-*bway*) assign to

aube (oab) *f* dawn

auberge (oa-*behrzh*) *f* inn, hostel; roadhouse; roadside restaurant; **~ de jeunesse** youth hostel

aubergine (oa-behr-*zheen*) *f* eggplant

aucun (oa-*kurng*) *adj* no; *pron* none

audace (oa-*dahss*) *f* nerve

audacieux (oa-dah-*s^{y}ur*) *adj* bold

au-dessous (oa-der-*soo*) *adv* beneath; **~ de** below

au-dessus (oa-der-*sew*) *adv* over; **~ de** above; over

audible (oa-*deebl*) *adj* audible

auditeur (oa-dee-*turr*) *m*, **auditrice** *f* auditor, listener

augmentation (oag-mahng-tah-*s^{y}awng*) *f* increase, rise; **~ de salaire** rise; raise *Am*

augmenter (oag-mahng-*tay*) *v* increase

aujourd'hui (oa-zhoor-*dwee*) *adv* today

auparavant (oa-pah-rah-*vahng*) *adv* formerly

auprès de (oa-*pray* der) near

auriculaire (oa-ree-kew-*lair*) *m* little finger

aurore (oa-*rawr*) *f* dawn

aussi (oa-*see*) *adv* too, also; as; **~ bien** as well; **~ bien que** as well as; both … and

aussitôt (oa-see-*toa*) *adv* at once; **~ que** as soon as

Australie (oa-strah-*lee*) *f* Australia

australien (oa-strah-*l^{y}ang*) *adj* Australian

autant (oa-*tahng*) *adv* as much

autel (oa-*tehl*) *m* altar

auteur (oa-*turr*) *m* author
authentique (oa-tahng-*teek*) *adj* authentic, original, genuine
auto (oa-*toa*) *f* automobile
autobus (oa-toa-*bewss*) *m* bus
autocar (oa-toa-*kaar*) *m* coach
auto-école (oa-toa-ay-*kol*) *f* driving school
automatique (oa-toa-mah-*teek*) *adj* automatic
automatisation (oa-toa-mah-tee-zah-*s^{y}awng*) *f* automation
automne (oa-*ton*) *m* autumn; fall *Am*
automobile (oa-toa-mo-*beel*) *f* motorcar
automobiliste (oa-toa-mo-bee-*leest*) *m/f* motorist
autonome (oa-to-*nom*) *adj* autonomous; independent
autonomie (oa-to-no-*mee*) *f* self-government
autoradio (oa-toa-rah-*d^{y}oa*) *m* car radio
autorisation (oa-to-ree-zah-*s^{y}awng*) *f* authorization; permission
autoriser (oa-to-ree-*zay*) *v* allow; license; **~ à** allow to
autoritaire (oa-to-ree-*tair*) *adj* authoritarian
autorité (oa-to-ree-*tay*) *f* authority
autoroute (oa-toa-*root*) *f* motorway; highway *Am*
auto-stop (oa-toa-*stop*): ***faire de l'auto-stop** hitchhike
auto-stoppeur (oa-toa-sto-*purr*) *m*, **-euse** *f* hitchhiker
autour (oa-*toor*) *adv* about; around; **~ de** around, about; round
autre (oatr) *adj* other; different; **entre autres** among other things
autrefois (oa-trer-*fwah*) *adv* formerly
autrement (oa-trer-*mahng*) *adv* otherwise, else
Autriche (oa-*treesh*) *f* Austria
Autrichien (oa-tree-*sh^{y}ang*) *m* Austrian
autrichien (oa-tree-*sh^{y}ang*) *adj* Austrian
autruche (oa-*trewsh*) *f* ostrich
aval: en ~ (ahng-nah-*vahl*) downstream
avalanche (ah-vah-*lahngsh*) *f* avalanche
avaler (ah-vah-*lay*) *v* swallow
avance (ah-*vahngss*) *f* lead; advance; **à l'avance** in advance; **d'avance** before; in advance
avancement (ah-vahng-*smahng*) *m* advance
avancer (ah-vahng-*say*) *v* advance
avant (ah-*vahng*) *prep* before; *adv* before; **~ que** before; **en ~** forward; ahead, onwards
avantage (ah-vahng-*taazh*) *m* profit, advantage, benefit
avantageux (ah-vahng-tah-*zhur*) *adj* advantageous; cheap
avant-dernier (ah-vahng-dehr-*n^{y}ay*) *adj* last but one
avant-hier (ah-vahng-*t^{y}air*) *adv* the day before yesterday
avant-saison (ah-vahng-seh-*zawng*) *f* off-peak season
avec (ah-*vehk*) *prep* with
avenir (ah-*vneer*) *m* future
aventure (ah-vahng-*tewr*) *f* adventure
avenue (ah-*vnew*) *f* avenue
averse (ah-*vehrs*) *f* shower; downpour
aversion (ah-vehr-*s^{y}awng*) *f* aversion, dislike
avertir (ah-vehr-*teer*) *v* warn, caution; notify
avertissement (ah-vehr-tee-*smahng*) *m* warning
aveugle (ah-*vurgl*) *adj* blind
aveugler (ah-vur-*glay*) *v* blind
aviation (ah-v^{y}ah-*s^{y}awng*) *f* aviation
avion (ah-*v^{y}awng*) *m* aeroplane; plane,

aircraft; airplane *Am*; **~ à réaction** jet
avis (ah-*vee*) *m* advice; notice
avocat (ah-vo-*kah*) *m* solicitor, attorney, lawyer, barrister
avoine (ah-*vwahn*) *f* oats *pl*
***avoir** (ah-*vwaar*) *v* *have
avoisinant (ah-vwah-zee-*nahng*) *adj* neighbo(u)ring
avortement (ah-vort-*mahng*) *m* abortion
avoué (ah-voo-*ay*) *m* solicitor
avouer (ah-voo-*ay*) *v* admit
avril (ah-*vreel*) April

B

babeurre (bah-*burr*) *m* buttermilk
bâbord (bah-*bawr*) *m* port
bac (bahk), **baccalauréat** (bah-kah-loa-ray-*ah*) *m* school-leaving certificate
bactérie (bahk-tay-*ree*) *f* bacterium
bagage (bah-*gaazh*) *m* baggage; luggage; **~ à main** hand luggage; hand baggage *Am*
bague (bahg) *f* ring; **~ de fiançailles** engagement ring
baguette (bah-geht) *f* stick, rod; stick of bread; baton; **~ magique** magic wand
baie (bay) *f* berry; bay, creek
baigner (bay-*ñay*)*v*: **se ~** bathe
baignoire (bay-*ñwaar*) *f* bath (tub); groundfloor box
bail (bigh) *m* (pl baux) lease
bâiller (bah-^{y}*ay*) *v* yawn
bain (bang) *m* bath; **~ turc** Turkish bath; **bonnet de ~** bathing cap; **caleçon de ~** bathing trunks
baiser (bay-*zay*) *m* kiss
baisse (behss) *f* drop, decline
baisser (bay-*say*) *v* lower
bal (bahl) *m* (pl ~s) ball
balai (bah-*lay*) *m* broom
balance (bah-*lahngss*) *f* scales *pl*
balancer (bah-lahng-*say*) *v* *swing; rock
balançoire (bah-lahng-*swaar*) *f* swing; seesaw
balayer (bah-lay-^{y}*ay*) *v* *sweep
balbutier (bahl-bew-*s^{y}ay*) *v* falter
balcon (bahl-*kawng*) *m* balcony; circle
baleine (bah-*lehn*) *f* whale
balle (bahl) *f* ball; bullet
ballet (bah-*lay*) *m* ballet
ballon (bah-*lawng*) *m* football, ball; balloon
balustrade (bah-lew-*strahd*) *f* rail
bambin (bahng-*bang*) *m* tot, toddler
bambou (bahng-*boo*) *m* bamboo
banane (bah-*nahn*) *f* banana
banc (bahng) *m* bench; **~ d'école** desk
bande (bahngd) *f* bunch, gang; tape, strip; **bandes dessinées** comics *pl*
bandit (bahng-*dee*) *m* bandit
banlieue (bahng-*l^{y}ur*) *f* suburb
bannière (bah-*n^{y}air*) *f* banner
banque (bahngk) *f* bank
banquet (bahng-*kay*) *m* banquet
baptême (bah-*tehm*) *m* christening, baptism
baptiser (bah-tee-*zay*) *v* christen, baptize
bar (baar) *m* bar
baratiner (bah-rah-tee-*nay*) *v* talk rubbish
barbe (bahrb) *f* beard
baril (bah-*ree*) *m* cask, barrel

bariton (bah-ree-*tawng*) *m* baritone
barman (bahr-*mahn*) *m* barman; bartender
baromètre (bah-ro-*mehtr*) *m* barometer
baroque (bah-*rok*) *adj* baroque
barque (bahrk) *f* boat
barrage (bah-*raazh*) *m* dam
barre (baar) *f* rod, bar, rail; helm; counter
barreau (bah-*roa*) *m* bar
barrière (bah-*r^yair*) *f* barrier; fence
bas[1] (bah) *adj* (f ~se) low; **en ~** down; downstairs; **en ~ de** under, below; **vers le ~** downwards, down
bas[2] (bah) *m* stocking; **~ élastiques** support hose
bas-côté (bah-koa-*tay*) *m* aisle
bascule (bah-*skewl*) *f* weighing machine
base (bahz) *f* basis, base
baser (bah-*zay*) *v* base
basilique (bah-zee-*leek*) *f* basilica
baskets (bah-*skeht*) *mpl* tennis shoes, plimsolls *pl*
basse (bahss) *f* bass
bassin (bah-*sang*) *m* pelvis, basin
bataille (bah-*tigh*) *f* battle
bateau (bah-*toa*) *m* boat; **~ à moteur** motor boat; **~ à rames** rowing boat; **~ à vapeur** steamer; **~ à voiles** sailing boat; **bateau-citerne** *m* tanker
bâtiment (bah-tee-*mahng*) *m* building; building trade
bâtir (bah-*teer*) *v* *build; construct
bâton (bah-*tawng*) *m* stick; **bâtons de ski** ski sticks; ski poles *Am*
***battre** (bahtr) *v* slap; *beat; shuffle; **se ~** *fight
bavard (bah-*vaar*) *adj* talkative
bavardage (bah-vahr-*daazh*) *m* chat
bavarder (bah-vahr-*day*) *v* chat
beau (boa) *adj* (bel; f belle) beautiful; fair, pretty, lovely, handsome
beaucoup (boa-*koo*) *adv* much; far; **~ de** much; many; **de ~** by far
beau-fils (boa-*feess*) *m* son-in-law
beau-frère (boa-*frair*) *m* brother-in-law
beau-père (boa-*pair*) *m* father-in-law; stepfather
beauté (boa-*tay*) *f* beauty; **produits de ~** cosmetics *pl*
beaux-arts (boa-*zaar*) *mpl* fine arts
beaux-parents (boa-pah-*rahng*) *mpl* parents-in-law *pl*
bébé (bay-*bay*) *m* baby
bec (behk) *m* beak; nozzle
bêche (behsh) *f* spade
beige (baizh) *adj* beige
beignet (bay-*ñay*) *m* doughnut
Belge (behlzh) *m* Belgian
belge (behlzh) *adj* Belgian
Belgique (behl-*zheek*) *f* Belgium
belle-fille (behl-*feey*) *f* daughter-in-law
belle-mère (behl-*mair*) *f* mother-in-law; stepmother
belle-sœur (behl-*sūrr*) *f* sister-in-law
bénédiction (bay-nay-deek-*s^yawng*) *f* blessing
bénéfice (bay-nay-*feess*) *m* profit, benefit
bénéficiaire (bay-nay-fee-*s^yair*) *m/f* payee
bénéficier de (bay-nay-fee-*s^yay*) profit by
bénir (bay-*neer*) *v* bless
béquille (bay-*keey*) *f* crutch
berceau (behr-*soa*) *m* cradle; **~ de voyage** carrycot
béret (bay-*ray*) *m* beret
berge (behrzh) *f* embankment
berger (behr-*zhay*) *m* shepherd
besogne (ber-*zoñ*) *f* work
besoin (ber-*zwang*) *m* need; want; ***avoir ~ de** need
bétail (bay-*tigh*) *m* cattle *pl*

bête (beht) *f* beast; *adj* silly, dumb; **~ de proie** beast of prey
bêtise (bay-*teez*) *f* stupidity; blunder; nonsense
béton (bay-*tawng*) *m* concrete
betterave (beh-*traav*) *f* beetroot, beet
beurre (burr) *m* butter
biberon (bee-*brawng*) *m* feeding (*Am* nursing) bottle; tippler
Bible (beebl) *f* bible
bibliothèque (bee-blee-o-*tehk*) *f* library
bicyclette (bee-see-*kleht*) *f* cycle, bicycle
bien (b^{y}ang) *adv* well; **bien!** well!; all right!; **~ que** though, although; **biens** *mpl* goods *pl*, possessions
bien-être (b^{y}ang-*naitr*) *m* welfare; comfort
bientôt (b^{y}ang-*toa*) *adv* soon; shortly
bienveillance (b^{y}ang-vay-^{y}*ahngss*) *f* goodwill
bienvenu (b^{y}ang-*vnew*) *adj* welcome
bière (b^{y}air) *f* beer; ale
bifteck (beef-*tehk*) *m* steak
bifurcation (bee-fewr-kah-*s^{y}awng*) *f* fork, road fork
bifurquer (bee-fewr-*kay*) *v* fork
bigorneau (bee-gor-*noa*) *m* winkle
bigoudi (bee-goo-*dee*) *m* curler
bijou (bee-*zhoo*) *m* (pl ~x) jewel; gem; **bijoux** jewellery, jewelry *Am*
bijoutier (bee-zhoo-*t^{y}ay*) *m* jewel(l)er
bikini (bee-kee-*nee*) *m* bikini
bilan (bee-*lahng*) *m* balance
bile (beel) *f* gall, bile
bilingue (bee-*langg*) *adj* bilingual
billard (bee-^{y}*aar*) *m* billiards *pl*
bille (beey) *f* marble
billet (bee-^{y}*ay*) *m* ticket; **~ de banque** banknote; **~ de quai** platform ticket; **~ gratuit** free ticket
biologie (bee-o-lo-*zhee*) *f* biology
biscotte (bee-*skot*) *f* rusk
biscuit (bee-*skwee*) *m* biscuit; cookie *Am*; cracker *Am*
bistrot (bee-*stroa*) *m* pub
bizarre (bee-*zaar*) *adj* funny, odd, strange
blague (blahg) *f* joke; **~ à tabac** tobacco pouch
blaireau (bleh-*roa*) *m* shaving brush
blâme (blaam) *m* blame
blâmer (blah-*may*) *v* blame
blanc (blahng) *adj* (f blanche) white; blank
blanchisserie (blahng-shee-*sree*) *f* laundry
blé (blay) *m* corn; wheat; grain
blesser (blay-*say*) *v* injure, *hurt, wound; offend
blessure (blay-*sewr*) *f* wound; injury
bleu (blur) *adj* (pl bleus) blue; *m* bruise
bloc (blok) *m* block
bloc-notes (blok-*not*) *m* pad, writing pad
blond (blawng) *adj* fair
blonde (blawngd) *f* blonde
bloquer (blo-*kay*) *v* block
bobine (bo-*been*) *f* spool; **~ d'allumage** ignition coil
bœuf (burf) *m* ox; beef
bohémien (bo-ay-*m^{y}ang*) *m* Bohemian
***boire** (bwaar) *v* *drink
bois (bwah) *m* wood; forest; **~ d'œuvre** timber; **en ~** wooden
boisé (bwah-*zay*) *adj* wooded
boisson (bwah-*sawng*) *f* drink, beverage; **~ non alcoolisée** soft drink; **boissons alcoolisées** spirits
boîte (bwaht) *f* box; can, tin; **~ à ordures** dustbin; trash can *Am*; **~ à outils** tool kit; **~ aux lettres** letterbox; mailbox *Am*; **~ d'allumettes** matchbox; **~ de couleurs** paintbox; **~ de nuit** nightclub; **~ de vitesse**

gearbox

boiter (bwah-*tay*) *v* limp

boiteux (bwah-*tur*) *adj* lame

bol (bol) *m* basin; bowl

Bolivie (bo-lee-*vee*) *f* Bolivia

Bolivien (bo-lee-*v*^{y}*ang*) *m* Bolivian

bolivien (bo-lee-*v*^{y}*ang*) *adj* Bolivian

bombarder (bawng-bahr-*day*) *v* bomb

bombe (bawngb) *f* bomb

bon[1] (bawng) *adj* good; enjoyable, nice; kind

bon[2] (bawng) *m* voucher; **~ de commande** order form

bonbon (bawng-*bawng*) *m* sweet; candy *Am*

bond (bawng) *m* jump

bondé (bawng-*day*) *adj* crowded

bondir (bawng-*deer*) *v* *leap

bonheur (bo-*nurr*) *m* happiness

bonjour! (bawng-*zhoor*) hello!

bonne (bon) *f* maid; housemaid; **~ d'enfants** nurse

bonne-maman (bon-mah-*mahng*) *f* grandmother

bonnet (bo-*nay*) *m* cap; **gros ~** bigwig, *Am* big shot

bon-papa (bawng-pah-*pah*) *m* grandfather

bonsoir! (bawng-*swaar*) good evening!

bonté (bawng-*tay*) *f* kindness

bord (bawr) *m* edge; brim, verge, border; **à ~** aboard; **~ de la mer** seaside, seashore; **~ de la rivière** riverside; **~ de la route** roadside; wayside; **~ du trottoir** curb

bordel (bor-*dehl*) *m* brothel

borne routière (born roo-*t*^{y}*air*) milestone

borné (bor-*nay*) *adj* narrow-minded

bosquet (bo-*skay*) *m* grove

bosse (boss) *f* dent, lump

botanique (bo-tah-*neek*) *f* botany

botte (bot) *f* boot

bottin (bo-*tang*) *m* telephone directory

bouc (book) *m* goat; **~ émissaire** scapegoat

bouche (boosh) *f* mouth

bouchée (boo-*shay*) *f* bite

boucher[1] (boo-*shay*) *m*, **-ère** *f* butcher

boucher[2] (boo-*shay*) *v* stop up

boucherie (boo-*shree*) *f* butcher's shop

bouchon (boo-*shawng*) *m* cork; stopper

boucle (bookl) *f* buckle; curl; loop; **~ d'oreille** earring

boucler (boo-*klay*) *v* curl; **bouclé** curly

boudin (boo-*dang*) *m* black pudding, *Am* blood sausage

boue (boo) *f* mud; slush

bouée (boo-*ay*) *f* buoy; **~ de sauvetage** lifebelt

boueux (boo-*ur*) *adj* muddy

bouger (boo-*zhay*) *v* move; stir

bougie (boo-*zhee*) *f* candle; **~ d'allumage** sparking plug

***bouillir** (boo-^{y}*eer*) *v* boil

bouilloire (boo-^{y}*waar*) *f* kettle

bouillotte (boo-^{y}*ot*) *f* hot-water bottle

boulanger (boo-lahng-*zhay*) *m*, **boulangère** *f* baker

boulangerie (boo-lahng-*zhree*) *f* bakery

boule (bool) *f* ball

bouleau (boo-*loa*) *m* birch

boulevard (bool-*vaar*) *m* boulevard

bouleversé (bool-vehr-*say*) *adj* upset

boulon (boo-*lawng*) *m* bolt

boulot (boo-*loa*) *m* job

bouquet (boo-*kay*) *m* bunch, bouquet

bouquin (boo-*kang*) *m* book

bourdon (boor-*dawng*) *m* great bell; bumblebee; **faux ~** drone

bourg (boor) *m* town

bourgeois (boor-*zhwah*) *adj* bourgeois, middle-class

bourgeon (boor-*zhawng̅*) *m* bud
bourré (boo-*ray*) *adj* chock-full
bourse (boors) *f* purse; **~ des valeurs** stock exchange; **~ d'études** scholarship
boussole (boo-*sol*) *f* compass
bout (boo) *m* end; tip
bouteille (boo-*tay*) *f* bottle
boutique (boo-*teek*) *f* boutique; shop
bouton (boo-*tawng̅*) *m* button, knob; **~ de col** collar stud; **boutons de manchettes** cuff links *pl*
boutonner (boo-to-*nay*) *v* button
boutonnière (boo-to-*nʸair*) *f* buttonhole
bowling (boa-*leeng*) *m* bowling; bowling alley
boxer (bok-*say*) *v* box
bracelet (brah-*slay*) *m* bracelet; bangle; **bracelet-montre** *m* wristwatch; **~ pour montre** watchstrap
braconner (brah-ko-*nay*) *v* poach
braguette (brah-*geht*) *f* fly
branche (brahng̅sh) *f* branch
brancher (brahng̅-*shay*) *v* connect; plug in
branchie (brahng̅-*shee*) *f* gill
branlant (brahng̅-*lahng̅*) *adj* unsteady
bras (brah) *m* arm; **bras-dessus brasdessous** arm-in-arm
brasse (brahss) *f* breaststroke; **~ papillon** butterfly stroke
brasser (brah-*say*) *v* brew
brasserie (brah-*sree*) *f* brewery
brave (brahv) *adj* brave, courageous; good
brèche (brehsh) *f* breach; gap
bref (brehf) *adj* (f brève) brief
Brésil (bray-*zeel*) *m* Brazil
brésilien (bray-zee-*lʸang̅*) *adj* Brazilian
bretelles (brer-*tehl*) *fpl* braces *pl*; suspenders *plAm*
breton (brer-*tawn*) *adj* Breton
brevet (brer-*vay*) *m* patent
bricoler (bree-ko-*lay*) do odd jobs; potter
bridge (breej) *m* bridge
brillant (bree-*ʸahng̅*) *adj* bright; brilliant
briller (bree-*ʸay*) *v* *shine; glow
brin d'herbe (brang̅ dehrb) blade of grass
brindille (brang̅-*deey*) *f* twig
brioche (bree-*osh*) *f* bun
brique (breek) *f* brick
briquet (bree-*kay*) *m* cigarette lighter, lighter
brise (breez) *f* breeze
briser (bree-*zay*) *v* *break; **brisé** broken
Britannique (bree-tah-*neek*) *m* Briton
britannique (bree-tah-*neek*) *adj* British
broche (brosh) *f* brooch; spit
brochet (bro-*shay*) *m* pike
brochette (bro-*sheht*) *f* skewer; pin
brochure (bro-*shewr*) *f* brochure
brocoli (bro-ko-*lee*) *m* broccoli
broder (bro-*day*) *v* embroider
broderie (bro-*dree*) *f* embroidery
bronchite (brawng̅-*sheet*) *f* bronchitis
bronze (brawng̅z) *m* bronze; **en ~** bronze
bronzer (brawng̅-*zay*) *v* bronze; tan
brosse (bross) *f* brush; **~ à cheveux** hairbrush; **~ à dents** toothbrush; **~ à ongles** nailbrush
brosser (bro-*say*) *v* brush
brouette (broo-*eht*) *f* wheelbarrow
brouillard (broo-*ʸaar*) *m* fog, mist
brouiller (broo-*ʸay*) *v* mix; mix up; *sow discord
bruit (brwee) *m* noise
brûler (brew-*lay*) *v* *burn
brûlure (brew-*lewr*) *f* burn; **brûlures d'estomac** heartburn

brume (brewm) *f* mist; haze
brumeux (brew-*mur*) *adj* misty; hazy, foggy
brun (brurn͞g) *adj* brown
brunette (brew-*neht*) *f* brunette
brusque (brewsk) *adj* sudden; rude
brut (brewt) *adj* gross
brutal (brew-*tahl*) *adj* brutal
bruyant (brwee-*ʸahn͞g*) *adj* noisy
bruyère (brwee-*ʸair*) *f* heather; moor
bûche (bewsh) *f* log
bûcher (bew-*shay*) *v* labo(u)r
budget (bew-*jay*) *m* budget
buffet (bew-*fay*) *m* buffet
buisson (bwee-*sawn͞g*) *m* bush, scrub
bulbe (bewlb) *m* bulb
bulgare (bewl-*gaar*) *adj* Bulgarian
Bulgarie (bewl-gah-*ree*) *f* Bulgaria
bulle (bewl) *f* bubble
bulletin météorologique (bewl-tan͞g may-tay-o-ro-lo-*zheek*) weather forecast
bureau (bew-*roa*) *m* office; bureau; desk, agency; **~ de change** exchange office; **~ de l'emploi** employment exchange; **~ de poste** post-office; **~ de renseignements** information bureau; **~ des objets trouvés** lost property office; **~ de tabac** tobacconist's; **~ de voyages** travel agency; **employé(e) de ~** clerk; **heures de ~** business hours
bureaucratie (bew-roa-krah-*see*) *f* bureaucracy
bus (bewss) *m* bus
buste (bewst) *m* bust
but (bew) *m* purpose, aim; goal
butte (bewt) *f* mound

C

ça (sah) *pron* that
cabane (kah-*bahn*) *f* cabin
cabaret (kah-bah-*ray*) *m* cabaret
cabine (kah-*been*) *f* cabin, booth; **~ de pont** deck cabin; **~ d'essayage** fitting room; **~ téléphonique** telephone booth
cabinet (kah-bee-*nay*) *m* lavatory; cabinet; study; **~ de consultations** surgery
câble (kahbl) *m* cable
cacahuète (kah-kah-*weht*) *f* peanut
cachemire (kahsh-*meer*) *m* cashmere
cacher (kah-*shay*) *v* *hide
cachet (kah-*shay*) *m* stamp; capsule
cactus (kahk-*tewss*) *m* cactus
cadavre (kah-*daavr*) *m* corpse
cadeau (kah-*doa*) *m* present, gift
cadenas (kahd-*nah*) *m* padlock
cadet (kah-*day*) *adj* junior
cadre (kaadr) *m* frame; setting; cadre
café (kah-*fay*) *m* coffee; café, public house, saloon
caféine (kah-fay-*een*) *f* caffeine
cafétéria (kah-fay-tay-*rʸah*) *f* cafeteria
cafetière (kahf-*tʸair*) *f* coffee-pot
cage (kaazh) *f* cage
cahier (kah-*ʸay*) *m* notebook; **~ de croquis** sketch-book
cahoteux (kah-o-*tur*) *adj* bumpy
caille (kigh) *f* quail
caillou (kah-*ʸoo*) *m* (pl ~x) pebble
caisse (kehss) *f* crate; pay desk, cashier *Am*; **~ d'épargne** savings bank
caissier (kay-*sʸay*) *m* cashier
caissière (keh-*sʸair*) *f* cashier
calamité (kah-lah-mee-*tay*) *f* calamity,

disaster
calcium (kahl-*s^yom*) *m* calcium
calcul (kahl-*kewl*) *m* calculation; **~ biliaire** gallstone
calculatrice (kahl-kew-lah-*treess*) *f* calculator
calculer (kahl-kew-*lay*) *v* reckon; calculate
caleçon (kahl-*sawn̅g̅*) *m* drawers; briefs *pl*, shorts *plAm*, pants *pl*; underpants *plAm*; **~ de bain** swimmingtrunks
calendrier (kah-lahn̅g̅-dree-*ay*) *m* calendar
câliner (kah-lee-*nay*) *v* cuddle
calmant (kahl-*mahn̅g̅*) *m* tranquillizer
calme (kahlm) *adj* calm, quiet
calmer (kahl-*may*) *v* calm down
calomnie (kah-lom-*nee*) *f* slander
calorie (kah-lo-*ree*) *f* calorie
camarade (kah-mah-*rahd*) *m/f* comrade; **~ de classe** classmate
cambrioler (kahn̅g̅-bree-o-*lay*) *v* burgle
cambrioleur (kahn̅g̅-bree-o-*lūrr*) *m*, **-euse** *f* burglar
caméra (kah-may-*rah*) *f* camera; **~ vidéo** video camera
camion (kah-*m^yawn̅g̅*) *m* lorry; truck *Am*; **~ de livraison** delivery van
camionnette (kah-m^yo-*neht*) *f* pick-up van
camomille (kah-mo-*meey*) *f* camomile
camp (kahn̅g̅) *m* camp; **~ de vacances** holiday camp
campagne (kahn̅g̅-*pahñ*) *f* countryside, country; campaign
camper (kahn̅g̅-*pay*) *v* camp
campeur (kahn̅g̅-*pūrr*) *m*, **-euse** *f* camper
camping (kahn̅g̅-*peeng*) *m* camping; **terrain de ~** camping site
Canada (kah-nah-*dah*) *m* Canada
canadien (kah-nah-*d^yan̅g̅*) *adj* Canadian
canal (kah-*nahl*) *m* canal; channel
canapé (kah-nah-*pay*) *m* sofa, couch
canard (kah-*naar*) *m* duck
canari (kah-nah-*ree*) *m* canary
cancer (kahn̅g̅-*sair*) *m* cancer
candidat (kahn̅g̅-dee-*dah*) *m*, **-e** *f* candidate
candidature (kahn̅g̅-dee-dah-*te̅w̅r*) *f* application
caniche (kah-*neesh*) *m* poodle
canif (kah-*neef*) *m* penknife
caniveau (kah-nee-*voa*) *m* gutter
canne (kahn) *f* cane; walking stick; **~ à pêche** fishing rod
cannelle (kah-*nehl*) *f* cinnamon
canoë (kah-no-*ay*) *m canoe*
canon (kah-*nawn̅g̅*) *m* gun
canot (kah-*noa*) *m* canoe; dinghy; **~ automobile** motorboat
cantine (kahn̅g̅-*teen*) *f* canteen
caoutchouc (kah-oo-*choo*) *m* rubber; **~ mousse** foam rubber
cap (kahp) *m* cape; course
capable (kah-*pahbl*) *adj* capable; able; ***être ~ de** *be able to
capacité (kah-pah-see-*tay*) *f* ability; capacity
cape (kahp) *f* cape
capitaine (kah-pee-*tehn*) *m* captain
capital (kah-pee-*tahl*) *m* capital; *adj* capital
capitale (kah-pee-*tahl*) *f* capital
capitalisme (kah-pee-tah-*leesm*) *m* capitalism
capitulation (kah-pee-tew-lah-*s^yawn̅g̅*) *f* capitulation
capot (kah-*poa*) *m* bonnet; hood *Am*
caprice (kah-*preess*) *m* fancy; whim
capsule (kah-*psewl*) *f* capsule
capture (kahp-*te̅w̅r*) *f* capture
capturer (kahp-tew-*ray*) *v* capture
capuchon (kah-pew-*shawn̅g̅*) *m* hood

car[1] (kaar) *conj* for
car[2] (kaar) *m* coach
caractère (kah-rahk-*tair*) *m* character
caractériser (kah-rahk-tay-ree-*zay*) *v* characterize; mark
caractéristique (kah-rahk-tay-ree-*steek*) *f* feature, characteristic, quality; *adj* characteristic, typical
carambolage (kah-rahng̅-bo-*laazh*) *m* cannon, *Am* carom; collision, crash
caramel (kah-rah-*mehl*) *m* caramel; toffee
caravane (kah-rah-*vahn*) *f* caravan; trailer *Am*
carburateur (kahr-bew-rah-*tu̅rr*) *m* carburettor
cardigan (kahr-dee-*gahng̅*) *m* cardigan
cardinal (kahr-dee-*nahl*) *m* cardinal; *adj* cardinal
carence (kah-*rahng̅ss*) *f* shortage; want
cargaison (kahr-gay-*zawng̅*) *f* cargo
carillon (kah-ree-*ʸawng̅*) *m* chimes *pl*
carnaval (kahr-nah-*vahl*) *m* (pl ~s) carnival
carnet (kahr-*nay*) *m* notebook; **~ de chèques** chequebook; checkbook *Am*
carotte (kah-*rot*) *f* carrot
carpe (kahrp) *f* carp
carré (kah-*ray*) *m* square; *adj* square
carreau (kah-*roa*) *m* tile; pane; **à carreaux** chequered
carrefour (kahr-*fo̅o̅r*) *m* junction; crossroads
carrière (kah-*rʸair*) *f* career; quarry
carrosse (kah-*ross*) *m* carriage; coach
carrosserie (kah-ro-*sree*) *f* motor body *Am*
cartable (kahr-*tahbl*) *m* satchel
carte (kahrt) *f* card; map; menu; **~ d'abonnement** season ticket; **~ de crédit** credit card; charge card *Am*; **~ de jeu** playing card; **~ des vins** wine list; **~ de visite** visiting-card; **~ d'identité** identity card; **~ marine** chart; **~ postale** card, picture postcard, postcard; **~ routière** road map; **~ verte** green card
cartilage (kahr-tee-*laazh*) *m* cartilage
carton (kahr-*tawng̅*) *m* cardboard; carton; **en ~** cardboard
cartouche (kahr-*toosh*) *f* cartridge; carton
cas (kah) *m* case; instance, event; **au ~ où** in case; **~ d'urgence** emergency; **en aucun ~** by no means; **en ~ de** in case of
cascade (kah-*skahd*) *f* waterfall
case (kaaz) *f* section
caserne (kah-*zehrn*) *f* barracks *pl*
casino (kah-zee-*noa*) *m* casino
casque (kahsk) *m* helmet
casquette (kah-*skeht*) *f* cap
casse-croûte (kah-*skroot*) *m* snack
casse-noix (kah-*snwah*) *m* nutcrackers *pl*
casser (kah-*say*) *v* *break; **cassé** broken
casserole (kah-*srol*) *f* pan
casse-tête (kah-*steht*) *m* puzzle
cassette (kah-*seht*) *f* casket; cassette
cassis (kah-*seess*) *m* blackcurrant
castor (kah-*stawr*) *m* beaver
catacombe (kah-tah-*kawng̅b*) *f* catacomb
catalogue (kah-tah-*log*) *m* catalogue
catarrhe (kah-*taar*) *m* catarrh
catastrophe (kah-tah-*strof*) *f* calamity, disaster
catégorie (kah-tay-go-*ree*) *f* category; sort
cathédrale (kah-tay-*drahl*) *f* cathedral
catholique (kah-to-*leek*) *adj* catholic; Roman Catholic
cause (ko̅a̅z) *f* cause, reason; **à ~ de** because of; for, on account of

causer (koa-*zay*) *v* cause; chat
causette (koa-*zeht*) *f* chat
caution (koa-*s^{y}awng*) *f* bail, security, guarantee; **sujet à ~** untrustworthy
cavalier (kah-vah-*l^{y}ay*) *m* horseman; rider
cave (kahv) *f* cellar; wine cellar
caverne (kah-*vehrn*) *f* cavern
caviar (kah-*v^{y}aar*) *m* caviar
cavité (kah-vee-*tay*) *f* cavity
ce (ser) *adj* (cet; f cette, pl ces) that; this
ceci (ser-*see*) *pron* this
céder (say-*day*) *v* *give in; indulge
ceinture (sang-*tewr*) *f* belt; **~ de sécurité** safety belt; seat belt
cela (ser-*lah*) *pron* that
célébration (say-lay-brah-*s^{y}awng*) *f* celebration
célèbre (say-*lehbr*) *adj* famous
célébrer (say-lay-*bray*) *v* celebrate
célébrité (say-lay-bree-*tay*) *f* fame, celebrity
céleri (sehl-*ree*) *m* celery
célibataire (say-lee-bah-*tair*) *m* bachelor; *adj* single
cellule (seh-*lewl*) *f* cell
celui-là (ser-lwee-*lah*) *pron* (f celle-là, pl ceux-là, celles-là) that
cendre (sahngdr) *f* ash
cendrier (sahng-dree-*ay*) *m* ashtray
censure (sahng-*sewr*) *f* censorship
cent (sahng) *num* hundred; **pour ~** percent
centigrade (sahng-tee-*grahd*) *adj* centigrade
centimètre (sahng-tee-*mehtr*) *m* centimeter *Am*, centimetre
central (sahng-*trahl*) *adj* central; **~ téléphonique** telephone exchange
centrale (sahng-*trahl*) *f* power station
centraliser (sahng-trah-lee-*zay*) *v* centralize
centre (sahngtr) *m* center *Am*, centre; **~ commercial** shopping centre; mall; **~ de la ville** town centre; **~ de loisirs** recreation centre
cependant (ser-pahng-*dahng*) *conj* however; but, yet, only
céramique (say-rah-*meek*) *f* ceramics *pl*
cercle (sehrkl) *m* circle, ring; club
céréale (say-ray-*ahl*) *f* grain; corn
cérémonie (say-ray-mo-*nee*) *f* ceremony
cérémonieux (say-ray-mo-*n^{y}ur*) *adj* formal
cerf (sair) *m* stag, hart
cerise (ser-*reez*) *f* cherry
certain (sehr-*tang*) *adj* certain; **certains** *pron* some
certificat (sehr-tee-fee-*kah*) *m* certificate; **~ médical** health certificate
cerveau (sehr-*voa*) *m* brain
ces (say) *adj* these; those
cesser (say-*say*) *v* cease; discontinue, quit, stop
c'est-à-dire (say-tah-*deer*) *conj* that is (to say), namely
ceux-là (sur-*lah*) *pron* (f celles-là) those
chacun (shah-*kurng*) *pron* everyone; anyone
chagrin (shah-*grang*) *m* sorrow; grief
chaîne (shehn) *f* chain; **~ de montagnes** mountain range
chair (shair) *f* flesh; **~ de poule** goose flesh
chaire (shair) *f* pulpit
chaise (shaiz) *f* chair; **~ longue** deck chair
chalet (shah-*lay*) *m* chalet
chaleur (shah-*lurr*) *f* heat; warmth
chambre (shahngbr) *f* room; **~ à air** inner tube; **~ à coucher** bedroom; **~ d'ami** spare room, guest room; **~ d'enfants** nursery; **~ et petit déjeuner**

bed and breakfast; ~ **forte** vault
chameau (shah-*moa*) *m* camel
champ (shahng̅) *m* field; ~ **de blé** cornfield; ~ **de courses** racecourse; **sur-le-champ** immediately
champagne (shahng̅-*pahñ*) *m* champagne
champignon (shahng̅-pee-*ñawng̅*) *m* mushroom, toadstool
champion (shahng̅-*p*ʸ*awng̅*) *m*, **-ne** *f* champion
chance (shahng̅ss) *f* luck; fortune; chance
chanceux (shahng̅-*sur*) *adj* lucky
chandail (shahng̅-*digh*) *m* jersey, jumper, sweater
change (shahng̅zh) *m* change; **bureau de** ~ money exchange
changement (shahng̅zh-*mahng̅*) *m* change; variation, alteration
changer (shahng̅-*zhay*) *v* vary, change, alter; exchange, switch; ~ **de vitesse** change gear; ~ **en** turn into; **se** ~ change
chanson (shahng̅-*sawng̅*) *f* song; ~ **populaire** folk song
chant (shahng̅) *m* song, singing
chantage (shahng̅-*taazh*) *m* blackmail
chanter (shahng̅-*tay*) *v* *sing; ***faire** ~ blackmail
chanteur (shahng̅-*tūrr*) *m*, **-euse** *f* singer; vocalist
chantier (shahng̅-*t*ʸ*ay*) *m* building site; yard; roadwork, ~ **naval** (shahng̅-tʸay nah-*vahl*) shipyard
chanvre (shahng̅vr) *m* hemp
chaos (kah-*oa*) *m* chaos
chaotique (kah-o-*teek*) *adj* chaotic
chapeau (shah-*poa*) *m* hat
chapelain (shah-*plang̅*) *m* chaplain
chapelet (shah-*play*) *m* beads *pl*
chapelle (shah-*pehl*) *f* chapel
chapitre (shah-*peetr*) *m* chapter
chaque (shahk) *adj* each; every
charbon (shahr-*bawng̅*) *m* coal; ~ **de bois** charcoal
charcuterie (shahr-kew-*tree*) *f* delicatessen; butcher's shop
chardon (shahr-*dawng̅*) *m* thistle
charge (shahrzh) *f* charge
chargement (shahr-zher-*mahng̅*) *m* cargo, load, charge, freight
charger (shahr-*zhay*) *v* charge; load; **chargé de** in charge of; **se** ~ **de** *take charge of
charité (shah-ree-*tay*) *f* charity
charmant (shahr-*mahng̅*) *adj* graceful; glamorous
charme (shahrm) *m* charm, glamour
charmer (shahr-*may*) *v* charm, enchant
charnière (shahr-*n*ʸ*air*) *f* hinge
charrette (shah-*reht*) *f* cart
charrue (shah-*rew*) *f* plough
chasse (shahss) *f* chase; hunt
chasser (shah-*say*) *v* chase; hunt
chasseur (shah-*sūrr*) *m* hunter; bellboy
châssis (shah-*see*) *m* chassis
chaste (shahst) *adj* chaste
chat (shah) *m* cat
château (shah-*toa*) *m* castle
chatouiller (shah-too-ʸ*ay*) *v* tickle
chaud (shoa) *adj* hot; warm
chaudière (shoa-*d*ʸ*air*) *f* boiler
chauffage (shoa-*faazh*) *m* heating; ~ **central** central heating
chauffer (shoa-*fay*) *v* heat; warm
chauffeur (shoa-*fūrr*) *m* chauffeur; ~ **de taxi** cab driver
chaussée (shoa-*say*) *f* causeway; carriageway; roadway *Am*
chaussette (shoa-*seht*) *f* sock
chaussure (shoa-*sēwr*) *f* shoe; **chaussures** footwear; **chaussures de basket** plimsolls *pl*; **chaussures de gymnastique** gym shoes; sneakers *plAm*; **chaussures de ski** ski boots;

chaussures de tennis tennis shoes
chauve (shoav) *adj* bald
chaux (shoa) *f* lime
chef (shehf) *m* chief; manager, boss; chieftain; **~ cuisinier** chef; **~ d'Etat** head of state; **~ d'orchestre** conductor
chef-d'œuvre (sheh-*durvr*) *m* masterpiece
chemin (sher-*mang*) *m* lane; **à michemin** halfway; **~ de fer** railroad *Am*; railway; **~ du retour** way back
chemineau (sher-mee-*noa*) *m* tramp
cheminée (sher-mee-*nay*) *f* chimney; fireplace; hearth
chemise (sher-*meez*) *f* shirt; vest; **~ de nuit** nightdress
chemisier (sher-mee-*z^{y}ay*) *m* blouse
chêne (shehn) *m* oak
chenil (sher-*nee*) *m* kennel
chèque (shehk) *m* cheque, check *Am*; **~ de voyage** traveler's check *Am*, traveller's cheque
cher (shair) *adj* dear; expensive
chercher (shehr-*shay*) *v* *seek, search; hunt for, look up, look for; ***aller ~** fetch
chère (shair) *f* fare
chéri (shay-*ree*) *m* darling, sweetheart
cheval (sher-*vahl*) *m* horse; **~ de bois** wooden horse; **~ de course** racehorse; **cheval-vapeur** *m* horsepower; **monter à ~** *ride
chevalier (sher-vah-*l^{y}ay*) *m* knight
chevelu (sher-*vlew*) *adj* hairy
cheveu (sher-*vur*) *m* hair; **coupe de cheveux** haircut
cheville (sher-*veey*) *f* ankle
chèvre (shaivr) *f* goat
chevreau (sher-*vroa*) *m* kid
chevreuil (sher-*vrur^{ee}*) *m* roebuck
chez (shay) *prep* at; to; with; **~ soi** home
chic (sheek) *adj* (f ~) smart
chichi (shee-*shee*) *m* fuss
chien (sh^{y}ang) *m* dog; **~ d'aveugle** guide dog
chienne (sh^{y}ehn) *f* bitch
chiffon (shee-*fawng*) *m* cloth; rag
chiffre (sheefr) *m* figure; digit, number
Chili (shee-*lee*) *m* Chile
chilien (shee-*l^{y}ang*) *adj* Chilean
chimie (shee-*mee*) *f* chemistry
chimique (shee-*meek*) *adj* chemical
Chine (sheen) *f* China
chinois (shee-*nwah*) *adj* Chinese
chirurgien (shee-rewr-*zh^{y}ang*) *m* surgeon
chlore (klawr) *m* chlorine
choc (shok) *m* shock
chocolat (sho-ko-*lah*) *m* chocolate
chœur (kurr) *m* choir
choisir (shwah-*zeer*) *v* *choose; pick, select; **choisi** select
choix (shwah) *m* choice; pick, selection
chômage (shoa-*maazh*) *m* unemployment; **en ~** unemployed
chômeur (shoa-*murr*) *m*, **-euse** *f* unemployed worker
chope (shop) *f* mug
choquer (sho-*kay*) *v* shock
chose (shoaz) *f* thing; **quelque ~** something
chou (shoo) *m* (pl ~x) cabbage; **chou-fleur** cauliflower; **choux de Bruxelles** Brussels sprouts *pl*
chouchou (shoo-*shoo*) *m* pet
choucroute (shoo-*kroot*) *f* sauerkraut
chouette (shweht) *f* owl; *adj* fine, splendid
chrétien (kray-*t^{y}ang*) *adj* Christian; *m*, **-ne** *f* Christian
chronique (kro-*neek*) *adj* chronic
chronologique (kro-no-lo-*zheek*) *adj* chronological
chuchotement (shew-shot-*mahng*) *m* whisper

chuchoter (shew-sho-*tay*) *v* whisper

chute (shewt) *f* fall

cible (seebl) *f* target; mark

ciboulette (see-boo-*leht*) *f* chives *pl*

cicatrice (see-kah-*treess*) *f* scar

cidre (seedr) *m* cider

ciel (s^{y}ehl) *m* (pl cieux) heaven; sky

cigare (see-*gaar*) *m* cigar

cigarette (see-gah-*reht*) *f* cigarette

cigogne (see-*goñ*) *f* stork

cil (seel) *m* eyelash

ciment (see-*mahng*) *m* cement

cimetière (seem-*t^{y}air*) *m* graveyard, cemetery, churchyard

cinéma (see-nay-*mah*) *m* cinema; pictures; movie theater *Am*, movies *Am*

cinq (sangk) *num* five

cinquante (sang-*kahngt*) *num* fifty

cinquième (sang-*k^{y}ehm*) *num* fifth

cintre (sangtr) *m* coat hanger, hanger

cirage (see-*raazh*) *m* shoe polish

circonstance (seer-kawng-*stahngss*) *f* circumstance; condition

circuit (seer-*kwee*) *m* circumference; circuit

circulation (seer-kew-lah-*s^{y}awng*) *f* circulation; traffic

cire (seer) *f* wax; **musée des figures de ~** waxworks *pl*

cirque (seerk) *m* circus

ciseaux (see-*zoa*) *mpl* scissors *pl*; **~ à ongles** nail scissors *pl*

citation (see-tah-*s^{y}awng*) *f* quotation

cité (see-*tay*) *f* city

citer (see-*tay*) *v* quote

citoyen (see-twah-*^{y}ang*) *m*, **-ne** *f* citizen

citoyenneté (see-twah-^{y}ehn-*tay*) *f* citizenship

citron (see-*trawng*) *m* lemon

civil (see-*veel*) *m* civilian; *adj* civilian, civil

civilisation (see-vee-lee-zah-*s^{y}awng*) *f* civilization

civilisé (see-vee-lee-*zay*) *adj* civilized

civique (see-*veek*) *adj* civic

clair (klair) *adj* clear; plain, light, serene

clairière (kleh-*r^{y}air*) *f* clearing

claque (klahk) *f* slap; smack, blow; **donner une ~** smack

claquer (klah-*kay*) *v* slam

clarifier (klah-ree-*f^{y}ay*) *v* clarify

clarté (klahr-*tay*) *f* light, clearness

classe (klahss) *f* class; form; **~ moyenne** middle class; **~ touriste** tourist class

classer (klah-*say*) *v* classify; assort, grade, arrange, sort

classique (klah-*seek*) *adj* classical

clavecin (klahv-*sang*) *m* harpsichord

clavicule (klah-vee-*kewl*) *f* collarbone

clavier (klah-*v^{y}ay*) *m* keyboard; range

clé (klay) *f* key; wrench; **~ à écrous** spanner, wrench *Am*; **~ de la maison** latchkey

clémence (klay-*mahngss*) *f* mercy; grace

client (klee-*ahng*) *m* client; customer

clientèle (klee-ahng-*tehl*) *f* customers *pl*

clignotant (klee-ño-*tahng*) *m* indicator

climat (klee-*mah*) *m* climate

climatisation (klee-mah-tee-zah-*s^{y}awng*) *f* air conditioning

climatisé (klee-mah-tee-*zay*) *adj* airconditioned

clinique (klee-*neek*) *f* clinic

cliquer (klee-*kay*) *v* click

cloche (klosh) *f* bell

clocher (klo-*shay*) *m* steeple

cloison (klwah-*zawng*) *f* partition; wall

cloître (klwaatr) *m* cloister

cloque (klok) *f* blister

clos (kloa) *adj* closed; shut
clôture (kloa-*tewr*) *f* fence
clou (kloo) *m* nail
clown (kloon) *m* clown
club (klurb) *m* club; **~ automobile** automobile club; **~ de golf** golfclub
cocaïne (ko-kah-*een*) *f* cocaine
cochon (ko-*shawng*) *m* pig; **~ de lait** piglet; **~ d'Inde** guinea pig
cocktail (kok-*tehl*) *m* cocktail
code (kod) *m* code; **~ postal** zip code *Am*
cœur (kurr) *m* heart; core; **par ~** by heart
coffre (kofr) *m* chest; boot; trunk *Am*; **coffre-fort** safe
cognac (ko-*ñahk*) *m* cognac
cogner (ko-*ñay*) *v* bump; **~ contre** knock against
cohérence (koa-ay-*rahngss*) *f* coherence
coiffeur (kwah-*furr*) *m* hairdresser; barber
coiffeuse (kwah-*furz*) *f* dressing table
coiffure (kwah-*fewr*) *f* hairdo
coin (kwang) *m* corner
coïncidence (koa-ang-see-*dahngss*) *f* concurrence
coïncider (koa-ang-see-*day*) *v* coincide
col (kol) *m* collar; mountain pass
coléoptère (ko-lay-op-*tair*) *m* bug
colère (ko-*lair*) *f* anger; temper, passion; **en ~** angry
coléreux (ko-lay-*rur*) *adj* hot-tempered
colis (ko-*lee*) *m* parcel, package
collaboration (ko-lah-borah-*s^{y}awng*) *f* cooperation
collant (ko-*lahng*) *adj* sticky; close-fitting, (skin)tight; clinging
collants (ko-*lahng*) *mpl* tights *pl*; panty hose
colle (kol) *f* glue, gum
collectif (ko-lehk-*teef*) *adj* collective
collection (ko-lehk-*s^{y}awng*) *f* collection; **~ d'art** art collection
collectionner (ko-lehk-s^{y}o-*nay*) *v* gather
collectionneur (ko-lehk-s^{y}o-*nurr*) *m*, **-euse** *f* collector
collège (ko-*laizh*) *m* college
collègue (ko-*lehg*) *m* colleague
coller (ko-*lay*) *v* paste, *stick
collier (ko-*l^{y}ay*) *m* necklace; collar, beads *pl*
colline (ko-*leen*) *f* hill
collision (ko-lee-*z^{y}awng*) *f* collision; crash; **entrer en ~** collide, crash
Colombie (ko-lawng-*bee*) *f* Colombia
colombien (ko-lawng-*b^{y}ang*) *adj* Colombian
colonel (ko-lo-*nehl*) *m* colonel
colonie (ko-lo-*nee*) *f* colony
colonne (ko-*lon*) *f* column; pillar; **~ de direction** steering column
coloré (ko-lo-*ray*) *adj* colo(u)rful
coma (ko-*mah*) *m* coma
combat (kawng-*bah*) *m* struggle; fight, combat, contest, battle
***combattre** (kawng-*bahtr*) *v* *fight; combat, battle
combien (kawng-*b^{y}ang*) *adv* how much; how many
combinaison (kawng-bee-nay-*zawng*) *f* combination; slip
combiner (kawng-bee-*nay*) *v* combine
comble (kawngbl) *m* roof; height; *adj* full
combler (kawng-*blay*) *v* fill up; overload
combustible (kawng-bew-*steebl*) *m* fuel
comédie (ko-may-*dee*) *f* comedy; **~ musicale** musical
comédien (ko-may-*d^{y}ang*) *m*, **-ne** *f* comedian
comestible (ko-meh-*steebl*) *adj* edible

comique (ko-*meek*) *m* comedian; *adj* comic, humorous
comité (ko-mee-*tay*) *m* committee
commandant (ko-mahng-*dahng*) *m* commander; captain
commande (ko-*mahngd*) *f* order; **fait sur ~** made to order
commandement (ko-mahngd-*mahng*) *m* order
commander (ko-mahng-*day*) *v* command; order
comme (kom) *conj* as; like; since; **~ si** as if
commémoration (ko-may-mo-rah-s^y*awng*) *f* commemoration
commencement (ko-mahng-*smahng*) *m* beginning
commencer (ko-mahng-*say*) *v* *begin; commence, start
comment (ko-*mahng*) *adv* how; **n'importe ~** anyhow
commentaire (ko-mahng-*tair*) *m* comment
commenter (ko-mahng-*tay*) *v* comment
commerçant (ko-mehr-*sahng*) *m*, **-e** *f* merchant; trader, shopkeeper
commerce (ko-*mehrs*) *m* commerce; business, trade; **~ de détail** retail trade; ***faire du ~** trade
commercial (ko-mehr-s^y*ahl*) *adj* commercial
***commettre** (ko-*mehtr*) *v* commit
commission (ko-mee-s^y*awng*) *f* committee, commission; errand, message
commode (ko-*mod*) *f* chest of drawers; bureau *Am*; *adj* convenient, easy, handy
commodité (ko-mo-dee-*tay*) *f* comfort
commotion (ko-moa-s^y*awng*) *f* shock; **~ cérébrale** concussion
commun (ko-*murng*) *adj* common; ordinary
communauté (ko-mew-noa-*tay*) *f* community
communication (ko-mew-nee-kah-s^y*awng*) *f* communication; information; connection; **~ locale** local call; ***mettre en ~** connect
communiqué (ko-mew-nee-*kay*) *m* communiqué
communiquer (ko-mew-nee-*kay*) *v* communicate; inform
communisme (ko-mew-*neesm*) *m* communism
commutateur (ko-mew-tah-*turr*) *m* switch
compact (kawng-*pahkt*) *adj* compact
compact-disc (kawng-*pahkt* deesk) *m* compact disc; **lecteur de ~** compact disc player
compagne (kawng-*pah*-ñe) *f* companion
compagnie (kawng-pah-*ñee*) *f* company; society; **~ de navigation** shipping line
compagnon (kawng-pah-*ñawng*) *m* companion
comparaison (kawng-pah-ray-*zawng*) *f* comparison
comparer (kawng-pah-*ray*) *v* compare
compartiment (kawng-pahr-tee-*mahng*) *m* compartment; **~ fumeurs** smoking compartment
compassion (kawng-pah-s^y*awng*) *f* compassion
compatir (kawng-pah-*teer*) *v* sympathize
compatissant (kawng-pah-tee-*sahng*) *adj* sympathetic
compatriote (kawng-pah-tree-*ot*) *m/f* fellow countryman
compensation (kawng-pahng-sah-s^y*awng*) *f* compensation
compenser (kawng-pahng-*say*) *v* compensate for; *make good
compétence (kawng-pay-*tahngss*) *f*

capacity
compétent (kawn͞g-pay-*tahn͞g*) *adj* qualified; expert
compétition (kawn͞g-pay-tee-*s*ʸ*awn͞g*) *f* competition
compiler (kawn͞g-pee-*lay*) *v* compile
complémentaire (kawn͞g-play-mahn͞g-*tair*) *adj* further
complet[1] (kawn͞g-*play*) *adj* (f -plète) whole, complete; total, utter; full up
complet[2] (kawn͞g-*play*) *m* suit
complètement (kawn͞g-pleht-*mahn͞g*) *adv* completely
complexe (kawn͞g-*plehks*) *m* complex; *adj* complex
compliment (kawn͞g-plee-*mahn͞g*) *m* compliment
complimenter (kawn͞g-plee-mahn͞g-*tay*) *v* compliment
compliqué (kawn͞g-plee-*kay*) *adj* complicated
complot (kawn͞g-*ploa*) *m* plot
comportement (kawn͞g-por-ter-*mahn͞g*) *m* behavio(u)r
comporter (kawn͞g-por-*tay*) *v* imply; **se ~** behave
composer (kawn͞g-poa-*zay*) *v* compose
compositeur (kawn͞g-po-zee-*tūrr*) *m*, **-trice** *f* composer
composition (kawn͞g-po-zee-*s*ʸ*awn͞g*) *f* composition; essay
composter (kawn͞g-po-*stay*) *v* punch (*a* ticket)
compote (kawn͞g-*pot*) *f* stewed fruit; **en ~** stewed; to *or* in a pulp
compréhension (kawn͞g-pray-ahn͞g-*s*ʸ*awn͞g*) *f* understanding; insight
***comprendre** (kawn͞g-*prahn͞gdr*) *v* *understand; *see; comprise, include, contain
comprimé (kawn͞g-pree-*may*) *m* tablet
compris (kawn͞g-*pree*) *adj* inclusive; **tout ~** all in
compromis (kawn͞g-pro-*mee*) *m* compromise
comptable (kawn͞g-*tahbl*) *m* accountant
compte (kawn͞gt) *m* account; **~ en banque** bank account; **~ rendu** report; minutes; **en fin de ~** at last; **rendre ~ de** account for; **se rendre ~** realize; *see
compter (kawn͞g-*tay*) *v* count; **~ sur** rely on
compteur (kawn͞g-*tūrr*) *m* meter
comptoir (kawn͞g-*twaar*) *m* counter
comte (kawn͞gt) *m* count; earl
comté (kawn͞g-*tay*) *m* county
comtesse (kawn͞g-*tehss*) *f* countess
concéder (kawn͞g-say-*day*) *v* grant
concentration (kawn͞g-sahn͞g-trah-*s*ʸ*awn͞g*) *f* concentration
concentrer (kawn͞g-sahn͞g-*tray*) *v* concentrate
concept (kawn͞g-*sehpt*) *m* idea
conception (kawn͞g-seh-*ps*ʸ*awn͞g*) *f* conception
concernant (kawn͞g-sehr-*nahn͞g*) *prep* concerning; as regards, about, regarding
concerner (kawn͞g-sehr-*nay*) *v* concern; **en ce qui concerne** as regards, regarding
concert (kawn͞g-*sair*) *m* concert
concession (kawn͞g-seh-*s*ʸ*awn͞g*) *f* concession
concessionnaire (kawn͞g-seh-sʸo-*nair*) *m* distributor
***concevoir** (kawn͞g-*svwaar*) *v* conceive; devise
concierge (kawn͞g-*s*ʸ*ehrzh*) *m/f* concierge; janitor
concis (kawn͞g-*see*) *adj* concise
***conclure** (kawn͞g-*klewr*) *v* finish; conclude
conclusion (kawn͞g-klew-*z*ʸ*awn͞g*) *f* conclusion, end; issue

concombre (kawng-*kawngbr*) *m* cucumber
concorder (kawng-kor-*day*) *v* agree
***concourir** (kawng-koo-*reer*) *v* compete
concours (kawng-*koor*) *m* contest
concret (kawng-*kray*) *adj* (f -crète) concrete
concurrence (kawng-kew-*rahngss*) *f* rivalry
concurrent (kawng-kew-*rahng*) *m* competitor; rival
condamnation (kawng-dah-nah-*s^{y}awng*) *f* condemnation; sentence
condamné (kawng-dah-*nay*) *m* convict
condamner (kawng-dah-*nay*) *v* sentence
condition (kawng-dee-*s^{y}awng*) *f* condition; term
conducteur (kawng-dewk-*turr*) *m* driver; conductor
***conduire** (kawng-*dweer*) *v* conduct, guide; *drive; carry, *take; **se ~** act
conduite (kawng-*dweet*) *f* conduct; lead
confédération (kawng-fay-day-rah-*s^{y}awng*) *f* confederation
conférence (kawng-fay-*rahngss*) *f* conference; lecture; **~ de presse** press conference
confesser (kawng-fay-*say*) *v* confess
confession (kawng-feh-*s^{y}awng*) *f* confession
confiance (kawng-*f^{y}ahngss*) *f* confidence; faith, trust; **digne de ~** reliable, trustworthy; ***faire ~** trust
confiant (kawng-*f^{y}ahng*) *adj* confident
confidentiel (kawng-fee-dahng-*s^{y}ehl*) *adj* confidential
confier (kawng-*f^{y}ay*) *v* confide
confirmation (kawng-feer-mah-*s^{y}awng*) *f* confirmation
confirmer (kawng-feer-*may*) *v* confirm; acknowledge
confiserie (kawng-fee-*zree*) *f* sweetshop; candy *Am*; candy store *Am*
confiseur (kawng-fee-*zurr*) *m*, **-euse** *f* confectioner
confisquer (kawng-fee-*skay*) *v* confiscate
confiture (kawng-fee-*tewr*) *f* jam
conflit (kawng-*flee*) *m* conflict
confondre (kawng-*fawngdr*) *v* confuse; *mistake
***être conforme** (aitr kawng-*form*) correspond
conformément à (kawng-for-may-*mahng*) in accordance with, according to
confort (kawng-*fawr*) *m* comfort
confortable (kawng-*for-tahbl*) *adj* comfortable; cosy, cozy *Am*
confus (kawng-*few*) *adj* confused; embarrassed
confusion (kawng-few-*z^{y}awng*) *f* confusion; disorder, muddle
congé (kawng-*zhay*) *m* vacation
congélateur (kawng-zhay-lah-*turr*) *m* deep-freeze
congelé (kawng-*zhlay*) *adj* frozen
congratuler (kawng-grah-tew-*lay*) *v* congratulate
congrès (kawng-*gray*) *m* congress
conifère (ko-nee-*fair*) *m* conifer
conjecture (kawng-zhehk-*tewr*) *f* conjecture, guess
conjoint (kawng-*zhwang*) *adj* joint
conjointement (kawng-zhwangt-*mahng*) *adv* jointly
connaissance (ko-nay-*sahngss*) *f* knowledge; acquaintance
connaisseur (ko-nay-*surr*) *m* connoisseur
***connaître** (ko-*naitr*) *v* *know; **connu** well-known
connotation (ko-no-tah-*s^{y}awng*) *f*

connotation
conquérant (kawng-kay-*rahng*) *m* conqueror
***conquérir** (kawng-kay-*reer*) *v* conquer
conquête (kawng-*keht*) *f* conquest
consacrer (kawng-sah-*kray*) *v* devote
conscience (kawng-*s^{y}ahngss*) *f* conscience; consciousness
conscient (kawng-*s^{y}ahng*) *adj* conscious; aware
conscrit (kawng-*skree*) *m* conscript
conseil (kawng-*say*) *m* advice; counsel, council; board; **donner des conseils** advise
conseiller (kawng-say-*^{y}ay*) *v* advise; recommend; *m* councillor; counsellor
consentement (kawng-sahngt-*mahng*) *m* consent, approval
***consentir** (kawng-sahng-*teer*) *v* consent, agree
conséquence (kawng-say-*kahngss*) *f* consequence; result
conséquent: par ~ (pahr kawng-say-*kahng*) consequently
conservateur (kawng-sehr-vah-*turr*) *adj* conservative
conservation (kawng-sehr-vah-*s^{y}awng*) *f* preservation
conservatoire (kawng-sehr-vah-*twaar*) *m* music academy
conserver (kawng-sehr-*vay*) *v* preserve
conserves (kawng-*sehrv*) *fpl* tinned food, canned food *Am*; ***mettre en conserve** preserve
considérable (kawng-see-day-*rahbl*) *adj* considerable; extensive
considération (kawng-see-day-rah-*s^{y}awng*) *f* consideration; respect
considérer (kawng-see-day-*ray*) *v* consider; **~ comme** regard as
consigne (kawng-*seeñ*) *f* deposit; left luggage office; checkroom, baggage check *Am*
consister (kawng-see-*stay*) v: **~ en** consist of
consoler (kawng-so-*lay*) *v* comfort
consommateur (kawng-so-mah-*turr*) *m* consumer
consommation (kawng-so-mah-*s^{y}awng*) *f* consumption; drink
consommer (kawng-so-*may*) *v* consume
conspiration (kawng-spee-rah-*s^{y}awng*) *f* plot
conspirer (kawng-spee-*ray*) *v* conspire
constant (kawng-*stahng*) *adj* constant; even
constater (kawng-stah-*tay*) *v* note, notice; certify
constipation (kawng-stee-pah-*s^{y}awng*) *f* constipation
constituer (kawng-stee-*tway*) *v* constitute
constitution (kawng-stee-tew-*s^{y}awng*) *f* constitution
construction (kawng-strewk-*s^{y}awng*) *f* construction; building
***construire** (kawng-*strweer*) *v* construct
consulat (kawng-sew-*lah*) *m* consulate
consultation (kawng-sewl-tah-*s^{y}awng*) *f* consultation
consulter (kawng-sewl-*tay*) *v* consult
contact (kawng-*tahkt*) *m* contact; touch
contacter (kawng-tahk-*tay*) *v* contact
contagieux (kawng-tah-*zh^{y}ur*) *adj* contagious
conte (kawngt) *m* tale; **~ de fées** fairytale
contempler (kawng-tahng-*play*) *v* view
contemporain (kawng-tahng-po-*rang*) *m* contemporary; *adj* contemporary

conteneur (kawngt-*nurr*) *m* container
***contenir** (kawngt-*neer*) *v* contain; restrain
content (kawng-*tahng*) *adj* glad; pleased, happy
contenu (kawngt-*new*) *m* contents *pl*
contester (kawng-teh-*stay*) *v* dispute
continent (kawng-tee-*nahng*) *m* continent
continental (kawng-tee-nahng-*tahl*) *adj* continental
continu (kawng-tee-*new*) *adj* continuous
continuel (kawng-tee-*nwehl*) *adj* continual; continuous
continuellement (kawng-tee-nwehl-*mahng*) *adv* all the time, continually
continuer (kawng-tee-*nway*) *v* continue; carry on, *keep on, *keep, *go on, *go ahead
contour (kawng-*toor*) *m* outline, contour
contourner (kawng-toor-*nay*) *v* by-pass
contraceptif (kawng-trah-sehp-*teef*) *m* contraceptive
contradictoire (kawng-trah-deek-*twaar*) *adj* contradictory
***contraindre** (kawng-*trangdr*) *v* compel
contraire (kawng-*trair*) *adj* opposite; *m* reverse, contrary; **au ~** on the contrary
contralto (kawng-trahl-*toa*) *m* contralto
contraste (kawng-*trahst*) *m* contrast
contrat (kawng-*trah*) *m* agreement, contract
contravention (kawng-trah-vahng-*s^yawng*) *f* ticket
contre (kawngtr) *prep* against; versus
contrecœur: à ~ (ah kawng-trer-*kurr*) reluctantly
***contredire** (kawng-trer-*deer*) *v* contradict
***contrefaire** (kawng-trer-*fair*) *v* counterfeit
contrefait (kawng-trer-*fay*) *adj* deformed
contremaître (kawng-trer-*maitr*) *m* foreman
contribution (kawng-tree-bew-*s^yawng*) *f* contribution
contrôle (kawng-*troal*) *m* control; inspection; **~ des passeports** passport control
contrôler (kawng-troa-*lay*) *v* control; check
contrôleur (kawng-troa-*lurr*) *m* ticket collector
controversé (kawng-troa-vehr-*say*) *adj* controversial
contusion (kawng-tew-*z^yawng*) *f* bruise
contusionner (kawng-tew-z^yo-*nay*) *v* bruise
***convaincre** (kawng-*vangkr*) *v* convince; persuade
convenable (kawng-*vnahbl*) *adj* proper; fit
***convenir** (kawng-*vneer*) *v* fit, suit
conversation (kawng-vehr-sah-*s^yawng*) *f* conversation; discussion, talk
convertir (kawng-vehr-*teer*) *v* convert
conviction (kawng-veek-*s^yawng*) *f* conviction; persuasion
convulsion (kawng-vewl-*s^yawng*) *f* convulsion
coopérant (koa-o-pay-*rahng*) *adj* cooperative
coopératif (koa-o-pay-rah-*teef*) *adj* cooperative
coopération (koa-o-pay-rah-*s^yawng*) *f* co-operation
coopérative (koa-o-pay-rah-*teev*) *f* cooperative
coordination (koa-or-dee-nah-

s^{y}awn̅g̅) *f* coordination
coordonner (koa-or-do-*nay)* *v* coordinate
copain (ko-*pan̅g̅*) *m* pal
copie (ko-*pee)* *f* copy; carbon copy
copier (ko-*p^{y}ay)* *v* copy
copine (ko-*peen)* *f* pal; girlfriend
coq (kok) *m* cock; **~ de bruyère** black grouse
coquelicot (ko-klee-*koa)* *m* poppy
coquetier (kok-*t^{y}ay)* *m* eggcup
coquillage (ko-kee-*^{y}aazh)* *m* seashell
coquille (ko-*keey)* *f* shell; **~ de noix** nutshell
coquin (ko-*kan̅g̅*) *m* rascal
corail (ko-*righ)* *m* (pl coraux) coral
corbeau (kor-*boa)* *m* raven
corbeille à papier (kor-bay ah pah-*p^{y}ay)* wastepaper basket
corde (kord) *f* rope; cord; string
cordial (kor-*d^{y}ahl)* *adj* hearty, cordial; warm
cordon (kor-*dawn̅g̅*) *m* cord; string
cordonnier (kor-do-*n^{y}ay)* *m* shoemaker
coriace (ko-*r^{y}ahss)* *adj* tough
corne (korn) *f* horn
corneille (kor-*nay)* *f* crow
cornichon (kor-nee-*shawn̅g̅*) *m* gherkin; colloquial nitwit
corps (kawr) *m* body
corpulent (kor-pew-*lahn̅g̅*) *adj* corpulent; stout
correct (ko-*rehkt)* *adj* correct; right
correction (ko-rehk-*s^{y}awn̅g̅*) *f* correction
correspondance (ko-reh-spawn̅g̅-*dahn̅g̅ss)* *f* correspondence; connection
correspondant (ko-reh-spawn̅g̅-*dahn̅g̅*) *m* correspondent
correspondre (ko-reh-*spawn̅g̅dr)* *v* correspond
corrida (ko-ree-*dah)* *f* bullfight
corridor (ko-ree-*dawr)* *m* corridor
corriger (ko-ree-*zhay)* *v* correct
***corrompre** (ko-*rawn̅g̅pr)* *v* corrupt; bribe; **corrompu** corrupt
corruption (ko-rew-*ps^{y}awn̅g̅*) *f* corruption; bribery
corset (kor-*say)* *m* corset
cortège (kor-*taizh)* *m* procession
cosmétiques (ko-smay-*teek)* *mpl* cosmetics *pl*
costume (ko-*stewm)* *m* suit; costume; **~ national** national dress
côte (ko̅a̅t) *f* coast; rib; chop
côté (koa-*tay)* *m* side; way; **à ~** next-door; **à ~ de** next to, beside; **de ~** aside, sideways; **de l'autre ~ de** across; **passer à ~** pass by
coteau (ko-*toa)* *m* hillside
côtelette (ko-*tleht)* *f* chop, cutlet
coton (ko-*tawn̅g̅*) *m* cotton; **en ~** cotton
cou (koo) *m* neck
couche (koosh) *f* layer; nappy; diaper *Am*; **fausse ~** miscarriage
coucher (koo-*shay)* *v*: **se ~** *lie down
couchette (koo-*sheht)* *f* couchette, bunk
coucou (koo-*koo)* *m* cuckoo
coude (kood) *m* elbow
***coudre** (koodr) *v* sew
couler (koo-*lay)* *v* flow, stream
couleur (koo-*l̅u̅r̅r̅)* *f* colo(u)r; **~ à l'eau** watercolo(u)r; **de ~** colo(u)red
couloir (koo-*lwaar)* *m* corridor
coup (koo) *m* blow; bump, tap, push, knock; **~ de feu** shot; **~ d'envoi** kickoff; **~ de pied** kick; **~ de poing** punch; **~ de téléphone** call; **jeter un ~ d'œil à** glance at
coupable (koo-*pahbl)* *adj* guilty; **déclarer ~** convict
coupe (koop) *f* cup
coupe-papier (koop-pah-*p^{y}ay)* *m* paper knife, letter opener *Am*

couper (koo-*pay*) *v* *cut; *cut off
couple (koopl) *m* couple; **~ marié** married couple
coupon (koo-*pawng*) *m* coupon
coupure (koo-*pewr*) *f* cut
cour (koor) *f* court; yard
courage (koo-*raazh*) *m* courage
courageux (koo-rah-*zhur*) *adj* courageous; plucky, brave
couramment (koo-rah-*mahng*) *adv* fluently
courant (koo-*rahng*) *m* current, stream; undercurrent; *adj* frequent, current; **~ alternatif** alternating current; **~ continu** direct current; **~ d'air** draught, draft *Am*; ***mettre au ~** inform
courbatures (koor-bah-*tewr*) *fpl* sore muscles
courbe (koorb) *f* bend, curve; *adj* curved
courbé (koor-*bay*) *adj* curved
courber (koor-*bay*) *v* *bend; bow
courgette (koor-*zheht*) *f* courgette, zucchini *Am*
***courir** (koo-*reer*) *v* *run
couronne (koo-*ron*) *f* crown
couronner (koo-ro-*nay*) *v* crown
courrier (koo-r^y*ay*) *m* mail
courroie (koo-*rwah*) *f* strap; **~ de ventilateur** fan belt
cours (koor) *m* course; lecture; **~ accéléré** crash course; **~ du change** foreign exchange rate
course (koors) *f* race; ride; **~ de chevaux** horserace
court (koor) *adj* short; **~ de tennis** tennis court
court-circuit (koor-seer-*kwee*) *m* short circuit
courtier (koor-t^y*ay*) *m* broker
courtois (koor-*twah*) *adj* courteous
cousin (koo-*zang*) *m* cousin
cousine (koo-*zeen*) *f* cousin
coussin (koo-*sang*) *m* cushion
coût (koo) *m* cost
couteau (koo-*toa*) *m* knife; **~ de poche** pocketknife
coûter (koo-*tay*) *v* *cost
coûteux (koo-*tur*) *adj* expensive
coutume (koo-*tewm*) *f* custom
couture (koo-*tewr*) *f* seam; **sans ~** seamless
couturière (koo-tew-r^y*air*) *f* dressmaker
couvent (koo-*vahng*) *m* convent; nunnery
couvercle (koo-*vehrkl*) *m* top, lid, cover
couvert (koo-*vair*) *m* cutlery; cover charge; *adj* overcast
couverture (koo-vehr-*tewr*) *f* blanket; cover
***couvrir** (koo-*vreer*) *v* cover
crabe (krahb) *m* crab
cracher (krah-*shay*) *v* *spit
crachin (krah-*shang*) *m* drizzle
craie (kray) *f* chalk
***craindre** (krangdr) *v* fear, dread
crainte (krangt) *f* fear, dread
cramoisi (krah-mwah-*zee*) *adj* crimson
crampe (krahngp) *f* cramp
crampon (krahng-*pawng*) *m* clamp
cran (krahng) *m* guts
crâne (kraan) *m* skull
crapaud (krah-*poa*) *m* toad
craquement (krahk-*mahng*) *m* crack
craquer (krah-*kay*) *v* crack
cratère (krah-*tair*) *m* crater
cravate (krah-*vaht*) *f* necktie, tie
crawl (kroal) *m* crawl
crayon (kreh-^{y}*awng*) *m* pencil; **~ à bille** Biro; **~ pour les yeux** eyebrow pencil
création (kray-ah-s^y*awng*) *f* creation
créature (kray-ah-*tewr*) *f* creature
crèche (krehsh) *f* nursery
crédit (kray-*dee*) *m* credit

créditer (kray-dee-*tay*) *v* credit
créditeur (kray-dee-*türr*) *m* creditor
crédule (kray-*dewl*) *adj* credulous
créer (kray-*ay*) *v* create; design
crème (krehm) *f* cream; *adj* cream; **~ à raser** shaving cream; **~ capillaire** hair cream; **~ de beauté** face cream; skin cream; **~ de nuit** night cream; **~ fraîche** crème fraîche; **~ glacée** ice cream; **~ hydratante** moisturizing cream
crémeux (kray-*mur*) *adj* creamy
crêpe (krehp) *f* pancake
crépi (kray-*pee*) *m* roughcast
crépuscule (kray-pew-*skewl*) *m* dusk, twilight
cresson (kreh-*sawng*) *m* watercress
creuser (krur-*zay*) *v* *dig
creux (krur) *adj* hollow
crevaison (krer-vay-*zawng*) *f* puncture; flat
crevasse (krer-*vahss*) *f* crack, fissure
crever (krer-*vay*) *v* *burst; die; **crevé** punctured
crevette (krer-*veht*) *f* shrimp; prawn; **~ rose** prawn
cri (kree) *m* shout, yell, scream, cry; **pousser des cris** shriek
cric (kreek) *m* jack
cricket (kree-*keht*) *m* cricket
crier (kree-*ay*) *v* cry; shout, scream
crime (kreem) *m* crime
criminalité (kree-mee-nah-lee-*tay*) *f* criminality
criminel (kree-mee-*nehl*) *m* criminal; *adj* criminal
crique (kreek) *f* inlet, creek
crise (kreez) *f* crisis; **~ cardiaque** heart attack
cristal (kree-*stahl*) *m* crystal; **en ~** crystal
critique (kree-*teek*) *f* criticism; review; *m/f* critic; *adj* critical
critiquer (kree-tee-*kay*) *v* criticize
crochet (kro-*shay*) *m* hook; ***faire du ~** crochet
crocodile (kro-ko-*deel*) *m* crocodile
***croire** (krwaar) *v* believe; guess
croisement (krwahz-*mahng*) *m* crossing
croisière (krwah-*z^{y}air*) *f* cruise
croissance (krwah-*sahngss*) *f* growth
***croître** (krwaatr) *v* increase
croix (krwah) *f* cross
croque-monsieur (krok-mer-*s^{y}ur*) *m* toasted ham and cheese sandwich
croustillant (kroo-stee-*^{y}ahng*) *adj* crisp
croûte (kroot) *f* crust
croyable (krwah-*^{y}aabl*) *adj* credible
croyance (krwah-*^{y}ahngss*) *f* belief
cru (krew) *adj* raw
cruche (krewsh) *f* pitcher; jug
crucifier (krew-see-*f^{y}ay*) *v* crucify
crucifix (krew-see-*fee*) *m* crucifix
crucifixion (krew-see-fee-*ks^{y}awng*) *f* crucifixion
crudités (krew-dee-*tay*) *fpl* crudités
cruel (krew-*ehl*) *adj* cruel; harsh
crustacé (krew-stah-*say*) *m* shellfish
Cuba (kew-*bah*) *m* Cuba
cubain (kew-*bang*) *adj* Cuban
cube (kewb) *m* cube
***cueillir** (kur-*^{y}eer*) *v* pick
cuillère (kwee-*^{y}air*) *f* spoon; tablespoon; **~ à thé** teaspoon
cuillerée (kwee-^{y}er-*ray*) *f* spoonful
cuir (kweer) *m* leather; **en ~** leather
***cuire** (kweer) *v* cook; **~ au four** bake
cuisine (kwee-*zeen*) *f* kitchen
cuisinier (kwee-zee-*n^{y}ay*) *m* cook
cuisinière (kwee-zee-*n^{y}air*) *f* cooker; stove; **~ à gaz** gas cooker
cuisse (kweess) *f* thigh
cuit (kwee) *adj* cooked
cuivre (kweevr) *m* brass, copper
cul-de-sac (kewd-*sahk*) *m* cul-de-sac
culotte (kew-*lot*) *f* panties *pl*; **culottes**

courtes short trousers *pl*
culpabilité (kewl-pah-bee-lee-*tay*) *f* guilt
culte (kewlt) *m* worship
cultiver (kewl-tee-*vay*) *v* cultivate; *grow, raise; **cultivé** cultured
culture (kewl-*tewr*) *f* culture
cupide (kew-*peed*) *adj* greedy
cupidité (kew-pee-dee-*tay*) *f* greed
cure (kewr) *f* cure
cure-dent (kewr-*dahng*) *m* toothpick
cure-pipe (kewr-*peep*) *m* pipe cleaner
curieux (kew-*r^{y}ur*) *adj* inquisitive, curious
curiosité (kew-r^{y}o-zee-*tay*) *f* curiosity; sight
curry (kur-*ree*) *m* curry
cycle (seekl) *m* cycle
cycliste (see-*kleest*) *m* cyclist
cygne (seeñ) *m* swan
cylindre (see-*langdr*) *m* cylinder; **tête de ~** cylinder head
cystite (see-*steet*) *f* cystitis

D

dactylographier (dahk-tee-loa-grah-*f^{y}ay*) *v* type
daltonien (dahl-to-*n^{y}ang*) *adj* colo(u)r-blind
dame (dahm) *f* lady
damier (dah-*m^{y}ay*) *m* check; **à damiers** chequered
Danemark (dahn-*mahrk*) *m* Denmark
danger (dahng-*zhay*) *m* risk, danger
dangereux (dahng-*zhrur*) *adj* dangerous; risky
danois (dah-*nwah*) *adj* Danish
dans (dahng) *prep* into, inside, in, within
danse (dahngss) *f* dance; **~ folklorique** folk dance
danser (dahng-*say*) *v* dance
date (daht) *f* date
datte (daht) *f* date
davantage (dah-vahng-*taazh*) *adv* more
de (der) *prep* of; out of, from, off; about; with
dé (day) *m* thimble
déballer (day-bah-*lay*) *v* unwrap, unpack
débarquer (day-bahr-*kay*) *v* disembark, land
débarrasser(day-bah-rah-*say*) *v*: **se ~ de** *get rid of
débat (day-*bah*) *m* debate; discussion
***débattre** (day-*bahtr*) *v* discuss
débit (day-*bee*) *m* debit
déboucher (day-boo-*shay*) *v* uncork
debout (der-*boo*) *adv* standing up, up
déboutonner (day-boo-to-*nay*) *v* unbutton
débrancher (day-brahng-*shay*) *v* disconnect
débrouiller (day-broo-*^{y}ay*): *v*: **se ~ avec** *make do with
début (day-*bew*) *m* start, beginning; **au ~** at first
débutant (day-bew-*tahng*) *m* learner, beginner
débuter (day-bew-*tay*) *v* *begin
décaféiné (day-kah-fay-ee-*nay*) *adj* decaffeinated
décalage (day-kah-*laazh*) *m* shifting; gap, discrepancy
décapsuleur (day-kah-psew-*lurr*) *m* bottle opener

décédé (day-say-*day*) *adj* dead, deceased
décembre (day-*sahngbr*) December
décence (day-*sahngss*) *f* decency
décent (day-*sahng*) *adj* decent
déception (day-seh-*ps^{y}awng*) *f* disap**décerner** (day-sehr-*nay*) *v* award
***décevoir** (day-*svwaar*) *v* disappoint
déchaînement (day-shehn-*mahng*) *m* outbreak
décharger (day-shahr-*zhay*) *v* discharge; unload
déchets (day-*shay*) *mpl* scraps, waste
déchirer (day-shee-*ray*) *v* rip, *tear
déchirure (day-shee-*rewr*) *f* tear
décider (day-see-*day*) *v* decide
décision (day-*see-z^y*awng) *f* decision
déclaration (day-klah-rah-*s^{y}awng*) *f* declaration, statement
déclarer (day-klah-*ray*) *v* declare, state
décliner (day-klee-*nay*) *v* slope
décollage (day-ko-*laazh*) *m* take-off
décoller (day-ko-*lay*) *v* *take off
décolorer (day-ko-lo-*ray*) *v* fade; bleach
déconcerter (day-kawng-sehr-*tay*) *v* discomfort; confound
décontracté (day-kawng-trahk-*tay*) *adj* easy-going
décoration (day-ko-rah-*s^{y}awng*) *f* decoration
décorer (day-ko-*ray*) *v* decorate
découper (day-koo-*pay*) *v* carve; *cut up; *cut out
décourager (day-koo-rah-*zhay*) *v* discourage
découverte (day-koo-*vehrt*) *f* discovery
***découvrir** (day-koo-*vreer*) *v* discover; uncover
***décrire** (day-*kreer*) *v* describe
déçu (day-*sew*) *adj* disappointed
dédain (day-*dang*) *m* contempt; scorn
dedans (der-*dahng*) *adv* in; inside
dédier (day-*d^{y}ay*) *v* dedicate
dédommagement (day-do-mahzh-*mahng*) *m* indemnity
***déduire** (day-*dweer*) *v* infer, deduce; deduct
défaillant (day-fah-*^{y}ahng*) *adj* faint
***défaire** (day-*fair*) *v* *undo
défaite (day-*feht*) *f* defeat
défaut (day-*foa*) *m* fault
défavorable (day-fah-vo-*rahbl*) *adj* unfavo(u)rable
défectueux (day-fehk-*twur*) *adj* faulty, defective
défendre (day-*fahngdr*) *v* defend
défense (day-*fahngss*) *f* defence, defense *Am*; **~ de doubler** no overtaking; no passing *Am*; **~ de fumer** no smoking; **~ d'entrer** no entry
défi (day-*fee*) *m* challenge
défiance (day-*f^{y}ahngss*) *f* mistrust, distrust
déficience (day-fee-*s^{y}ahngss*) *f* deficiency
déficit (day-fee-*seet*) *m* deficit
défier (day-*f^{y}ay*) *v* challenge; defy
définir (day-fee-*neer*) *v* determine, define
définition (day-fee-nee-*s^{y}awng*) *f* definition
dégât (day-*gah*) *m* waste
dégel (day-*zhehl*) *m* thaw
dégeler (day-*zhlay*) *v* thaw
dégoût (day-*goo*) *m* disgust
dégoûtant (day-goo-*tahng*) *adj* disgusting, revolting
dégoûté (day-goo-*tay*) *adj* fed up with
degré (der-*gray*) *m* degree
déguisement (day-geez-*mahng*) *m* disguise
déguiser (day-gee-*zay*) *v*: **se ~** disguise
dehors (der-*awr*) *adv* outside, outdoors, out; **en ~ de** out of

déjà (day-*zhah*) *adv* already
déjeuner (day-zhur-*nay*) *m* lunch; **petit ~** breakfast
delà: au ~ de (oa der-*lah* der) past, beyond
délabré (day-lah-*bray*) *adj* dilapidated
délai (day-*lay*) *m* time limit; **dans les plus brefs délais** as soon as possible
délégation (day-lay-gah-*s^y awn͞g*) *f* delegation
délégué (day-lay-*gay*) *m*, **-e** *f* delegate
délibération (day-lee-bay-rah-*s^y awn͞g*) *f* deliberation; discussion
délibérer (day-lee-bay-*ray*) *v* deliberate; **délibéré** deliberate
délicat (day-lee-*kah*) *adj* tender, delicate; gentle; critical
délicatesse (day-lee-kah-*tehss*) *f* delicacy
délice (day-*leess*) *m* delight
délicieux (day-lee-*s^y ur*) *adj* delightful, delicious, wonderful, lovely
délinquant (day-lan͞g-*kahn͞g*) *m*, **-e** *f* criminal
délivrance (day-lee-*vrahn͞gss*) *f* delivery
délivrer (day-lee-*vray*) *v* deliver
demain (der-*man͞g*) *adv* tomorrow
demande (der-*mahn͞gd*) *f* demand; application, request
demander (der-mahn͞g-*day*) *v* ask, beg; **se ~** wonder
démangeaison (day-mahn͞g-zhay-*zawn͞g*) *f* itching
démanger (day-mahn͞g-zhay) *v* itch
démarche (day-*mahrsh*) *f* walk, gait; step, move
déménagement (day-may-nahzh-*mahn͞g*) *m* move
déménager (day-may-nah-*zhay*) *v* move
démence (day-*mahn͞gss*) *f* madness
dément (day-*mahn͞g*) *adj* mad
demeure (der-*m͞urr*) *f* home
demeurer (der-mur-*ray*) *v* stay; live
demi (der-*mee*) *adj* half
demi-heure (der-mee-*͞urr*) *f* **une ~** half an hour
demi-pension (der-mee-pahn͞g-*s^y awn͞g*) *f* part board
démission (day-mee-*s^y awn͞g*) *f* resignation
démissionner (day-mee-s^y o-*nay*) *v* resign
demi-tour (der-mee-*t͞oor*) *m* half-turn, U-turn; **faire demi-tour** turn back
démocratie (day-mo-krah-*see*) *f* democracy
démocratique (day-mo-krah-*teek*) *adj* democratic
démodé (day-mo-*day*) *adj* out of date, old-fashioned
demoiselle (der-mwah-*zehl*) *f* miss
démolir (day-mo-*leer*) *v* demolish
démolition (day-mo-lee-*s^y awn͞g*) *f* demolition
démonstration (day-mawn͞g-strah-*s^y awn͞g*) *f* demonstration
démontrer (day-mawn͞g-*tray*) *v* *show, demonstrate, prove
dénier (day-*n^y ay*) *v* deny
dénomination (day-no-mee-nah-*s^y awn͞g*) *f* denomination
dénouer (day-*nway*) *v* untie
dense (dahn͞gss) *adj* dense
dent (dahn͞g) *f* tooth
dentelle (dahn͞g-*tehl*) *f* lace
dentier (dahn͞g-*t^y ay*) *m* false teeth, denture
dentifrice (dahn͞g-teh-*freess*) *m* toothpaste
dentiste (dahn͞g-*teest*) *m/f* dentist
dénudé (day-new-*day*) *adj* naked
dénutrition (day-new-tree-*s^y awn͞g*) *f* malnutrition
déodorant (day-o-do-*rahn͞g*) *m* deodorant

départ (day-*paar*) *m* departure
département (day-pahr-ter-*mahn̅g̅*) *m* division, department
dépasser (day-pah-*say*) *v* *overtake; pass
dépêcher (day-pay-*shay*): **se ~** hurry
dépendant (day-pahn̅g̅-*dahn̅g̅*) *adj* dependent
dépendre de (day-*pahn̅g̅dr*) depend on
dépense (day-*pahn̅g̅ss*) *f* expense, expenditure
dépenser (day-pahn̅g̅-*say*) *v* *spend
dépit: en ~ de (ahn̅g̅ day-*pee* der) in spite of
déplacement (day-plah-*smahn̅g̅*) *m* moving
déplacer (day-plah-*say*) *v* move
***déplaire** (day-*plair*) *v* displease
déplaisant (day-play-*zahn̅g̅*) *adj* unpleasant
déplier (day-plee-*ay*) *v* unfold
déployer (day-plwah-^{y}*ay*) *v* expand
déposer (day-poa-*zay*) *v* deposit
dépôt (day-*poa*) *m* deposit; warehouse, depot
dépression (day-preh-*s^{y}awn̅g̅*) *f* depression
déprimer (day-pree-*may*) *v* depress; **déprimé** down; blue; low
depuis (der-*pwee*) *prep* since; *adv* since; **~ que** since
député (day-pew-*tay*) *m/f* deputy; Member of Parliament
déraisonnable (day-ray-zo-*nahbl*) *adj* unreasonable
dérangement (day-rahn̅g̅zh-*mahn̅g̅*) *m* trouble; disturbance; **en ~** broken, out of order
déranger (day-rahn̅g̅-*zhay*) *v* disturb, upset, trouble
déraper (day-rah-*pay*) *v* slip, skid
dermatologue (dehr-mah-to-*log*) *m/f* dermatologist
dernier (dehr-*n^{y}ay*) *adj* last; past
dernièrement (dehr-n^{y}ehr-*mahn̅g̅*) *adv* lately
derrière (deh-*r^{y}air*) *prep* after, behind; *m* bottom
dès que (day ker) as soon as
désaccord: *être en ~ (aitr ahn̅g̅ day-zah-*kawr*) disagree
désagréable (day-zah-gray-*ahbl*) *adj* nasty, disagreeable, unpleasant, unkind
désagrément (day-zah-gray-*mahn̅g̅*) *m* inconvenience
***désapprendre** (day-zah-*prahn̅g̅dr*) *v* unlearn
désapprouver (day-zah-proo-*vay*) *v* disapprove
désastre (day-*zahstr*) *m* disaster
désastreux (day-zah-*strur*) *adj* disastrous
désavantage (day-zah-vahn̅g̅-*taazh*) *m* disadvantage
descendance (day-sahn̅g̅-*dahn̅g̅ss*) *f* origin
descendant (day-sahn̅g̅-*dahn̅g̅*) *m*, **-e** *f* descendant
descendre (day-*sahn̅g̅dr*) *v* descend; *get off
descente (day-*sahn̅g̅t*) *f* descent
description (day-skree-*ps^{y}awn̅g̅*) *f* description
désenchanter (day-zahn̅g̅-shahn̅g̅-*tay*) *v* disillusion
désert (day-*zair*) *m* desert; *adj* desert
déserter (day-zehr-*tay*) *v* desert
désespérer (day-zeh-spay-*ray*) *v* despair; **désespéré** desperate; hopeless
désespoir (day-zeh-*spwaar*) *m* despair
déshabiller (day-zah-bee-^{y}*ay*) *v*: **se ~** undress
déshonneur (day-zo-*nu̅r̅r̅*) *m* disgrace, shame
désigner (day-zee-*ñay*) *v* designate;

appoint
désinfectant (day-zan̅g̅-fehk-*tahn̅g̅*) *m* disinfectant
désinfecter (day-zan̅g̅-fehk-*tay*) *v* disinfect
désintéressé (day-zan̅g̅-tay-ray-*say*) *adj* unselfish
désir (day-*zeer*) *m* desire, wish
désirable (day-zee-*rahbl*) *adj* desirable
désirer (day-zee-*ray*) *v* want, desire, wish, long for
désireux (day-zee-*rur*) *adj* eager, anxious
désobligeant (day-zo-blee-*zhahn̅g̅*) *adj* disagreeable
désodorisant (day-zo-do-ree-*zahn̅g̅*) *m* deodorant
désoler (day-zo-*lay*) *v* grieve; **désolé** sorry
désordonné (day-zor-do-*nay*) *adj* disorderly, untidy
désordre (day-*zordr*) *m* disorder, mess
désormais (day-zawr-*may*) *adv* from now on, henceforth
désosser (day-zo-*say*) *v* bone
dessein (day-*san̅g̅*) *m* design
desserrer (day say-*ray*) *v* loosen
dessert (day-*sair*) *m* dessert, sweet
dessin (day-*san̅g̅*) *m* sketch, drawing; pattern; **dessins animés** cartoon
dessiner (day-see-*nay*) *v* sketch, *draw
dessous (der-*soo*) *adv* underneath; **en ~** below; **en ~ de** beneath
dessus (der-*sew*) *m* top; **au-dessus de** on top of; **sens ~ dessous** upside-down
destin (day-*stan̅g̅*) *m* destiny; fate
destinataire (day-stee-nah-*tair*) *m* addressee
destination (day-stee-nah-s^{y}*awn̅g̅*) *f* destination
destiner (day-stee-*nay*) *v* destine
destruction (day-strewk-s^{y}*awn̅g̅*) *f* destruction
détachant (day-tah-*shahn̅g̅*) *m* cleaning fluid, stain remover
détacher (day-tah-*shay*) *v* unfasten, detach
détail (day-*tigh*) *m* detail; **commerce de ~** retail trade
détaillant (day-tah-^{y}*ahn̅g̅*) *m*, **-e** *f* retailer
détaillé (day-tah-^{y}*ay*) *adj* detailed
détailler (day-tah-^{y}*ay*) *v* retail
détecter (day-tehk-*tay*) *v* detect
détective (day-tehk-*teev*) *m* detective
***déteindre** (day-*tan̅g̅dr*) *v* fade
détendre (day-*tahn̅g̅dr*) *v*: **se ~** relax
détente (day-*tahn̅g̅t*) *f* relaxation
détention (day-tahn̅g̅-s^{y}*awn̅g̅*) *f* detention
détenu (dayt-*new*) *m* prisoner
détergent (day-tehr-*zhahn̅g̅*) *m* detergent
déterminer (day-tehr-mee-*nay*) *v* determine, define; **déterminé** *adj* definite; resolute
détester (day-teh-*stay*) *v* dislike, hate
détour (day-*to͞or*) *m* detour
détourner (day-toor-*nay*) *v* divert; hijack
détresse (day-*trehss*) *f* distress; misery
détritus (day-tree-*tewss*) *m* litter, garbage, rubbish
***détruire** (day-*trweer*) *v* destroy, wreck
dette (deht) *f* debt
deuil (dur^{ee}) *m* mourning
deux (dur) *num* two; **les ~** either, both
deuxième (dur-z^{y}*ehm*) *num* second
deux-pièces (dur-p^{y}*ehss*) *m* two-piece
dévaluation (day-vah-lwah-s^{y}*awn̅g̅*) *f* devaluation
dévaluer (day-vah-*lway*) *v* devalue
devant (der-*vahn̅g̅*) *prep* in front of, ahead of, before
dévaster (day-vah-*stay*) *v* destroy

développement (day-vlop-*mahng*) *m* development
développer (day-vlo-*pay*) *v* develop
***devenir** (der-*vneer*) *v* *become, *go, *get
déviation (day-v^{y}ah-*s^{y}awng*) *f* diversion, detour
dévier (day-*v^{y}ay*) *v* deviate
deviner (der-vee-*nay*) *v* guess
devise (der-*veez*) *f* slogan, motto
dévisser (day-vee-*say*) *v* unscrew
devoir (der-*vwaar*) *m* duty
***devoir** (der-*vwaar*) *v* *be obliged to, *be bound to, *have to; need to, *should, *ought to, *shall; owe
dévorer (day-vo-*ray*) *v* devour
dévouement (day-voo-*mahng*) *m* devotion
diabète (d^{y}ah-*beht*) *m* diabetes
diabétique (d^{y}ah-bay-*teek*) *m/f* diabetic
diable (d^{y}aabl) *m* devil
diagnostic (d^{y}ahg-no-*steek*) *m* diagnosis
diagnostiquer (d^{y}ahg-no-stee-*kay*) *v* diagnose
diagonale (d^{y}ah-go-*nahl*) *f* diagonal; *adj* diagonal
diagramme (d^{y}ah-*grahm*) *m* graph, diagram
dialecte (d^{y}ah-*lehkt*) *m* dialect
diamant (d^{y}ah-*mahng*) *m* diamond
diapositive (d^{y}ah-po-zee-*teev*) *f* slide
diarrhée (d^{y}ah-*ray*) *f* diarrh(o)ea
dictée (deek-*tay*) *f* dictation
dicter (deek-*tay*) *v* dictate
dictionnaire (deek-s^{y}o-*nair*) *m* dictionary
diesel (d^{y}ay-*zehl*) *m* diesel
dieu (d^{y}ur) *m* god
différence (dee-fay-*rahngss*) *f* difference, contrast
différent (dee-fay-*rahng*) *adj* different
différer (dee-fay-*ray*) *v* delay; vary, differ
difficile (dee-fee-*seel*) *adj* difficult, hard
difficulté (dee-fee-kewl-*tay*) *f* difficulty
difforme (dee-*form*) *adj* deformed
digérer (dee-zhay-*ray*) *v* digest
digestible (dee-zheh-*steebl*) *adj* digestible
digestif (dee-zheh-*steef*) *adj*, *m* digestive
digestion (dee-zheh-*st^{y}awng*) *f* digestion
digne (deeñ) *adj* dignified; **~ de** worthy of
digue (deeg) *f* dike, dam
diluer (dee-*lway*) *v* dissolve, dilute
dimanche (dee-*mahngsh*) *m* Sunday
dimension (dee-mahng-*s^{y}awng*) *f* size, extent
diminuer (dee-mee-*nway*) *v* decrease, lessen, reduce
diminution (dee-mee-new-*s^{y}awng*) *f* decrease
dinde (dangd) *f* turkey
dîner (dee-*nay*) *v* dine, *have dinner; *m* dinner
diphtérie (deef-tay-*ree*) *f* diphtheria
diplomate (dee-plo-*maht*) *m* diplomat
diplôme (dee-*ploam*) *m* certificate, diploma
***dire** (deer) *v* *tell, *say
direct (dee-*rehkt*) *adj* direct
directement (dee-rehk-ter-*mahng*) *adv* straight away, straight
directeur (dee-rehk-*turr*) *m* manager, director; **~ d'école** headmaster, head teacher
direction (dee-rehk-*s^{y}awng*) *f* management, direction, leadership; way; **indicateur de ~** indicator, blinker *Am*
directive (dee-rehk-*teev*) *f* directive
directrice (dee-rehk-*trees*) *f* director; ~

d'école headmistress, head teacher
dirigeant (dee-ree-*zhahn͞g*) *m*, **-e** *f* leader, ruler
diriger (dee-ree-*zhay*) *v* direct; head, conduct, *lead; manage
discerner (dee-sehr-*nay*) *v* distinguish
discipline (dee-see-*pleen*) *f* discipline
discours (dee-*sko͞or*) *m* speech
discret (dee-*skray*) *adj* (*f* discrète) discreet, reserved; unobtrusive
discussion (dee-skew-*s^y^awn͞g*) *f* discussion, argument, deliberation; dispute
discuter (dee-skew-*tay*) *v* discuss, argue, deliberate
***disjoindre** (deess-*zhwan͞gdr*) *v* disconnect
disloqué (dee-slo-*kay*) *adj* dislocated
***disparaître** (dee-spah-*raitr*) *v* vanish, disappear
disparu (dee-spah-*rew*) *adj* lost; *m* missing person
dispensaire (dee-spahn͞g-*sair*) *m* health center *Am*, health centre
dispenser (dee-spahn͞g-*say*) *v* exempt; **~ de** discharge of
disperser (dee-spehr-*say*) *v* scatter
disponible (dee-spo-*neebl*) *adj* available; obtainable; spare
disposé (dee-spoa-*zay*) *adj* inclined, willing
disposer de (dee-spoa-*zay*) dispose of
dispositif (dee-spoa-zee-*teef*) *m* apparatus
disposition (dee-spoa-zee-*s^y^awn͞g*) *f* disposal
dispute (dee-*spewt*) *f* argument
disputer (dee-spew-*tay*) *v* argue; **se ~** dispute, quarrel
disque (deesk) *m* disc; record
dissertation (dee-sehr-tah-*s^y^awn͞g*) *f* essay
dissimuler (dee-see-mew-*lay*) *v* *hide, conceal
***dissoudre** (dee-*soodr*) *v* dissolve; **se ~** dissolve
dissuader (dee-swah-*day*) *v* dissuade from
distance (dee-*stahn͞gss*) *f* way, distance, space
distinct (dee-*stan͞g*) *adj* distinct, separate
distinction (dee-stan͞gk-*s^y^awn͞g*) *f* distinction, difference
distinguer (dee-stan͞g-*gay*) *v* distinguish
distraction (dee-strahk-*s^y^awn͞g*) *f* diversion; inadvertence
distrait (dee-*stray*) *adj* absent-minded
distribuer (dee-stree-*bway*) *v* distribute, *deal
distributeur (dee-stree-bew-*t͞urr*) *m* distributor; **~ de billets** ticket machine; **~ d'essence** fuel pump *Am*; **~ de timbres** stamp machine; **~ automatique** cash dispenser, ATM
distribution (dee-stree-bew-*s^y^awn͞g*) *f* distribution
district (dee-*stree*) *m* district
divers (dee-*vair*) *adj* various, several; miscellaneous
diversion (dee-vehr-*s^y^awn͞g*) *f* diversion
divertir (dee-vehr-*teer*) *v* entertain, amuse
divertissant (dee-vehr-tee-*sahn͞g*) *adj* entertaining
divertissement (dee-vehr-tee-*smahn͞g*) *m* pleasure, fun, entertainment, amusement
divin (dee-*van͞g*) *adj* divine
diviser (dee-vee-*zay*) *v* divide; **~ en deux** halve
division (dee-vee-*z^y^awn͞g*) *f* division; department
divorce (dee-*vors*) *m* divorce
divorcer (dee-vor-*say*) *v* divorce
dix (deess) *num* ten

dix-huit (dee-*zweet*) *num* eighteen
dix-huitième (dee-zwee-*t^{y}ehm*) *num* eighteenth
dixième (dee-*z^{y}ehm*) *num* tenth
dix-neuf (deez-*nurf*) *num* nineteen
dix-neuvième (deez-nur-*v^{y}ehm*) *num* nineteenth
dix-sept (dee-*seht*) *num* seventeen
dix-septième (dee-seh-*t^{y}ehm*) *num* seventeenth
dock (dok) *m* dock
docteur (dok-*tūrr*) *m* doctor
document (do-kew-*mahng*) *m* document, certificate
doigt (dwah) *m* finger
domaine (do-*mehn*) *m* field
dôme (dōam) *m* dome
domestique (do-meh-*steek*) *adj* domestic; *m/f* domestic, servant
domestiqué (do-meh-stee-*kay*) *adj* tame
domicile (do-mee-*seel*) *m* domicile
domicilié (do-mee-see-*l^{y}ay*) *adj* resident
domination (do-mee-nah-*s^{y}awng*) *f* domination
dominer (do-mee-*nay*) *v* dominate; prevail; **dominant** leading
dommage (do-*maazh*) *m* mischief, damage; **dommage!** what a pity!
don (dawng) *m* faculty, talent; donation, gift
donateur (do-nah-*tūrr*) *m*, **-trice** *f* donor
donation (do-nah-*s^{y}awng*) *f* donation
donc (dawngk) *conj* therefore; so
données (do-*nay*) *fpl* data *pl*
donner (do-*nay*) *v* *give; donate; **étant donné que** given that
dont (dawng) *pron* of which; of whom
doré (do-*ray*) *adj* gilt
***dormir** (dor-*meer*) *v* *sleep; **~ trop longtemps** *oversleep
dortoir (dor-*twaar*) *m* dormitory
dos (doa) *m* back
dose (dōaz) *f* dose
dossier (do-*s^{y}ay*) *m* file, record
douane (dwahn) *f* Customs *pl*; **droit de ~** Customs duty
douanier (dwah-*n^{y}ay*) *m* Customs officer
double (dōobl) *adj* double
doubler (doo-*blay*) *v* pass *Am*
doublure (doo-*blēwr*) *f* lining
doucement (doos-*mahng*) *adv* gently; softly; smoothly; carefully
douceurs (doo-*sūrr*) *fpl* sweets
douche (doosh) *f* shower
doué (doo-*ay*) *adj* talented, gifted
douleur (doo-*lūrr*) *f* ache, pain; sorrow, grief; **sans ~** painless; **douleurs** labo(u)r
douloureux (doo-loo-*rur*) *adj* painful; distressing
doute (doot) *m* doubt; ***mettre en ~** query; **sans ~** doubtless, probably
douter (doo-*tay*) *v* doubt; **~ de** doubt
douteux (doo-*tur*) *adj* doubtful; unreliable
douve (dōov) *f* moat
doux (doo) *adj* (f douce) mild; smooth, gentle
douzaine (doo-*zehn*) *f* dozen
douze (dōoz) *num* twelve
douzième (doo-*z^{y}ehm*) *num* twelfth
dragon (drah-*gawng*) *m* dragon
drainer (dray-*nay*) *v* drain
dramatique (drah-mah-*teek*) *adj* dramatic
dramaturge (drah-mah-*tewrzh*) *m* dramatist; playwright
drame (drahm) *m* drama
drap (drah) *m* sheet
drapeau (drah-*poa*) *m* flag
dresser (dray-*say*) *v* *draw up; train
drogue (drog) *f* drug
droguerie (dro-*gree*) *f* hardware shop; hardware store *Am*

droit (drwah) *m* right, law, justice; *adj* right, straight; erect, upright; ~ **administratif** administrative law; ~ **civil** civil law; ~ **commercial** commercial law; ~ **de douane** Customs duty; ~ **de stationnement** parking fee; ~ **de vote** right to vote; ~ **d'importation** duty; ~ **pénal** criminal law; **droits** duties *pl*; **tout** ~ straight ahead
droite: de ~ (der drwaht) right-hand
drôle (drōal) *adj* humorous, funny, queer
dû (dew) *adj* (f due; pl dus, dues) due
duc (dewk) *m* duke
duchesse (dew-*shehss*) *f* duchess
dune (dewn) *f* dune
dupe (dewp) *f* victim
duper (dew-*pay*) *v* cheat
dur (dēwr) *adj* hard
durable (dew-*rahbl*) *adj* permanent, lasting
durant (dew-*rahng*) *prep* during
durée (dew-*ray*) *f* duration
durer (dew-*ray*) *v* continue, last
duvet (dew-*vay*) *m* down
dynamo (dee-nah-*moa*) *f* dynamo

E

eau (oa) *f* water; ~ **courante** running water; ~ **de mer** sea water; ~ **dentifrice** mouthwash; ~ **de Seltz** soda water; ~ **douce** fresh water; ~ **gazeuse** sparkling mineral water; ~ **glacée** iced water; ~ **minérale** mineral water; ~ **oxygénée** hydrogen peroxide; ~ **potable** drinking water
eau-de-vie (oa-der-*vee*) *f* brandy; spirits
eau-forte (oa-*fort*) *f* etching
ébène (ay-*behn*) *f* ebony
éblouissant (ay-bloo-ee-*sahng*) *adj* glaring
éblouissement (ay-bloo-ee-*smahng*) *m* glare
ébrécher (ay-bray-*shay*) *v* chip
écaille (ay-*kigh*) *f* scale
écarlate (ay-kahr-*laht*) *adj* scarlet
écarter (ay-kahr-*tay*) *v* *spread, part; remove; **écarté** out of the way
ecclésiastique (ay-klay-z^{y}ah-*steek*) *m* clergyman
échafaudage (ay-shah-foa-*daazh*) *m* scaffolding
échange (ay-*shahngzh*) *m* exchange
échanger (ay-shahng-*zhay*) *v* exchange
échantillon (ay-shahng-tee-^{y}*awng*) *m* sample
échappement (ay-shahp-*mahng*) *m* exhaust
échapper (ay-shah-*pay*) *v* escape; **s'échapper** slip
écharde (ay-*shahrd*) *f* splinter
écharpe (ay-*shahrp*) *f* scarf
échec (ay-*shehk*) *m* failure; **échec!** check!; **échecs** chess
échelle (ay-*shehl*) *f* ladder; scale
échiquier (ay-shee-*k^{y}ay*) *m* checkerboard *Am*
écho (ay-*koa*) *m* echo
échoppe (ay-*shop*) *f* booth
échouer (ay-*shway*) *v* fail
éclabousser (ay-klah-boo-*say*) *v* splash
éclair (ay-*klair*) *m* flash; lightning
éclairage (ay-kleh-*raazh*) *m* lighting

éclaircir (ay-klehr-*seer*) *v* clarify
éclaircissement (ay-klehr-see-*smahng*) *m* explanation
éclairer (ay-klay-*ray*) *v* illuminate
éclat (ay-*klah*) *m* glow; glare; chip
éclatant (ay-klah-*tahng*) *adj* bright, gay
éclater (ay-klah-*tay*) *v* *burst
éclipse (ay-*kleeps*) *f* eclipse
éclisse (ay-*kleess*) *f* splint
écluse (ay-*klewz*) *f* sluice, lock
écœurant (ay-kur-*rahng*) *adj* repellent
école (ay-*kol*) *f* school; **~ maternelle** kindergarten; **~ secondaire** secondary school; ***faire l'école buissonnière** play truant
écolier (ay-ko-*l^{y}ay*) *m* schoolboy
écolière (ay-ko-*l^{y}air*) *f* schoolgirl
économe (ay-ko-*nom*) *adj* economical
économie (ay-ko-no-*mee*) *f* economy; **économies** savings *pl*
économique (ay-ko-no-*meek*) *adj* economic
économiser (ay-ko-no-mee-*zay*) *v* economize
économiste (ay-ko-no-*meest*) *m* economist
écorce (ay-*kors*) *f* bark
écossais (ay-ko-*say*) *adj* Scotch; Scottish
Ecosse (ay-*koss*) *f* Scotland
écouler (ay-koo-*lay*): **s'~** flow
écouter (ay-koo-*tay*) *v* listen
écouteur (ay-koo-*turr*) *m* earpiece
écran (ay-*krahng*) *m* screen
écraser (ay-krah-*zay*) *v* mash; overwhelm; **s'écraser** crash
***écrire** (ay-*kreer*) *v* *write; **par écrit** in writing, written
écriture (ay-kree-*tewr*) *f* handwriting
écrivain (ay-kree-*vang*) *m*, **-e** *f* writer
écrouler (ay-kroo-*lay*): **s'~** collapse
Ecuadorien (ay-kwah-do-*r^{y}ang*) *m* Ecuadorian
écume (ay-*kewm*) *f* froth, lather
écureuil (ay-kew-*rur^{ee}*) *m* squirrel
eczéma (ehg-zay-*mah*) *m* eczema
édification (ay-dee-fee-kah-*s^{y}awng*) *f* construction
édifice (ay-dee-*feess*) *m* construction
édifier (ay-dee-*f^{y}ay*) *v* construct
éditeur (ay-dee-*turr*) *m* publisher
édition (ay-dee-*s^{y}awng*) *f* edition; **~ du matin** morning edition
éditrice (ay-dee-*trees*) *f* publisher
édredon (ay-drer-*dawng*) *m* eiderdown
éducation (ehr-*tsee*-oong) *f* education
éduquer (ay-dew-*kay*) *v* educate
effacer (ay-fah-*say*) *v* wipe out
effectif (ay-fehk-*teef*) *adj* effective
effectivement (ay-fehk-teev-*mahng*) *adv* as a matter of fact
effectuer (ay-fehk-*tway*) *v* effect
effet (ay-*fay*) *m* result; consequence, effect; **en ~** indeed
efficace (ay-fee-*kahss*) *adj* effective; efficient
effilocher (ay-fee-lo-*shay*): **s'~** fray
effondrer (ay-fawng-*dray*): **s'~** collapse
efforcer (ay-for-*say*): **s'~** try hard, endeavour
effort (ay-*fawr*) *m* effort, strain
effrayé (ay-fray-*^{y}ay*) *adj* frightened, afraid
effrayer (ay-fray-*^{y}ay*) *v* frighten; scare
effronté (ay-frawng-*tay*) *adj* bold; impertinent
égal (ay-*gahl*) *adj* even, level, equal
également (ay-gahl-*mahng*) *adv* as well, likewise, equally, also
égaler (ay-gah-*lay*) *v* equal
égaliser (ay-gah-lee-*zay*) *v* level, equalize
égalité (ay-gah-lee-*tay*) *f* equality
égards (ay-*gaar*) *mpl* consideration
égarer (ay-gah-*ray*) *v* mislay
égayer (ay-gay-*^{y}ay*) *v* cheer up

église (ay-*gleez*) *f* chapel, church
égocentrique (ay-go-sahng-*treek*) *adj* self-centred
égoïsme (ay-go-*eesm*) *m* selfishness, ego(t)ism
égoïste (ay-go-*eest*) *adj* ego(t)istic, selfish
égout (ay-*goo*) *m* drain, sewer
égratignure (ay-grah-tee-*ñewr*) *f* graze, scratch
Egypte (ay-*zheept*) *f* Egypt
égyptien (ay-zhee-*ps^{y}ang*) *adj* Egyptian
élaborer (ay-lah-bo-*ray*) *v* elaborate
élan (ay-*lahng*) *m* vigour; moose
élargir (ay-lahr-*zheer*) *v* widen
élasticité (ay-lah-stee-see-*tay*) *f* elasticity
élastique (ay-lah-*steek*) *adj* elastic; *m* elastic, rubber band
électeur (ay-lehk-*turr*) *m*, **-trice** *f* voter
élection (ay-lehk-*s^{y}awng*) *f* election
électricien (ay-lehk-tree-*s^{y}ang*) *m* electrician
électricité (ay-lehk-tree-see-*tay*) *f* electricity
électrique (ay-lehk-*treek*) *adj* electric
électronique (ay-lehk-tro-*neek*) *adj* electronic
élégance (ay-lay-*gahngss*) *f* elegance
élégant (ay-lay-*gahng*) *adj* smart, elegant
élément (ay-lay-*mahng*) *m* element
élémentaire (ay-lay-mahng-*tair*) *adj* primary
éléphant (ay-lay-*fahng*) *m* elephant
élevage (ehl-*vaazh*) *m* breeding
élévation (ay-lay-vah-*s^{y}awng*) *f* rise
élève (ay-*laiv*) *m/f* pupil, scholar
élever (ehl-*vay*) *v* *bring up, rear, raise; *breed
éliminer (ay-lee-mee-*nay*) *v* eliminate
***élire** (ay-*leer*) *v* elect
elle (ehl) *pron* she
elle-même (ehl-*mehm*) *pron* herself
éloge (ay-*lozh*) *m* praise
éloigner (ay-lwah-*ñay*) *v* remove; **éloigné** distant, far-away, remote
élucider (ay-lew-see-*day*) *v* elucidate
émail (ay-*migh*) *m* (pl émaux) enamel
émaillé (ay-mah-*^{y}ay*) *adj* enamelled
émancipation (ay-mahng-see-pah-*s^{y}awng*) *f* emancipation
emballage (ahng-bah-*laazh*) *m* packing
emballer (ahng-bah-*lay*) *v* pack up, pack
embargo (ahng-bahr-*goa*) *m* embargo
embarquement (ahng-bahr-ker-*mahng*) *m* embarkation
embarquer (ahng-bahr-*kay*) *v* embark
embarras (ahng-bah-*rah*) *m* fuss
embarrassant (ahng-bah-rah-*sahng*) *adj* awkward, embarrassing; puzzling
embarrasser (ahng-bah-rah-*say*) *v* embarrass
embêtant (ahng-bay-*tahng*) *adj* annoying
emblème (ahng-*blehm*) *m* emblem
embouchure (ahng-boo-*shewr*) *f* mouth
embouteillage (ahng-boo-teh-*^{y}aazh*) *m* traffic jam, jam
embrasser (ahng-brah-*say*) *v* kiss
embrayage (ahng-breh-*^{y}aazh*) *m* clutch
embrouiller (ahng-broo-*^{y}ay*) *v* muddle
émeraude (aym-*road*) *f* emerald
émerveiller (ay-mehr-vay-*^{y}ay*): **s'~** marvel
émetteur (ay-meh-*turr*) *m* transmitter
***émettre** (ay-*mehtr*) *v* utter; transmit, *broadcast
émeute (ay-*murt*) *f* riot
émigrant (ay-mee-*grahng*) *m* emigrant
émigration (ay-mee-grah-*s^{y}awng*) *f* emigration
émigrer (ay-mee-*gray*) *v* emigrate

éminent (ay-mee-*nahn̄g*) *adj* outstanding
émission (ay-mee-*s*ʸ*awn̄g*) *f* issue; transmission, broadcast
emmagasiner (ahn̄g-mah-gah-zee-*nay*) *v* store
emmener (ahn̄g-mer-*nay*) *v* *take along
émoi (ay-*mwah*) *m* emotion
émotion (ay-moa-*s*ʸ*awn̄g*) *f* emotion
émoussé (ay-moo-*say*) *adj* dull, blunt
***émouvoir** (ay-moo-*vwaar*) *v* move
empêcher (ahn̄g-pay-*shay*) *v* prevent
empereur (ahn̄g-*prūrr*) *m* emperor
empiéter (ahn̄g-pʸay-*tay*) *v* trespass
empire (ahn̄g-*peer*) *m* empire
emploi (ahn̄g-*plwah*) *m* use; job, employment; **solliciter un ~** apply
employé (ahn̄g-plwah-ʸ*ay*) *m*, **-e** *f* employee; **~ de bureau** clerk
employer (ahn̄g-plwah-ʸ*ay*) *v* use; employ
employeur (ahn̄g-plwah-ʸ*ūrr*) *m*, **-euse** *f* employer
empoisonner (ahn̄g-pwah-zo-*nay*) *v* poison
emporter (ahn̄g-por-*tay*) *v* *take away
empreinte digitale (ahn̄g-pran̄gt dee-zhee-*tahl*) fingerprint
emprisonnement (ahn̄g-pree-zon-*mahn̄g*) *m* imprisonment
emprisonner (ahn̄g-pree-zo-*nay*) *v* imprison
emprunt (ahn̄g-*prurn̄g*) *m* loan
emprunter (ahn̄g-prurn̄g-*tay*) *v* borrow
en (ahn̄g) *prep* in; by; *pron* of it
encaisser (ahn̄g-kay-*say*) *v* cash
enceinte (ahn̄g-*san̄gt*) *adj* pregnant
encens (ahn̄g-*sahn̄g*) *m* incense
encercler (ahn̄g-sehr-*klay*) *v* circle, encircle
enchanté (ahn̄g-shahn̄g-*tay*) *adj* enchanted; delightful; **~ de** delighted at, with
enchantement (ahn̄g-shahn̄gt-*mahn̄g*) *m* spell
enchanter (ahn̄g-shahn̄g-*tay*) *v* delight; bewitch
enchanteur (ahn̄g-shahn̄g-*tūrr*) *adj* (f -teresse) glamorous
enclin (ahn̄g-*klan̄g*) *adj* inclined
encore (ahn̄g-*kawr*) *adv* again; still, yet; **~ que** though; **~ un** another; **~ un peu** some more
encourager (ahn̄g-koo-rah-*zhay*) *v* encourage
encre (ahn̄gkr) *f* ink
encyclopédie (ahn̄g-see-klo-pay-*dee*) *f* encyclop(a)edia
endive (ahn̄g-*deev*) *f* chicory
endommager (ahn̄g-do-mah-*zhay*) *v* damage
endormir (ahn̄g-dor-*meer*) *v* send to sleep; numb; deaden; bore; lull
endormi (ahn̄g-dor-*mee*) *adj* asleep
endosser (ahn̄g-do-*say*) *v* endorse
endroit (ahn̄g-*drwah*) *m* spot
endurer (ahn̄g-dew-*ray*) *v* endure, sustain; *go through
énergie (ay-nehr-*zhee*) *f* energy; power; **~ nucléaire** nuclear energy
énergique (ay-nehr-*zheek*) *adj* energetic
énerver (ay-nehr-*vay*) *v* *get on someone's nerves; **s'énerver** *get excited
enfance (ahn̄g-*fahn̄gss*) *f* childhood
enfant (ahn̄g-*fahn̄g*) *m* child, kid
enfer (ahn̄g-*fair*) *m* hell
enfermer (ahn̄g-fehr-*may*) *v* lock up, *shut in
enfiler (ahn̄g-fee-*lay*) *v* thread
enfin (ahn̄g-*fan̄g*) *adv* at last
enfler (ahn̄g-*flay*) *v* *swell
enflure (ahn̄g-*flewr*) *f* swelling
enfoncer (ahn̄g-fawn̄g-*say*): **s'~** *sink
engagement (ahn̄g-gahzh-*mahn̄g*) *m* engagement

engager (ahng-gah-*zhay*) *v* engage; **s'engager** engage

engourdi (ahng-goor-*dee*) *adj* numb

engrais (ahng-*gray*) *m* fertilizer

énigme (ay-*neegm*) *f* mystery, riddle, puzzle, enigma

enjeu (ahng-*zhur*) *m* stake

enlacement (ahng-lah-*smah*) *m* embrace

enlever (ahngl-*vay*) *v* remove; *take away

ennemi (ehn-*mee*) *m*, **-e** *f* enemy

ennui (ahng-*nwee*) *m* annoyance, trouble; nuisance

ennuyer (ahng-nwee-*^{y}ay*) *v* annoy, bore

ennuyeux (ahng-nwee-*^{y}ur*) *adj* annoying; dull, unpleasant, boring

énorme (ay-*norm*) *adj* tremendous, immense, huge, enormous

enquête (ahng-*keht*) *f* inquiry; enquiry

enquêter (ahng-kay-*tay*) *v* investigate, enquire

enragé (ahng-rah-*zhay*) *adj* mad

enregistrement (ahngr-zhee-strer-*mahng*) *m* recording

enregistrer (ahngr-zhee-*stray*) *v* book; record

enrhumer (ahng-rew-*may*): **s'~** catch a cold

enroué (ahng-roo-*ay*) *adj* hoarse

enrouler (ahng-roo-*lay*) *v* *wind

enseignement (ahng-sehñ-*mahng*) *m* education; teaching

enseigner (ahng-say-*ñay*) *v* *teach

ensemble (ahng-*sahngbl*) *adv* together; *m* whole

ensoleillé (ahng-so-lay-*^{y}ay*) *adj* sunny

ensorceler (ahng-sor-ser-*lay*) *v* bewitch

ensuite (ahng-*sweet*) *adv* then, afterwards

entailler (ahng-tah-*^{y}ay*) *v* carve

entasser (ahng-tah-*say*) *v* pile

entendre (ahng-*tahngdr*) *v* *hear

entente (ahng-*tahngt*) *f* agreement

enterrement (ahng-tehr-*mahng*) *m* burial

enterrer (ahng-tay-*ray*) *v* bury

enthousiasme (ahng-too-*z^{y}ahsm*) *m* enthusiasm

enthousiaste (ahng-too-*z^{y}ahst*) *adj* enthusiastic

entier (ahng-*t^{y}ay*) *adj* whole, complete, entire

entièrement (ahng-t^{y}ehr-*mahng*) *adv* wholly, completely, entirely, altogether

entonnoir (ahng-to-*nwaar*) *m* funnel

entourer (ahng-too-*ray*) *v* encircle; surround

entracte (ahng-*trahkt*) *m* interval, intermission

entrailles (ahng-*trigh*) *fpl* entrails, guts

entrain (ahng-*trang*) *m* zest

entraînement (ahng-trehn-*mahng*) *m* training

entraîner (ahng-tray-*nay*) *v* drill

entraîneur (ahng-treh-*nurr*) *m* coach

entrave (ahng-*traav*) *f* impediment

entraver (ahng-trah-*vay*) *v* impede

entre (ahngtr) *prep* between, among, amid

entrée (ahng-*tray*) *f* way in, entry, entrance; appearance; **~ interdite** no admittance

entrepôt (ahng-trer-*poa*) *m* depository

***entreprendre** (ahng-trer-*prahngdr*) *v* *undertake

entrepreneur (ahng-trer-prer-*nurr*) *m*, **-euse** *f* contractor

entreprise (ahng-trer-*preez*) *f* enterprise; business, company, undertaking

entrer (ahng-*tray*) *v* enter, *go in

entre-temps (ahng-trer-*tahng*) *adv* meanwhile, in the meantime

***entretenir** (ahng-trer-*tneer*) *v*

maintain; support
entretien (ahng-trer-*t^{y}ang*) *m* upkeep, maintenance; conversation
***entrevoir** (ahng-trer-*vwaar*) *v* glimpse
entrevue (ahng-trer-*vew*) *f* interview
envahir (ahng-vah-*eer*) *v* invade
enveloppe (ahng-*vlop*) *f* envelope
envelopper (ahng-vlo-*pay*) *v* wrap
envers (ahng-*vair*) *prep* towards; **à l'envers** inside out
envie (ahng-*vee*) *f* longing, desire; envy; ***avoir ~ de** *feel like; fancy, desire
envier (ahng-*v^{y}ay*) *v* grudge, envy
envieux (ahng-*v^{y}ur*) *adj* envious
environ (ahng-vee-*rawng*) *adv* about
environnant (ahng-vee-ro-*nahng*) *adj* surrounding
environnement (ahng-vee-ron-*mahng*) *m* environment
environs (ahng-vee-*rawng*) *mpl* environment
envisager (ahng-vee-zah-*zhay*) *v* consider
envoyé (ahng-vwah-*^{y}ay*) *m* envoy
***envoyer** (ahng-vwah-*^{y}ay*) *v* *send; dispatch
épais (ay-*pay*) *adj* (f ~se) thick
épaisseur (ay-peh-*surr*) *f* thickness
épaissir (ay-pay-*seer*) *v* thicken
épargner (ay-pahr-*ñay*) *v* save
épaule (ay-*poal*) *f* shoulder
épave (ay-*paav*) *f* wreck
épée (ay-*pay*) *f* sword
épeler (eh-*play*) *v* *spell
épice (ay-*peess*) *f* spice
épicé (ay-pee-*say*) *adj* spicy, spiced
épicerie (ay-pee-*sree*) *f* grocer's; **~ fine** delicatessen
épicier (ay-pee-*s^{y}ay*) *m*, **-ière** *f* grocer
épidémie (ay-pee-day-*mee*) *f* epidemic
épier (ay-*p^{y}ay*) *v* peep
épilepsie (ay-pee-leh-*psee*) *f* epilepsy
épinards (ay-pee-*naar*) *mpl* spinach
épine (ay-*peen*) *f* thorn; **~ dorsale** backbone, spine
épingle (ay-*panggl*) *f* pin; **~ à cheveux** hairpin; **~ de sûreté** safetypin
épingler (ay-pang-*glay*) *v* pin
épisode (ay-pee-*zod*) *m* episode
éplucher (ay-plew-*shay*) *v* peel; clean; examine closely, sift
éponge (ay-*pawngzh*) *f* sponge
époque (ay-*pok*) *f* period; **de l'époque** contemporary
épouse (ay-*pooz*) *f* wife
épouser (ay-poo-*zay*) *v* marry
épouvantable (ay-poo-vahng-*tahbl*) *adj* terrible
épouvante (ay-poo-*vahngt*) *f* horror
époux (ay-*poo*) *m* husband
épreuve (ay-*prurv*) *f* test, experiment; print
éprouver (ay-proo-*vay*) *v* experience; test
épuiser (ay-pwee-*zay*) *v* exhaust; use up; **épuisé** sold out
Equateur (ay-kwah-*turr*) *m* Ecuador
équateur (ay-kwah-*turr*) *m* equator
équilibre (ay-kee-*leebr*) *m* balance
équipage (ay-kee-*paazh*) *m* crew
équipe (ay-*keep*) *f* shift, team, gang; soccer team
équipement (ay-keep-*mahng*) *m* outfit, gear, equipment
équiper (ay-kee-*pay*) *v* equip
équitable (ay-kee-*tahbl*) *adj* right; reasonable
équitation (ay-kee-tah-*s^{y}awng*) *f* riding
équivalent (ay-kee-vah-*lahng*) *adj* equivalent
équivoque (ay-kee-*vok*) *adj* ambiguous
érable (ay-*rahbl*) *m* maple
érafler (ay-rah-*flay*) *v* scratch
ériger (ay-ree-*zhay*) *v* erect
errer (ay-*ray*) *v* err; wander

erreur (eh-*rūrr*) *f* error; mistake
erroné (eh-ro-*nay*) *adj* mistaken
érudit (ay-rew-*dee*) *m* scholar
éruption (ay-rew-*ps^{y}awn͞g*) *f* rash
escale (eh-*skahl*) *f* port of call; stop; call
escalier (eh-skah-*l^{y}ay*) *m* staircase; stairs *pl*; ~ **de secours** fire escape; ~ **roulant** escalator
escalope (eh-skah-*lop*) *f* escalope
escargot (eh-skahr-*goa*) *m* snail
escarpé (eh-skahr-*pay*) *adj* steep
escorte (eh-*skort*) *f* escort
escorter (eh-skor-*tay*) *v* escort
escrime: *faire de l'escrime (fair der leh-*skreem*) fence
escroc (eh-*skroa*) *m* swindler
escroquer (eh-skro-*kay*) *v* swindle
escroquerie (eh-skro-*kree*) *f* swindle
espace (eh-*spahss*) *m* space; room
espacer (eh-spah-*say*) *v* space
Espagne (eh-*spahñ*) *f* Spain
espagnol (eh-spah-*ñol*) *adj* Spanish
espèce (eh-*spehss*) *f* species; breed
espérance (eh-spay-*rahn͞gss*) *f* expectation
espérer (eh-spay-*ray*) *v* hope
espièglerie (eh-sp^{y}eh-gler-*ree*) *f* piece of mischief, prank
espion (eh-*sp^{y}awn͞g*) *m* spy
esplanade (eh-splah-*nahd*) *f* esplanade
espoir (eh-*spwaar*) *m* hope
esprit (eh-*spree*) *m* spirit; soul, mind; ghost
esquisse (eh-*skeess*) *f* sketch
esquisser (eh-skee-*say*) *v* sketch
essai (ay-*say*) *m* trial, essay; **à l'essai** on approval
essayer (ay-say-*^{y}ay*) *v* try; attempt, test; try on
essence (ay-*sahn͞gss*) *f* essence; petrol, fuel; gasoline *Am*, gas *Am*
essentiel (ay-sahn͞g-*s^{y}ehl*) *adj* capital, essential
essentiellement (ay-sahn͞g-s^{y}ehl-*mahn͞g*) *adv* essentially
essieu (ay-*s^{y}ur*) *m* axle
essor (ay-*sawr*) *m* rise
essuie-glace (ay-swee-*glahss*) *m* windscreen wiper, windshield wiper *Am*
essuyer (ay-swee-*^{y}ay*) *v* wipe; dry
est (ehst) *m* east
estampe (eh-*stahn͞gp*) *f* print; engraving
estimation (eh-stee-mah-*s^{y}awn͞g*) *f* estimate
estime (eh-*steem*) *f* esteem; respect
estimer (eh-stee-*may*) *v* consider, esteem, reckon; value, estimate
estomac (eh-sto-*mah*) *m* stomach
estropié (eh-stro-*p^{y}ay*) *adj* crippled
estuaire (eh-*stwair*) *m* estuary
et (ay) *conj* and
étable (ay-*tahbl*) *f* stable
établir (ay-tah-*bleer*) *v* establish; found; **s'établir** settle down
étage (ay-*taazh*) *m* floor, stor(e)y; apartment *Am*
étagère (ay-tah-*zhair*) *f* shelf
étain (ay-*tan͞g*) *m* pewter, tin
étal (ay-*tahl*) *m* stall
étalage (ay-tah-*laazh*) *m* shop-window
étaler (ay-tah-*lay*) *v* display
étang (ay-*tahn͞g*) *m* pond
étape (ay-*tahp*) *f* stage
Etat (ay-*tah*) *m* state; **Etats-Unis** United States; the States
état (ay-*tah*) *m* state; condition; ~ **d'urgence** emergency
et cætera (eht-say-tay-*rah*) etcetera
été (ay-*tay*) *m* summer; **en plein** ~ in midsummer
***éteindre** (ay-*tan͞gdr*) *v* *put out; switch off; extinguish
étendre (ay-*tahn͞gdr*) *v* expand, *spread, enlarge; extend

étendu (ay-tahng-*dew*) *adj* broad, extensive; comprehensive
éternel (ay-tehr-*nehl*) *adj* eternal
éternité (ay-tehr-nee-*tay*) *f* eternity
éternuer (ay-tehr-*nway*) *v* sneeze
Ethiopie (ay-t^{y}o-*pee*) *f* Ethiopia
éthiopien (ay-t^{y}o-*p^{y}ang*) *adj* Ethiopian
étincelle (ay-tang-*sehl*) *f* spark
étiqueter (ay-teek-*tay*) *v* label
étiquette (ay-tee-*keht*) *f* tag, label
étoffes (ay-*tof*) *fpl* drapery
étoile (ay-*twahl*) *f* star
étole (ay-*tol*) *f* stole
étonnant (ay-to-*nahng*) *adj* astonishing
étonnement (ay-ton-*mahng*) *m* astonishment, wonder, amazement
étonner (ay-to-*nay*) *v* amaze; astonish
étouffant (ay-too-*fahng*) *adj* stifling
étouffer (ay-too-*fay*) *v* choke
étourdi (ay-toor-*dee*) *adj* dizzy, giddy
étourneau (ay-toor-*noa*) *m* starling
étrange (ay-*trahngzh*) *adj* strange; quaint, curious, queer
étranger (ay-trahng-*zhay*) *m*, **-ère** *f* foreigner, alien, stranger; *adj* foreign, alien; **à l'étranger** abroad
étrangler (ay-trahng-*glay*) *v* choke, strangle
être (aitr) *m* being; creature; **~ humain** human being
***être** (aitr) *v* *be
***étreindre** (ay-*trangdr*) *v* hug, embrace
étreinte (ay-*trangt*) *f* grip; hug
étroit (ay-*trwah*) *adj* narrow, tight
étude (ay-*tewd*) *f* study
étudiant (ay-tew-*d^{y}ahng*) *m* student
étudiante (ay-tew-*d^{y}ahngt*) *f* student
étudier (ay-tew-*d^{y}ay*) *v* study
étui (ay-*twee*) *m* case; **~ à cigarettes** cigarette case
Europe (ur-*rop*) *f* Europe
Européen (ur-ro-pay-*ang*) *m*, **-ne** *f* European
européen (ur-ro-pay-*ang*) *adj* European
eux (ur) *pron* them; **eux-mêmes** *pron* themselves
évacuer (ay-vah-*kway*) *v* evacuate, clear
évaluer (ay-vah-*lway*) *v* evaluate; appreciate, estimate
évangile (ay-vahng-*zheel*) *m* gospel
évanouir (ay-vah-*nweer*): **s'~** faint
évaporer (ay-vah-po-*ray*) *v* evaporate
évasion (ay-vah-*z^{y}awng*) *f* escape
éveillé (ay-vay-*^{y}ay*) *adj* clever
éveiller (ay-vay-*^{y}ay*): **s'~** wake up
événement (ay-vehn-*mahng*) *m* event; occurrence
éventail (ay-vahng-*tigh*) *m* fan
éventuel (ay-vahng-*twehl*) *adj* possible, eventual
évêque (ay-*vehk*) *m* bishop
évidemment (ay-vee-dah-*mahng*) *adv* of course
évident (ay-vee-*dahng*) *adj* obvious, evident; self-evident
évier (ay-*v^{y}ay*) *m* sink
éviter (ay-vee-*tay*) *v* avoid
évolution (ay-vo-lew-*s^{y}awng*) *f* evolution
évoquer (ay-vo-*kay*) *v* call to mind; evoke
exact (ehg-*zahkt*) *adj* just, precise, exact
exactement (ehg-zahk-ter-*mahng*) *adv* exactly
exactitude (ehg-zahk-tee-*tewd*) *f* correctness
exagérer (ehg-zah-zhay-*ray*) *v* exaggerate
examen (ehg-zah-*mang*) *m* examination; checkup
examiner (ehg-zah-mee-*nay*) *v* examine
excéder (ehk-say-*day*) *v* exceed
excellent (ehk-seh-*lahng*) *adj* excellent

exceller (ehk-say-*lay*) *v* excel
excentrique (ehk-sahng-*treek*) *adj* eccentric
excepté (ehk-sehp-*tay*) *prep* except
exception (ehk-sehp-*s^{y}awng*) *f* exception
exceptionnel (ehk-sehp-s^{y}o-*nehl*) *adj* exceptional
excès (ehk-*say*) *m* excess; **~ de vitesse** speeding
excessif (ehk-say-*seef*) *adj* excessive
excitation (ehk-see-tah-*s^{y}awng*) *f* excitement
exciter (ehk-see-*tay*) *v* excite
exclamation (ehk-sklah-mah-*s^{y}awng*) *f* exclamation
exclamer (ehk-sklah-*may*) *v* exclaim
***exclure** (ehk-*sklewr*) *v* exclude
exclusif (ehk-sklew-*zeef*) *adj* exclusive
exclusivement (ehk-sklew-zeev-*mahng*) *adv* solely, exclusively
excursion (ehk-skewr-*s^{y}awng*) *f* trip, excursion; day trip; tour
excuse (ehk-*skewz*) *f* excuse, apology
excuser (ehk-skew-*zay*) *v* excuse; **excusez-moi!** sorry!; **s'excuser** apologize
exécuter (ehg-zay-kew-*tay*) *v* execute
exécutif (ehg-zay-kew-*teef*) *m* executive; *adj* executive
exécution (ehg-zay-kew-*s^{y}awng*) *f* execution
exemplaire (ehg-zahng-*plair*) *m* copy
exemple (ehg-*zahngpl*) *m* instance, example; **par ~** for instance, for example
exempt (ehg-*zahng*) *adj* exempt; **~ de droits** duty-free; **~ d'impôts** tax-free
exempter (ehg-zahng-*tay*) *v* exempt
exemption (ehg-zahng-*ps^{y}awng*) *f* exemption
exercer (ehg-zehr-*say*) *v* exercise; **s'exercer** practise
exercice (ehg-zehr-*seess*) *m* exercise
exhiber (ehg-zee-*bay*) *v* exhibit
exhibition (ehg-zee-bee-*s^{y}awng*) *f* exhibition
exhorter (ehg-zor-*tay*) *v* urge
exigeant (ehg-zee-*zhahng*) *adj* particular
exigence (ehg-zee-*zhahngss*) *f* requirement
exiger (ehg-zee-*zhay*) *v* demand, require
exile (ehg-*zeel*) *m* exile
exilé (ehg-zee-*lay*) *m* exile
existence (ehg-zee-*stahngss*) *f* existence
exister (ehg-zee-*stay*) *v* exist
exotique (ehg-zo-*teek*) *adj* exotic
expédier (ehk-spay-*d^{y}ay*) *v* dispatch, despatch, *send off, *send; ship
expéditeur (ehk-spay-dee-*turr*) *m* sender; shipper; forwarding agent
expédition (ehk-spay-dee-*s^{y}awng*) *f* expedition; consignment
expeditrice (ehk-spay-dee-*trees*) *f* sender
expérience (ehk-spay-*r^{y}ahngss*) *f* experience; experiment; ***faire l'expérience de** experience
expérimenter (ehk-spay-ree-mahng-*tay*) *v* test; experiment with; **expérimenté** experienced
expert (ehk-*spair*) *adj* skilled; *m* expert
expirer (ehk-spee-*ray*) *v* breathe out, expire
explicable (ehk-splee-*kahbl*) *adj* explicable, explainable
explication (ehk-splee-kah-*s^{y}awng*) *f* explanation
explicite (ehk-splee-*seet*) *adj* explicit
expliquer (ehk-splee-*kay*) *v* explain
exploitation (ehk-splwah-tah-*s^{y}awng*) *f* exploitation; concern; **~ minière** mining development
exploiter (ehk-splwah-*tay*) *v* exploit
explorer (ehk-splo-*ray*) *v* explore

exploser (ehk-sploa-*zay*) *v* explode
explosif (ehk-sploa-*zeef*) *m* explosive; *adj* explosive
explosion (ehk-sploa-*z^{y}awng*) *f* explosion, blast
exportation (ehk-spor-tah-*s^{y}awng*) *f* exports *pl*, exportation, export
exporter (ehk-spor-*tay*) *v* export
exposer (ehk-spoa-*zay*) *v* exhibit, *show
exposition (ehk-spoa-zee-*s^{y}awng*) *f* display, exposition, exhibition, show; exposure; **~ d'art** art exhibition
exprès[1] (ehk-*spray*) *adv* on purpose
exprès[2] (ehk-*sprehss*) *adj* express; special delivery
expression (ehk-spreh-*s^{y}awng*) *f* expression
exprimer (ehk-spree-*may*) *v* express
expulser (ehk-spewl-*say*) *v* expel
exquis (ehk-*skee*) *adj* delicious; exquisite; select
extase (ehk-*staaz*) *m* ecstasy
exténuer (ehk-stay-*nway*) *v* exhaust
extérieur (ehk-stay-*r^{y}urr*) *m* exterior, outside; *adj* external, exterior; **vers l'extérieur** outwards
externe (ehk-*stehrn*) *adj* outward
extincteur (ehk-stangk-*turr*) *m* fire extinguisher
extorquer (ehk-stor-*kay*) *v* extort
extorsion (ehk-stor-*s^{y}awng*) *f* extortion
extrader (ehk-strah-*day*) *v* extradite
***extraire** (ehk-*strair*) *v* extract
extrait (ehk-*stray*) *m* excerpt
extraordinaire (ehk-strah-or-dee-*nair*) *adj* extraordinary, exceptional
extravagant (ehk-strah-vah-*gahng*) *adj* extravagant
extrême (ehk-*strehm*) *adj* extreme, utmost; *m* extreme
exubérant (ehg-zew-bay-*rahng*) *adj* exuberant

F

fable (fahbl) *f* fable
fabricant (fah-bree-*kahng*) *m* manufacturer
fabriquer (fah-bree-*kay*) *v* manufacture
façade (fah-*sahd*) *f* façade
face (fahss) *f* front; **en ~ de** facing, opposite
fâcher (fah-*shay*) *v* annoy; **fâché** cross
facile (fah-*seel*) *adj* easy
façon (fah-*sawng*) *f* way; **de la même ~** alike; **de toute ~** anyway; at any rate
façonner (fah-so-*nay*) *v* model
facteur (fahk-*turr*) *m* factor; postman
facture (fahk-*tewr*) *f* invoice, bill
facturer (fahk-tew-*ray*) *v* bill
facultatif (fah-kewl-tah-*teef*) *adj* optional
faculté (fah-kewl-*tay*) *f* faculty
faible (fehbl) *adj* feeble, weak; small, slight; faint
faiblesse (feh-*blehss*) *f* weakness
faïence (fah-^{y}*ahngss*) *f* crockery
faillite: en ~ (ahng fah-^{y}*eet*) bankrupt
faim (fang) *f* hunger
***faire** (fair) *v* *do; *make; cause to, *have
faisable (fer-*zahbl*) *adj* feasible
faisan (fer-*zahng*) *m* pheasant
fait (fay) *m* fact; **de ~** in fact; **en ~** as a matter of fact, in effect
falaise (fah-*laiz*) *f* cliff

***falloir** (fah-*lwaar*) *v* need, *must
falsification (fahl-see-fee-kah-*s*ʸ*awng̅*) *f* fake
falsifier (fahl-see-*f*ʸ*ay*) *v* forge
fameux (fah-*mur*) *adj* famous
familial (fah-mee-*l*ʸ*ahl*) *adj* of the family
familiariser (fah-mee-lʸah-ree-*zay*) *v* familiarize, accustom
familier (fah-mee-*l*ʸ*ay*) *adj* familiar
famille (fah-*meey*) *f* family
fan (fahn) *m/f* fan
fanatique (fah-nah-*teek*) *adj* fanatical
faner (fah-*nay*) *v*: **se ~** fade
fanfare (fahng̅-*faar*) *f* brass band
fantaisie (fahng̅-tay-*zee*) *f* fantasy
fantastique (fahng̅-tah-*steek*) *adj* fantastic
fantôme (fahng̅-*tōam*) *m* phantom, ghost; spook
faon (fahng̅) *m* fawn
farce (fahrs) *f* filling, stuffing
farci (fahr-*see*) *adj* stuffed
fardeau (fahr-*doa*) *m* burden, load
farine (fah-*reen*) *f* flour
farouche (fah-*roosh*) *adj* shy
fasciner (fah-see-*nay*) *v* fascinate
fascisme (fah-*sheesm*) *m* fascism
fasciste (fah-*sheest*) *m* fascist; *adj* fascist
fastidieux (fah-stee-*d*ʸ*ur*) *adj* tedious, tiresome, boring
fatal (fah-*tahl*) *adj* (pl ~s) fatal, mortal
fatigant (fah-tee-*gahng̅*) *adj* tiring
fatigue (fah-*teeg*) *f* fatigue
fatiguer (fah-tee-*gay*) *v* tire; **fatigué** weary
faubourg (foa-*bōor*) *m* outskirts *pl*, suburb
fauché (foa-*shay*) *adj* broke
faucon (foa-*kawng̅*) *m* hawk
faute (fōat) *f* mistake, error; fault; **donner la ~ à** blame; **sans ~** without fail
fauteuil (foa-*tur*ᵉᵉ) *m* armchair, easy chair; **~ d'orchestre** orchestra seat *Am*; **~ roulant** wheelchair
faux (foa) *adj* (f fausse) false; untrue
faveur (fah-*vūrr*) *f* favo(u)r; **en ~ de** on behalf of
favorable (fah-vo-*rahbl*) *adj* favo(u)rable
favori (fah-vo-*ree*) *m*, **-rite** *f* favo(u)rite; *adj* favo(u)rite; **favoris** whiskers *pl*, sideburns *pl*
favoriser (fah-vo-ree-*zay*) *v* favo(u)r
favorite (fah-vo-*reet*) *f* favo(u)rite
fax (fahks) *m* fax; **envoyer un ~** send a fax
fédéral (fay-day-*rahl*) *adj* federal
fédération (fay-day-rah-*s*ʸ*awng̅*) *f* federation
***feindre** (fang̅dr) *v* pretend
félicitations (fay-lee-see-tah-*s*ʸ*awng̅*) *fpl* congratulations
féliciter (fay-lee-see-*tay*) *v* congratulate, compliment
femelle (fer-*mehl*) *f* female
féminin (fay-mee-*nang̅*) *adj* feminine, female
femme (fahm) *f* woman, wife
fendre (fahng̅dr) *v* *split; crack
fenêtre (fer-*naitr*) *f* window
fenouil (fer-*noo*ᵉᵉ) *m* fennel
fente (fahng̅t) *f* slot, cleft
fer (fair) *m* iron; **en ~** iron; **~ à cheval** horseshoe; **~ à repasser** iron
ferme (fehrm) *f* farmhouse, farm; *adj* firm, steady; steadfast
fermenter (fehr-mahng̅-*tay*) *v* ferment
fermer (fehr-*may*) *v* close, *shut; fasten; turn off; **fermé** closed shut; **~ à clé** lock
fermeture (fehrm-*tēwr*) *f* fastener; **~ éclair** zip, zipper *Am*
fermier (fehr-*m*ʸ*ay*) *m* farmer
fermière (fehr-*m*ʸ*air*) *f* farmer's wife
féroce (fay-*ross*) *adj* fierce, wild

ferraille (feh-*righ*) *f* scrap-iron
ferry-boat (feh-ree-*boat*) *m* ferryboat; train ferry
fertile (fehr-*teel*) *adj* fertile
fesse (fehss) *f* buttock
fessée (fay-*say*) *f* spanking
festival (feh-stee-*vahl*) *m* (pl ~s) festival
fête (feht) *f* feast
Fête-Dieu (feht-*d^{y}ur*) *m* Corpus Christi
feu (fur) *m* fire; ~ **arrière** taillight, rear light; ~ **de circulation** traffic light; ~ **de position** parking light
feuille (fur^{ee}) *f* leaf; sheet
feuilleton (fur^{ee}-*tawng*) *m* serial
feutre (furtr) *m* felt
février (fay-vree-*ay*) February
fiançailles (f^{y}ahng-*sigh*) *fpl* engagement
fiancé (f^{y}ahng-*say*) *m* fiancé; *adj* engaged
fiancée (f^{y}ahng-*say*) *f* fiancée, bride
fibre (feebr) *f* fibre
ficelle (fee-*sehl*) *f* twine, string
fiche (feesh) *f* plug
fiction (feek-*s^{y}awng*) *f* fiction
fidèle (fee-*dehl*) *adj* faithful, true
fier (f^{y}air) *adj* proud
fièvre (f^{y}aivr) *f* fever
fiévreux (f^{y}ay-*vrur*) *adj* feverish
figue (feeg) *f* fig
figure (fee-*gewr*) *f* figure; shape, form; face; appearance; court-card
se figurer (fee-gew-*ray*) imagine
fil (feel) *m* thread; line, yarn; ~ **de fer** wire; ~ **électrique** electric wire
file (feel) *f* line
filer (fee-*lay*) *v* *spin
filet (fee-*lay*) *m* net; ~ **à bagage** luggage rack; ~ **de pêche** fishing net
fille (feey) *f* girl; daughter; **vieille** ~ spinster
film (feelm) *m* film, movie; ~ **en couleurs** colo(u)r film
filmer (feel-*may*) *v* film
fils (feess) *m* son
filtre (feeltr) *m* filter; ~ **à air** air-filter; ~ **à huile** oil filter
filtrer (feel-*tray*) *v* filter
fin (fang) *f* finish, ending, end; issue; *adj* fine, thin
final (fee-*nahl*) *adj* (pl ~s) final
financer (fee-nahng-*say*) *v* finance
finances (fee-*nahngss*) *fpl* finances *pl*
financier (fee-nahng-*s^{y}ay*) *adj* financial
finir (fee-*neer*) *v* finish, end; **fini** finished, over
Finlandais (fang-lahng-*day*) *m* Finn
finlandais (fang-lahng-*day*) *adj* Finnish
Finlande (fang-*lahngd*) *f* Finland
fissure (fee-*sewr*) *f* crack, fissure
fixateur (feek-sah-*turr*) *m* setting lotion
fixe (feeks) *adj* fixed; permanent
fixer (feek-*say*) *v* attach; gaze, stare; ~ **le prix** price
flacon (flah-*kawng*) *m* flask
flamant (flah-*mahng*) *m* flamingo
flamme (flahm) *f* flame
flanelle (flah-*nehl*) *f* flannel
flâner (flah-*nay*) *v* stroll
flaque (flahk) *f* puddle
flash (flahsh) *m* flash-light
flasque (flahsk) *adj* limp
fléau (flay-*oa*) *m* plague
flèche (flehsh) *f* arrow
flétan (flay-*tahng*) *m* halibut
fleur (flurr) *f* flower
fleuriste (flur-*reest*) *m/f* flower shop, florist
fleuve (flurv) *m* river
flexible (flehk-*seebl*) *adj* flexible, elastic
flic (fleek) *m* cop, policeman
flotte (flot) *f* fleet

flotter (flo-*tay*) *v* float
flotteur (flo-*t̅u̅r̅r*) *m* float
fluide (flew-*eed*) *adj* fluid
flûte (flewt) *f* flute
foi (fwah) *f* faith
foie (fwah) *m* liver
foin (fwan̅g̅) *m* hay
foire (fwaar) *f* fair
fois (fwah) *f* time; *prep* times; **à la ~** at the same time; **deux ~** twice; **une ~** once; some time; **une ~ de plus** once more
folie (fo-*lee*) *f* lunacy
folklore (fol-*klawr*) *m* folklore
foncé (fawn̅g̅-*say*) *adj* dark
foncer (fawn̅g̅-*say*) *v* *speed
fonction (fawn̅g̅k-*s^{y}awn̅g̅*) *f* function; office
fonctionnaire (fawn̅g̅k-s^{y}o-*nair*) *m* civil servant
fonctionnement (fawn̅g̅k-s^{y}on-*mahn̅g̅*) *m* working, operation
fonctionner (fawn̅g̅k-s^{y}o-*nay*) *v* work, operate
fond (fawn̅g̅) *m* ground, bottom; essence; background; **à ~** thoroughly; **au ~** fundamentally; **~ de teint** foundation cream
fondamental (fawn̅g̅-dah-mahn̅g̅-*tahl*) *adj* fundamental, basic, essential
fondation (fawn̅g̅-dah-*s^{y}awn̅g̅*) *f* foundation
fondement (fawn̅g̅d-*mahn̅g̅*) *m* base
fonder (fawn̅g̅-*day*) *v* found; **bien fondé** well-founded
fondre (fawn̅g̅dr) *v* melt; thaw
fonds (fawn̅g̅) *mpl* fund
fontaine (fawn̅g̅-*tehn*) *f* fountain
fonte (fawn̅g̅t) *f* cast iron
football (foot-*bol*) *m* soccer
force (fors) *f* force, power, strength; **~ armée** military force; **~ motrice** driving force
forcément (for-say-*mahn̅g̅*) *adv* by force
forcer (for-*say*) *v* force; strain
forer (fo-*ray*) *v* drill, bore
forestier (fo-reh-*st^{y}ay*) *m* forester
forêt (fo-*ray*) *f* forest
foreuse (fo-*r̅u̅r̅z*) *f* drill
forgeron (for-zher-*rawn̅g̅*) *m* smith, blacksmith
formalité (for-mah-lee-*tay*) *f* formality
format (for-*mah*) *m* size
formation (for-mah-*s^{y}awn̅g̅*) *f* formation, forming; training
forme (form) *f* shape, form; figure
formel (for-*mehl*) *adj* explicit
former (for-*may*) *v* shape, form; train, educate
formidable (for-mee-*dahbl*) *adj* fine, swell; terrific
formulaire (for-mew-*lair*) *m* form; **~ d'inscription** registration form
formule (for-*mewl*) *f* formula
fort (fawr) *adj* powerful, strong; loud
fortement (for-ter-*mahn̅g̅*) *adv* tight
forteresse (for-ter-*rehss*) *f* fortress
fortuit (for-*twee*) *adj* casual, incidental
fortune (for-*tewn*) *f* fortune
fosse (foass) *f* pit
fossé (foa-*say*) *m* ditch
fou[1] (foo) *adj* (fol; f folle) crazy, mad; insane, lunatic
fou[2] (foo) *m* fool
foudre (foodr) *f* lightning
fouet (fway) *m* whip
fouetter (fway-*tay*) *v* whip
fouille (foo^{ee}) *f* search
fouiller (foo-*^{y}ay*) *v* search; *dig
foulard (foo-*laar*) *m* scarf
foule (fool) *f* crowd
fouler (foo-*lay*) *v* press; **se ~ la cheville** sprain one's ankle
foulure (foo-*l̅e̅w̅r*) *f* sprain
four (fo̅o̅r) *m* oven; **~ à micro-ondes** microwave oven
fourbe (foorb) *adj* hypocritical

fourchette (foor-*sheht*) *f* fork
fourgon (foor-*gawng*) *m* luggage van; van
fourmi (foor-*mee*) *f* ant
fournaise (foor-*naiz*) *f* furnace
fourneau (foor-*noa*) *m* stove; **~ à gaz** gas stove
fournir (foor-*neer*) *v* provide, furnish, supply
fourniture (foor-nee-*tewr*) *f* supply
fourreur (foo-*rurr*) *m* furrier
fourrure (foo-*rewr*) *f* fur
foyer (fwah-^{y}*ay*) *m* foyer, lounge; home; focus
fracas (frah-*kah*) *m* noise
fraction (frahk-*s^{y}awng*) *f* fraction
fracture (frahk-*tewr*) *f* break, fracture
fracturer (frahk-tew-*ray*) *v* fracture
fragile (frah-*zheel*) *adj* fragile
fragment (frahg-*mahng*) *m* extract, fragment
frais[1] (fray) *adj* (f fraîche) fresh; chilly, cool
frais[2] (fray) *mpl* expenses *pl*, expenditure; **~ de voyage** travel(l)ing expenses
fraise (fraiz) *f* strawberry
framboise (frahng-*bwaaz*) *f* raspberry
franc (frahng) *adj* (f franche) open
français (frahng-*say*) *adj* French
France (frahngss) *f* France
franchir (frahng-*sheer*) *v* cross
frange (frahngzh) *f* fringe
frappant (frah-*pahng*) *adj* striking
frappé (frah-*pay*) *m* milkshake
frapper (frah-*pay*) *v* *beat; *hit, bump, tap, knock, *strike
fraternité (frah-tehr-nee-*tay*) *f* fraternity
fraude (froad) *f* fraud
frayeur (freh-^{y}*urr*) *f* fright
fredonner (frer-do-*nay*) *v* hum
frein (frang) *m* brake; **~ à main** handbrake; **~ à pédale** foot brake
freiner (fray-*nay*) *v* slow down, curb
fréquemment (fray-kah-*mahng*) *adv* frequently
fréquence (fray-*kahngss*) *f* frequency
fréquent (fray-*kahng*) *adj* frequent
fréquenter (fray-kahng-*tay*) *v* see frequently, mix with
frère (frair) *m* brother
fret (fray) *m* freight
friction (freek-*s^{y}awng*) *f* friction
frigidaire (free-zhee-*dair*) *m* refrigerator
frigo (free-*goa*) *m* fridge
fripon (free-*pawng*) *m* rascal
***frire** (freer) *v* fry
friser (free-*zay*) *v* curl
frisson (free-*sawng*) *m* shudder, chill, shiver
frissonnant (free-so-nahng) *adj* shivery
frissonner (free-so-*nay*) *v* tremble, shiver
frites (freet) *fpl* chips, *Am* French fries
froid (frwah) *m* cold; *adj* cold
froisser (frwah-*say*) *v* crease
fromage (fro-*maazh*) *m* cheese
front (frawng) *m* forehead
frontière (frawng-*t^{y}air*) *f* border; frontier, boundary
frotter (fro-*tay*) *v* rub, scrub
fruit (frwee) *m* fruit
fugitif (few-zhee-*teef*) *m* runaway
***fuir** (fweer) *v* escape; leak
fuite (fweet) *f* flight; leak
fumée (few-*may*) *f* smoke
fumer (few-*may*) *v* smoke
fumeur (few-*murr*) *m*, **-euse** *f* smoker; **compartiment fumeurs** smoker
fumier (few-*m^{y}ay*) *m* manure; dung; **tas de ~** dunghill
funérailles (few-nay-*righ*) *fpl* funeral
fureur (few-*rurr*) *f* anger, rage
furibond (few-ree-*bawng*) *adj* furious
furieux (few-*r^{y}ur*) *adj* furious

furoncle (few-*rawngkl*) *m* boil
fusée (few-*zay*) *f* rocket
fusible (few-*zeebl*) *m* fuse
fusil (few-*zee*) *m* rifle, gun
fusion (few-*z^yawng*) *f* merger
futile (few-*teel*) *adj* petty, insignificant, idle
futur (few-*tewr*) *adj* future

G

gâcher (gah-*shay*) *v* mess up
gâchette (gah-*sheht*) *f* trigger
gâchis (gah-*shee*) *m* mess
gadget (gah-*jeht*) *m* gadget
gadoue (gah-*doo*) *f* muck
gages (gaazh) *mpl* wages *pl*; **donner en gage** pawn
gagner (gah-*ñay*) *v* *win; *make, earn, gain
gai (gay) *adj* jolly, cheerful, gay
gain (gang) *m* gain; **gains** earnings *pl*; winnings *pl*
gaine (gehn) *f* girdle
galerie (gahl-*ree*) *f* gallery; **~ d'art** art gallery
galet (gah-*lay*) *m* pebble
galop (gah-*loa*) *m* gallop
gamin (gah-*mang*) *m* little boy
gamine (gah-*meen*) *f* little girl
gamme (gahm) *f* scale; range
gant (gahng) *m* glove
garage (gah-*raazh*) *m* garage
garagiste (gah-rah-*zheest*) *m* garage proprietor
garantie (gah-rahng-*tee*) *f* guarantee
garantir (gah-rahng-*teer*) *v* guarantee
garçon (gahr-*sawng*) *m* boy; lad; waiter
garde (gahrd) *m* guard; *f* custody; **~ du corps** bodyguard; ***prendre ~** watch out
garder (gahr-*day*) *v* *keep; *hold
garde-robe (gahr-*drob*) *f* wardrobe; closet *Am*
gardien (gahr-*d^yang*) *m* attendant, warden; caretaker; **~ de but** goalkeeper
gardon (gahr-*dawng*) *m* roach
gare (gaar) *f* station; depot *Am*
garer (gah-*ray*) *v* garage; **se ~** park
se gargariser (gahr-gah-ree-*zay*) gargle
gars (gah) *m* fellow
gaspillage (gah-spee-*^yaazh*) *m* waste
gaspiller (gah-spee-*^yay*) *v* waste
gaspilleur (gah-spee-*^yurr*) *adj* wasteful
gastrique (gah-*streek*) *adj* gastric
gastro-entérite (gah-stroa-ahng-tay-*reet*) *f* gastroenteritis
gâteau (gah-*toa*) *m* cake
gâter (gah-*tay*) *v* *spoil
gauche (goash) *adj* left; **de ~** left-hand
gaucher (goa-*shay*) *adj* left-handed
gaufre (goafr) *f* waffle
gaufrette (goa-*freht*) *f* wafer
gaz (gaaz) *m* gas; **~ d'échappement** exhaust gases
gazeux (gah-*zur*) *adj* gaseous; aerated, fizzy
gazole (gah-*zol*) *m* diesel
gazon (gah-*zawng*) *m* lawn
géant (zhay-*ahng*) *m* giant
gel (zhehl) *m* frost
gelée (zher-*lay*) *f* jelly
geler (zher-*lay*) *v* *freeze
gémir (zhay-*meer*) *v* groan, moan
gênant (zheh-*nahng*) *adj*

inconvenient, troublesome
gencive (zhahn̅g̅-*seev*) *f* gum
gendre (zhahn̅g̅dr) *m* son-in-law
gêner (zhay-*nay*) *v* hinder; embarrass, bother; **se ~** *be embarrassed
général (zhay-nay-*rahl*) *m* general; *adj* universal, public, general; **en ~** as a rule, in general
généralement (zhay-nay-rahl-*mahn̅g̅*) *adv* as a rule
générateur (zhay-nay-rah-*tūrr*) *m* generator
génération (zhay-nay-rah-*s^{y}awn̅g̅*) *f* generation
généreux (zhay-nay-*rur*) *adj* liberal, generous
générosité (zhay-nay-ro-zee-*tay*) *f* generosity
génie (zhay-*nee*) *m* genius
génital (zhay-nee-*tahl*) *adj* genital
genou (zher-*noo*) *m* (pl ~x) knee
genre (zhahn̅g̅r) *m* kind; gender
gens (zhahn̅g̅) *mpl/fpl* people *pl*
gentil (zhahn̅g̅-*tee*) *adj* friendly, kind; nice; sweet
gentillesse (zhahn̅g̅-tee-*^{y}ehss*) *f* politeness; **avoir la ~ de** be so kind as to
géographie (zhay-o-grah-*fee*) *f* geography
géologie (zhay-o-lo-*zhee*) *f* geology
géométrie (zhay-o-may-*tree*) *f* geometry
germe (zhehrm) *m* germ
geste (zhehst) *m* sign
gesticuler (zheh-stee-kew-*lay*) *v* gesticulate
gestion (zheh-*st^{y}awn̅g̅*) *f* management, administration
gibier (zhee-*b^{y}ay*) *m* game
gigantesque (zhee-gahn̅g̅-*tehsk*) *adj* gigantic, enormous
gifle (zheefl) *f* slap in the face; box on the ear
gilet (zhee-*lay*) *m* waistcoat; vest *Am*
gingembre (zhan̅g̅-*zhahn̅g̅br*) *m* ginger
gîte (zheet) *m* resting-place, lodging; form; vein
glace (glahss) *f* ice; ice cream
glacial (glah-*s^{y}ahl*) *adj* freezing
glacier (glah-*s^{y}ay*) *m* glacier
glaçon (glah-*sawn̅g̅*) *m* icicle; ice cube; ice floe
glande (glahn̅g̅d) *f* gland
glissade (glee-*sahd*) *f* slide
glissant (glee-*sahn̅g̅*) *adj* slippery
glisser (glee-*say*) *v* *slide, glide; slip
global (glo-*bahl*) *adj* global, total, comprehensive
globe (glob) *m* globe
gloire (glwaar) *f* glory
glousser (gloo-*say*) *v* chuckle; giggle
gluant (glew-*ahn̅g̅*) *adj* sticky
gobelet (go-*blay*) *m* mug, tumbler
goéland (go-ay-*lahn̅g̅*) *m* seagull
golf (golf) *m* golf; **terrain de ~** golf links, golf course
golfe (golf) *m* gulf
gomme (gom) *f* gum; rubber, eraser
gondole (gawn̅g̅-*dol*) *f* gondola
gonflable (gawn̅g̅-*flahbl*) *adj* inflatable
gonfler (gawn̅g̅-*flay*) *v* inflate
gorge (gorzh) *f* throat; gorge
gorgée (gor-*zhay*) *f* sip
gosse (goss) *m* kid, boy
goudron (goo-*drawn̅g̅*) *m* tar
goulot d'étranglement (goo-lo day-trahn̅g̅-gler-*mahn̅g̅*) bottleneck
gourdin (goor-*dan̅g̅*) *m* club
gourmand (goor-*mahn̅g̅*) *adj* greedy
gourmet (goor-*may*) *m* gourmet
goût (goo) *m* taste; ***avoir ~ de** taste
goûter (goo-*tay*) *v* taste
goutte (goot) *f* drop; gout
gouvernail (goo-vehr-*nigh*) *m* rudder
gouvernante (goo-vehr-*nahn̅g̅t*) *f*

governess; housekeeper
gouvernement (goo-vehr-ner-*mahng*) *m* rule, government
gouverner (goo-vehr-*nay*) *v* rule, govern
gouverneur (goo-vehr-*nurr*) *m* governor
grâce (graass) *f* grace; pardon; **~ à** thanks to
gracieux (grah-*s^{y}ur*) *adj* graceful; **à titre ~** free of charge
grade (grahd) *m* grade; degree, rank
graduel (grah-*dwehl*) *adj* gradual
graduellement (grah-dwehl-*mahng*) *adv* gradually
grain (grang) *m* corn, grain
graisse (grehss) *f* grease, fat
graisser (gray-*say*) *v* grease
graisseux (greh-*sur*) *adj* greasy
grammaire (grah-*mair*) *f* grammar
grammatical (grah-mah-tee-*kahl*) *adj* grammatical
gramme (grahm) *m* gram
grand (grahng) *adj* great; tall, big, major
Grande-Bretagne (grahngd-brer-*tahñ*) *f* Great Britain
grandeur (grahng-*durr*) *f* size
grandiose (grahng-*d^{y}oaz*) *adj* superb, magnificent
grandir (grahng-*deer*) *v* *grow
grand-mère (grahng-*mair*) *f* grandmother
grand-papa (grahng-pah-*pah*) *m* granddad
grand-père (grahng-*pair*) *m* grandfather
grands-parents (grahng-pah-*rahng*) *mpl* grandparents *pl*
grange (grahngzh) *f* barn
granit (grah-*neet*) *m* granite
graphique (grah-*feek*) *adj* graphic; *m* diagram; chart
gras (grah) *adj* (f ~se) fatty, fat
gratitude (grah-tee-*tewd*) *f* gratitude
gratte-ciel (grah-*ts^{y}ehl*) *m* skyscraper
gratter (grah-*tay*) *v* scratch
gratuit (grah-*twee*) *adj* gratis, free of charge, free
grave (graav) *adj* grave; bad, severe
graver (grah-*vay*) *v* engrave
graveur (grah-*vurr*) *m* engraver
gravier (grah-*v^{y}ay*) *m* gravel
gravillon (grah-vee-*^{y}awng*) *m* grit
gravité (grah-vee-*tay*) *f* gravity
gravure (grah-*vewr*) *f* engraving; carving
grec (grehk) *adj* (f grecque) Greek
Grèce (grehss) *f* Greece
grêle (grehl) *f* hail
grenier (grer-*n^{y}ay*) *m* attic
grenouille (grer-*noo^{ee}*) *f* frog
grève (graiv) *f* strike; ***faire ~** *strike
gréviste (gray-*veest*) *m/f* striker
griffe (greef) *f* claw
grill (greel) *m* steakhouse
grillade (gree-*^{y}ahd*) *f* grilled meat
grille (greey) *f* gate; grate
griller (gree-*^{y}ay*) *v* roast; grill
grillon (gree-*^{y}awng*) *m* cricket
grimper (grang-*pay*) *v* climb
grincer (grang-*say*) *v* creak
grippe (greep) *f* flu, influenza
gris (gree) *adj* grey
grive (greev) *f* thrush
grogner (gro-*ñay*) *v* grumble, growl
grondement (grawngd-*mahng*) *m* roar
gronder (grawng-*day*) *v* rumble; scold
gros (groa) *adj* (f -se) big; thick, fat, corpulent, stout
groseille (groa-*zay*) *f* currant; **~ à maquereau** gooseberry
grosse (groass) *f* gross
grossesse (groa-*sehss*) *f* pregnancy
grossier (groa-*s^{y}ay*) *adj* coarse, gross, rude
grossir (gro-*seer*) *v* increase; *put on weight

grossiste (groa-*seest*) *m* wholesale dealer
grotesque (gro-*tehsk*) *adj* ludicrous
grotte (grot) *f* cave; grotto
groupe (groop) *m* group; party
grouper (groo-*pay*) *v* group
grue (grew) *f* crane
grumeau (grew-*moa*) *m* lump
grumeleux (grewm-*lur*) *adj* lumpy
gruyère (grew-*ʸair*) *m* Swiss cheese
guêpe (gehp) *f* wasp
guère: ne ... ~ (ner ... gair) scarcely
guérir (gay-*reer*) *v* cure; heal, recover
guérison (gay-ree-*zawng*) *f* recovery, cure
guérisseur (gay-ree-*sūrr*) *m* quack
guerre (gair) *f* war; **d'avant-guerre** pre-war; **~ mondiale** world war
guetter (gay-*tay*) *v* watch for
gueule (gurl) *f* mouth; **~ de bois** hangover
guichet (gee-*shay*) *m* box office; **~ de location** box office
guide (geed) *m* guidebook; *m/f* guide
guider (gee-*day*) *v* *lead
guidon (gee-*dawng*) *m* handlebars *pl*
guillemets (geey-*may*) *mpl* quotation marks
guitare (gee-*taar*) *f* guitar
gymnase (zheem-*naaz*) *m* gymnasium
gymnaste (zheem-*nahst*) *m/f* gymnast
gymnastique (zheem-nah-*steek*) *f* gymnastics *pl*
gynécologue (zhee-nay-ko-*log*) *m/f* gyn(a)ecologist

H

habile (ah-*beel*) *adj* skil(l)ful; skilled
habileté (ah-beel-*tay*) *f* skill, art
habiller (ah-bee-*ʸay*) *v* dress
habitable (ah-bee-*tahbl*) *adj* inhabitable, habitable
habitant (ah-bee-*tahng*) *m* inhabitant
habitation (ah-bee-tah-*sʸawng*) *f* house
habiter (ah-bee-*tay*) *v* inhabit, live
habits (ah-*bee*) *mpl* clothes *pl*
habitude (ah-bee-*tewd*) *f* habit; custom; ***avoir l'habitude de** would; **d'habitude** usually
habitué (ah-bee-*tway*) *adj* accustomed; ***être ~ à** *be used to
habituel (ah-bee-*twehl*) *adj* common, habitual, ordinary
habituellement (ah-bee-twehl-*mahng*) *adv* usually
habituer (ah-bee-*tway*): **s'~** *get accustomed
hache ('ahsh) *f* axe
hacher ('ah-*shay*) *v* chop, mince
haie ('ay) *f* hedge
haine ('ehn) *f* hatred, hate
***haïr** ('ah-*eer*) *v* hate
hâlé ('ah-*lay*) *adj* tanned
haleter ('ahl-*tay*) *v* pant
hamac ('ah-*mahk*) *m* hammock
hameau ('ah-*moa*) *m* hamlet
hameçon (ahm-*sawng*) *m* fishing hook
hanche ('ahngsh) *f* hip
handicapé ('ahng-dee-kah-*pay*) *adj* disabled, handicapped
hardi ('ahr-*dee*) *adj* bold
hareng ('ah-*rahng*) *m* herring
haricot ('ah-ree-*koa*) *m* bean
harmonie (ahr-mo-*nee*) *f* harmony
harmonieux (ahr-mo-*nʸur*) *adj* tuneful
harpe ('ahrp) *f* harp

hasard ('ah-*zaar*) *m* chance, luck; hazard; **par ~** by chance
hâte ('aat) *f* hurry, speed, haste
hâter ('ah-*tay*) *v*: **se ~** hasten
hausse ('ōass) *f* rise
haut ('oa) *m* top side; *adj* high, tall; **en ~** upstairs, above, overhead; up; **vers le ~** upwards
hautain ('oa-*tang̅*) *adj* haughty
hauteur ('oa-*tūrr*) *f* height; ***être à la ~ de** *keep up with
haut-parleur ('oa-pahr-*lūrr*) *m* loudspeaker
hebdomadaire (ehb-do-mah-*dair*) *adj* weekly
héberger (ay-behr-*zhay*) *v* accommodate, put up, take in
hébreu (ay-*brur*) *m* Hebrew
hélas ('ay-*laass*) *adv* unfortunately
hélice (ay-*leess*) *f* propeller
hémorragie (ay-mo-rah-*zhee*) *f* h(a)emorrhage
hémorroïdes (ay-mo-ro-*eed*) *fpl* piles *pl*, h(a)emorrhoids *pl*
herbe (ehrb) *f* grass; herb; **mauvaise ~** weed
héréditaire (ay-ray-dee-*tair*) *adj* hereditary
hérisson ('ay-ree-*sawng̅*) *m* hedgehog
héritage (ay-ree-*taazh*) *m* inheritance
hériter (ay-ree-*tay*) *v* inherit
hermétique (ehr-may-*teek*) *adj* airtight
hernie ('ehr-*nee*) *f* hernia; **~ discale** slipped disc
héron ('ay-*rawng̅*) *m* heron
héros ('ay-*roa*) *m* hero
hésiter (ay-zee-*tay*) *v* hesitate
hétérosexuel (ay-tay-ro-sehk-*swehl*) *adj* heterosexual
hêtre ('aitr) *m* beech
heure (ūrr) *f* hour; **à ... heures** at ... o'clock; **~ d'arrivée** time of arrival; **~ de départ** time of departure; **~ de pointe** rush hour; **~ d'été** summer time; **heures de bureau** office hours; **heures de consultation** consultation hours; **heures de visite** visiting hours; **heures d'ouverture** business hours; **tout à l'heure** a short while ago; shortly; **toutes les heures** hourly
heureux (ur-*rur*) *adj* fortunate, happy
heurter ('urr-*tay*) *v* knock
hibou ('ee-*boo*) *m* (pl ~x) owl
hideux ('ee-*dur*) *adj* hideous
hier ('ʸair) *adv* yesterday
hiérarchie ('ʸay-rahr-*shee*) *f* hierarchy
hippodrome (ee-po-*drom*) *m* racecourse
hirondelle (ee-rawng̅-*dehl*) *f* swallow
hisser ('ee-*say*) *v* hoist
histoire (ee-*stwaar*) *f* history; story; **~ d'amour** love story; **~ de l'art** art history
historien (ee-sto-*rʸang̅*) *m*, **-ne** *f* historian
historique (ee-sto-*reek*) *adj* historic; historical
hiver (ee-*vair*) *m* winter
H.L.M. (ahsh-ehl-*ehm*) *f or m* council flat
hobby ('o-*bee*) *m* hobby
hockey ('o-*kay*) *m* hockey
hollandais ('o-lahng̅-*day*) *adj* Dutch
Hollande ('o-*lahng̅d*) *f* Holland
homard ('o-*maar*) *m* lobster
hommage (o-*maazh*) *m* homage, tribute; **rendre ~** hono(u)r
homme (om) *m* man; **~ d'affaires** businessman; **~ d'Etat** statesman
homosexuel (o-mo-sehk-*swehl*) *adj* homosexual
Hongrie ('awng̅-*gree*) *f* Hungary
hongrois ('awng̅-*grwah*) *adj* Hungarian
honnête (o-*neht*) *adj* hono(u)rable, honest; fair
honnêteté (o-neht-*tay*) *f* honesty

honneur (o-*nūrr*) *m* hono(u)r, glory
honorable (o-no-*rahbl*) *adj* hono(u)rable, respectable
honoraires (o-no-*rair*) *mpl* fee
honorer (o-no-*ray*) *v* hono(u)r
honte ('awn̄gt) *f* shame; ***avoir ~** *be ashamed; **quelle honte!** shame!
honteux ('awn̄g-*tur*) *adj* ashamed
hôpital (o-pee-*tahl*) *m* hospital
hoquet ('o-*kay*) *m* hiccup
horaire (o-*rair*) *m* timetable, schedule
horizon (o-ree-*zawn̄g*) *m* horizon
horizontal (o-ree-zawn̄g-*tahl*) *adj* horizontal
horloge (or-*lawzh*) *f* clock
horloger (or-lo-*zhay*) *m* watchmaker
horreur (o-*rūrr*) *f* horror
horrible (o-*reebl*) *adj* horrible
horrifiant (o-ree-*f'ahn̄g*) *adj* horrible
hors ('awr) *adv* out; **~ de** outside
hors d'œuvre ('or-*dūrvr*) *m* hors-d'œuvre
horticulture (or-tee-kewl-*tewr*) *f* horticulture
hospice (o-*speess*) *m* home
hospitalier (o-spee-tah-*l'ay*) *adj* hospitable
hospitalité (o-spee-tah-lee-*tay*) *f* hospitality
hostile (o-*steel*) *adj* hostile
hôte (ōat) *m* host; guest
hôtel (oa-*tehl*) *m* hotel; **~ de ville** town hall
hôtel-Dieu (oa-tehl-*d'ur*) *m* general hospital
hôtesse (oa-*tehss*) *f* hostess; receptionist; **~ de l'air** stewardess
houblon ('oo-*blawn̄g*) *m* hop
housse ('ooss) *f* sleeve
hublot ('ew-*bloa*) *m* porthole
huile (weel) *f* oil; **~ capillaire** hair oil; **~ de table** salad oil; **~ d'olive** olive oil; **~ solaire** suntan oil
huiler (wee-*lay*) *v* lubricate
huileux (wee-*lur*) *adj* oily
huit ('weet) *num* eight
huitième ('wee-*t'ehm*) *num* eighth
huître (weetr) *f* oyster
humain (ew-*man̄g*) *adj* human
humanité (ew-mah-nee-*tay*) *f* mankind, humanity
humble (urn̄gbl) *adj* humble
humecter (ew-mehk-*tay*) *v* moisten
humeur (ew-*mūrr*) *f* mood, spirit
humide (ew-*meed*) *adj* humid; wet, damp
humidifier (ew-mee-dee-*f'ay*) *v* damp
humidité (ew-mee-dee-*tay*) *f* humidity, moisture, damp
humour (ew-*mōōr*) *m* humo(u)r
hurler ('ewr-*lay*) *v* yell, scream
hutte ('ewt) *f* hut
hydrogène (ee-dro-*zhehn*) *m* hydrogen
hygiène (ee-*zh'ehn*) *f* hygiene
hygiénique (ee-zh'ay-*neek*) *adj* hygienic
hymne (eemn) *m* hymn; **~ national** national anthem
hypermarché (ee-pehr-mahr-*shay*) *m* superstore, hypermarket
hypocrisie (ee-po-kree-*zee*) *f* hypocrisy
hypocrite (ee-po-*kreet*) *m* hypocrite; *adj* hypocritical
hypothèque (ee-po-*tehk*) *f* mortgage
hystérique (ee-stay-*reek*) *adj* hysterical

I

ici (ee-*see*) *adv* here
icône (ee-*kōan*) *f* icon
idéal[1] (ee-day-*ahl*) *adj* (pl -aux) ideal
idéal[2] (ee-day-*ahl*) *m* (pl ~s, -aux) ideal
idée (ee-*day*) *f* idea; opinion; ~ **lumineuse** brain wave
identification (ee-dahng-tee-fee-kah-*s^{y}awng*) *f* identification
identifier (ee-dahng-tee-*f^{y}ay*) *v* identify
identique (ee-dahng-*teek*) *adj* identical
identité (ee-dahng-tee-*tay*) *f* identity
idiot (ee-*d^{y}oa*) *adj* idiotic; *m*, **-e** *f* fool, idiot
idole (ee-*dol*) *f* idol
idylle (ee-*deel*) *f* romance
ignorant (ee-ño-*rahng*) *adj* ignorant; uneducated
ignorer (ee-ño-*ray*) *v* ignore; overlook
il (eel) *pron* he
île (eel) *f* island
illégal (ee-lay-*gahl*) *adj* illegal
illettré (ee-leh-*tray*) *m* illiterate
illicite (ee-lee-*seet*) *adj* unlawful, unauthorized
illimité (ee-lee-mee-*tay*) *adj* unlimited
illisible (ee-lee-*zeebl*) *adj* illegible
illumination (ee-lew-mee-nah-*s^{y}awng*) *f* illumination
illuminer (ee-lew-mee-*nay*) *v* illuminate
illusion (ee-lew-*z^{y}awng*) *f* illusion
illustration (ee-lew-strah-*s^{y}awng*) *f* illustration; picture
illustre (ee-*lewstr*) *adj* noted
illustré (ee-lew-*stray*) *m* comic
illustrer (ee-lew-*stray*) *v* illustrate
ils (eel) *pron* they
image (ee-*maazh*) *f* picture, image
imaginaire (ee-mah-zhee-*nair*) *adj* imaginary
imagination (ee-mah-zhee-nah-*s^{y}awng*) *f* fancy, imagination
imaginer (ee-mah-zhee-*nay*) *v* fancy, imagine; **s'imaginer** fancy, imagine
imitation (ee-mee-tah-*s^{y}awng*) *f* imitation
imiter (ee-mee-*tay*) *v* imitate, copy
immaculé (ee-mah-kew-*lay*) *adj* stainless, spotless
immangeable (ang-mahng-*zhahbl*) *adj* inedible
immédiat (ee-may-*d^{y}ah*) *adj* immediate
immédiatement (ee-may-d^{y}aht-*mahng*) *adv* at once, instantly, immediately
immense (ee-*mahngss*) *adj* immense; vast, huge
immérité (ee-may-ree-*tay*) *adj* unearned
immeuble (ee-*murbl*) *m* house; ~ **d'habitation** block of flats; apartment house *Am*
immigrant (ee-mee-*grahng*) *m*, **-e** *f* immigrant
immigration (ee-mee-grah-*s^{y}awng*) *f* immigration
immigrer (ee-mee-*gray*) *v* immigrate
immobile (ee-mo-*beel*) *adj* motionless
immodeste (ee-mo-*dehst*) *adj* immodest
immuniser (ee-mew-nee-*zay*) *v* immunize
immunité (ee-mew-nee-*tay*) *f* immunity
impair (ang-*pair*) *adj* odd
imparfait (ang-pahr-*fay*) *adj* imperfect; faulty
impartial (ang-pahr-*s^{y}ahl*) *adj* impartial
impasse (ang-*pahss*) *f* dead end,

blind alley; deadlock
impatient (ang-pah-s^y*ahng*) *adj* impatient; eager
impeccable (ang-peh-*kahbl*) *adj* faultless
impératrice (ang-pay-rah-*treess*) *f* empress
imperfection (ang-pehr-fehk-*s^yawng*) *f* fault
impérial (ang-pay-*r^yahl*) *adj* imperial
imperméable (ang-pehr-may-*ahbl*) *m* mackintosh, raincoat; *adj* waterproof, rainproof
impersonnel (ang-pehr-so-*nehl*) *adj* impersonal
impertinence (ang-pehr-tee-*nahngss*) *f* impertinence
impertinent (ang-pehr-tee-*nahng*) *adj* impertinent
impétueux (ang-pay-*twur*) *adj* impetuous, fiery; raging
impliquer (ang-plee-*kay*) *v* involve, imply
impoli (ang-po-*lee*) *adj* impolite
impopulaire (ang-po-pew-*lair*) *adj* unpopular
importance (ang-por-*tahngss*) *f* importance; ***avoir de l'importance** matter; **sans ~** insignificant
important (ang-por-*tahng*) *adj* important; considerable, big
importateur (ang-por-tah-*turr*) *m* importer
importation (ang-por-tah-*s^yawng*) *f* import; **taxe d'importation** import duty
importer (ang-por-*tay*) *v* import
imposable (ang-poa-zahbl) *adj* dutiable
imposant (ang-poa-*zahng*) *adj* imposing
imposer (ang-poa-*zay*) *v* tax
impossible (ang-po-*seebl*) *adj* impossible
impôt (ang-*poa*) *m* tax; **~ sur le chiffre d'affaires** turnover tax; **~ sur le revenu** income tax
impotence (ang-po-*tahngss*) *f* impotence
impotent (ang-po-*tahng*) *adj* impotent
impraticable (ang-prah-tee-*kahbl*) *adj* impassable
impression (ang-*preh-s^yawng*) *f* impression; ***faire ~ sur** impress
impressionnant (ang-preh-s^yo-*nahng*) *adj* impressive
impressionner (ang-preh-s^yo-*nay*) *v* impress
imprévu (ang-pray-*vew*) *adj* unexpected
imprimé (ang-pree-*may*) *m* printed matter
imprimer (ang-pree-*may*) *v* print
imprimerie (ang-preem-*ree*) *f* printing office
improbable (ang-pro-*bahbl*) *adj* improbable, unlikely
impropre (ang-*propr*) *adj* improper, unfit; wrong
improviser (ang-pro-vee-*zay*) *v* improvise
imprudent (ang-prew-*dahng*) *adj* unwise
impuissant (ang-pwee-*sahng*) *adj* powerless
impulsif (ang-pewl-*seef*) *adj* impulsive
impulsion (ang-pewl-*s^yawng*) *f* urge, impulse
inabordable (ee-nah-bor-*dahbl*) *adj* prohibitive
inacceptable (ee-nahk-sehp-*tahbl*) *adj* unacceptable
inaccessible (ee-nahk-say-*seebl*) *adj* inaccessible
inadéquat (ee-nah-day-*kwah*) *adj* inadequate, unsuitable
inadvertance (ee-nahd-vehr-*tahngss*) *f* oversight

inattendu (ee-nah-tahng-*dew*) *adj* unexpected

inattentif (ee-nah-tahng-*teef*) *adj* careless

incapable (ang-kah-*pahbl*) *adj* incapable, unable

incassable (ang-kah-*sahbl*) *adj* unbreakable

incendie (ang-sahng-*dee*) *m* fire; **alarme d'incendie** fire alarm

incertain (ang-sehr-*tang*) *adj* doubtful, uncertain

incident (ang-see-*dahng*) *m* incident

incinérer (ang-see-nay-*ray*) *v* cremate

incision (ang-see-*z^{y}awng*) *f* cut

inciter (ang-see-*tay*) *v* incite

inclinaison (ang-klee-neh-*zawng*) *f* gradient

inclination (ang-klee-nah-*s^{y}awng*) *f* tendency; **~ de la tête** nod

incliné (ang-klee-*nay*) *adj* slanting

incliner (ang-klee-*nay*): **s'~** slant

***inclure** (ang-*klewr*) *v* include, enclose; comprise, count

incompétent (ang-kawng-pay-*tahng*) *adj* incompetent, unqualified

incomplet (ang-kawng-*play*) *adj* (f -plète) incomplete

inconcevable (ang-kawng-*svahbl*) *adj* inconceivable

inconditionnel (ang-kawng-dee-s^{y}o-*nehl*) *adj* unconditional

inconfortable (ang-kawng-for-*tahbl*) *adj* uncomfortable

inconnu (ang-ko-*new*) *adj* unknown; *m* stranger

inconscient (ang-kawng-*s^{y}ahng*) *adj* unconscious; unaware

inconsidéré (ang-kawng-see-day-*ray*) *adj* rash

inconvénient (ang-kawng-vay-*n^{y}ahng*) *m* inconvenience

incorrect (ang-ko-*rehkt*) *adj* incorrect, inaccurate, wrong

incroyable (ang-krwah-*^{y}ahbl*) *adj* incredible

inculte (ang-*kewlt*) *adj* uncultivated

incurable (ang-kew-*rahbl*) *adj* incurable

Inde (angd) *f* India

indécent (ang-day-*sahng*) *adj* indecent

indéfini (ang-day-fee-*nee*) *adj* indefinite

indemne (ang-*dehmn*) *adj* unhurt

indemnité (ang-dehm-nee-*tay*) *f* compensation, indemnity

indépendance (ang-day-pahng-*dahngss*) *f* independence

indépendant (ang-day-pahng-*dahng*) *adj* independent; self-employed

indésirable (ang-day-zee-*rahbl*) *adj* undesirable

index (ang-*dehks*) *m* index finger; index

indicatif (ang-dee-kah-*teef*) *m* area code

indication (ang-dee-kah-*s^{y}awng*) *f* indication

Indien (ang-*d^{y}ang*) *m* Indian

indien (ang-*d^{y}ang*) *adj* Indian

indifférent (ang-dee-fay-*rahng*) *adj* indifferent

indigène (ang-dee-*zhehn*) *m/f* native; *adj* native

indigent (ang-dee-*zhahng*) *adj* poor

indigestion (ang-dee-zheh-*st^{y}awng*) *f* indigestion

indignation (ang-dee-ñah-*s^{y}awng*) *f* indignation

indiquer (ang-dee-*kay*) *v* point out, indicate; declare

indirect (ang-dee-*rehkt*) *adj* indirect

indispensable (ang-dee-spahng-*sahbl*) *adj* essential

indisposé (ang-dee-spoa-*zay*) *adj* unwell

indistinct (ang-dee-*stang*) *adj* indistinct, vague

individu (ang-dee-vee-*dew*) *m* individual
individuel (ang-dee-vee-*dwehl*) *adj* individual
Indonésie (ang-do-nay-*zee*) *f* Indonesia
Indonésien (ang-do-nay-*z*^{y}*ang*) *m* Indonesian
indonésien (ang-do-nay-*z*^{y}*ang*) *adj* Indonesian
industrie (ang-dew-*stree*) *f* industry
industriel (ang-dew-stree-*ehl*) *adj* industrial
inefficace (ee-nay-fee-*kahss*) *adj* inefficient
inégal (ee-nay-*gahl*) *adj* uneven, unequal
inéquitable (ee-nay-kee-*tahbl*) *adj* unfair
inestimable (ee-neh-stee-*mahbl*) *adj* priceless
inévitable (ee-nay-vee-*tahbl*) *adj* inevitable, unavoidable
inexact (ee-nehg-*zahkt*) *adj* inaccurate, inexact
inexpérimenté (ee-nehk-spay-ree-mahng-*tay*) *adj* inexperienced
inexplicable (ee-nehk-splee-*kahbl*) *adj* inexplicable
infâme (ang-*faam*) *adj* foul
infanterie (ang-fahng-*tree*) *f* infantry
infecter (ang-fehk-*tay*) *v* infect; **s'infecter** *become septic
infectieux (ang-fehk-*s*^{y}*ur*) *adj* infectious
infection (ang-fehk-*s*^{y}*awng*) *f* infection
inférieur (ang-fay-*r*^{y}*urr*) *adj* inferior, bottom
infidèle (ang-fee-*dehl*) *adj* unfaithful
infini (ang-fee-*nee*) *adj* infinite, endless
infinitif (ang-fee-nee-*teef*) *m* infinitive
infirme (ang-*feerm*) *m* invalid; *adj* invalid
infirmière (ang-feer-*m*^{y}*air*) *f* nurse
inflammable (ang-flah-*mahbl*) *adj* inflammable
inflammation (ang-flah-mah-*s*^{y}*awng*) *f* inflammation
inflation (ang-flah-*s*^{y}*awng*) *f* inflation
influence (ang-flew-*ahngss*) *f* influence
influencer (ang-flew-ahng-*say*) *v* influence
influent (ang-flew-*ahng*) *adj* influential
information (ang-for-mah-*s*^{y}*awng*) *f* information; enquiry
informer (ang-for-*may*) *v* inform; **s'informer** inquire, enquire, query
infortune (ang-for-*tewn*) *f* misfortune
infortuné (ang-for-tew-*nay*) *adj* unlucky
infraction (ang-frahk-*s*^{y}*awng*) *f* offence, offense *Am*
infrarouge (ang-frah-*roozh*) *adj* infrared
infructueux (ang-frewk-*twur*) *adj* unsuccessful
infusion (ang-few-*z*^{y}*awng*) *f* infusion; herb tea
ingénieur (ang-zhay-*n*^{y}*urr*) *m* engineer
ingénu (ang-zhay-*new*) *adj* simple
ingérence (ang-zhay-*rahngss*) *f* interference
ingrat (ang-*grah*) *adj* ungrateful
ingrédient (ang-gray-*d*^{y}*ahng*) *m* ingredient
inhabitable (ee-nah-bee-*tahbl*) *adj* uninhabitable
inhabité (ee-nah-bee-*tay*) *adj* uninhabited
inhabitué (ee-nah-bee-*tway*) *adj* unaccustomed
inhabituel (ee-nah-bee-*twehl*) *adj* unusual, uncommon
inhaler (ee-nah-*lay*) *v* inhale
ininterrompu (ee-nang-teh-rawng-

pew) adj continuous
initial (ee-nee-*s^{y}ahl*) *adj* initial
initiale (ee-nee-*s^{y}ahl*) *f* initial
initiative (ee-nee-s^{y}ah-*teev*) *f* initiative
injecter (an̄ḡ-zhehk-*tay*) *v* inject
injection (an̄ḡ-zhehk-*s^{y}awn̄ḡ*) *f* injection
injurier (an̄ḡ-zhew-*r^{y}ay*) *v* abuse, insult
injuste (an̄ḡ-*zhewst*) *adj* unjust, unfair
injustice (an̄ḡ-zhew-*steess*) *f* injustice
inné (ee-*nay*) *adj* natural
innocence (ee-no-*sahn̄ḡss*) *f* innocence
innocent (ee-no-*sahn̄ḡ*) *adj* innocent
inoculer (ee-no-kew-*lay*) *v* inoculate
inoffensif (ee-no-fahn̄ḡ-*seef*) *adj* harmless
inondation (ee-nawn̄ḡ-dah-*s^{y}awn̄ḡ*) *f* flood
inopportun (ee-no-por-*turn̄ḡ*) *adj* inconvenient, misplaced
inquiet (an̄ḡ-*k^{y}ay*) *adj* (f -ète) anxious; restless
inquiétant (an̄ḡ-k^{y}ay-*tahn̄ḡ*) *adj* scary
inquiéter (an̄ḡ-k^{y}ay-*tay*): **s'~** worry
inquiétude (an̄ḡ-k^{y}ay-*tewd*) *f* worry; unrest
insatisfaisant (an̄ḡ-sah-teess-fer-*zahn̄ḡ*) *adj* unsatisfactory
insatisfait (an̄ḡ-sah-tee-*sfay*) *adj* dissatisfied
inscription (an̄ḡ-skree-*ps^{y}awn̄ḡ*) *f* inscription; registration; entry
***inscrire** (an̄ḡ-*skreer*) *v* enter, book; list; **s'*inscrire** check in, register
insecte (an̄ḡ-*sehkt*) *m* insect; bug *Am*
insecticide (an̄ḡ-sehk-tee-*seed*) *m* insecticide
insensé (an̄ḡ-sahn̄ḡ-*say*) *adj* crazy, senseless, mad
insensible (an̄ḡ-sahn̄ḡ-*seebl*) *adj* insensitive; imperceptible
insérer (an̄ḡ-say-*ray*) *v* insert
insignifiant (an̄ḡ-see-ñee-*f^{y}ahn̄ḡ*) *adj* petty, insignificant, unimportant
insipide (an̄ḡ-see-*peed*) *adj* tasteless
insister (an̄ḡ-see-*stay*) *v* insist
insolation (an̄ḡ-so-lah-*s^{y}awn̄ḡ*) *f* sunstroke
insolence (an̄ḡ-so-*lahn̄ḡss*) *f* insolence
insolent (an̄ḡ-so-*lahn̄ḡ*) *adj* insolent, impudent, impertinent
insolite (an̄ḡ-so-*leet*) *adj* unusual
insomnie (an̄ḡ-som-*nee*) *f* insomnia
insonorisé (an̄ḡ-so-noa-ree-*zay*) *adj* soundproof
insouciant (an̄ḡ-soo-*s^{y}ahn̄ḡ*) *adj* carefree
inspecter (an̄ḡ-spehk-*tay*) *v* inspect
inspecteur (an̄ḡ-spehk-*tūrr*) *m* (*f* **-trice**) inspector
inspection (an̄ḡ-spehk-*s^{y}awn̄ḡ*) *f* inspection
inspectrice (an̄ḡ-spehk-*trees*) *f* inspector
inspirer (an̄ḡ-spee-*ray*) *v* inspire
instable (an̄ḡ-*stahbl*) *adj* unsteady, unstable
installation (an̄ḡ-stah-lah-*s^{y}awn̄ḡ*) *f* installation
installer (an̄ḡ-stah-*lay*) *v* instal(l;) furnish
instant (an̄ḡ-*stahn̄ḡ*) *m* instant, moment; second
instantané (an̄ḡ-stahn̄ḡ-tah-*nay*) *m* snapshot; *adj* prompt
instantanément (an̄ḡ-stahn̄ḡ-tah-nay-*mahn̄ḡ*) *adv* instantly
instinct (an̄ḡ-*stan̄ḡ*) *m* instinct
instituer (an̄ḡ-stee-*tway*) *v* institute
institut (an̄ḡ-stee-*tew*) *m* institute; **~ de beauté** beauty parlo(u)r
instituteur (an̄ḡ-stee-tew-*tūrr*) *m* master, teacher, schoolteacher, schoolmaster
institution (an̄ḡ-stee-tew-*s^{y}awn̄ḡ*) *f* institution; institute
instructeur (an̄ḡ-strewk-*tūrr*) *m*

instructor
instructif (an̅g̅-strewk-*teef*) *adj* instructive
instruction (an̅g̅-strewk-*s^{y}awn̅g̅*) *f* instruction, direction
***instruire** (an̅g̅-*strweer*) *v* instruct
instrument (an̅g̅-strew-*mahn̅g̅*) *m* instrument; tool, implement; **~ de musique** musical instrument
insuffisant (an̅g̅-sew-fee-*zahn̅g̅*) *adj* insufficient
insulte (an̅g̅-*sewlt*) *f* insult
insulter (an̅g̅-sewl-*tay*) *v* insult; scold
insupportable (an̅g̅-sew-por-*tahbl*) *adj* unbearable
insurrection (an̅g̅-sew-rehk-*s^{y}awn̅g̅*) *f* revolt, uprising
intact (an̅g̅-*tahkt*) *adj* whole, intact, unbroken
intellect (an̅g̅-teh-*lehkt*) *m* intellect
intellectuel (an̅g̅-teh-lehk-*twehl*) *adj* intellectual
intelligence (an̅g̅-teh-lee-*zhahn̅g̅ss*) *f* intelligence, intellect, brain
intelligent (an̅g̅-teh-lee-*zhahn̅g̅*) *adj* intelligent, bright, clever
intense (an̅g̅-*tahn̅g̅ss*) *adj* intense; heavy
intention (an̅g̅-tahn̅g̅-*s^{y}awn̅g̅*) *f* intention, purpose; ***avoir l'intention de** intend
intentionnel (an̅g̅-tahn̅g̅-s^{y}o-*nehl*) *adj* intentional, on purpose
interdiction (an̅g̅-tehr-deek-*s^{y}awn̅g̅*) *f* prohibition
***interdire** (an̅g̅-tehr-*deer*) *v* *forbid, prohibit
interdit (an̅g̅-tehr-*dee*) *adj* prohibited; **~ aux piétons** no pedestrians
intéressant (an̅g̅-tay-reh-*sahn̅g̅*) *adj* interesting
intéresser (an̅g̅-tay-ray-*say*) *v* interest
intérêt (an̅g̅-tay-*ray*) *m* interest
intérieur (an̅g̅-tay-*r^{y}u̅r̅r̅*) *m* interior, inside; *adj* internal, inside, inner; indoor; domestic; **à l'intérieur** inside; indoors, within; **à l'intérieur de** inside; **vers l'intérieur** inwards
intérim (an̅g̅-tay-*reem*) *m* interim
interloqué (an̅g̅-tehr-lo-*kay*) *adj* speechless
interlude (an̅g̅-tehr-*lewd*) *m* interlude
intermédiaire (an̅g̅-tehr-may-*d^{y}air*) *m/f* intermediary; ***servir d'intermédiaire** mediate
internat (an̅g̅-tehr-*nah*) *m* boarding school
international (an̅g̅-tehr-nah-s^{y}o-*nahl*) *adj* international
interne (an̅g̅-*tehrn*) *adj* internal, resident
Internet (an̅g̅-tehr-*neht*) *m* internet
interprète (an̅g̅-tehr-*preht*) *m/f* interpreter
interpréter (an̅g̅-tehr-pray-*tay*) *v* interpret
interrogatif (an̅g̅-teh-ro-gah-*teef*) *adj* interrogative
interrogatoire (an̅g̅-teh-ro-gah-*twaar*) *m* interrogation, examination
interroger (an̅g̅-teh-ro-*zhay*) *v* interrogate
***interrompre** (an̅g̅-teh-*rawn̅g̅pr*) *v* interrupt; **s'*interrompre** *break off
interruption (an̅g̅-teh-rew-*ps^{y}awn̅g̅*) *f* interruption
intersection (an̅g̅-tehr-sehk-*s^{y}awn̅g̅*) *f* intersection
intervalle (an̅g̅-tehr-*vahl*) *m* interval; space
***intervenir** (an̅g̅-tehr-ver-*neer*) *v* intervene, interfere
intervertir (an̅g̅-tehr-vehr-*teer*) *v* invert
interview (an̅g̅-tehr-*v^{y}oo*) *f* interview
intestin (an̅g̅-teh-*stan̅g̅*) *m* intestine, gut; **intestins** bowels *pl*
intime (an̅g̅-*teem*) *adj* intimate, cosy, cozy *Am*

intimité (ang-tee-mee-*tay*) *f* privacy
intolérable (ang-to-lay-*rahbl*) *adj* intolerable
intoxication alimentaire (ang-tok-see-kah-s^{y}awng ah-lee-mahng-*tair*) food poisoning
intrigue (ang-*treeg*) *f* intrigue; plot
introduction (ang-tro-dewk-*s^{y}awng*) *f* introduction
***introduire** (ang-tro-*dweer*) *v* introduce
intrus (ang-*trew*) *m* trespasser
inutile (ee-new-*teel*) *adj* useless
inutilement (ee-new-teel-*mahng*) *adv* in vain
invalide (ang-vah-*leed*) *adj* disabled, handicapped
invasion (ang-vah-*z^{y}awng*) *f* invasion
inventaire (ang-vahng-*tair*) *m* inventory
inventer (ang-vahng-*tay*) *v* invent
inventeur (ang-vahng-*turr*) *m* inventor
inventif (ang-vahng-*teef*) *adj* inventive
invention (ang-vahng-*s^{y}awng*) *f* invention
inverse (ang-*vehrs*) *adj* reverse
investigation (ang-veh-stee-gah-*s^{y}awng*) *f* investigation, enquiry
investir (ang-veh-*steer*) *v* invest
investissement (ang-veh-stee-*smahng*) *m* investment
investisseur (ang-veh-stee-*surr*) *m* investor
invisible (ang-vee-*zeebl*) *adj* invisible
invitation (ang-vee-tah-*s^{y}awng*) *f* invitation
invité (ang-vee-*tay*) *m* guest
inviter (ang-vee-*tay*) *v* invite
involontaire (ang-vo-lawng-*tair*) *adj* unintentional
iode (^{y}od) *m* iodine
Irak (ee-*rahk*) *m* Iraq
Irakien (ee-rah-*k^{y}ang*) *m* Iraqi
irakien (ee-rah-*k^{y}ang*) *adj* Iraqi
Iran (ee-*rahng*) *m* Iran
iranien (ee-rah-*n^{y}ang*) *adj* Iranian
irascible (ee-rah-*seebl*) *adj* quick-tempered
irlandais (eer-lahng-*day*) *adj* Irish
Irlande (eer-*lahngd*) *f* Ireland
ironie (ee-ro-*nee*) *f* irony
ironique (ee-ro-*neek*) *adj* ironical
irréel (ee-ray-*ehl*) *adj* unreal
irrégulier (ee-ray-gew-*l^{y}ay*) *adj* irregular, uneven
irréparable (ee-ray-pah-*rahbl*) *adj* irreparable
irrétrécissable (ee-ray-tray-see-*sahbl*) *adj* shrinkproof
irrévocable (ee-ray-vo-*kahbl*) *adj* irrevocable
irritable (ee-ree-*tahbl*) *adj* irritable
irrité (ee-ree-*tay*) *adj* angry, annoyed
irriter (ee-ree-*tay*) *v* irritate
islandais (ee-slahng-*day*) *adj* Icelandic
Islande (ee-*slahngd*) *f* Iceland
isolateur (ee-zo-lah-*turr*) *m* insulator
isolation (ee-zo-lah-*s^{y}awng*) *f* isolation, insulation
isolement (ee-zol-*mahng*) *m* isolation
isoler (ee-zo-*lay*) *v* isolate, insulate
Israël (ee-srah-*ehl*) *m* Israel
israélien (ee-srah-ay-*l^{y}ang*) *adj* Israeli
issue (ee-*sew*) *f* issue
Italie (ee-tah-*lee*) *f* Italy
italien (ee-tah-*l^{y}ang*) *adj* Italian
itinéraire (ee-tee-nay-*rair*) *m* itinerary
ivoire (ee-*vwaar*) *m* ivory
ivre (eevr) *adj* drunk; intoxicated

J

jadis (zhah-*deess*) *adv* formerly
jalousie (zhah-loo-*zee*) *f* jealousy
jaloux (zhah-*loo*) *adj* jealous, envious
jamais (zhah-*may*) *adv* ever; **ne ... ~** never
jambe (zhahngb) *f* leg
jambon (zhahng-*bawng*) *m* ham
jante (zhahngt) *f* rim
janvier (zhahng-*v^{y}ay*) January
Japon (zhah-*pawng*) *m* Japan
Japonais (zhah-po-*nay*) *m* Japanese
japonais (zhah-po-*nay*) *adj* Japanese
jaquette (zhah-*keht*) *f* jacket
jardin (zhahr-*dang*) *m* garden; **~ potager** kitchen garden; **~ public** public garden; **~ zoologique** zoological gardens
jardinier (zhahr-dee-*n^{y}ay*) *m* gardener
jarre (zhaar) *f* jar
jauge (zhōazh) *f* gauge
jaune (zhōan) *adj* yellow; **~ d'œuf** yolk, egg yolk
jaunisse (zhoa-*neess*) *f* jaundice
je (zher) *pron* I
jersey (zhehr-*zay*) *m* jersey
jet (zhay) *m* cast; jet, squirt, spout
jetée (zher-*tay*) *f* jetty, pier
jeter (zher-*tay*) *v* *cast, *throw; **à ~** disposable
jeton (zher-*tawng*) *m* token, chip
jeu (zhur) *m* play, game; set; **carte de ~** playing card; **~ concours** quiz; **~ de dames** draughts; checkers *plAm*; **~ de quilles** ninepins, skittles; **terrain de jeux** playground
jeudi (zhur-*dee*) *m* Thursday
jeune (zhurn) *adj* young
jeunesse (zhur-*nehss*) *f* youth
joaillerie (zhwigh-*ree*) *f* jewellery, jewelry *Am*
joaillier (zhwigh-*yay*) *m*, **-ière** *f* jewel(l)er
jockey (zho-*kay*) *m* jockey
joie (zhwah) *f* joy, gladness
***joindre** (zhwangdr) *v* join, connect; attach, enclose
jointure (zhwang-*tewr*) *f* knuckle
joli (zho-*lee*) *adj* fine, nice, pretty, good-looking
jonc (zhawng) *m* rush
jonction (zhawngk-*s^{y}awng*) *f* junction
jonquille (zhawng-*keey*) *f* daffodil
Jordanie (zhor-dah-*nee*) *f* Jordan
jordanien (zhor-dah-*n^{y}ang*) *adj* Jordanian
joue (zhoo) *f* cheek
jouer (zhoo-*ay*) *v* play; act
jouet (zhoo-*ay*) *m* toy
joueur (zhoo-*ūrr*) *m*, **-euse** *f* player
joug (zhoo) *m* yoke
jouir de (zhoo-*eer*) enjoy
jour (zhōor) *m* day; **de ~** by day; **~ de fête** holiday; **~ de la semaine** weekday; **~ ouvrable** working day; **l'autre ~** recently; **par ~** per day; **un ~ ou l'autre** some day
journal (zhoor-*nahl*) *m* newspaper, paper; diary; **~ du matin** morning paper
journalier (zhoor-nah-*l^{y}ay*) *adj* daily
journalisme (zhoor-nah-*leesm*) *m* journalism
journaliste (zhoor-nah-*leest*) *m/f* journalist
journée (zhoor-*nay*) *f* day
joyau (zhwah-^{y}*oa*) *m* gem
joyeux (zhwah-^{y}*ur*) *adj* joyful, cheerful, merry, glad
juge (zhēwzh) *m* judge
jugement (zhewzh-*mahng*) *m* judgment; sentence
juger (zhew-*zhay*) *v* judge
juif (zhweef) *adj* Jewish; *m* Jew
juillet (zhwee-^{y}*ay*) July

juin (zhwang̅) June
juive (zhweef) *adj* Jewish; *f* Jew
jumeaux (zhew-*moa*) *mpl* twins *pl*
jumelage (zhew-mer-*laazh*) *m* twinning
jumelles (zhew-*mehl*) *fpl* field glasses, binoculars *pl*
jument (zhew-*mahng̅*) *f* mare
jungle (zhawng̅gl) *f* jungle
jupe (zhewp) *f* skirt
jupon (zhew-*pawng̅*) *m* underskirt
jurer (zhew-*ray*) *v* vow, *swear; curse
juridique (zhew-ree-*deek*) *adj* legal
juriste (zhew-*reest*) *m* lawyer
juron (zhew-*rawng̅*) *m* curse
jury (zhew-*ree*) *m* jury
jus (zhew) *m* juice; gravy; **~ de fruits** fruit juice
jusque (zhewsk) *prep* to; **jusqu'à** *prep* till; until; **jusqu'à ce que** till
juste (zhewst) *adj* just, righteous, right, fair; appropriate, proper, correct, exact; tight; *adv* just
justement (zhew-ster-*mahng̅*) *adv* rightly
justice (zhew-*steess*) *f* justice
justifier (zhew-stee-*f*ʸ*ay*) *v* justify
juteux (zhew-*tur*) *adj* juicy
juvénile (zhew-vay-*neel*) *adj* juvenile

K

kaki (kah-*kee*) *m* khaki
kangourou (kahng̅-goo-*roo*) *m* kangaroo
Kenya (kay-*n*ʸ*ah*) *m* Kenya
kilo (kee-*loa*) *m* kilogram
kilométrage (kee-lo-may-*traazh*) *m* distance in kilometres (kilometers *Am*)
kilomètre (kee-lo-*mehtr*) *m* kilometre, kilometer *Am*
kiosque (kʸosk) *m* kiosk; **~ à journaux** newsstand
klaxon (klahk-*sawng̅*) *m* hooter; horn
klaxonner (klahk-so-*nay*) *v* hoot; toot *Am*, honk *Am*

L

la (lah) *art* the; *pron* her
là (lah) *adv* there
là-bas (lah-*bah*) *adv* over there
labeur (lah-*būrr*) *m* labo(u)r
laboratoire (lah-bo-rah-*twaar*) *m* laboratory; **~ de langues** language laboratory
labourer (lah-boo-*ray*) *v* plough
labyrinthe (lah-bee-*rang̅t*) *m* maze, labyrinth
lac (lahk) *m* lake
lacet (lah-*say*) *m* shoelace, lace
lâche (laash) *m* coward; *adj* cowardly; loose
lâcher (lah-*shay*) *v* *let go
lagune (lah-*gewn*) *f* lagoon
laid (lay) *adj* ugly
laine (lehn) *f* wool; **en ~** wool(l)en; **~ à**

repriser darning wool
laisse (lehss) *f* leash, lead
laisser (lay-*say*) *v* *let, *leave; *leave behind
lait (lay) *m* milk
laiterie (leh-*tree*) *f* dairy
laiteux (lay-*tur*) *adj* milky
laitier (lay-*t^y ay*) *m* milkman
laiton (lay-*tawng*) *m* brass
laitue (lay-*tew*) *f* lettuce
lame (lahm) *f* blade; **~ de rasoir** razor blade
lamentable (lah-mahng-*tahbl*) *adj* lamentable
lampadaire (lahng-pah-*dair*) *m* lamppost
lampe (lahngp) *f* lamp; **~ de poche** torch; **~ de travail** reading lamp; **lampe-tempête** *f* hurricane lamp
lance (lahngss) *f* spear
lancement (lahng-*smahng*) *m* throw; launching
lancer (lahng-*say*) *v* *cast, toss, *throw; launch
lande (lahngd) *f* heath, moor
langage (lahng-*gaazh*) *m* language
langue (lahngg) *f* tongue; language; **~ maternelle** native language, mother tongue
lanterne (lahng-*tehrn*) *f* lantern
lapin (lah-*pang*) *m* rabbit
laque (lahk) *f* varnish; **~ capillaire** hair spray
lard (laar) *m* bacon
lardon (lahr-*dawng*) *m* piece of larding bacon; kid, baby
large (lahrzh) *adj* wide, broad; generous, liberal
largeur (lahr-*zhurr*) *f* width, breadth
larme (lahrm) *f* tear
laryngite (lah-rang-*zheet*) *f* laryngitis
las (lah) *adj* (f ~se) weary; **~ de** tired of
latitude (lah-tee-*tewd*) *f* latitude
lavable (lah-*vahbl*) *adj* washable
lavabo (lah-vah-*boa*) *m* washbasin
lavage (lah-*vaazh*) *m* washing
laver (lah-*vay*) *v* wash
laverie automatique (lah-vree oa-toa-mah-*teek*) launderette
lave-vaisselle (lahv-veh-*sehl*) *m* dish washer
laxatif (lahk-sah-*teef*) *m* laxative
le[1] (ler) *art* (f la, pl les) the
le[2] (ler) *pron* (f la) him; it
leader (lee-*dair*) *m* leader
lécher (lay-*shay*) *v* lick
lèche-vitrines (lehsh-vee-*treen*) *m*windowshopping
leçon (ler-*sawng*) *f* lesson
lecteur (lehk-*turr*) *m*, **-trice** *f* reader
lecture (lehk-*tewr*) *f* reading
légal (lay-*gahl*) *adj* legal, lawful
léger (lay-*zhay*) *adj* (f légère) slight, light; weak, gentle
légitime (lay-zhee-*teem*) *adj* legitimate, legal; just
légume (lay-*gewm*) *m* vegetable
lendemain (lahngd-*mang*) *m* next day
lent (lahng) *adj* slow; sluggish
lentille (lahng-*teey*) *f* lens
lèpre (lehpr) *f* leprosy
lequel (ler-*kehl*) *pron* (f laquelle; pl lesquels, lesquelles) which
les (lay) *art* the; *pron* them
lésion (lay-*z^y awng*) *f* injury
lessive (lay-*seev*) *f* washing, laundry
lettre (lehtr) *f* letter; **boîte aux lettres** letterbox, mailbox *Am*; **~ de crédit** letter of credit; **~ de recommandation** letter of recommendation; **~ recommandée** registered letter
leur (lurr) *adj* their; *pron* them
levée (ler-*vay*) *f* collection
lever (ler-*vay*) *v* lift; **~ du jour** daybreak; **se ~** *rise, *get up
levier (ler-*v^y ay*) *m* lever; **~ de vitesse** gear lever

lèvre (laivr) *f* lip
lévrier (lay-*vr^{y}ay*) *m* greyhound
levure (ler-*vewr*) *f* yeast
liaison (l^{y}ay-*zawng*) *f* connection; affair
Liban (lee-*bahng*) *m* Lebanon
libanais (lee-bah-*nay*) *adj* Lebanese
libéral (lee-bay-*rahl*) *adj* liberal
libération (lee-bay-rah-*s^{y}awng*) *f* liberation
libérer (lee-bay-*ray*) *v* release; liberate
Libéria (lee-bay-*r^{y}ah*) *m* Liberia
libérien (lee-bay-*r^{y}ang*) *adj* Liberian
liberté (lee-behr-*tay*) *f* freedom, liberty
libraire (lee-*brair*) *m/f* bookseller
librairie (lee-bray-*ree*) *f* bookstore
libre (leebr) *adj* free
libre-service (leebr-sehr-*veess*) *m* self-service
licence (lee-*sahngss*) *f* permission, licence, license *Am*
licencier (lee-sahng-*s^{y}ay*) *v* fire
lien (l^{y}ang) *m* band; link
lier (lee-*ay*) *v* *bind
lierre (l^{y}air) *m* ivy
lieu (l^{y}ur) *m* spot; **au ~ de** instead of; ***avoir ~** *take place; **~ de naissance** place of birth; **~ de rencontre** meeting place
lièvre (l^{y}aivr) *m* hare
ligne (leeñ) *f* line; **~ aérienne** airline; **~ d'arrivée** finish; **~ de pêche** fishing line; **~ intérieure** extension; **~ principale** main line
ligue (leeg) *f* union, league
lime (leem) *f* file; **~ à ongles** nail file
limette (lee-*meht*) *f* lime
limite (lee-*meet*) *f* limit, boundary, bound; **~ de vitesse** speed limit
limiter (lee-mee-*tay*) *v* limit
limonade (lee-mo-*nahd*) *f* lemonade
linge (langzh) *m* linen
lingerie (lang-*zhree*) *f* lingerie
lion (l^{y}awng) *m* lion
liqueur (lee-*kurr*) *f* liqueur
liquide (lee-*keed*) *m* fluid; *adj* liquid
***lire** (leer) *v* *read
lis (leess) *m* lily
lisible (lee-*zeebl*) *adj* legible
lisse (leess) *adj* smooth
liste (leest) *f* list; **~ d'attente** waiting list
lit (lee) *m* bed; **~ de camp** camp bed; cot *Am*; **lits jumeaux** twin beds
literie (lee-*tree*) *f* bedding
litige (lee-*teezh*) *m* dispute
litre (leetr) *m* liter *Am*, litre
littéraire (lee-tay-*rair*) *adj* literary
littérature (lee-tay-rah-*tewr*) *f* literature
littoral (lee-to-*rahl*) *m* sea-coast
livraison (lee-vreh-*zawng*) *f* delivery
livre^1 (leevr) *m* book; **~ de cuisine** cookery book; cookbook *Am*; **~ de poche** paperback
livre^2 (leevr) *f* pound
livrer (lee-*vray*) *v* deliver
local (lo-*kahl*) *adj* local
localiser (lo-kah-lee-*zay*) *v* locate
localité (lo-kah-lee-*tay*) *f* locality
locataire (lo-kah-*tair*) *m* tenant
location (lo-kah-*s^{y}awng*) *f* lease; **donner en ~** lease; **~ de voitures** car hire; car rental *Am*
locomotive (lo-ko-mo-*teev*) *f* locomotive, engine
locution (lo-kew-*s^{y}awng*) *f* phrase
loge (lozh) *f* dressing room
logement (lozh-*mahng*) *m* lodgings *pl*, accommodation
loger (lo-*zhay*) *v* accommodate; lodge
logeur (lo-*zhurr*) *m* landlord
logeuse (lo-*zhurz*) *f* landlady
logique (lo-*zheek*) *f* logic; *adj* logical
loi (lwah) *f* law
loin (lwang) *adv* away, far; **plus ~** further

lointain (lwang-*tang*) *adj* far-off, remote
loisir (lwah-*zeer*) *m* leisure
long (lawng) *adj* (f longue) long; **en ~** lengthways; **le ~ de** past, along
longitude (lawng-zhee-*tewd*) *f* longitude
longtemps (lawng-*tahng*) *adv* long
longueur (lawng-*gurr*) *f* length; **~ d'onde** wavelength
lopin (lo-*pang*) *m* plot
lors de (lor der) at the time of
lorsque (lorsk) *conj* when
lot (loa) *m* batch
loterie (lo-*tree*) *f* lottery
lotion (lo-*s^{y}awng*) *f* lotion
louange (loo-*ahngzh*) *f* glory
louche (loosh) *adj* cross-eyed
louer (loo-*ay*) *v* hire, rent, lease; *let; praise; **à ~** for hire
loup (loo) *m* wolf
lourd (loor) *adj* heavy
loyal (lwah-*^{y}ahl*) *adj* true, loyal
loyer (lwah-*^{y}ay*) *m* rent
lubie (lew-*bee*) *f* whim
lubrifiant (lew-bree-*f^{y}ahng*) *m* lubrication oil
lubrification (lew-bree-fee-kah-*s^{y}awng*) *f* lubrication
lubrifier (lew-bree-*f^{y}ay*) *v* lubricate
lueur (lwurr) *f* gleam
luge (lewzh) *f* sleigh, sled(ge)
lugubre (lew-*gewbr*) *adj* creepy
lui (lwee) *pron* him; her; **lui-même** *pron* himself
luisant (lwee-*zahng*) *adj* glossy
lumbago (lawng-bah-*goa*) *m* lumbago
lumière (lew-*m^{y}air*) *f* light; **~ du jour** daylight; **~ du soleil** sunlight; **~ latérale** sidelight
lumineux (lew-mee-*nur*) *adj* luminous
lundi (lurng-*dee*) *m* Monday
lune (lewn) *f* moon; **clair de ~** moonlight; **~ de miel** honeymoon
lunettes (lew-*neht*) *fpl* spectacles, glasses; **~ de plongée** goggles *pl*; **~ de soleil** sunglasses *pl*
lustre (lewstr) *m* gloss
lustrer (lew-*stray*) *v* lustre; *shine
lutte (lewt) *f* fight, combat, battle, struggle
lutter (lew-*tay*) *v* struggle; combat
luxe (lewks) *m* luxury
luxueux (lewk-*swur*) *adj* luxurious
lycée (lee-*say*) *m* (state) secondary school

M

mâcher (mah-*shay*) *v* chew
machine (mah-*sheen*) *f* engine, machine; **~ à coudre** sewing machine; **~ à écrire** typewriter; **~ à laver** washing machine
machinerie (mah-sheen-*ree*) *f* machinery
mâchoire (mah-*shwaar*) *f* jaw
maçon (mah-*sawng*) *m* bricklayer
madame (mah-*dahm*) madam
mademoiselle (mahd-mwah-*zehl*) miss
magasin (mah-gah-*zang*) *m* store; warehouse, store house; **grand ~** department store; **~ de chaussures** shoe shop; **~ de jouets** toyshop; **~ de spiritueux** off-licence, liquor store *Am*
magazine (mah-gah-*zeen*) *m* magazine

magie (mah-*zhee*) *f* magic
magique (mah-*zheek*) *adj* magic
magistrat (mah-zhee-*strah*) *m* magistrate
magnétique (mah-ñay-*teek*) *adj* magnetic
magnéto (mah-ñay-*toa*) *f* magneto
magnétophone (mah-ñay-to-*fon*) *m* tape recorder
magnétoscope (mah-ñay-to-*skop*) *m* video recorder
magnifique (mah-ñee-*feek*) *adj* splendid, gorgeous, magnificent
mai (may) May
maigre (maigr) *adj* thin, lean
maigrir (meh-*greer*) *v* slim
maille (migh) *f* mesh
maillet (mah-*ʸay*) *m* mallet
maillot de bain (mah-ʸoa der bang̅) bathing suit, swimsuit
main (mang̅) *f* hand; **fait à la ~** hand-made
main-d'œuvre (mang̅-*dūrvr*) *f* manpower
maintenant (mang̅t-*nahng̅*) *adv* now; **jusqu'à ~** so far
***maintenir** (mang̅t-*neer*) *v* maintain
maire (mair) *m* mayor
mairie (may-*ree*) *f* town hall
mais (may) *conj* but
maïs (mah-*eess*) *m* maize, corn *Am*; **~ en épi** corn on the cob
maison (may-*zawng̅*) *f* house; home; **à la ~** at home; **fait à la ~** home-made; **maison-bateau** houseboat; **~ de campagne** country house; **~ de repos** rest home
maître (maitr) *m* master; **~ d'école** teacher, schoolmaster; **~ d'hôtel** head waiter
maîtresse (meh-*trehss*) *f* mistress; **~ de maison** mistress
maîtriser (meh-tree-*zay*) *v* master
majeur (mah-*zhūrr*) *adj* major; superior, main; of age
majorité (mah-zho-ree-*tay*) *f* bulk, majority
majuscule (mah-zhew-*skewl*) *f* capital letter
mal (mahl) *m* (pl maux) evil, harm; mischief; ***faire du ~** harm; ***faire ~** ache; *hurt; **~ à l'aise** uneasy; **~ au cœur** sickness; **~ au dos** backache; **~ au ventre** stomachache; **~ aux dents** toothache; **~ de gorge** sore throat; **~ de l'air** airsickness; **~ de mer** seasickness; **~ d'estomac** stomach ache; **~ de tête** headache; **~ d'oreille** earache; **~ du pays** homesickness
malade (mah-*lahd*) *adj* sick, ill
maladie (mah-lah-*dee*) *f* sickness, illness, disease; **~ vénérienne** venereal disease
maladroit (mah-lah-*drwah*) *adj* clumsy, awkward
Malais (mah-*lay*) *m* Malay
malaisien (mah-lay-*zʸang̅*) *adj* Malaysian
malaria (mah-lah-*rʸah*) *f* malaria
malchance (mahl-*shahng̅ss*) *f* bad luck
mâle (maal) *adj* male
malentendu (mah-lahng̅-tahng̅-*dew*) *m* misunderstanding
malgré (mahl-*gray*) *prep* in spite of, despite
malheur (mah-*lūrr*) *m* misfortune
malheureusement (mah-lur-rurz-*mahng̅*) *adv* unfortunately
malheureux (mah-lur-*rur*) *adj* unhappy, unfortunate; miserable, sad
malhonnête (mah-lo-*neht*) *adj* dishonest, crooked
malice (mah-*leess*) *f* mischief
malicieux (mah-lee-*sʸur*) *adj* mischievous
malin (mah-*lang̅*) *adj* (f maligne) malignant; sly; bright
malle (mahl) *f* trunk

mallette (mah-*leht*) *f* suitcase; **~ de voyage** grip *Am*
malodorant (mah-lo-do-*rahng*) *adj* smelly
malpropre (mahl-*propr*) *adj* foul, unclean
malsain (mahl-*sang*) *adj* unsound, unhealthy
malveillant (mahl-veh-*ʸahng*) *adj* spiteful; malicious
maman (mah-*mahng*) *f* mum
mammifère (mah-mee-*fair*) *m* mammal
manche (mahngsh) *m* handle; *f* sleeve; **La Manche** English Channel
manchette (mahng-*sheht*) *f* cuff; headline
mandarine (mahng-dah-*reen*) *f* tangerine, mandarin
mandat (mahng-*dah*) *m* mandate
manège (mah-*naizh*) *m* riding school
mangeoire (mahng-*zhwaar*) *f* manger
manger (mahng-*zhay*) *v* *eat; *m* food
maniable (mah-*nʸahbl*) *adj* manageable
manier (mah-*nʸay*) *v* handle
manière (mah-*nʸair*) *f* way, manner; **de la même ~** likewise; **de ~ que** so that
manifestation (mah-nee-feh-stah-*sʸawng*) *f* demonstration
manifestement (mah-nee-feh-ster-*mahng*) *adv* apparently
manifester (mah-nee-feh-*stay*) *v* express; demonstrate
manipuler (mah-nee-pew-*lay*) *v* handle
mannequin (mahn-*kang*) *m* model, mannequin
manoir (mah-*nwaar*) *m* mansion, manor house
manquant (mahng-*kahng*) *adj* missing
manque (mahngk) *m* want, shortage, lack
manquer (mahng-*kay*) *v* fail, lack; miss
manteau (mahng-*toa*) *m* coat, cloak; **~ de fourrure** fur coat
manucure (mah-new-*kewr*) *f* manicure
manuel (mah-*nwehl*) *m* textbook, handbook; *adj* manual; **~ de conversation** phrase book
manuscrit (mah-new-*skree*) *m* manuscript
maquereau (mah-*kroa*) *m* mackerel
maquillage (mah-kee-*ʸaazh*) *m* make-up
marais (mah-*ray*) *m* marsh, swamp, bog
marbre (mahrbr) *m* marble
marchand (mahr-*shahng*) *m*, **-e** *f* merchant; tradesman, dealer; **~ de journaux** newsagent; **~ de légumes** greengrocer; vegetable merchant; **~ de volaille** poulterer
marchander (mahr-shahng-*day*) *v* bargain
marchandise (mahr-shahng-*deez*) *f* merchandise; wares *pl*, goods *pl*
marche (mahrsh) *f* march; step; ***faire ~ arrière** reverse
marché (mahr-*shay*) *m* market; **bon ~** cheap; inexpensive; **~ des valeurs** stock market; **~ noir** black market; **place du ~** marketplace
marcher (mahr-*shay*) *v* walk, step, *go; march; ***faire ~** fool
mardi (mahr-*dee*) *m* Tuesday
marée (mah-*ray*) *f* tide; **~ basse** low tide; **~ haute** flood; high tide
margarine (mahr-gah-*reen*) *f* margarine
marge (mahrzh) *f* margin
mari (mah-*ree*) *m* husband
mariage (mah-*rʸaazh*) *m* matrimony, marriage; wedding
marié (mah-*rʸay*) *m* bridegroom
marier: se ~ (mah-*rʸay*) marry

marin (mah-*rang*) *m* sailor; seaman
marinade (mah-ree-*nahd*) *f* marinade *f*
marine (mah-*reen*) *f* navy; seascape
maritime (mah-ree-*teem*) *adj* maritime
marmelade (mahr-mer-*lahd*) *f* marmalade
marmite (mahr-*meet*) *f* pot
Maroc (mah-*rok*) *m* Morocco
marocain (mah-ro-*kang*) *adj* Moroccan
maroquinerie (mah-ro-keen-*ree*) *f* leather goods *pl*
marque (mahrk) *f* mark; sign, brand; **~ de fabrique** trademark
marquer (mahr-*kay*) *v* mark
marquise (mahr-*keez*) *f* awning
marrant (mah-*rahng*) *adj* funny; odd
marron (mah-*rawng*) *m* chestnut
mars (mahrs) March
marteau (mahr-*toa*) *m* hammer
marteler (mahr-ter-*lay*) *v* thump
martyr (mahr-*teer*) *m*, **-e** *f* martyr
masculin (mah-skew-*lang*) *adj* masculine
masque (mahsk) *m* mask; **~ de beauté** face pack
massage (mah-*saazh*) *m* massage; **~ facial** face massage
masse (mahss) *f* mass; bulk; crowd
masser (mah-*say*) *v* massage
masseur (mah-*sūrr*) *m* masseur
massif (mah-*seef*) *adj* massive, solid
massue (mah-*sew*) *f* club
mat (maht) *adj* mat, dull, dim
mât (mah) *m* mast
match (mahch) *m* match; **~ de boxe** boxing match; **~ de football** football match
matelas (mah-*tlah*) *m* mattress
matériau (mah-tay-*r^{y}oa*) *m* material
matériel (mah-tay-*r^{y}ehl*) *m* material; *adj* material; substantial
maternel (mah-tehr-*nehl*) *adj* motherly
mathématique (mah-tay-mah-*teek*) *adj* mathematical
mathématiques (mah-tay-mah-*teek*) *fpl* mathematics
matière (mah-*t^{y}air*) *f* matter; **~ première** raw material
matin (mah-*tang*) *m* morning; **ce ~** this morning
matinée (mah-tee-*nay*) *f* morning
maturité (mah-tew-ree-*tay*) *f* maturity
***maudire** (moa-*deer*) *v* curse
mausolée (moa-zo-*lay*) *m* mausoleum
mauvais (moa-*vay*) *adj* bad; wicked, ill, evil; **le plus ~** worst
mauve (mōav) *adj* mauve
maximum (mahk-see-*mom*) *m* maximum; **au ~** at most
mayonnaise (mah-^{y}o-*naiz*) *f* mayonnaise
mazout (mah-*zoot*) *m* fuel oil
me (mer) *pron* me; myself
mécanicien (may-kah-nee-*s^{y}ang*) *m* mechanic
mécanique (may-kah-*neek*) *adj* mechanical
mécanisme (may-kah-*neesm*) *m* mechanism, machinery
méchant (may-*shahng*) *adj* evil; naughty, nasty, ill
mèche (mehsh) *f* fuse
mécontent (may-kawng-*tahng*) *adj* discontented
médaille (may-*digh*) *f* medal
médecin (may-*dsang*) *m* physician, doctor; **~ généraliste** general practitioner
médecine (may-*dseen*) *f* medicine
médiateur (may-d^{y}ah-*tūrr*) *m*, **-trice** *f* mediator
médical (may-dee-*kahl*) *adj* medical
médicament (may-dee-kah-*mahng*) *m* medicine, drug
médiéval (may-d^{y}ay-*vahl*) *adj*

mediaeval
méditer (may-dee-*tay*) *v* meditate
Méditerranée (may-dee-tay-rah-*nay*) *f* Mediterranean
méduse (may-*dewz*) *f* jellyfish
méfiance (may-*f^{y}ahngss*) *f* suspicion
méfiant (may-*f^{y}ahng*) *adj* suspicious
méfier (may-*f^{y}ay*) *v*: **se ~ de** mistrust
meilleur (meh-*^{y}urr*) *adj* better; **le ~** best
mélancolie (may-lahng-ko-*lee*) *f* melancholy
mélancolique (may-lahng-ko-*leek*) *adj* melancholy
mélange (may-*lahngzh*) *m* mixture
mélanger (may-lahng-*zhay*) *v* mix
mêler (may-*lay*) *v* mix; **se ~ de** interfere with
mélo (may-*loa*) *m* tear-jerker
mélodie (may-lo-*dee*) *f* melody
mélodrame (may-lo-*drahm*) *m* melodrama
melon (mer-*lawng*) *m* melon
membre (mahngbr) *m* member, associate; limb
mémé (may-*may*) *f* granny
même (mehm) *adj* same; *adv* even; **de ~** also
mémoire (may-*mwaar*) *f* memory
mémorable (may-mo-*rahbl*) *adj* memorable
mémorandum (may-mo-rahng-*dom*) *m* memo
mémorial (may-mo-*r^{y}ahl*) *m* memorial
menaçant (mer-nah-*sahng*) *adj* threatening
menace (mer-*nahss*) *f* threat
menacer (mer-nah-*say*) *v* threaten
ménage (may-*naazh*) *m* housekeeping, household
ménagère (may-nah-*zhair*) *f* housewife
mendiant (mahng-*d^{y}ahng*) *m*, **-e** *f* beggar
mendier (mahng-*d^{y}ay*) *v* beg
mener (mer-*nay*) *v* *take, *lead
menottes (mer-*not*) *fpl* handcuffs *pl*
mensonge (mahng-*sawngzh*) *m* lie
menstruation (mahng-strew-ah-*s^{y}awng*) *f* menstruation
mensuel (mahng-*swehl*) *adj* monthly
mental (mahng-*tahl*) *adj* mental; **aliéné ~** lunatic
menthe (mahngt) *f* peppermint, mint
mention (mahng-*s^{y}awng*) *f* mention
mentionner (mahng-s^{y}o-*nay*) *v* mention
***mentir** (mahng-*teer*) *v* lie
menton (mahng-*tawng*) *m* chin
menu[1] (mer-*new*) *m* menu; **~ fixe** set menu
menu[2] (mer-*new*) *adj* minor
menuisier (mer-nwee-*z^{y}ay*) *m* carpenter
mépris (may-*pree*) *m* contempt, scorn
méprise (may-*preez*) *f* mistake
mépriser (may-pree-*zay*) *v* despise, scorn
mer (mair) *f* sea
merci (mehr-*see*) thank you
mercredi (mehr-krer-*dee*) *m* Wednesday
mercure (mehr-*kewr*) *m* mercury
merde (mehrd) *f* shit
mère (mair) *f* mother
méridional (may-ree-d^{y}o-*nahl*) *adj* southern, southerly
mérite (may-*reet*) *m* merit
mériter (may-ree-*tay*) *v* merit, deserve
merlan (mehr-*lahng*) *m* whiting
merle (mehrl) *m* blackbird
merveille (mehr-*vay*) *f* marvel
merveilleux (mehr-veh-*^{y}ur*) *adj* marvel(l)ous; fine, wonderful
mesquin (meh-*skang*) *adj* mean, stingy
message (meh-*saazh*) *m* message

messager (meh-sah-*zhay*) *m* messenger
messe (mehss) *f* mass
mesure (mer-*zewr*) *f* measure; size; **en ~** able; **fait sur ~** tailor-made
mesurer (mer-zew-*ray*) *v* measure
métal (may-*tahl*) *m* metal
métallique (may-tah-*leek*) *adj* metal
météo (may-tay-*oa*) *f* weather report; *m* meteorologist
méthode (may-*tod*) *f* method
méthodique (may-to-*deek*) *adj* methodical
méticuleux (may-tee-kew-*lur*) *adj* meticulous
métier (may-*t^{y}ay*) *m* trade, profession
mètre (mehtr) *m* meter *Am*, metre
métrique (may-*treek*) *adj* metric
métro (may-*troa*) *m* underground; subway *Am*
***mettre** (mehtr) *v* *put; *put on
meuble (murbl) *m* piece of furniture; **meubles** furniture
meubler (mur-*blay*) *v* furnish
meunier (mur-*n^{y}ay*) *m* miller
meurtrier (murr-tree-*ay*) *m*, **-ière** *f* murderer
mexicain (mehk-see-*kang*) *adj* Mexican
Mexique (mehk-*seek*) *m* Mexico
mi-bas (mee-*bah*) *m* knee-length sock
miche (meesh) *f* loaf
microbe (mee-*krob*) *m* germ
microphone (mee-kro-*fon*) *m* microphone
microsillon (mee-kro-see-*^{y}awng*) *m* long-playing record
midi (mee-*dee*) *m* midday, noon
miel (m^{y}ehl) *m* honey
mien: le ~ (ler m^{y}ang) mine
miette (m^{y}eht) *f* crumb
mieux (m^{y}ur) *adv* better
mignon (mee-*ñawng*) *adj* dainty, nice, sweet; **péché ~** little weakness
migraine (mee-*grehn*) *f* migraine
milieu (mee-*l^{y}ur*) *m* middle, midst; milieu; **au ~ de** among, amid; **du ~** middle
militaire (mee-lee-*tair*) *adj* military
mille (meel) *num* thousand; *m* mile
million (mee-*l^{y}awng*) *m* million
millionnaire (mee-l^{y}o-*nair*) *m/f* millionaire
mince (mangss) *adj* slim, thin
mine[1] (meen) *f* pit, mine; **~ d'or** goldmine
mine[2] (meen) *f* look
minerai (meen-*ray*) *m* ore
minéral (mee-nay-*rahl*) *m* mineral
minet (mee-*nay*) *m* pussy-cat
mineur (mee-*nurr*) *m* miner; minor; *adj* minor; under age
miniature (mee-n^{y}ah-*tewr*) *f* miniature
mini-jupe (mee-nee-*zhewp*) *f* miniskirt
minimum (mee-nee-*mom*) *m* minimum
ministère (mee-nee-*stair*) *m* ministry
ministre (mee-*neestr*) *m* minister; **premier ~** Prime Minister
minorité (mee-no-ree-*tay*) *f* minority
minuit (mee-*nwee*) midnight
minuscule (mee-new-*skewl*) *adj* tiny, minute
minute (mee-*newt*) *f* minute
minutieux (mee-new-*s^{y}ur*) *adj* thorough
miracle (mee-*raakl*) *m* miracle, wonder
miraculeux (mee-rah-kew-*lur*) *adj* miraculous
miroir (mee-*rwaar*) *m* looking-glass, mirror
misérable (mee-zay-*rahbl*) *adj* miserable
misère (mee-*zair*) *f* misery
miséricorde (mee-zay-ree-*kord*) *f* mercy

miséricordieux (mee-zay-ree-kor-*d^{y}ur*) *adj* merciful
mite (meet) *f* moth
mi-temps (mee-*tahng*) *f* half time
mixeur (meek-*surr*) *m* mixer
mobile (mo-*beel*) *adj* mobile; movable
mode[1] (mod) *f* fashion; **à la ~** fashionable
mode[2] (mod) *m* fashion, manner; **~ d'emploi** directions for use
modèle (mo-*dehl*) *m* model
modeler (mo-*dlay*) *v* model
modéré (mo-day-*ray*) *adj* moderate
moderne (mo-*dehrn*) *adj* modern
modeste (mo-*dehst*) *adj* modest
modestie (mo-deh-*stee*) *f* modesty
modification (mo-dee-fee-kah-*s^{y}awng*) *f* change, alteration
modifier (mo-dee-*f^{y}ay*) *v* change, modify, alter
moelle (mwahl) *f* marrow
moelleux (mwah-*lur*) *adj* mellow
mœurs (murrs) *fpl* morals
mohair (mo-*air*) *m* mohair
moi (mwah) *pron* me; **moi-même** *pron* myself
moindre (mwangdr) *adj* least; inferior
moine (mwahn) *m* monk
moineau (mwah-*noa*) *m* sparrow
moins (mwang) *adv* less; *prep* minus; **à ~ que** unless; **au ~** at least
mois (mwah) *m* month
moisi (mwah-*zee*) *adj* mouldy
moisissure (mwah-zee-*sewr*) *f* mildew
moisson (mwah-*sawng*) *f* harvest
moite (mwaht) *adj* moist; damp
moitié (mwah-*t^{y}ay*) *f* half; **à ~** half
molaire (mo-*lair*) *f* molar
mollet (mo-*lay*) *m* calf
moment (mo-*mahng*) *m* moment; while
momentané (mo-mahng-tah-*nay*) *adj* momentary
mon (mawng) *adj* (f ma, pl mes) my
monarchie (mo-nahr-*shee*) *f* monarchy
monarque (mo-*nahrk*) *m* monarch, ruler
monastère (mo-nah-*stair*) *m* monastery
monde (mawngd) *m* world; **tout le ~** everyone
mondial (mawng-*d^{y}ahl*) *adj* worldwide; global
monétaire (mo-nay-*tair*) *adj* monetary
monnaie (mo-*nay*) *f* currency; **~ étrangère** foreign currency; **petite ~** petty cash, change; **pièce de ~** coin
monopole (mo-no-*pol*) *m* monopoly
monotone (mo-no-*ton*) *adj* monotonous
monsieur (mer-*s^{y}ur*) *m* (pl messieurs) gentleman; mister; sir
mont (mawng) *m* mount
montagne (mawng-*tahñ*) *f* mountain
montagneux (mawng-tah-*ñur*) *adj* mountainous
montant (mawng-*tahng*) *m* amount
montée (mawng-*tay*) *f* rise; ascent
monter (mawng-*tay*) *v* *rise; ascend; *get on; assemble; mount; **se ~ à** amount to
monteur (mawng-*turr*) *m* mechanic
monticule (mawng-tee-*kewl*) *m* hillock
montre (mawngtr) *f* watch; **~ à affichage numérique** digital watch
montrer (mawng-*tray*) *v* *show; display; **~ du doigt** point
monture (mawng-*tewr*) *f* frame
monument (mo-new-*mahng*) *m* monument
moquer (mo-*kay*): **se ~ de** mock
moquerie (mo-*kree*) *f* mockery
moral (mo-*rahl*) *adj* moral; *m* spirits
morale (mo-*rahl*) *f* moral
moralité (mo-rah-lee-*tay*) *f* morality

morceau (mor-*soa*) *m* piece, part; morsel, fragment, scrap, bit, lump; ~ **de sucre** lump of sugar
mordre (mordr) *v* *bite
morphine (mor-*feen*) *f* morphine, morphia
morsure (mor-*sewr*) *f* bite
mort (mawr) *f* death; *adj* dead
mortel (mor-*tehl*) *adj* fatal; mortal
morue (mo-*rew*) *f* cod
mosaïque (mo-zah-*eek*) *f* mosaic
mosquée (mo-*skay*) *f* mosque
mot (moa) *m* word; ~ **de passe** password
motel (mo-*tehl*) *m* motel
moteur (mo-*tūrr*) *m* motor, engine
motif (mo-*teef*) *m* cause, motive; pattern
moto (mo-*toa*) *f* motor bike
motocyclette (mo-to-see-*kleht*) *f* motorcycle
mou (moo) *adj* (f molle) soft
moucher (moo-*shay*) wipe (*s.o.'s*) nose; snuff; snub
mouche (moosh) *f* fly
mouchoir (moo-*shwaar*) *m* handkerchief; ~ **de papier** tissue
***moudre** (moodr) *v* *grind
mouette (mweht) *f* gull; seagull
moufles (moofl) *fpl* mittens *pl*
mouiller (moo-*ʸay*) *v* wet; **mouillé** wet, moist
moule (mool) *f* mussel
moulin (moo-*lang*) *m* mill; ~ **à paroles** chatterbox; ~ **à vent** windmill
***mourir** (moo-*reer*) *v* die
mousse (mooss) *f* foam; moss
mousser (moo-*say*) *v* foam
mousseux (moo-*sur*) *adj* sparkling
moustache (moo-*stahsh*) *f* moustache
moustiquaire (moo-stee-*kair*) *f* mosquito net
moustique (moo-*steek*) *m* mosquito
moutarde (moo-*tahrd*) *f* mustard
mouton (moo-*tawng*) *m* sheep; mutton
mouvement (moov-*mahng*) *m* motion, movement
***mouvoir** (moo-*vwaar*): **se ~** move
moyen (mwah-*ʸang*) *m* means; *adj* medium, average
moyen-âge (mwah-ʸeh-*naazh*) *m* Middle Ages
moyenne (mwah-*ʸehn*) *f* mean, average; **en ~** on the average
muet (mway) *adj* dumb, mute
mugir (mew-*zheer*) *v* roar
muguet (mew-*gay*) *m* lily of the valley; thrush
mule (mewl) *f* mule
mulet (mew-*lay*) *m* mule
multiplication (mewl-tee-plee-kah-*sʸawng*) *f* multiplication
multiplier (mewl-tee-plee-*ay*) *v* multiply
municipal (mew-nee-see-*pahl*) *adj* municipal
municipalité (mew-nee-see-pah-lee-*tay*) *f* municipality
munir (mew-*neer*): **~ de** provide with
mur (mewr) *m* wall
mûr (mewr) *adj* mature, ripe
mûre (mewr) *f* blackberry
muscade (mew-*skahd*) *f* nutmeg
muscle (mewskl) *m* muscle
musclé (mew-*sklay*) *adj* muscular
museau (mew-*zoa*) *m* snout
musée (mew-*zay*) *m* museum
musical (mew-zee-*kahl*) *adj* musical
musicien (mew-zee-*sʸang*) *m*, **-ne** *f* musician
musique (mew-*zeek*) *f* music; **~ pop** pop music
musulman (mew-zewl-*mahng*) *adj* Moslem; *m*, **-e** *f* Moslem, Muslim
mutinerie (mew-teen-*ree*) *f* mutiny
mutuel (mew-*twehl*) *adj* mutual
myope (mʸop) *adj* short-sighted

mystère (mee-*stair*) *m* mystery
mystérieux (mee-stay-*r^{y}ur*) *adj* mysterious
mythe (meet) *m* myth

N

nacre (nahkr) *f* mother of pearl
nager (nah-*zhay*) *v* *swim
nageur (nah-*zhurr*) *m* swimmer
naïf (nah-*eef*) *adj* naïve
nain (nang) *m* dwarf
naissance (nay-*sahngss*) *f* birth
***naître** (naitr) *v* *be born
nappe (nahp) *f* tablecloth
narcose (nahr-*koaz*) *f* narcosis
narcotique (nahr-ko-*teek*) *m* narcotic
narine (nah-*reen*) *f* nostril
natation (nah-tah-*s^{y}awng*) *f* swimming
nation (nah-*s^{y}awng*) *f* nation
national (nah-s^{y}o-*nahl*) *adj* national
nationaliser (nah-s^{y}o-nah-lee-*zay*) *v* nationalize
nationalité (nah-s^{y}o-nah-lee-*tay*) *f* nationality
nature (nah-*tewr*) *f* nature; essence
naturel (nah-tew-*rehl*) *adj* natural
naturellement (nah-tew-rehl-*mahng*) *adv* naturally
naufrage (noa-*fraazh*) *m* shipwreck
nausée (noa-*zay*) *f* nausea
naval (nah-*vahl*) *adj* (pl ~s) naval
navette (nah-*veht*) *f* shuttle (service); **~ spatiale** space shuttle; **faire la ~** commute
navigable (nah-vee-*gahbl*) *adj* navigable
navigation (nah-vee-gah-*s^{y}awng*) *f* navigation
naviguer (nah-vee-*gay*) *v* navigate; sail
navire (nah-*veer*) *m* ship; **~ de guerre** man-of-war
né (nay) *adj* born
néanmoins (nay-ahng-*mwang*) *adv* nevertheless
nébuleux (nay-bew-*lur*) *adj* hazy
nécessaire (nay-say-*sair*) *adj* necessary; **~ de toilette** toilet case
nécessité (nay-say-see-*tay*) *f* need, necessity
nécessiter (nay-say-see-*tay*) *v* require
néerlandais (nay-ehr-lahng-*day*) *adj* Dutch
néfaste (nay-*fahst*) *adj* fatal
négatif (nay-gah-*teef*) *m* negative; *adj* negative
négligé (nay-glee-*zhay*) *m* negligee
négligence (nay-glee-*zhahngss*) *f* neglect
négligent (nay-glee-*zhahng*) *adj* careless, neglectful
négliger (nay-glee-*zhay*) *v* neglect
négociant (nay-go-*s^{y}ahng*) *m* dealer; **~ en vins** wine merchant
négociation (nay-go-s^{y}ah-*s^{y}awng*) *f* negotiation
négocier (nay-go-*s^{y}ay*) *v* negotiate
neige (naizh) *f* snow
neiger (nay-*zhay*) *v* snow
neigeux (neh-*zhur*) *adj* snowy
néon (nay-*awng*) *m* neon
nerf (nair) *m* nerve
nerveux (nehr-*vur*) *adj* nervous
n'est-ce pas? (nehss-pah) *adv* isn't it
net (neht) *adj* distinct; net
nettoyage (neh-twah-*^{y}aazh*) *m* cleaning
nettoyer (neh-twah-*^{y}ay*) *v* clean; **~ à sec** dry-clean

neuf[1] (nurf) *adj* (f neuve) new
neuf[2] (nurf) *num* nine
neutre (nurtr) *adj* neuter; neutral
neuvième (nur-*v^{y}ehm*) *num* ninth
neveu (ner-*vur*) *m* nephew
névralgie (nay-vrahl-*zhee*) *f* neuralgia
névrose (nay-*vroaz*) *f* neurosis
nez (nay) *m* nose; **saignement de ~** nosebleed
ni ... ni (nee) neither ... nor
nickel (nee-*kehl*) *m* nickel
nicotine (nee-ko-*teen*) *f* nicotine
nid (nee) *m* nest
nièce (n^{y}ehss) *f* niece
nier (nee-*ay*) *v* deny
Nigeria (nee-zhay-*r^{y}ah*) *m* Nigeria
nigérien (nee-zhay-*r^{y}ang*) *adj* Nigerian
niveau (nee-*voa*) *m* level; **~ de vie** standard of living; **passage à ~** level crossing
niveler (nee-*vlay*) *v* level
noble (nobl) *adj* noble
noblesse (no-*blehss*) *f* nobility
nocturne (nok-*tewrn*) *adj* nightly
Noël (no-*ehl*) Christmas, Xmas
nœud (nur) *m* knot; **~ papillon** bow tie
Noir (nwaar) *m* black
noir (nwaar) *adj* black
noisette (nwah-*zeht*) *f* hazelnut
noix (nwah) *f* nut; walnut; **~ de coco** coconut
nom (nawng) *m* name; noun; denomination; **au ~ de** in the name of, on behalf of; **~ de famille** family name, surname; **~ de jeune fille** maiden name
nombre (nawngbr) *m* number; quantity; numeral
nombreux (nawng-*brur*) *adj* numerous
nombril (nawng-*bree*) *m* navel
nomination (no-mee-nah-*s^{y}awng*) *f* nomination, appointment
nommer (no-*may*) *v* name; nominate, appoint
non (nawng) no
non-fumeur (nawng-few-murr)* *m* nonsmoker
nord (nawr) *m* north
nord-est (no-*rehst*) *m* north-east
nord-ouest (no-*rwehst*) *m* north-west
normal (nor-*mahl*) *adj* normal, regular
norme (norm) *f* standard
Norvège (nor-*vaizh*) *f* Norway
norvégien (nor-vay-*zh^{y}ang*) *adj* Norwegian
notaire (no-*tair*) *m* notary
notamment (no-tah-*mahng*) *adv* namely
note (not) *f* note; mark; bill; check *Am*
noter (no-*tay*) *v* note, *write down; notice
notifier (no-tee-*f^{y}ay*) *v* notify
notion (noa-*s^{y}awng*) *f* notion; idea
notoire (no-*twaar*) *adj* notorious
notre (notr) *adj* our
nouer (noo-*ay*) *v* tie, knot
nougat (noo-*gah*) *m* nougat
nourrir (noo-*reer*) *v* *feed; **nourrissant** nourishing
nourrisson (noo-ree-*sawng*) *m* infant
nourriture (noo-ree-*tewr*) *f* food
nous (noo) *pron* we; ourselves, us; **nous-mêmes** *pron* ourselves
nouveau (noo-*voa*) *adj* (nouvel; f nouvelle) new; **de ~** again; **Nouvel An** New Year
nouvelle (noo-*vehl*) *f* notice; **nouvelles** news
Nouvelle-Zélande (noo-vehl-zay-*lahngd*) *f* New Zealand
novembre (no-*vahngbr*) November
noyau (nwah-*^{y}oa*) *m* stone; nucleus
noyer (nwah-*^{y}ay*) *v* drown; **se ~** *be drowned
nu (new) *adj* naked, nude; bare; *m* nude

nuage (nwaazh) *m* cloud; **nuages** clouds
nuageux (nwah-*zhur*) *adj* cloudy, overcast
nuance (nwahn͞gss) *f* nuance; shade
nucléaire (new-klay-*air*) *adj* atomic, nuclear
***nuire** (nweer) *v* harm
nuisible (nwee-*zeebl*) *adj* harmful
nuit (nwee) *f* night; **boîte de ~** cabaret; **cette ~** tonight; **de ~** by night, overnight; **tarif de ~** night rate
nul (newl) *adj* (f nulle) invalid, void
numéro (new-may-*roa*) *m* number; act; **~ d'immatriculation** registration number; license number *Am*
nuque (newk) *f* nape of the neck
nutritif (new-tree-*teef*) *adj* nutritious
nylon (nee-*lawn͞g*) *m* nylon

O

oasis (oa-ah-*zeess*) *f* oasis
obéir (o-bay-*eer*) *v* obey
obéissance (o-bay-ee-*sahn͞gss*) *f* obedience
obéissant (o-bay-ee-*sahn͞g*) *adj* obedient
obèse (o-*baiz*) *adj* stout, corpulent
obésité (o-bay-zee-*tay*) *f* fatness
objecter (ob-zhehk-*tay*) *v* object
objectif (ob-zhehk-*teef*) *m* target, objective, object, goal; *adj* objective
objection (ob-zhehk-*s^{y}awn͞g*) *f* objection; ***faire ~ à** object to
objet (ob-*zhay*) *m* object; **objets de valeur** valuables *pl*; **objets trouvés** lost and found
obligation (o-blee-gah-*s^{y}awn͞g*) *f* bond
obligatoire (o-blee-gah-*twaar*) *adj* compulsory, obligatory
obligeant (o-blee-*zhahn͞g*) *adj* obliging
obliger (o-blee-*zhay*) *v* oblige; force
oblique (o-*bleek*) *adj* slanting
oblong (o-*blawn͞g*) *adj* (f oblongue) oblong
obscène (o-*psehn*) *adj* obscene
obscur (op-*skewr*) *adj* obscure; dim, dark
obscurité (op-skew-ree-*tay*) *f* dark
observation (o-psehr-vah-*s^{y}awn͞g*) *f* observation
observatoire (o-psehr-vah-*twaar*) *m* observatory
observer (o-psehr-*vay*) *v* watch, observe; notice, note
obsession (o-pseh-*s^{y}awn͞g*) *f* obsession
obstacle (op-*stahkl*) *m* obstacle
obstiné (op-stee-*nay*) *adj* stubborn, obstinate; dogged
obstruer (op-strew-*ay*) *v* block
***obtenir** (op-ter-*neer*) *v* *get; obtain
occasion (o-kah-*z^{y}awn͞g*) *f* chance, opportunity; occasion; **d'occasion** second-hand
occident (ok-see-*dahn͞g*) *m* west
occidental (ok-see-dahn͞g-*tahl*) *adj* western, westerly
occupant (o-kew-*pahn͞g*) *m* occupant
occupation (o-kew-pah-*s^{y}awn͞g*) *f* occupation; business
occuper (o-kew-*pay*) *v* occupy; *take up; **occupé** busy, engaged, occupied; **s'occuper de** attend to, look after; *take care of, see to, *deal with
océan (o-say-*ahn͞g*) *m* ocean; **Océan**

Atlantique Atlantic; **Océan Pacifique** Pacific Ocean
octobre (ok-*tobr*) October
oculiste (o-kew-*leest*) *m/f* oculist
odeur (o-*dūrr*) *f* smell, odo(u)r
œil (ur^{ee}) *m* (pl yeux) eye; **coup d'œil** look; glance; glimpse
œuf (urf) *m* egg; **œufs de poisson** roe
œuvre (ūrvr) *m* work; **~ d'art** work of art
offense (o-*fahn̅g̅ss*) *f* offence, offense *Am*
offenser (o-fahn̅g̅-*say*) *v* injure, *hurt, wound, offend; **s'offenser de** resent
offensif (o-fahn̅g̅-*seef*) *adj* offensive
offensive (o-fahn̅g̅-*seev*) *f* offensive
office (o-*fees*)* *m* office; agency; service
officiel (o-fee-*s^{y}ehl*) *adj* official
officier (o-fee-*s^{y}ay*) *m* officer
officieux (o-fee-*s^{y}ur*) *adj* unofficial
offre (ofr) *f* offer; supply
***offrir** (o-*freer*) *v* offer
oie (wah) *f* goose
oignon (o-*ñawn̅g̅*) *m* onion; bulb
oiseau (wah-*zoa*) *m* bird; **~ de mer** seabird
oisif (wah-*zeef*) *adj* idle
olive (o-*leev*) *f* olive
ombragé (awn̅g̅-brah-*zhay*) *adj* shady
ombre (awn̅g̅br) *f* shadow, shade; **~ à paupières** eye shadow
omelette (om-*leht*) *f* omelette
***omettre** (o-*mehtr*) *v* *leave out, omit; fail
omnibus (om-nee-*bewss*) *m* slow train
omnipotent (om-nee-po-*tahn̅g̅*) *adj* omnipotent
on (awn̅g̅) *pron* one
oncle (awn̅g̅kl) *m* uncle
ondulation (awn̅g̅-dew-lah-*s^{y}awn̅g̅*) *f* wave
ondulé (awn̅g̅-dew-*lay*) *adj* wavy, undulating
ongle (awn̅g̅gl) *m* nail
onguent (awn̅g̅-*gahn̅g̅*) *m* ointment, salve
onze (awn̅g̅z) *num* eleven
onzième (awn̅g̅-*z^{y}ehm*) *num* eleventh
opéra (o-pay-*rah*) *m* opera; opera house
opération (o-pay-rah-*s^{y}awn̅g̅*) *f* operation, surgery
opérer (o-pay-*ray*) *v* operate
opérette (o-pay-*reht*) *f* operetta
opiniâtre (o-pee-*n^{y}aatr*) *adj* obstinate
opinion (o-pee-*n^{y}awn̅g̅*) *f* view, opinion
opposé (o-poa-*zay*) *adj* contrary, opposite
opposer (o-poa-*zay*): **s'~** oppose
opposition (o-poa-zee-*s^{y}awn̅g̅*) *f* opposition
oppresser (o-pray-*say*) *v* oppress
opprimer (o-pree-*may*) *v* oppress
opticien (op-tee-*s^{y}an̅g̅*) *m*, **-ne** *f* optician
optimisme (op-tee-*meesm*) *m* optimism
optimiste (op-tee-*meest*) *m/f* optimist; *adj* optimistic
or (awr) *m* gold; **en ~** golden; **~ en feuille** gold leaf
orage (o-*raazh*) *m* thunderstorm
orageux (o-rah-*zhur*) *adj* thundery, stormy
oral (o-*rahl*) *adj* oral
orange (o-*rahn̅g̅zh*) *f* orange; *adj* orange
orchestre (or-*kehstr*) *m* orchestra; band; **fauteuil d'orchestre** seat in the stalls
ordinaire (or-dee-*nair*) *adj* plain, simple, usual, regular, customary; common
ordinateur (or-dee-nah-*tūrr*) *n* computer; **~ portable** lap-top computer

ordonnance (or-do-*nahn̄gss*)* f arrangement, layout, organisation; prescription
ordonner (or-do-*nay*) *v* arrange; order; **ordonné** *adj* tidy
ordre (ordr) *m* order; method; command; **~ du jour** agenda
ordures (or-*dewr*) *fpl* garbage
oreille (o-*ray*) *f* ear
oreiller (o-ray-*yay*) *m* pillow; **taie d'oreiller** pillowcase
oreillons (o-reh-*yawn̄g*) *mpl* mumps
orfèvre (or-*faivr*) *m* goldsmith; silversmith
organe (or-*gahn*) *m* organ
organique (or-gah-*neek*) *adj* organic
organisation (or-gah-nee-zah-*syawn̄g*) *f* organization
organiser (or-gah-nee-*zay*) *v* organize
orgue (org) *m* (pl f) organ; **~ de Barbarie** street-organ
orgueil (or-*guree*) *m* pride
orgueilleux (or-gur-*yur*) *adj* proud
Orient (o-*ryahn̄g*) *m* Orient
oriental (o-ryahn̄g-*tahl*) *adj* oriental; eastern, easterly
orienter (o-ryahn̄g-*tay*): **s'~** orientate
originairement (o-ree-zhee-nehr-*mahn̄g*) *adv* originally
original (o-ree-zhee-*nahl*) *adj* original
origine (o-ree-*zheen*) *f* origin
ornement (or-ner-*mahn̄g*) *m* ornament
ornemental (or-ner-mahn̄g-*tahl*) *adj* ornamental
orphelin (or-fer-*lan̄g*) *m*, **-e** *f* orphan
orteil (or-*tay*) *m* toe
orthodoxe (or-to-*doks*) *adj* orthodox
orthographe (or-to-*grahf*) *f* spelling
os (oss) *m* (pl ~) bone
oser (oa-*zay*) *v* dare
otage (o-*taazh*) *m* hostage
ôter (oa-*tay*) *v* *take out; wipe
ou (oo) *conj* or; **~ ... ou** either ... or
où (oo) *adv* where; *pron* where; **n'importe ~** anywhere
ouate (waht) *f* cotton wool
oublier (oo-blee-*ay*) *v* *forget
oublieux (oo-blee-*ur*) *adj* forgetful
ouest (wehst) *m* west
oui (wee) yes
ouïe (oo-*ee*) *f* hearing
ouragan (oo-rah-*gahn̄g*) *m* hurricane
ourlet (oor-*lay*) *m* hem
ours (oors) *m* bear
oursin (oor-*san̄g*) *m* sea urchin
outil (oo-*tee*) *m* tool, utensil, implement
outrage (oo-*traazh*) *m* outrage; offence, offense *Am*
outrager (oo-trah-*zhay*) *v* offend
outre (ootr) *prep* beyond, besides; **d'outre-mer** overseas; **en ~** furthermore, besides
ouvert (oo-*vair*) *adj* open
ouverture (oo-vehr-*tewr*) *f* opening; overture
ouvrage (oo-*vraazh*) *m* work
ouvre-boîte (oo-vrer-*bwaht*) *m* tin opener, can opener *Am*
ouvre-bouteille (oo-vrer-boo-*tay*) *m* bottle opener
ouvreur (oo-*vrūrr*) *m* usher
ouvreuse (oo-*vrūrz*) *f* usherette
ouvrier (oo-vree-*ay*) *m*, **-ière** *f* worker
***ouvrir** (oo-*vreer*) *v* open; unlock; turn on
ovale (o-*vahl*) *adj* oval
oxygène (ok-see-*zhehn*) *m* oxygen

P

pacifisme (pah-see-*feesm*) *m* pacifism
pacifiste (pah-see-*feest*) *adj* pacifist; *m/f* pacifist
pagaie (pah-*gay*) *f* paddle
pagaille (pah-*gigh*) *f* muddle
page (paazh) *f* page; *m* pageboy
paie (pay) *f* salary
paiement (pay-*mahn̅g̅*) *m* payment; **~ échelonné** payment by insta(l)lments
païen (pah-^{y}*an̅g̅*) *m* pagan, heathen; *adj* pagan, heathen
paille (pigh) *f* straw
pain (pan̅g̅) *m* bread; **~ complet** wholemeal bread; **petit ~** roll
pair (pair) *adj* even
paire (pair) *f* pair
paisible (pay-*zeebl*) *adj* peaceful, quiet
paix (pay) *f* peace
Pakistan (pah-kee-*stahn̅g̅*) *m* Pakistan
pakistanais (pah-kee-stah-*nay*) *adj* Pakistani
palais (pah-*lay*) *m* palace; palate
pâle (paal) *adj* pale
palmier (pahl-*m^{y}ay*) *m* palm (tree)
palper (pahl-*pay*) *v* *feel
palpitation (pahl-pee-tah-*s^{y}awn̅g̅*) *f* palpitation
pamplemousse (pahn̅g̅-pler-*mooss*) *m* grapefruit
panier (pah-*n^{y}ay*) *m* basket
panique (pah-neek) *f* panic; scare
panne (pahn) *f* breakdown; **tomber en ~** *break down
panneau (pah-*noa*) *m* panel
pansement (pahn̅g̅-*smahn̅g̅*) *m* bandage
panser (pahn̅g̅-*say*) *v* dress
pantalon (pahn̅g̅-tah-*lawn̅g̅*) *m* trousers *pl*, slacks *pl*; pants *plAm*; **ensemble-pantalon** pant suit; **~ de ski** ski pants
pantoufle (pahn̅g̅-*toofl*) *f* slipper
paon (pahn̅g̅) *m* peacock
papa (pah-*pah*) *m* daddy
pape (pahp) *m* pope
papeterie (pah-peh-*tree*) *f* stationer's; stationery
papier (pah-*p^{y}ay*) *m* paper; **en ~** paper; **~ de brouillon** rough paper; **~ à lettres** notepaper, writing paper; **~ à machine** typing paper; **~ buvard** blotting paper; **~ carbone** carbon paper; **~ d'emballage** wrapping paper; **~ d'étain** tinfoil; **~ de verre** sandpaper; **~ hygiénique** toilet paper; **~ peint** wallpaper
papillon (pah-pee-^{y}*awn̅g̅*) *m* butterfly
paquebot (pahk-*boa*) *m* liner
Pâques (paak) Easter
paquet (pah-*kay*) *m* parcel, packet; bundle
par (pahr) *prep* by; for
parade (pah-*rahd*) *f* parade
paragraphe (pah-rah-*grahf*) *m* paragraph
***paraître** (pah-*raitr*) *v* seem, appear
parallèle (pah-rah-*lehl*) *m* parallel; *adj* parallel
paralyser (pah-rah-lee-*zay*) *v* paralyze; **paralysé** paralyzed
parapluie (pah-rah-*plwee*) *m* umbrella
parasol (pah-rah-*sol*) *m* sunshade
parc (pahrk) *m* park; **~ de stationnement** car park; **~ national** national park
parce que (pahr-sker) as, because
parcmètre (pahrk-mehtr) *m* parking meter
***parcourir** (pahr-koo-*reer*) *v* *go through; cover
parcours (pahr-*ko̅o̅r*) *m* distance; route; course

par-dessus (pahr-der-*sew*) *prep* over

pardessus (pahr-der-*sew*) *m* coat, overcoat

pardon (pahr-*dawng*) *m* pardon; **pardon!** sorry!

pardonner (pahr-do-*nay*) *v* *forgive

pare-brise (pahr-*breez*) *m* windscreen, windshield *Am*

pare-choc (pahr-*shok*) *m* bumper

pareil (pah-*ray*) *adj* alike, like; **sans ~** unsurpassed

parent (pah-*rahng*) *m* relative, relation; **parents** parents *pl*; **parents nourriciers** foster parents *pl*

paresseux (pah-reh-*sur*) *adj* lazy

parfait (pahr-*fay*) *adj* perfect; faultless

parfois (pahr-*fwah*) *adv* sometimes

parfum (pahr-*furng*) *m* scent; perfume

parfumerie (pahr-fewm-*ree*) *f* perfumery

pari (pah-*ree*) *m* bet

parier (pah-*r^{y}ay*) *v* *bet

parking (pahr-*keeng*) *m* parking lot *Am*

parlement (pahr-ler-*mahng*) *m* parliament

parlementaire (pahr-ler-mahng-*tair*) *adj* parliamentary

parler (pahr-*lay*) *v* talk, *speak

parmi (pahr-*mee*) *prep* among, amid

paroisse (pah-*rwahss*) *f* parish

parole (pah-*rol*) *f* speech

parrain (pah-*rang*) *m* godfather

part (paar) *f* part, share; **à ~** separately, apart; aside; **nulle ~** nowhere; **quelque ~** somewhere

partager (pahr-tah-*zhay*) *v* share

partenaire (pahr-ter-*nair*) *m/f* associate, partner

parti (pahr-*tee*) *m* party; side

partial (pahr-*s^{y}ahl*) *adj* partial

participant (pahr-tee-see-*pahng*) *m*, **-e** *f* participant

participer (pahr-tee-see-*pay*) *v* participate

particularité (pahr-tee-kew-lah-ree-*tay*) *f* particularity, characteristic

particulier (pahr-tee-kew-*l^{y}ay*) *adj* particular, special; individual, private; peculiar; *m* private individual; **en ~** in particular

particulièrement (pahr-tee-kew-l^{y}ehr-*mahng*) *adv* specially

partie (pahr-*tee*) *f* part; **en ~** partly

partiel (pahr-*s^{y}ehl*) *adj* partial

partiellement (pahr-s^{y}ehl-*mahng*) *adv* partly

***partir** (pahr-*teer*) *v* *leave, *go away; *set out, depart, pull out; **à partir de** as from, from; **parti** gone

partisan (pahr-tee-*zahng*) *m* advocate

partout (pahr-*too*) *adv* throughout, everywhere; **~ où** wherever

***parvenir à** (pahr-ver-*neer*) achieve

pas (pah) *m* step; pace, move; **faux ~** slip; **ne … ~** not

passablement (pah-sah-bler-*mahng*) *adv* pretty, rather, fairly

passage (pah-*saazh*) *m* passage; crossing; aisle; **~ à niveau** crossing; **~ clouté** pedestrian crossing; **~ pour piétons** crosswalk *Am*

passager (pah-sah-*zhay*) *m*, **-ère** *f* passenger

passant (pah-*sahng*) *m* passer-by

passé (pah-*say*) *m* past; *adj* past; *prep* over

passeport (pah-*spawr*) *m* passport

passer (pah-*say*) *v* pass; *give; **en passant** casually; **~ à côté** pass by; **~ en contrebande** smuggle; **se ~** occur; **se ~ de** spare

passerelle (pah-*srehl*) *f* gangway

passe-temps (pah-*stahng*) *m* hobby

passif (pah-*seef*) *adj* passive

passion (pah-*s^{y}awng*) *f* passion

passionnant (pah-s^{y}o-*nahng*) *adj* exciting

passionné (pah-s^yo-*nay*) *adj* passionate; keen
passoire (pah-*swaar*) *f* sieve; strainer
pastèque (pah-*stehk*) *f* watermelon
pasteur (pah-*sturr*) *m* clergyman; parson, minister, rector
pastille (pah-*steey*) *f* pastille, lozenge
patauger (pah-toa-*zhay*) *v* wade
pâte (paat) *f* paste; dough, batter; pie; ~ **dentifrice** toothpaste
patère (pah-*tair*) *f* peg
paternel (pah-tehr-*nehl*) *adj* fatherly
patience (pah-*s^yahngss*) *f* patience
patient (pah-*s^yahng*) *adj* patient; *m*, **-e** *f* patient
patin (pah-*tang*) *m* skate
patinage (pah-tee-*naazh*) *m* skating; ~ **à roulettes** roller-skating
patiner (pah-tee-*nay*) *v* skate
patinette (pah-tee-*neht*) *f* scooter
patinoire (pah-tee-*nwaar*) *f* skating rink
pâtisserie (pah-tee-*sree*) *f* cake, pastry; pastry shop
patrie (pah-*tree*) *f* native country
patriote (pah-tree-*ot*) *m* patriot
patron (pah-*trawng*) *m* master, boss
patronne (pah-*tron*) *f* mistress
patrouille (pah-*troo^{ee}*) *f* patrol
patrouiller (pah-troo-*^{y}ay*) *v* patrol
patte (paht) *f* paw
pâture (pah-*tewr*) *f* pasture
paume (poam) *f* palm
paupière (poa-*p^yair*) *f* eyelid
pause (poaz) *f* pause; break
pauvre (poavr) *adj* poor
pauvreté (poa-vrer-*tay*) *f* poverty
paver (pah-*vay*) *v* pave
pavillon (pah-vee-*^{y}awng*) *m* pavilion; ~ **de chasse** lodge
pavot (pah-*voa*) *m* poppy
payable (pay-*^{y}ahbl*) *adj* due
paye (pay) *f* pay
payer (pay-*^{y}ay*) *v* *pay; ~ **comptant** *pay cash
pays (pay-*ee*) *m* country, land; ~ **boisé** woodland; ~ **natal** native country
paysage (pay-ee-*zaazh*) *m* landscape, scenery
paysan (pay-ee-*zahng*) *m* peasant
Pays-Bas (pay-ee-*bah*) *mpl* the Netherlands
péage (pay-*aazh*) *m* toll
peau (poa) *f* skin; hide; ~ **de porc** pigskin
péché (pay-*shay*) *m* sin
pêche[1] (pehsh) *f* peach
pêche[2] (pehsh) *f* fishing industry; **attirail de** ~ fishing tackle, fishing gear
pêcher (pay-*shay*) *v* fish; ~ **à la ligne** angle
pêcheur (peh-*shurr*) *m* fisherman
pédale (pay-*dahl*) *f* pedal
pédiatre (pay-*dyaatr*) *m* p(a)ediatrist
peigne (pehñ) *m* comb
peigner (pay-*ñay*) *v* comb
peignoir (peh-*ñwaar*) *m* bathrobe
***peindre** (pangdr) *v* paint
peine (pehn) *f* trouble, pains, difficulty; penalty; **à** ~ hardly; just, barely, scarcely; ***avoir de la** ~ grieve; ~ **de mort** death penalty
peiner (pay-*nay*) *v* labo(u)r
peintre (pangtr) *m* painter
peinture (pang-*tewr*) *f* paint; picture, painting; ~ **à l'huile** oil painting
peler (per-*lay*) *v* peel
pèlerin (pehl-*rang*) *m* pilgrim
pèlerinage (pehl-ree-*naazh*) *m* pilgrimage
pélican (pay-lee-*kahng*) *m* pelican
pelle (pehl) *f* spade, shovel
pellicule (peh-lee-*kewl*) *f* film; **pellicules** dandruff
pelouse (per-*looz*) *f* lawn
pelure (per-*lewr*) *f* peel
penchant (pahng-*shahng*) *m*

inclination
pencher (pahng-*shay*) *v*: **se ~** *bend down
pendant (pahng-*dahng*) *prep* for, during; **~ que** while
pendentif (pahng-dahng-*teef*) *m* pendant
pendre (pahngdr) *v* *hang
pénétrer (pay-nay-*tray*) *v* penetrate
pénible (pay-*neebl*) *adj* laborious; painful
pénicilline (pay-nee-see-*leen*) *f* penicillin
péninsule (pay-nang-*sewl*) *f* peninsula
pensée (pahng-*say*) *f* thought; idea
penser (pahng-*say*) *v* *think; **~ à** *think of
pensif (pahng-*seef*) *adj* thoughtful
pension (pahng-*s^{y}awng*) *f* guesthouse, pension, boardinghouse; board; **~ complète** room and board, full board, bed and board, board and lodging
pensionnaire (pahng-s^{y}o-*nair*) *m/f* boarder
pente (pahngt) *f* incline; ramp; **en ~** sloping, slanting
Pentecôte (pahngt-*koat*) *f* Whitsun, Pentecost *Am*
pénurie (pay-new-*ree*) *f* scarcity
pépé (pay-*pay*) *m* grandad
pépin (pay-*pang*) *m* pip
pépinière (pay-pee-*n^{y}air*) *f* nursery
perceptible (pehr-sehp-*teebl*) *adj* noticeable, perceptible
perception (pehr-seh-*ps^{y}awng*) *f* perception
percer (pehr-*say*) *v* pierce
***percevoir** (pehr-ser-*vwaar*) *v* perceive; sense
perche (pehrsh) *f* perch, bass
percolateur (pehr-ko-lah-*turr*) *m* percolator
perdre (pehrdr) *v* *lose
perdrix (pehr-*dree*) *f* partridge
père (pair) *m* father
perfection (pehr-fehk-*s^{y}awng*) *f* perfection
performance (pehr-for-*mahngss*) *f* achievement; performance
péril (pay-*reel*) *m* peril
périlleux (pay-ree-*^{y}ur*) *adj* perilous
périmé (pay-ree-*may*) *adj* expired
période (pay-*r^{y}od*) *f* period; term
périodique (pay-r^{y}o-*deek*) *adj* periodical; *m* journal, periodical
périr (pay-*reer*) *v* perish
périssable (pay-ree-*sahbl*) *adj* perishable
perle (pehrl) *f* pearl; bead
permanent (pehr-mah-*nahng*) *adj* permanent
permanente (pehr-mah-*nahngt*) *f* permanent wave
***permettre** (pehr-*mehtr*) *v* permit, allow; enable; **se ~** afford
permis (pehr-*mee*) *m* permit; permission, licence; **~ de conduire** driver's license *Am*, driving licence; **~ de pêche** fishing licence; **~ de séjour** residence permit; **~ de travail** work permit; labor permit *Am*
permission (pehr-mee-*s^{y}awng*) *f* authorization, permission; leave
perpendiculaire (pehr-pahng-dee-kew-*lair*) *adj* perpendicular
perroquet (peh-ro-*kay*) *m* parrot
perruche (peh-*rewsh*) *f* parakeet
perruque (peh-*rewk*) *f* wig
persan (pehr-*sahng*) *adj* Persian
Perse (pehrs) *f* Persia
persévérer (pehr-say-vay-*ray*) *v* *keep up
persienne (pehr-*s^{y}ehn*) *f* blind; shutter
persil (pehr-*see*) *m* parsley
persister (pehr-see-*stay*) *v* insist
personnalité (pehr-so-nah-lee-*tay*) *f* personality

personne (pehr-*son*) *f* person; **ne ... personne** nobody, no one; **par ~** per person
personnel (pehr-so-*nehl*) *m* personnel, staff; *adj* personal, private
perspective (pehr-spehk-*teev*) *f* perspective, prospect
persuader (pehr-swah-*day*) *v* persuade
perte (pehrt) *f* loss
pertinent (pehr-tee-*nahng*) *adj* proper
peser (per-*zay*) *v* weigh
pessimisme (peh-see-*meesm*) *m* pessimism
pessimiste (peh-see-*meest*) *m/f* pessimist; *adj* pessimistic
pétale (pay-*tahl*) *m* petal
pétanque (pay-*tahngk*) *f* petanque
pétillement (pay-teey-*mahng*) *m* fizz
petit (per-*tee*) *adj* small, little; petty, short, minor
petite-fille (per-teet-*feey*) *f* granddaughter
petit-fils (per-tee-*feess*) *m* grandson
pétition (pay-tee-*s*^{y}*awng*) *f* petition
petits pois (per-tee-*pwah*)* *pl* peas
pétrole (pay-*trol*) *m* petroleum, oil; kerosene, paraffin; **gisement de ~** oil well
peu (pur) *adj* little; *m* bit; **à ~ près** approximately, about; almost; **~ de** few; **quelque ~** somewhat; **sous ~** soon, shortly; **un ~** some
peuple (purpl) *m* people; nation
peur (purr) *f* fear, fright; ***avoir ~** *be afraid
peut-être (pur-*taitr*) *adv* maybe, perhaps
phare (faar) *m* lighthouse; headlight, headlamp; **~ anti-brouillard** foglamp
pharmacie (fahr-mah-*see*) *f* pharmacy, chemist's; drugstore *Am*
pharmacien (fahr-mah-*s*^{y}*ang*) *m*, **-ne** *f* chemist, pharmacist *Am*
pharmacologie (fahr-mah-ko-lo-*zhee*) *f* pharmacology
phase (faaz) *f* phase, stage
philippin (fee-lee-*pang*) *adj* Philippine
Philippines (fee-lee-*peen*) *fpl* Philippines *pl*
philosophe (fee-lo-*zof*) *m* philosopher
philosophie (fee-lo-zo-*fee*) *f* philosophy
phonétique (fo-nay-*teek*) *adj* phonetic
phoque (fok) *m* seal
photo (fo-*toa*) *f* photo; **~ d'identité** passport photograph
photocopie (fo-to-ko-*pee*) *f* photocopy
photographe (fo-to-*grahf*) *m/f* photographer
photographie (fo-to-grah-*fee*) *f* photography; photograph
photographier (fo-to-grah-*f*^{y}*ay*) *v* photograph
phrase (fraaz) *f* sentence
physicien (fee-zee-*s*^{y}*ang*) *m*, **-ne** *f* physicist
physique (fee-*zeek*) *f* physics; *adj* physical
pianiste (p^{y}ah-*neest*) *m/f* pianist
piano (p^{y}ah-*noa*) *m* piano; **~ à queue** grand piano
pickpocket (peek-po-*keht*)* *m* pickpocket
pie (pee) *f* magpie
pièce (p^{y}ehss) *f* piece; room, chamber; **~ de monnaie** coin; **~ de rechange** spare part; **~ détachée** spare part; **~ de théâtre** play
pied (p^{y}ay) *m* foot; leg; **à ~** walking, on foot
piège (p^{y}aizh) *m* trap
pierre (p^{y}air) *f* stone; **en ~** stone; **~ à briquet** flint; **~ ponce** pumice stone; **~ précieuse** gem; stone; **~ tombale** tombstone, gravestone
piétiner (p^{y}ay-tee-*nay*) *v* stamp

piéton (p^{y}ay-*tawng*) *m* pedestrian
piètre (p^{y}ehtr) *adj* poor
pieuvre (p^{y}urvr) *f* octopus
pieux (p^{y}ur) *adj* pious
pigeon (pee-*zhawng*) *m* pigeon
pignon (pee-*ñawng*) *m* gable
pile (peel) *f* stack; battery
pilier (pee-*l^{y}ay*) *m* pillar
pilote (pee-*lot*) *m* pilot
pilule (pee-*lewl*) *f* pill
piment (pee-*mahng*)* *m* red pepper; spice
pin (pang) *m* pine
pince (pangss) *f* pliers *pl*, tongs *pl*; tweezers *pl*; **~ à cheveux** hairgrip; bobby pin *Am*
pinceau (pang-*soa*) *m* brush; paintbrush
pincer (pang-*say*) *v* pinch
pincettes (pang-*seht*) *fpl* tweezers *pl*
pingouin (pang-*gwang*) *m* penguin
ping-pong (peeng-*pong*) *m* table tennis
pion (p^{y}awng) *m* pawn
pionnier (p^{y}o-*n^{y}ay*) *m* pioneer
pipe (peep) *f* pipe
piquant (pee-*kahng*) *adj* savo(u)ry
pique-nique (peek-*neek*) *m* picnic
pique-niquer (peek-nee-*kay*) *v* picnic
piquer (pee-*kay*) *v* *sting, prick
piqûre (pee-*kewr*) *f* shot; sting, bite
pirate (pee-*raht*) *m* pirate
pire (peer) *adj* worse; **le ~** worst
pis (pee) *adv* worse; **tant pis!** never mind!
piscine (pee-*seen*) *f* swimming pool
pissenlit (pee-sahng-*lee*) *m* dandelion
pistache (pee-*stahsh*)* *f* pistachio nut
piste (peest) *f* trail; track; ring; **~ de courses** racetrack; **~ de décollage** runway
pistolet (pee-sto-*lay*) *m* pistol
piston (pee-*stawng*) *m* piston; **segment de ~** piston ring
pitié (pee-*t^{y}ay*) *f* pity; ***avoir ~ de** pity
pittoresque (pee-to-*rehsk*) *adj* picturesque, scenic
pizza (pee-*tsah*)* *f* pizza
placard (plah-*kaar*) *m* closet, cupboard
place (plahss) *f* place; seat; room; square; **~ forte** stronghold
placement (plah-*smahng*) *m* investment
placer (plah-*say*) *v* place; *put, *lay; invest
plafond (plah-*fawng*) *m* ceiling
plage (plaazh) *f* beach; **~ pour nudistes** nudist beach
plaider (play-*day*) *v* plead
plaidoyer (pleh-dwah-*^{y}ay*) *m* plea
plaie (play) *f* wound
***plaindre** (plangdr) *v*: **se ~** complain
plaine (plehn) *f* plain, lowlands *pl*
plainte (plangt) *f* complaint
***plaire** (plair) *v* please; **s'il vous plaît** please
plaisant (pleh-*zahng*) *adj* pleasant; nice, enjoyable, amusing
plaisanter (pleh-zahng-*tay*) *v* joke
plaisanterie (play-zahng-*tree*) *f* joke
plaisir (play-*zeer*) *m* pleasure; joy, delight, fun, enjoyment; **avec ~** gladly; ***prendre ~** enjoy
plan (plahng) *m* plan, project; map; scheme; *adj* flat, level, even; **premier ~** foreground
planche (plahngsh) *f* plank, board
plancher (plahng-*shay*) *m* floor
planétarium (plah-nay-tah-*r^{y}om*) *m* planetarium
planète (plah-*neht*) *f* planet
planeur (plah-*nurr*) *m* glider
planifier (plah-nee-*f^{y}ay*) *v* plan
plantation (plahng-tah-*s^{y}awng*) *f* plantation
plante (plahngt) *f* plant
planter (plahng-*tay*) *v* plant

plaque (plahk) *f* plate; sheet; ~ **d'immatriculation** registration plate; license plate *Am*
plastique (plah-*steek*) *adj* plastic; *m* plastic
plat (plah) *m* dish; course; *adj* flat, plane, smooth, level
plateau (plah-*toa*) *m* plateau; tray
plate-bande (plaht-*bahngd*) *f* flowerbed
platine (plah-*teen*) *m* platinum
plâtre (plaatr) *m* plaster
plein (plang) *adj* full; ***faire le** ~ fill up; **pleine saison** high season
pleurer (plur-*ray*) *v* *weep, cry
***pleuvoir** (plur-*vwaar*) *v* rain
pli (plee) *m* fold; crease; ~ **permanent** permanent press
plie (plee) *f* plaice
plier (plee-*ay*) *v* fold
plomb (plawng) *m* lead; **sans** ~ unleaded
plombage (plawng-*baazh*) *m* filling
plombier (plawng-*b^{y}ay*) *m* plumber
plonger (plawng-*zhay*) *v* dive
pluie (plwee) *f* rain
plume (plewm) *f* feather; pen
plupart (plew-*paar*): **(la)** ~ most
pluriel (plew-*r^{y}ehl*) *m* plural
plus (plewss) *adj* more; *prep* plus; **de** ~ moreover; **le** ~ most; **ne ...** ~ no longer; ~ **... plus** the ... the
plusieurs (plew-*z^{y}urr*) *adj* several
plutôt (plew-*toa*) *adv* fairly, pretty, rather, quite; sooner
pluvieux (plew-*v^{y}ur*) *adj* rainy
pneu (pnur) *m* (pl ~s) tire *Am*, tyre; ~ **crevé** flat tyre (tire *Am*); ~ **de rechange** spare tyre (tire *Am*)
pneumatique (pnur-mah-*teek*) *adj* pneumatic
pneumonie (pnur-mo-*nee*) *f* pneumonia
poche (posh) *f* pocket; **lampe de** ~ flashlight
pochette (po-*sheht*) *f* pouch
poêle (pwahl) *f* saucepan; *m* stove; ~ **à frire** frying pan
poème (po-*ehm*) *m* poem; ~ **épique** epic
poésie (po-ay-*zee*) *f* poetry
poète (po-*eht*) *m* poet
poids (pwah) *m* weight
poignée (pwah-*ñay*) *f* handle; handful; ~ **de main** handshake
poignet (pwah-*ñay*) *m* wrist
poil (pwahl) *m* hair
poing (pwang) *m* fist
point (pwang) *m* point; item; period, full stop; stitch; ~ **de congélation** freezing point; ~ **de départ** starting point; ~ **de repère** landmark; ~ **de vue** view, outlook; ~ **d'interrogation** question mark; **point-virgule** *m* semicolon
pointe (pwangt) *f* point; **heure de** ~ peak hour
pointer (pwang-*tay*) *v* tick off
pointu (pwang-*tew*) *adj* pointed
pointure (pwang-*tewr*)* *f* size
poire (pwaar) *f* pear
poireau (pwah-*roa*) *m* leek
pois (pwah) *m* pea
poison (pwah-*zawng*) *m* poison
poisson (pwah-*sawng*) *m* fish
poissonnerie (pwah-son-*ree*) *f* fish shop
poitrine (pwah-*treen*) *f* chest; bosom
poivre (pwaavr) *m* pepper
pôle nord (poal nawr) North Pole
pôle sud (poal sewd) South Pole
poli (po-*lee*) *adj* polite; civil
police (po-*leess*) *f* police *pl*; policy; **commissariat de** ~ police station; ~ **d'assurance** insurance policy
policier (po-lee-*s^{y}ay*) *m* policeman
poliomyélite (po-l^{y}o-m^{y}ay-*leet*) *f* polio
polir (po-*leer*) *v* polish

polisson (po-lee-*sawn̄ḡ*) *adj* naughty
politicien (po-lee-tee-*s^{y}an̄ḡ*) *m*, **-ne** *f* politician
politique (po-lee-*teek*) *f* politics; policy; *adj* political
pollution (po-lew-*s^{y}awn̄ḡ*) *f* pollution
Pologne (po-*loñ*) *f* Poland
Polonais (po-lo-*nay*) *m* Pole
polonais (po-lo-*nay*) *adj* Polish
pomme (pom) *f* apple; **~ de terre** potato; **pommes frites** chips, French fries *Am*
pompe (pawn̄ḡp) *f* pump; **~ à eau** water pump; **~ à essence** petrol pump, gas pump *Am*
pomper (pawn̄ḡ-*pay*) *v* pump
pompier (pawn̄ḡ-*p^{y}ay*) *m* fireman; **pompiers** fire brigade, fire department *Am*
ponctuel (pawn̄ḡk-*twehl*) *adj* punctual
pondéré (pawn̄ḡ-day-*ray*) *adj* level-minded
pondre (pawn̄ḡdr) *v* *lay
poney (po-*nay*) *m* pony
pont (pawn̄ḡ) *m* bridge; deck; **pontlevis** *m* drawbridge; **~ principal** main deck; **~ suspendu** suspension bridge
populaire (po-pew-*lair*) *adj* popular
population (po-pew-lah-*s^{y}awn̄ḡ*) *f* population
populeux (po-pew-*lur*) *adj* populous
porc (pawr) *m* pork
porcelaine (por-ser-*lehn*) *f* porcelain, china
porc-épic (por-kay-*peek*) *m* porcupine
port[1] (pawr) *m* port, harbo(u)r; **~ de mer** seaport
port[2] (pawr) *m* postage; **~ payé** postage paid, post-paid
portatif (por-tah-*teef*) *adj* portable
porte (port) *f* door; gate; **~ coulissante** sliding door; **~ tournante** revolving door
porte-bagages (port-bah-*gaazh*) *m* luggage rack
porte-bonheur (port-bo-*nūrr*) *m* lucky charm
portée (por-*tay*) *f* reach; litter
portefeuille (por-ter-*fur^{ee}*) *m* wallet, billfold *Am*
porte-manteau (port-mahn̄ḡ-*toa*) *m* hat rack
porte-monnaie (port-mo-*nay*) *m* purse
porter (por-*tay*) *v* carry, *bear; *wear; **~ sur** concern; **se ~ bien** *be in good health
porteur (por-*tūrr*) *m* bearer; porter
portier (por-*t^{y}ay*) *m* porter, doorman, doorkeeper
portière (por-*t^{y}air*)* *f* door
portion (por-*s^{y}awn̄ḡ*) *f* helping, portion
portrait (por-*tray*) *m* portrait
Portugais (por-tew-*gay*) *m* Portuguese
portugais (por-tew-*gay*) *adj* Portuguese
Portugal (por-tew-*gahl*) *m* Portugal
poser (poa-*zay*) *v* place; *put, *lay, *set
positif (poa-zee-*teef*) *m* positive; *adj* positive
position (poa-zee-*s^{y}awn̄ḡ*) *f* position
posséder (po-say-*day*) *v* possess, own
possession (po-seh-*s^{y}awn̄ḡ*) *f* possession
possibilité (po-see-bee-lee-*tay*) *f* possibility
possible (po-*seebl*) *adj* possible
poste[1] (post) *f* post; ***mettre à la ~** mail; **~ aérienne** airmail; **~ restante** poste restante
poste[2] (post) *m* station; post; **~ de secours** first aid post; **~ d'essence** petrol station, gas station *Am*
poster (po-*stay*) *v* post
postérieur (po-stay-*r^{y}ūrr*) *m* bottom;

adj subsequent
postiche (po-*steesh*) *m* hair piece
pot (poa) *m* pot
potable (po-*tahbl*) *adj* for drinking
potage (po-*taazh*) *m* soup
poteau (po-*toa*) *m* post, pole; ~ **indicateur** milepost, signpost
potelé (po-*tlay*) *adj* plump
poterie (po-*tree*) *f* pottery, crockery
pou (poo) *m* (pl ~x) louse
poubelle (poo-*behl*) *f* rubbish bin
pouce (pooss) *m* thumb
poudre (poodr) *f* powder; ~ **à canon** gunpowder; ~ **dentifrice** toothpowder; ~ **de riz** face powder; ~ **pour les pieds** foot powder; **savon en** ~ soap powder
poudrier (poo-dree-*ay*) *m* powder compact
poule (pool) *f* hen
poulet (poo-*lay*) *m* chicken
pouls (poo) *m* pulse
poumon (poo-*mawng̅*) *m* lung
poupée (poo-*pay*) *f* doll
pour (po̅o̅r) *prep* for, to; ~ **que** so that
pourboire (poor-*bwaar*) *m* tip, gratuity
pourcentage (poor-sahng̅-*taazh*) *m* percentage
pourchasser (poor-shah-*say*) *v* chase
pourpre (poorpr) *adj* purple
pourquoi (poor-*kwah*) *adv* why; what for
pourrir (poo-*reer*) *v* rot; **pourri** rotten
***poursuivre** (poor-*sweevr*) *v* carry on, continue, pursue
pourtant (poor-*tahng̅*) *adv* however, yet; though
pourvu que (poor-vew ker) provided that
poussée (poo-*say*) *f* push
pousser (poo-*say*) *v* push
poussette (poo-*seht*) *f* baby carriage *Am*
poussière (poo-*s^yair*) *f* dust
poussiéreux (poo-s^yay-*rur*) *adj* dusty
poutre (pootr) *f* beam
pouvoir (poo-*vwaar*) *m* power; authority; ~ **exécutif** executive
***pouvoir** (poo-*vwaar*) *v* *can, *be able to; *might, *may
praline (prah-*leen*) *f* chocolate
pratique (prah-*teek*) *f* practice; *adj* practical, convenient
pratiquer (prah-tee-*kay*) *v* practise
pré (pray) *m* meadow
préalable (pray-ah-*lahbl*) *adj* previous
précaire (pray-*kair*) *adj* precarious, critical
précaution (pray-koa-*s^yawng̅*) *f* precaution
précédemment (pray-say-dah-*mahng̅*) *adv* before
précédent (pray-say-*dahng̅*) *adj* preceding, previous, last; former
précéder (pray-say-*day*) *v* precede
prêcher (pray-*shay*) *v* preach
précieux (pray-*s^yur*) *adj* valuable; precious
précipice (pray-see-*peess*) *m* precipice
précipitation (pray-see-pee-tah-*s^yawng̅*) *f* precipitation
précipité (pray-see-pee-*tay*) *adj* hasty
se précipiter (pray-see-pee-*tay*) dash
précis (pray-*see*) *adj* precise; accurate
préciser (pray-see-*zay*) *v* specify
précision (pray-see-*z^yawng̅*) *f* precision; **précisions** points *pl*
***prédire** (pray-*deer*) *v* predict
préférable (pray-fay-*rahbl*) *adj* preferable
préférence (pray-fay-*rahng̅ss*) *f* preference
préférer (pray-fay-*ray*) *v* prefer; **préféré** favo(u)rite
préjudiciable (pray-zhew-dee-*s^yahbl*) *adj* harmful
préjugé (pray-zhew-*zhay*) *m* prejudice

prélever (prayl-*vay*) *v* impose; deduct; *withdraw

préliminaire (pray-lee-mee-*nair*) *adj* preliminary

prématuré (pray-mah-tew-*ray*) *adj* premature

premier (prer-*m^{y}ay*) *num* first; *adj* foremost, primary; **~ ministre** premier

***prendre** (prahngdr) *v* *take; collect; *v* *catch; capture; **~ garde** look out, beware; **~ soin de** look after

prénom (pray-*nawng*) *m* first name, Christian name

préparation (pray-pah-rah-*s^{y}awng*) *f* preparation

préparer (pray-pah-*ray*) *v* prepare; arrange; cook

préposition (pray-poa-zee-*s^{y}awng*) *f* preposition

près (pray) *adv* near; **à peu ~** about; **~ de** by, near

prescription (preh-skree-*ps^{y}awng*) *f* prescription

***prescrire** (preh-*skreer*) *v* prescribe

présence (pray-*zahngss*) *f* presence

présent (pray-*zahng*) *m* present; *adj* present; **jusqu'à ~** so far

présentation (pray-zahng-tah-*s^{y}awng*) *f* introduction

présenter (pray-zahng-*tay*) *v* present; introduce; **se ~** appear; report

préservatif (pray-sehr-vah-*teef*) *m* condom

président (pray-zee-*dahng*) *m*, **-e** *f* president, chairman

présomptueux (pray-zawngp-*twur*) *adj* presumptuous

presque (prehsk) *adv* nearly, almost

presqu'île (preh-*skeel*) *f* peninsula

pressant (preh-*sahng*) *adj* pressing

presse (prehss) *f* press

presser (pray-*say*) *v* press; **se ~** hurry, rush

pression (preh-*s^{y}awng*) *f* pressure; **~ atmosphérique** atmospheric pressure; **~ des pneus** tyre (tire *Am*) pressure; **~ d'huile** oil pressure

prestidigitateur (preh-stee-dee-zhee-tah-*turr*) *m* magician

prestige (preh-*steezh*) *m* prestige

présumer (pray-zew-*may*) *v* assume

prêt (pray) *m* loan; *adj* ready; prepared

prétendre (pray-*tahngdr*) *v* claim, pretend

prétentieux (pray-tahng-*s^{y}ur*) *adj* conceited

prétention (pray-tahng-*s^{y}awng*) *f* claim

prêter (pray-*tay*) *v* *lend; **~ attention à** attend to, mind

prétexte (pray-*tehkst*) *m* pretence, pretext

prêtre (praitr) *m* priest

preuve (prurv) *f* proof, evidence

prévenant (preh-*vnahng*) *adj* considerate, thoughtful

***prévenir** (preh-*vneer*) *v* warn; prevent, anticipate

préventif (preh-vahng-*teef*) *adj* preventive

prévenu (pray-*vnew*) *m*, **-e** *f* accused

prévision (pray-vee-*z^{y}awng*) *f* forecast, outlook

***prévoir** (pray-*vwaar*) *v* forecast; anticipate

prier (pree-*ay*) *v* pray; ask

prière (pree-*air*) *f* prayer

primaire (pree-*mair*) *adj* primary

prime (preem) *f* premium

primordial (pree-mor-*d^{y}ahl*) *adj* primary

prince (prangss) *m* prince

princesse (prang-*sehss*) *f* princess

principal (prang-see-*pahl*) *adj* principal; cardinal, chief, leading, main

principalement (prang-see-pahl-

mahng) *adv* especially, mainly
principe (prang-*seep*) *m* principle
printemps (prang-*tahng*) *m* spring; springtime
priorité (pree-o-ree-*tay*) *f* priority; ~ **de passage** right of way
prise (preez) *f* grip, clutch, grasp; capture; ~ **de vue** shot
prison (pree-*zawng*) *f* prison; jail
prisonnier (pree-zo-*n^{y}ay*) *m*, **-ière** *f* prisoner; ***faire** ~ capture; ~ **de guerre** prisoner of war
privation (pree-vah-*s^{y}awng*) *f* deprivation, deprival
privé (pree-*vay*) *adj* private
priver de (pree-*vay*) deprive of
privilège (pree-vee-*laizh*) *m* privilege
prix (pree) *m* price; charge, cost; award, prize; ~ **courant** *m* price list; ~ **d'achat** purchase price; ~ **de consolation** consolation prize; ~ **d'entrée** entrance fee; ~ **du voyage** fare
probable (pro-*bahbl*) *adj* probable; presumable, likely
probablement (pro-bah-bler-*mahng*) *adv* probably
problème (pro-*blehm*) *m* problem; question
procédé (pro-say-*day*) *m* process
procéder (pro-say-*day*) *v* proceed
procédure (pro-say-*dewr*) *f* procedure
procès (pro-*say*) *m* process; trial, lawsuit
procession (pro-seh-*s^{y}awng*) *f* procession
processus (pro-say-*sewss*) *m* process
prochain (pro-*shang*) *adj* following, next
prochainement (pro-shehn-*mahng*) *adv* soon, shortly
proche (prosh) *adj* close, near; nearby; oncoming
proclamer (pro-klah-*may*) *v* proclaim
procurer (pro-kew-*ray*) *v* furnish; **se** ~ obtain
prodigue (pro-*deeg*) *adj* extravagant; generous
producteur (pro-dewk-*turr*) *m*, **-trice** *f* producer
production (pro-dewk-*s^{y}awng*) *f* production; output; ~ **en série** mass production
***produire** (pro-*dweer*) *v* produce; generate; **se** ~ occur, happen
produit (pro-*dwee*) *m* product; produce
prof (prof) *m or f* teacher
profane (pro-*fahn*) *m* layman
professer (pro-fay-*say*) *v* confess
professeur (pro-feh-*surr*) *m* teacher; professor
profession (pro-feh-*s^{y}awng*) *f* profession
professionnel (pro-feh-s^{y}o-*nehl*) *adj* professional
profit (pro-*fee*) *m* profit, benefit
profitable (pro-fee-*tahbl*) *adj* profitable
profiter (pro-fee-*tay*) *v* profit, benefit
profond (pro-*fawng*) *adj* deep; low; profound
profondeur (pro-fawng-*durr*) *f* depth
programme (pro-*grahm*) *m* programme
progrès (pro-*gray*) *m* progress
progresser (pro-gray-*say*) *v* *get on
progressif (pro-gray-*seef*) *adj* progressive
projecteur (pro-zhehk-*turr*) *m* spotlight; searchlight
projet (pro-*zhay*) *m* project; scheme
prolongation (pro-lawng-gah-*s^{y}awng*) *f* extension
prolonger (pro-lawng-*zhay*) *v* prolong, extend
promenade (prom-*nahd*) *f* walk, stroll; promenade; ~ **en voiture** drive

promener (prom-*nay*) *v*: **se ~** go for a walk
promeneur (prom-*nurr*) *m* walker
promesse (pro-*mehss*) *f* promise
***promettre** (pro-*mehtr*) *v* promise
promontoire (pro-mawng-*twaar*) *m* headland
promotion (pro-mo-*s^{y}awng*) *f* promotion
***promouvoir** (pro-moo-*vwaar*) *v* promote
prompt (prawng) *adj* prompt; fast
prononcer (pro-nawng-*say*) *v* pronounce
prononciation (pro-nawng-s^{y}ah-*s^{y}awng*) *f* pronunciation
proportion (pro-por-*s^{y}awng*) *f* proportion
proportionnel (pro-por-s^{y}o-*nehl*) *adj* proportional
propos (pro-*poa*) *m* intention; **à ~** by the way; **à ~ de** regarding
proposer (pro-poa-*zay*) *v* propose
proposition (pro-poa-zee-*s^{y}awng*) *f* proposition, proposal
propre (propr) *adj* clean; own
propriétaire (pro-pree-*ay*-tair) *m/f* owner, proprietor; landlord
propriété (pro-pree-ay-*tay*) *f* property; estate
propulser (pro-pewl-*say*) *v* propel
prospectus (pro-spehk-*tewss*) *m* prospectus
prospère (pro-*spair*) *adj* prosperous
prospérité (pro-spay-ree-*tay*) *f* prosperity
prostituée (pro-stee-*tway*) *f* prostitute
protection (pro-tehk-*s^{y}awng*) *f* protection
protéger (pro-tay-*zhay*) *v* protect
protestant (pro-teh-*stahng*) *adj* Protestant
protestation (pro-teh-stah-*s^{y}awng*) *f* protest
protester (pro-teh-*stay*) *v* protest
prouver (proo-*vay*) *v* prove
provenance (pro-*vnahngss*) *f* origin
***provenir de** (pro-*vneer*) *come from
proverbe (pro-*vehrb*) *m* proverb
province (pro-*vangss*) *f* province
provincial (pro-vang-*s^{y}ahl*) *adj* provincial
proviseur (pro-vee-*zurr*) *m* principal
provision (pro-vee-*z^{y}awng*) *f* store; provisions *pl*
provisoire (pro-vee-*zwaar*) *adj* temporary, provisional
provoquer (pro-vo-*kay*) *v* cause
prudence (prew-*dahngss*) *f* caution
prudent (prew-*dahng*) *adj* careful; cautious, wary
prune (prewn) *f* plum
pruneau (prew-*noa*) *m* prune
prurit (prew-*reet*) *m* pruritus
psychiatre (psee-*k^{y}aatr*) *m* psychiatrist
psychique (psee-*sheek*) *adj* psychic
psychologie (psee-ko-lo-*zhee*) *f* psychology
psychologique (psee-ko-lo-*zheek*) *adj* psychological
psychologue (psee-ko-*log*) *m/f* psychologist
public (pew-*bleek*) *m* audience, public; *adj* public
publication (pew-blee-kah-*s^{y}awng*) *f* publication
publicité (pew-blee-see-*tay*) *f* advertising, publicity; advertisement
publier (pew-blee-*ay*) *v* publish
puer (pway) *v* *stink
puis (pwee) *adv* then
puisque (pweesk) *conj* as
puissance (pwee-*sahngss*) *f* might, force; power, energy
puissant (pwee-*sahng*) *adj* powerful, mighty; strong
puits (pwee) *m* well; **~ de pétrole** oil well

pull(-over) (pew-lo-*vair*) *m* pullover
pulvérisateur (pewl-vay-ree-zah-*tūrr*) *m* atomizer
pulvériser (pewl-vay-ree-*zay*) *v* *grind
punaise (pew-*naiz*) *f* bug; drawing pin; thumbtack *Am*
punir (pew-*neer*) *v* punish
punition (pew-nee-*s^y awnḡ*) *f* punishment
pupitre (pew-*peetr*) *m* desk; pulpit
pur (pēwr) *adj* pure; clean; sheer, neat
pus (pew) *m* pus
pustule (pew-*stewl*) *f* pimple
putain (pew-*tanḡ*) *f* whore
puzzle (purzl) *m* jigsaw puzzle
pyjama (pee-zhah-*mah*) *m* pyjamas *pl*

Q

quai (kay) *m* wharf, dock, quay; platform
qualification (kah-lee-fee-kah-*s^y awnḡ*) *f* qualification
qualifié (kah-lee-*f^y ay*) *adj* qualified; ***être ~** qualify; **non ~** unskilled
qualité (kah-lee-*tay*) *f* quality; **de première ~** first-class; first-rate
quand (kahnḡ) *adv* when; *conj* when; **n'importe ~** whenever
quant à (kahnḡ-*tah*) as regards
quantité (kahnḡ-tee-*tay*) *f* quantity, amount; lot
quarantaine (kah-rahnḡ-*tehn*) *f* quarantine
quarante (kah-*rahnḡt*) *num* forty
quart (kaar) *m* quarter; **~ d'heure** quarter of an hour
quartier (kahr-*t^y ay*) *m* district, quarter; **bas ~** slum; **~ général** headquarters *pl*
quatorze (kah-*torz*) *num* fourteen
quatorzième (kah-tor-*z^y ehm*) *num* fourteenth
quatre (kahtr) *num* four
quatre-vingt-dix (kah-trer-vanḡ-*deess*) *num* ninety
quatre-vingts (kah-trer-*vanḡ*) *num* eighty
quatrième (kah-*tr^y ehm*) *num* fourth
que (ker) *conj* that; as, than; *adv* how; **ce ~** what
quel (kehl) *pron* which; **n'importe ~** any; whichever
quelquefois (kehl-ker-*fwah*) *adv* sometimes
quelques (kehlk) *adj* some, some
quelqu'un (kehl-*kurnḡ*) *pron* someone, somebody
querelle (ker-*rehl*) *f* dispute, row, quarrel
question (keh-*st^y awnḡ*) *f* question; inquiry, query; matter, issue, problem
quêter (kay-*tay*) *v* collect
queue (kur) *f* tail; queue; ***faire la ~** queue; stand in line *Am*
qui (kee) *pron* who; which, that; **à ~** whom; **n'importe ~** anybody
quiche (keesh) *f* quiche
quille (keey) *f* keel
quincaillerie (kanḡ-kigh-*ree*) *f* hardware; hardware store
quinze (kanḡz) *num* fifteen; **~ jours** fortnight
quinzième (kanḡ-*z^y ehm*) *num* fifteenth
quitter (kee-*tay*) *v* *leave
quoi (kwah) *pron* what; **n'importe ~** anything
quoique (kwahk) *conj* though,

although; **quoiqu'il en soit** at any rate

quote-part (kot-*paar*) *f* quota

quotidien (ko-tee-*d^{y}ang*) *adj* everyday, daily; *m* daily

R

rabais (rah-*bay*) *m* discount, reduction, rebate

raccourcir (rah-koor-*seer*) *v* shorten

racial (rah-*s^{y}ahl*) *adj* racial

racine (rah-*seen*) *f* root

racler (rah-*klay*) *v* scrape

raconter (rah-kawng-*tay*) *v* *tell

radeau (rah-*doa*) *m* raft

radiateur (rah-d^{y}ah-*turr*) *m* radiator

radical (rah-dee-*kahl*) *adj* radical

radio (rah-*d^{y}oa*) *f* wireless, radio

radiographie (rah-d^{y}oa-grah-*fee*) *f* X-ray

radiographier (rah-d^{y}oa-grah-*f^{y}ay*) *v* X-ray

radis (rah-*dee*) *m* radish

radotage (rah-do-*taazh*) *m* rubbish

rafale (rah-*fahl*) *f* gust

raffinerie (rah-feen-*ree*) *f* refinery; **~ de pétrole** oil refinery

rafraîchir (rah-fray-*sheer*) *v* refresh

rafraîchissement (rah-freh-shee-*smahng*) *m* refreshment

rage (raazh) *f* rabies; rage; craze

rager (rah-*zhay*) *v* rage

raide (rehd) *adj* stiff

raie (ray) *f* stripe; parting

raifort (ray-*fawr*) *m* horseradish

rail (righ) *m* rail

raisin (ray-*zang*) *m* grapes *pl*; **~ sec** currant, raisin

raison (ray-*zawng*) *f* reason; cause; wits *pl*, sense; ***avoir ~** * be right; **en ~ de** for, owing to, because of

raisonnable (ray-zo-*nahbl*) *adj* reasonable; sensible

raisonner (ray-zo-*nay*) *v* reason

ralentir (rah-lahng-*teer*) *v* slow down

rallonge (rah-*lawngzh*) *f* extension cord

ramasser (rah-mah-*say*) *v* pick up

rame (rahm) *f* oar

ramener (rahm-*nay*) *v* *bring back

ramer (rah-*may*) *v* row

rampe (rahngp) *f* railing

ramper (rahng-*pay*) *v* *creep, crawl

rance (rahngss) *adj* rancid

rançon (rahng-*sawng*) *f* ransom

randonnée (rahng-do-*nay*) *f* tour, excursion; (long) trip; outing; hike

rang (rahng) *m* row, rank

rangée (rahng-*zhay*) *f* line

ranger (rahng-*zhay*) *v* sort; tidy up, *put away

râpe (raap) *f* grater

râper (rah-*pay*) *v* grate

rapide (rah-*peed*) *adj* quick; fast, swift, rapid; *m* rapids *pl*

rapidement (rah-peed-*mahng*) *adv* soon

rapidité (rah-pee-dee-*tay*) *f* speed

rappeler (rah-*play*) *v* remind; recall; **se ~** remember, recall

rapport (rah-*pawr*) *m* report; connection, relation; **rapports** intercourse

rapporter (rah-por-*tay*) *v* *bring back; report

rapprocher (rah-pro-*shay*) *v* *bring closer

rare (raar) *adj* rare; uncommon, scarce
rarement (rahr-*mahng*) *adv* seldom, rarely
raser (rah-*zay*): **se ~** shave
raseur (rah-*zurr*) *m* bore
rasoir (rah-*zwaar*) *m* razor; **~ électrique** electric razor; shaver
rassemblement (rah-sahng-bler-*mahng*) *m* rally
rassembler (rah-sahng-*blay*) *v* assemble; collect
rassis (rah-*see*) *adj* stale
rassurer (rah-sew-*ray*) *v* reassure
rat (rah) *m* rat
râteau (rah-*toa*) *m* rake
ration (rah-*s^{y}awng*) *f* ration
rauque (roak) *adj* hoarse
ravissant (rah-vee-*sahng*) *adj* lovely, delightful, enchanting
rayé (ray-*^{y}ay*) *adj* striped
rayon (ray-*^{y}awng*) *m* beam, ray; radius; spoke
rayure (ray-*^{y}ewr*) *f* scratch
réaction (ray-ahk-*s^{y}awng*) *f* reaction
réalisable (ray-ah-lee-*zahbl*) *adj* feasible; realizable
réalisation (ray-ah-lee-zah-*s^{y}awng*) *f* realization; direction
réaliser (ray-ah-lee-*zay*) *v* realize; carry out, implement
réaliste (ray-ah-*leest*) *adj* matter-of-fact
réalité (ray-ah-lee-*tay*) *f* reality; **en ~** actually; really
rébellion (ray-beh-*l^{y}awng*) *f* revolt, rebellion
rebord (rer-*bawr*) *m* edge, rim; **~ de fenêtre** windowsill
rebut (rer-*bew*) *m* junk, refuse
récemment (ray-sah-*mahng*) *adv* lately, recently
récent (ray-*sahng*) *adj* recent
réception (ray-seh-*ps^{y}awng*) *f* receipt; reception; reception office
recette (rer-*seht*) *f* recipe; **recettes** revenue
***recevoir** (rer-*svwaar*) *v* receive; entertain
recharge (rer-*shahrzh*) *f* refill
réchaud (ray-*shoa*)* *m* (portable) stove
réchauffer (ray-shoa-*fay*) *v* warm up
recherche (rer-*shehrsh*) *f* research
rechercher (rer-shehr-*shay*) *v* search for
récif (ray-*seef*) *m* reef
récipient (ray-see-*p^{y}ahng*) *m* container, vessel
réciproque (ray-see-*prok*) *adj* mutual
récit (ray-*see*) *m* tale; account
récital (ray-see-*tahl*) *m* (pl ~s) recital
réclamation (ray-klah-mah-*s^{y}awng*) *f* claim
réclame (ray-*klahm*) *f* publicity
réclamer (ray-klah-*may*) *v* claim
récolte (ray-*kolt*) *f* crop
recommandation (rer-ko-mahng-dah-*s^{y}awng*) *f* recommendation
recommander (rer-ko-mahng-*day*) *v* recommend; register
recommencer (rer-ko-mahng-*say*) *v* recommence
récompense (ray-kawng-*pahngss*) *f* reward, prize
récompenser (ray-kawng-pahng-*say*) *v* reward
réconciliation (ray-kawng-see-l^{y}ah-*s^{y}awng*) *f* reconciliation
réconfort (ray-kawng-*fawr*) *m* comfort
reconnaissance (rer-ko-nay-*sahngss*) *f* recognition
reconnaissant (rer-ko-nay-*sahng*) *adj* thankful, grateful
***reconnaître** (rer-ko-*naitr*) *v* recognize; acknowledge; admit
record (rer-*kawr*) *m* record
***recouvrir** (rer-koo-*vreer*) *v* cover; re-cover

récréation (ray-kray-ah-*s^{y}awn̅g̅*) *f* recreation
rectangle (rehk-*tahn̅g̅gl*) *m* rectangle; oblong
rectangulaire (rehk-tahn̅g̅-gew-*lair*) *adj* rectangular
rectification (rehk-tee-fee-kah-*s^{y}awn̅g̅*) *f* correction
reçu (rer-*sew*) *m* receipt; voucher
***recueillir** (rer-kur-*^{y}eer*) *v* gather
reculer (rer-kew-*lay*) *v* step back; back up
récupérer (ray-kew-pay-*ray*) *v* recover
rédacteur (ray-dahk-*tūrr*) *m* editor
rédiger (ray-dee-*zhay*) *v* *draw up
redouter (rer-doo-*tay*) *v* fear
réduction (ray-dewk-*s^{y}awn̅g̅*) *f* discount, reduction
***réduire** (ray-*dweer*) *v* reduce; decrease, *cut
réduit (ray-*dwee*) *m* shed
rééducation (ray-ay-dew-kah-*s^{y}awn̅g̅*) *f* rehabilitation
réel (ray-*ehl*) *adj* real; true, factual, actual, substantial
réellement (ray-ehl-*mahn̅g̅*) *adv* really
référence (ray-fay-*rahn̅g̅ss*) *f* reference
réfléchir (ray-flay-*sheer*) *v* *think; **~ à** *think over
réflecteur (ray-flehk-*tūrr*) *m* reflector
reflet (rer-*flay*) *m* reflection
refléter (rer-flay-*tay*) *v* reflect
réforme (ray-*form*) *f* reformation
réfrigérateur (ray-free-zhay-rah-*tūrr*) *m* fridge, refrigerator
refroidir (rer-frwah-*deer*) *v* cool off
refuge (rer-*fēwzh*) *m* refuge
réfugié (ray-few-*zh^{y}ay*) *m*, **-e** *f* refugee
refus (rer-*few*) *m* refusal
refuser (rer-few-*zay*) *v* refuse; deny, reject
regard (rer-*gaar*) *m* look
regarder (rer-gahr-*day*) *v* look; watch, look at; concern
régime (ray-*zheem*) *m* régime; rule, government; diet
région (ray-*zh^{y}awn̅g̅*) *f* region; area, zone
régional (ray-zh^{y}o-*nahl*) *adj* regional
règle (raigl) *f* rule; ruler; **en ~** in order
règlement (reh-gler-*mahn̅g̅*) *m* regulation; arrangement, settlement
régler (ray-*glay*) *v* regulate; settle
réglisse (ray-*gleess*) *f* liquorice
règne (rehñ) *m* reign; dominion, rule
régner (ray-*ñay*) *v* reign; rule
regret (rer-*gray*) *m* regret
regretter (rer-gray-*tay*) *v* regret
régulier (ray-gew-*l^{y}ay*) *adj* regular
rein (ran̅g̅) *m* kidney
reine (rehn) *f* queen
rejeter (rerzh-*tay*) *v* reject; turn down
***rejoindre** (rer-*zhwan̅g̅dr*) *v* rejoin
relater (rer-lah-*tay*) *v* relate; report
relatif (rer-lah-*teef*) *adj* relative; comparative; **~ à** with reference to, concerning
relation (rer-lah-*s^{y}awn̅g̅*) *f* connection; relation
relayer (rer-lay-*^{y}ay*) *v* relieve
relèvement (rer-lehv-*mahn̅g̅*) *m* increase
relever (rerl-*vay*) *v* raise
relief (rer-*l^{y}ehf*) *m* relief
relier (rer-*l^{y}ay*) *v* link; *bind
religieuse (rer-lee-*zh^{y}ūrz*) *f* nun
religieux (rer-lee-*zh^{y}ur*) *adj* religious
religion (rer-lee-*zh^{y}awn̅g̅*) *f* religion
relique (rer-*leek*) *f* relic
reliure (rer-*l^{y}ēwr*) *f* binding
remarquable (rer-mahr-*kahbl*) *adj* remarkable; noticeable, striking
remarque (rer-*mahrk*) *f* remark
remarquer (rer-mahr-*kay*) *v* notice; remark
remboursement (rahn̅g̅-boor-ser-*mahn̅g̅*) *m* repayment, refund
rembourser (rahn̅g̅-boor-*say*) *v*

*repay, reimburse, refund
remède (rer-*mehd*) *m* remedy
remerciement (rer-mehr-see-*mahng*) *m* thanks *pl*
remercier (rer-mehr-*s^{y}ay*) *v* thank
***remettre** (rer-*mehtr*) *v* deliver; commit; hand over; remit; **se ~** recover
remise (rer-*meez*) *f* delivery
remonter (rer-mawng-*tay*) *v* *wind up
remorque (rer-*mork*) *f* trailer
remorquer (rer-mor-*kay*) *v* tow, tug
remorqueur (rer-mor-*kurr*) *m* tug
rémoulade (ray-moo-*lahd*) *f* remoulade-sauce
remplacer (rahng-plah-*say*) *v* replace
remplir (rahng-*pleer*) *v* fill; fill in; fill out *Am*
remue-ménage (rer-mew-may-*naazh*) *m* bustle
remuer (rer-*mway*) *v* stir
rémunération (ray-mew-nay-rah-*s^{y}awng*) *f* remuneration
rémunérer (ray-mew-nay-*ray*) *v* remunerate
renard (rer-*naar*) *m* fox
rencontre (rahng-*kawngtr*) *f* meeting, encounter; **aller à la ~** *go and *meet
rencontrer (rahng-kawng-*tray*) *v* *meet; *come across, run into, encounter
rendement (rahng-der-*mahng*) *m* profit
rendez-vous (rahng-day-*voo*) *m* appointment, date
rendre (rahngdr) *v* refund; *make; **~ compte de** account for; **~ visite à** call on; **se ~** surrender; *go; **se ~ compte** realize
renommée (rer-no-*may*) *f* fame
renoncer (rer-nawng-*say*) *v* *give up
renouveler (rer-noo-*vlay*) *v* renew
renseignement (rahng-sehñ-*mahng*) *m* information; **bureau des renseignements** inquiry office
renseigner (rahng-say-*ñay*) *v*: **se ~** inquire
rentable (rahng-*tahbl*) *adj* paying
rentrée (rahng-*tray*) *f* return; home-coming; re-entry
rentrer (rahng-*tray*) *v* *go home; reassemble
renverser (rahng-vehr-*say*) *v* knock down
***renvoyer** (rahng-vwah-*^{y}ay*) *v* *send back; dismiss; **~ à** refer to; postpone
répandre (ray-*pahngdr*) *v* *shed; *spill
réparation (ray-pah-rah-*s^{y}awng*) *f* reparation, repair
réparer (ray-pah-*ray*) *v* repair; mend, fix
répartir (ray-pahr-*teer*) *v* divide
repas (rer-*pah*) *m* meal
repassage *m* ironing
repasser (rer-pah-*say*) *v* press, iron
repentir (rer-pahng-*teer*) *m* repentance
répertoire (ray-pehr-*twaar*) *m* repertory
répéter (ray-pay-*tay*) *v* repeat; rehearse
répétition (ray-pay-tee-*s^{y}awng*) *f* repetition; rehearsal
répit (ray-*pee*) *m* respite
répondre (ray-*pawngdr*) *v* reply, answer
réponse (ray-*pawngss*) *f* reply, answer; **en ~** in reply; **sans ~** unanswered
reporter (rer-por-*tay*) *m* reporter
repos (rer-*poa*) *m* rest
reposant (rer-poa-*zahng*) *adj* restful
reposer (rer-poa-*zay*) *v*: **se ~** rest
repousser (rer-poo-*say*) *v* turn down; repel; **repoussant** repulsive
***reprendre** (rer-*prahngdr*) *v* resume; *take over
représentant (rer-pray-zahng-*tahng*) *m*, **-e** *f* agent

représentatif (rer-pray-zahng-tah-*teef*) *adj* representative
représentation (rer-pray-zahng-tah-*s^y awng*) *f* show; representation
représenter (rer-pray-zahng-*tay*) *v* represent
réprimander (ray-pree-mahng-*day*) *v* reprimand
réprimer (ray-pree-*may*) *v* suppress
reprise (rer-*preez*) *f* revival; round
repriser (rer-pree-*zay*) *v* darn
reproche (rer-*prosh*) *m* reproach
reprocher (rer-pro-*shay*) *v* reproach
reproduction (rer-pro-dewk-*s^y awng*) *f* reproduction
***reproduire** (rer-pro-*dweer*) *v* reproduce
reptile (rehp-*teel*) *m* reptile
républicain (ray-pew-blee-*kang*) *adj* republican
république (ray-pew-*bleek*) *f* republic
répugnance (ray-pew-*ñahngss*) *f* dislike
répugnant (ray-pew-*ñahng*) *adj* repellent; filthy, disgusting, revolting
réputation (ray-pew-tah-*s^y awng*) *f* fame, reputation
***requérir** (rer-kay-*reer*) *v* request
requête (rer-*keht*) *f* request
requin (rer-*kang*) *m* shark
requis (rer-*kee*) *adj* requisite
R.E.R. (ehr-er-*ehr*) *m* high-speed train service between Paris and the suburbs
réseau (ray-*zoa*) *m* network; **~ routier** road system
réservation (ray-zehr-vah-*s^y awng*) *f* reservation; booking
réserve (ray-*zehrv*) *f* reserve; qualification; **de ~** spare; **~ zoologique** game reserve
réserver (ray-zehr-*vay*) *v* reserve; book
réservoir (ray-zehr-*vwaar*) *m* reservoir; tank; **~ d'essence** petrol tank, gas tank *Am*
résidence (ray-zee-*dahngss*) *f* residence
résident (ray-zee-*dahng*) *m* resident
résider (ray-zee-*day*) *v* reside
résille (ray-*zeey*) *f* hair net
résine (ray-*zeen*) *f* resin
résistance (ray-zee-*stahngss*) *f* resistance
résister (ray-zee-*stay*) *v* resist
résolu (ray-zo-*lew*) *adj* determined, resolute
***résoudre** (ray-*zoodr*) *v* solve
respect (reh-*spay*) *m* respect; esteem, regard
respectable (reh-spehk-*tahbl*) *adj* respectable
respecter (reh-spehk-*tay*) *v* respect
respectif (reh-spehk-*teef*) *adj* respective
respectueux (reh-spehk-*twur*) *adj* respectful
respiration (reh-spee-rah-*s^y awng*) *f* breathing, respiration
respirer (reh-spee-*ray*) *v* breathe
resplendir (reh-splahng-*deer*) *v* *shine
responsabilité (reh-spawng-sah-bee-lee-*tay*) *f* responsibility; liability
responsable (reh-spawng-*sahbl*) *adj* responsible; in charge; liable
ressemblance (rer-sahng-*blahngss*) *f* resemblance
ressembler à (rer-sahng-*blay*) resemble
resserrer (rer-say-*ray*) *v* tighten; **se ~** tighten
ressort (rer-*sawr*) *m* spring
ressource (rer-*soors*) *f* option; **ressources** resources *pl*; means *pl*
restant (reh-*stahng*) *adj* remaining; *m* remnant, remainder
restaurant (reh-stoa-*rahng*) *m* restaurant; **~ libre service** self-

service restaurant
reste (rehst) *m* rest; remnant, remainder
rester (reh-*stay*) *v* stay; remain
restituer (reh-stee-*tway*) *v* reimburse
restriction (reh-streek-*s*^{y}*aw̅n̅g̅*) *f* restriction; qualification
résultat (ray-zewl-*tah*) *m* result; issue, effect, outcome
résulter (ray-zewl-*tay*) *v*: **~ de** result from
résumé (ray-zew-*may*) *m* résumé, summary; survey
retard (rer-*taar*) *m* delay; **en ~** overdue, late
retarder (rer-tahr-*day*) *v* delay
***retenir** (rert-*neer*) *v* reserve, book; remember; restrain
rétine (ray-*teen*) *f* retina
retirer (rer-tee-*ray*) *v* *withdraw
retour (rer-*t͞o͞or*) *m* return; **voyage de ~** return journey
retourner (rer-toor-*nay*) *v* *get back; return, turn back, *go back; turn over, turn, turn round; **se ~** turn round
retracer (rer-trah-*say*) *v* trace
retraite (rer-*treht*) *f* retirement; pension
retraité (rer-tray-*tay*) *adj* retired
rétrécir (ray-tray-*seer*) *v* *shrink
rétroviseur (ray-tro-vee-*zūrr*) *m* driving mirror, rear-view mirror
réunion (ray-ew-*n*^{y}*aw̅n̅g̅*) *f* meeting, assembly
réunir (ray-ew-*neer*) *v* join; reunite; **se ~** gather
réussir (ray-ew-*seer*) *v* manage, succeed; pass, *make; **réussi** successful
rêve (raiv) *m* dream
réveil (ray-*vay*) *m* alarm clock
réveiller (ray-vay-^{y}*ay*) *v* *awake, *wake; **réveillé** awake; **se ~** wake up
révélation (ray-vay-lah-*s*^{y}*aw̅n̅g̅*) *f* revelation
révéler (ray-vay-*lay*) *v* reveal; *give away; **se ~** prove
revendication (rer-vahn̅g̅-dee-kah-*s*^{y}*aw̅n̅g̅*) *f* claim
revendiquer (rer-vahn̅g̅-dee-*kay*) *v* claim
***revenir** (rer-*vneer*) *v* return
revenu (rer-*vnew*) *m* earnings *pl*, income, revenue
rêver (ray-*vay*) *v* *dream
revers (rer-*vair*) *m* reverse; lapel
revirement (rer-veer-*mahn̅g̅*) *m* reverse, turn
reviser (rer-vee-*zay*) *v* revise; overhaul
révision (ray-vee-*z*^{y}*aw̅n̅g̅*) *f* revision
***revoir** (rer-*vwaar*) *v* *see again; review; **au revoir!** goodbye!
révoltant (ray-vol-*tahn̅g̅*) *adj* revolting
révolte (ray-*volt*) *f* revolt, rebellion
révolter (ray-vol-*tay*) *v*: **se ~** revolt
révolution (ray-vo-lew-*s*^{y}*aw̅n̅g̅*) *f* revolution
revolver (ray-vol-*vair*) *m* gun, revolver
révoquer (ray-vo-*kay*) *v* recall
revue (rer-*vew*) *f* revue; review, magazine; **~ mensuelle** monthly magazine
rez-de-chaussée (reh-dshoa-*say*) *m* ground floor
rhinocéros (ree-no-say-*ross*) *m* rhinoceros
rhubarbe (rew-*bahrb*) *f* rhubarb
rhum (rom) *m* rum
rhumatisme (rew-mah-*teesm*) *m* rheumatism
rhume (rewm) *m* cold; **~ des foins** hay fever
riche (reesh) *adj* rich; wealthy
richesse (ree-*shehss*) *f* wealth; riches *pl*
ride (reed) *f* wrinkle
rideau (ree-*doa*) *m* curtain

ridicule (ree-dee-*kewl*) *adj* ridiculous; ludicrous
ridiculiser (ree-dee-kew-lee-*zay*) *v* ridicule
rien (r^{y}ang) *pron* nothing; nil; **ne ... ~** nothing; **~ que** only
rigoler (ree-go-*lay*) *v* laugh; have fun; be joking
rime (reem) *f* rhyme
rinçage (rang-*saazh*) *m* rinse
rincer (rang-*say*) *v* rinse
rire (reer) *m* laughter, laugh
***rire** (reer) *v* laugh
risque (reesk) *m* risk; chance
risquer (ree-*skay*) *v* venture, risk; **risqué** risky
rivage (ree-*vaazh*) *m* shore
rival (ree-*vahl*) *m* rival
rivaliser (ree-vah-lee-*zay*) *v* rival
rivalité (ree-vah-lee-*tay*) *f* rivalry
rive (reev) *f* bank, shore
rivière (ree-*v^{y}air*) *f* river
riz (ree) *m* rice
robe (rob) *f* dress; robe, frock, gown; **~ de chambre** dressing gown
robinet (ro-bee-*nay*) *m* tap; faucet *Am*
robuste (ro-*bewst*) *adj* solid, robust
rocade (ro-*kahd*) *f* bypass
rocher (ro-*shay*) *m* rock, boulder
rocheux (ro-*shur*) *adj* rocky
roi (rwah) *m* king
rôle (roal) *m* role
roman (ro-*mahng*) *m* novel; **~ policier** detective story
romantique (ro-mahng-*teek*) *adj* romantic
rompre (rawngpr) *v* *break
rond (rawng) *adj* round
rond-point (rawng-*pwang*) *m* roundabout
ronfler (rawng-*flay*) *v* snore
rosaire (roa-*zair*) *m* rosary
rose (roaz) *f* rose; *adj* pink, rose
roseau (roa-*zoa*) *m* reed
rosée (roa-*zay*) *f* dew
rossignol (ro-see-*ñol*) *m* nightingale
rotation (ro-tah-*s^{y}awng*) *f* revolution
rôti (roa-*tee*) *m* roast (meat)
rotin (ro-*tang*) *m* rattan
rôtir (roa-*teer*) *v* roast
rôtisserie (ro-tee-*sree*) *f* grillroom
rotule (ro-*tewl*) *f* kneecap
roue (roo) *f* wheel; **~ de secours** spare wheel
rouge (roozh) *adj* red; *m* rouge; **~ à lèvres** lipstick
rouge-gorge (roozh-*gorzh*) *m* robin
rougeole (roo-*zhol*) *f* measles
rougir (roo-*zheer*) *v* blush
rouille (roo^{ee}) *f* rust
rouillé (roo-^{y}*ay*) *adj* rusty
rouleau (roo-*loa*) *m* roll
rouler (roo-*lay*) *v* roll; *go
roulette (roo-*leht*) *f* roulette
roulotte (roo-*lot*) *f* caravan
roumain (roo-*mang*) *adj* Rumanian
Roumanie (roo-mah-*nee*) *f* Rumania
route (root) *f* drive, road; route; **en ~ pour** bound for; **~ à péage** turnpike *Am*; **~ d'évitement** by-pass; **~ principale** thoroughfare, main road
routine (roo-*teen*) *f* routine
royal (rwah-^{y}*ahl*) *adj* royal
royaume (rwah-^{y}*oam*) *m* kingdom
ruban (rew-*bahng*) *m* ribbon; **~ adhésif** adhesive tape, scotch tape
rubrique (rew-*breek*) *f* column
ruche (rewsh) *f* beehive
rude (rewd) *adj* rough
rue (rew) *f* street; road; **~ principale** main street; **~ transversale** side street
ruelle (rwehl) *f* alley, lane
rugir (rew-*zheer*) *v* roar
rugissement (rew-zhee-*smahng*) *m* roar
rugueux (rew-*gur*) *adj* rough
ruine (rween) *f* ruins; ruin
ruiner (rwee-*nay*) *v* ruin

ruisseau (rwee-*soa*) *m* brook, stream
rumeur (rew-*mūrr*) *f* rumo(u)r
rural (rew-*rahl*) *adj* rural
rusé (rew-*zay*) *adj* cunning
russe (rewss) *adj* Russian
Russie (rew-*see*) *f* Russia
rustique (rew-*steek*) *adj* rustic
rythme (reetm) *m* rhythm; pace

S

sable (sahbl) *m* sand
sableux (sah-*blur*) *adj* sandy
sabot (sah-*boa*) *m* wooden shoe; hoof
sac (sahk) *m* bag; sack; **~ à dos** rucksack; **~ à glace** ice bag; **~ à main** bag, handbag; **~ à provisions** shopping bag; **~ de couchage** sleeping bag; **~ en papier** paper bag
sachet (sah-*shay*) *m* small bag; **~ de thé** teabag
sacoche (sah-*kosh*) *f* bag
sacré (sah-*kray*) *adj* holy, sacred
sacrifice (sah-kree-*feess*) *m* sacrifice
sacrifier (sah-kree-*f*ʸ*ay*) *v* sacrifice
sacrilège (sah-kree-*laizh*) *m* sacrilege
sage (saazh) *adj* wise; good
sage-femme (sahzh-*fahm*) *f* midwife
sagesse (sah-*zhehss*) *f* wisdom
saigner (say-*ñay*) *v* *bleed
sain (sang̅) *adj* healthy; wholesome, well
saint (sang̅) *m* saint
saisir (say-*zeer*) *v* seize; *catch, grip, *take, grasp
saison (seh-*zawng̅*) *f* season; **hors ~** off season; **morte-saison** *f* low season; **pleine ~** peak season
salade (sah-*lahd*) *f* salad
salaire (sah-*lair*) *m* salary, pay
salaud (sah-*loa*) *m* bastard
sale (sahl) *adj* dirty; filthy
salé (sah-*lay*) *adj* salty
saleté (sahl-*tay*) *f* dirt
salière (sah-*l*ʸ*air*) *f* salt cellar, salt shaker *Am*
salir (sah-*leer*) *v* soil
salive (sah-*leev*) *f* spit
salle (sahl) *f* hall; **~ à manger** dining room; **~ d'attente** waiting room; **~ de bains** bathroom; **~ de bal** ballroom; **~ de classe** classroom; **~ de concert** concert hall; **~ de lecture** reading room; **~ de séjour** living room; **~ d'exposition** showroom
salon (sah-*lawng̅*) *m* sitting room; drawing room, salon; **~ de beauté** beauty salon; **~ de thé** tearoom
salopette (sah-lo-*peht*) *f* overalls *pl*
saluer (sah-*lway*) *v* greet; salute
salut (sah-*lew*) *m* welfare
salutation (sah-lew-tah-*s*ʸ*awng̅*) *f* greeting
samedi (sahm-*dee*) *m* Saturday
S.A.M.U. (sah-*mew*) *m* mobile accident unit
sanatorium (sah-nah-to-*r*ʸ*om*) *m* sanatorium
sanctuaire (sahng̅k-*twair*) *m* shrine
sandale (sahng̅-*dahl*) *f* sandal
sandwich (sahng̅-*dweech*) *m* sandwich
sang (sahng̅) *m* blood
sanitaire (sah-nee-*tair*) *adj* sanitary
sans (sahng̅) *prep* without
santé (sahng̅-*tay*) *f* health
sapin (sah-*pang̅*) *m* fir-tree
sardine (sahr-*deen*) *f* sardine
satellite (sah-tay-*leet*) *m* satellite
satin (sah-*tang̅*) *m* satin

satisfaction (sah-teess-fahk-*s^{y}awng*) *f* satisfaction
***satisfaire** (sah-tee-*sfair*) *v* satisfy; **satisfait** satisfied; content
sauce (soass) *f* sauce
saucisse (soa-*seess*) *f* sausage
saucisson (soa-see-*sawng*) *m* sausage
sauf (soaf) *prep* but
saumon (soa-*mawng*) *m* salmon
sauna (soa-*nah*) *m* sauna
saut (soa) *m* jump; hop, leap; **~ à ski** ski jump
sauter (soa-*tay*) *v* jump; skip; ***faire ~** fry
sauterelle (soa-*trehl*) *f* grasshopper
sautiller (soa-tee-*^{y}ay*) *v* hop, skip
sauvage (soa-*vaazh*) *adj* savage; wild, fierce
sauver (soa-*vay*) *v* rescue, save
sauvetage (soav-*taazh*) *m* rescue
sauveur (soa-*vurr*) *m* savio(u)r
savant (sah-*vahng*) *m* scientist
saveur (sah-*vurr*) *f* flavour
***savoir** (sah-*vwaar*) *v* *know; *be able to
savoir-vivre (sah-vwahr-*veevr*) *m* manners *pl*
savon (sah-*vawng*) *m* soap; **~ à barbe** shaving soap; **~ en poudre** soap powder
savoureux (sah-voo-*rur*) *adj* tasty, savo(u)ry
scandale (skahng-*dahl*) *m* scandal
scandinave (skahng-dee-*naav*) *adj* Scandinavian
Scandinavie (skahng-dee-nah-*vee*) *f* Scandinavia
sceau (soa) *m* seal
scène (sehn) *f* scene; stage; **metteur en ~** director; ***mettre en ~** direct
scie (see) *f* saw
science (s^{y}ahngss) *f* science
scientifique (s^{y}ahng-tee-*feek*) *adj* scientific
scierie (see-*ree*) *f* sawmill
scintillant (sang-tee-*^{y}ahng*) *adj* sparkling
scolaire (sko-*lair*) *adj* school-
scooter (skoo-*tair*) *m* scooter
scout (skoot) *m* scout; boy scout
sculpteur (skewl-*turr*) *m* sculptor
sculpture (skewl-*tewr*) *f* sculpture
se (ser) *pron* himself; herself; themselves
séance (say-*ahngss*) *f* session
seau (soa) *m* bucket, pail
sec (sehk) *adj* (f sèche) dry
sèche-cheveux (sehsh-sher-*vur*) *m* hairdrier, hairdryer
sécher (say-*shay*) *v* dry
sécheresse (say-*shrehss*) *f* drought
séchoir (say-*shwaar*) *m* dryer
second (ser-*gawng*) *adj* second
secondaire (ser-gawng-*dair*) *adj* secondary; subordinate
seconde (ser-*gawngd*) *f* second
secouer (ser-*kway*) *v* *shake
secours (ser-*koor*) *m* assistance; **premier ~** first aid
secousse (ser-*kooss*) *f* jolt; jerk
secret[1] (ser-*kray*) *m* secret
secret[2] (ser-*kray*) *adj* (f secrète) secret
secrétaire (ser-kray-*tair*) *m/f* clerk, secretary
section (sehk-*s^{y}awng*) *f* section; stretch
sécurité (say-kew-ree-*tay*) *f* safety, security; **glissière de ~** crash barrier
sédatif (say-dah-*teef*) *m* sedative
***séduire** (say-*dweer*) *v* seduce
séduisant (say-dwee-*zahng*) *adj* attractive, charming
sein (sang) *m* breast; bosom
seize (saiz) *num* sixteen
seizième (seh-*z^{y}ehm*) *num* sixteenth
séjour (say-*zhoor*) *m* stay
séjourner (say-zhoor-*nay*) *v* stay
sel (sehl) *m* salt; **sels de bain** bath

salts
sélection (say-lehk-*s^{y}awng*) *f* choice, selection
sélectionner (say-lehk-s^{y}o-*nay*) *v* select
selle (sehl) *f* saddle
selon (ser-*lawng*) *prep* according to
semaine (ser-*mehn*) *f* week
semblable (sahng-*blahbl*) *adj* alike
sembler (sahng-*blay*) *v* seem; look, appear
semelle (ser-*mehl*) *f* sole
semence (ser-*mahngss*) *f* seed
semer (ser-*may*) *v* *sow
semi- (ser-*mee*) semi-
sénat (say-*nah*) *m* senate
sénateur (say-nah-*turr*) *m* senator
sénile (say-*neel*) *adj* senile
sens (sahngss) *m* sense; reason; **bon ~** sense; **en ~ inverse** the other way round; **~ unique** one-way traffic
sensation (sahng-sah-*s^{y}awng*) *f* sensation; feeling
sensationnel (sahng-sah-s^{y}o-*nehl*) *adj* sensational
sensible (sahng-*seebl*) *adj* sensitive; considerable
sentence (sahng-*tahngss*) *f* verdict
sentier (sahng-*t^{y}ay*) *m* path; trail; **~ pour piétons** footpath
sentiment (sahng-tee-*mahng*) *m* feeling; emotion; consciousness, sense
sentimental (sahng-tee-mahng-*tahl*) *adj* sentimental
***sentir** (sahng-*teer*) *v* *feel; *smell; **~ mauvais** *smell
séparation (say-pah-rah-*s^{y}awng*) *f* division
séparé (say-pah-*ray*) *adj* separate
séparément (say-pah-ray-*mahng*) *adv* apart
séparer (say-pah-*ray*) *v* separate; divide, part
sept (seht) *num* seven
septembre (sehp-*tahngbr*) September
septentrional (sehp-tahng-tree-o-*nahl*) *adj* northern, north
septicémie (sehp-tee-say-*mee*) *f* bloodpoisoning
septième (seh-*t^{y}ehm*) *num* seventh
septique (sehp-*teek*) *adj* septic
sépulture (say-pewl-*tewr*) *f* burial
serein (ser-*rang*) *adj* serene
série (say-*ree*) *f* sequence; series
sérieux (say-*r^{y}ur*) *adj* serious; *m* seriousness
seringue (ser-*ranggg*) *f* syringe
serment (sehr-*mahng*) *m* vow, oath; **faux ~** perjury
sermon (sehr-*mawng*) *m* sermon
serpent (sehr-*pahng*) *m* snake
serpentant (sehr-pahng-*tahng*) *adj* winding
serpenter (sehr-pahng-*tay*) *v* *wind
serre (sair) *f* greenhouse
serrer (say-*ray*) *v* tighten; **serré** tight, narrow
serrure (say-*rewr*) *f* lock; **trou de la ~** keyhole
sérum (say-*rom*) *m* serum
serveuse (sehr-*vurz*) *f* waitress
serviable (sehr-*v^{y}ahbl*) *adj* helpful
service (sehr-*veess*) *m* service; service charge; section; **~ à thé** tea set; **~ de table** dinner service; **~ d'étage** room service; **services postaux** postal service
serviette (sehr-*v^{y}eht*) *f* towel; napkin, serviette; briefcase; **~ de bain** bath towel; **~ de papier** paper napkin; **~ hygiénique** sanitary towel, sanitary napkin *Am*
***servir** (sehr-*veer*) *v* serve; attend on, wait on; *be of use; **se ~ de** apply
serviteur (sehr-vee-*turr*) *m* servant
seuil (sur^{ee}) *m* threshold
seul (surl) *adv* alone; *adj* single, only

seulement (surl-*mahng*) *adv* only; merely
sévère (say-*vair*) *adj* strict; harsh; severe
sévir (say-*veer*) *v* rage
sexe (sehks) *m* sex
sexualité (sehk-swah-lee-*tay*) *f* sexuality
sexuel (sehk-*swehl*) *adj* sexual
shampooing (shahng-*pwang*) *m* shampoo
short (short) *m* shorts
si (see) *conj* if; whether; *adv* so; **si … ou** whether … or
Siamois (s^{y}ah-*mwah*) *m* Siamese
siamois (s^{y}ah-*mwah*) *adj* Siamese
sida (see-*dah*) *m* Aids, AIDS
siècle (s^{y}ehkl) *m* century
siège (s^{y}aizh) *m* chair, seat; siege
sien: le ~ (ler s^{y}ang) his
sieste (s^{y}ehst) *f* siesta; nap
siffler (see-*flay*) *v* whistle
sifflet (see-*flay*) *m* whistle
signal (see-*ñahl*) *m* signal; **~ de détresse** distress signal
signalement (see-ñahl-*mahng*) *m* description
signaler (see-ñah-*lay*) *v* signal; indicate
signature (see-ñah-*tewr*) *f* signature
signe (seeñ) *m* sign; token, signal, indication; ***faire ~** *make a sign, wave
signer (see-*ñay*) *v* sign
significatif (see-ñee-fee-kah-*teef*) *adj* significant
signification (see-ñee-fee-kah-*s^{y}awng*) *f* meaning, sense
signifier (see-ñee-*f^{y}ay*) *v* *mean
silence (see-*lahngss*) *m* silence; quiet
silencieux (see-lahng-*s^{y}ur*) *adj* silent; *m* silencer; muffler *Am*
sillon (see-*^{y}awng*) *m* groove
similaire (see-mee-*lair*) *adj* similar
similitude (see-mee-lee-*tewd*) *f* similarity
simple (sangpl) *adj* simple; plain
simplement (sang-pler-*mahng*) *adv* simply
simuler (see-mew-*lay*) *v* simulate
simultané (see-mewl-tah-*nay*) *adj* simultaneous
sincère (sang-*sair*) *adj* honest, sincere
singe (sangzh) *m* monkey
singulier (sang-gew-*l^{y}ay*) *m* singular; *adj* remarkable, singular, uncommon
sinistre (see-*neestr*) *adj* sinister, ominous; *m* catastrophe
sinon (see-*nawng*) *conj* otherwise
sirène (see-*rehn*) *f* siren
sirop (see-*roa*) *m* syrup
site (seet) *m* site
situation (see-twah-*s^{y}awng*) *f* situation; position, location
situé (see-*tway*) *adj* situated
six (seess) *num* six
sixième (see-*z^{y}ehm*) *num* sixth
ski (skee) *m* ski; skiing; **~ nautique** water ski
skier (skee-*ay*) *v* ski
skieur (skee-*urr*) *m* skier
slip (sleep) *m* briefs *pl*
smoking (smo-*keeng*) *m* dinner jacket; tuxedo *Am*
S.N.C.F. (eh-sehn-say-*ehf*) *f* French national railway company
snob (snob) *adj* snooty
sobre (sobr) *adj* sober
social (so-*s^{y}ahl*) *adj* social
socialisme (so-s^{y}ah-*leesm*) *m* socialism
socialiste (so-s^{y}ah-*leest*) *adj* socialist; *m* socialist
société (so-s^{y}ay-*tay*) *f* community, society; company
sœur (surr) *f* sister
soi (swah) *pron* oneself; **soi-même** *pron* oneself

soi-disant (swah-dee-*zahng*) *adj* socalled
soie (swah) *f* silk
soif (swahf) *f* thirst
soigné (swah-*ñay*) *adj* neat; thorough
soigner (swah-*ñay*) *v* treat; nurse
soigneux (swah-*ñur*) *adj* careful
soin (swang) *m* care; ***prendre ~ de** *take care of; **soins de beauté** beauty treatment
soir (swaar) *m* night, evening; **ce ~** tonight
soirée (swah-*ray*) *f* evening
soit ... soit (swah) either ... or
soixante (swah-*sahngt*) *num* sixty
soixante-dix (swah-sahngt-*deess*) *num* seventy
sol (sol) *m* floor; soil, earth, ground
soldat (sol-*dah*) *m* soldier
solde (sold) *m* balance; **soldes** sales, clearance sale
sole (sol) *f* sole
soleil (so-*lay*) *m* sun; sunshine; **coucher du ~** sunset; **coup de ~** sunburn; **lever du ~** sunrise
solennel (so-lah-*nehl*) *adj* solemn
solide (so-*leed*) *adj* solid; firm, sound; *m* solid
solitaire (so-lee-*tair*) *adj* lonely
solitude (so-lee-*tewd*) *f* loneliness
soluble (so-*lewbl*) *adj* soluble
solution (so-lew-*s^yawng*) *f* solution
sombre (sawngbr) *adj* somber *Am*, sombre, obscure; gloomy
sommaire (so-*mair*) *m* summary
somme (som) *f* sum; amount; *m* nap; **~ globale** lump sum
sommeil (so-*may*) *m* sleep
sommelier (so-mer-*l^yay*) *m* winewaiter
sommet (so-*may*) *m* summit; top, peak, height; **~ de colline** hilltop
somnifère (som-nee-*fair*) *m* sleeping pill
somnolent (som-no-*lahng*) *adj* sleepy
son[1] (sawng) *adj* (f sa, pl ses) his; her
son[2] (sawng) *m* sound
songer (sawng-*zhay*) *v* *dream; **~ à** *think of
sonner (so-*nay*) *v* sound; *ring
sonnette (so-*neht*) *f* bell; doorbell
sorcière (sor-*s^yair*) *f* witch
sort (sawr) *m* fortune, lot, destiny
sorte (sort) *f* sort; **toutes sortes de** all sorts of
sortie (sor-*tee*) *f* way out, exit; **~ de secours** emergency exit
***sortir** (sor-*teer*) *v* *go out
sot (soa) *adj* (f sotte) foolish, silly
sottise (so-*teez*) *f* nonsense, rubbish
souche (soosh) *f* stub
souci (soo-*see*) *m* concern, worry; care
soucier (soo-*s^yay*) *v*: **se ~ de** care about
soucieux (soo-*s^yur*) *adj* concerned, worried
soucoupe (soo-*koop*) *f* saucer
soudain (soo-*dang*) *adj* sudden; *adv* suddenly
souder (soo-*day*) *v* weld
souffle (soofl) *m* breath
souffler (soo-*flay*) *v* *blow
souffrance (soo-*frahngss*) *f* suffering
***souffrir** (soo-*freer*) *v* suffer
souhait (sweh) *m* wish
souhaiter (sway-*tay*) *v* wish
souillé (soo-*^{y}ay*) *adj* soiled, dirty
soulagement (soo-lahzh-*mahng*) *m* relief
soulager (soo-lah-*zhay*) *v* relieve
soulever (sool-*vay*) *v* lift; *bring up
soulier (soo-*l^yay*) *m* shoe
souligner (soo-lee-*ñay*) *v* underline; stress, emphasize
***soumettre** (soo-*mehtr*) *v* subject; **se ~** submit
soupape (soo-*pahp*) *f* valve
soupçon (soop-*sawng*) *m* suspicion
soupçonner (soop-so-*nay*) *v* suspect

soupçonneux (soop-so-*nur*) *adj* suspicious
soupe (soop) *f* soup
souper (soo-*pay*) *m* supper
souple (soopl) *adj* supple; flexible
source (soors) *f* well; fountain, source, spring
sourcil (soor-*see*) *m* eyebrow
sourd (sōōr) *adj* deaf
sourire (soo-*reer*) *m* smile; ~ **forcé** forced smile
***sourire** (soo-*reer*) *v* smile
souris (soo-*ree*) *f* mouse
sous (soo) *prep* under
sous-estimer (soo-zeh-stee-*may*) *v* underestimate
sous-locataire (soo-lo-kah-*tair*) *m* lodger
sous-marin (soo-mah-*rang̅*) *adj* underwater
soussigné (soo-see-*ñay*) *m* undersigned
sous-sol (soo-*sol*) *m* basement
sous-titre (soo-*teetr*) *m* subtitle
***soustraire** (soo-*strair*) *v* subtract
sous-vêtements (soo-veht-*mahng̅*) *mpl* underwear
***soutenir** (soot-*neer*) *v* support; *hold up
souterrain (soo-teh-*rang̅*) *adj* underground
soutien (soo-*tʸang̅*) *m* support; relief
soutien-gorge (soo-tʸang̅-*gorzh*) *m* bra
souvenir (soo-*vneer*) *m* memory, remembrance; souvenir; **se *souvenir** recollect
souvent (soo-*vahng̅*) *adv* often; **le plus** ~ mostly
souverain (soo-*vrang̅*) *m* sovereign
spacieux (spah-*sʸur*) *adj* spacious, roomy, large
sparadrap (spah-rah-*drah*) *m* adhesive plaster
spécial (spay-*sʸahl*) *adj* special; peculiar, particular
spécialement (spay-sʸahl-*mahng̅*) *adv* especially
spécialiser (spay-sʸah-lee-*zay*) *v*: **se** ~ specialize
spécialiste (spay-sʸah-*leest*) *m/f* specialist, expert
spécialité (spay-sʸah-lee-*tay*) *f* speciality
spécifique (spay-see-*feek*) *adj* specific
spectacle (spehk-*tahkl*) *m* spectacle; show; sight; ~ **de variétés** floor show, variety show
spectaculaire (spehk-tah-kew-*lair*) *adj* sensational
spectateur (spehk-tah-*tūrr*) *m*, **-trice** *f* spectator
spectre (spehktr) *m* spook
spéculer (spay-kew-*lay*) *v* speculate
sphère (sfair) *f* sphere
spirituel (spee-ree-*twehl*) *adj* spiritual; witty
spiritueux (spee-ree-*twur*) *mpl* liquor, spirits
splendeur (splahng̅-*dūrr*) *f* splendo(u)r
splendide (splahng̅-*deed*) *adj* splendid; wonderful, glorious, enchanting, magnificent
sport (spawr) *m* sport; **sports d'hiver** winter sports
sportif (spor-*teef*) *m* sportsman
square (skwaar) *m* square
stable (stahbl) *adj* permanent, stable; solid, fixed
stade (stahd) *m* stadium
stand (stahng̅) *m* stand; ~ **de livres** bookstand
standard (stahng̅-*daar*) *adj* standard
starter (stahr-*tair*) *m* choke
station (stah-*sʸawng̅*) *f* station; ~ **balnéaire** seaside resort; ~ **de taxis** taxi rank; taxi stand *Am*; ~ **thermale**

spa
stationnaire (stah-s^{y}o-*nair*) *adj* stationary
stationnement (stah-s^{y}on-*mahng*) *m* parking; ~ **interdit** no parking
station-service (stah-s^{y}on-sehr-*veess*) *f* filling station, service station; gas station *Am*
statistique (stah-tee-*steek*) *f* statistics *pl*
statue (stah-*tew*) *f* statue
stature (stah-*tewr*) *f* figure
steak (stehk) *m* steak
stéréo (*stay*-ray-oa) *f* stereo
stérile (stay-*reel*) *adj* sterile
stériliser (stay-ree-lee-*zay*) *v* sterilize
stimulant (stee-mew-*lahng*) *m* impulse; stimulant
stimuler (stee-mew-*lay*) *v* stimulate
stock (stok) *m* stock; supply; ***avoir en** ~ stock
stop! (stop) stop!
store (stawr) *m* blind
strophe (strof) *f* stanza
structure (strewk-*tewr*) *f* structure; fabric
studio (stew-*d^{y}oa*) *m* studio; flatlet, one-room apartment
stupide (stew-*peed*) *adj* foolish, stupid
style (steel) *m* style
stylo (stee-*loa*) *m* fountain pen; ~ **à bille** ballpoint pen
subir (sew-*beer*) *v* suffer
sublime (sew-*bleem*) *adj* grand
subordonné (sew-bor-do-*nay*) *adj* subordinate
subsistance (sewb-zee-*stahngss*) *f* livelihood
substance (sewb-*stahngss*) *f* substance
substantiel (sewb-stahng-*s^{y}ehl*) *adj* substantial
substantif (sewb-stahng-*teef*) *m* noun
substituer (sewb-stee-*tway*) *v* substitute
substitut (sewb-stee-*tew*) *m* substitute; deputy
subtil (sewb-*teel*) *adj* subtle
suburbain (sew-bewr-*bang*) *adj* suburban
subvention (sewb-vahng-*s^{y}awng*) *f* subsidy; grant
succéder (sewk-say-*day*) *v* succeed
succès (sewk-*say*) *m* success; hit
succession (sewk-seh-*s^{y}awng*) *f* sequence
succomber (sew-kawng-*bay*) *v* succumb
succulent (sew-kew-*lahng*) *adj* tasty
succursale (sew-kewr-*sahl*) *f* branch
sucer (sew-*say*) *v* suck
sucre (sewkr) *m* sugar
sucrer (sew-*kray*) *v* sweeten; **sucré** sweet
sud (sewd) *m* south
sud-américain (sew-dah-may-ree-*kang*) *adj* Latin-American
sud-est (sew-*dehst*) *m* southeast
sud-ouest (sew-*dwehst*) *m* southwest
Suède (swehd) *f* Sweden
suédois (sway-*dwah*) *adj* Swedish
suer (sway) *v* perspire, sweat
sueur (swurr) *f* perspiration, sweat
***suffire** (sew-*feer*) *v* *do, suffice
suffisant (sew-fee-*zahng*) *adj* enough, sufficient
suffrage (sew-*fraazh*) *m* vote
suggérer (sewg-zhay-*ray*) *v* suggest
suggestion (sewg-zheh-*st^{y}awng*) *f* suggestion
suicide (swee-*seed*) *m* suicide
Suisse (sweess) *f* Switzerland; *m/f* Swiss
suisse (sweess) *adj* Swiss
suite (sweet) *f* sequel; series; **et ainsi de** ~ and so on; **par la** ~ afterwards; **tout de** ~ at once, instantly
suivant (swee-*vahng*) *adj* following, next

***suivre** (sweevr) *v* follow; ***faire ~** forward
sujet (sew-*zhay*) *m* subject; issue, topic, theme; **~ à** liable to, subject to
superbe (sew-*pehrb*) *adj* superb
superficiel (sew-pehr-fee-*s^{y}ehl*) *adj* superficial
superflu (sew-pehr-*flew*) *adj* superfluous; unnecessary, redundant
supérieur (sew-pay-*r^{y}urr*) *adj* superior; top, upper; excellent
supermarché (sew-pehr-mahr-*shay*) *m* supermarket
superstition (sew-pehr-stee-*s^{y}awng*) *f* superstition
superviser (sew-pehr-vee-*zay*) *v* supervise
supervision (sew-pehr-vee-*z^{y}awng*) *f* supervision
supplément (sew-play-*mahng*) *m* supplement; surcharge
supplémentaire (sew-play-mahng-*tair*) *adj* additional; extra
supplier (sew-plee-*ay*) *v* beg
supporter[1] (sew-por-*tay*) *v* *bear; support
supporter[2] (sew-por-*tair*) *m* supporter
supposer (sew-poa-*zay*) *v* suppose; guess, assume, reckon
suppositoire (sew-poa-zee-*twaar*) *m* suppository
supprimer (sew-pree-*may*) *v* *do away with
suprême (sew-*prehm*) *adj* supreme
sur (sewr) *prep* upon, on; in; about
sûr (sewr) *adj* sure; safe, secure; **bien ~** naturally
surcharge (sewr-*shahrzh*) *f* overweight
sûrement (sewr-*mahng*) *adv* surely
surface (sewr-*fahss*) *f* surface, surface area
surgelé (sewr-zher-*lay*) *adj* deep- *or* quick-frozen
surgir (sewr-*zheer*) *v* *arise
surmené (sewr-mer-*nay*) *adj* overworked
surmener (sewr-mer-*nay*) *v*: **se ~** overwork
surnom (sewr-*nawng*) *m* nickname
surpasser (sewr-pah-*say*) *v* *outdo, exceed
surplus (sewr-*plew*) *m* surplus
***surprendre** (sewr-*prahngdr*) *v* surprise; amaze; *catch
surprise (sewr-*preez*) *f* surprise
surprise-partie (sewr-preez-pahr-*tee*) *f* party
surtout (sewr-*too*) *adv* most of all
surveillance (sewr-veh-^{y}*ahngss*) *f* supervision
surveillant (sewr-veh-^{y}*ahng*) *m* warden, supervisor
surveiller (sewr-vay-^{y}*ay*) *v* watch; guard, patrol
***survenir** (sewr-ver-*neer*) *v* occur
survie (sewr-*vee*) *f* survival
***survivre** (sewr-*veevr*) *v* survive
suspect (sew-*spehkt*) *adj* suspicious; *m* suspect
suspecter (sew-spehk-*tay*) *v* suspect
suspendre (sew-*spahngdr*) *v* *hang; discontinue, suspend
suspension (sew-spahng-*s^{y}awng*) *f* suspension
suture (sew-*tewr*) *f* stitch
svelte (svehlt) *adj* slender
syllabe (see-*lahb*) *f* syllable
symbole (sang-*bol*) *m* symbol
sympathie (sang-pah-*tee*) *f* sympathy
sympathique (sang-pah-*teek*) *adj* nice; pleasant
symphonie (sang-fo-*nee*) *f* symphony
symptôme (sangp-*toam*) *m* symptom
synagogue (see-nah-*gog*) *f* synagogue
syndicat (sang-dee-*kah*) *m* trade union; **~ d'initiative** tourist office
synonyme (see-no-*neem*) *m* synonym

synthétique (sa$\overline{ng}$-tay-*teek*) *adj* synthetic
Syrie (see-*ree*) *f* Syria
syrien (see-*r*^{y}*a$\overline{ng}$*) *adj* Syrian
systématique (see-stay-mah-*teek*) *adj* systematic
système (see-*stehm*) *m* system; **~ décimal** decimal system; **~ de lubrification** lubrication system

T

tabac (tah-*bah*) *m* tobacco; **bureau de ~** tobacconist's; **débitant de ~** tobacconist; **~ à rouler** cigarette tobacco; **tabac pour pipe** pipe tobacco
table (tahbl) *f* table; **~ des matières** table of contents
tableau (tah-*bloa*) *m* chart; board; **~ de bord** dashboard; **~ de conversions** conversion chart; **~ de distribution** switchboard; **~ noir** blackboard
tablette (tah-*bleht*) *f* tablet
tablier (tah-blee-*ay*) *m* apron
tabou (tah-*boo*) *m* taboo
tache (tahsh) *f* speck, stain, spot, blot
tâche (taash) *f* duty, task
tacher (tah-*shay*) *v* stain
tâcher (tah-*shay*) *v* try
tacheté (tahsh-*tay*) *adj* spotted
tactique (tahk-*teek*) *f* tactics *pl*
taille (tigh) *f* waist; size
taille-crayon (tigh-kreh-^{y}*aw$\overline{ng}$*) *m* pencil sharpener
tailler (tah-^{y}*ay*) *v* trim, chip; carve
tailleur (tah-^{y}*$\overline{ur}$r*) *m* tailor
***taire** (tair): **se ~** *keep quiet, *be silent
talc (tahlk) *m* talc powder
talent (tah-*lah$\overline{ng}$*) *m* talent; faculty, gift
talon (tah-*law$\overline{ng}$*) *m* heel; counterfoil
tambour (tah$\overline{ng}$-*b$\overline{oo}$r*) *m* drum; **~ de frein** brake drum
tamiser (tah-mee-*zay*) *v* sift, sieve
tampon (tah$\overline{ng}$-*paw$\overline{ng}$*) *m* tampon
tamponner (tah$\overline{ng}$-po-*nay*) *v* bump
tandis que (tah$\overline{ng}$-dee ker) while; whilst
tangible (tah$\overline{ng}$-*zheebl*) *adj* tangible
tanière (tah-*n*^{y}*air*) *f* den
tante (tah$\overline{ng}$t) *f* aunt
tapageur (tah-pah-*zh$\overline{ur}$r*) *adj* rowdy
taper (tah-*pay*) *v* slap; **~ à la machine** type
tapis (tah-*pee*) *m* carpet; rug, mat
taquiner (tah-kee-*nay*) *v* kid, tease
tard (taar) *adj* late
tarif (tah-*reef*) *m* rate
tarte (tahrt) *f* tart; flan
tartine (tahr-*teen*) *f* sandwich
tas (tah) *m* pile, lot, heap
tasse (tahss) *f* cup; **~ à thé** teacup
taureau (toa-*roa*) *m* bull
taux (toa) *m* tariff; **~ d'escompte** bankrate
taverne (tah-*vehrn*) *f* tavern
taxe (tahks) *f* tax
taxi (tahk-*see*) *m* taxi; cab; **chauffeur de ~** taxi driver
taximètre (tahk-see-*mehtr*) *m* taximeter
tchèque (chehk) *adj* Czech
te (ter) *pron* you; yourself
technicien (tehk-nee-*s*^{y}*a$\overline{ng}$*) *m* technician
technique (tehk-*neek*) *f* technique; *adj*

technical
technologie (tehk-no-lo-*zhee*) *f* technology
***teindre** (tan̅g̅dr) *v* dye
teint (tan̅g̅) *m* complexion
teinture (tan̅g̅-*tewr*) *f* dye
teinturerie (tan̅g̅-tewr-*ree*) *f* dry cleaner's
tel (tehl) *adj* such; **~ que** such as
télé (tay-*lay*) *f* television
télécarte (tay-lay-*kahrt*) *f* phonecard
télégramme (tay-lay-*grahm*) *m* cable, telegram
télé-objectif (tay-lay-ob-zhehk-*teef*) *m* telephoto lens
téléphone (tay-lay-*fon*) *m* telephone; phone; **coup de ~** telephone call
téléphoner (tay-lay-fo-*nay*) *v* phone; call, ring up; call up *Am*
téléski (tay-lay-*skee*) *m* ski lift
téléviseur (tay-lay-vee-*zu̅r̅r*) *m* television set
télévision (tay-lay-vee-*z^{y}awn̅g̅*) *f* television; television set; **~ par câble** cable television; **~ par satellite** satellite television
télex (tay-*lehks*) *m* telex
tellement (tehl-*mahn̅g̅*) *adv* such; so
téméraire (tay-may-*rair*) *adj* daring
témoignage (tay-mwah-*n^{y}aazh*) *m* testimony
témoigner (tay-mwah-*ñay*) *v* testify
témoin (tay-*mwan̅g̅*) *m* witness; **~ oculaire** eye-witness
tempe (tahn̅g̅p) *f* temple
température (tahn̅g̅-pay-rah-*te̅w̅r*) *f* temperature; **~ ambiante** room temperature
tempête (tahn̅g̅-*peht*) *f* storm; tempest, gale; **~ de neige** snowstorm, blizzard
temple (tahn̅g̅pl) *m* temple
temporaire (tahn̅g̅-po-*rair*) *adj* temporary
temps (tahn̅g̅) *m* time; weather; **à ~** in time; **ces derniers ~** lately; **de temps en ~** now and then, occasionally; **~ libre** spare time
tenailles (ter-*nigh*) *fpl* pincers *pl*
tendance (tahn̅g̅-*dahn̅g̅ss*) *f* tendency; ***avoir ~** *be inclined to, tend
tendon (tahn̅g̅-*dawn̅g̅*) *m* sinew, tendon
tendre[1] (tahn̅g̅dr) *adj* delicate, tender
tendre[2] (tahn̅g̅dr) *v* stretch; **~ à** tend to; **tendu** tense
tendresse (tahn̅g̅-*drehss*) *f* tenderness
ténèbres (tay-*nehbr*) *fpl* dark; gloom
***tenir** (ter-*neer*) *v* *hold; *keep; **se ~ debout** *stand; **~ à** care for
tennis (tay-*neess*) *m* tennis; **~ de table** table tennis
tension (tahn̅g̅-*s^{y}awn̅g̅*) *f* tension; stress, strain; pressure; **~ artérielle** blood pressure
tentation (tahn̅g̅-tah-*s^{y}awn̅g̅*) *f* temptation
tentative (tahn̅g̅-tah-*teev*) *f* try, attempt
tente (tahn̅g̅t) *f* tent
tenter (tahn̅g̅-*tay*) *v* try; attempt; tempt
tenue (ter-*new*) *f* conduct; dress; **~ de soirée** evening dress
térébenthine (tay-ray-bahn̅g̅-*teen*) *f* turpentine
terme (tehrm) *m* term
terminer (tehr-mee-*nay*) *v* finish; **se ~** expire
terminus (tehr-mee-*newss*) *m* terminal
terne (tehrn) *adj* dull, colo(u)rless
terrain (teh-*ran̅g̅*) *m* terrain; grounds; **~ d'aviation** airfield; **~ de camping** camping site; **~ de golf** golf course; **~ de jeux** recreation ground
terrasse (teh-*rahss*) *f* terrace
terre (tair) *f* earth; soil, land; **à ~** ashore; **hautes terres** uplands *pl*; **par ~** down; **~ cuite** terracotta; **~ ferme**

mainland
terreur (teh-*rurr*) *f* terror
terrible (tay-*reebl*) *adj* terrible; awful, dreadful, frightful
terrifiant (teh-ree-*f^{y}ahng*) *adj* terrifying; horrible, creepy
terrifier (teh-ree-*f^{y}ay*) *v* terrify
territoire (teh-ree-*twaar*) *m* territory
terroir (teh-*rwaar*) *m* soil
terrorisme (teh-ro-*reesm*) *m* terrorism
terroriste (teh-ro-*reest*) *m* terrorist
test (tehst) *m* test
testament (teh-stah-*mahng*) *m* will
tête (teht) *f* head
têtu (tay-*tew*) *adj* head-strong, stubborn
texte (tehkst) *m* text
textile (tehk-*steel*) *m* textile
T.G.V. (tay-zhay-*vay*) *m* high-speed train
thaïlandais (tah-ee-lahng-*day*) *adj* Thai
Thaïlande (tah-ee-*lahngd*) *f* Thailand
thé (tay) *m* tea
théâtre (tay-*aatr*) *m* theater *Am*, theatre; drama; **~ de marionnettes** puppet-show; **~ de variétés** variety theatre (theater *Am*)
théière (tay-*^{y}air*) *f* teapot
thème (tehm) *m* theme
théologie (tay-o-lo-*zhee*) *f* theology
théorie (tay-o-*ree*) *f* theory
théorique (tay-o-*reek*) *adj* theoretical
thérapie (tay-rah-*pee*) *f* therapy
thermomètre (tehr-mo-*mehtr*) *m* thermometer
thermoplongeur (tehr-moa-plawng-*zhurr*) *m* immersion heater
thermos (tehr-*moss*) *m* thermos flask, vacuum flask
thermostat (tehr-mo-*stah*) *m* thermostat
thèse (taiz) *f* thesis
thon (tawng) *m* tuna
thym (tang) *m* thyme
ticket (tee-*kay*) *m* ticket
tiède (t^{y}ehd) *adj* lukewarm, tepid
tien: le ~ (ler t^{y}ang) yours
tiers (t^{y}air) *adj* (f tierce) third
tige (teezh) *f* stem; rod
tigre (teegr) *m* tiger
tilleul (tee-*^{y}url*) *m* limetree, lime
timbre (tangbr) *m* stamp; tone
timbre-poste (tang-brer-*post*) *m* postage stamp
timide (tee-*meed*) *adj* timid, shy
timidité (tee-mee-dee-*tay*) *f* timidity, shyness
tirage (tee-*raazh*) *m* draw; issue
tire-bouchon (teer-boo-*shawng*) *m* corkscrew
tirer (tee-*ray*) *v* *draw, pull; fire, *shoot
tiroir (tee-*rwaar*) *m* drawer
tisane (tee-*zahn*) *f* infusion; tea
tisser (tee-*say*) *v* *weave
tissu (tee-*sew*) *m* tissue; fabric, cloth, material
tissu-éponge (tee-sew-ay-*pawngz*) *m* towel(l)ing
titre (teetr) *m* title; heading
toast (toast) *m* toast
toboggan (to-bo-*gahng*) *m* slide
toi (twah) *pron* you
toile (twahl) *f* linen; **grosse ~** canvas
toilettes (twah-*leht*) *fpl* toilet, bathroom; washroom *Am*; **~ pour dames** ladies' room; powder room; **~ pour hommes** men's room
toi-même (twah-*mehm*) *pron* yourself
toit (twah) *m* roof; **~ de chaume** *m* thatched roof
tolérable (to-lay-*rahbl*) *adj* tolerable
tolérer (to-lay-*ray*) *v* *bear
tomate (to-*maht*) *f* tomato
tombe (tawngb) *f* tomb, grave
tomber (tawng-*bay*) *v* *fall
tome (tom) *m* volume

ton[1] (tawng̅) *adj* (f ta, pl tes) your
ton[2] (tawng̅) *m* note, tone
tonique (to-*neek*) *m* tonic; **~ capillaire** hair tonic
tonne (ton) *f* ton
tonneau (to-*noa*) *m* barrel; cask
tonnerre (to-*nair*) *m* thunder
torche (torsh) *f* torch
torchon (tor-*shawng̅*) *m* tea towel, kitchen towel *Am*
tordre (tordr) *v* twist; wrench
tordu (tor-*dew*) *adj* crooked
torsion (tor-*s*ʸ*awng̅*) *f* twist
tort (tawr) *m* wrong; harm; ***avoir ~** *be wrong; ***faire du ~** harm
tortue (tor-*tew*) *f* turtle
torture (tor-*tewr*) *f* torture
torturer (tor-tew-*ray*) *v* torture
tôt (toa) *adv* early
total (to-*tahl*) *adj* total; utter, overall; *m* total
totalement (to-tahl-*mahng̅*) *adv* completely
totalitaire (to-tah-lee-*tair*) *adj* totalitarian
touchant (too-*shahng̅*) *adj* touching
toucher (too-*shay*) *v* touch; affect; *hit; cash; *m* touch
toujours (too-*zhoor*) *adv* always; ever; **~ et encore** again and again
tour (toor) *m* turn; move; *f* tower
tourisme (too-*reesm*) *m* tourism
touriste (too-*reest*) *m/f* tourist
tourment (toor-*mahng̅*) *m* torment
tourmenter (toor-mahng̅-*tay*) *v* torment
tournant (toor-*nahng̅*) *m* turn, curve; turning point
tourne-disque (toor-ner-*deesk*) *m* record player
tourner (toor-*nay*) *v* turn; *spin
tournevis (toor-ner-*veess*) *m* screwdriver
tournoi (toor-*nwah*) *m* tournament
tousser (too-*say*) *v* cough
tout (too) *adj* all; every; entire; *pron* everything; **du ~** at all; **en ~** altogether; **~ à fait** quite; **~ à l'heure** presently; **~ au plus** at most; **~ ce que** whatever; **~ de suite** immediately, straight away; **~ droit** straight on; **~ le monde** everybody
toutefois (toot-*fwah*) *adv* still
toux (too) *f* cough
toxique (tok-*seek*) *adj* toxic
tracas (trah-*kah*) *m* bother
tracasser (trah-kah-*say*) *v* bother
trace (trahss) *f* trace
tracer (trah-*say*) *v* trace
tracteur (trahk-*turr*) *m* tractor
tradition (trah-dee-*s*ʸ*awng̅*) *f* tradition
traditionnel (trah-dee-sʸo-*nehl*) *adj* traditional
traducteur (trah-dewk-*turr*) *m*, **-trice** *f* translator
traduction (trah-dewk-*s*ʸ*awng̅*) *f* translation
***traduire** (trah-*dweer*) *v* translate
trafic (trah-*feek*) *m* traffic
tragédie (trah-zhay-*dee*) *f* tragedy; drama
tragique (trah-*zheek*) *adj* tragic
trahir (trah-*eer*) *v* betray
trahison (trah-ee-*zawng̅*) *f* treason
train (trang̅) *m* train; **~ de marchandises** goods train; freight train *Am*; **~ de nuit** night train; **~ de voyageurs** passenger train; **~ direct** through train; **~ express** fast train; **~ local** local train
traîneau (treh-*noa*) *m* sled(ge); sleigh
traîner (tray-*nay*) *v* drag, haul
trait (tray) *m* line; trait; **~ de caractère** characteristic; **~ d'union** hyphen; **~ du visage** feature
traite (treht) *f* draft
traité (tray-*tay*) *m* treaty
traitement (treht-*mahng̅*) *m* treatment

traiter (tray-*tay*) *v* treat; handle
traître (traitr) *m* traitor
trajet (trah-*zhay*) *m* way
tram (trahm) *m* tram; streetcar *Am*
tranche (trahn̅g̅sh) *f* slice
trancher (trahn̅g̅-*shay*) *v* *cut off; settle
tranquille (trahn̅g̅-*keel*) *adj* calm; tranquil, quiet, still
tranquillité (trahn̅g̅-kee-lee-*tay*) *f* quietness
transaction (trahn̅g̅-zahk-*s*^{y}*awn̅g̅*) *f* transaction, deal
transatlantique (trahn̅g̅-zaht-lahn̅g̅-*teek*) *adj* transatlantic
transférer (trahn̅g̅-sfay-*ray*) *v* transfer
transformateur (trahn̅g̅-sfor-mah-*ūrr*) *m* transformer
transformer (trahn̅g̅-sfor-*may*) *v* transform
transition (trahn̅g̅-zee-*s*^{y}*awn̅g̅*) *f* transition
transparent (trahn̅g̅-spah-*rahn̅g̅*) *adj* transparent
transpiration (trahn̅g̅-spee-rah-*s*^{y}*awn̅g̅*) *f* perspiration
transpirer (trahn̅g̅-spee-*ray*) *v* perspire
transport (trahn̅g̅-*spawr*) *m* transportation, transport
transporter (trahn̅g̅-spor-*tay*) *v* transport
travail (trah-*vigh*) *m* (pl travaux) work, labo(u)r, job; **~ artisanal** handwork; **~ manuel** handicraft; **travaux ménagers** housekeeping, housework
travailler (trah-vah-^{y}*ay*) *v* work
travailleur (trah-vah-^{y}*ūrr*) *m*, **-euse** *f* worker
travers: à ~ (ah trah-*vair*) through; across
traversée (trah-vehr-*say*) *f* passage, crossing
traverser (trah-vehr-*say*) *v* cross; pass through
trébucher (tray-bew-*shay*) *v* stumble
trèfle (trehfl) *m* clover; shamrock
treize (traiz) *num* thirteen
treizième (treh-*z*^{y}*ehm*) *num* thirteenth
trembler (trahn̅g̅-*blay*) *v* tremble; shiver
tremper (trahn̅g̅-*pay*) *v* soak
trente (trahn̅g̅t) *num* thirty
trentième (trahn̅g̅-*t*^{y}*ehm*) *num* thirtieth
trépasser (tray-pah-*say*) *v* pass away
très (tray) *adv* very
trésor (tray-*zawr*) *m* treasure; darling; **Trésor** treasury
triangle (tree-*ahn̅g̅gl*) *m* triangle
triangulaire (tree-ahn̅g̅-gew-*lair*) *adj* triangular
tribord (tree-*bawr*) *m* starboard
tribu (tree-*bew*) *f* tribe
tribunal (tree-bew-*nahl*) *m* court, law court
tribune (tree-*bewn*) *f* stand
tricher (tree-*shay*) *v* cheat
tricot (tree-*koa*) *m* knitted wear; jersey; **~ de corps** undershirt
tricoter (tree-ko-*tay*) *v* *knit
trier (tree-*ay*) *v* sort
trimestre (tree-*mehstr*) *m* quarter
trimestriel (tree-meh-stree-*ehl*) *adj* quarterly
triomphant (tree-awn̅g̅-*fahn̅g̅*) *adj* triumphant
triomphe (tree-*awn̅g̅f*) *m* triumph
triompher (tree-awn̅g̅-*fay*) *v* triumph
triste (treest) *adj* sad
tristesse (tree-*stehss*) *f* sorrow, sadness
trivial (tree-*v*^{y}*ahl*) *adj* coarse, crude
trognon (tro-*ñawn̅g̅*) *m* core
trois (trwah) *num* three; **~ quarts** three-quarter
troisième (trwah-*z*^{y}*ehm*) *num* third
tromper (trawn̅g̅-*pay*) *v* deceive; **se ~** *be mistaken; err

tromperie (trawng-*pree*) *f* deceit
trompette (trawng-*peht*) *f* trumpet
tronc (trawng) *m* trunk
trône (troan) *m* throne
trop (troa) *adv* too
tropical (tro-pee-*kahl*) *adj* tropical
tropiques (tro-*peek*) *mpl* tropics *pl*
troquer (tro-*kay*) *v* swap
trottoir (tro-*twaar*) *m* pavement, sidewalk *Am*
trou (troo) *m* hole
trouble (troobl) *adj* turbid; dubious; *m* perturbation
troubler (troo-*blay*) *v* disturb
troupeau (troo-*poa*) *m* herd; flock
troupes (troop) *fpl* troops *pl*
trousseau (troo-*soa*) *m* kit
trousse de secours (trooss der ser-*koor*) first aid kit
trouver (troo-*vay*) *v* *find; *come across; consider
truc (trewk) *m* trick
truite (trweet) *f* trout
tu (tew) *pron* you
tube (tewb) *m* tube; **~ de plongée** snorkel
tuberculose (tew-behr-kew-*loaz*) *f* tuberculosis
tuer (tway) *v* kill
tuile (tweel) *f* tile
tulipe (tew-*leep*) *f* tulip
tumeur (tew-*murr*) *f* tumo(u)r; growth
tunique (tew-*neek*) *f* tunic
Tunisie (tew-nee-*zee*) *f* Tunisia
tunisien (tew-nee-*z^{y}ang*) *adj* Tunisian
tunnel (tew-*nehl*) *m* tunnel
turbine (tewr-*been*) *f* turbine
turc (tewrk) *adj* Turkish; **Turc** *m* Turk
Turquie (tewr-*kee*) *f* Turkey
tuteur (tew-*turr*) *m* guardian, tutor
tuyau (twee-*^{y}oa*) *m* tube, pipe; **~ d'échappement** exhaust
tympan (tang-*pahng*) *m* eardrum
type (teep) *m* type; guy, chap
typhoïde (tee-fo-*eed*) *f* typhoid
typique (tee-*peek*) *adj* typical

U

ulcère (ewl-*sair*) *m* ulcer; **~ à l'estomac** gastric ulcer
ultime (ewl-*teem*) *adj* ultimate
ultra-violet (ewl-trah-v^{y}o-*lay*) *adj* ultraviolet
un (urng) *art* (f une) a *art*; *num* one; **l'un l'autre** each other; **l'un ou l'autre** either; **ni l'un ni l'autre** neither
unanime (ew-nah-*neem*) *adj* unanimous
uni (ew-*nee*) *adj* joint; smooth
uniforme (ew-nee-*form*) *m* uniform; *adj* uniform
unilatéral (ew-nee-lah-tay-*rahl*) *adj* one-sided
union (ew-*n^{y}awng*) *f* union
unique (ew-*neek*) *adj* unique; sole
uniquement (ew-neek-*mahng*) *adv* exclusively
unir (ew-*neer*) *v* unite
unité (ew-nee-*tay*) *f* unity; unit; **~ monétaire** monetary unit
univers (ew-nee-*vair*) *m* universe
universel (ew-nee-vehr-*sehl*) *adj* universal; all-round
université (ew-nee-vehr-see-*tay*) *f* university
urbain (ewr-*bang*) *adj* urban
urgence (ewr-*zhahngss*) *f* urgency; emergency

urgent (ewr-*zhahng*) *adj* pressing, urgent

urine (ew-*reen*) *f* urine

Uruguay (ew-rew-*gay*) *m* Uruguay

uruguayen (ew-rew-gay-^{y}*ang*) *adj* Uruguayan

usage (ew-*zaazh*) *m* usage

usager (ew-zah-*zhay*) *m* user

user (ew-*zay*) *v* use up; wear out; **usé** worn; threadbare, worn-out

usine (ew-*zeen*) *f* factory; mill, plant, works *pl*; **~ à gaz** gasworks

ustensile (ew-stahng-*seel*) *m* utensil

usuel (ew-*zwehl*) *adj* customary

utile (ew-*teel*) *adj* useful

utilisable (ew-tee-lee-*zahbl*) *adj* usable

utilisateur (ew-tee-lee-zah-*turr*) *m* consumer

utilisation (ew-tee-lee-zah-*s^{y}awng*) *f* utilization

utiliser (ew-tee-lee-*zay*) *v* utilize, employ

utilité (ew-tee-lee-*tay*) *f* utility, use

V

vacance (vah-*kahngss*) *f* vacancy; **vacances** holiday

vacant (vah-*kahng*) *adj* vacant, unoccupied

vacarme (vah-*kahrm*) *m* noise, racket

vaccination (vahk-see-nah-*s^{y}awng*) *f* vaccination

vacciner (vahk-see-*nay*) *v* vaccinate

vache (vahsh) *f* cow

vaciller (vah-see-^{y}*ay*) *v* falter

vagabond (vah-gah-*bawng*) *m* tramp

vagabonder (vah-gah-bawng-*day*) *v* tramp, roam

vague (vahg) *f* wave; *adj* vague; faint, obscure

vaillance (vah-^{y}*ahngss*) *f* courage

vain (vang) *adj* vain; **en ~** in vain

***vaincre** (vangkr) *v* *overcome; conquer, defeat

vainqueur (vang-*kurr*) *m* winner

vaisseau (vay-*soa*) *m* vessel; **~ sanguin** blood vessel

vaisselle (veh-*sehl*) *f* crockery; dishes *pl*; ***faire la ~** wash up

valable (vah-*lahbl*) *adj* valid

valeur (vah-*lurr*) *f* value, worth; **sans ~** worthless

valise (vah-*leez*) *f* case, bag, suitcase

vallée (vah-*lay*) *f* valley

***valoir** (vah-*lwaar*) *v* *be worth; **~ la peine** *be worth-while

valse (vahls) *f* waltz

vanille (vah-*neey*) *f* vanilla

vaniteux (vah-nee-*tur*) *adj* vain

vanneau (vah-*noa*) *m* peewit

vanter (vahng-*tay*): **se ~** boast

vapeur (vah-*purr*) *f* steam; vapo(u)r

vaporisateur (vah-po-ree-zah-*turr*) *m* atomizer

variable (vah-*r^{y}ahbl*) *adj* variable

variation (vah-r^{y}ah-*s^{y}awng*) *f* variation

varice (vah-*reess*) *f* varicose vein

varicelle (vah-ree-*sehl*) *f* chickenpox

varier (vah-*r^{y}ay*) *v* vary

variété (vah-r^{y}ay-*tay*) *f* variety

variole (vah-*r^{y}ol*) *f* smallpox

vase (vaaz) *m* vase; *f* mud *m*

vaseline (vah-*zleen*) *f* vaseline

vaste (vahst) *adj* large; wide, broad, vast; extensive

vautour (voa-*toor*) *m* vulture

veau (voa) *m* calf; veal; calf skin

végétarien (vay-zhay-tah-*r^{y}ahng*) *m* vegetarian
végétation (vay-zhay-tah-*s^{y}awng*) *f* vegetation
véhicule (vay-ee-*kewl*) *m* vehicle
veille (vay^y) *f* day before
veiller (vay-*^{y}ay*) *v* stay awake; **~ sur** watch over
veine (vain) *f* vein
vélo (vay-*loa*) *m* bicycle, cycle
vélomoteur (vay-loa-mo-*turr*) *m* motorbike *Am*, moped
velours (ver-*loor*) *m* velvet; **~ côtelé** corduroy; **~ de coton** cotton velvet
vendable (vahng-*dahbl*) *adj* saleable
vendange (vahng-*dahngzh*) *f* vintage
vendeur (vahng-*durr*) *m*, **-euse** *f* vendor; seller; sales clerk *Am*, shop assistant
vendre (vahngdr) *v* *sell; **à ~** for sale
vendredi (vahng-drer-*dee*) *m* Friday
vénéneux (vay-nay-*nur*) *adj* poisonous
vénérable (vay-nay-*rahbl*) *adj* venerable
Venezuela (vay-nay-zway-*lah*) *m* Venezuela
vénézuélien (vay-nay-zway-*l^{y}ahng*) *adj* Venezuelan
vengeance (vahng-*zhahngss*) *f* revenge
venger (vahng-*zhay*) *v* avenge
***venir** (ver-*neer*) *v* *come; ***faire ~** *send for
vent (vahng) *m* wind; **coup de ~** blow
vente (vahngt) *f* sale; **~ aux enchères** auction; **~ en gros** wholesale
venteux (vahng-*tur*) *adj* windy, gusty
ventilateur (vahng-tee-lah-*turr*) *m* fan, ventilator
ventilation (vahng-tee-lah-*s^{y}awng*) *f* ventilation
ventiler (vahng-tee-*lay*) *v* ventilate
ventre (vahngtr) *m* belly
venue (ver-*new*) *f* arrival
ver (vair) *m* worm
véranda (vay-rahng-*dah*) *f* veranda
verbal (vehr-*bahl*) *adj* verbal
verbe (vehrb) *m* verb
verdict (vehr-*deekt*) *m* verdict
verger (vehr-*zhay*) *m* orchard
véridique (vay-ree-*deek*) *adj* truthful
vérifier (vay-ree-*f^{y}ay*) *v* verify; check
véritable (vay-ree-*tahbl*) *adj* real
vérité (vay-ree-*tay*) *f* truth
vernir (vehr-*neer*) *v* varnish; glaze
vernis (vehr-*nee*) *m* varnish; lacquer; **~ à ongle** nail polish
verre (vair) *m* glass; **~ de couleur** stained glass; **~ grossissant** magnifying glass; **verres de contact** contact lenses
verrou (veh-*roo*) *m* bolt
vers (vair) *m* verse; *prep* towards, at; **~ le bas** downwards; **~ le haut** up
versant (vehr-*sahng*) *m* slope
versement (vehr-ser-*mahng*) *m* deposit, remittance
verser (vehr-*say*) *v* pour; *shed
version (vehr-*s^{y}awng*) *f* version
vert (vair) *adj* green
vertical (vehr-tee-*kahl*) *adj* vertical
vertige (vehr-*teezh*) *m* dizziness, giddiness
vertu (vehr-*tew*) *f* virtue
vessie (vay-*see*) *f* bladder
veste (vehst) *f* jacket; **~ de sport** blazer
vestiaire (veh-*st^{y}air*) *m* cloakroom; checkroom *Am*
vestibule (veh-stee-*bewl*) *m* hall, lobby
veston (veh-*stawng*) *m* jacket; **~ sport** sports jacket
vêtements (veht-*mahng*) *mpl* clothes *pl*; **~ de sport** sportswear
vétérinaire (vay-tay-ree-*nair*) *m/f* veterinary surgeon
***vêtir** (vay-*teer*) *v* dress
veuf (vurf) *m* widower

veuve (vurv) *f* widow
via (vee-*ah*) *prep* via
viaduc (v^{y}ah-*dewk*) *m* viaduct
viande (v^{y}ahngd) *f* meat
vibration (vee-brah-*s^{y}awng*) *f* vibration
vibrer (vee-*bray*) *v* vibrate; tremble
vicaire (vee-*kair*) *m* vicar
vice-président (vee-spray-zee-*dahng*) *m* vice president
vicieux (vee-*s^{y}ur*) *adj* vicious
victime (veek-*teem*) *f* victim; casualty
victoire (veek-*twaar*) *f* victory
vide (veed) *adj* empty; *m* vacuum
vider (vee-*day*) *v* empty
vie (vee) *f* life; lifetime; **en ~** alive; **~ privée** privacy
vieillard (v^{y}eh-*^{y}aar*) *m* old man
vieillesse (v^{y}eh-*^{y}ehss*) *f* age, old age
vieilli (v^{y}ay-*^{y}ee*) *adj* ancient
vieillot (v^{y}eh-*^{y}oa*) *adj* quaint
vierge (v^{y}ehrzh) *f* virgin
vieux (v^{y}ur) *adj* (vieil; f vieille) old; aged, ancient
vif (veef) *adj* vivid; intense, brisk, lively
vigilant (vee-zhee-*lahng*) *adj* vigilant
vigne (veeñ) *f* vine
vignoble (vee-*ñobl*) *m* vineyard
vigoureux (vee-goo-*rur*) *adj* vigorous
vigueur (vee-*gurr*) *f* strength
vilain (vee-*lang*) *adj* bad
villa (vee-*lah*) *f* villa; cottage
village (vee-*laazh*) *m* village
ville (veel) *f* town
vin (vang) *m* wine
vinaigre (vee-*naigr*) *m* vinegar
vingt (vang) *num* twenty
vingtième (vang-*t^{y}ehm*) *num* twentieth
violation (v^{y}o-lah-*s^{y}awng*) *f* violation
violence (v^{y}o-*lahngss*) *f* violence
violent (v^{y}o-*lahng*) *adj* violent; fierce, severe
violer (v^{y}o-*lay*) *v* assault, rape
violet (v^{y}o-*lay*) *adj* violet
violette (v^{y}o-*leht*) *f* violet
violon (v^{y}o-*lawng*) *m* violin
virage (vee-*raazh*) *m* turning, bend
virer (vee-*ray*) *v* turn
virgule (veer-*gewl*) *f* comma
vis (veess) *f* screw
visa (vee-*zah*) *m* visa
visage (vee-*zaazh*) *m* face
viser (vee-*zay*) *v* aim at
viseur (vee-*zurr*) *m* viewfinder
visibilité (vee-zee-bee-lee-*tay*) *f* visibility
visible (vee-*zeebl*) *adj* visible
vision (vee-*z^{y}awng*) *f* vision
visite (vee-*zeet*) *f* visit; call; **rendre ~ à** call on
visiter (vee-zee-*tay*) *v* visit
visiteur (vee-zee-*turr*) *m* visitor
vital (vee-*tahl*) *adj* vital
vitamine (vee-tah-*meen*) *f* vitamin
vite (veet) *adv* quickly
vitesse (vee-*tehss*) *f* speed; gear; **en ~** in a hurry; **indicateur de ~** speedometer; **limitation de ~** speed limit; **~ de croisière** cruising speed
vitre (veetr) *f* window-pane
vitrine (vee-*treen*) *f* showcase, shopwindow
vivant (vee-*vahng*) *adj* alive; live
***vivre** (veevr) *v* live; experience
vocabulaire (vo-kah-bew-*lair*) *m* vocabulary
vocal (vo-*kahl*) *adj* vocal
vœu (vur) *m* desire; vow
voici (vwah-*see*) *adv* here is
voie (vwah) *f* way; track; lane; **~ d'eau** waterway; **~ ferrée** railway line; railroad line *Am*
voilà (vwah-*lah*) *adv* there is; here you are
voile (vwahl) *f* sail; *m* veil
***voir** (vwaar) *v* *see

voisin (vwah-*zang*) *m* neighbo(u)r
voisinage (vwah-zee-*naazh*) *m* vicinity, neighbo(u)rhood
voisine (vwah-*zeen*) *f* neighbo(u)r
voiture (vwah-*tewr*) *f* car; carriage; **~ d'enfant** pram; **~ de sport** sports car; **~ Pullman** Pullman
voix (vwah) *f* voice; **à haute ~** aloud
vol (vol) *m* flight; robbery, theft; **~ charter** charter flight; **~ de nuit** night flight; **~ de retour** return flight
volaille (vo-*ligh*) *f* poultry, fowl
volant (vo-*lahng*) *m* steering wheel
volcan (vol-*kahng*) *m* volcano
voler (vo-*lay*) *v* *fly; *steal; rob
volet (vo-*lay*) *m* shutter
voleur (vo-*lurr*) *m* thief; robber
volontaire (vo-lawng-*tair*) *adj* voluntary; *m* volunteer
volonté (vo-lawng-*tay*) *f* will; willpower
volontiers (vo-lawng-*t^{y}ay*) *adv* willingly, gladly
volt (volt) *m* volt
voltage (vol-*taazh*) *m* voltage
volume (vo-*lewm*) *m* volume
volumineux (voa-lew-mee-*nur*) *adj* bulky, big
vomir (vo-*meer*) *v* vomit
vote (vot) *m* vote; **droit de ~** franchise
voter (vo-*tay*) *v* vote
votre (votr) *adj* (pl vos) your
***vouloir** (voo-*lwaar*) *v* want; *will; **en ~ à** resent; **~ dire** *mean
vous (voo) *pron* you; yourselves; **vous-même** *pron* yourself; **vousmêmes** *pron* yourselves
voûte (voot) *f* vault, arch
voyage (vwah-^{y}*aazh*) *m* journey; trip, voyage; **~ d'affaires** business trip; **~ de retour** return journey
voyager (vwah-^{y}ah-*zhay*) *v* travel; **~ en auto** motor
voyageur (vwah-^{y}ah-*zhurr*) *m*, **-euse** *f* travel(l)er
voyelle (vwah-^{y}*ehl*) *f* vowel
vrai (vray) *adj* true; very
vraiment (vray-*mahng*) *adv* really
vraisemblable (vray-sahng-*blahbl*) *adj* probable
vu (vew) *prep* considering
vue (vew) *f* sight; view; **point de ~** point of view
vulgaire (vewl-*gair*) *adj* vulgar
vulnérable (vewl-nay-*rahbl*) *adj* vulnerable

W

wagon (vah-*gawng*) *m* carriage; wag(g)on, coach; passenger car *Am*; **wagon-lit** sleeping car; **wagon-restaurant** dining car

Y

y (ee) *pron* there; to it

yacht (^{y}ot) *m* yacht

Z

zèbre (zaibr) *m* zebra
zélé (zay-*lay*) *adj* zealous
zèle (zehl) *m* zeal
zéro (zay-*roa*) *m* zero; nought
zinc (zan͞gg) *m* zinc
zodiaque (zo-*d^{y}ahk*) *m* zodiac
zone (zōān) *f* zone; area; ~ **de stationnement** parking zone; ~ **industrielle** industrial area
zoo (zoa) *m* zoo
zoom (zoom) *m* zoom lens

Menu Reader

Food

à la, à l', au, aux in the manner of, as in, with
abats, abattis giblets, innards
abricot apricot
agneau lamb
aiglefin haddock
ail garlic
ailloli garlic mayonnaise
airelle a kind of cranberry
alouette sans tête slice of veal rolled and generally stuffed with minced meat, garlic and parsley
(à l')alsacienne usually garnished with sauerkraut, ham and sausages
amande almond
amuse-gueule appetizer
ananas pineapple
anchois anchovy
(à l')ancienne old style; usually with wine-flavoured cream sauce of mushrooms, onions or shallots
(à l')andalouse usually with green peppers, aubergines and tomatoes
andouille a kind of tripe sausage
andouillette smaller kind of tripe sausage
(à l')anglaise 1) usually boiled or steamed vegetables, especially potatoes 2) breaded and fried vegetables, meat, fish or fowl
anguille eel
~ **au vert** eel braised in a white sauce served with minced parsley and other greens
anis aniseed
artichaut (globe) artichoke
asperge asparagus
assiette plate
~ **anglaise** cold meat (US cold cuts)
~ **de charcuterie** assorted pork and other meat products
assorti assorted
aubergine aubergine (US eggplant)
ballottine (de volaille) boned fowl which is stuffed, rolled, cooked and served in gelatine
banane banana
bar bass
barbue brill
basilic basil
béarnaise sauce of egg-yolk, butter, vinegar, shallots, tarragon and white wine
bécasse woodcock
béchamel white sauce
beignet fritter generally filled with fruit, vegetables or meat
(à la) Bercy butter sauce of white wine and shallots
betterave beetroot
beurre butter
~ **blanc** white butter sauce of shallots, vinegar and white wine
~ **maître d'hôtel** butter with chopped parsley and lemon juice
~ **noir** browned butter sauce of vinegar and parsley
bifteck beef steak
(à la) bigarade brown sauce generally with oranges, sugar and vinegar
biscotte rusk (US zwieback)
biscuit biscuit (US cookie)
bisque cream soup of lobster or crayfish (US chowder)
blanc de volaille boned breast of fowl
blanchaille whitebait
blanquette de veau veal stew in white sauce
(au) bleu 1) of fish (usually trout), boiled very fresh 2) of cheese, blue-

veined 3) of meat, very underdone (US rare)
bœuf beef
~ **bourguignon** chunks of beef stewed in red wine with onions, bacon and mushrooms
~ **en daube** larded chunks of beef marinated in red wine with vegetables and stewed
~ **miro(n)ton** cold boiled beef or beef stew with onion sauce
~ **mode** larded chunks of beef braised in red wine with carrots and onions
bolet boletus mushroom
bombe glacée moulded ice-cream dessert
(à la) bordelaise red wine sauce with shallots, beef marrow and boletus mushrooms
bouchée à la reine vol-au-vent; puff-pastry shell filled with meat, sweetbreads or seafood and sometimes mushrooms
boudin black pudding (US blood sausage)
bouillabaisse assorted fish and shellfish stewed in white wine, garlic, saffron and olive oil
bouilli 1) boiled 2) boiled beef
bouillon bouillon, broth, stock
(à la) bourguignonne button mushrooms, pearl onions or shallots braised in rich red wine
braisé braised
brandade (de morue) prepared cod with cream, oil and garlic
brie white, mellow cheese
brioche small roll or cake
(à la) broche (on a) spit
brochet pike
(en) brochette (cooked on a) skewer
cabillaud fresh cod
café glacé coffee-flavoured ice-cream dessert
caille quail
camembert soft cheese with a thin white rind and a yellow interior
canard (caneton) duck (duckling)
~ **à l'orange** roast duck braised with oranges and orange liqueur
cannelle cinnamon
cantal smooth, firm cheese not unlike Cheddar
câpre caper
carbonnade charcoal-grilled meat
~ **flamande** beef slices, onions and herbs braised in beer
cardon cardoon (vegetable)
carotte carrot
carottes Vichy steamed carrots
carpe carp
carré loin, rack
~ **de l'Est** usually square-shaped soft, mild, fermented cheese
carrelet plaice
carte des vins wine list
cassis blackcurrant
cassoulet toulousain butter-bean stew of goose or with mutton, pork and sometimes sausage
céleri celery (usually celery root)
~ **en branche** branch celery
~**-rave** celeriac, celery root
cèpe boletus mushroom
cerfeuil chervil
cerise cherry
cervelle brains
champignon mushroom
~ **de Paris** button mushroom
chanterelle chanterelle mushroom
charbonnade charcoal-grilled meat
charcuterie various kinds of cold pork products
charlotte fruit dessert (usually apples) made in a deep, round mould
chasse venison
chasseur hunter's style; sauce of mushrooms, tomatoes, wine and

garlic herbs
chateaubriand thick slice of beef taken from the fillet
chaud warm
chaudrée fish and seafood stew, often with garlic, herbs, onions and white wine
chausson aux pommes apple dumpling (US turnover)
chevreuil deer
chicorée endive (US chicory)
chou cabbage
~ de Bruxelles brussels sprouts
~ à la crème cream puff
~-fleur cauliflower
~ rouge red cabbage
choucroute sauerkraut
~ garnie usually with ham, bacon and sausage
ciboulette chive
citron lemon
civet de lapin (lièvre) jugged rabbit (hare)
clafoutis fruit baked in pancake batter, brandy often added
clémentine pipless (US seedless) tangerine
cochon de lait suck(l)ing pig
(en) cocotte casserole
cœur heart
~ d'artichaut artichoke heart
(à la) Colbert dipped in egg batter and breadcrumbs, fried
colin hake
concombre cucumber
confit d'oie pieces of goose preserved in its own fat
confiture jam
consommation general word for drinks
consommé clear soup served hot or cold
~ Célestine with chicken and noodles
~ aux cheveux d'ange with thin noodles
~ Colbert with poached eggs, spring vegetables
~ julienne with shredded vegetables
~ madrilène cold and flavoured with tomatoes
~ princesse with diced chicken and asparagus tips
~ aux vermicelles with thin noodles
contre-filet sirloin
coq au vin chicken stewed in red wine with mushrooms, bacon, onions and herbs
coquelet cockerel
coquillage shellfish
coquille Saint-Jacques scallop gratinéed in its shell
corbeille de fruits basket of assorted fruit
cornichon small gherkin (US pickle)
côte chop or rib
~ de bœuf rib of beef
~ de veau veal chop
côtelette cutlet, chop
~ d'agneau lamb chop
~ de porc pork chop
coupe a metal or glass dish usually for individual desserts
~ glacée ice-cream dessert
courgette a long vegetable with a dark green skin (US zucchini)
couvert cover charge
~, vin et service compris price includes wine, service and cover charges
crabe crab
crème 1) a dessert with cream or a creamy dessert
~ anglaise custard
~ caramel caramel custard
~ Chantilly whipped cream
~ glacée ice-cream
crème 2) a creamy soup
crêpe large, paper-thin pancake

~ **Suzette** pancake with orange sauce, flamed with brandy and often orange liqueur
cresson (water)cress
crevette shrimp
croissant crescent-shaped flaky roll (usually served for breakfast)
croque-monsieur grilled or baked ham-and-cheese sandwich
croustade pie, pastry shell filled with fish, seafood, meat or vegetables
(en) croûte (in a) pastry crust
croûton small piece of bread, toasted or fried
cru raw
crudités raw vegetables usually served sliced, grated or diced as an hors d'œuvre
crustacé shellfish
cuisse leg or thigh
cuisses de grenouilles frogs' legs
cuit cooked
bien ~ well-done
cumin caraway, cumin
darne thick fillet of fish, usually of salmon
datte date
daurade gilt-head
déjeuner lunch
délice often used to describe a dessert speciality of the chef
demi half
~-sel soft cream cheese, slightly salty
demoiselle de Cherbourg small rock lobster
(à la) dieppoise garnish of mussels and shrimp served in white-wine sauce
dinde, dindon turkey
dindonneau young turkey
dîner dinner
diplomate moulded custard dessert with crystallized fruit and lined with sponge fingers steeped in liqueur
dodine de canard boned duck, rolled, stuffed, sometimes served cold in gelatine
(à la) du Barry garnish of cauliflower and cheese sauce, gratinéed
(aux) duxelles with minced mushrooms sautéed with butter, white wine and herbs
échalote shallot
écrevisse (freshwater) crayfish
~ à la nage simmered in white wine, aromatic vegetables and herbs
églefin haddock
émincé slices of cooked meat in gravy or thick cream sauce
endive chicory (US endive)
~ à la bruxelloise steamed chicory rolled in a slice of ham
entrecôte rib-eye steak
entrée dish served between the hors d'oeuvre or soup and the main course; the first course in a smaller dinner (US starter)
entremets small dish served before cheese; today it often means dessert
épaule shoulder
éperlan smelt
épice spice
épicé hot, peppered
épinard spinach
escalope de veau veal scallop, thin slice of veal
escalope viennoise wiener schnitzel; breaded veal cutlet
escargot snail
estouffade braised or steamed in tightly sealed vessel with minimum of cooking liquid
estragon tarragon
étuvé steamed, stewed with minimum of cooking liquid
faisan pheasant
farci stuffed
fenouil fennel
féra dace (fish)

fève broad bean
filet meat or fish fillet
~ de bœuf fillet of beef (US tenderloin)
~ mignon small round veal or pork fillet
~ de sole fillet of sole
(à la) financière rich sauce of pike dumplings, truffles, mushrooms, Madeira wine, sometimes with olives and crayfish
(aux) fines herbes with herbs
(à la) flamande Flemish style; usually a garnish of braised potatoes, carrots, cabbage, turnips, bacon and sausage (sometimes simmered in beer)
flambé dish flamed usually with brandy
flétan halibut
foie liver
~ gras goose or duck liver
fond d'artichaut artichocke heart (US bottom)
fondue (au fromage) melted-cheese mixture in a pot into which pieces of bread are dipped
fondue bourguignonne bite-size pieces of meat dipped into boiling oil at the table and eaten with a variety of sauces
fondue chinoise paper-thin slices of beef dipped into boiling bouillon and eaten with a variety of sauces
(à la) forestière forester's style; generally sautéed in butter with morel mushrooms, potatoes and bacon
(au) four baked
frais, fraîche fresh
fraise strawberry
~ des bois wild strawberry
framboise raspberry
frappé chilled, iced
friand patty with meat filling
fricandeau braised, larded veal
fricassée browned pieces of meat braised with seasonings and vegetables and served in a thick sauce
frit fried
frites chips (US french fries)
friture (de poisson) fried fish
fromage cheese
~ frais fresh curd cheese
~ de tête brawn (US headcheese)
fruit confit candied fruit
fruits de mer mussels, oysters, clams
fumé smoked
galette flat, plain cake
garbure thick cabbage soup made of salted pork, spices and *confit d'oie*
garni garnished
(avec) garniture (with) vegetables
gâteau cake, flan, tart
gaufre waffle
gaufrette small, crisp, sweet wafer
(en) gelée jellied
gélinotte hazel-hen, hazel-grouse (US prairie chicken)
gibelotte de lapin rabbit stew in wine sauce
gibier game
~ de saison game in season
gigot d'agneau leg of lamb
girolle chanterelle mushroom
glace ice-cream
~ (à la) napolitaine ice-cream layers of different flavours
glacé iced, glazed
goujon gudgeon
gras-double tripe simmered in wine and onions
(au) gratin browned with breadcrumbs or cheese
gratin dauphinois sliced potatoes gratinéed in the oven with eggs, cream and cheese
gratin de fruits de mer shellfish in

heavy cream sauce and gratinéed
grillade grilled meat
grillé grilled
grive thrush
groseille à maquereau gooseberry
groseille rouge redcurrant
gruyère a hard cheese rich in flavour
haché minced, hashed
hachis mince, hash
hareng herring
haricot bean
~ **de mouton** stew of mutton with beans and potatoes
~ **vert** French bean (US green bean)
Henri IV artichoke hearts garnished with béarnaise sauce
hollandaise sauce of egg-yolks, butter and lemon juice or vinegar
homard lobster
~ **à l'américaine** (or **à l'armoricaine**) lobster flamed in brandy, simmered in white wine with garlic, tomatoes and herbs
~ **cardinal** flamed in brandy, diced, served in its shell with truffles and chopped mushrooms and gratinéed
~ **Newburg** cut into sections, cooked in brandy and fish stock
~ **Thermidor** simmered in white wine, sautéed in butter with mushrooms, herbs, spices, mustard, flamed in brandy and gratinéed with cheese**huile** oil
huître oyster
~ **belon** flat, pinkish oyster
~ **de claire** similar to bluepoint oyster
~ **portugaise** small, fat oyster
jambon ham
~ **de Bayonne** raw, with a slightly salty flavour
~ **cru** raw, cured
~ **à l'os** baked ham
jardinière cooked assorted vegetables
jarret shank, shin
julienne vegetables cut into fine strips
jus gravy, juice
lamproie lamprey
langouste spiny lobster
langoustine Norway lobster, prawn, crawfish
langue tongue
lapin rabbit
lard bacon
légume vegetable
lentille lentil
levraut young hare, leveret
lièvre hare
limande dab
livarot small, round cheese from Normandy
longe de veau loin of veal
(**à la**) **lorraine** usually braised in red wine with red cabbage
loup (de mer) (sea) bass
(**à la**) **lyonnaise** generally sautéed with onions
macédoine mixed, diced vegetables or fruit
(**au**) **madère** with Madeira wine
maigre lean
maïs maize (US corn)
maître d'hôtel sautéed in butter with chopped parsley and lemon juice
maquereau mackerel
marcassin young boar
marchand de vin red wine sauce seasoned with shallots
mariné marinated
marinière sailor's style; garnish of mussels with other seafood simmered in white wine and spices
marjolaine marjoram
maroilles strong, semi-hard cheese from Picardy
marron chestnut
matelote freshwater-fish stew (especially of eel) with wine, onions, mushrooms

médaillon small, round cut of meat
menthe mint
menu in France, generally means *menu à prix fixe*, set meal at a fixed price
merguez very spicy sausage
merlan whiting
merluche dried hake
meunière floured and sautéed in butter with lemon juice and chopped parsley
miel honey
mijoté simmered
millefeuille flaky pastry with cream filling (US napoleon)
(**à la**) **Mirabeau** with anchovies, olives, tarragon
mirabelle small yellow plum
(**à la**) **mode** in the style (of); often means made according to a local recipe
moelle marrow (bone)
morille morel mushroom
Mornay *béchamel* sauce with cheese
moule mussel
moules marinière mussels simmered in white wine with shallots, thyme and parsley
mousse 1) any frothy cream dish 2) chopped or pounded meat or fish with eggs and cream
mousseline 1) frothy mixture containing cream, usually whipped 2) variation of hollandaise sauce with whipped cream
moutarde mustard
mouton mutton
munster soft cheese with a pungent flavour
mûre mulberry or blackberry
myrtille bilberry (US blueberry)
nature/au naturel plain, without dressing, sauce or stuffing
navarin mutton stew with turnips
navet turnip
(**à la/en**) **neige** snow-like; i.e. with beaten egg-whites
(**à la**) **niçoise** Riviera style; usually with garlic, anchovies, olives, onions, tomatoes
(**à la**) **nivernaise** a garnish of carrots, onions, potatoes
noisette 1) hazelnut 2) boneless round piece of meat usually taken from loin or rib
noix walnut
~ **de coco** coconut
~ **(de) muscade** nutmeg
~ **de veau** pope's eye of veal
(**à la**) **normande** usually cooked with gudgeon, shrimps, mushrooms, cream and sometimes truffles
nouilles noodles
œuf egg
~ **brouillé** scrambled
~ **à la coque** soft-boiled
~ **dur** hard-boiled
~ **farci** stuffed
~ **en gelée** lightly poached and served in gelatine
~ **au jambon** ham and eggs
~ **au/sur le plat** fried
~ **poché** poached
~ **Rossini** with truffles and Madeira wine
oie goose
oignon onion
omble-chevalier freshwater fish of the char family
omelette omelet
~ **norvégienne** ice-cream dessert covered with beaten egg-whites, quickly browned in oven and served flaming (US baked Alaska)
ortolan small game bird like a finch
os bone
~ **à moelle** marrow bone
oseille sorrel

oursin sea urchin
pain bread
palourde clam
pamplemousse grapefruit
panaché mixed; two or more kinds of something
pané breaded, rolled in breadcrumbs
(**en**) **papillote** encased in greased paper and baked
parfait ice-cream dessert
Parmentier containing potatoes
pastèque watermelon
pâté 1) a moulded pastry case which holds meat or fish 2) a thickish paste often of liver (contained in an earthenware dish)
~ **ardennais** a purée of pork and seasonings encased in a loaf of bread, served in slices
~ **de campagne** strongly flavoured with a variety of meat
~ **en croûte** in a pastry crust
~ **de foie gras** goose (or duck) liver paste
pâtes noodles, macaroni, spaghetti
paupiette (**de veau**) veal bird, thin slice of veal rolled around stuffing
(**à la**) **paysanne** country style; usually containing various vegetables
pêche peach
perche perch
perdreau young partridge
perdrix partridge
(**à la**) **périgourdine** preparation with truffles
persil parsley
petit small
~ **déjeuner** breakfast
~ **four** small, fancy cake (US fancy cookie)
~ **pain** roll
~ **pois** green pea
~ **salé** (**au chou**) salt pork (with cabbage)
~**-suisse** a mild-flavoured, double-cream cheese
pied de porc pig's trotter (US pig's foot)
pigeonneau squab
piment pimento
pintade guinea hen
piperade omelet with green peppers, garlic, tomatoes, ham
piquant sharp-tasting, spicy (e.g. of a sauce)
pissaladière onion and anchovy tart with black olives
plat plate
~ **du jour** speciality of the day
~ **principal** main dish
plateau de fromages cheese board
plie plaice
poché poached
(**à la**) **poêle** fried
(**à**) **point** medium
pointe d'asperge asparagus tip
poire pear
~ **à la Condé** served hot on a bed of vanilla-flavoured rice
~ **Belle Hélène** with vanilla ice-cream and chocolate sauce
poireau leek
pois pea
~ **chiche** chick pea
poisson fish
~ **d'eau douce** freshwater fish
~ **de mer** saltwater fish
poitrine breast
~ **de bœuf** brisket
(**au**) **poivre** (with) pepper
poivron sweet pepper
pomme apple
pommes (**de terre**) potatoes
~ **allumettes** matchstick potatoes
~ **chips** crisps (US potato chips)
~ **dauphine** potatoes mashed in butter and egg-yolks, mixed in seasoned flour and deep-fried

~ **duchesse** potatoes mashed with butter and egg-yolks
~ **en robe des champs** potatoes in their jackets
~ **frites** chips (US french fries)
~ **mousseline** mashed potatoes
~ **nature** boiled, steamed potatoes
~ **nouvelles** new potatoes
~ **vapeur** steamed, boiled potatoes
pont-l'évêque soft cheese, firmer and yellower than camembert
porc pork
port-salut soft cheese, yellow in colour, mild in taste
potage soup
~ **bonne femme** potato, leek, mushroom, onion, rice and sometimes bacon
~ **cancalais** fish consommé (often with oysters or other seafood)
~ **Condé** mashed red beans
~ **Crécy** carrots
~ **cultivateur** mixed vegetables and bacon or pork
~ **du Barry** cream of cauliflower
~ **julienne** vegetables
~ **Longchamp** peas, sorrel and chervil
~ **Saint-Germain** split-pea, leek and onion
~ **soissonnais** haricot bean
pot-au-feu 1) stockpot of beef, potatoes and aromatic vegetables 2) stew
potée boiled pork or beef with vegetables, especially cabbage
potiron pumpkin
poularde fat pullet
~ **de Bresse** grain-fed; reputedly the finest available
~ **demi-deuil** with truffles inserted under the skin and simmered in broth
poule hen
~ **au pot** stewed with vegetables
~ **au riz** stewed in bouillon and served with rice
poulet chicken
~ **Marengo** sautéed in olive oil, cooked with white wine, tomatoes, garlic, shallots and mushrooms
pourboire tip (but *service* is the percentage added to the bill)
praire clam
pré-salé lamb pastured in the salt meadows on the Atlantic seashore
(à la) **printanière** with spring vegetables
prix price
~ **fixe** at a fixed price
profiterole au chocolat puff pastry filled with whipped cream or custard and covered with hot chocolate
(à la) **provençale** often with garlic, onions, herbs, olives, oil and tomatoes
prune plum
pruneau (blue) plum
~ **sec** prune
pudding plum pudding
puits d'amour pastry shell filled with liqueur-flavoured custard
purée pulped and strained fruit or vegetables
~ **de pommes de terre** mashed potatoes
quenelle light dumpling made of fish, fowl or meat
queue tail
quiche flan, open tart with meat or vegetable filling, eggs and cream
~ **lorraine** tart with cheese, bacon, eggs and cream
râble de lièvre saddle of hare
raclette hot, melted cheese scraped from a block of cheese; accompanied with boiled potatoes and gherkins
radis radish

(en) ragoût stew(ed)
raie skate, ray
raisin grape
~ **sec** raisin, sultana
ramequin small cheese tart
rascasse a Mediterranean fish, an essential ingredient of *bouillabaisse*
ratatouille Mediterranean stew of tomatoes, peppers, onions, garlic and aubergines, served hot or cold
ravigote vinegar sauce with chopped hard-boiled eggs, capers and herbs
reblochon soft, mild cheese, pale cream colour (Savoy)
(à la) reine with mince meat or fowl
reine-claude greengage
repas meal
rhubarbe rhubarb
(à la) Richelieu garnish of tomatoes, peas, bacon and potatoes
rillettes usually minced pork (sometimes goose or duck) baked in its own fat
ris de veau calf sweetbread
rissole fritter, pasty
riz rice
~ **pilaf** rice boiled in a bouillon, sometimes with onions
rognon kidney
romarin rosemary
roquefort blue-veined cheese made from ewe's milk; strong, salty with piquant flavour
rosbif roast beef
rôti roast(ed)
rouelle de veau shank of veal (usually a round cut)
roulade 1) a rolled slice of meat or fish with stuffing 2) dessert with cream or jam stuffing (Swiss roll)
sabayon creamy dessert of egg-yolks, sugar and white wine flavoured with a citrus fruit, served warm
safran saffron
saignant underdone (US rare)
saint-pierre John Dory (fish)
salade salad
~ **chiffonnade** shredded lettuce and sorrel in melted butter, served with a dressing
~ **de fruits** fruit salad (US fruit cocktail)
~ **niçoise** lettuce, tomatoes, green beans, hard-boiled eggs, tunny, olives, green pepper, potatoes and anchovies
~ **russe** cooked vegetables in mayonnaise
~ **verte** green
salé salted
salmis game or fowl partially roasted, then simmered in wine and vegetable *purée*
salpicon garnish or stuffing of one or various elements held together by sauce
salsifis salsify
sandre pikeperch
sanglier wild boar
sarcelle teal, small freshwater duck
sauce sauce
~ **béarnaise** vinegar, egg-yolks, butter, shallots and tarragon
~ **béchamel** white sauce
~ **au beurre blanc** butter, shallots, vinegar or lemon juice
~ **au beurre noir** browned butter
~ **bordelaise** brown sauce with boletus mushrooms, red wine, shallots and beef marrow
~ **bourguignonne** red wine sauce with herbs, onions and spices (sometimes tarragon)
~ **café de Paris** cream, mustard and herbs
~ **chasseur** brown sauce with wine, mushrooms, onions, shallots and herbs

~ **diable** hot, spicy sauce with white wine, herbs, vinegar and cayenne pepper
~ **financière** cream, Madeira wine, herbs, spices, mushrooms, truffles and olives
~ **hollandaise** butter, egg-yolks and vinegar or lemon juice
~ **lyonnaise** onions, white wine and butter
~ **madère** brown sauce with Madeira wine base
~ **Mornay** *béchamel* sauce with cheese
~ **ravigote** vinegar sauce with chopped hardboiled eggs, capers and herbs; served cold
~ **rémoulade** mayonnaise enriched with mustard and herbs
~ **suprême** chicken-stock base, thick and bland, served with fowl
~ **tartare** mayonnaise base with gherkins, chives, capers and olives
~ **vinaigrette** oil, vinegar and herbs (sometimes mustard)
saucisse sausage
~ **de Francfort** frankfurter
saucisson a large sausage
saumon salmon
sauté lightly browned in hot butter, oil or fat, sautéed
savarin sponge cake steeped in rum and usually topped with cream
sel salt
selle saddle
selon grosseur (or **grandeur**) price according to size, e.g. of a lobster, often abbreviated **s.g. service (non) compris** service (not) included
sorbet water ice (US sherbet)
soufflé à la reine soufflé with finely chopped poultry or meat
soufflé Rothschild vanilla-flavoured soufflé with candied fruit
soupe soup
~ **au pistou** vegetables, noodles, garlic, basil and cheese
~ **à l'oignon** onion
~ **à l'oignon gratinée** onion soup topped with toast and grated cheese; gratinéed
spécialité (du chef) (chef's) speciality
steak steak
~ **haché** hamburger
~ **au poivre** broiled with crushed peppercorns (often flamed in brandy)
~ **tartare** minced beef, eaten raw, with sauce of egg-yolks, mustard, capers, onions, oil and parsley
sucre sugar
suprême de volaille boned chicken breast with creamy sauce
sur commande to your special order
(en) sus in addition, additional charge
tarte open(-faced) flan, tart
~ **Tatin** upside-down tart of caramelized apples
tartelette small tart
tendrons de veau breast of veal
(en) terrine a preparation of meat, fish, fowl or game baked in an earthenware dish called a *terrine*, served cold
tête head
thon tunny (US tuna)
(en) timbale meat, fish, seafood, fruit or vegetables cooked in a pastry case or mould
tomate tomato
tomme a mild soft cheese
topinambour Jerusalem artichoke
tortue turtle
tournedos round cut of prime beef
~ **Rossini** garnished with foie gras and truffles, served with Madeira wine sauce
tout compris all-inclusive (price of a

meal)
tranche slice
~ **napolitaine** cassata; slice of layered ice-cream and crystallized fruit
tripes tripe
~ **à la mode de Caen** baked with calf's trotters (US calf's feet), vegetables, apple brandy or cider
truffe truffle
truite trout
vacherin a mellow cheese
~ **glacé** an ice-cream dessert with meringue
vanille vanilla
(à la) vapeur steamed
varié assorted
veau veal
velouté a creamy soup (of vegetables or poultry), thickened with butter and flour
vert-pré a garnish of cress
viande meat
~ **séchée** dried beef served as hors d'oeuvre in paper-thin slices
viandes froides various cold slices of meat and ham (US cold cuts)
vinaigre vinegar
vinaigrette salad sauce of vinegar, oil, herbs and mustard
volaille fowl
vol-au-vent puff-pastry shell filled with meat, sweetbreads or fish and sometimes mushrooms
waterzoï de poulet chicken poached in white wine and shredded vegetables, cream and egg-yolks
yaourt yoghurt

Drinks

Alsace (93 communes situated on the River Rhine) produces virtually only dry white wine, notably *Gewurztraminer*, *Riesling*, *Sylvaner*, *Traminer*; the terms *grand vin* and *grand cru* are sometimes employed to indicate a wine of exceptional quality
Amer Picon an aperitif with wine and brandy base and quinine flavouring
Anjou a region of the Loire district producing fine rosé and white wine
apéritif often bittersweet, some aperitifs have a wine and brandy base with herbs and bitters (like *Amer Picon*, *Byrrh*, *Dubonnet*), others, called *pastis*, have an aniseed base (like *Pernod* or *Ricard*); an aperitif may also be simply vermouth (like *Noilly Prat*) or a liqueur drink like *blanc-cassis*
appellation d'origine contrôlée (A.O.C.) officially recognized wines of which there are over 250 in France; standards of quality are rigidly checked by government inspectors
armagnac a wine-distilled brandy from the Armagnac region, west of Toulouse
Beaujolais Burgundy's most southerly and extensive vineyards which produce mainly red wine, e.g., *Brouilly*, *Chénas*, *Chiroubles*, *Côte de Brouilly*, *Fleurie*, *Juliénas*, *Morgon*, *Moulin-à-Vent*
Belgique Belgium; though the Romans introduced wine-making to Belgium, the kingdom today only incidentally produces wine, primarily

white, sometimes rosé and sparkling wine

bénédictine forest-green liqueur; brandy base, herbs and orange peel, reputedly secret formula

Berry a region of the Loire district producing red, white and rosé wine; e.g., *Châteaumeillant*, *Menetou-Salon*, *Quincy*, *Reuilly*, *Sancerre*, *Sauvignon*

bière beer

~ **blonde** light

~ **(en) bouteille** bottled

~ **brune** dark

~ **pression** draught (US draft)

~ **des Trappistes** malt beer brewed by Trappist monks

blanc-cassis white wine mixed with blackcurrant liqueur

Blayais a region of Bordeaux producing mainly red and white wine

boisson drink

Bordeaux divided into several regions: Blayais, Bourgeais, Entre-Deux-Mers, Fronsac, Graves, Médoc, Pomerol, St-Emilion, Sauternais; among the officially recognized wines are 34 reds, 23 whites and two rosés divided into three categories: general (e.g., *Bordeaux* or *Bordeaux supérieur*), regional (e.g., *Entre-Deux-Mers*, *Graves*, *Médoc*) and communal (e.g., *Margaux*, *Pauillac*, *Sauternes*); Bordeaux red wine is known as claret in America and Britain

Bourgeais a region of Bordeaux producing red and white table wine

Bourgogne Burgundy, divided into five regions: Beaujolais, Chablis, Côte Chalonnaise, Côte d'Or (which comprises the Côte de Beaune and the Côte de Nuits) and Mâconnais; Burgundy counts the largest number of officially recognized wines of France's wine-growing districts; there are four categories of wine: generic or regional (e.g., *Bourgogne* red, white or rosé), subregional (e.g., *Beaujolais*, *Beaujolais supérieur*, *Beaujolais-Villages*, *Côte de Beaune-Villages*, *Mâcon*, *Mâcon supérieur*, *Mâcon-Villages*), communal (e.g., *Beaune*, *Chablis*, *Fleurie*, *Meursault*, *Nuits-St-Georges*, *Volnay*) and vineyard (*climat*) (e.g., *Chambertin*, *Clos de Vougeot*, *Musigny*)

brut extra dry, refers to *Champagne*

Byrrh an aperitif with wine base and quinine, fortified with brandy

cacao cocoa

café coffee

~ **complet** with bread, roll, butter and jam; the Continental breakfast

~ **crème** with cream

~ **espresso** espresso

~ **filtre** percolated or dripped through a filter

~ **frappé** iced

~ **au lait** white (with milk)

~ **liégeois** cold with ice-cream, topped with whipped cream

~ **nature, noir** simple, black

~ **sans caféine** caffeine-free

calvados an apple brandy from Normandy

cassis blackcurrant liqueur

Chablis a region of Burgundy noted for its white wine

chambrer to bring wine gently to room (*chambre*) temperature

Champagne district divided into three large regions: Côte des Blancs, Montagne de Reims and Vallée de la Marne with some 200 kilometres (120 miles) of underground caves where the wine ferments; there are ordinary red, white and rosé wines but the production is overwhelmingly centered upon the sparkling white and rosé (usually referred to in English as pink Champagne) for which the region is universally known; vineyards are of little importance in classifying wines from Champagne since, according to tradition, certain varieties of Champagne are produced by blending wine from different vineyards in proportions which are carefully-guarded secrets; sparkling Champagne is sold according to the amount of sugar added: *brut* (extra dry) contains up to 1.5 per cent sugar additive, *extra-sec* (very dry), 1.5–2.5 per cent, *sec* (dry), 2.5–5 per cent, *demi-sec* (slightly sweet), 5–8 per cent and *doux* (sweet), 8–15 per cent

Chartreuse a yellow or green liqueur of herbs and spices produced by monks of Grande Chartreuse in the French Alps

château castle; term employed traditionally in the district of Bordeaux to indicate a wine of exceptional quality; synonyms: *clos*, *domaine*

chocolat chocolate

cidre cider

citron pressé freshly squeezed lemon juice

citronnade lemon squash (US lemon drink)

claret see *Bordeaux*

clos vineyard; generally indicates a wine of exceptional quality

cognac cognac; the famed winedistilled brandy from the Charente and Charente-Maritime regions

Cointreau orange liqueur

Corse Corsica; this Mediterranean island, a French department, produces fine wine, particularly from the hilly areas and Cape Corsica; red, white and rosé wine is characterized by a rich, full-bodied taste; the best wine, grown near Bastia, is the rosé *Patrimonio*

Côte de Beaune the southern half of Burgundy's celebrated Côte d'Or producing chiefly red wine; e.g., the prestigious *Aloxe-Corton* as well as *Beaune*, *Blagny*, *Chassagne-Montrachet*, *Meursault*, *Pernand-Vergelesses*, *Puligny-Montrachet*, *Santenay*, *Savigny-lès-Beaune*, *Volnay*

Côte de Nuits a region of Burgundy especially noted for its red wine, e.g., *Chambolle-Musigny*, *Fixin*, *Gevrey-Chambertin*, *Morey-St-Denis*, *Nuits-St-Georges*, *Vosne-Romanée*

Côte d'Or a famed region of Burgundy composed of the Côte de Beaune and de Nuits which is noted for its red and white wine

Côtes du Rhône extend from Vienne to Avignon along the banks of the River Rhone between the Burgundy and Provence wine districts; over a hundred communes offer a wide diversity in white, red and rosé wine of varying character; divided into a northern and southern region with notable wine: *Château-Grillet*, *Châteauneuf-du-Pape*, *Condrieu*, *Cornas*, *Côte-Rôtie*, *Crozes-Hermitage*, *Hermitage*, *Lirac*, *St-Joseph*, *St-Péray*, *Tavel*

crème 1) cream 2) sweetened liqueur like *crème de menthe*, *crème de cacao*

cru growth 1) refers to a particular vineyard and its wine 2) a system of grading wine; *premier cru*, *grand cru*, *cru classé*

curaçao originally from the name of the island of the Dutch Antilles, now applied to liqueur made from orange peel
cuvée a blend of wine from various vineyards, especially, according to tradition, in the making of Champagne
domaine estate; used on a wine label it indicates a wine of exceptional quality
eau water
 ~ **gazeuse** fizzy (US carbonated)
 ~ **minérale** mineral
Entre-Deux-Mers a vast Bordeaux region called "between two seas"—actually it's between two rivers—which produces white and red wine
extra-sec very dry (of Champagne)
framboise raspberry liqueur or brandy
frappé 1) iced 2) milk shake
Fronsac a Bordeaux region producing chiefly red wine
Gueuzelambic a strong Flemish bitter beer brewed from wheat and barley
grand cru, grand vin indicates a wine of exceptional quality
Grand Marnier an orange liqueur
Graves a Bordeaux region especially noted for its white wine but also its red
Jura a six-kilometre- (four-mile-) wide strip which runs 80 kilometres (50 miles) parallel to the western Swiss border and Burgundy; offers white, red, rosé, golden and sparkling wine; there are four formally recognized wines: *Arbois*, *Château-Chalon*, *Côtes du Jura* and *l'Etoile*
kirsch spirit distilled from cherries
Kriekenlambic a strong Brussels bitter beer flavoured with morello cherries
lait milk
 ~ **écrémé** skimmed
Languedoc district, formerly a French province, to the south-west of the Rhone delta; its ordinary table wine is often referred to as *vin du Midi* but other officially recognized wines, mostly white, are produced, including *Blanquette de Limoux* (sparkling), *Clairette du Languedoc*, *Fitou* and the *Muscats* from Frontignan, Lunel, Mireval and St-Jean-de-Minervois
limonade 1) lemonade 2) soft drink
Loire a district of 200, 000 hectares (80,000 acres) sprawled over the vicinity of France's longest river, the Loire; produces much fine red, white and rosé wine in four regions: Anjou (e.g., *Coteaux-de-l'Aubance*, *Coteaux-du-Layon*, *Coteaux-de-la-Loire*, *Saumur*), Berry and Nivernais (*Menetou-Salon*, *Pouilly-sur-Loire*, *Quincy*, *Reuilly*, *Sancerre*), Nantais (*Muscadet*) and Touraine (*Bourgueil*, *Chinon*, *Montlouis*, *Vouvray*)
Lorraine a flourishing and renowned wine district up to the 18th century, today it is of minor importance; good red, white and rosé wine continue to be produced (e.g., *Vins de la Moselle*, *Côtes-de-Toul*)
Mâcon a region of Burgundy producing basically red wine
marc spirit distilled from grape residue
Médoc a Bordeaux region producing highly reputed red wine including *Listrac*, *Margaux*, *Moulis*, *Pauillac*, *St-Estèphe*, *St-Julien*
mirabelle a brandy made from small yellow plums, particularly produced in the Alsace-Lorraine area
Muscadet a white wine from the Nantes area (Loire)
muscat 1) a type of grape 2) name

given to dessert wine; especially renowned is the muscat from Frontignan (Languedoc)

Nantais a region of the Loire chiefly renowned for its *Muscadet* white wine but offers other wine, e.g., *Coteaux d'Ancenis*, *Gros-Plant*

Neuchâtel a Swiss region producing primarily white wine (e.g., *Auvernier*, *Cormondrèche*, *Cortaillod*, *Hauterive*)

Noilly Prat a French vermouth

orange pressée freshly squeezed orange juice

pastis aniseed-flavoured aperitif

Pernod an aniseed-flavoured aperitif

pétillant slightly sparkling

Pomerol a Bordeaux region producing red wine (e.g., *Château Pétrus*, *Lalande-de-Pomerol*, *Néac*)

Provence France's most ancient wine-producing district; it traces its history back over two-and-a-half milleniums when Greek colonists planted the first vineyards on the Mediterranean coast of Gaul; red, white and rosé wine is produced, e.g., *Bandol*, *Bellet*, *Cassis*, *Coteaux-d'Aix-en-Provence*, *Coteaux-des-Baux*, *Coteaux-de-Pierrevert*, *Côtes-de-Provence*, *Palette*

quetsche spirit distilled from plums

rancio dessert wine, especially from Roussillon, which is aged in oak casks under the Midi sun

Ricard an aniseed-flavoured aperitif

Roussillon district which was a French province with Perpignan as its capital; its wine is similar in character to that of the Languedoc to the immediate north; good red, white and rosé table wine, e.g., *Corbières du Roussillon* and *Roussillon Dels Aspres*; this region produces three quarters of France's naturally sweet wine, usually referred to as *rancio*, which is aged in oak casks under the Midi sun; notable examples among them are *Banyuls*, *Côtes-d'Agly*, *Côtes-du-Haut-Roussillon*; *Grand-Roussillon*, *Muscat de Rivesaltes*, *Rivesaltes*

St-Emilion a Bordeaux region producing red wine including *Lussac*, *Montagne*, *Parsac*, *Puisseguin*, *St-Georges*

St-Raphaël a quinine-flavoured aperitif

Sauternais a Bordeaux region noted for its white wine (*Sauternes*), notably the prestigious *Château d'Yquem*

Savoie Savoy; the Alpine district producing primarily dry, light and often slightly acid white wine (e.g., *Crépy*, *Seyssel*) but also good red, rosé and sparkling wine which is chiefly produced around Chambéry

Sud-Ouest a district in southwestern France producing quite varying types of wine, mostly white but some red and even rosé; the district includes the former province of Aquitaine, Béarn, Basque Country and Languedoc; wines of particular note are *Bergerac*, *Côtes-de-Duras*, *Gaillac*, *Jurançon*, *Madiran*, *Monbazillac*, *Montravel*

Suisse Switzerland; two-thirds of the nation's wine production consists of white wine; some 230 different vineyards are scattered over a dozen of Switzerland's 23 cantons though only four have a special significance: Neuchâtel, Tessin, Valais and Vaud

Suze an aperitif based on gentian

thé tea

Touraine for 14 centuries a celebrated wine district of the Loire producing red, white and rosé wine (e.g.,

Bourgueil, *Chinon*, *Montlouis*, *St-Nicolas-de-Bourgueil*, *Vouvray*)

Triple Sec an orange liqueur

Valais sometimes referred to as the California of Switzerland, this Swiss region produces nearly a quarter of the nation's wine; the region in the Rhone Valley is noted for providing Switzerland's best red wine (e.g., *Dôle*) and much of its finest white wine (e.g., *Arvine*, *Ermitage*, *Fendant*, *Johannisberg*, *Malvoisie*)

Vaud a Swiss region producing primarily white wine (e.g., *Aigle*, *Dézaley*, *Mont-sur-Rolle*, *Lavaux*, *Yvorne*)

V.D.Q.S. (**vin délimité de qualité supérieure**) regional wine of exceptional quality, produced according to carefully defined specifications and checked by government inspectors

Vieille Cure a wine-distilled liqueur

vin wine

~ **blanc** white

~ **chambré** wine at room temperature

~ **doux** sweet, dessert

~ **gris** pinkish

~ **mousseux** sparkling

~ **ordinaire** table

~ **du pays** local

~ **rosé** rosé (pink in reference to Champagne)

~ **rouge** red

~ **sec** dry

V.S.O.P. (**very special old pale**) in reference to cognac, indicates that it has been aged at least 5 years

(**vin de**) **xérès** sherry

Mini French Grammar

Articles

All nouns in French are either masculine or feminine.

1. Definite article (the):

masc. le **train**	the train	*fem. la* **voiture**	the car

Le and **la** are contracted to **l'** when followed by a vowel or a silent **h***.

l'avion	the plane	**l'hôtel**	the hotel

Plural (masc. and fem.):

les **trains**	*les* **voitures**	*les* **avions**

2. Indefinite article (a/an):

masc. *un* **timbre**	a stamp	fem. *une* **lettre**	a letter

Plural (masc. and fem.):

des **timbres**	stamps	*des* **lettres**	letters

3. Some/any (partitive)

Expressed by **de, du, de la, de l', des** as follows:

masc. **du** (= **de** + **le**) fem. **de la**	de l' when followed by a vowel or a silent **h***

Plural (masc. and fem.): **des** (= **de** + **les**)

du **sel**	some salt	*de la* **moutarde**	some mustard
*de l'***ail**	some garlic	*des* **oranges**	some oranges

In negatives sentences, **de** is generally used.

Il n'y a pas *de* **taxis.**	There aren't any taxis.
Je n'ai pas *d'***argent.**	I haven't any money.

Note the contraction **d'** before a vowel.

* In French the letter *h* at the beginning of a word is not pronounced. However, in several words the *h* is what is called "aspirate", i.e., no liaison is made with the word preceding it. E.g., *le héros*. See also Guide to Pronunciation, p. 10.

Nouns

1. As already noted, nouns are either masculine or feminine. There are no short cuts for determining gender (though, note that most nouns ending in **-e, -té, -tion** are feminine). So always learn a noun together with its accompanying article.

2. The plural of the majority of nouns is formed by adding **s** to the singular. (The final **s** is not pronounced.)

3. To show possession, use the preposition **de** (of).

la fin *de* **la semaine**	the end of the week
le début *du* **mois**	the beginning of the month
le patron *de* **l'hôtel**	the owner of the hotel
les valises *des* **voyageurs**	the travellers' luggage

Adjectives

1. Adjectives agree with the noun in gender and number. Most of them form the feminine by adding **e** to the masculine (unless the word already ends in **e**). For the plural, add **s.**

a. **un grand magasin**	a big shop	**des grands magasins**
b. **une auto anglaise**	an English car	**des autos anglaises**

2. As can be seen from the above, adjectives can come (a) before the noun or (b) after the noun. Since it is basically a question of sound and idiom, rules are difficult to formulate briefly; but adjectives more often follow nouns.

3. **Demonstrative adjectives:**

this/that	**ce** (*masc.*)	these/those	**ces** (*masc. and fem.*)
	cet (*masc. before a vowel or silent* **h**)		
	cette (*fem.*)		

4. **Possessive adjectives:** These agree in number and gender with *the noun they modify*, i.e., with the thing possessed and not the possessor.

	masc.	fem.	plur.
my	**mon**	**ma**	**mes**
your	**ton**	**ta**	**tes**
his/her/its	**son**	**sa**	**ses**
our	**notre**	**notre**	**nos**
your	**votre**	**votre**	**vos**
their	**leur**	**leur**	**leurs**

Thus, depending on the context:

son **fils**	can mean *his* son or *her* son
sa **chambre**	can mean *his* room or *her* room
ses **vêtements**	can mean *his* clothes or *her* clothes

Personal pronouns

	Subject	Direct object	Indirect object	After a preposition
I	**je**	**me**	**me**	**moi**
you	**tu**	**te**	**te**	**toi**
he/it (masc.)	**il**	**le**	**lui**	**lui**
she/it (fem.)	**elle**	**la**	**lui**	**elle**
we	**nous**	**nous**	**nous**	**nous**
you	**vous**	**vous**	**vous**	**vous**
they (masc.)	**ils**	**les**	**leur**	**eux**
they (fem.)	**elles**	**les**	**leur**	**elles**

Note: There are two forms for "you" in French: **tu** is used when talking to relatives, close friends and children (and between young people); **vous** is used in all other cases, and is also the plural form of **tu.**

Adverbs

Adverbs are generally formed by adding **-ment** to the feminine form of the adjective.

masc.:	fem.:	adverb:
lent (slow)	**lente**	lentement
sérieux (serious)	**sérieuse**	sérieusement

Verbs

Three regular conjugations appear below, grouped by families according to their infinitive endings, *-er*, *-ir* and *-re*. Verbs with the ending *-er* are considered as the true regular conjugation in French. Verbs which do not follow the conjugations below are considered irregular (see irregular verb list). Note that there are some verbs which follow the regular conjugation of the category they belong to, but present some minor changes in the spelling of the stem. Example: *acheter, j'achète*; *broyer, je broie*.

		1st conj.	2nd conj.	3rd conj.
Infinitive		**chant er** (*sing*)	**fin ir** (*finish*)	**vend re**[1] (*sell*)
Present	je	chant **e**	fin **is**	vend **s**
	tu	chant **es**	fin **is**	vend **s**
	il	chant **e**	fin **it**	vend
	nous	chant **ons**	fin **issons**	vend **ons**
	vous	chant **ez**	fin **issez**	vend **ez**
	ils	chant **ent**	fin **issent**	vend **ent**
Imperfect	je	chant **ais**	fin **issais**	vend **ais**
	tu	chant **ais**	fin **issais**	vend **ais**
	il	chant **ait**	fin **issait**	vend **ait**
	nous	chant **ions**	fin **issions**	vend **ions**
	vous	chant **iez**	fin **issiez**	vend **iez**
	ils	chant **aient**	fin **issaient**	vend **aient**
Future	je	chant **erai**	fin **irai**	vend **rai**
	tu	chant **eras**	fin **iras**	vend **ras**
	il	chant **era**	fin **ira**	vend **ra**
	nous	chant **erons**	fin **irons**	vend **rons**
	vous	chant **erez**	fin **irez**	vend **rez**
	ils	chant **eront**	fin **iront**	vend **ront**
Conditional	je	chant **erais**	fin **irais**	vend **rais**
	tu	chant **erais**	fin **irais**	vend **rais**
	il	chant **erait**	fin **irait**	vend **rait**
	nous	chant **erions**	fin **irions**	vend **rions**
	vous	chant **eriez**	fin **iriez**	vend **riez**
	ils	chant **eraient**	fin **iraient**	vend **raient**

[1]conjugated in the same way: all verbs ending in *-andre*, *-endre*, *-ondre*, *-erdre*, *-ordre* (except *prendre* and its compounds).

Pres. subj.[2]	je	chant **e**	fin **isse**	vend **e**
	tu	chant **es**	fin **isses**	vend **es**
	il	chant **e**	fin **isse**	vend **e**
	nous	chant **ions**	fin **issions**	vend **ions**
	vous	chant **iez**	fin **issiez**	vend **iez**
	ils	chant **ent**	fin **issent**	vend **ent**
Past part.		chant **é(e)**	fin **i(e)**	vend **u(e)**

[2]French verbs are always preceded by *que* when conjugated in all tenses of subjonctive. Examples: *que je chante*, *que nous finissions*, *qu'ils aient.*

Auxiliary verbs

	avoir (*to have*)		**être** (*to be*)	
Present	*Imperfect*	*Present*	*Imperfect*	
j', je	ai	avais	suis	étais
tu	as	avais	es	étais
il	a	avait	est	était
nous	avons	avions	sommes	étions
vous	avez	aviez	êtes	étiez
ils	ont	avaient	sont	étaient
	Future	*Conditional*	*Future*	*Conditional*
j', je	aurai	aurais	serai	serais
tu	auras	aurais	seras	serais
il	aura	aurait	sera	serait
nous	aurons	aurions	serons	serions
vous	aurez	auriez	serez	seriez
ils	auront	auraient	seront	seraient
	Pres. subj. [1]	*Pres. perf*	*Pres. subj.*[1]	*Pres. perf.*
j', je	aie	ai eu	sois	ai été
tu	aies	as eu	sois	as été
il	ait	a eu	soit	a été
nous	ayons	avons eu	soyons	avons été
vous	ayez	avez eu	soyez	avez été
ils	aient	ont eu	soient	ont été

[1]French verbs are always preceded by *que* when conjugated in all tenses of subjonctive. Examples: *que je chante*, *que nous finissions*, *qu'ils aient.*

Irregular verbs

Below is a list of the verbs and tenses commonly used in spoken French. In the listing a) stands for the present tense, b) for the imperfect, c) for the future, d) for the conditional, e) for the present subjonctive and f) for the past participle. In the present tense we have given the whole conjugation, for the other tenses the first person singular, as the conjugations for tenses other than present are similar to those used in the regular verbs. Unless otherwise indicated, verbs with prefixes (*ab-*, *ac-*, *com-*, *con-*, *contre-*, *de-*, *dé-*, *dis-*, *é-*, *en-*, *entr(e)-*, *ex-*, *in-*, *o-*, *par-*, *pré-*, *pour-*, *re-*, *ré-*, *sous-*, etc.) are conjugated like the stem verb.

absoudre *absolve* — a) absous, absous, absout, absolvons, absolvez, absolvent; b) absolvais; c) absoudrai; d) absoudrais; e) absolve; f) absous, absoute

accroître *increase* — a) accrois, accrois, accroît, accroissons, accroissez, accroissent; b) accroissais; c) accroîtrai; d) accroîtrais; e) accroisse; f) accru(e)

acquérir *acquire* — a) acquiers, acquiers, acquiert, acquérons, acquérez, acquièrent; b) acquérais; c) acquerrai; d) acquerrais; e) acquière; f) acquis(e)

aller *go* — a) vais, vas, va, allons, allez, vont; b) allais; c) irai; d) irais; e) aille; f) allé(e)

apercevoir *perceive* — → recevoir

apparaître *appear* — → connaître

assaillir *assail* — a) assaille, assailles, assaille, assaillons, assaillez, assaillent; b) assaillais; c) assaillirai; d) assaillirais; e) assaille; f) assailli(e)

asseoir *set* — a) assieds, assieds, assied, asseyons, asseyez, asseyent; b) asseyais; c) assiérai; d) assiérais; e) asseye; f) assis(e)

astreindre *compel* — → peindre

battre *beat* — a) bats, bats, bat, battons, battez, battent; b) battais; c) battrai; d) battrais; e) batte; f) battu(e)

boire *drink* — a) bois, bois, boit, buvons, buvez, boivent; b) buvais; c) boirai; d) boirais; e) boive; f) bu(e)

bouillir *boil* — a) bous, bous, bout, bouillons, bouillez, bouillent; b) bouillais; c) bouillirai; d) bouillirais; e) bouille; f) bouilli(e)

ceindre *gird* — → peindre

circoncire *circumcise* — → suffire

circonscrire *limit* — → écrire

clore *close*	a) je clos, tu clos, il clôt, ils closent; b) –; c) clorai; d) clorais; e) close; f) clos(e)
concevoir *conceive*	→ recevoir
conclure *conclude*	a) conclus, conclus, conclut, concluons, concluez, concluent; b) concluais; c) conclurai; d) conclurais; e) conclue; f) conclu(e)
conduire *drive*	→ cuire
connaître *know*	a) connais, connais, connaît, connaissons, connaissez, connaissent; b) connaissais; c) connaîtrai; d) connaîtrais; e) connaisse; f) connu(e)
conquérir *conquer*	→ acquérir
construire *build*	→ cuire
contraindre *constrain*	→ craindre
contredire *contradict*	→ médire
coudre *sew*	a) couds, couds, coud, cousons, cousez, cousent; b) cousais; c) coudrai; d) coudrais; e) couse; f) cousu(e)
courir *run*	a) cours, cours, court, courons, courez, courent; b) courais; c) courrai; d) courrais; e) coure; f) couru(e)
couvrir *cover*	a) couvre, couvres, couvre, couvrons, couvrez, couvrent; b) couvrais; c) couvrirai; d) couvrirais; e) couvre; f) couvert(e)
craindre *fear*	a) crains, crains, craint, craignons, craignez, craignent; b) craignais; c) craindrai; d) craindrais; e) craigne; f) craint(e)
croire *believe*	a) crois, crois, croit, croyons, croyez, croient; b) croyais; c) croirai; d) croirais; e) croie; f) cru(e)
croître *grow*	a) croîs, croîs, croît, croissons, croissez, croissent; b) croissais; c) croîtrai; d) croîtrais; e) croisse; f) crû, crue
cueillir *pick*	a) cueille, cueilles, cueille, cueillons, cueillez, cueillent; b) cueillais; c) cueillerai; d) cueillerais; e) cueille; f) cueilli(e)
cuire *cook*	a) cuis, cuis, cuit, cuisons, cuisez, cuisent; b) cuisais; c) cuirai; d) cuirais; e) cuise; f) cuit(e)
décevoir *deceive*	→ recevoir
décrire *describe*	→ écrire
déduire *deduct*	→ cuire
détruire *destroy*	→ cuire

devoir *have to*	a) dois, dois, doit, devons, devez, doivent; b) devais; c) devrai; d) devrais; e) doive; f) dû, due
dire *say*	a) dis, dis, dit, disons, dites, disent; b) disais; c) dirai; d) dirais; e) dise; f) dit(e)
dissoudre *dissolve*	→ absoudre
dormir *sleep*	a) dors, dors, dort, dormons, dormez, dorment; b) dormais; c) dormirai; d) dormirais; e) dorme; f) dormi
échoir *fall to*	a) il échoit; b) –; c) il échoira; d) il échoirait; e) qu'il échoie; f) échu(e)
écrire *write*	a) écris, écris, écrit, écrivons, écrivez, écrivent; b) écrivais; c) écrirai; d) écrirais; e) écrive; f) écrit(e)
élire *elect*	→ lire
émettre *emit*	→ mettre
émouvoir *affect*	→ mouvoir; f) ému(e)
empreindre *imprint*	→ peindre
enduire *coat*	→ cuire
enfreindre *infringe*	→ craindre
envoyer *send*	a) envoie, envoies, envoie, envoyons, envoyez, envoient; b) envoyais; c) enverrai; d) enverrais; e) envoie; f) envoyé(e)
éteindre *switch off*	→ peindre
étreindre *embrace*	→ peindre
exclure *exclude*	→ conclure
faillir *fail*	a) –; b) –; c) faillirai; d) faillirais; e) faille; f) failli
faire *do*, *make*	a) fais, fais, fait, faisons, faites, font; b) faisais; c) ferai; d) ferais; e) fasse; f) fait(e)
falloir *have to*	a) il faut; b) il fallait; c) il faudra; d) il faudrait; e) qu'il faille; f) il a fallu
feindre *feign*	→ peindre
frire *fry*	→ confire
fuir *escape*	a) fuis, fuis, fuit, fuyons, fuyez, fuient; b) fuyais; c) fuirai; d) fuirais; e) fuie; f) fui

geindre *whine*	→ craindre
haïr *hate*	a) hais, hais, hait, haïssons, haïssez, haïssent; b) haïssais; c) haïrai; d) haïrais; e) haïsse; f) haï(e)
inclure *include*	→ conclure
induire *induce*	→ cuire
inscrire *register*	→ écrire
instruire *instruct*	→ cuire
interdire *forbid*	→ médire
introduire *introduce*	→ cuire
joindre *join*	a) joins, joins, joint, joignons, joignez, joignent; b) joignais; c) joindrai; d) joindrais; e) joigne; f) joint(e)
lire *read*	a) lis, lis, lit, lisons, lisez, lisent; b) lisais; c) lirai; d) lirais; e) lise; f) lu(e)
luire *shine*	a) luis, luis, luit, luisons, luisez, luisent; b) luisais; c) luirai; d) luirais; e) luise; f) lui
maudire *curse*	a) maudis, maudis, maudit, maudissons, maudissez, maudissent; b) maudissais; c) maudirai; d) maudirais; e) maudisse; f) maudit(e)
médire *speak ill of*	a) médis, médis, médit, médisons, médisez, médisent; b) médisais; c) médirai; d) médirais; e)médise; f) médit(e)
mentir *lie*	a) mens, mens, ment, mentons, mentez, mentent; b) mentais; c) mentirai; d) mentirais; e) mente; f) menti
mettre *put*	a) mets, mets, met, mettons, mettez, mettent; b) mettais; c) mettrai; d) mettrais; e) mette; f) mis(e)
moudre *grind*	a) mouds, mouds, moud, moulons, moulez, moulent; b) moulais; c) moudrai; d) moudrais; e) moule; f) moulu(e)
mourir *die*	a) meurs, meurs, meurt, mourons, mourez, meurent; b) mourais; c) mourrai; d) mourrais; e) meure; f) mort(e)
mouvoir *set in motion*	a) meus, meus, meut, mouvons, mouvez, meuvent; b) mouvais; c) mouvrai; d) mouvrais; e) meuve; f) mû, mue
naître *be born*	a) nais, nais, naît, naissons, naissez, naissent; b) naissais; c) naîtrai; d) naîtrais; e) naisse; f) né(e)
nuire *harm*	→ cuire; f) nui
offrir *offer*	→ couvrir

ouvrir → couvrir
open

paître a) pais, pais, paît, paissons, paissez, paissent; b) paissais; c) paîtrai; d) paîtrais; e) paisse; f) –
graze

paraître → connaître
appear

partir → mentir; f) parti(e)
leave

peindre a) peins, peins, peint, peignons, peignez, peignent; b) peignais; c) peindrai; d) peindrais; e) peigne; f) peint(e)
paint

percevoir → recevoir
perceive

plaindre → craindre
pity

plaire a) plais, plais, plaît, plaisons, plaisez, plaisent; b) plaisais; c) plairai; d) plairais; e) plaise; f) plu
please

pleuvoir a) il pleut; b) il pleuvait; c) il pleuvra; d) il pleuvrait; e) qu'il pleuve; f) il a plu
rain

pourvoir a) pourvois, pourvois, pourvoit, pourvoyons, pourvoyez, pourvoient; b) pourvoyais; c) pourvoirai; d) pourvoirais; e) pourvoie; f) pourvu(e)
provide

pouvoir a) peux (puis), peux, peut, pouvons, pouvez, peuvent; b) pouvais, c) pourrai; d) pourrais; e) puisse; f) pu
be able to

prédire a) prédis, prédis, prédit, prédisons, prédisez, prédisent; b) prédisais; c) prédirai; d) prédirais; e) prédise; f) prédit(e)
foretell

prendre a) prends, prends, prend, prenons, prenez, prennent; b) prenais; c) prendrai; d) prendrais; e) prenne; f) pris(e)
take

prescrire → écrire
prescribe

prévoir a) prévois, prévois, prévoit, prévoyons, prévoyez, prévoient; b) prévoyais; c) prévoirai; d) prévoirais; e) prévoie; f) prévu(e)
foresee

produire → cuire
produce

proscrire → écrire
outlaw

recevoir a) reçois, reçois, reçoit, recevons, recevez, reçoivent; b) recevais; c) recevrai; d) recevrais; e) reçoive; f) reçu(e)
receive

requérir → acquérir
require

restreindre → peindre
restrict

rire a) ris, ris, rit, rions, riez, rient; b) riais; c) rirai; d) rirais; e) rie; f) ri
laugh

savoir *know*	a) sais, sais, sait, savons, savez, savent; b) savais; c) saurai; d) saurais; e) sache; f) su(e)
séduire *seduce*	→ cuire
sentir *feel*	→ mentir; f) senti(e)
servir *serve*	a) sers, sers, sert, servons, servez, servent; b) servais; c) servirai; d) servirais; e) serve; f) servi(e)
sortir *go out*	→ mentir; f) sorti(e)
souffrir *suffer*	→ couvrir
souscrire *subscribe*	→ écrire
suffire *be enough*	a) suffis, suffis, suffit, suffisons, suffisez, suffisent; b) suffisais; c) suffirai; d) suffirais; e) suffise; e) suffi
suivre *follow*	a) suis, suis, suit, suivons, suivez, suivent; b) suivais; c) suivrai; d) suivrais; e) suive; f) suivi(e)
taire *be silent*	a) tais, tais, tait, taisons, taisez, taisent; b) taisais; c) tairai; d) tairais; e) taise; f) tu(e)
teindre *dye*	→ peindre
tenir *hold*	a) tiens, tiens, tient, tenons, tenez, tiennent; b) tenais; c) tiendrai; d) tiendrais; e) tienne; f) tenu(e)
traduire *translate*	→ cuire
traire *milk (cow)*	a) trais, trais, trait, trayons, trayez, traient; b) trayais; c) trairai; d) trairais; e) traie; f) trait(e)
transcrire *transcribe*	→ écrire
tressaillir *startle*	→ assaillir
vaincre *defeat*	a) vaincs, vaincs, vainc, vainquons, vainquez, vainquent; b) vainquais; c) vaincrai; d) vaincrais; e) vainque; f) vaincu(e)
valoir *be worth*	a) vaux, vaux, vaut, valons, valez, valent; b) valais; c) vaudrai; d) vaudrais; e) vaille; f) valu(e)
venir *come*	→ tenir
vêtir *dress*	a) vêts, vêts, vêt, vêtons, vêtez, vêtent; b) vêtais; c) vêtirai; d) vêtirais; e) vête; f) vêtu(e)
vivre *live*	a) vis, vis, vit, vivons, vivez, vivent; b) vivais; c) vivrai; d) vivrais; e) vive; f) vécu(e)

voir *see*	a) vois, vois, voit, voyons, voyez, voient; b) voyais; c) verrai; d) verrais; e) voie; f) vu(e)
vouloir *want*	a) veux, veux, veut, voulons, voulez, veulent; b) voulais; c) voudrai; d) voudrais; e) veuille; f) voulu(e)

French Abbreviations

ACF	*Automobile-Club de France*	Automobile Association of France
ACS	*Automobile-Club de Suisse*	Swiss Automobile Association
AELE	*Association européenne de libre-échange*	EFTA, European Free Trade Association
apr. J.-C.	*après Jésus-Christ*	A.D.
av. J.-C.	*avant Jésus-Christ*	B.C.
bd	*boulevard*	boulevard
c.-à-d.	*c'est-à-dire*	i.e.
c/c	*compte courant*	current account
CCP	*compte de chèques postaux*	postal account
CFF	*Chemins de fer fédéraux*	Swiss Federal Railways
ch	*chevaux-vapeur*	horsepower
Cie, Co.	*compagnie*	company
CRS	*Compagnies républicaines de sécurité*	French order and riot police
ct	*courant*	of the month
CV	*chevaux-vapeur*	horsepower
EU	*Etats-Unis*	United States
exp.	*expéditeur*	sender
Fs/Fr.s.	*franc suisse*	Swiss franc
h.	*heure*	hour, o'clock
hab.	*habitants*	inhabitants, population
M.	*Monsieur*	Mr.
Me	*Maître*	title for barrister or lawyer
Mgr	*Monseigneur*	ecclesiastic title for the rank of bishop
Mlle	*Mademoiselle*	Miss
MM.	*Messieurs*	gentlemen, Messrs.
Mme	*Madame*	Mrs.
n°	*numéro*	number
ONU	*Organisation des Nations Unies*	UN
OTAN	*Organisation du Traité de l'Atlantique Nord*	NATO, North Atlantic Treaty Organization
PCV	*paiement contre vérification*	reverse-charge call (collect call)
PDG	*président-directeur général*	chairman of the board
p.ex.	*par exemple*	e.g.
PJ	*police judiciaire*	criminal investigation department
p.p.	*port payé*	postage paid

P & T	*Postes et Télécommunications*	post and telecommunications (France)
PTT	*Postes, Télégraphes, Téléphones*	Post, Telegraph, Telephone (Belgium and Switzerland)
RATP	*Régie autonome des transports parisiens*	Parisian transport authority
RF	*République française*	the French Republic
RN	*route nationale*	national highway
RP	*Révérend Père*	Reverend Father
RSVP	*répondez, s'il vous plaît*	RSVP, please reply
s/	*sur*	on, at
SA	*société anonyme*	Ltd., Inc.
S.A.R.L.	*société à responsabilité limitée*	limited liability company
SE	*Son Eminence; Son Excellence*	His Eminence; His/Her Excellency
SI	*Syndicat d'Initiative*	tourist office
SIDA	*syndrome immuno-déficitaire acquis*	AIDS
SM	*Sa Majesté*	His/Her Majesty
SNCB	*Société nationale des chemins de fer belges*	Belgian National Railways
SNCF	*Société nationale des chemins de fer français*	French National Railways
St, Ste	*saint, sainte*	saint
succ.	*successeur; succursale*	successor; branch office
s. v. p.	*s'il vous plaît*	please
TCB	*Touring-Club royal de Belgique*	Royal Touring Club of Belgium
TCF	*Touring-Club de France*	Touring Club of France
TCS	*Touring-Club Suisse*	Swiss Touring Club
TGV	*train à grande vitesse*	high-speed train
t. s. v. p.	*tournez, s'il vous plaît*	please turn over
TVA	*taxe à la valeur ajoutée*	VAT, value added tax
UE	*Union européenne*	European Union
Vve	*veuve*	widow

Numerals

Cardinal numbers

0	zéro
1	un
2	deux
3	trois
4	quatre
5	cinq
6	six
7	sept
8	huit
9	neuf
10	dix
11	onze
12	douze
13	treize
14	quatorze
15	quinze
16	seize
17	dix-sept
18	dix-huit
19	dix-neuf
20	vingt
21	vingt et un
22	vingt-deux
30	trente
40	quarante
50	cinquante
60	soixante
70	soixante-dix
71	soixante et onze
72	soixante-douze
80	quatre-vingts
81	quatre-vingt-un
90	quatre-vingt-dix
100	cent
101	cent un
230	deux cent trente
1 000	mille
1 107	onze cent sept
2 000	deux mille
1 000 000	un million

Ordinal numbers

1er	premier
2^{e}	deuxième (second)
3^{e}	troisième
4^{e}	quatrième
5^{e}	cinquième
6^{e}	sixième
7^{e}	septième
8^{e}	huitième
9^{e}	neuvième
10^{e}	dixième
11^{e}	onzième
12^{e}	douzième
13^{e}	treizième
14^{e}	quatorzième
15^{e}	quinzième
16^{e}	seizième
17^{e}	dix-septième
18^{e}	dix-huitième
19^{e}	dix-neuvième
20^{e}	vingtième
21^{e}	vingt et unième
22^{e}	vingt-deuxième
23^{e}	vingt-troisième
30^{e}	trentième
40^{e}	quarantième
50^{e}	cinquantième
60^{e}	soixantième
70^{e}	soixante-dixième
71^{e}	soixante et onzième
72^{e}	soixante-douzième
80^{e}	quatre-vingtième
81^{e}	quatre-vingt-unième
90^{e}	quatre-vingt-dixième
100^{e}	centième
101^{e}	cent unième
200^{e}	deux centième
330^{e}	trois cent trentième
$1\,000^{e}$	millième
$1\,107^{e}$	onze cent septième
$2\,000^{e}$	deux millième

Time

Although official time in France is based on the 24-hour clock, the 12-hour system is used in conversation.

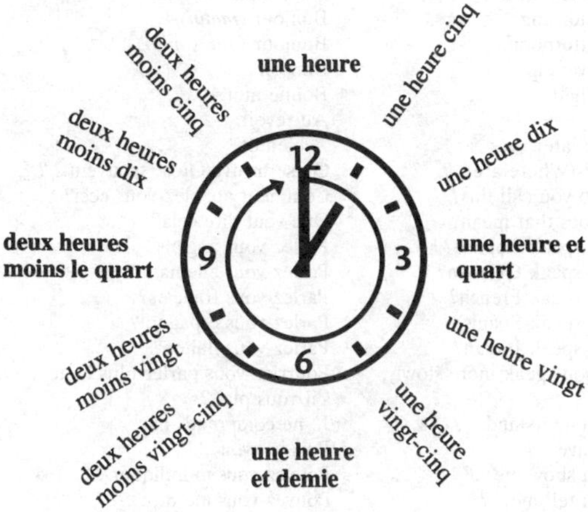

If you have to indicate that it is a.m. or p.m., add *du matin*, *de l'après-midi* or *du soir.*

Thus:

huit heures du matin	8 a.m.
deux heures de l'après-midi	2 p.m.
huit heures du soir	8 p.m.

Days of the Week

dimanche	Sunday	*jeudi*	Thursday
lundi	Monday	*vendredi*	Friday
mardi	Tuesday	*samedi*	Saturday
mercredi	Wednesday		

Some Basic Phrases	Quelques expressions utiles
Please.	S'il vous plaît.
Thank you very much.	Merci beaucoup.
Don't mention it.	Il n'y a pas de quoi.
Good morning.	Bonjour (*matin*).
Good afternoon.	Bonjour (*après-midi*).
Good evening.	Bonsoir.
Good night.	Bonne nuit.
Good-bye.	Au revoir.
See you later.	A bientôt.
Where is/Where are…?	Où se trouve/Où se trouvent…?
What do you call this?	Comment appelez-vous ceci?
What does that mean?	Que veut dire cela?
Do you speak English?	Parlez-vous anglais?
Do you speak German?	Parlez-vous allemand?
Do you speak French?	Parlez-vous français?
Do you speak Spanish?	Parlez-vous espagnol?
Do you speak Italian?	Parlez-vous italien?
Could you speak more slowly, please?	Pourriez-vous parler plus lentement, s'il vous plaît?
I don't understand.	Je ne comprends pas.
Can I have…?	Puis-je avoir…?
Can you show me…?	Pouvez-vous m'indiquer…?
Can you tell me…?	Pouvez-vous me dire…?
Can you help me, please?	Pouvez-vous m'aider, s'il vous plaît?
I'd like…	Je voudrais…
We'd like…	Nous voudrions…
Please give me…	S'il vous plaît, donnez-moi…
Please bring me…	S'il vous plaît, apportez-moi…
I'm hungry.	J'ai faim.
I'm thirsty.	J'ai soif.
I'm lost.	Je me suis perdu.
Hurry up!	Dépêchez-vous!
There is/There are…	Il y a…
There isn't/There aren't…	Il n'y a pas…

Arrival	**Arrivée**
Your passport, please.	Votre passeport, s'il vous plaît.
Have you anything to declare?	Avez-vous quelque chose à déclarer?
No, nothing at all.	Non, rien du tout.

Can you help me with my luggage, please?	Pouvez-vous prendre mes bagages, s'il vous plaît?
Where's the bus to the centre of town, please?	Où est le bus pour le centre de la ville, s'il vous plaît?
This way, please.	Par ici, s'il vous plaît.
Where can I get a taxi?	Où puis-je trouver un taxi?
What's the fare to…?	Quel est le tarif pour…?
Take me to this address, please.	Conduisez-moi à cette adresse, s'il vous plaît.
I'm in a hurry.	Je suis pressé.

Hotel	**Hôtel**
My name is…	Je m'appelle…
Have you a reservation?	Avez-vous réservé?
I'd like a room with a bath.	J'aimerais une chambre avec bains.
What's the price per night?	Quel est le prix pour une nuit?
May I see the room?	Puis-je voir la chambre?
What's my room number, please?	Quel est le numéro de ma chambre, s'il vous plaît?
There's no hot water.	Il n'y a pas d'eau chaude.
May I see the manager, please?	Puis-je voir le directeur, s'il vous plaît?
Did anyone telephone me?	Y a-t-il eu des appels pour moi?
Is there any mail for me?	Y a-t-il du courrier pour moi?
May I have my bill (check), please?	Puis-je avoir ma note, s'il vous plaît?

Eating out	**Restaurant**
Do you have a fixed-price menu?	Avez-vous un menu?
May I see the menu?	Puis-je voir la carte?
May we have an ashtray, please?	Pouvons-nous avoir un cendrier, s'il vous plaît?
Where's the toilet, please?	Où sont les toilettes, s'il vous plaît?
I'd like an hors d'uvre (starter).	Je voudrais un hors-d'uvre.
Have you any soup?	Avez-vous du potage?
I'd like some fish.	J'aimerais du poisson.
What kind of fish do you have?	Qu'avez-vous comme poisson?
I'd like a steak.	Je voudrais un steak.
What vegetables have you got?	Quels légumes servez-vous?
Nothing more, thanks.	Je suis servi, merci.
What would you like to drink?	Qu'aimeriez-vous boire?
I'll have a beer, please.	J'aimerais une bière, s'il vous plaît.
I'd like a bottle of wine.	Je voudrais une bouteille de vin.
May I have the bill (check), please?	Puis-je avoir l'addition, s'il vous plaît?
Is service included?	Le service est-il compris?
Thank you, that was a very good meal.	Merci, c'était très bon.

Travelling	Voyages
Where's the railway station, please?	Où se trouve la gare, s'il vous plaît?
Where's the ticket office, please?	Où est le guichet, s'il vous plaît?
I'd like a ticket to...	J'aimerais un billet pour...
First or second class?	Première ou deuxième classe?
First class, please.	Première classe, s'il vous plaît.
Single or return (one way or roundtrip)?	Aller simple ou aller et retour?
Do I have to change trains?	Est-ce que je dois changer de train?
What platform does the train for ... leave from?	De quel quai part le train pour...?
Where's the nearest underground (subway) station?	Où est la station de métro la plus proche?
Where's the bus station, please?	Où est la gare routière, s'il vous plaît?
When's the first bus to...?	A quelle heure part le premier autobus pour...?
Please let me off at the next stop.	S'il vous plaît, déposez-moi au prochain arrêt.

Relaxing	Distractions
What's on at the cinema (movies)?	Que joue-t-on au cinéma?
What time does the film begin?	A quelle heure commence le film?
Are there any tickets for tonight?	Reste-t-il encore des places pour ce soir?
Where can we go dancing?	Où pouvons-nous aller danser?

Meeting people	Rencontres
How do you do.	Bonjour, Madame/Mademoiselle/Monsieur.
How are you?	Comment allez-vous?
Very well, thank you. And you?	Très bien, merci. Et vous?
May I introduce...?	Puis-je vous présenter...?
My name is...	Je m'appelle...
I'm very pleased to meet you.	Enchanté de faire votre connaissance.
How long have you been here?	Depuis combien de temps êtes-vous ici?
It was nice meeting you.	Enchanté d'avoir fait votre connaissance.
Do you mind if I smoke?	Est-ce que ça vous dérange que je fume?
Do you have a light, please?	Avez-vous du feu, s'il vous plaît?
May I get you a drink?	Puis-je vous offrir un verre?
May I invite you for dinner tonight?	Puis-je vous inviter à dîner ce soir?
Where shall we meet?	Où nous retrouverons-nous?

Shops, stores and services	**Magasins et services**
Where's the nearest bank, please?	Où se trouve la banque la plus proche, s'il vous plaît?
Where can I cash some travellers' cheques?	Où puis-je changer des chèques de voyage?
Can you give me some small change, please?	Pouvez-vous me donner de la monnaie, s'il vous plaît?
Where's the nearest chemist's (pharmacy)?	Où est la pharmacie la plus proche?
How do I get there?	Comment puis-je m'y rendre?
Is it within walking distance?	Peut-on y aller à pied?
Can you help me, please?	Pouvez-vous m'aider, s'il vous plaît?
How much is this? And that?	Combien coûte ceci? Et cela?
It's not quite what I want.	Ce n'est pas exactement ce que je désire.
I like it.	Cela me plaît.
Can you recommend something for sunburn?	Pouvez-vous me conseiller quelque chose contre les coups de soleil?
I'd like a haircut, please.	Je voudrais me faire couper les cheveux, s'il vous plaît.
I'd like a manicure, please.	Je voudrais une manucure, s'il vous plaît.

Street directions	**Directions**
Can you show me on the map where I am?	Pouvez-vous me montrer sur la carte où je me trouve?
You are on the wrong road.	Vous n'êtes pas sur la bonne route.
Go/Walk straight ahead.	Continuez tout droit.
It's on the left/on the right.	C'est à gauche/à droite.

Emergencies	**Urgences**
Call a doctor quickly.	Appelez vite un médecin.
Call an ambulance.	Appelez une ambulance.
Please call the police.	Appelez la police, s'il vous plaît.

Shops, stores and services — **Magasins et services**

[illegible]

Directions

[illegible]

Anglais-Français

English-French

Introduction

Ce dictionnaire a été conçu dans un but pratique. Vous n'y trouverez donc pas d'information linguistique inutile. Les adresses sont classées par ordre alphabétique, sans tenir compte du fait qu'un mot peut être simple ou composé, avec ou sans trait d'union.

Lorsqu'une adresse est suivie d'adresses secondaires (p. ex. expressions usuelles ou locutions), ces dernières sont également rangées par ordre alphabétique sous le mot vedette.

Chaque mot souche est suivi d'une transcription phonétique (voir le Guide de prononciation) et, s'il y a lieu, de l'indication de la catégorie grammaticale (substantif, verbe, adjectif, etc.). Lorsqu'un mot souche peut appartenir à plusieurs catégories grammaticales, les traductions qui s'y réfèrent sont groupées derrière chacune d'elles.

Les pluriels irréguliers des substantifs sont toujours donnés, de même que certains pluriels pouvant prêter à hésitation.

Pour éviter toute répétition, nous avons utilisé un tilde (~) en lieu et place de l'adresse principale.

Dans le pluriel des mots composés, le tiret (-) remplace la partie du mot qui demeure inchangée.

Un astérisque (*) signale les verbes irréguliers. Pour plus de détails, consulter la liste de ces verbes.

Ce dictionnaire tient compte de l'épellation anglaise. Les mots et les définitions des termes typiquement américains ont été indiqués comme tels (voir la liste des abréviations utilisées dans le texte).

Abréviations

adj	adjectif	*num*	numéral
adv	adverbe	*p*	imparfait
Am	américain	*pl*	pluriel
art	article	*plAm*	pluriel (américain)
conj	conjonction	*pp*	participe passé
f	féminin	*pr*	présent
fpl	féminin pluriel	*pref*	préfixe
m	masculin	*prep*	préposition
mpl	masculin pluriel	*pron*	pronom
n	nom	*v*	verbe
nAm	nom (américain)	*vAm*	verbe (américain)

Guide de prononciation

Chaque article de cette partie du dictionnaire est accompagné d'une transcription phonétique qui vous indique la prononciation des mots. Vous la lirez comme si chaque lettre ou groupe de lettres avait la même valeur qu'en français. Au-dessous figurent uniquement les lettres et les symboles ambigus ou particulièrement difficiles à comprendre. *Toutes* les consonnes, y compris celles placées à la fin d'une syllabe ou d'un mot, doivent être prononcées.

Les traits d'union séparent chaque syllabe. Celles que l'on doit accentuer sont imprimées en *italique*.

Les sons de deux langues ne coïncident jamais parfaitement; mais si vous suivez soigneusement nos indications, vous pourrez prononcer les mots étrangers de façon à vous faire comprendre. Pour faciliter votre tâche, nos transcriptions simplifient parfois légèrement le système phonétique de la langue, mais elles reflètent néanmoins les différences de son essentielles.

Consonnes

ð	le **th** anglais de **th**e; **z** dit en zézayant
gh	comme **g** dans **g**ai
h	doit être prononcé en expirant fortement; rappelle le **h** de l'interjection **h**ue!
ng/nng	comme dans campi**ng**; ou comme le dernier son de pai**n**, prononcé avec l'accent du Midi
s	toujours comme dans **s**i
θ	le **th** anglais de **th**ink; **s** dit en zézayant
y	toujours comme dans **y**eux

Au début ou à la fin d'un mot anglais, **b, d, v, z** sont moins sonores qu'en français. C'est également le cas avec **gh** et **ð.**

Voyelles et diphtongues

æ	entre **a** et **è**
i	entre **i** et **é**
ii	comme **i** dans l**i**re
o	proche du **o** de p**o**mme, mais avec la langue placée plus bas et plus retirée dans la bouche et avec les lèvres plus arrondies

1) Les voyelles longues sont indiquées par un dédoublement (p.ex. **oo**) ou par un accent circonflexe placé sur le second élément (p.ex. **eû**).
2) Nos transcriptions comprenant un **ï** doivent être lues comme des diphtongues; le **ï** ne doit pas être séparé de la voyelle qui le précède (comme dans tr**ahi**), mais doit se fondre dans celle-ci (comme dans **ai**l).
3) Les lettres imprimées en petits caractères et dans une position surélevée doivent être prononcées d'une façon assez faible et rapide (p.ex. ^{ou}**i**, **i**^{eu}).

Prononciation américaine

Notre transcription correspond à la prononciation anglaise habituelle. Si la langue américaine varie grandement d'une région à l'autre, elle présente tout de même quelques différences marquantes par rapport à l'anglais de Grande-Bretagne. Ainsi par exemple:
1) Le **r**, qu'il soit placé devant une consonne ou à la fin d'un mot, se prononce toujours (contrairement à l'habitude anglaise).
2) Le **ââ** devient **ææ** dans certains mots, tels que *ask*, *castle*, *laugh*, etc.
3) Le **o** anglais se prononce **a** ou souvent **oo.**
4) Placé devant **oû,** le son **y** est fréquemment omis (ainsi: *duty*, *tune*, *new*, etc.)
5) Enfin, l'accent tonique de certains mots peut varier considérablement.

A

a (éï, eu) *art* (an) un *art*
abbey (*æ*-bi) *n* abbaye *f*
abbreviation (eu-brii-vi-*éï*-cheunn) *n* abréviation *f*
ability (eu-*bi*-leu-ti) *n* capacité *f*
able (*éï*-beul) *adj* en mesure; capable; ***be ~ to** *être capable de; *savoir, *pouvoir
aboard (eu-*bood*) *adv* à bord
abolish (eu-*bo*-lich) *v* abolir
abortion (eu-*boo*-cheunn) *n* avortement *m*
about (eu-*baout*) *prep* de; concernant, sur; autour de; *adv* à peu près; autour
above (eu-*bav*) *prep* au-dessus de; *adv* en haut
abroad (eu-*brood*) *adv* à l'étranger
abscess (*æb*-sèss) *n* abcès *m*
absence (*æb*-seunns) *n* absence *f*
absent (*æb*-seunnt) *adj* absent
absolutely (*æb*-seu-loût-li) *adv* absolument
abstain from (eub-*stéïn*) s'*abstenir de
abstract (*æb*-strækt) *adj* abstrait
absurd (eub-*seûd*) *adj* absurde
abundance (eu-*bann*-deunns) *n* abondance *f*
abundant (eu-*bann*-deunnt) *adj* abondant
abuse (eu-*byoûss*) *n* abus *m*
abyss (eu-*biss*) *n* abîme *m*
academy (eu-*kæ*-deu-mi) *n* académie *f*
accelerate (euk-*sè*-leu-réït) *v* accélérer
accelerator (euk-*sè*-leu-réï-teu) *n* accélérateur *m*
accent (*æk*-seunnt) *n* accent *m*
accept (euk-*sèpt*) *v* accepter
access (*æk*-sèss) *n* accès *m*
accessible (euk-*sè*-seu-beul) *adj* accessible
accessories (euk-*sè*-seu-riz) *pl* accessoires *mpl*
accident (*æk*-si-deunnt) *n* accident *m*
accidental (æk-si-*dèn*-teul) *adj* accidentel
accommodate (eu-*ko*-meu-déït) *v* loger
accommodation (eu-ko-meu-*déï*-cheunn) *n* accommodation *f*, logement *m*
accompany (eu-*kamm*-peu-ni) *v* accompagner
accomplish (eu-*kamm*-plich) *v* achever; accomplir
accordance: in ~ with (inn eu-*koo*-deunns ouið) conformément à
according to (eu-*koo*-dinng toû) d'après, selon; conformément à
account (eu-*kaount*) *n* compte *m*; récit *m*; **~ for** rendre compte de; **on ~ of** à cause de
accountable (eu-*kaoun*-teu-beul) *adj* responsable
accurate (*æ*-kyou-reut) *adj* précis
accuse (eu-*kyoûz*) *v* accuser
accused (eu-*kyoûzd*) *n* prévenu *m*, -e *f*
accustom (eu-*ka*-steumm) *v* familiariser; **accustomed** accoutumé, habitué
ache (éïk) *v* *faire mal; *n* douleur *f*
achieve (eu-*tchiiv*) *v* *parvenir à; accomplir
achievement (eu-*tchiiv*-meunnt) *n* performance *f*
acid (*æ*-sid) *n* acide *m*
acknowledge (euk-*no*-lidj) *v* *reconnaître; *admettre; confirmer
acne (*æk*-ni) *n* acné *f*
acquaintance (eu-*kouéïn*-teunns) *n* connaissance *f*

acquire (eu-*kouaïeu*) *v* *acquérir
acquisition (æ-k^{ou}i-*zi*-cheunn) *n* acquisition *f*
acquittal (eu-*koui*-teul) *n* acquittement *m*
across (eu-*kross*) *prep* à travers; de l'autre côté de; *adv* de l'autre côté
act (ækt) *n* acte *m*; numéro *m*; *v* agir; se *conduire; jouer
action (*æk*-cheunn) *n* action *f*
active (*æk*-tiv) *adj* actif; animé
activity (æk-*ti*-veu-ti) *n* activité *f*
actor (*æk*-teu) *n* acteur *m*
actress (*æk*-triss) *n* actrice *f*
actual (*æk*-tchou-eul) *adj* véritable, réel
actually (*æk*-tchou-eu-li) *adv* en réalité
acute (eu-*kyoût*) *adj* aigu
adapt (eu-*dæpt*) *v* adapter
add (æd) *v* additionner; ajouter
addition (eu-*di*-cheunn) *n* addition *f*
additional (eu-*di*-cheu-neul) *adj* supplémentaire; accessoire
address (eu-*drèss*) *n* adresse *f*; *v* adresser; s'adresser à
addressee (æ-drè-*sii*) *n* destinataire *m*
adequate (*æ*-di-k^{ou}eut) *adj* adéquat; approprié
adjective (*æ*-djik-tiv) *n* adjectif *m*
adjourn (eu-*djeûnn*) *v* ajourner
adjust (eu-*djast*) *v* ajuster; rectifier; régler
administer (eud-*mi*-ni-steu) *v* administrer
administration (eud-mi-ni-*stréï*-cheunn) *n* administration *f*; gestion *f*
administrative (eud-*mi*-ni-streu-tiv) *adj* administratif; **~ law** droit administratif
admiration (æd-meu-*réï*-cheunn) *n* admiration *f*
admire (eud-*maïeu*) *v* admirer
admission (eud-*mi*-cheunn) *n* admission *f*
admit (eud-*mit*) *v* *admettre; *reconnaître
admittance (eud-*mi*-teunns) *n* accès *m*; **no ~** entrée interdite
adopt (eu-*dopt*) *v* adopter
adoption (eu-*dop*-cheunn) *n* adoption *f*
adorable (eu-*doo*-reu-beul) *adj* adorable
adult (*æ*-dalt) *n* adulte *m*; *adj* adulte
advance (eud-*vââns*) *n* avancement *m*; avance *f*; *v* avancer; **in ~** à l'avance, d'avance
advanced (eud-*vâânst*) *adj* avancé
advantage (eud-*vâân*-tidj) *n* avantage *m*
advantageous (æd-veunn-*téï*-djeuss) *adj* avantageux
adventure (eud-*vèn*-tcheu) *n* aventure *f*
advertise (*æd*-veu-taïz) *v* faire de la réclame (pour), annoncer, faire connaître; insérer une annonce
advertisement (eud-*veû*-tiss-meunnt) *n* annonce *f*; publicité *f*
advertising (*æd*-veu-taï-zinng) *n* publicité *f*
advice (eud-*vaïss*) *n* avis *m*, conseil *m*
advise (eud-*vaïz*) *v* donner des conseils, conseiller
advocate (*æd*-veu-keut) *n* partisan *m*
aerial (*èeu*-ri-eul) *n* antenne *f*
aeroplane (*èeu*-reu-pléïn) *n* avion *m*
affair (eu-*fèeu*) *n* affaire *f*; liaison *f*, affaire de cœur
affect (eu-*fèkt*) *v* affecter; toucher
affected (eu-*fèk*-tid) *adj* affecté
affection (eu-*fèk*-cheunn) *n* affection *f*
affectionate (eu-*fèk*-cheu-nit) *adj* affectueux
affiliated (eu-*fi*-li-éï-tid) *adj* affilié
affirm (eu-*feûm*) *v* affirmer, soutenir

affirmative (eu-*feû*-meu-tiv) *adj* affirmatif
afford (eu-*food*) *v* se *permettre
afraid (eu-*frëïd*) *adj* apeuré, effrayé; ***be ~** *avoir peur
Africa (*æ*-fri-keu) Afrique *f*
African (*æ*-fri-keunn) *adj* africain; *n* Africain *m*
after (*ââf*-teu) *prep* après; derrière; *conj* après que
afternoon (ââf-teu-*noûn*) *n* après-midi *m/f*
afterwards (*ââf*-teu-^{ou}eudz) *adv* après; par la suite, ensuite
again (eu-*ghèn*) *adv* encore; de nouveau; **~ and again** toujours et encore
against (eu-*ghènst*) *prep* contre
age (ëïdj) *n* âge *m*; vieillesse *f*; **of ~** majeur; **under ~** mineur
aged (*ëï*-djid) *adj* âgé; vieux
agency (*ëï*-djeunn-si) *n* agence *f*; bureau *m*
agenda (eu-*djèn*-deu) *n* ordre du jour
agent (*ëï*-djeunnt) *n* agent *m*, représentant *m*
aggressive (eu-*ghrè*-siv) *adj* agressif
ago (eu-*ghôou*) *adv* il y a
agree (eu-*ghrii*) *v* *être d'accord; *consentir; concorder
agreeable (eu-*ghrii*-eu-beul) *adj* agréable
agreement (eu-*ghrii*-meunnt) *n* contrat *m*; accord *m*; entente *f*
agriculture (*æ*-ghri-kal-tcheu) *n* agriculture *f*
ahead (eu-*hèd*) *adv* en avant; **~ of** devant; ***go ~** continuer; **straight ~** tout droit
aid (ëïd) *n* aide *f*; *v* assister, aider
aim (ëïm) *n* but *m*; **~ at** viser; aspirer à
air (è^{eu}) *n* air *m*; *v* aérer; **~ conditioning** climatisation *f*
air-conditioned *adj* climatisé
aircraft (*èeu*-krââft) *n* (pl ~) avion *m*; appareil *m*
airfield (*èeu*-fiild) *n* terrain d'aviation
air-filter (*èeu*-fil-teu) *n* filtre à air
airline (*èeu*-laïn) *n* ligne aérienne
airmail (*èeu*-méïl) *n* poste aérienne
airplane (*èeu*-pléïn) *nAm* avion *m*
airport (*èeu*-poot) *n* aéroport *m*
airsickness (*èeu*-sik-neuss) *n* mal de l'air
airtight (*èeu*-taït) *adj* hermétique
airy (*èeu*-ri) *adj* aéré
aisle (aïl) *n* bas-côté *m*; passage *m*
alarm (eu-*lââm*) *n* alerte *f*; *v* alarmer; **~ clock** réveil *m*
album (*æl*-beumm) *n* album *m*
alcohol (*æl*-keu-hol) *n* alcool *m*
alcoholic (æl-keu-*ho*-lik) *adj* alcoolique
ale (ëïl) *n* bière *f*
Algeria (æl-*djieu*-ri-eu) Algérie *f*
Algerian (æl-*djieu*-ri-eunn) *adj* algérien; *n* Algérien *m*
alien (*ëï*-li-eunn) *n* étranger *m*, -ère *f*; *adj* étranger
alike (eu-*laïk*) *adj* pareil, semblable; *adv* de la même façon
alive (eu-*laïv*) *adj* en vie, vivant
all (ool) *adj* tout; **~ in** tout compris; **~ right!** bien!; **at ~** du tout
allergy (*æ*-leu-dji) *n* allergie *f*
alley (*æ*-li) *n* ruelle *f*
alliance (eu-*laï*-eunns) *n* alliance *f*
Allies (*æ*-laïz) *pl* Alliés
allot (eu-*lot*) *v* assigner
allow (eu-*laou*) *v* autoriser, *permettre; **~ to** autoriser à; ***be allowed** *être autorisé
allowance (eu-*laou*-eunns) *n* allocation *f*
all-round (ool-*raound*) *adj* universel
almond (*ââ*-meunnd) *n* amande *f*
almost (*ool*-mô^{ou}st) *adv* presque; à peu près

alone (eu-*lôoun*) *adv* seul
along (eu-*lonng*) *prep* le long de
aloud (eu-*laoud*) *adv* à haute voix
alphabet (*æl*-feu-bèt) *n* alphabet *m*
already (ool-*rè*-di) *adv* déjà
also (*ool*-sô^{ou}) *adv* aussi; de même, également
altar (*ool*-teu) *n* autel *m*
alter (*ool*-teu) *v* changer, modifier
alteration (ool-teu-*réï*-cheunn) *n* changement *m*, modification *f*
alternate (ool-*teû*-neut) *adj* alternatif
alternative (ool-*teû*-neu-tiv) *n* alternative *f*
although (ool-*ðôou*) *conj* quoique, bien que
altitude (*æl*-ti-tyoûd) *n* altitude *f*
alto (*æl*-tô^{ou}) *n* (pl ~s) contralto *m*
altogether (ool-teu-*ghè*-ðeu) *adv* entièrement; en tout
always (*ool*-^{ou}éïz) *adv* toujours
am (æm) *v* (pr be)
amaze (eu-*méïz*) *v* étonner, *surprendre
amazement (eu-*méïz*-meunnt) *n* étonnement *m*
amazing (eu-*méï*-zinng) *adj* stupéfiant, étonnant
ambassador (æm-*bæ*-seu-deu) *n* ambassadeur *m*
amber (*æm*-beu) *n* ambre *m*
ambiguous (æm-*bi*-ghyou-euss) *adj* ambigu; équivoque
ambition (æm-*bi*-cheunn) *n* ambition *f*
ambitious (æm-*bi*-cheuss) *adj* ambitieux
ambulance (*æm*-byou-leunns) *n* ambulance *f*
America (eu-*mè*-ri-keu) Amérique *f*
American (eu-*mè*-ri-keunn) *adj* américain; *n* Américain *m*
amid (eu-*mid*) *prep* entre; parmi, au milieu de
ammonia (eu-*môou*-ni-eu) *n* ammoniaque *f*
amnesty (*æm*-ni-sti) *n* amnistie *f*
among (eu-*manng*) *prep* parmi; au milieu de, entre; **~ other things** entre autres
amount (eu-*maount*) *n* quantité *f*; montant *m*, somme *f*; **~ to** se monter à
amuse (eu-*myoûz*) *v* divertir, amuser
amusement (eu-*myoûz*-meunnt) *n* amusement *m*, divertissement *m*
amusing (eu-*myoû*-zinng) *adj* plaisant
anaemia (eu-*nii*-mi-eu) *n* anémie *f*
anaesthesia (æ-niss-*θii*-zi-eu) *n* anesthésie *f*
anaesthetic (æ-niss-*θè*-tik) *n* anesthésique *m*
analyse (*æ*-neu-laïz) *v* analyser
analysis (eu-*næ*-leu-siss) *n* (pl -ses) analyse *f*
analyst (*æ*-neu-list) *n* analyste *m/f*; psychanalyste *m/f*
anarchy (*æ*-neu-ki) *n* anarchie *f*
anatomy (eu-*næ*-teu-mi) *n* anatomie *f*
ancestor (*æn*-sè-steu) *n* ancêtre *m/f*
anchor (*æng*-keu) *n* ancre *f*
anchovy (*æn*-tcheu-vi) *n* anchois *m*
ancient (*éïn*-cheunnt) *adj* vieux, ancien; antique
and (ænd, eunnd) *conj* et
angel (*éïn*-djeul) *n* ange *m*
anger (*æng*-gheu) *n* colère *f*; fureur *f*
angle (*æng*-gheul) *v* pêcher à la ligne; *n* angle *m*
angry (*æng*-ghri) *adj* en colère
animal (*æ*-ni-meul) *n* animal *m*
ankle (*æng*-keul) *n* cheville *f*
annex[1] (*æ*-nèks) *n* annexe *f*
annex[2] (eu-*nèks*) *v* annexer
anniversary (æ-ni-*veû*-seu-ri) *n* anniversaire *m*
announce (eu-*naouns*) *v* annoncer
announcement (eu-*naouns*-meunnt)

n annonce *f*
annoy (eu-*noï*) *v* agacer, fâcher; ennuyer
annoyance (eu-*noï*-eunns) *n* ennui *m*
annoying (eu-*noï*-inng) *adj* ennuyeux
annual (*æ*-nyou-eul) *adj* annuel; *n* annuaire *m*
annum: per ~ (peur *æ*-neumm) par an
anonymous (eu-*no*-ni-meuss) *adj* anonyme
another (eu-*na*-ðeu) *adj* encore un; un autre
answer (*âân*-seu) *v* répondre à; *n* réponse *f*
ant (ænt) *n* fourmi *f*
antibiotic (æn-ti-baï-*o*-tik) *n* antibiotique *m*
anticipate (æn-*ti*-si-péït) *v* *prévoir, anticiper; *prévenir
antifreeze (*æn*-ti-friiz) *n* antigel *m*
antipathy (æn-*ti*-peu-θi) *n* antipathie *f*
antique (æn-*tiik*) *adj* antique; *n* antiquité *f*; **~ dealer** antiquaire *m/f*
antiquity (æn-*ti*-k^ou^eu-ti) *n* Antiquité; **antiquities** *pl* antiquités
anxiety (æng-*zaï*-eu-ti) *n* anxiété *f*
anxious (*ængk*-cheuss) *adj* désireux; inquiet
any (*è*-ni) *adj* n'importe quel
anybody (*è*-ni-bo-di) *pron* n'importe qui
anyhow (*è*-ni-haou) *adv* n'importe comment
anyone (*è*-ni-^ou^ann) *pron* chacun
anything (*è*-ni-θinng) *pron* n'importe quoi
anyway (*è*-ni-^ou^éï) *adv* de toute façon
anywhere (*è*-ni-^ou^è^eu^) *adv* n'importe où
apart (eu-*pâât*) *adv* à part, séparément; **~ from** abstraction faite de
apartment (eu-*pâât*-meunnt) *nAm* appartement *m*; étage *m*; **~ house** *Am* immeuble d'habitation
aperitif (eu-*pè*-reu-tiv) *n* apéritif *m*
apologize (eu-*po*-leu-djaïz) *v* s'excuser
apology (eu-*po*-leu-dji) *n* excuse *f*
apparatus (æ-peu-*réï*-teuss) *n* dispositif *m*, appareil *m*
apparent (eu-*pæ*-reunnt) *adj* apparent
apparently (eu-*pæ*-reunnt-li) *adv* apparemment; manifestement
appeal (eu-*piil*) *n* appel *m*
appear (eu-*pieu*) *v* sembler, *paraître; *apparaître; se présenter
appearance (eu-*pieu*-reunns) *n* apparence *f*; aspect *m*; entrée *f*
appendicitis (eu-pèn-di-*saï*-tiss) *n* appendicite *f*
appendix (eu-*pèn*-diks) *n* (pl -dices, -dixes) appendice *m*
appetite (*æ*-peu-taït) *n* appétit *m*
appetizer (*æ*-peu-taï-zeu) *n* amusegueule *m*
appetizing (*æ*-peu-taï-zinng) *adj* appétissant
applaud (eu-*plood*) *v* applaudir
applause (eu-*plooz*) *n* applaudissements *mpl*
apple (*æ*-peul) *n* pomme *f*
appliance (eu-*plaï*-eunns) *n* appareil *m*
application (æ-pli-*kéï*-cheunn) *n* application *f*; demande *f*; candidature *f*
apply (eu-*plaï*) *v* appliquer; se *servir de; solliciter un emploi; s'appliquer à
appoint (eu-*poïnt*) *v* désigner, nommer
appointment (eu-*poïnt*-meunnt) *n* rendez-vous *m*; nomination *f*
appreciate (eu-*prii*-chi-éït) *v* évaluer; apprécier
appreciation (eu-prii-chi-*éï*-cheunn) *n* appréciation *f*
apprentice (eu-*prèn*-tiss) *n* apprenti

m, -e *f*
approach (eu-*prôoutch*) *v* approcher; *n* approche *f*; accès *m*
appropriate (eu-*prôou*-pri-eut) *adj* juste, approprié, adéquat
approval (eu-*proû*-veul) *n* approbation *f*; consentement *m*, accord *m*; **on ~** à l'essai
approve (eu-*proûv*) *v* approuver; **~ of** *être d'accord avec
approximate (eu-*prok*-si-meut) *adj* approximatif
approximately (eu-*prok*-si-meut-li) *adv* à peu près, approximativement
apricot (*éï*-pri-kot) *n* abricot *m*
April (*éï*-preul) avril
apron (*éï*-preunn) *n* tablier *m*
Arab (*æ*-reub) *adj* arabe; *n* Arabe *m/f*
arbitrary (*ââ*-bi-treu-ri) *adj* arbitraire
arcade (ââ-*kéïd*) *n* arcade *f*
arch (ââtch) *n* arche *f*; voûte *f*
arch(a)eologist (ââ-ki-*o*-leu-djist) *n* archéologue *m/f*
arch(a)eology (ââ-ki-*o*-leu-dji) *n* archéologie *f*
archbishop (ââtch-*bi*-cheup) *n* archevêque *m*
arched (ââtcht) *adj* arqué
architect (*ââ*-ki-tèkt) *n* architecte *m/f*
architecture (*ââ*-ki-tèk-tcheu) *n* architecture *f*
archives (*ââ*-kaïvz) *pl* archives *fpl*
are (ââ) *v* (pr be)
area (*èeu*-ri-eu) *n* région *f*; zone *f*; **~ code** indicatif *m*
Argentina (ââ-djeunn-*tii*-neu) Argentine *f*
Argentinian (ââ-djeunn-*ti*-ni-eunn) *adj* argentin; *n* Argentin *m*
argue (*ââ*-ghyoû) *v* argumenter, discuter; disputer
argument (*ââ*-ghyou-meunnt) *n* argument *m*; discussion *f*; dispute *f*
***arise** (eu-*raïz*) *v* surgir
arm (ââm) *n* bras *m*; arme *f*; *v* armer
armchair (*ââm*-tchè^eu^) *n* fauteuil *m*
armed (ââmd) *adj* armé; **~ forces** forces armées
armour (*ââ*-meu) *n* armure *f*
army (*ââ*-mi) *n* armée *f*
aroma (eu-*rôou*-meu) *n* arôme *m*
around (eu-*raound*) *prep* autour de; *adv* autour
arrange (eu-*réïndj*) *v* classer, arranger; préparer
arrangement (eu-*réïndj*-meunnt) *n* règlement *m*
arrest (eu-*rèst*) *v* arrêter; *n* arrestation *f*
arrival (eu-*raï*-veul) *n* arrivée *f*; venue *f*
arrive (eu-*raïv*) *v* arriver
arrow (*æ*-rô^ou^) *n* flèche *f*
art (âât) *n* art *m*; habileté *f*; **~ collection** collection d'art; **~ exhibition** exposition d'art; **~ gallery** galerie d'art; **~ history** histoire de l'art; **arts and crafts** arts et métiers; **~ school** académie des beaux-arts
artery (*ââ*-teu-ri) *n* artère *f*
artichoke (*ââ*-ti-tchô^ou^k) *n* artichaut *m*
article (*ââ*-ti-keul) *n* article *m*
artificial (ââ-ti-*fi*-cheul) *adj* artificiel
artist (*ââ*-tist) *n* artiste *m/f*
artistic (ââ-*ti*-stik) *adj* artistique
as (æz) *conj* comme; aussi; que; puisque, parce que; **~ from** à partir de; **~ if** comme si
asbestos (æz-*bè*-stoss) *n* amiante *m*
ascend (eu-*sènd*) *v* monter; *faire l'ascension de
ascent (eu-*sènt*) *n* montée *f*
ascertain (æ-seu-*téïn*) *v* établir; vérifier
ash (æch) *n* cendre *f*
ashamed (eu-*chéïmd*) *adj* honteux; ***be ~** *avoir honte

ashore (eu-*choo*) *adv* à terre
ashtray (*æch*-tréï) *n* cendrier *m*
Asia (*éï*-cheu) Asie *f*
Asian (*éï*-cheunn) *adj* asiatique; *n* Asiatique *m/f*
aside (eu-*saïd*) *adv* de côté, à part
ask (ââsk) *v* demander; prier
asleep (eu-*sliip*) *adj* endormi
asparagus (eu-*spæ*-reu-gheuss) *n* asperge *f*
aspect (*æ*-spèkt) *n* aspect *m*
asphalt (*æss*-fælt) *n* asphalte *m*
aspire (eu-*spaïeu*) *v* aspirer
aspirin (*æ*-speu-rinn) *n* aspirine *f*
assassination (eu-sæ-si-*néï*-cheunn) *n* assassinat *m*
assault (eu-*soolt*) *v* attaquer; violer
assemble (eu-*sèm*-beul) *v* rassembler; monter, assembler
assembly (eu-*sèm*-bli) *n* réunion *f*, assemblée *f*
assignment (eu-*saïn*-meunnt) *n* tâche assignée
assign to (eu-*saïn*) assigner à; attribuer à
assist (eu-*sist*) *v* assister
assistance (eu-*si*-steunns) *n* secours *m*; aide *f*, assistance *f*
assistant (eu-*si*-steunnt) *n* assistant *m*, -e *f*
associate (eu-*sôou*-chi-eut) *n* partenaire *m/f*, associé *m*, -e *f*; allié *m*; membre *m*; *v* associer; **~ with** fréquenter
association (eu-sô^{ou}-si-*éï*-cheunn) *n* association *f*
assort (eu-*soot*) *v* classer
assortment (eu-*soot*-meunnt) *n* assortiment *m*
assume (eu-*syoûm*) *v* supposer, présumer
assure (eu-*choueu*) *v* assurer
asthma (*æss*-meu) *n* asthme *m*
astonish (eu-*sto*-nich) *v* étonner
astonishing (eu-*sto*-ni-chinng) *adj* étonnant
astonishment (eu-*sto*-nich-meunnt) *n* étonnement *m*
astronaut (*æss*-treu-noot) *n* astronaute *m/f*
astronomy (eu-*stro*-neu-mi) *n* astronomie *f*
asylum (eu-*saï*-leumm) *n* asile *m*
at (æt) *prep* à, chez; vers
ate (èt) *v* (p eat)
athlete (*æθ*-liit) *n* athlète *m*
athletics (æθ-*lè*-tiks) *pl* athlétisme *m*
Atlantic (eut-*læn*-tik) Océan Atlantique
atmosphere (*æt*-meuss-fi^{eu}) *n* atmosphère *f*; ambiance *f*
atomic (eu-*to*-mik) *adj* atomique; nucléaire
attach (eu-*tætch*) *v* attacher; fixer; *joindre
attack (eu-*tæk*) *v* attaquer; *n* attaque *f*
attain (eu-*téïn*) *v* *atteindre
attainable (eu-*téï*-neu-beul) *adj* accessible
attempt (eu-*tèmpt*) *v* tenter; essayer; *n* tentative *f*
attend (eu-*tènd*) *v* assister à; **~ on** *servir; **~ to** s'occuper de; *faire attention à, prêter attention à
attendance (eu-*tèn*-deunns) *n* assistance *f*
attendant (eu-*tèn*-deunnt) *n* gardien *m*, gardienne *f*
attention (eu-*tèn*-cheunn) *n* attention *f*; ***pay ~** *faire attention
attentive (eu-*tèn*-tiv) *adj* attentif
attest (eu-*tèst*) *v* attester; **~ to** témoigner de
attic (*æ*-tik) *n* grenier *m*
attitude (*æ*-ti-tyoûd) *n* attitude *f*
attorney (eu-*teû*-ni) *n* avocat *m*, -e *f*
attract (eu-*trækt*) *v* attirer
attraction (eu-*træk*-cheunn) *n*

attraction *f*; attrait *m*
attractive (eu-*træk*-tiv) *adj* séduisant
auction (*ook*-cheunn) *n* vente aux enchères
audible (*oo*-di-beul) *adj* audible
audience (*oo*-di-eunns) *n* public *m*
auditor (*oo*-di-teu) *n* auditeur *m*, -trice *f*
August (*oo*-gheust) août
aunt (âânt) *n* tante *f*
Australia (o-*stréï*-li-eu) Australie *f*
Australian (o-*stréï*-li-eunn) *adj* australien; *n* Australien *m*
Austria (*o*-stri-eu) Autriche *f*
Austrian (*o*-stri-eunn) *adj* autrichien; *n* Autrichien *m*
authentic (oo-*θèn*-tik) *adj* authentique
author (*oo*-θeu) *n* auteur *m*
authoritarian (oo-θo-ri-*tèeu*-ri-eunn) *adj* autoritaire
authority (oo-*θo*-reu-ti) *n* autorité *f*; pouvoir *m*
authorization (oo-θeu-raï-*zéï*-cheunn) *n* autorisation *f*; permission *f*
authorize (*oo*-θeu-raïz) *v* autoriser
automatic (oo-teu-*mæ*-tik) *adj* automatique
automation (oo-teu-*méï*-cheunn) *n* automatisation *f*
automobile (*oo*-teu-meu-biil) *n* auto *f*; ~ **club** club automobile
autonomous (oo-*to*-neu-meuss) *adj* autonome
autumn (*oo*-teumm) *n* automne *m*
available (eu-*véï*-leu-beul) *adj* disponible
avalanche (*æ*-veu-lâânch) *n* avalanche *f*
avenue (*æ*-veu-nyoû) *n* avenue *f*
average (*æ*-veu-ridj) *adj* moyen; *n* moyenne *f*; **on the** ~ en moyenne
averse (eu-*veûss*) *adj* ennemi, peu disposé
aversion (eu-*veû*-cheunn) *n* aversion *f*
avert (eu-*veût*) *v* détourner
avoid (eu-*voïd*) *v* éviter
await (eu-*ouéït*) *v* attendre
awake (eu-*ouéïk*) *adj* réveillé
***awake** (eu-*ouéïk*) *v* réveiller
award (eu-*ouood*) *n* prix *m*; *v* décerner
aware (eu-*ouèeu*) *adj* conscient
away (eu-*ouéï*) *adv* loin; ***go** ~ s'en *aller
awful (*oo*-feul) *adj* terrible
awkward (*oo*-k^{ou}eud) *adj* embarrassant; maladroit
awning (*oo*-ninng) *n* marquise *f*
axe (æks) *n* hache *f*
axle (*æk*-seul) *n* essieu *m*

B

baby (*béï*-bi) *n* bébé *m*; ~ **carriage** *Am* poussette *f*
babysitter (*béï*-bi-si-teu) *n* baby-sitter *m*
bachelor (*bæ*-tcheu-leu) *n* célibataire *m*
back (bæk) *n* dos *m*; *adv* en arrière; ***go** ~ retourner
backache (*bæ*-kéïk) *n* mal au dos
backbone (*bæk*-bô^{ou}n) *n* épine dorsale
background (*bæk*-ghraound) *n* fond *m*
backwards (*bæk*-^{ou}eudz) *adv* en arrière
bacon (*béï*-keunn) *n* lard *m*

bacterium (bæk-*tii*-ri-eumm) *n* (pl -ria) bactérie *f*
bad (bæd) *adj* mauvais; grave; vilain
bag (bægh) *n* sac *m*; sac à main; valise *f*
baggage (*bæ*-ghidj) *n* bagage *m*; ~ **check** *Am* consigne *f*; **hand** ~ *Am* bagage à main
bail (béïl) *n* caution *f*
bait (béït) *n* amorce *f*
bake (béïk) *v* *cuire au four
baker (*béï*-keu) *n* boulanger *m*
bakery (*béï*-keu-ri) *n* boulangerie *f*
balance (*bæ*-leunns) *n* équilibre *m*; bilan *m*; solde *m*
balcony (*bæl*-keu-ni) *n* balcon *m*
bald (boold) *adj* chauve
ball (bool) *n* ballon *m*, balle *f*; bal *m*
ballet (*bæ*-léï) *n* ballet *m*
balloon (beu-*loûn*) *n* ballon *m*
ballpoint pen (*bool*-poïnt-pèn) *n* stylo à bille
ballroom (*bool*-roûm) *n* salle de bal
bamboo (bæm-*boû*) *n* (pl ~s) bambou *m*
banana (beu-*nââ*-neu) *n* banane *f*
band (bænd) *n* orchestre *m*; lien *m*
bandage (*bæn*-didj) *n* pansement *m*
bandit (*bæn*-dit) *n* bandit *m*
bangle (*bæng*-gheul) *n* bracelet *m*
bank (bængk) *n* rive *f*, banque *f*; *v* déposer en banque; ~ **account** compte en banque
banknote (*bængk*-nô^{ou}t) *n* billet de banque
bank rate (*bængk*-réït) *n* taux d'escompte
bankrupt (*bængk*-rapt) *adj* en faillite
banner (*bæ*-neu) *n* bannière *f*
banquet (*bæng*-k^{ou}it) *n* banquet *m*
baptism (*bæp*-ti-zeumm) *n* baptême *m*
baptize (bæp-*taïz*) *v* baptiser
bar (bââ) *n* bar *m*; barre *f*, barreau *m*
barbecue (*bââ*-bi-kyoû) *n* barbecue *m*; *v* griller au charbon de bois; rôtir tout entier
barber (*bââ*-beu) *n* coiffeur *m*
bare (bè^{eu}) *adj* nu
barely (*bèeu*-li) *adv* à peine
bargain (*bââ*-ghinn) *n* bonne affaire; *v* marchander
baritone (*bæ*-ri-tô^{ou}n) *n* bariton *m*
bark (bââk) *n* écorce *f*; *v* aboyer
barley (*bââ*-li) *n* orge *f*
barman (*bââ*-meunn) *n* (pl -men) barman *m*
barn (bâân) *n* grange *f*
barometer (beu-*ro*-mi-teu) *n* baromètre *m*
baroque (beu-*rok*) *adj* baroque
barracks (*bæ*-reuks) *pl* caserne *f*
barrel (*bæ*-reul) *n* tonneau *m*, baril *m*
barrier (*bæ*-ri-eu) *n* barrière *f*
barrister (*bæ*-ri-steu) *n* avocat *m*
bartender (*bââ*-tèn-deu) *n* barman *m*
base (béïss) *n* base *f*; fondement *m*; *v* baser
baseball (*béïss*-bool) *n* base-ball *m*
basement (*béïss*-meunnt) *n* sous-sol *m*
basic (*béï*-sik) *adj* fondamental
basilica (beu-*zi*-li-keu) *n* basilique *f*
basin (*béï*-seunn) *n* bol *m*, bassin *m*
basis (*béï*-siss) *n* (pl bases) base *f*
basket (*bââ*-skit) *n* panier *m*
bass[1] (béïss) *n* basse *f*
bass[2] (bæss) *n* (pl ~) perche *f*
bastard (*bââ*-steud) *n* bâtard *m*; salaud *m*
batch (bætch) *n* lot *m*
bath (bââθ) *n* bain *m*; ~ **salts** sels de bain; ~ **towel** serviette de bain
bathe (béïð) *v* se baigner
bathing cap (*béï*-ðinng-kæp) *n* bonnet de bain
bathing suit (*béï*-ðinng-soût) *n* maillot de bain
bathing trunks (*béï*-ðinng-tranngks)

n caleçon de bain
bathrobe (*bââθ*-rô^{ou}b) *n* peignoir *m*
bathroom (*bââθ*-roûm) *n* salle de bains
batter (*bæ*-teu) *n* pâte *f*
battery (*bæ*-teu-ri) *n* pile *f*; accumulateur *m*
battle (*bæ*-teul) *n* bataille *f*; lutte, combat *m*; *v* *combattre
bay (béï) *n* baie *f*; *v* aboyer
***be** (bii) *v* *être
beach (biitch) *n* plage *f*; **nudist ~** plage pour nudistes
bead (biid) *n* perle *f*; **beads** *pl* collier *m*; chapelet *m*
beak (biik) *n* bec *m*
beam (biim) *n* rayon *m*; poutre *f*
bean (biin) *n* haricot *m*
bear (bè^{eu}) *n* ours *m*
***bear** (bè^{eu}) *v* porter; tolérer; supporter
beard (bi^{eu}d) *n* barbe *f*
bearer (*bèeu*-reu) *n* porteur *m*
beast (biist) *n* bête *f*; **~ of prey** bête de proie
***beat** (biit) *v* frapper; *battre
beautiful (*byoû*-ti-feul) *adj* beau
beauty (*byoû*-ti) *n* beauté *f*; **~ parlo(u)r** institut de beauté; **~ salon** salon de beauté; **~ treatment** soins de beauté
beaver (*bii*-veu) *n* castor *m*
because (bi-*koz*) *conj* parce que; **~ of** en raison de, à cause de
***become** (bi-*kamm*) *v* *devenir
bed (bèd) *n* lit *m*; **~ and board** pension complète; **~ and breakfast** chambre et petit déjeuner
bedding (*bè*-dinng) *n* literie *f*
bedroom (*bèd*-roûm) *n* chambre à coucher
bee (bii) *n* abeille *f*
beech (bii-tch) *n* hêtre *m*
beef (biif) *n* bœuf *m*
beehive (*bii*-haïv) *n* ruche *f*
been (biin) *v* (pp be)
beer (bi^{eu}) *n* bière *f*
beet (biit) *n* betterave *f*
beetroot (*biit*-roût) *n* betterave *f*
before (bi-*foo*) *prep* avant; devant; *conj* avant que; *adv* d'avance; précédemment, avant
beg (bègh) *v* mendier; supplier; demander
beggar (*bè*-gheu) *n* mendiant *m*, -e *f*
***begin** (bi-*ghinn*) *v* commencer; débuter
beginner (bi-*ghi*-neu) *n* débutant *m*, -e *f*
beginning (bi-*ghi*-ninng) *n* commencement *m*; début *m*
behalf: on ~ of (onn bi-*hââf* ov) au nom de; en faveur de
behave (bi-*héïv*) *v* se comporter
behavio(u)r (bi-*héï*-vyeu) *n* comportement *m*
behind (bi-*haïnd*) *prep* derrière; *adv* en arrière
beige (béïj) *adj* beige
being (*bii*-inng) *n* être *m*
Belgian (*bèl*-djeunn) *adj* belge; *n* Belge *m*
Belgium (*bèl*-djeumm) Belgique *f*
belief (bi-*liif*) *n* croyance *f*
believe (bi-*liiv*) *v* *croire
bell (bèl) *n* cloche *f*; sonnette *f*
bellboy (*bèl*-boï) *n* chasseur *m*
belly (*bè*-li) *n* ventre *m*
belong (bi-*lonng*) *v* *appartenir
belongings (bi-*lonng*-inngz) *pl* affaires *fpl*
beloved (bi-*lavd*) *adj* aimé
below (bi-*lôou*) *prep* au-dessous de; en bas de; *adv* en dessous
belt (bèlt) *n* ceinture *f*
bench (bèntch) *n* banc *m*
bend (bènd) *n* virage *m*, courbe *f*
***bend** (bènd) *v* courber; **~ down** se

pencher
beneath (bi-*niiθ*) *prep* en dessous de; *adv* au-dessous
benefit (*bè*-ni-fit) *n* profit *m*, bénéfice *m*; avantage *m*; *v* profiter
bent (bènt) *adj* (pp bend) tordu
beret (*bè*-réï) *n* béret *m*
berry (*bè*-ri) *n* baie *f*
beside (bi-*saïd*) *prep* à côté de
besides (bi-*saïdz*) *adv* en outre; d'ailleurs; *prep* outre
best (bèst) *adj* le meilleur
bet (bèt) *n* pari *m*
***bet** (bèt) *v* parier
betray (bi-*tréï*) *v* trahir
better (*bè*-teu) *adj* meilleur
between (bi-*touiin*) *prep* entre
beverage (*bè*-veu-ridj) *n* boisson *f*
beware (bi-*ouèeu*) *v* *prendre garde, *faire attention
bewitch (bi-*ouitch*) *v* ensorceler, enchanter
beyond (bi-*yonnd*) *prep* au delà de; outre; *adv* au delà
bible (*baï*-beul) *n* Bible *f*
bicycle (*baï*-si-keul) *n* bicyclette *f*; vélo *m*
bid (bid) *v* commander; dire; faire une offre de; **a ~ to** un effort pour
big (bigh) *adj* grand; volumineux; gros; important
bike (baïk) *n* vélo *m*
bile (baïl) *n* bile *f*
bilingual (baï-*linng*-gh^{ou}eul) *adj* bilingue
bill (bil) *n* facture *f*, addition *f*, note *f*; *v* facturer
billiards (*bil*-yeudz) *pl* billard *m*
billion (*bil*-yeunn) *n* billion *m*, *Am* milliard *m*
***bind** (baïnd) *v* lier
binding (*baïn*-dinng) *n* reliure *f*
binoculars (bi-*no*-kyeu-leuz) *pl* jumelles *fpl*
biology (baï-*o*-leu-dji) *n* biologie *f*
birch (beûtch) *n* bouleau *m*
bird (beûd) *n* oiseau *m*
Biro (*baï*-rô^{ou}) *n* crayon à bille
birth (beûθ) *n* naissance *f*
birthday (*beûθ*-déï) *n* anniversaire *m*
biscuit (*biss*-kit) *n* biscuit *m*
bishop (*bi*-cheup) *n* évêque *m*
bit (bit) *n* morceau *m*; peu *m*
bitch (bitch) *n* chienne *f*
bite (baït) *n* bouchée *f*; morsure *f*; piqûre *f*
***bite** (baït) *v* mordre
bitter (*bi*-teu) *adj* amer
black (blæk) *adj* noir; **~ market** marché noir
blackberry (*blæk*-beu-ri) *n* mûre *f*
blackbird (*blæk*-beûd) *n* merle *m*
blackboard (*blæk*-bood) *n* tableau noir
blackcurrant (blæk-*ka*-reunnt) *n* cassis *m*
blackmail (*blæk*-méïl) *n* chantage *m*; *v* *faire chanter
blacksmith (*blæk*-smiθ) *n* forgeron *m*
bladder (*blæ*-deu) *n* vessie *f*
blade (bléïd) *n* lame *f*; **~ of grass** brin d'herbe
blame (bléïm) *n* blâme *m*; *v* donner la faute à, blâmer
blank (blængk) *adj* blanc
blanket (*blæng*-kit) *n* couverture *f*
blast (blââst) *n* explosion *f*
blazer (*bléï*-zeu) *n* veste de sport, blazer *m*
bleach (bliitch) *v* décolorer
bleak (bliik) *adj* morne; désolé
***bleed** (bliid) *v* saigner
bless (blèss) *v* bénir
blessing (*blè*-sinng) *n* bénédiction *f*
blind (blaïnd) *n* store *m*, persienne *f*; *adj* aveugle; *v* aveugler
blinker (*blinng*-keu) *n* clignotant *m*
blister (*bli*-steu) *n* ampoule *f*, cloque *f*

blizzard (*bli*-zeud) *n* tempête de neige
block (blok) *v* obstruer, bloquer; *n* bloc *m*; ~ **of flats** immeuble d'habitation
blond(e) (blonnd) *n* blonde *f*
blood (blad) *n* sang *m*; ~ **poisoning** septicémie *f*;~ **pressure** tension artérielle; ~ **vessel** vaisseau sanguin**bloody** (*bla*-di) *adj* ensanglanté; sanguinaire; sacré; vachement
blossom (*blo*-seum) *n* fleur *f* ; *v* fleurir
blot (blot) *n* tache *f*; **blotting paper** papier buvard
blouse (blaouz) *n* chemisier *m*
blow (blô^{ou}) *n* claque *f*, coup *m*; coup de vent
***blow** (blô^{ou}) *v* souffler
blowout (*blôou*-aout) *n* éclatement *m*
blue (bloû) *adj* bleu; déprimé
blunt (blannt) *adj* émoussé
blush (blach) *v* rougir
board (bood) *n* planche *f*; tableau *m*; pension *f*; conseil *m*; ~ **and lodging** pension complète
boarder (*boo*-deu) *n* pensionnaire *m/f*
boardinghouse (*boo*-dinng-haouss) *n* pension *f*
boarding school (*boo*-dinng-skoûl) *n* internat *m*
boast (bô^{ou}st) *v* se vanter
boat (bô^{ou}t) *n* navire *m*, bateau *m*
body (*bo*-di) *n* corps *m*
bodyguard (*bo*-di-ghââd) *n* garde du corps
bog (bogh) *n* marais *m*
boil (boïl) *v* *bouillir; *n* furoncle *m*
bold (bô^{ou}ld) *adj* audacieux; effronté, hardi
Bolivia (beu-*li*-vi-eu) Bolivie *f*
Bolivian (beu-*li*-vi-eunn) *adj* bolivien; *n* Bolivien *m*
bolt (bô^{ou}lt) *n* verrou *m*; boulon *m*
bomb (bomm) *n* bombe *f*; *v* bombarder
bond (bonnd) *n* obligation *f*
bone (bô^{ou}n) *n* os *m*; arête *f*; *v* désosser
bonnet (*bo*-nit) *n* capot *m*
book (bouk) *n* livre *m*; *v* *retenir, réserver; *inscrire, enregistrer
booking (*bou*-kinng) *n* réservation *f*
bookseller (*bouk*-sè-leu) *n* libraire *m/f*
bookstand (*bouk*-stænd) *n* stand de livres
bookstore (*bouk*-stoo) *n* librairie *f*
boot (boût) *n* botte *f*; coffre *m*
booth (boûð) *n* échoppe *f*; cabine *f*
border (*boo*-deu) *n* frontière *f*; bord *m*
bore[1] (boo) *v* ennuyer; forer; *n* raseur *m*
bore[2] (boo) *v* (p bear)
boring (*boo*-rinng) *adj* ennuyeux
born (boon) *adj* né
borrow (*bo*-rô^{ou}) *v* emprunter
bosom (*bou*-zeumm) *n* poitrine *f*; sein *m*
boss (boss) *n* chef *m*, patron *m*
botany (*bo*-teu-ni) *n* botanique *f*
both (bô^{ou}θ) *adj* les deux; **both … and** aussi bien que
bother (*bo*-ðeu) *v* gêner, tracasser; *n* tracas *m*
bottle (*bo*-teul) *n* bouteille *f*; ~ **opener** ouvre-bouteilles *m*; **hotwater ~** bouillotte *f*
bottleneck (*bo*-teul-nèk) *n* goulot d'étranglement
bottom (*bo*-teumm) *n* fond *m*; postérieur *m*, derrière *m*; *adj* inférieur
bought (boot) *v* (p, pp buy)
boulder (*bôoul*-deu) *n* rocher *m*
bound (baound) *n* limite *f*; ***be ~ to** *devoir; ~ **for** en route pour
boundary (*baoun*-deu-ri) *n* limite *f*;

frontière *f*
bouquet (bou-*kéï*) *n* bouquet *m*
bourgeois (*boueu*-j^{ou}ââ) *adj* bourgeois
boutique (bou-*tiik*) *n* boutique *f*
bow[1] (baou) *v* courber
bow[2] (bô^{ou}) *n* arc *m*; **~ tie** nœud papillon
bowels (baou^{eu}lz) *pl* intestins
bowl (bô^{ou}l) *n* bol *m*
bowling (*bôou*-linng) *n* bowling *m*; **~ alley** bowling *m*
box[1] (boks) *v* boxer; **boxing match** match de boxe
box[2] (boks) *n* boîte *f*
box office (*boks*-o-fiss) *n* guichet de location, guichet *m*
boy (boï) *n* garçon *m*; gamin *m*, gosse *m*; serviteur *m*; **~ scout** scout *m*
bra (brââ) *n* soutien-gorge *m*
bracelet (*bréïss*-lit) *n* bracelet *m*
braces (*bréï*-siz) *pl* bretelles *fpl*
brain (bréïn) *n* cerveau *m*; intelligence *f*; **~ wave** idée lumineuse
brake (bréïk) *n* frein *m*; **~ drum** tambour de frein
branch (brââintch) *n* branche *f*; succursale *f*
brand (brænd) *n* marque *f*
brand-new (brænd-*nyoû*) *adj* flambant neuf
brass (brââss) *n* laiton *m*; cuivre *m*, cuivre jaune; **~ band** *n* fanfare *f*
brave (bréïv) *adj* courageux, brave
Brazil (breu-*zil*) Brésil *m*
Brazilian (breu-*zil*-yeunn) *adj* brésilien; *n* Brésilien *m*
breach (briitch) *n* brèche *f*
bread (brèd) *n* pain *m*; **wholemeal ~** pain complet
breadth (brèdθ) *n* largeur *f*
break (bréïk) *n* fracture *f*; pause *f*
***break** (bréïk) *v* rompre, casser; **~ down** tomber en panne; analyser
breakdown (*bréïk*-daoun) *n* panne *f*
breakfast (*brèk*-feust) *n* petit déjeuner
breast (brèst) *n* sein *m*
breaststroke (*brèst*-strô^{ou}k) *n* brasse *f*
breath (brèθ) *n* souffle *m*
breathe (briið) *v* respirer
breathing (*brii*-ðinng) *n* respiration *f*
breed (briid) *n* race *f*; espèce *f*
***breed** (briid) *v* élever
breeze (briiz) *n* brise *f*
brew (broû) *v* brasser
brewery (*broû*-eu-ri) *n* brasserie *f*
bribe (braïb) *v* *corrompre
bribery (*braï*-beu-ri) *n* corruption *f*
brick (brik) *n* brique *f*
bricklayer (*brik*-léï^{eu}) *n* maçon *m*
bride (braïd) *n* fiancée *f*
bridegroom (*braïd*-ghroûm) *n* marié *m*
bridge (bridj) *n* pont *m*; bridge *m*
brief (briif) *adj* bref
briefcase (*briif*-kéïss) *n* serviette *f*
briefs (briifs) *pl* slip *m*, caleçon *m*
bright (braït) *adj* brillant; malin, intelligent
brighten (*braï*-teunn) *v* faire briller; éclairer; égayer; *v* s'éclaicir; s'allumer; s'animer
brilliant (*bril*-yeunnt) *adj* brillant
brim (brimm) *n* bord *m*
***bring** (brinng) *v* apporter; amener; **~ back** rapporter, ramener; **~ up** élever; soulever
brisk (brisk) *adj* vif
Britain (*bri*-teunn) Angleterre *f*
British (*bri*-tich) *adj* britannique
Briton (*bri*-teunn) *n* Britannique *m*; Anglais *m*
broad (brood) *adj* large; vaste, étendu
broadcast (*brood*-kââst) *n* émission *f*
***broadcast** (*brood*-kââst) *v* *émettre
brochure (*brôou*-chou^{eu}) *n* brochure *f*
broke[1] (brô^{ou}k) *v* (p break)
broke[2] (brô^{ou}k) *adj* fauché

broken (*brôou*-keunn) *adj* (pp break) cassé, brisé; en dérangement
broker (*brôou*-keu) *n* courtier *m*
bronchitis (bronng-*kaï*-tiss) *n* bronchite *f*
bronze (bronnz) *n* bronze *m*; *adj* en bronze
brooch (brô^{ou}tch) *n* broche *f*
brook (brouk) *n* ruisseau *m*
broom (broûm) *n* balai *m*
brothel (*bro*-θeul) *n* bordel *m*
brother (*bra*-ðeu) *n* frère *m*
brother-in-law (*bra*-ðeu-rinn-loo) *n* (pl brothers-) beau-frère *m*
brought (broot) *v* (p, pp bring)
brown (braoun) *adj* brun
bruise (broûz) *n* bleu *m*, contusion *f*; *v* contusionner
brunette (broû-*nèt*) *n* brunette *f*
brush (brach) *n* brosse *f*; pinceau *m*; *v* lustrer, brosser
brutal (*broû*-teul) *adj* brutal
bubble (*ba*-beul) *n* bulle *f*
buck (bak) *m* mâle; *Am colloquial* dollar *m*; chevalet; *v* ruer; ~ **off** jeter, désarçonner; *colloquial* ~ **up** se remuer; prendre courage; résister à, opposer; remonter le moral à
bucket (*ba*-kit) *n* seau *m*
buckle (*ba*-keul) *n* boucle *f*
bud (bad) *n* bourgeon *m*
buddy (*ba*-di) *n Am colloquial* ami *m*; copain *m*
budget (*ba*-djit) *n* budget *m*
buffet (*bou*-féï) *n* buffet *m*
bug (bagh) *n* punaise *f*; coléoptère *m*; *nAm* insecte *m*
***build** (bild) *v* bâtir
building (*bil*-dinng) *n* construction *f*
bulb (balb) *n* bulbe *m*; oignon *m*; **light** ~ ampoule *f*
Bulgaria (bal-*ghèeu*-ri-eu) Bulgarie *f*
Bulgarian (bal-*ghèeu*-ri-eunn) *adj* bulgare; *n* Bulgare *m*
bulk (balk) *n* masse *f*; majorité *f*
bulky (*bal*-ki) *adj* volumineux
bull (boul) *n* taureau *m*
bullet (*bou*-lit) *n* balle *f*
bulletin (*bou*-li-tinn) *n* bulletin *m*, communiqué *m*; informations *pl*; *Am* **bulletin board** tableau *m* d'affichage
bullfight (*boul*-faït) *n* corrida *f*
bullring (*boul*-rinng) *n* arène *f*
bump (bammp) *v* cogner; tamponner; frapper; *n* coup *m*
bumper (*bamm*-peu) *n* pare-choc *m*
bumpy (*bamm*-pi) *adj* cahoteux
bun (bann) *n* brioche *f*
bunch (banntch) *n* bouquet *m*; bande *f*
bundle (*bann*-deul) *n* paquet *m*; *v* empaqueter, lier ensemble
bunk (banngk) *n* couchette *f*
buoy (boï) *n* bouée *f*
burden (*beû*-deunn) *n* fardeau *m*
bureau (*byoueu*-rô^{ou}) *n* (pl ~x, ~s) bureau *m*; *nAm* commode *f*
bureaucracy (byou^{eu}-*ro*-kreu-si) *n* bureaucratie *f*
burglar (*beû*-ghleu) *n* cambrioleur *m*, -euse *f*
burgle (*beû*-gheul) *v* cambrioler
burial (*bè*-ri-eul) *n* sépulture *f*, enterrement *m*
burn (beûnn) *n* brûlure *f*
***burn** (beûnn) *v* brûler
***burst** (beûst) *v* éclater
bury (*bè*-ri) *v* enterrer
bus (bass) *n* autobus *m*
bush (bouch) *n* buisson *m*
business (*biz*-neuss) *n* affaires *fpl*, commerce *m*; entreprise *f*, affaire *f*; occupation *f*; ~ **hours** heures d'ouverture, heures de bureau; ~ **trip** voyage d'affaires; **on** ~ pour affaires
businessman (*biz*-neuss-meunn) *n* (pl -men) homme d'affaires

businesswoman (*biz*-neuss-^{ou}ou-meunn) *n* (pl -women) femme d'affaires
bust (bast) *n* buste *m*
bustle (*ba*-seul) *n* remue-ménage *m*
busy (*bi*-zi) *adj* occupé; animé, affairé
but (bat) *conj* mais; cependant; *prep* sauf
butcher (*bou*-tcheu) *n* boucher *m*
butter (*ba*-teu) *n* beurre *m*
butterfly (*ba*-teu-flaï) *n* papillon *m*; **~ stroke** brasse papillon
buttock (*ba*-teuk) *n* fesse *f*
button (*ba*-teunn) *n* bouton *m*; *v* boutonner
buttonhole (*ba*-teunn-hô^{ou}l) *n* boutonnière *f*
***buy** (baï) *v* acheter; *acquérir
buyer (*baï*-eu) *n* acheteur *m*, -euse *f*
buzz (baz) *n* bourdonnement *m*; *Am* **~ saw** scie *f* circulaire; *colloquial* **give someone a ~** donner un coup de fil à quelqu'un; bourdonner
by (baï) *prep* par; en; près de
bye-bye (*baï-baï*) *colloquial* au revoir!; adieu!
by-pass (*baï*-pââss) *n* route d'évitement; *v* contourner

C

cab (kæb) *n* taxi *m*
cabaret (*kæ*-beu-réï) *n* cabaret *m*; boîte de nuit
cabbage (*kæ*-bidj) *n* chou *m*
cab driver (*kæb*-draï-veu) *n* chauffeur de taxi
cabin (*kæ*-binn) *n* cabine *f*; cabane *f*
cabinet (*kæ*-bi-neut) *n* cabinet *m*
cable (*kéï*-beul) *n* câble *m*; télégramme *m*
café (*kæ*-féï) *n* café *m*
cafeteria (kæ-feu-*tieu*-ri-eu) *n* cafétéria *f*
caffeine (*kæ*-fiin) *n* caféine *f*
cage (kéïdj) *n* cage *f*
cake (kéïk) *n* gâteau *m*; pâtisserie *f*
calamity (keu-*læ*-meu-ti) *n* calamité *f*, catastrophe *f*
calcium (*kæl*-si-eumm) *n* calcium *m*
calculate (*kæl*-kyou-léït) *v* calculer
calculation (kæl-kyou-*léï*-cheunn) *n* calcul *m*
calculator (*kæl*-kyou-léï-teu) *n* calculatrice *f*
calendar (*kæ*-leunn-deu) *n* calendrier *m*
calf (kââf) *n* (pl calves) veau *m*; mollet *m*; **~ skin** veau *m*
call (kool) *v* appeler; téléphoner; *n* appel *m*; visite *f*; coup de téléphone; ***be called** s'appeler; **~ names** injurier; **~ on** rendre visite à; **~ up** *Am* téléphoner
calm (kââm) *adj* tranquille, calme; **~ down** calmer
calorie (*kæ*-leu-ri) *n* calorie *f*
came (kéïm) *v* (p come)
camel (*kæ*-meul) *n* chameau *m*
camera (*kæ*-meu-reu) *n* appareil photographique; caméra *f*; **~ shop** magasin de photographe
camp (kæmp) *n* camp *m*; *v* camper; **~ bed** lit de camp
campaign (kæm-*péïn*) *n* campagne *f*
camper (*kæm*-peu) *n* campeur *m*
camping (*kæm*-pinng) *n* camping *m*; **~ site** terrain de camping
can (kæn) *n* boîte *f*; **~ opener**

ouvreboîte *m*; **canned food** conserves *fpl*

***can** (kæn) *v* *pouvoir

Canada (*kæ*-neu-deu) Canada *m*

Canadian (keu-*néï*-di-eunn) *adj* canadien; *n* Canadien *m*

canal (keu-*næl*) *n* canal *m*

canary (keu-*nèeu*-ri) *n* canari *m*

cancel (*kæn*-seul) *v* annuler

cancellation (kæn-seu-*léï*-cheunn) *n* annulation *f*

cancer (*kæn*-seu) *n* cancer *m*

candidate (*kæn*-di-deut) *n* candidat *m*

candle (*kæn*-deul) *n* bougie *f*

candy (*kæn*-di) *nAm* bonbon *m*; confiserie *f*; ~ **store** *Am* confiserie *f*

cane (kéïn) *n* canne *f*

canister (*kæ*-ni-steu) *n* boîte métallique

canoe (keu-*noû*) *n* canot *m*

canteen (kæn-*tiin*) *n* cantine *f*

canvas (*kæn*-veuss) *n* grosse toile

cap (kæp) *n* casquette *f*

capable (*kéï*-peu-beul) *adj* capable

capacity (keu-*pæ*-seu-ti) *n* capacité *f*; compétence *f*

cape (kéïp) *n* cape *f*; cap *m*

capital (*kæ*-pi-teul) *n* capitale *f*; capital *m*; *adj* capital, essentiel; ~ **letter** majuscule *f*

capitalism (*kæ*-pi-teu-li-zeumm) *n* capitalisme *m*

capitulation (keu-pi-tyou-*léï*-cheunn) *n* capitulation *f*

capsule (*kæp*-syoûl) *n* capsule *f*

captain (*kæp*-tinn) *n* capitaine *m*; commandant *m*

capture (*kæp*-tcheu) *v* *faire prisonnier, capturer; *prendre; *n* capture *f*; prise *f*

car (kââ) *n* voiture *f*; ~ **hire** location de voitures; ~ **park** parc de stationnement; ~ **rental** *Am* location de voitures

caramel (*kæ*-reu-meul) *n* caramel *m*

caravan (*kæ*-reu-væn) *n* caravane *f*; roulotte *f*

carburettor (kââ-byou-*rè*-teu) *n* carburateur *m*

card (kââd) *n* carte *f*; carte postale

cardboard (*kââd*-bood) *n* carton *m*; *adj* en carton

cardigan (*kââ*-di-gheunn) *n* cardigan *m*

cardinal (*kââ*-di-neul) *n* cardinal *m*; *adj* cardinal, principal

care (kè^{eu}) *n* soin *m*; souci *m*; ~ **about** se soucier de; ~ **for** *tenir à; ***take** ~ **of** *prendre soin de, s'occuper de

career (keu-*rieu*) *n* carrière *f*

carefree (*kèeu*-frii) *adj* insouciant

careful (*kèeu*-feul) *adj* prudent; soigneux, attentif

careless (*kèeu*-leuss) *adj* inattentif, négligent

caretaker (*kèeu*-téï-keu) *n* gardien *m*

cargo (*kââ*-ghô^{ou}) *n* (pl ~es) chargement *m*, cargaison *f*

carnival (*kââ*-ni-veul) *n* carnaval *m*

carp (kââp) *n* (pl ~) carpe *f*

carpenter (*kââ*-pinn-teu) *n* menuisier *m*

carpet (*kââ*-pit) *n* tapis *m*

carriage (*kæ*-ridj) *n* wagon *m*; carrosse *m*, voiture *f*

carrot (*kæ*-reut) *n* carotte *f*

carry (*kæ*-ri) *v* porter; *conduire; ~ **on** continuer; *poursuivre; ~ **out** réaliser

carrycot (*kæ*-ri-kot) *n* berceau de voyage

cart (kâât) *n* charrette *f*

cartilage (*kââ*-ti-lidj) *n* cartilage *m*

carton (*kââ*-teunn) *n* carton *m*; cartouche *f*

cartoon (kââ-*toûn*) *n* dessins animés

cartridge (*kââ*-tridj) *n* cartouche *f*

carve (kââv) *v* découper; entailler, tailler

carving (*kââ*-vinng) *n* gravure *f*
case (kéïss) *n* cas *m*; affaire *f*; valise *f*; étui *m*; **in ~** au cas où; **in ~ of** en cas de
cash (kæch) *n* argent liquide, argent comptant; *v* toucher, encaisser; **~ dispenser** distributeur automatique *m*
cashier (kæ-*chieu*) *n* caissier *m*, caissière *f*
cashmere (*kæch*-mi^{eu}) *n* cachemire *m*
casino (keu-*sii*-nô^{ou}) *n* (pl ~s) casino *m*
cask (kââsk) *n* baril *m*, tonneau *m*
cassette (kæ-*sèt*) *n* cassette *f*; **~ player** lecteur *m* de cassettes; **~ recorder** magnétophone *m* à cassettes
cast (kââst) *n* jet *m*
***cast** (kââst) *v* lancer, jeter; **cast iron** fonte *f*
castle (*kââ*-seul) *n* château *m*
casual (*kæ*-jou-eul) *adj* sans façons; fait en passant, fortuit
casualty (*kæ*-jou-eul-ti) *n* victime *f*
cat (kæt) *n* chat *m*
catacomb (*kæ*-teu-kô^{ou}m) *n* catacombe *f*
catalogue (*kæ*-teu-logh) *n* catalogue *m*
catarrh (keu-*tââ*) *n* catarrhe *m*
catastrophe (keu-*tæ*-streu-fi) *n* sinistre *m*
***catch** (kætch) *v* attraper; saisir; *surprendre; *prendre
category (*kæ*-ti-gheu-ri) *n* catégorie *f*
cathedral (keu-*θii*-dreul) *n* cathédrale *f*
catholic (*kæ*-θeu-lik) *adj* catholique
cattle (*kæ*-teul) *pl* bétail *m*
caught (koot) *v* (p, pp catch)
cauliflower (*ko*-li-flaou^{eu}) *n* choufleur
cause (kooz) *v* causer; provoquer; *n* cause *f*; raison *f*, motif *m*; **~ to** *faire
causeway (*kooz*-^{ou}éï) *n* chaussée *f*
caution (*koo*-cheunn) *n* prudence *f*; *v* avertir
cautious (*koo*-cheuss) *adj* prudent
cave (kéïv) *n* grotte *f*
cavern (*kæ*-veunn) *n* caverne *f*
caviar (*kæ*-vi-ââ) *n* caviar *m*
cavity (*kæ*-veu-ti) *n* cavité *f*
cd (sii-*dii*) *n* cd *m*; **~ player** lecteur de cd
cease (siiss) *v* cesser
cease-fire (*siiss*-faï^{eu}) *n* cessez-le-feu *m*
ceiling (*sii*-linng) *n* plafond *m*
celebrate (*sè*-li-bréït) *v* célébrer
celebration (sè-li-*bréï*-cheunn) *n* célébration *f*
celebrity (si-*lè*-breu-ti) *n* célébrité *f*
celery (*sè*-leu-ri) *n* céleri *m*
cell (sèl) *n* cellule *f*
cellar (*sè*-leu) *n* cave *f*
cell phone (*sèl*-fô^{ou}n) *n* (téléphone) portable
cement (si-*mènt*) *n* ciment *m*
cemetery (*sè*-mi-tri) *n* cimetière *m*
censorship (*sèn*-seu-chip) *n* censure *f*
center (*sèn*-teu) *n* centre *m*
centigrade (*sèn*-ti-ghréïd) *adj* centigrade
centimetre, *Am* **centimeter** (*sèn*-ti-mii-teu) *n* centimètre *m*
central (*sèn*-treul) *adj* central; **~ heating** chauffage central; **~ station** gare centrale
centralize (*sèn*-treu-laïz) *v* centraliser
centre (*sèn*-teu) *n* centre *m*
century (*sèn*-tcheu-ri) *n* siècle *m*
ceramics (si-*ræ*-miks) *pl* céramique *f*
ceremony (*sè*-reu-meu-ni) *n* cérémonie *f*
certain (*seû*-teunn) *adj* certain
certificate (seu-*ti*-fi-keut) *n* certificat *m*; attestation *f*, document *m*, diplôme *m*

chain (tchéïn) *n* chaîne *f*
chair (tchè^{eu}) *n* chaise *f*; siège *m*
chairman (*tchèeu*-meunn) *n* (pl -men) président *m*
chalet (*chæ*-léï) *n* chalet *m*
chalk (tchook) *n* craie *f*
challenge (*tchæ*-leunndj) *v* défier; *n* défi *m*
chamber (*tchéïm*-beu) *n* pièce *f*
champagne (chæm-*péïn*) *n* champagne *m*
champion (*tchæm*-pyeunn) *n* champion *m*, -ne *f*; défenseur *m*
chance (tchââns) *n* hasard *m*; chance *f*, occasion *f*; risque *m*; **by ~** par hasard
change (tchéïndj) *v* modifier, changer; se changer; *n* modification *f*, changement *m*; petite monnaie, change *m*
channel (*tchæ*-neul) *n* canal *m*; **English Channel** La Manche
chaos (*kéï*-oss) *n* chaos *m*
chaotic (kéï-*o*-tik) *adj* chaotique
chap (tchæp) *n* type *m*
chapel (*tchæ*-peul) *n* église *f*, chapelle *f*
chaplain (*tchæ*-plinn) *n* chapelain *m*
character (*kæ*-reuk-teu) *n* caractère *m*
characteristic (kæ-reuk-teu-*ri*-stik) *adj* caractéristique; *n* caractéristique *f*; trait de caractère
characterize (*kæ*-reuk-teu-raïz) *v* caractériser
charcoal (*tchââ*-kô^{ou}l) *n* charbon de bois
charge (tchââdj) *v* demander; charger; accuser; *n* prix *m*; charge *f*, chargement *m*; accusation *f*; **~ card** *Am* carte de crédit; **free of ~** à titre gracieux; **in ~ of** chargé de; ***take ~ of** se charger de
charity (*tchæ*-reu-ti) *n* charité *f*
charm (tchââm) *n* attraits, charme *m*; amulette *f*
charming (*tchââ*-minng) *adj* séduisant
chart (tchâât) *n* tableau *m*; graphique *m*; carte marine; **conversion ~** tableau de conversions
chase (tchéïss) *v* pourchasser; poursuivre, chasser; *n* chasse *f*
chasm (*kæ*-zeumm) *n* gouffre *m*, abîme *m*
chassis (*chæ*-si) *n* (pl ~) châssis *m*
chaste (tchéïst) *adj* chaste
chat (tchæt) *v* bavarder, causer; *n* causette *f*, bavardage *m*
chatterbox (*tchæ*-teu-boks) *n* moulin à paroles
cheap (tchiip) *adj* bon marché; avantageux
cheat (tchiit) *v* tricher; duper
check (tchèk) *v* contrôler, vérifier; *n* damier *m*; *nAm* note *f*; chèque *m*; **check!** échec!; **~ in** s'*inscrire; **~ out** *partir
checkbook (*tchèk*-bouk) *nAm* carnet de chèques
checkerboard (*tchè*-keu-bood) *nAm* échiquier *m*
checkers (*tchè*-keuz) *plAm* jeu de dames
checkroom (*tchèk*-roûm) *nAm* vestiaire *m*
checkup (*tchè*-kap) *n* examen *m*
cheek (tchiik) *n* joue *f*
cheeky (*tchii*-ki) *adj colloquial* insolent, effronté
cheer (tchi^{eu}) *v* acclamer; **~ up** égayer
cheerful (*tchieu*-feul) *adj* joyeux, gai
cheese (tchiiz) *n* fromage *m*
chef (chèf) *n* chef cuisinier
chemical (*kè*-mi-keul) *adj* chimique
chemist (*kè*-mist) *n* pharmacien *m*, pharmacienne *f*; **chemist's** pharmacie *f*
chemistry (*kè*-mi-stri) *n* chimie *f*

cheque (tchèk) *n* chèque *m*
chequebook (*tchèk*-bouk) *n* carnet de chèques
chequered (*tchè*-keud) *adj* à carreaux, à damiers
cherry (*tchè*-ri) *n* cerise *f*
chess (tchèss) *n* échecs
chest (tchèst) *n* poitrine *f*; coffre *m*; **~ of drawers** commode *f*
chestnut (*tchèss*-nat) *n* marron *m*
chew (tchoû) *v* mâcher
chewing gum (*tchoû*-inng-ghamm) *n* chewing gum *m*
chicken (*tchi*-kinn) *n* poulet *m*
chickenpox (*tchi*-kinn-poks) *n* varicelle *f*
chief (tchiif) *n* chef *m*; *adj* principal
chieftain (*tchiif*-teunn) *n* chef *m*
child (tchaïld) *n* (pl children) enfant *m*
childbirth (*tchaïld*-beûθ) *n* accouchement *m*
childhood (*tchaïld*-houd) *n* enfance *f*
Chile (*tchi*-li) Chili *m*
Chilean (*tchi*-li-eunn) *adj* chilien; *n* Chilien *m*
chill (tchil) *n* frisson *m*
chilly (*tchi*-li) *adj* frais
chimes (tchaïmz) *pl* carillon *m*
chimney (*tchimm*-ni) *n* cheminée *f*
chin (tchinn) *n* menton *m*
China (*tchaï*-neu) Chine *f*
china (*tchaï*-neu) *n* porcelaine *f*
Chinese (tchaï-*niiz*) *adj* chinois; *n* Chinois *m*
chip (tchip) *n* éclat *m*; jeton *m*; *v* tailler, ébrécher; **chips** pommes frites
chives (tchaïvz) *pl* ciboulette *f*
chlorine (*kloo*-riin) *n* chlore *m*
chock-full (tchok-*foul*) *adj* plein à craquer, bourré
chocolate (*tcho*-kleut) *n* chocolat *m*; praline *f*
choice (tchoïss) *n* choix *m*; sélection *f*
choir (k[ou]ai[eu]) *n* chœur *m*
choke (tchô[ou]k) *v* étrangler, étouffer; *n* starter *m*
***choose** (tchoûz) *v* choisir
chop (tchop) *n* côte *f*, côtelette *f*; *v* hacher
christen (*kri*-seunn) *v* baptiser
christening (*kri*-seu-ninng) *n* baptême *m*
Christian (*kriss*-tcheunn) *adj* chrétien; **~ name** prénom *m*
Christmas (*kriss*-meuss) Noël
chronic (*kro*-nik) *adj* chronique
chronological (kro-neu-*lo*-dji-keul) *adj* chronologique
chuckle (*tcha*-keul) *v* glousser
chunk (tchanngk) *n* gros morceau
church (tcheûtch) *n* église *f*
churchyard (*tcheûtch*-yââd) *n* cimetière *m*
cigar (si-*ghââ*) *n* cigare *m*; **~ shop** bureau de tabac
cigarette (si-gheu-*rèt*) *n* cigarette *f*; **~ case** étui à cigarettes; **~ lighter** briquet *m*
cinema (*si*-neu-meu) *n* cinéma *m*
cinnamon (*si*-neu-meunn) *n* cannelle *f*
circle (*seû*-keul) *n* cercle *m*; balcon *m*; *v* encercler, entourer
circulation (seû-kyou-*léï*-cheunn) *n* circulation *f*
circumstance (*seû*-keumm-stæns) *n* circonstance *f*
circus (*seû*-keuss) *n* cirque *m*
citizen (*si*-ti-zeunn) *n* citoyen *m*, -ne *f*
citizenship (*si*-ti-zeunn-chip) *n* citoyenneté *f*
city (*si*-ti) *n* cité *f*
civic (*si*-vik) *adj* civique
civil (*si*-veul) *adj* civil; poli; **~ law** droit civil; **~ servant** fonctionnaire *m*
civilian (si-*vil*-yeunn) *adj* civil; *n* civil *m*

civilization (si-veu-laï-*zéï*-cheunn) *n* civilisation *f*
civilized (*si*-veu-laïzd) *adj* civilisé
claim (kléïm) *v* revendiquer, réclamer; prétendre; *n* revendication *f*, prétention *f*
clamp (klæmp) *n* mordache *f*; crampon *m*
clap (klæp) *v* applaudir
clarify (*klæ*-ri-faï) *v* éclaircir, clarifier
class (klâââss) *n* classe *f*
classical (*klæ*-si-keul) *adj* classique
classify (*klæ*-si-faï) *v* classer
classmate (*klâââss*-méït) *n* camarade de classe
classroom (*klâââss*-roûm) *n* salle de classe
claw (kloo) *n* griffe *f*
clay (kléï) *n* argile *f*
clean (kliin) *adj* pur, propre; *v* nettoyer
cleaning (*klii*-ninng) *n* nettoyage *m*; ~ **fluid** détachant *m*
clear (kli^eu^) *adj* clair; *v* nettoyer
clearing (*klieu*-rinng) *n* clairière *f*
cleft (klèft) *n* fente *f*
clergyman (*kleû*-dji-meunn) *n* (pl -men) pasteur *m*; ecclésiastique *m*
clerk (klââk) *n* employé(e) de bureau; greffier *m*; secrétaire *m*/*f*
clever (*klè*-veu) *adj* intelligent; astucieux, éveillé
click (klik) *n* cliquetis *m*, bruit *m* sec; cliquet *m*; déclic *m*; *v* cliqueter; faire un déclic; *colloquial* become clear; ~ **with** plaire à
client (*klaï*-eunnt) *n* client *m*, -e *f*
cliff (klif) *n* falaise *f*
climate (*klaï*-mit) *n* climat *m*
climb (klaïm) *v* grimper; *n* ascension *f*
cling (klinng) *v* s'accrocher, se cramponner; adhérer (**to** à)
clinic (*kli*-nik) *n* clinique *f*
cloak (klô^{ou}k) *n* manteau *m*
cloakroom (*klôouk*-roûm) *n* vestiaire *m*
clock (klok) *n* horloge *f*; **at ... o'clock** à ... heures
cloister (*kloï*-steu) *n* cloître *m*
close[1] (klô^{ou}z) *v* fermer; **closed** *adj* fermé, clos
close[2] (klô^{ou}ss) *adj* proche
closet (*klo*-zit) *n* placard *m*; *nAm* garde-robe *f*
cloth (kloθ) *n* tissu *m*; chiffon *m*
clothes (klô^{ou}ðz) *pl* habits *mpl*, vêtements *mpl*
clothing (*klôou*-ðinng) *n* habillement *m*
cloud (klaoud) *n* nuage *m*
cloudy (*klaou*-di) *adj* nuageux
clover (*klôou*-veu) *n* trèfle *m*
clown (klaoun) *n* clown *m*
club (klab) *n* club *m*; cercle *m*, association *f*; gourdin *m*, massue *f*
clumsy (*klamm*-zi) *adj* maladroit
clutch (klatch) *n* embrayage *m*; prise *f*
coach (kô^{ou}tch) *n* car *m*; wagon *m*; carrosse *m*; entraîneur *m*
coal (kô^{ou}l) *n* charbon *m*
coarse (kooss) *adj* grossier
coast (kô^{ou}st) *n* côte *f*
coat (kô^{ou}t) *n* pardessus *m*, manteau *m*; ~ **hanger** cintre *m*
cocaine (kô^{ou}-*kéïn*) *n* cocaïne *f*
cock (kok) *n* coq *m*
cocktail (*kok*-téïl) *n* cocktail *m*
coconut (*kôou*-keu-nat) *n* noix de coco
cod (kod) *n* (pl ~) morue *f*
code (kô^{ou}d) *n* code *m*
coffee (*ko*-fi) *n* café *m*
coherence (kô^{ou}-*hieu*-reunns) *n* cohérence *f*
coin (koïn) *n* pièce de monnaie
coincide (kô^{ou}-inn-*saïd*) *v* coïncider
cold (kô^{ou}ld) *adj* froid; *n* froid *m*; rhume *m*; **catch a** ~ s'enrhumer
collaborate (keu-*læ*-beu-réït) *v*

collaborer
collapse (keu-*læps*) *v* s'effondrer, s'écrouler
collar (*ko*-leu) *n* collier *m*; col *m*; ~ **stud** bouton de col
collarbone (*ko*-leu-bô^{ou}n) *n* clavicule *f*
colleague (*ko*-liigh) *n* collègue *m*
collect (keu-*lèkt*) *v* rassembler; *prendre, *aller chercher; quêter
collection (keu-*lèk*-cheunn) *n* collection *f*; levée *f*
collective (keu-*lèk*-tiv) *adj* collectif
collector (keu-*lèk*-teu) *n* collectionneur
college (*ko*-lidj) *n* collège *m*
collide (keu-*laïd*) *v* entrer en collision
collision (keu-*li*-jeunn) *n* collision *f*; abordage *m*
colloquial (ko-*lô^{ou}*-k^{ou}i-eul) *adj* familier
Colombia (keu-*lomm*-bi-eu) Colombie *f*
Colombian (keu-*lomm*-bi-eunn) *adj* colombien; *n* Colombien *m*
colonel (*keû*-neul) *n* colonel *m*
colony (*ko*-leu-ni) *n* colonie *f*
colo(u)r (*ka*-leu) *n* couleur *f*; *v* colorer; ~ **film** film en couleurs
colo(u)r-blind (*ka*-leu-blaïnd) *adj* daltonien
colo(u)red (*ka*-leud) *adj* de couleur
colo(u)rful (*ka*-leu-feul) *adj* coloré
column (*ko*-leumm) *n* colonne *f*; rubrique *f*
coma (*kôou*-meu) *n* coma *m*
comb (kô^{ou}m) *v* peigner; *n* peigne *m*
combat (*komm*-bæt) *n* lutte *f*, combat *m*; *v* *combattre, lutter
combination (komm-bi-*néï*-cheunn) *n* combinaison *f*
combine (keumm-*baïn*) *v* combiner
***come** (kamm) *v* *venir; ~ **across** rencontrer; trouver
comedian (keu-*mii*-di-eunn) *n* comédien *m*, -ne *f*; comique *m*
comedy (*ko*-meu-di) *n* comédie *f*; **musical** ~ comédie musicale
comfort (*kamm*-feut) *n* bien-être *m*, commodité *f*, confort *m*; réconfort *m*; *v* consoler
comfortable (*kamm*-feu-teu-beul) *adj* confortable
comic (*ko*-mik) *adj* comique
comics (*ko*-miks) *pl* bandes dessinées
coming (*ka*-minng) *n* arrivée *f*
comma (*ko*-meu) *n* virgule *f*
command (keu-*mâând*) *v* commander; *n* ordre *m*
commander (keu-*mâân*-deu) *n* commandant *m*
commemoration (keu-mè-meu-*réï*-cheunn) *n* commémoration *f*
commence (keu-*mèns*) *v* commencer
comment (*ko*-mènt) *n* commentaire *m*; *v* commenter
commerce (*ko*-meûss) *n* commerce *m*
commercial (keu-*meû*-cheul) *adj* commercial; *n* annonce publicitaire; ~ **law** droit commercial
commission (keu-*mi*-cheunn) *n* commission *f*
commit (keu-*mit*) *v* *remettre, confier; *commettre
committee (keu-*mi*-ti) *n* commission *f*, comité *m*
common (*ko*-meunn) *adj* commun; habituel; ordinaire
communicate (keu-*myoû*-ni-kéït) *v* communiquer
communication (keu-myoû-ni-*kéï*-cheunn) *n* communication *f*
communism (*ko*-myou-ni-zeumm) *n* communisme *m*
community (keu-*myoû*-neu-ti) *n* société *f*, communauté *f*
commuter (keu-*myoû*-teu) *n* navetteur *m*

compact (*komm*-pækt) *adj* compact
compact disc (*komm*-pækt disk) *n* compact disc *m*; ~ **player** lecteur de compact disc *m*
companion (keumm-*pæ*-nyeunn) *n* compagnon *m*, compagne *f*
company (*kamm*-peu-ni) *n* compagnie *f*; entreprise *f*, société *f*
comparative (keumm-*pæ*-reu-tiv) *adj* relatif
compare (keumm-*pèeu*) *v* comparer
comparison (keumm-*pæ*-ri-seunn) *n* comparaison *f*
compartment (keumm-*pâât*-meunnt) *n* compartiment *m*
compass (*kamm*-peuss) *n* boussole *f*
compel (keumm-*pèl*) *v* *contraindre
compensate (*komm*-peunn-séït) *v* compenser
compensation (komm-peunn-*séï*-cheunn) *n* compensation *f*; indemnité *f*
compete (keumm-*piit*) *v* *concourir
competition (komm-peu-*ti*-cheunn) *n* compétition *f*
competitor (keumm-*pè*-ti-teur) *n* concurrent *m*
compile (keumm-*païl*) *v* compiler
complain (keumm-*plëïn*) *v* se *plaindre
complaint (keumm-*plëïnt*) *n* plainte *f*; **complaints book** cahier de doléances
complete (keumm-*pliit*) *adj* entier, complet; *v* achever
completely (keumm-*pliit*-li) *adv* entièrement, totalement, complètement
complex (*komm*-plèks) *n* complexe *m*; *adj* complexe
complexion (keumm-*plèk*-cheunn) *n* teint *m*
complicated (*komm*-pli-kéï-tid) *adj* compliqué
compliment (*komm*-pli-meunnt) *n* compliment *m*; *v* complimenter, féliciter
compose (keumm-*pôouz*) *v* composer
composer (keumm-*pôou*-zeu) *n* compositeur *m*, -trice *f*
comprehensive (komm-pri-*hèn*-siv) *adj* étendu
comprise (keumm-*praïz*) *v* *comprendre, *inclure
compromise (*komm*-preu-maïz) *n* compromis *m*
compulsory (keumm-*pal*-seu-ri) *adj* obligatoire
computer (komm-*pyou*-teu) *n* ordinateur *m*; **lap-top** ~ ordinateur portable
comrade (*komm*-réïd) *n* camarade *m*
conceal (keunn-*siil*) *v* dissimuler
conceited (keunn-*sii*-tid) *adj* prétentieux
conceive (keunn-*siiv*) *v* *concevoir
concentrate (*konn*-seunn-tréït) *v* concentrer
concentration (konn-seunn-*tréï*-cheunn) *n* concentration *f*
conception (keunn-*sèp*-cheunn) *n* conception *f*
concern (keunn-*seûnn*) *v* regarder, concerner; *n* souci *m*; affaire *f*
concerned (keunn-*seûnnd*) *adj* soucieux; concerné
concerning (keunn-*seû*-ninng) *prep* relatif à, concernant
concert (*konn*-seut) *n* concert *m*; ~ **hall** salle de concert
concession (keunn-*sè*-cheunn) *n* concession *f*
concierge (kon-si-*èeuj*) *n* concierge *m*
concise (keunn-*saïss*) *adj* concis
conclusion (keunng-*kloû*-jeunn) *n* conclusion *f*
concrete (*konng*-kriit) *adj* concret; *n*

béton *m*
concussion (keunng-*ka*-cheunn) *n* commotion cérébrale
condition (keunn-*di*-cheunn) *n* condition *f*; état *m/f*; circonstance *f*
condom (*konn*-dom) *n* préservatif *m*
conduct[1] (*konn*-dakt) *n* conduite *f*
conduct[2] (keunn-*dakt*) *v* *conduire; diriger
conductor (keunn-*dak*-teu) *n* conducteur *m*, -trice *f*; chef d'orchestre
confectioner (keunn-*fèk*-cheu-neu) *n* confiseur *m*, -seuse *f*
conference (*konn*-feu-reunns) *n* conférence *f*
confess (keunn-*fèss*) *v* *reconnaître; confesser; professer
confession (keunn-*fè*-cheunn) *n* confession *f*
confidence (*konn*-fi-deunns) *n* confiance *f*
confident (*konn*-fi-deunnt) *adj* confiant
confidential (konn-fi-*dèn*-cheul) *adj* confidentiel
confirm (keunn-*feûmm*) *v* confirmer
confirmation (konn-feu-*méï*-cheunn) *n* confirmation *f*
confiscate (*konn*-fi-skéït) *v* confisquer
conflict (*konn*-flikt) *n* conflit *m*
confuse (keunn-*fyoûz*) *v* confondre; **confused** *adj* confus
confusion (keunn-*fyoû*-jeunn) *n* confusion *f*
congratulate (keunng-*ghræ*-tchou-léït) *v* congratuler, féliciter
congratulations (keunng-ghræ-tchou-*léï*-cheunnz) *n* félicitations *fpl*
congregation (konng-ghri-*ghéï*-cheunn) *n* congrégation *f*
congress (*konng*-ghrèss) *n* congrès *m*
connect (keu-*nèkt*) *v* *joindre; *mettre en communication; brancher
connection (keu-*nèk*-cheunn) *n* relation *f*; rapport *m*; communication *f*, correspondance *f*
connoisseur (ko-neu-*seû*) *n* connaisseur *m*
connotation (ko-neu-*téï*-cheunn) *n* connotation *f*
conquer (*konng*-keu) *v* *conquérir; *vaincre
conqueror (*konng*-keu-reu) *n* conquérant *m*
conquest (*konng*-k^ou^èst) *n* conquête *f*
conscience (*konn*-cheunns) *n* conscience *f*
conscious (*konn*-cheuss) *adj* conscient
consciousness (*konn*-cheuss-neuss) *n* conscience *f*
conscript (*konn*-skript) *n* conscrit *m*
consent (keunn-*sènt*) *v* *consentir; approuver; *n* assentiment *m*, consentement *m*
consequence (*konn*-si-k^ou^eunns) *n* effet *m*, conséquence *f*
consequently (*konn*-si-k^ou^eunnt-li) *adv* par conséquent
conservative (keunn-*seû*-veu-tiv) *adj* conservateur
consider (keunn-*si*-deu) *v* considérer; envisager; trouver, estimer
considerable (keunn-*si*-deu-reu-beul) *adj* considérable; important, sensible
considerate (keunn-*si*-deu-reut) *adj* prévenant
consideration (keunn-si-deu-*réï*-cheunn) *n* considération *f*; égards *mpl*, attention *f*
considering (keunn-*si*-deu-rinng) *prep* vu
consignment (keunn-*saïn*-meunnt) *n* expédition *f*
consist (keunn-*sist*) *v* ~ **in** consister

en; consister à; ~ **of** se composer de
conspire (keunn-*spaïeu*) *v* conspirer
constant (*konn*-steunnt) *adj* constant
constipation (konn-sti-*péï*-cheunn) *n* constipation *f*
constituency (keunn-*sti*-tchou-eunn-si) *n* circonscription électorale
constitution (konn-sti-*tyoû*-cheunn) *n* constitution *f*
construct (keunn-*strakt*) *v* *construire; bâtir, édifier
construction (keunn-*strak*-cheunn) *n* construction *f*; édification *f*; édifice *m*
consulate (*konn*-syou-leut) *n* consulat *m*
consult (keunn-*salt*) *v* consulter
consultation (konn-seul-*téï*-cheunn) *n* consultation *f*; ~ **hours** *n* heures de consultation
consume (keunn-*syoûm*) *v* consommer; consumer
consumer (keunn-*syoû*-meu) *n* utilisateur *m*, consommateur *m*, -trice *f*
contact (*konn*-tækt) *n* contact *m*; *v* contacter; ~ **lenses** verres de contact
contagious (keunn-*téï*-djeuss) *adj* contagieux
contain (keunn-*téïn*) *v* *contenir; *comprendre
container (keunn-*téï*-neu) *n* récipient *m*; conteneur *m*
contemporary (keunn-*tèm*-peu-reu-ri) *adj* contemporain; de l'époque; *n* contemporain *m*
contempt (keunn-*tèmpt*) *n* dédain *m*, mépris *m*
content (keunn-*tènt*) *adj* satisfait
contents (*konn*-tènts) *pl* contenu *m*
contest (*konn*-tèst) *n* combat *m*; concours *m*
continent (*konn*-ti-neunnt) *n* continent *m*
continental (konn-ti-*nèn*-teul) *adj* continental
continual (keunn-*ti*-nyou-eul) *adj* continuel
continue (keunn-*ti*-nyoû) *v* continuer; *poursuivre, durer
continuous (keunn-*ti*-nyou-euss) *adj* continuel, continu, ininterrompu
contour (*konn*-tou^{eu}) *n* contour *m*
contraceptive (konn-treu-*sèp*-tiv) *n* contraceptif *m*
contract[1] (*konn*-trækt) *n* contrat *m*
contract[2] (keunn-*trækt*) *v* attraper
contractor (keunn-*træk*-teu) *n* entrepreneur *m*
contradict (konn-treu-*dikt*) *v* *contredire
contradictory (konn-treu-*dik*-teu-ri) *adj* contradictoire
contrary (*konn*-treu-ri) *n* contraire *m*; *adj* opposé; **on the** ~ au contraire
contrast (*konn*-trââst) *n* contraste *m*; différence *f*
contribution (konn-tri-*byoû*-cheunn) *n* contribution *f*
control (keunn-*trôoul*) *n* contrôle *m*; *v* contrôler
controversial (konn-treu-*veû*-cheul) *adj* discuté, controversé
convenience (keunn-*vii*-nyeunns) *n* commodité *f*
convenient (keunn-*vii*-nyeunnt) *adj* pratique; approprié, qui convient, commode
convent (*konn*-veunnt) *n* couvent *m*
conversation (konn-veu-*séï*-cheunn) *n* entretien *m*, conversation *f*
convert (keunn-*veût*) *v* convertir
convict[1] (keunn-*vikt*) *v* déclarer coupable
convict[2] (*konn*-vikt) *n* condamné *m*
conviction (keunn-*vik*-cheunn) *n* conviction *f*; condamnation *f*
convince (keunn-*vinns*) *v*

*convaincre
convulsion (keunn-*val*-cheunn) *n* convulsion *f*
cook (kouk) *n* cuisinier *m*; *v* *cuire; préparer
cookbook (*kouk*-bouk) *nAm* livre de cuisine
cooker (*kou*-keu) *n* cuisinière *f*; **gas ~** cuisinière à gaz
cookery book (*kou*-keu-ri-bouk) *n* livre de cuisine
cookie (*kou*-ki) *nAm* biscuit *m*
cool (koûl) *adj* frais
cooperation (kô^ou-o-peu-*réï*-cheunn) *n* coopération *f*; collaboration *f*
cooperative (kô^ou-*o*-peu-reu-tiv) *adj* coopératif; coopérant; *n* coopérative *f*
coordinate (kô^ou-*oo*-di-néït) *v* coordonner
coordination (kô^ou-oo-di-*néï*-cheunn) *n* coordination *f*
cope (kô^oup) *v* se débrouiller, s'en tirer, *colloquial* se défendre; **~ with** tenir tête à, faire face à; s'occuper de; venir à bout de
copper (*ko*-peu) *n* cuivre *m*
copy (*ko*-pi) *n* copie *f*; exemplaire *m*; *v* copier; imiter; **carbon ~** copie *f*
coral (*ko*-reul) *n* corail *m*
cord (kood) *n* corde *f*; cordon *m*
cordial (*koo*-di-eul) *adj* cordial
corduroy (*koo*-deu-roï) *n* velours côtelé
core (koo) *n* cœur *m*; trognon *m*
cork (kook) *n* bouchon *m*
corkscrew (*kook*-skroû) *n* tire-bouchon *m*
corn (koon) *n* grain *m*; céréale *f*, blé *m*; durillon *m*, cor au pied; **~ on the cob** maïs en épi
corner (*koo*-neu) *n* coin *m*
cornfield (*koon*-fiild) *n* champ de blé
corpse (koops) *n* cadavre *m*
corpulent (*koo*-pyou-leunnt) *adj* corpulent; gros, obèse
correct (keu-*rèkt*) *adj* juste, correct; *v* corriger
correction (keu-*rèk*-cheunn) *n* correction *f*; rectification *f*
correctness (keu-*rèkt*-neuss) *n* exactitude *f*
correspond (ko-ri-*sponnd*) *v* correspondre; *être conforme
correspondence (ko-ri-*sponn*-deunns) *n* correspondance *f*
correspondent (ko-ri-*sponn*-deunnt) *n* correspondant *m*, -e *f*
corridor (*ko*-ri-doo) *n* corridor *m*
corrupt (keu-*rapt*) *adj* corrompu; *v* *corrompre
corruption (keu-*rap*-cheunn) *n* corruption *f*
corset (*koo*-sit) *n* corset *m*
cosmetics (koz-*mè*-tiks) *pl* cosmétiques *mpl*, produits de beauté
cost (kost) *n* coût *m*; prix *m*
***cost** (kost) *v* coûter
cosy (*kôou*-zi) *adj* intime, confortable
cot (kot) *nAm* lit de camp
cottage (*ko*-tidj) *n* villa *f*
cotton (*ko*-teunn) *n* coton *m*; en coton; **~ wool** ouate *f*
couch (kaoutch) *n* canapé *m*
cough (kof) *n* toux *f*; *v* tousser
could (koud) *v* (p can)
council (*kaoun*-seul) *n* conseil *m*
councillor (*kaoun*-seu-leu) *n* conseiller *m*
counsel (*kaoun*-seul) *n* conseil *m*
counsellor (*kaoun*-seu-leu) *n* conseiller *m*
count (kaount) *v* compter; *inclure; *n* comte *m*
counter (*kaoun*-teu) *n* comptoir *m*; barre *f*
counterfeit (*kaoun*-teu-fiit) *v* *contrefaire

counterfoil (*kaoun*-teu-foïl) *n* talon *m*
countess (*kaoun*-tiss) *n* comtesse *f*
country (*kann*-tri) *n* pays *m*; campagne *f*; région *f*; ~ **house** maison de campagne
countryman (*kann*-tri-meunn) *n* (pl -men) **fellow** ~ compatriote *m*
countryside (*kann*-tri-saïd) *n* campagne *f*
county (*kaoun*-ti) *n* comté *m*
couple (*ka*-peul) *n* couple *m*
coupon (*koû*-ponn) *n* coupon *m*
courage (*ka*-ridj) *n* vaillance *f*, courage *m*
courageous (keu-*réï*-djeuss) *adj* brave, courageux
course (kooss) *n* cap *m*; plat *m*; cours *m*; **crash** ~ cours accéléré; **of** ~ évidemment
court (koot) *n* tribunal *m*; cour *f*
courteous (*keû*-ti-euss) *adj* courtois
cousin (*ka*-zeunn) *n* cousine *f*, cousin *m*
cover (*ka*-veu) *v* *couvrir; *n* abri *m*; couvercle *m*; couverture *f*
cow (kaou) *n* vache *f*
coward (*kaou*-eud) *n* lâche *m*
cowardly (*kaou*-eud-li) *adj* lâche
crab (kræb) *n* crabe *m*
crack (kræk) *n* craquement *m*; fissure *f*; *v* craquer; fendre
cracker (*kræ*-keu) *nAm* biscuit *m*
cradle (*kréï*-deul) *n* berceau *m*
cramp (kræmp) *n* crampe *f*
crane (kréïn) *n* grue *f*
crash (kræch) *n* collision *f*; *v* entrer en collision; s'écraser; ~ **barrier** glissière de sécurité
crate (kréït) *n* caisse *f*
crater (*kréï*-teu) *n* cratère *m*
crawl (krool) *v* ramper; *n* crawl *m*
craze (kréïz) *n* rage *f*
crazy (*kréï*-zi) *adj* fou; insensé
creak (kriik) *v* grincer
cream (kriim) *n* crème *f*; crème fraîche; *adj* crème
creamy (*krii*-mi) *adj* crémeux
crease (kriiss) *v* froisser; *n* pli *m*; faux pli
create (kri-*éït*) *v* créer
creative (kri-*éï*-tiv) *adj* créateur, créatif
creature (*krii*-tcheu) *n* créature *f*; être *m*
credible (*krè*-di-beul) *adj* croyable
credit (*krè*-dit) *n* crédit *m*; *v* créditer; ~ **card** carte de crédit
creditor (*krè*-di-teu) *n* créditeur *m*
credulous (*krè*-dyou-leuss) *adj* crédule
creek (kriik) *n* baie *f*, crique *f*
***creep** (kriip) *v* ramper
creepy (*krii*-pi) *adj* lugubre, terrifiant
cremate (kri-*méït*) *v* incinérer
crew (kroû) *n* équipage *m*
cricket (*kri*-kit) *n* cricket *m*; grillon *m*
crime (kraïm) *n* crime *m*
criminal (*kri*-mi-neul) *n* délinquant *m*, criminel *m*; *adj* criminel; ~ **law** droit pénal
criminality (kri-mi-*næ*-leu-ti) *n* criminalité *f*
crimson (*krimm*-zeunn) *adj* cramoisi
crippled (*kri*-peuld) *adj* estropié
crisis (*kraï*-siss) *n* (pl crises) crise *f*
crisp (krisp) *adj* croustillant
critic (*kri*-tik) *n* critique *m/f*
critical (*kri*-ti-keul) *adj* critique; précaire, délicat
criticism (*kri*-ti-si-zeumm) *n* critique *f*
criticize (*kri*-ti-saïz) *v* critiquer
crochet (*krôou*-chéï) *v* *faire du crochet
crockery (*kro*-keu-ri) *n* poterie *f*, faïence *f*
crocodile (*kro*-keu-daïl) *n* crocodile *m*
crooked (*krou*-kid) *adj* tordu;

malhonnête

crop (krop) *n* récolte *f*

cross (kross) *v* traverser; *adj* en colère, fâché; *n* croix *f*

cross-eyed (*kross*-aïd) *adj* louche

crossing (*kro*-sinng) *n* traversée *f*; croisement *m*; passage *m*; passage à niveau

crossroads (*kross*-rô^{ou}dz) *n* carrefour *m*

crosswalk (*kross*-^{ou}ook) *nAm* passage pour piétons

crow (krô^{ou}) *n* corneille *f*

crowd (kraoud) *n* masse *f*, foule *f*

crowded (*kraou*-did) *adj* animé; bondé

crown (kraoun) *n* couronne *f*; *v* couronner

crucifix (*kroû*-si-fiks) *n* crucifix *m*

crucifixion (kroû-si-*fik*-cheunn) *n* crucifixion *f*

crucify (*kroû*-si-faï) *v* crucifier

cruel (krou^{eu}l) *adj* cruel

cruise (kroûz) *n* croisière *f*

crumb (kramm) *n* miette *f*

crust (krast) *n* croûte *f*

crutch (kratch) *n* béquille *f*

cry (kraï) *v* pleurer; crier; appeler; *n* cri *m*; appel *m*

crystal (*kri*-steul) *n* cristal *m*; *adj* en cristal

Cuba (*kyoû*-beu) Cuba *m*

Cuban (*kyoû*-beunn) *adj* cubain; *n* Cubain *m*

cube (kyoûb) *n* cube *m*

cuckoo (*kou*-koû) *n* coucou *m*

cucumber (*kyoû*-keumm-beu) *n* concombre *m*

cuddle (*ka*-deul) *v* câliner

cuff (kaf) *n* manchette *f*; **~ links** boutons de manchettes

cuff-links (*kaf*-linngks) *pl* boutons de manchettes

cultivate (*kal*-ti-véït) *v* cultiver

culture (*kal*-tcheu) *n* culture *f*

cultured (*kal*-tcheud) *adj* cultivé

cunning (*ka*-ninng) *adj* rusé

cup (kap) *n* tasse *f*, coupe *f*

cupboard (*ka*-beud) *n* placard *m*

curb (keûb) *n* bord du trottoir; *v* freiner

cure (kyou^{eu}) *v* guérir; *n* cure *f*; guérison *f*

curiosity (kyou^{eu}-ri-*o*-seu-ti) *n* curiosité *f*

curious (*kyoueu*-ri-euss) *adj* curieux; étrange

curl (keûl) *v* boucler; friser; *n* boucle *f*

curler (*keû*-leu) *n* bigoudi *m*

curly (*keû*-li) *adj* bouclé

currant (*ka*-reunnt) *n* raisin sec; groseille *f*

currency (*ka*-reunn-si) *n* monnaie *f*; **foreign ~** monnaie étrangère

current (*ka*-reunnt) *n* courant *m*; *adj* courant; **alternating ~** courant alternatif; **direct ~** courant continu

curry (*ka*-ri) *n* curry *m*

curse (keûss) *v* jurer; *maudire; *n* juron *m*

curtain (*keû*-teunn) *n* rideau *m*

curve (keûv) *n* courbe *f*; tournant *m*

curved (keûvd) *adj* courbe, courbé

cushion (*kou*-cheunn) *n* coussin *m*

custody (*ka*-steu-di) *n* garde *f* à vue; garde *f*

custom (*ka*-steumm) *n* coutume *f*; habitude *f*

customary (*ka*-steu-meu-ri) *adj* usuel, coutumier, ordinaire

customer (*ka*-steu-meu) *n* client *m*

Customs (*ka*-steummz) *pl* douane *f*; **~ duty** droit de douane; **~ officer** douanier *m*

cut (kat) *n* incision *f*; coupure *f*

***cut** (kat) *v* couper; *réduire; **~ off** couper; **~ out** découper

cutlery (*kat*-leu-ri) *n* couvert *m*

cutlet (*kat*-leut) *n* côtelette *f*
cycle (*saï*-keul) *n* vélo *m*; bicyclette *f*; cycle *m*
cyclist (*saï*-klist) *n* cycliste *m*
cylinder (*si*-linn-deu) *n* cylindre *m*; ~ **head** tête de cylindre
cystitis (si-*staï*-tiss) *n* cystite *f*
Czech (tchèk) *adj* tchèque; *n* Tchèque *m*
Czech Republic (tchèk ri-*pa*-blik) République Tchèque

D

dad (dæd) *n* papa *m*
daddy (*dæ*-di) *n* papa *m*
daffodil (*dæ*-feu-dil) *n* jonquille *f*
daily (*déï*-li) *adj* journalier, quotidien; *n* quotidien *m*
dairy (*dèeu*-ri) *n* laiterie *f*
dam (dæm) *n* barrage *m*; digue *f*
damage (*dæ*-midj) *n* dommage *m*; *v* endommager
damn (dæm) *v* condamner; maudire
damned (dæmd) *adj* sacré, fichu
damp (dæmp) *adj* humide; moite; *n* humidité *f*; *v* humidifier
dance (dââns) *v* danser; *n* danse *f*
dandelion (*dæn*-di-laï-eunn) *n* pissenlit *m*
dandruff (*dæn*-dreuf) *n* pellicules
Dane (déïn) *n* Danois *m*
danger (*déïn*-djeu) *n* danger *m*
dangerous (*déïn*-djeu-reuss) *adj* dangereux
Danish (*déï*-nich) *adj* danois
dare (dè^{eu}) *v* oser
daring (*dèeu*-rinng) *adj* téméraire
dark (dââk) *adj* obscur; *n* obscurité *f*, ténèbres *fpl*
darling (*dââ*-linng) *n* trésor *m*, chéri *m*
darn (dâân) *v* repriser
dash (dæch) *v* se précipiter
dashboard (*dæch*-bood) *n* tableau de bord
data (*déï*-teu) *pl* données *fpl*
date[1] (déït) *n* date *f*; rendez-vous *m*; *v* dater; **out of ~** démodé
date[2] (déït) *n* datte *f*
daughter (*doo*-teu) *n* fille *f*; **~-in-law** belle-fille *f*
dawn (doon) *n* aube *f*; aurore *f*
day (déï) *n* jour *m*; **by ~** de jour; **~ trip** excursion *f*; **per ~** par jour; **the ~ before yesterday** avant-hier
daybreak (*déï*-bréïk) *n* lever du jour
daylight (*déï*-laït) *n* lumière du jour
dead (dèd) *adj* mort; décédé
deaf (dèf) *adj* sourd
deal (diil) *n* transaction *f*, affaire *f*
***deal** (diil) *v* distribuer; **~ with** *v* s'occuper de; *faire des affaires avec
dealer (*dii*-leu) *n* négociant *m*; marchand *m*, -e *f*
dear (di^{eu}) *adj* cher
death (dèθ) *n* mort *f*; **~ penalty** peine de mort
debate (di-*béït*) *n* débat *m*
debit (*dè*-bit) *n* débit *m*
debt (dèt) *n* dette *f*
decaffeinated (dii-*kæ*-fi-néï-tid) *adj* décaféiné
deceit (di-*siit*) *n* tromperie *f*
deceive (di-*siiv*) *v* tromper
December (di-*sèm*-beu) décembre
decency (*dii*-seunn-si) *n* décence *f*
decent (*dii*-seunnt) *adj* décent
decide (di-*saïd*) *v* décider

decision (di-*si*-jeunn) *n* décision *f*
deck (dèk) *n* pont *m*; ~ **cabin** cabine de pont; ~ **chair** chaise longue
declaration (dè-kleu-*réï*-cheunn) *n* déclaration *f*
declare (di-*klèeu*) *v* déclarer; indiquer
decorate (*dè*-keu-réït) *v* décorer; orner; peindre (et tapisser)
decoration (dè-keu-*réï*-cheunn) *n* décoration *f*
decrease (dii-*kriiss*) *v* *réduire; diminuer; *n* diminution *f*
dedicate (*dè*-di-kéït) *v* dédier
deduce (di-*dyoûss*) *v* *déduire
deduct (di-*dakt*) *v* *déduire
deed (diid) *n* action *f*, acte *m*
deep (diip) *adj* profond
deep-freeze (diip-*friiz*) *n* congélateur *m*
deer (di^{eu}) *n* (pl ~) daim *m*
defeat (di-*fiit*) *v* *vaincre; *n* défaite *f*
defective (di-*fèk*-tiv) *adj* défectueux
defence (di-*fèns*) *n* défense *f*
defend (di-*fènd*) *v* défendre
defense *Am* (di-*fèns*) *n* défense *f*
deficiency (di-*fi*-cheunn-si) *n* déficience *f*
deficit (*dè*-fi-sit) *n* déficit *m*
define (di-*faïn*) *v* définir, déterminer
definite (*dè*-fi-nit) *adj* déterminé
definition (dè-fi-*ni*-cheunn) *n* définition *f*
deformed (di-*foomd*) *adj* contrefait, difforme
degree (di-*ghrii*) *n* degré *m*; grade *m*
delay (di-*léï*) *v* retarder; différer; *n* retard *m*; ajournement *m*
delegate (*dè*-li-gheut) *n* délégué *m*
delegation (dè-li-*ghéï*-cheunn) *n* délégation *f*
deliberate¹ (di-*li*-beu-réït) *v* discuter, délibérer
deliberate² (di-*li*-beu-reut) *adj* délibéré
deliberation (di-li-beu-*réï*-cheunn) *n* discussion *f*, délibération *f*
delicacy (*dè*-li-keu-si) *n* délicatesse *f*
delicate (*dè*-li-keut) *adj* délicat; tendre
delicatessen (dè-li-keu-*tè*-seunn) *n* épicerie fine
delicious (di-*li*-cheuss) *adj* exquis, délicieux
delight (di-*laït*) *n* délice *m*, plaisir *m*; *v* enchanter
delightful (di-*laït*-feul) *adj* délicieux, ravissant
deliver (di-*li*-veu) *v* *remettre, livrer; délivrer
delivery (di-*li*-veu-ri) *n* remise *f*, livraison *f*; accouchement *m*; délivrance *f*; ~ **van** camion de livraison
demand (di-*mâând*) *v* exiger, réclamer; *n* demande *f*
democracy (di-*mo*-kreu-si) *n* démocratie *f*
democratic (dè-meu-*kræ*-tik) *adj* démocratique
demolish (di-*mo*-lich) *v* démolir
demolition (dè-meu-*li*-cheunn) *n* démolition *f*
demonstrate (*dè*-meunn-stréït) *v* démontrer; manifester
demonstration (dè-meunn-*stréï*-cheunn) *n* démonstration *f*; manifestation *f*
den (dèn) *n* tanière *f*
Denmark (*dèn*-mââk) Danemark *m*
denomination (di-no-mi-*néï*-cheunn) *n* dénomination *f*
dense (dèns) *adj* dense
dent (dènt) *n* bosse *f*
dentist (*dèn*-tist) *n* dentiste *m*
denture (*dèn*-tcheu) *n* dentier *m*
deny (di-*naï*) *v* nier; dénier, refuser
deodorant (dii-*ôou*-deu-reunnt) *n* désodorisant *m*
depart (di-*pâât*) *v* s'en *aller, *partir; ~

this world trépasser
department (di-*pâât*-meunnt) *n* division *f*, département *m*; ~ **store** grand magasin
departure (di-*pââ*-tcheu) *n* départ *m*
depend (di-*pènd*): ~ **on** dépendre de
dependent (di-*pèn*-deunnt) *adj* dépendant
deposit (di-*po*-zit) *n* versement *m*; consigne *f*; dépôt *m*; *v* déposer
depository (di-*po*-zi-teu-ri) *n* entrepôt *m*
depot (*dè*-pô^{ou}) *n* dépôt *m*; *nAm* gare *f*
depress (di-*prèss*) *v* déprimer
depression (di-*prè*-cheunn) *n* dépression *f*
deprive of (di-*praïv*) priver de
depth (dèpθ) *n* profondeur *f*
deputy (*dè*-pyou-ti) *n* député *m/f*; substitut *m*
descend (di-*sènd*) *v* descendre
descendant (di-*sèn*-deunnt) *n* descendant *m*, -e *f*
descent (di-*sènt*) *n* descente *f*
describe (di-*skraïb*) *v* *décrire
description (di-*skrip*-cheunn) *n* description *f*; signalement *m*
desert[1] (*dè*-zeut) *n* désert *m*; *adj* désert
desert[2] (di-*zeût*) *v* déserter; abandonner
deserve (di-*zeûv*) *v* mériter
design (di-*zaïn*) *v* créer; *n* dessein *m*
designate (*dè*-zigh-néït) *v* désigner
desirable (di-*zaïeu*-reu-beul) *adj* désirable
desire (di-*zaïeu*) *n* vœu *m*; envie *f*, désir *m*; *v* *avoir envie de, désirer
desk (dèsk) *n* bureau *m*; pupitre *m*; banc d'école
despair (di-*spèeu*) *n* désespoir *m*; *v* désespérer
despatch (di-*spætch*) *v* expédier
desperate (*dè*-speu-reut) *adj* désespéré
despise (di-*spaïz*) *v* mépriser
despite (di-*spaït*) *prep* malgré
dessert (di-*zeût*) *n* dessert *m*
destination (dè-sti-*néï*-cheunn) *n* destination *f*
destine (*dè*-stinn) *v* destiner
destiny (*dè*-sti-ni) *n* destin *m*, sort *m*
destroy (di-*stroï*) *v* dévaster, *détruire
destruction (di-*strak*-cheunn) *n* destruction *f*; anéantissement *m*
detach (di-*tætch*) *v* détacher
detail (*dii*-téïl) *n* détail *m*
detailed (*dii*-téïld) *adj* détaillé
detect (di-*tèkt*) *v* détecter
detective (di-*tèk*-tiv) *n* détective *m*; ~ **story** roman policier
detergent (di-*teû*-djeunnt) *n* détergent *m*
determine (di-*teû*-minn) *v* définir, déterminer
determined (di-*teû*-minnd) *adj* résolu
detest (di-*tèst*) *v* détester
detour (*dii*-tou^{eu}) *n* détour *m*; déviation *f*
devaluation (dii-væl-you-*éï*-cheunn) *n* dévaluation *f*
devalue (dii-*væl*-yoû) *v* dévaluer
develop (di-*vè*-leup) *v* développer
development (di-*vè*-leup-meunnt) *n* développement *m*
deviate (*dii*-vi-éït) *v* dévier
devil (*dè*-veul) *n* diable *m*
devise (di-*vaïz*) *v* *concevoir
devote (di-*vôout*) *v* consacrer
dew (dyoû) *n* rosée *f*
diabetes (daï-eu-*bii*-tiiz) *n* diabète *m*
diabetic (daï-eu-*bè*-tik) *n* diabétique *m/f*
diagnose (daï-eugh-*nôouz*) *v* diagnostiquer
diagnosis (daï-eugh-*nôou*-siss) *n* (pl -ses) diagnostic *m*

diagonal (daï-*æ*-gheu-neul) *n* diagonale *f*; *adj* diagonale
diagram (*daï*-eu-ghræm) *n* diagramme *m*; graphique *m*
dial (daï^{eu}l) *n* cadran *m*; *v* composer, faire
dial(l)ing tone (*daï*-eu-linng-tô^{ou}n) *n* tonalité *f*
dialect (*daï*-eu-lèkt) *n* dialecte *m*
diamond (*daï*-eu-meunnd) *n* diamant *m*
diaper (*daï*-eu-peu) *nAm* couche *f*
diarrh(o)ea (daï-eu-*ri*-eu) *n* diarrhée *f*
diary (*daï*-eu-ri) *n* agenda *m*; journal *m*
dictate (dik-*téït*) *v* dicter
dictation (dik-*téï*-cheunn) *n* dictée *f*
dictionary (*dik*-cheu-neu-ri) *n* dictionnaire *m*
did (did) *v* (p do)
die (daï) *v* *mourir
diesel (*dii*-zeul) *n* diesel *m*
diet (*daï*-eut) *n* régime *m*
differ (*di*-feu) *v* différer
difference (*di*-feu-reunns) *n* différence *f*; distinction *f*
different (*di*-feu-reunnt) *adj* différent; autre
difficult (*di*-fi-keult) *adj* difficile
difficulty (*di*-fi-keul-ti) *n* difficulté *f*; peine *f*
***dig** (digh) *v* creuser; fouiller
digest (di-*djèst*) *v* digérer
digestible (di-*djè*-steu-beul) *adj* digestible
digestion (di-*djèss*-tcheunn) *n* digestion *f*
digit (*di*-djit) *n* chiffre *m*
dignified (*digh*-ni-faïd) *adj* digne
dignity (*digh*-ni-ti) *n* dignité *f*
dike (daïk) *n* digue *f*
dilapidated (di-*læ*-pi-déï-tid) *adj* délabré
diligence (*di*-li-djeunns) *n* assiduité *f*, application *f*
diligent (*di*-li-djeunnt) *adj* laborieux, assidu
dilute (daï-*lyoût*) *v* allonger, diluer
dim (dimm) *adj* terne, mat; obscur
dine (daïn) *v* dîner
dinghy (*dinng*-ghi) *n* canot *m*
dining car (*daï*-ninng-kââ) *n* wagon-restaurant
dining room (*daï*-ninng-roûm) *n* salle à manger
dinner (*di*-neu) *n* dîner *m*; **~ jacket** smoking *m*; **~ service** service de table
diphtheria (dif-*θieu*-ri-eu) *n* diphtérie *f*
diploma (di-*plôou*-meu) *n* diplôme *m*
diplomat (*di*-pleu-mæt) *n* diplomate *m*
direct (di-*rèkt*) *adj* direct; *v* diriger; administrer; *mettre en scène
direction (di-*rèk*-cheunn) *n* direction *f*; instruction *f*; réalisation *f*; **directions for use** mode d'emploi
directive (di-*rèk*-tiv) *n* directive *f*
director (di-*rèk*-teu) *n* directeur *m*, -trice *f*; metteur en scène
directory (di-*rèk*-teu-ri) *n* répertoire *m* d'adresses; annuaire *m* (des téléphones); **~ assistance, ~ enquiry** renseigements *pl*
dirt (deût) *n* saleté *f*
dirty (*deû*-ti) *adj* sale, souillé
disabled (di-*séï*-beuld) *adj* handicapé, invalide
disadvantage (di-seud-*vâân*-tidj) *n* désavantage *m*
disagree (di-seu-*ghrii*) *v* *être en désaccord
disagreeable (di-seu-*ghrii*-eu-beul) *adj* désagréable
disappear (di-seu-*pieu*) *v* *disparaître
disappoint (di-seu-*poïnt*) *v* *décevoir
disappointment (di-seu-*poïnt*-

meunnt) *n* déception *f*
disapprove (di-seu-*proûv*) *v* désapprouver
disaster (di-*zââ*-steu) *n* désastre *m*; catastrophe *f*, calamité *f*
disastrous (di-*zââ*-streuss) *adj* désastreux
disc (disk) *n* disque *m*; **slipped ~** hernie discale
discard (di-*skââd*) *v* se débarrasser de
discharge (diss-*tchââdj*) *v* décharger; **~ of** dispenser de
discipline (*di*-si-plinn) *n* discipline *f*
discolo(u)r (di-*ska*-leu) *v* décolorer
disconnect (di-skeu-*nèkt*) *v* *disjoindre; débrancher
discontented (di-skeunn-*tèn*-tid) *adj* mécontent
discontinue (di-skeunn-*ti*-nyoû) *v* suspendre, cesser
discount (*di*-skaount) *n* réduction *f*, rabais *m*
discourage (di-*ska*-ridj *v* décourager (**from** de)
discover (di-*ska*-veu) *v* *découvrir
discovery (di-*ska*-veu-ri) *n* découverte *f*
discuss (di-*skass*) *v* discuter; *débattre
discussion (di-*ska*-cheunn) *n* discussion *f*; conversation *f*, délibération *f*, débat *m*
disease (di-*ziiz*) *n* maladie *f*
disembark (di-simm-*bââk*) *v* débarquer
disgrace (diss-*ghréïss*) *n* déshonneur *m*
disguise (diss-*ghaïz*) *v* se déguiser; *n* déguisement *m*
disgust (diss-*ghast*) *n* dégoût *m*; répugnance *f*; *v* dégoûter
disgusting (diss-*gha*-stinng) *adj* répugnant, dégoûtant
dish (dich) *n* assiette *f*; plat *m*
dishonest (di-*so*-nist) *adj* malhonnête
dishwasher (*dich*-ᵒᵘo-cheu) *n* laveur *m* de vaisselle; lave-vaisselle *m*
disinfect (di-sinn-*fèkt*) *v* désinfecter
disinfectant (di-sinn-*fèk*-teunnt) *n* désinfectant *m*
dislike (di-*slaïk*) *v* détester, ne pas aimer; *n* répugnance *f*, aversion *f*, antipathie *f*
dislocated (*di*-sleu-kéï-tid) *adj* disloqué
dismiss (diss-*miss*) *v* *renvoyer
disorder (di-*soo*-deu) *n* désordre *m*; confusion *f*
dispatch (di-*spætch*) *v* *envoyer, expédier
display (di-*spléï*) *v* étaler; montrer; *n* exposition *f*
displease (di-*spliiz*) *v* *déplaire
disposable (di-*spôou*-zeu-beul) *adj* à jeter
disposal (di-*spôou*-zeul) *n* disposition *f*
dispose of (di-*spôouz*) disposer de
dispute (di-*spyoût*) *n* discussion *f*; querelle *f*, litige *m*; *v* se disputer, contester
dissatisfied (di-*sæ*-tiss-faïd) *adj* insatisfait
dissolve (di-*zolv*) *v* *dissoudre, diluer
dissuade from (di-*souéïd*) dissuader
distance (*di*-steunns) *n* distance *f*; **~ in kilometres,** *Am* **kilometers** kilométrage *m*
distant (*di*-steunnt) *adj* éloigné
distinct (di-*stinngkt*) *adj* net; distinct
distinction (di-*stinngk*-cheunn) *n* distinction *f*
distinguish (di-*stinng*-ghᵒᵘich) *v* distinguer, discerner
distinguished (di-*stinng*-ghᵒᵘicht) *adj* distingué
distress (di-*strèss*) *n* détresse *f*; **~ signal** signal de détresse

distribute (di-*stri*-byoût) *v* distribuer
distributor (di-*stri*-byou-teu) *n* concessionnaire *m*; distributeur *m*
district (*di*-strikt) *n* district *m*; région *f*; quartier *m*
disturb (di-*steûb*) *v* déranger
disturbance (di-*steû*-beunns) *n* dérangement *m*; agitation *f*
ditch (ditch) *n* fossé *m*
dive (daïv) *v* plonger
diversion (daï-*veû*-cheunn) *n* déviation *f*; diversion *f*
divide (di-*vaïd*) *v* diviser; répartir; séparer
divine (di-*vaïn*) *adj* divin
division (di-*vi*-jeunn) *n* division *f*; séparation *f*; département *m*
divorce (di-*vooss*) *n* divorce *m*; *v* divorcer
dizziness (di-*zi*-neuss) *n* vertige *m*
dizzy (*di*-zi) *adj* étourdi
***do** (doû) *v* *faire; *suffire
dock (dok) *n* dock *m*; quai *m*; *v* accoster
docker (*do*-keu) *n* docker *m*
doctor (*dok*-teu) *n* médecin *m*, docteur *m*
document (*do*-kyou-meunnt) *n* document *m*
dog (dogh) *n* chien *m*
dogged (*do*-ghid) *adj* obstiné
doll (dol) *n* poupée *f*
dollar (*do*-leu) *n* dollar *m*
dome (dô^{ou}m) *n* dôme *m*
domestic (deu-*mè*-stik) *adj* domestique; intérieur; *n* domestique *m*
domicile (*do*-mi-saïl) *n* domicile *m*
domination (do-mi-*néï*-cheunn) *n* domination *f*
dominion (deu-*mi*-nyeunn) *n* règne *m*
donate (dô^{ou}-*néït*) *v* donner
donation (dô^{ou}-*néï*-cheunn) *n* don *m*, donation *f*
done (dann) *v* (pp do)
donkey (*donng*-ki) *n* âne *m*
donor (*dôou*-neu) *n* donateur *m*
door (doo) *n* porte *f*; **revolving ~** porte tournante; **sliding ~** porte coulissante
doorbell (*doo*-bèl) *n* sonnette *f*
doorkeeper (*doo*-kii-peu) *n* portier *m*
doorman (*doo*-meunn) *n* (pl -men) portier *m*
dormitory (*doo*-mi-tri) *n* dortoir *m*
dose (dô^{ou}ss) *n* dose *f*
dot (dot) *n* point *m*
double (*da*-beul) *adj* double
doubt (daout) *v* douter de, douter; *n* doute *m*; **without ~** sans aucun doute
doubtful (*daout*-feul) *adj* douteux; incertain
dough (dô^{ou}) *n* pâte *f*
down[1] (daoun) *adv* en bas; vers le bas, par terre; *adj* déprimé; *prep* le long de, en bas de; **~ payment** acompte *m*
down[2] (daoun) *n* duvet *m*
downpour (*daoun*-poo) *n* averse *f*
downstairs (daoun-*stèeuz*) *adv* en bas
downstream (daoun-*striim*) *adv* en aval
downwards (*daoun*-^{ou}eudz) *adv* vers le bas
dozen (*da*-zeunn) *n* (pl ~, ~s) douzaine *f*
draft[1] (drââft) *n* traite *f*
draft[2] (drââft) *n* courant *m* d'air
drag (drægh) *v* traîner
dragon (*dræ*-gheunn) *n* dragon *m*
drain (dréïn) *v* assécher; drainer; *n* égout *m*
drama (*drââ*-meu) *n* drame *m*; tragédie *f*; théâtre *m*
dramatic (dreu-*mæ*-tik) *adj* dramatique
dramatist (*dræ*-meu-tist) *n* dramaturge *m*
drank (drængk) *v* (p drink)

drapery (*dréï*-peu-ri) *n* étoffes *fpl*
draught (drââft) *n* courant d'air; **draughts** jeu de dames
draw (droo) *n* tirage *m*
***draw** (droo) *v* dessiner; tirer; ~ **up** rédiger
drawbridge (*droo*-bridj) *n* pont-levis *m*
drawer (*droo*-eu) *n* tiroir *m*; **drawers** caleçon *m*
drawing (*droo*-inng) *n* dessin *m*; ~ **pin** punaise *f*; ~ **room** (*droo*-inng-roûm) *n* salon *m*
dread (drèd) *v* *craindre; *n* crainte *f*
dreadful (*drèd*-feul) *adj* terrible, affreux
dream (driim) *n* rêve *m*
***dream** (driim) *v* rêver, songer
dress (drèss) *v* habiller; se *vêtir, s'habiller, *vêtir; panser; *n* robe *f*
dressing gown (*drè*-sinng-ghaoun) *n* robe de chambre
dressing room (*drè*-sinng-roûm) *n* loge *f*
dressing table (*drè*-sinng-téï-beul) *n* coiffeuse *f*
dressmaker (*drèss*-méï-keu) *n* couturière *f*
drill (dril) *v* forer; entraîner; *n* foreuse *f*
drink (drinngk) *n* apéritif *m*, boisson *f*
***drink** (drinngk) *v* *boire
drinking water (*drinng*-kinng-ouoo-teu) *n* eau potable
drip-dry (drip-*draï*) *adj* qui ne nécessite aucun repassage
drive (draïv) *n* route *f*; promenade en voiture
***drive** (draïv) *v* *conduire
driver (*draï*-veu) *n* conducteur *m*
drizzle (*dri*-zeul) *n* crachin *m*
drop (drop) *v* laisser tomber; *n* goutte *f*
drought (draout) *n* sécheresse *f*
drown (draoun) *v* noyer; ***be drowned** se noyer
drug (dragh) *n* drogue *f*; médicament *m*
drugstore (*dragh*-stoo) *nAm* drugstore *m*
drum (dramm) *n* tambour *m*
drunk (dranngk) *adj* (pp drink) ivre
dry (draï) *adj* sec; *v* sécher; essuyer
dry-clean (draï-*kliin*) *v* nettoyer à sec
dry cleaner's (draï-*klii*-neuz) *n* teinturerie *f*
dryer (*draï*-eu) *n* séchoir *m*
duchess (da-tchiss) *n* duchesse *f*
duck (dak) *n* canard *m*
due (dyoû) *adj* attendu; payable; dû
dues (dyoûz) *pl* droits
dug (dagh) *v* (p, pp dig)
duke (dyoûk) *n* duc *m*
dull (dal) *adj* ennuyeux; terne, mat; émoussé
dumb (damm) *adj* muet; bête
dune (dyoûn) *n* dune *f*
dung (danng) *n* fumier *m*
dunghill (*danng*-hil) *n* tas de fumier
duration (dyou-*réï*-cheunn) *n* durée *f*
during (*dyoueu*-rinng) *prep* durant, pendant
dusk (dask) *n* crépuscule *m*
dust (dast) *n* poussière *f*
dustbin (*dast*-binn) *n* boîte à ordures
dusty (*da*-sti) *adj* poussiéreux
Dutch (datch) *adj* néerlandais, hollandais
duty (*dyoû*-ti) *n* devoir *m*; tâche *f*; droit d'importation; **Customs** ~ droit de douane
duty-free (dyoû-ti-*frii*) *adj* exempt de droits
dwarf (douoof) *n* nain *m*
dye (daï) *v* *teindre; *n* teinture *f*
dynamo (*daï*-neu-môou) *n* (pl ~s) dynamo *f*

E

each (iitch) *adj* chaque; **~ other** l'un l'autre
eager (*ii*-gheu) *adj* désireux, impatient
eagle (*ii*-gheul) *n* aigle *m*
ear (i^{eu}) *n* oreille *f*
earache (*ieu*-réïk) *n* mal d'oreille
eardrum (*ieu*-dramm) *n* tympan *m*
earl (eûl) *n* comte *m*
early (*eû*-li) *adj* tôt
earn (eûnn) *v* gagner
earnest (*eû*-nist) *n* sérieux *m*
earnings (*eû*-ninngz) *pl* revenu *m*, gains
earring (*ieu*-rinng) *n* boucle d'oreille
earth (eûθ) *n* terre *f*; sol *m*
earthquake (*eûθ*-k^{ou}éïk) *n* tremblement de terre
ease (iiz) *n* aisance *f*; aise *f*
east (iist) *n* est *m*
Easter (*ii*-steu) Pâques
easterly (*ii*-steu-li) *adj* oriental
eastern (*ii*-steunn) *adj* oriental
easy (*ii*-zi) *adj* facile; commode; **~ chair** fauteuil *m*
easy-going (*ii*-zi-ghô^{ou}-inng) *adj* décontracté
***eat** (iit) *v* manger; dîner
eavesdrop (*iivz*-drop) *v* écouter aux portes
ebony (*è*-beu-ni) *n* ébène *f*
eccentric (ik-*sèn*-trik) *adj* excentrique
echo (*è*-kô^{ou}) *n* (pl ~es) écho *m*
eclipse (i-*klips*) *n* éclipse *f*
economic (ii-keu-*no*-mik) *adj* économique
economical (ii-keu-*no*-mi-keul) *adj* parcimonieux, économe
economist (i-*ko*-neu-mist) *n* économiste *m*
economize (i-*ko*-neu-maïz) *v* économiser
economy (i-*ko*-neu-mi) *n* économie *f*
ecstasy (*èk*-steu-zi) *n* extase *m*
Ecuador (*è*-k^{ou}eu-doo) Equateur *m*
Ecuadorian (è-k^{ou}eu-*doo*-ri-eunn) *n* Ecuadorien *m*
eczema (*èk*-si-meu) *n* eczéma *m*
edge (èdj) *n* rebord *m*, bord *m*
edible (*è*-di-beul) *adj* comestible
edit (*è*-dit) *v* éditer; diriger
edition (i-*di*-cheunn) *n* édition *f*; **morning ~** édition du matin
editor (*è*-di-teu) *n* rédacteur *m*
educate (*è*-djou-kéït) *v* former, éduquer
education (è-djou-*kéï*-cheunn) *n* éducation *f*
eel (iil) *n* anguille *f*
effect (i-*fèkt*) *n* résultat *m*, effet *m*; *v* effectuer; **in ~** en fait
effective (i-*fèk*-tiv) *adj* efficace, effectif
efficient (i-*fi*-cheunnt) *adj* efficace
effort (*è*-feut) *n* effort *m*
egg (ègh) *n* œuf *m*; **~ yolk** jaune d'œuf
eggcup (*ègh*-kap) *n* coquetier *m*
eggplant (*ègh*-plâânt) *n* aubergine *f*
ego(t)istic (è-ghô^{ou}-*i*-stik) *adj* égoïste
Egypt (*ii*-djipt) Egypte *f*
Egyptian (i-*djip*-cheunn) *adj* égyptien; *n* Egyptien *m*
eiderdown (*aï*-deu-daoun) *n* édredon *m*
eight (éït) *num* huit
eighteen (éï-*tiin*) *num* dix-huit
eighteenth (éï-*tiinθ*) *num* dix-huitième
eighth (éïtθ) *num* huitième
eighty (*éï*-ti) *num* quatre-vingts
either (*aï*-ðeu) *pron* l'un ou l'autre; **either ... or** ou ... ou, soit ... soit
elaborate (i-*læ*-beu-réït) *v* élaborer
elastic (i-*læ*-stik) *adj* élastique; flexible; élastique *m*

elasticity (è-læ-*sti*-seu-ti) *n* élasticité *f*
elbow (*èl*-bô^ou^) *n* coude *m*
elder (*èl*-deu) *adj* plus âgé
elderly (*èl*-deu-li) *adj* âgé
eldest (*èl*-dist) *adj* le plus âgé
elect (i-*lèkt*) *v* *élire
election (i-*lèk*-cheunn) *n* élection *f*
electric (i-*lèk*-trik) *adj* électrique; ~ **razor** rasoir électrique; ~ **wire** fil électrique
electrician (i-lèk-*tri*-cheunn) *n* électricien *m*
electricity (i-lèk-*tri*-seu-ti) *n* électricité *f*
electronic (i-lèk-*tro*-nik) *adj* électronique
elegance (*è*-li-gheunns) *n* élégance *f*
elegant (*è*-li-gheunnt) *adj* élégant
element (*è*-li-meunnt) *n* élément *m*
elephant (*è*-li-feunnt) *n* éléphant *m*
elevator (*è*-li-véï-teu) *nAm* ascenseur *m*
eleven (i-*lè*-veunn) *num* onze
eleventh (i-*lè*-veunnθ) *num* onzième
eliminate (i-*li*-mi-néït) *v* éliminer
else (èls) *adv* autrement
elsewhere (èl-*souèeu*) *adv* ailleurs
elucidate (i-*loû*-si-déït) *v* élucider
e-mail (i-méïl) *n* e-mail *m*; message électronique
emancipation (i-mæn-si-*péï*-cheunn) *n* émancipation *f*
embankment (imm-*bængk*-meunnt) *n* berge *f*
embargo (èm-*bââ*-ghô^ou^) *n* (pl ~es) embargo *m*
embark (imm-*bââk*) *v* embarquer
embarkation (èm-bââ-*kéï*-cheunn) *n* embarquement *m*
embarrass (imm-*bæ*-reuss) *v* embarrasser; gêner;
embarrassed (imm-*bæ*-reust) *adj* confus
embarrassment (imm-*bæ*-reuss-meunnt) *n* embarras *m*; gêne *f*
embassy (*èm*-beu-si) *n* ambassade *f*
emblem (*èm*-bleumm) *n* emblème *m*
embrace (imm-*bréïss*) *v* *étreindre; *n* enlacement *m*
embroider (imm-*broï*-deu) *v* broder
embroidery (imm-*broï*-deu-ri) *n* broderie *f*
emerald (*è*-meu-reuld) *n* émeraude *f*
emergency (i-*meû*-djeunn-si) *n* cas d'urgence, urgence *f*; état d'urgence; ~ **exit** sortie de secours
emigrant (*è*-mi-ghreunnt) *n* émigrant *m*
emigrate (*è*-mi-ghréït) *v* émigrer
emigration (è-mi-*ghréï*-cheunn) *n* émigration *f*
emotion (i-*môou*-cheunn) *n* émoi *m*, émotion *f*
emotional (i-*môou*-cheu-neul) *adj* émotionnel; émotif ; qui fait appel aux émotions, touchant, émouvant
emperor (*èm*-peu-reu) *n* empereur *m*
emphasize (*èm*-feu-saïz) *v* souligner
empire (*èm*-paï^eu^) *n* empire *m*
employ (imm-*ploï*) *v* employer; utiliser
employee (èm-ploï-*ii*) *n* employé *m*, -e *f*
employer (imm-*ploï*-eu) *n* employeur *m*, -se *f*
employment (imm-*ploï*-meunnt) *n* emploi *m*; ~ **exchange** bureau de l'emploi
empress (*èm*-priss) *n* impératrice *f*
empty (*èmp*-ti) *adj* vide; *v* vider
enable (i-*néï*-beul) *v* *permettre
enamel (i-*næ*-meul) *n* émail *m*
enamelled (i-*næ*-meuld) *adj* émaillé
enchanting (inn-*tchâân*-tinng) *adj* splendide, ravissant
encircle (inn-*seû*-keul) *v* encercler, entourer
enclose (inng-*klôouz*) *v* *inclure,

*joindre
enclosure (inng-*klôou*-jeu) *n* pièce jointe
encounter (inng-*kaoun*-teu) *v* rencontrer; *n* rencontre *f*
encourage (inng-*ka*-ridj) *v* encourager
encyclop(a)edia (èn-saï-kleu-*pii*-di-eu) *n* encyclopédie *f*
end (ènd) *n* fin *f*, bout *m*; conclusion *f*; *v* finir
ending (*èn*-dinng) *n* fin *f*
endless (*ènd*-leuss) *adj* infini
endorse (inn-*dooss*) *v* endosser
endure (inn-*dyoueu*) *v* endurer
enemy (*è*-neu-mi) *n* ennemi *m*, -e *f*
energetic (è-neu-*djè*-tik) *adj* énergique
energy (*è*-neu-dji) *n* énergie *f*; puissance *f*
engage (inng-*ghéïdj*) *v* engager; s'engager; **engaged** fiancé; occupé
engagement (inng-*ghéïdj*-meunnt) *n* fiançailles *fpl*; engagement *m*; **~ ring** bague de fiançailles
engine (*èn*-djinn) *n* machine *f*, moteur *m*; locomotive *f*
engineer (èn-dji-*nieu*) *n* ingénieur *m*
England (*inng*-ghleunnd) Angleterre *f*
English (*inng*-ghlich) *adj* anglais
Englishman (*inng*-ghlich-meunn) *n* (pl -men) Anglais *m*
Englishwoman (*inng*-ghlich-^{ou}ou-meunn) *n* (pl -women) Anglaise *f*
engrave (inng-*ghréïv*) *v* graver
engraver (inng-*ghréï*-veu) *n* graveur *m*
engraving (inng-*ghréï*-vinng) *n* estampe *f*; gravure *f*
enigma (i-*nigh*-meu) *n* énigme *f*
enjoy (inn-*djoï*) *v* jouir de, *prendre plaisir
enjoyable (inn-*djoï*-eu-beul) *adj* agréable, plaisant; bon
enjoyment (inn-*djoï*-meunnt) *n* plaisir *m*
enlarge (inn-*lââdj*) *v* agrandir; étendre
enlargement (inn-*lââdj*-meunnt) *n* agrandissement *m*
enormous (i-*noo*-meuss) *adj* gigantesque, énorme
enough (i-*naf*) *adv* assez; *adj* suffisant
enquire (inng-*kouaïeu*) *v* s'informer; enquêter
enquiry (inng-*kouaïeu*-ri) *n* information *f*; investigation *f*; enquête *f*
enter (*èn*-teu) *v* entrer; *inscrire
enterprise (*èn*-teu-praïz) *n* entreprise *f*
entertain (èn-teu-*téïn*) *v* divertir, amuser; *recevoir
entertainer (èn-teu-*téï*-neu) *n* animateur *m*
entertaining (èn-teu-*téï*-ninng) *adj* amusant, divertissant
entertainment (èn-teu-*téïn*-meunnt) *n* amusement *m*, divertissement *m*
enthusiasm (inn-*θyoû*-zi-æ-zeumm) *n* enthousiasme *m*
enthusiastic (inn-θyoû-zi-*æ*-stik) *adj* enthousiaste
entire (inn-*taïeu*) *adj* tout, entier
entirely (inn-*taïeu*-li) *adv* entièrement
entrance (*èn*-treunns) *n* entrée *f*; accès *m*; **~ fee** prix d'entrée
entry (*èn*-tri) *n* entrée *f*; admission *f*; inscription *f*; **no ~** défense d'entrer
envelop (inn- *vè*-leup) *v* envelopper
envelope (*èn*-veu-lô^{ou}p) *n* enveloppe *f*
envious (*èn*-vi-euss) *adj* envieux, jaloux
environment (inn-*vaïeu*-reunn-meunnt) *n* environnement *m*; environs *mpl*

envoy (*èn*-voï) *n* envoyé *m*
envy (*èn*-vi) *n* envie *f*; *v* envier
epic (*è*-pik) *n* poème épique; *adj* épique
epidemic (è-pi-*dè*-mik) *n* épidémie *f*
epilepsy (*è*-pi-lèp-si) *n* épilepsie *f*
episode (*è*-pi-sô^{ou}d) *n* épisode *m*
equal (*ii*-k^{ou}eul) *adj* égal; *v* égaler
equality (i-*kouo*-leu-ti) *n* égalité *f*
equalize (*ii*-k^{ou}eu-laïz) *v* égaliser
equally (*ii*-k^{ou}eu-li) *adv* également
equator (i-*kouéï*-teu) *n* équateur *m*
equip (i-*kouip*) *v* équiper
equipment (i-*kouip*-meunnt) *n* équipement *m*
equivalent (i-*koui*-veu-leunnt) *adj* équivalent
eraser (i-*réï*-zeu) *n* gomme *f*
erect (i-*rèkt*) *v* ériger; *adj* debout, droit
err (eû) *v* se tromper, errer
errand (*è*-reunnd) *n* commission *f*
error (*è*-reu) *n* faute *f*, erreur *f*
escalator (*è*-skeu-léï-teu) *n* escalier roulant
escape (i-*skéïp*) *v* échapper; *fuir; *n* évasion *f*
escort[1] (*è*-skoot) *n* escorte *f*
escort[2] (i-*skoot*) *v* escorter
especially (i-*spè*-cheu-li) *adv* principalement, spécialement
esplanade (è-spleu-*néïd*) *n* esplanade *f*
essay (*è*-séï) *n* essai *m*; dissertation *f*, composition *f*
essence (*è*-seunns) *n* essence *f*; fond *m*, nature *f*
essential (i-*sèn*-cheul) *adj* indispensable; fondamental, essentiel
essentially (i-*sèn*-cheu-li) *adv* essentiellement
establish (i-*stæ*-blich) *v* établir
estate (i-*stéït*) *n* propriété *f*
esteem (i-*stiim*) *n* respect *m*, estime *f*; *v* estimer
estimate[1] (*è*-sti-méït) *v* évaluer, estimer
estimate[2] (*è*-sti-meut) *n* estimation *f*
estuary (*èss*-tchou-eu-ri) *n* estuaire *m*
etcetera (èt-*sè*-teu-reu) et cætera
etching (*è*-tchinng) *n* eau-forte *f*
eternal (i-*teû*-neul) *adj* éternel
eternity (i-*teû*-neu-ti) *n* éternité *f*
Ethiopia (i-θi-*ôou*-pi-eu) Ethiopie *f*
Ethiopian (i-θi-*ôou*-pi-eunn) *adj* éthiopien; *n* Ethiopien *m*
Euro (*youeu*-reu) *n* euro *m*
Europe (*youeu*-reup) Europe *f*
European (you^{eu}-reu-*pii*-eunn) *adj* européen; *n* Européen *m*
evacuate (i-*væ*-kyou-éït) *v* évacuer
evade (i-*véïd*) *v* éviter, échapper à; éluder
evaluate (i-*væl*-you-éït) *v* évaluer
evaporate (i-*væ*-peu-réït) *v* évaporer
even (*ii*-veunn) *adj* plan, égal; constant; pair; *adv* même
evening (*iiv*-ninng) *n* soir *m*; **~ dress** tenue de soirée
event (i-*vènt*) *n* événement *m*; cas *m*
eventual (i-*vèn*-tchou-eul) *adj* éventuel
ever (*è*-veu) *adv* jamais; toujours
every (*èv*-ri) *adj* tout, chaque
everybody (*èv*-ri-bo-di) *pron* tout le monde
everyday (*èv*-ri-déï) *adj* quotidien
everyone (*èv*-ri-^{ou}ann) *pron* chacun, tout le monde
everything (*èv*-ri-θinng) *pron* tout
everywhere (*èv*-ri-^{ou}è^{eu}) *adv* partout
evidence (*è*-vi-deunns) *n* preuve *f*
evident (*è*-vi-deunnt) *adj* évident
evil (*ii*-veul) *n* mal *m*; *adj* méchant, mauvais
evolution (ii-veu-*loû*-cheunn) *n* évolution *f*
exact (igh-*zækt*) *adj* juste, exact

exactly (igh-*zækt*-li) *adv* exactement
exaggerate (igh-*zæ*-djeu-réït) *v* exagérer
exam (igh-*zæm*) *n colloquial* examen *m*
examination (igh-zæ-mi-*néï*-cheunn) *n* examen *m*; interrogatoire *m*
examine (igh-*zæ*-minn) *v* examiner
example (igh-*zââm*-peul) *n* exemple *m*; **for ~** par exemple
exceed (ik-*siid*) *v* excéder; surpasser
excel (ik-*sèl*) *v* exceller
excellent (*èk*-seu-leunnt) *adj* excellent
except (ik-*sèpt*) *prep* excepté
exception (ik-*sèp*-cheunn) *n* exception *f*
exceptional (ik-*sèp*-cheu-neul) *adj* extraordinaire, exceptionnel
excerpt (*èk*-seûpt) *n* extrait *m*
excess (ik-*sèss*) *n* excès *m*
excessive (ik-*sè*-siv) *adj* excessif
exchange (iks-*tchéïndj*) *v* échanger, changer; *n* bourse *f*; **~ office** bureau de change; **~ rate** taux de change
excite (ik-*saït*) *v* exciter
excitement (ik-*saït*-meunnt) *n* agitation *f*, excitation *f*
exciting (ik-*saï*-tinng) *adj* passionnant
exclaim (ik-*skléïm*) *v* exclamer
exclamation (èk-skleu-*méï*-cheunn) *n* exclamation *f*
exclude (ik-*skloûd*) *v* *exclure
exclusive (ik-*skloû*-siv) *adj* exclusif
exclusively (ik-*skloû*-siv-li) *adv* exclusivement, uniquement
excursion (ik-*skeû*-cheunn) *n* excursion *f*
excuse¹ (ik-*skyoûss*) *n* excuse *f*
excuse² (ik-*skyoûz*) *v* excuser
execute (*èk*-si-kyoût) *v* exécuter
execution (èk-si-*kyoû*-cheunn) *n* exécution *f*
executive (igh-*zè*-kyou-tiv) *adj* exécutif; *n* pouvoir exécutif; exécutif *m*
exempt (igh-*jèmpt*) *v* dispenser, exempter; *adj* exempt
exemption (igh-*zèmp*-cheunn) *n* exemption *f*
exercise (*èk*-seu-saïz) *n* exercice *m*; *v* exercer
exhale (èks-*héïl*) *v* expirer
exhaust (igh-*zoost*) *n* tuyau d'échappement, échappement *m*; *v* exténuer; **~ gases** gaz d'échappement
exhibit (igh-*zi*-bit) *v* exposer; exhiber
exhibition (èk-si-*bi*-cheunn) *n* exhibition *f*, exposition *f*
exile (*èk*-saïl) *n* exile *m*; exilé *m*
exist (igh-*zist*) *v* exister
existence (igh-*zi*-steunns) *n* existence *f*
exit (*èk*-sit) *n* sortie *f*
exotic (igh-*zo*-tik) *adj* exotique
expand (ik-*spænd*) *v* étendre; déployer
expansion (ik-*spæn*-cheunn) *n* expansion *f*; dilatation *f*; développement *m*
expect (ik-*spèkt*) *v* attendre
expectation (èk-spèk-*téï*-cheunn) *n* espérance *f*
expedition (èk-speu-*di*-cheunn) *n* expédition *f*
expel (ik-*spèl*) *v* expulser
expenditure (ik-*spèn*-di-tcheu) *n* dépense *f*
expense (ik-*spèns*) *n* dépense *f*; **expenses** *pl* frais *mpl*
expensive (ik-*spèn*-siv) *adj* cher; coûteux
experience (ik-*spieu*-ri-eunns) *n* expérience *f*; *v* éprouver, *vivre, *faire l'expérience de; **experienced** expérimenté
experiment (ik-*spè*-ri-meunnt) *n* épreuve *f*, expérience *f*; *v*

expérimenter
expert (*èk*-speût) *n* spécialiste *m*, expert *m*; *adj* compétent
expire (ik-*spaïeu*) *v* *venir à échéance, se terminer, expirer; **expired** périmé
expiry (ik-*spaïeu*-ri) *n* expiration *f*
explain (ik-*spléïn*) *v* expliquer
explanation (èk-spleu-*néï*-cheunn) *n* éclaircissement *m*, explication *f*
explicit (ik-*spli*-sit) *adj* formel, explicite
explode (ik-*splôoud*) *v* exploser
exploit (ik-*sploït*) *v* exploiter
explore (ik-*sploo*) *v* explorer
explosion (ik-*splôou*-jeunn) *n* explosion *f*
explosive (ik-*splôou*-siv) *adj* explosif; *n* explosif *m*
export[1] (ik-*spoot*) *v* exporter
export[2] (*èk*-spoot) *n* exportation *f*
exportation (èk-spoo-*téï*-cheunn) *n* exportation *f*
exports (*èk*-spoots) *n pl* exportation *f*
expose (ik-*spôouz*) *v* exposer; démasquer; dévoiler
exposition (èk-speu-*zi*-cheunn) *n* exposition *f*
exposure (ik-*spôou*-jeu) *n* exposition *f*
express (ik-*sprèss*) *v* exprimer; manifester; *adj* exprès; explicite; ~ **train** rapide *m*
expression (ik-*sprè*-cheunn) *n* expression *f*
exquisite (ik-*skoui*-zit) *adj* exquis
extend (ik-*stènd*) *v* étendre; agrandir
extension (ik-*stèn*-cheunn) *n* prolongation *f*; agrandissement *m*; ligne intérieure; ~ **cord** rallonge *f*
extensive (ik-*stèn*-siv) *adj* considérable; vaste, étendu
extent (ik-*stènt*) *n* dimension *f*
exterior (èk-*stieu*-ri-eu) *adj* extérieur; *n* extérieur *m*
external (èk-*steû*-neul) *adj* extérieur
extinguish (ik-*stinng*-gh^ou^ich) *v* *éteindre
extort (ik-*stoot*) *v* extorquer
extortion (ik-*stoo*-cheunn) *n* extorsion *f*
extra (*èk*-streu) *adj* supplémentaire
extract[1] (ik-*strækt*) *v* *arracher, *extraire
extract[2] (*èk*-strækt) *n* fragment *m*
extradite (*èk*-streu-daït) *v* extrader
extraordinary (ik-*stroo*-deunn-ri) *adj* extraordinaire
extravagant (ik-*stræ*-veu-gheunnt) *adj* exagéré, extravagant
extreme (ik-*striim*) *adj* extrême; *n* extrême *m*
exuberant (igh-*zyoû*-beu-reunnt) *adj* exubérant
eye (aï) *n* œil *m*; ~ **shadow** ombre à paupières
eyebrow (*aï*-braou) *n* sourcil *m*; ~ **pencil** crayon pour les yeux
eyelash (*aï*-læch) *n* cil *m*
eyelid (*aï*-lid) *n* paupière *f*
eyewitness (*aï*-^{ou}it-neuss) *n* témoin oculaire

F

fable (*féï*-beul) *n* fable *f*
fabric (*fæ*-brik) *n* tissu *m*; structure *f*
façade (feu-*sââd*) *n* façade *f*
face (féïss) *n* visage *m*; *v* affronter; ~ **cream** crème de beauté; ~ **massage** massage facial; ~ **pack** masque de

beauté; **~ powder** poudre de riz; **facing** en face de
fact (fækt) *n* fait *m*; **in ~** de fait
factor (*fæk*-teu) *n* facteur *m*
factory (*fæk*-teu-ri) *n* usine *f*
factual (*fæk*-tchou-eul) *adj* réel
faculty (*fæ*-keul-ti) *n* faculté *f*, don *m*, talent *m*, aptitude *f*
fade (féïd) *v* se faner, *déteindre
fail (féïl) *v* échouer; manquer; *omettre; **without ~** sans faute
failure (*féïl*-yeu) *n* échec *m*
faint (féïnt) *v* s'évanouir; *adj* faible, vague, défaillant
fair (fè[eu]) *n* foire *f*, *adj* honnête, juste; blond; beau
fairly (*fèeu*-li) *adv* assez, plutôt
fairy (*fèeu*-ri) *n* fée *f*
fairytale (*fèeu*-ri-téïl) *n* conte de fées
faith (féïθ) *n* foi *f*; confiance *f*
faithful (*féïθ*-foul) *adj* fidèle
fake (féïk) *n* falsification *f*
fall (fool) *n* chute *f*, *nAm* automne *m*
***fall** (fool) *v* tomber
false (fools) *adj* faux; **~ teeth** dentier *m*
falter (*fool*-teu) *v* vaciller; balbutier
fame (féïm) *n* renommée *f*, célébrité *f*, réputation *f*
familiar (feu-*mil*-yeu) *adj* familier
family (*fæ*-meu-li) *n* famille *f*; **~ name** nom de famille
famous (*féï*-meuss) *adj* fameux
fan (fæn) *n* ventilateur *m*; éventail *m*; fan *m/f*; **~ belt** courroie de ventilateur
fanatical (feu-*næ*-ti-keul) *adj* fanatique
fancy (*fæn*-si) *v* aimer, *avoir envie de; s'imaginer, imaginer; *n* caprice *m*; imagination *f*
fantastic (fæn-*tæ*-stik) *adj* fantastique
fantasy (*fæn*-teu-zi) *n* fantaisie *f*
far (fââ) *adj* loin; *adv* beaucoup; **by ~** de beaucoup; **so ~** jusqu'à maintenant
far-away (*fââ*-reu-[ou]éï) *adj* éloigné
fare (fè[eu]) *n* prix du voyage; chère *f*, nourriture *f*
farm (fââm) *n* ferme *f*
farmer (*fââ*-meu) *n* fermier *m*; **farmer's wife** fermière *f*
farmhouse (*fââm*-haouss) *n* ferme *f*
far-off (*fââ*-rof) *adj* lointain
fascinate (*fæ*-si-néït) *v* fasciner
fascism (*fæ*-chi-zeumm) *n* fascisme *m*
fascist (*fæ*-chist) *adj* fasciste
fashion (*fæ*-cheunn) *n* mode *f*; mode *m*
fashionable (*fæ*-cheu-neu-beul) *adj* à la mode
fast (fââst) *adj* prompt, rapide; ferme
fasten (*fââ*-seunn) *v* attacher; fermer
fastener (*fââ*-seu-neu) *n* fermeture *f*
fat (fæt) *adj* gras, gros; *n* graisse *f*
fatal (*féï*-teul) *adj* néfaste, mortel, fatal
fate (féït) *n* destin *m*
father (*fââ*-ðeu) *n* père *m*
father-in-law (*fââ*-ðeu-rinn-loo) *n* (pl fathers-) beau-père *m*
fatness (*fæt*-neuss) *n* obésité *f*
fatty (*fæ*-ti) *adj* gras
faucet (*foo*-sit) *nAm* robinet *m*
fault (foolt) *n* faute *f*; imperfection *f*, défaut *m*
faultless (*foolt*-leuss) *adj* impeccable; parfait
faulty (*fool*-ti) *adj* imparfait, défectueux
favo(u)r (*féï*-veu) *n* faveur *f*; *v* favoriser
favo(u)rable (*féï*-veu-reu-beul) *adj* favorable
favo(u)rite (*féï*-veu-rit) *n* favori *m*, -te *f*, *adj* préféré
fax (faks) *n* fax *m*; **send a ~** envoyer un fax
fear (fi[eu]) *n* crainte *f*, peur *f*; *v*

*craindre
feasible (*fii*-zeu-beul) *adj* faisable
feast (fiist) *n* fête *f*
feat (fiit) *n* exploit *m*, prouesse *f*
feather (*fè*-ðeu) *n* plume *f*
feature (*fii*-tcheu) *n* caractéristique *f*; trait du visage
February (*fè*-brou-eu-ri) février
federal (*fè*-deu-reul) *adj* fédéral
federation (fè-deu-*réï*-cheunn) *n* fédération *f*
fee (fii) *n* honoraires *mpl*
feeble (*fii*-beul) *adj* faible
***feed** (fiid) *v* nourrir; **fed up with** dégoûté
***feel** (fiil) *v* *sentir; palper; **~ like** *avoir envie de
feeling (*fii*-linng) *n* sensation *f*
feet (fiit) *n* (pl foot)
fell (fèl) *v* (p fall)
fellow (*fè*-lô^{ou}) *n* gars *m*
felt[1] (fèlt) *n* feutre *m*
felt[2] (fèlt) *v* (p, pp feel)
female (*fii*-méïl) *adj* féminin
feminine (*fè*-mi-ninn) *adj* féminin
fence (fèns) *n* clôture *f*; barrière *f*; *v* *faire de l'escrime
ferment (feû-*mènt*) *v* fermenter
ferry-boat (*fè*-ri-bô^{ou}t) *n* ferry-boat *m*
fertile (*feû*-taïl) *adj* fertile
festival (*fè*-sti-veul) *n* festival *m*
festive (*fè*-stiv) *adj* de fête
fetch (fètch) *v* apporter; *aller chercher
fever (*fii*-veu) *n* fièvre *f*
feverish (*fii*-veu-rich) *adj* fiévreux
few (fyoû) *adj* peu de
fiancé (fi-*an*-séï) *n* fiancé *m*
fiancée (fi-*an*-séï) *n* fiancée *f*
fibre (*faï*-beu) *n* fibre *f*
fiction (*fik*-cheunn) *n* fiction *f*
field (fiild) *n* champ *m*; domaine *m*; **~ glasses** jumelles *fpl*
fierce (fi^{eu}ss) *adj* féroce; sauvage, violent
fifteen (fif-*tiin*) *num* quinze
fifteenth (fif-*tiinθ*) *num* quinzième
fifth (fifθ) *num* cinquième
fifty (*fif*-ti) *num* cinquante
fig (figh) *n* figue *f*
fight (faït) *n* lutte *f*, combat *m*
***fight** (faït) *v* se *battre, *combattre
figure (*fi*-gheu) *n* stature *f*, forme *f*; chiffre *m*
file (faïl) *n* lime *f*; dossier *m*
fill (fil) *v* remplir; **~ in** remplir; **filling station** station-service *f*; **~ out** *Am* remplir; **~ up** *faire le plein
filling (*fi*-linng) *n* plombage *m*; farce *f*
film (film) *n* film *m*; pellicule *f*; *v* filmer
filter (*fil*-teu) *n* filtre *m*
filthy (*fil*-θi) *adj* répugnant, sale
final (*faï*-neul) *adj* final
finally (*faï*-neu-li) *adv* enfin; définitivement
finance (faï-*næns*) *v* financer
finances (faï-*næn*-siz) *pl* finances *fpl*
financial (faï-*næn*-cheul) *adj* financier
***find** (faïnd) *v* trouver
fine (faïn) *n* amende *f*; *adj* fin; joli; formidable, merveilleux; **~ arts** beaux-arts *mpl*
finger (*finng*-gheu) *n* doigt *m*; **little ~** auriculaire *m*
fingerprint (*finng*-gheu-prinnt) *n* empreinte digitale
finish (*fi*-nich) *v* achever, finir; terminer; *n* fin *f*; ligne d'arrivée
Finland (*finn*-leunnd) Finlande *f*
Finn (finn) *n* Finlandais *m*
Finnish (*fi*-nich) *adj* finlandais
fire (faï^{eu}) *n* feu *m*; incendie *m*; *v* tirer; licencier; **~ alarm** alarme d'incendie; **~ brigade,** *Am* **fire department** pompiers; **~ escape** escalier de secours; **~ extinguisher** extincteur *m*
fireplace (*faïeu*-pléïss) *n* cheminée *f*
fireproof (*faïeu*-proûf) *adj* ignifuge;

qui va au four
firm (feûmm) *adj* ferme; solide; *n* firme *f*
first (feûst) *num* premier; **at ~** d'abord; au début; **~ name** prénom *m*
first aid (feûst-*éïd*) *n* premier secours; **~ kit** trousse de secours; **~ post** poste de secours
first-class (feûst-*klââss*) *adj* de première qualité
first-rate (feûst-*réït*) *adj* de premier ordre, de première qualité
fir tree (*feû*-trii) *n* sapin *m*
fish[1] (fich) *n* (pl ~, ~es) poisson *m*; **~ shop** poissonnerie *f*
fish[2] (fich) *v* pêcher; **fishing gear** attirail de pêche; **fishing hook** hameçon *m*; **fishing industry** pêche *f*; **fishing licence (license** *Am***)** permis de pêche; **fishing line** ligne de pêche; **fishing net** filet de pêche; **fishing rod** canne à pêche; **fishing tackle** attirail de pêche
fishbone (*fich*-bô^{ou}n) *n* arête *f*
fisherman (*fi*-cheu-meunn) *n* (pl -men) pêcheur *m*
fist (fist) *n* poing *m*
fit (fit) *adj* convenable; *n* attaque *f*; *v* *convenir; **fitting room** cabine d'essayage
five (faïv) *num* cinq
fix (fiks) *v* réparer
fixed (fikst) *adj* fixe
fizz (fiz) *n* pétillement *m*
flag (flægh) *n* drapeau *m*
flame (fléïm) *n* flamme *f*
flamingo (fleu-*minng*-ghô^{ou}) *n* (pl ~s, ~es) flamant *m*
flannel (*flæ*-neul) *n* flanelle *f*
flash (flæch) *n* éclair *m*; **~ bulb** ampoule de flash
flashlight (*flæch*-laït) *n* lampe de poche
flask (flââsk) *n* flacon *m*; **thermos ~** thermos *m*
flat (flæt) *adj* plan, plat; *n* appartement *m*; **~ tire** *Am*, **~ tyre** pneu crevé
flavour (*fléï*-veu) *n* saveur *f*; *v* assaisonner
flee (flii) *v* s'enfuir; fuir
fleet (fliit) *n* flotte *f*
flesh (flèch) *n* chair *f*
flew (floû) *v* (p fly)
flex (flèks) *n* fil souple
flexible (*flèk*-si-beul) *adj* flexible; souple
flight (flaït) *n* vol *m*; **charter ~** vol charter
flint (flinnt) *n* pierre à briquet
float (flô^{ou}t) *v* flotter; *n* flotteur *m*
flock (flok) *n* troupeau *m*
flood (flad) *n* inondation *f*, marée haute
floor (floo) *n* sol *m*; étage *m*; **~ show** spectacle de variétés
florist (*flo*-rist) *n* fleuriste *m/f*
flour (flaou^{eu}) *n* farine *f*
flow (flô^{ou}) *v* s'écouler, couler
flower (flaou^{eu}) *n* fleur *f*; **~ shop** fleuriste *m*
flowerbed (*flaoueu*-bèd) *n* plate-bande *f*
flown (flô^{ou}n) *v* (pp fly)
flu (floû) *n* grippe *f*
fluently (*floû*-eunnt-li) *adv* couramment
fluid (*floû*-id) *adj* fluide; *n* liquide *m*
flute (floût) *n* flûte *f*
fly (flaï) *n* mouche *f*; braguette *f*
***fly** (flaï) *v* voler
foam (fô^{ou}m) *n* mousse *f*; *v* mousser; **~ rubber** caoutchouc mousse
focus (*fôou*-keuss) *n* foyer *m*
fog (fogh) *n* brouillard *m*
foggy (*fo*-ghi) *adj* brumeux
foglamp (*fogh*-læmp) *n* phare antibrouillard
fold (fô^{ou}ld) *v* plier; *n* pli *m*

folk (fô^{ou}k) *n* gens *mpl*; **~ dance** danse folklorique; **~ song** chanson populaire
folklore (*fôouk*-loo) *n* folklore *m*
follow (*fo*-lô^{ou}) *v* *suivre; **following** *adj* prochain, suivant
fond: *be ~ of (bii fonnd ov) aimer
food (foûd) *n* nourriture *f*; manger *m*; **~ poisoning** intoxication alimentaire
foodstuffs (*foûd*-stafs) *pl* aliments *mpl*
fool (foûl) *n* idiot *m*/fou *m*; *v* *faire marcher
foolish (*foû*-lich) *adj* sot, stupide; absurde
foot (fout) *n* (pl feet) pied *m*; **~ brake** frein à pédale; **~ powder** poudre pour les pieds; **on ~** à pied
football (*fout*-bool) *n* ballon *m*; **~ match** match de football
footpath (*fout*-pââθ) *n* sentier pour piétons
footwear (*fout*-^{ou}è^{eu}) *n* chaussures
for (foo, feu) *prep* pour; pendant; à cause de, en raison de, par; *conj* car
***forbid** (feu-*bid*) *v* *interdire
force (fooss) *v* obliger, forcer; *n* puissance *f*, force *f*; **by ~** forcément; **driving ~** force motrice
forecast (*foo*-kââst) *n* prévision *f*; *v* *prévoir
foreground (*foo*-ghraound) *n* premier plan
forehead (*fo*-rèd) *n* front *m*
foreign (*fo*-rinn) *adj* étranger
foreigner (*fo*-ri-neu) *n* étranger *m*
foreman (*foo*-meunn) *n* (pl -men) contremaître *m*
foremost (*foo*-mô^{ou}st) *adj* premier
forest (*fo*-rist) *n* bois *m*/forêt *f*
forester (*fo*-ri-steu) *n* forestier *m*
forge (foodj) *v* falsifier
***forget** (feu-*ghèt*) *v* oublier
forgetful (feu-*ghèt*-feul) *adj* oublieux
***forgive** (feu-*ghiv*) *v* pardonner
fork (fook) *n* fourchette *f*; bifurcation *f*; *v* bifurquer
form (foom) *n* forme *f*; formulaire *m*; classe *f*; *v* former
formal (*foo*-meul) *adj* cérémonieux
formality (foo-*mæ*-leu-ti) *n* formalité *f*
former (*foo*-meu) *adj* ancien; précédent; **formerly** antérieurement, auparavant
formula (*foo*-myou-leu) *n* (pl ~e, ~s) formule *f*
fortnight (*foot*-naït) *n* quinze jours
fortress (*foo*-triss) *n* forteresse *f*
fortunate (*foo*-tcheu-neut) *adj* heureux
fortunately (*foo*-tcheu-neut-li) *adv* par bonheur, heureusement
fortune (*foo*-tchoûn) *n* fortune *f*; sort *m*, chance *f*
forty (*foo*-ti) *num* quarante
forward (*foo*-^{ou}eud) *adv* en avant; *v* *faire suivre
foster parents (*fo*-steu-pè^{eu}-reunnts) *pl* parents nourriciers
fought (foot) *v* (p, pp fight)
foul (faoul) *adj* malpropre; infâme
found[1] (faound) *v* (p, pp find)
found[2] (faound) *v* fonder, établir
foundation (faoun-*déï*-cheunn) *n* fondation *f*; **~ cream** fond de teint
fountain (*faoun*-tinn) *n* fontaine *f*; source *f*; **~ pen** stylo *m*
four (foo) *num* quatre
fourteen (foo-*tiin*) *num* quatorze
fourteenth (foo-*tiinθ*) *num* quatorzième
fourth (fooθ) *num* quatrième
fowl (faoul) *n* (pl ~s, ~) volaille *f*
fox (foks) *n* renard *m*
fraction (*fræk*-cheunn) *n* fraction *f*
fracture (*fræk*-tcheu) *v* fracturer; *n* fracture *f*
fragile (*fræ*-djaïl) *adj* fragile

fragment (*frægh*-meunnt) *n* fragment *m*; morceau *m*
frame (fréïm) *n* cadre *m*; monture *f*
France (frââns) France *f*
franchise (*fræn*-tchaïz) *n* droit de vote
fraternity (freu-*teû*-neu-ti) *n* fraternité *f*
fraud (frood) *n* fraude *f*
fray (fréï) *v* s'effilocher
free (frii) *adj* libre; gratuit; **~ of charge** gratuit; **~ ticket** billet gratuit
freedom (*frii*-deumm) *n* liberté *f*
***freeze** (friiz) *v* geler
freezer (*frii*-zeu) *n* congélateur *m*
freezing (*frii*-zinng) *adj* glacial; **~ point** point de congélation
freight (fréït) *n* fret *m*, chargement *m*; **~ train** train de marchandises
French (frèntch) *adj* français
French fries (frèntch-*fraïz*) *nAm* pommes de terre frites *fpl*
frequency (*frii*-k^ou^eunn-si) *n* fréquence *f*
frequent (*frii*-k^ou^eunnt) *adj* courant, fréquent
fresh (frèch) *adj* frais; **~ water** eau douce
friction (*frik*-cheunn) *n* friction *f*
Friday (*fraï*-di) vendredi *m*
fridge (fridj) *n* réfrigérateur *m*, frigo *m*
friend (frènd) *n* ami *m*, -e *f*
friendly (*frènd*-li) *adj* gentil; amical
friendship (*frènd*-chip) *n* amitié *f*
fright (fraït) *n* peur *f*, frayeur *f*
frighten (*fraï*-teunn) *v* effrayer
frightened (*fraï*-teunnd) *adj* effrayé; ***be ~** *être effrayé
frightful (*fraït*-feul) *adj* terrible, affreux
fringe (frinndj) *n* frange *f*
frock (frok) *n* robe *f*
frog (frogh) *n* grenouille *f*
from (fromm) *prep* de; à partir de
front (frannt) *n* face *f*; **in ~ of** devant
frontier (*frann*-ti^{eu}) *n* frontière *f*
frost (frost) *n* gel *m*
froth (froθ) *n* écume *f*
frozen (*frôou*-zeunn) *adj* congelé; **~ food** aliments surgelés
fruit (froût) *n* fruits; fruit *m*
fry (fraï) *v* *faire sauter; *frire
frying pan (*fraï*-inng-pæn) *n* poêle à frire
fuel (*fyoû*-eul) *n* combustible *m*; essence *f*; **~ pump** *Am* distributeur d'essence
full (foul) *adj* plein; **~ board** pension complète; **~ stop** point *m*; **~ up** complet
fun (fann) *n* divertissement *m*, plaisir *m*
function (*fanngk*-cheunn) *n* fonction *f*
fund (fannd) *n* fonds *mpl*
fundamental (fann-deu-*mèn*-teul) *adj* fondamental
funeral (*fyoû*-neu-reul) *n* funérailles *fpl*
funnel (*fa*-neul) *n* entonnoir *m*
funny (*fa*-ni) *adj* drôle, amusant; bizarre
fur (feû) *n* fourrure *f*; **~ coat** manteau de fourrure
furious (*fyoueu*-ri-euss) *adj* furibond, furieux
furnace (*feû*-niss) *n* fournaise *f*
furnish (*feû*-nich) *v* fournir, procurer; installer, meubler; **~ with** approvisionner en
furniture (*feû*-ni-tcheu) *n* meubles
furrier (*fa*-ri-eu) *n* fourreur *m*
further (*feû*-ðeu) *adj* plus loin; complémentaire
furthermore (*feû*-ðeu-moo) *adv* en outre
furthest (*feû*-ðist) *adj* le plus éloigné
fuse (fyoûz) *n* fusible *m*; mèche *f*

fuss (fass) *n* agitation *f*; embarras *m*, chichi *m*

future (*fyoû*-tcheu) *n* avenir *m*; *adj* futur

G

gable (*ghéï*-beul) *n* pignon *m*
gadget (*ghæ*-djit) *n* gadget *m*
gain (ghéïn) *v* gagner; *n* gain *m*
gale (ghéïl) *n* tempête *f*
gall (ghool) *n* bile *f*; ~ **bladder** vésicule biliaire
gallery (*ghæ*-leu-ri) *n* galerie *f*
gallon (*ghæ*-leun) *n* gallon *m*
gallop (*ghæ*-leup) *n* galop *m*
gallstone (*ghool*-stô^{ou}n) *n* calcul biliaire
game (ghéïm) *n* jeu *m*; gibier *m*; ~ **reserve** réserve zoologique
gang (ghæng) *n* bande *f*; équipe *f*
gangway (*ghæng*-^{ou}éï) *n* passerelle *f*
gap (ghæp) *n* brèche *f*
garage (*ghæ*-rââj) *n* garage *m*; *v* garer
garbage (*ghââ*-bidj) *n* détritus *m*, ordures *fpl*
garden (*ghââ*-deunn) *n* jardin *m*; **public** ~ jardin public; **zoological gardens** jardin zoologique
gardener (*ghââ*-deu-neu) *n* jardinier *m*, -ière *f*
gargle (*ghââ*-gheul) *v* se gargariser
garlic (*ghââ*-lik) *n* ail *m*
gas (ghæss) *n* gaz *m*; *nAm* essence *f*; ~ **cooker** cuisinière à gaz; ~ **pump** *Am* pompe à essence; ~ **station** *Am* station-service *f*; ~ **stove** fourneau à gaz; ~ **tank** réservoir d'essence
gasoline (*ghæ*-seu-liin) *nAm* essence *f*
gastric (*ghæ*-strik) *adj* gastrique; ~ **ulcer** ulcère à l'estomac
gasworks (*ghæss*-^{ou}eûks) *n* usine à gaz
gate (ghéït) *n* porte *f*; grille *f*
gather (*ghæ*-ðeu) *v* collectionner; se réunir
gauge (ghéïdj) *n* jauge *f*
gave (ghéïv) *v* (p give)
gay (ghéï) *adj* gai; éclatant
gaze (ghéïz) *v* fixer
gear (ghi^{eu}) *n* vitesse *f*; équipement *m*; **change** ~ changer de vitesse; ~ **lever** levier de vitesse
gearbox (*ghieu*-boks) *n* boîte de vitesse
geese (ghiiz) *n* (pl goose)
gem (djèm) *n* joyau *m*, pierre précieuse; bijou *m*
gender (*djèn*-deu) *n* genre *m*
general (*djè*-neu-reul) *adj* général; *n* général *m*; ~ **practitioner** médecin généraliste; **in** ~ en général
generate (*djè*-neu-réït) *v* *produire
generation (djè-neu-*réï*-cheunn) *n* génération *f*
generator (*djè*-neu-réï-teur) *n* générateur *m*
generosity (djè-neu-*ro*-seu-ti) *n* générosité *f*
generous (*djè*-neu-reuss) *adj* large, généreux
genital (*djè*-ni-teul) *adj* génital
genius (*djii*-ni-euss) *n* génie *m*
gentle (*djèn*-teul) *adj* doux; léger; délicat
gentleman (*djèn*-teul-meunn) *n* (pl -men) monsieur *m*
genuine (*djè*-nyou-inn) *adj* authentique

geography (dji-*o*-ghreu-fi) *n* géographie *f*
geology (dji-*o*-leu-dji) *n* géologie *f*
geometry (dji-*o*-meu-tri) *n* géométrie *f*
germ (djeûmm) *n* microbe *m*; germe *m*
German (*djeû*-meunn) *adj* allemand; *n* Allemand *m*
Germany (*djeû*-meu-ni) Allemagne *f*
gesticulate (dji-*sti*-kyou-léït) *v* gesticuler
***get** (ghèt) *v* *obtenir; *aller prendre; *devenir; **~ back** retourner; **~ off** descendre; **~ on** monter; progresser; **~ up** se lever
ghost (ghô^{ou}st) *n* fantôme *m*; esprit *m*
giant (*djaï*-eunnt) *n* géant *m*
giddiness (*ghi*-di-neuss) *n* vertige *m*
giddy (*ghi*-di) *adj* étourdi
gift (ghift) *n* don *m*, cadeau *m*; talent *m*
gifted (*ghif*-tid) *adj* doué
gigantic (djaï-*ghæn*-tik) *adj* gigantesque
giggle (*ghi*-gheul) *v* glousser
gill (ghil) *n* branchie *f*
gilt (ghilt) *adj* doré
ginger (*djinn*-djeu) *n* gingembre *m*
girdle (*gheû*-deul) *n* gaine *f*
girl (gheûl) *n* fille *f*; **~ guide** scout *m*
girlfriend (*gheûl*-frènd) *n* amie *f*; petite amie *f*
***give** (ghiv) *v* donner; passer; **~ away** révéler; **~ in** céder; **~ up** renoncer
glacier (*ghlæ*-si-eu) *n* glacier *m*
glad (ghlæd) *adj* joyeux, content; **gladly** avec plaisir, volontiers
gladness (*ghlæd*-neuss) *n* joie *f*
glamorous (*ghlæ*-meu-reuss) *adj* enchanteur, charmant
glamour (*ghlæ*-meu) *n* charme *m*
glance (ghlââns) *n* coup d'œil; *v* jeter un coup d'œil
gland (ghlænd) *n* glande *f*
glare (ghlè^{eu}) *n* éclat *m*; éblouissement *m*
glaring (*ghlèeu*-rinng) *adj* éblouissant
glass (ghlââss) *n* verre *m*; de verre; **glasses** lunettes *fpl*; **magnifying ~** verre grossissant
glaze (ghléïz) *v* vernir
glide (ghlaïd) *v* glisser
glider (*ghlaï*-deu) *n* planeur *m*
glimpse (ghlimmps) *n* aperçu *m*; coup d'œil; *v* *entrevoir
global (*ghlôou*-beul) *adj* mondial
globe (ghlô^{ou}b) *n* globe *m*
gloom (ghloûm) *n* ténèbres *fpl*
gloomy (*ghloû*-mi) *adj* sombre
glorious (*ghloo*-ri-euss) *adj* splendide
glory (*ghloo*-ri) *n* gloire *f*; honneur *m*, louange *f*
gloss (ghloss) *n* lustre *m*
glossy (*ghlo*-si) *adj* luisant
glove (ghlav) *n* gant *m*
glow (ghlô^{ou}) *v* briller; *n* éclat *m*
glue (ghloû) *n* colle *f*
***go** (ghô^{ou}) *v* se rendre, *aller; marcher; *devenir; **~ ahead** continuer; **~ away** *partir; **~ back** retourner; **~ home** rentrer; **~ in** entrer; **~ on** continuer; **~ out** *sortir; **~ through** endurer
goal (ghô^{ou}l) *n* objectif *m*, but *m*
goalkeeper (*ghôoul*-kii-peu) *n* gardien de but
goat (ghô^{ou}t) *n* bouc *m*, chèvre *f*
god (ghod) *n* dieu *m*
godfather (*ghod*-fââ-ðeu) *n* parrain *m*
goggles (*gho*-gheulz) *pl* lunettes de plongée
gold (ghô^{ou}ld) *n* or *m*; **~ leaf** or en feuille
golden (*ghôoul*-deunn) *adj* en or
goldmine (*ghôould*-maïn) *n* mine d'or
goldsmith (*ghôould*-smiθ) *n* orfèvre

m

golf (gholf) *n* golf *m*; ~ **course** terrain de golf; ~ **links** terrain de golf

golfclub (*gholf*-klab) *n* club de golf

gondola (*ghonn*-deu-leu) *n* gondole *f*

gone (ghonn) *adv* (pp go) parti

good (ghoud) *adj* bon; sage, brave

goodbye! (ghoud-*baï*) au revoir!

good-humoured (ghoud-*hyoû*-meud) *adj* de bonne humeur

good-looking (ghoud-*lou*-kinng) *adj* joli

good-natured (ghoud-*néï*-tcheud) *adj* de bon caractère

goods (ghoudz) *pl* marchandise *f*, biens *mpl*; ~ **train** train de marchandises

good-tempered (ghoud-*tèm*-peud) *adj* de bonne humeur

goodwill (ghoud-*ouil*) *n* bienveillance *f*

goose (ghoûss) *n* (pl geese) oie *f*; ~ **bumps,** ~ **flesh,** ~ **pimples** chair de poule

gooseberry (*ghouz*-beu-ri) *n* groseille à maquereau

gorge (ghoodj) *n* gorge *f*

gorgeous (*ghoo*-djeuss) *adj* magnifique

gospel (*gho*-speul) *n* évangile *m*

gossip (*gho*-sip) *n* commérage *m*; *v* *faire des commérages

got (ghot) *v* (p, pp get)

gout (ghaout) *n* goutte *f*

govern (*gha*-veunn) *v* gouverner

governess (*gha*-veu-niss) *n* gouvernante *f*

government (*gha*-veunn-meunnt) *n* régime *m*, gouvernement *m*

governor (*gha*-veu-neu) *n* gouverneur *m*

gown (ghaoun) *n* robe *f*

grace (ghréïss) *n* grâce *f*; clémence *f*

graceful (*ghréïss*-feul) *adj* charmant, gracieux

grade (ghréïd) *n* grade *m*; *v* classer

gradient (*ghréï*-di-eunnt) *n* inclinaison *f*

gradual (*ghræ*-djou-eul) *adj* graduel

graduate (*ghræ*-djou-éït) *v* *obtenir un diplôme

grain (ghréïn) *n* grain *m*, blé *m*, céréale *f*

gram (ghræm) *n* gramme *m*

grammar (*ghræ*-meu) *n* grammaire *f*

grammatical (ghreu-*mæ*-ti-keul) *adj* grammatical

grand (ghrænd) *adj* sublime

grandchild (*ghræn*-tchaïld) *n* petit-fils *m*,-fille *f*

granddad (*ghræn*-dæd) *n* grand-papa *m*

granddaughter (*ghræn*-doo-teu) *n* petite-fille *f*

grandfather (*ghræn*-fââ-ðeu) *n* grandpère *m*

grandmother (*ghræn*-ma-ðeu) *n* grand-mère *f*

grandparents (*ghræn*-pè^{eu}-reunnts) *pl* grands-parents *mpl*

grandson (*ghræn*-sann) *n* petit-fils *m*

granite (*ghræ*-nit) *n* granit *m*

grant (ghrâânt) *v* accorder; concéder; *n* subvention *f*, bourse *f*

grapefruit (*ghréïp*-froût) *n* pamplemousse *m*

grapes (ghréïps) *pl* raisin *m*

graph (ghræf) *n* diagramme *m*

graphic (*ghræ*-fik) *adj* graphique

grasp (ghrââsp) *v* saisir; *n* prise *f*

grass (ghrââss) *n* herbe *f*

grasshopper (*ghrââss*-ho-peu) *n* sauterelle *f*

grate (ghréït) *n* grille *f*; *v* râper

grateful (*ghréït*-feul) *adj* reconnaissant

grater (*ghréï*-teu) *n* râpe *f*

gratis (*ghræ*-tiss) *adj* gratuit

gratitude (*ghræ*-ti-tyoûd) *n* gratitude *f*
gratuity (ghreu-*tyoû*-eu-ti) *n* pourboire *m*
grave (ghréïv) *n* tombe *f*; *adj* grave
gravel (*ghræ*-veul) *n* gravier *m*
gravestone (*ghréïv*-stô^{ou}n) *n* pierre tombale
graveyard (*ghréïv*-yââd) *n* cimetière *m*
gravity (*ghræ*-veu-ti) *n* gravité *f*
gravy (*ghréï*-vi) *n* jus *m*
graze (ghréïz) *v* *paître; *n* égratignure *f*
grease (ghriiss) *n* graisse *f*; *v* graisser
greasy (*ghrii*-si) *adj* graisseux
great (ghréït) *adj* grand; **Great Britain** Grande-Bretagne *f*
Greece (ghriiss) Grèce *f*
greed (ghriid) *n* cupidité *f*
greedy (*ghrii*-di) *adj* cupide; gourmand
Greek (ghriik) *adj* grec; *n* Grec *m*
green (ghriin) *adj* vert; **~ card** carte verte
greengrocer (*ghriin*-ghrô^{ou}-seu) *n* marchand de légumes
greenhouse (*ghriin*-haouss) *n* serre *f*
greens (ghriinz) *pl* légumes *mpl*
greet (ghriit) *v* saluer
greeting (*ghrii*-tinng) *n* salutation *f*
grey (ghréï) *adj* gris
greyhound (*ghréï*-haound) *n* lévrier *m*
grief (ghriif) *n* chagrin *m*; affliction *f*, douleur *f*
grieve (ghriiv) *v* *avoir de la peine
grill (ghril) *n* grill *m*; *v* griller
grillroom (*ghril*-roûm) *n* rôtisserie *f*
grim (ghrimm) *adj* sinistre; sévère; farouche
grin (ghrinn) *n* large sourire
***grind** (ghraïnd) *v* *moudre; pulvériser
grip (ghrip) *v* saisir; *n* prise *f*, étreinte *f*; *nAm* mallette de voyage
grit (ghrit) *n* gravillon *m*
groan (ghrô^{ou}n) *v* gémir
grocer (*ghrôou*-seu) *n* épicier *m*; **grocer's, grocery** épicerie *f*
groceries (*ghrôou*-seu-riz) *pl* articles d'épicerie
groin (ghroïn) *n* aine *f*
groom (ghroûm) *n* palefrenier *m*; marié *m*; *v* panser; soigner; former, façonner
groove (ghroûv) *n* sillon *m*
gross[1] (ghrô^{ou}ss) *n* (pl ~) grosse *f*
gross[2] (ghrô^{ou}ss) *adj* grossier; brut
grotto (*ghro*-tô^{ou}) *n* (pl ~es, ~s) grotte *f*
ground[1] (ghraound) *n* fond *m*, sol *m*; **~ floor** rez-de-chaussée *m*; **grounds** terrain *m*
ground[2] (ghraound) *v* (p, pp grind)
group (ghroûp) *n* groupe *m*
grouse (ghraouss) *n* (pl ~) grouse *f*
grove (ghrô^{ou}v) *n* bosquet *m*
***grow** (ghrô^{ou}) *v* grandir; cultiver
growl (ghraoul) *v* grogner
grown-up (*ghrôoun*-ap) *adj* adulte; *n* adulte *m/f*
growth (ghrô^{ou}θ) *n* croissance *f*; tumeur *f*
grudge (ghradj) *v* envier
grumble (*ghramm*-beul) *v* grogner
guarantee (ghæ-reunn-*tii*) *n* garantie *f*; caution *f*; *v* garantir
guard (ghââd) *n* garde *m*; *v* surveiller
guardian (*ghââ*-di-eunn) *n* tuteur *m*
guess (ghèss) *v* deviner; *croire, supposer; *n* conjecture *f*
guest (ghèst) *n* hôte *m*, invité *m*; **~ room** chambre d'ami
guesthouse (*ghèst*-haouss) *n* pension *f*
guide (ghaïd) *n* guide *m*; *v* *conduire; **~ dog** chien d'aveugle
guidebook (*ghaïd*-bouk) *n* guide *m*

guilt (ghilt) *n* culpabilité *f*
guilty (*ghil*-ti) *adj* coupable
guinea pig (*ghi*-ni-pigh) *n* cochon d'Inde
guitar (ghi-*tââ*) *n* guitare *f*
gulf (ghalf) *n* golfe *m*
gull (ghal) *n* mouette *f*
gum (ghamm) *n* gencive *f*; gomme *f*; colle *f*
gun (ghann) *n* fusil *m*, revolver *m*; canon *m*
gunpowder (*ghann*-paou-deu) *n* poudre à canon
gust (ghast) *n* rafale *f*
gusty (*gha*-sti) *adj* venteux
gut (ghat) *n* intestin *m*; **guts** cran *m*
gutter (*gha*-teu) *n* caniveau *m*
guy (ghaï) *n* type *m*
gym (djimm) *n colloquial* gymnase *f*; gym(nastique) *f*; de gymnastique; **~ shoes** tennis *pl*, baskets *pl*
gymnasium (djimm-*néï*-zi-eumm) *n* (pl ~s, -sia) gymnase *m*
gymnast (*djimm*-næst) *n* gymnaste *m*
gymnastics (djimm-*næ*-stiks) *pl* gymnastique *f*
gyn(a)ecologist (ghaï-neu-*ko*-leu-djist) *n* gynécologue *m*/*f*

H

habit (*hæ*-bit) *n* habitude *f*
habitable (*hæ*-bi-teu-beul) *adj* habitable
habitual (heu-*bi*-tchou-eul) *adj* habituel
had (hæd) *v* (p, pp have)
haddock (*hæ*-deuk) *n* (pl ~) aiglefin *m*
h(a)emorrhage (*hè*-meu-ridj) *n* hémorragie *f*
h(a)emorrhoids (*hè*-meu-roïdz) *pl* hémorroïdes *fpl*
hail (héïl) *n* grêle *f*
hair (hè^{eu}) *n* cheveu *m*; **~ cream** crème capillaire; **~ gel** gel pour les cheveux *m*; **~ net** résille *f*; **~ oil** huile capillaire; **~ piece** postiche *m*; **~ rollers** bigoudis *mpl*
hairbrush (*hèeu*-brach) *n* brosse à cheveux
haircut (*hèeu*-kat) *n* coupe de cheveux
hairdo (*hèeu*-doû) *n* coiffure *f*
hairdresser (*hèeu*-drè-seu) *n* coiffeur *m*, -se *f*
hairdrier, hairdryer (*hèeu*-draï-eu) *n* sèche-cheveux *m*
hairgrip (*hèeu*-ghrip) *n* pince à cheveux
hairpin (*hèeu*-pinn) *n* épingle à cheveux
hair spray (*hèeu*-spréï) *n* laque capillaire
hairy (*hèeu*-ri) *adj* chevelu
half[1] (hââf) *adj* demi; *adv* à moitié
half[2] (hââf) *n* (pl halves) moitié *f*
half time (hââf-*taïm*) *n* mi-temps *f*
halfway (hââf-*ouéï*) *adv* à mi-chemin
halibut (*hæ*-li-beut) *n* (pl ~) flétan *m*
hall (hool) *n* vestibule *m*; salle *f*
halt (hoolt) *v* s'arrêter
halve (hââv) *v* diviser en deux
ham (hæm) *n* jambon *m*
hamlet (*hæm*-leut) *n* hameau *m*
hammer (*hæ*-meu) *n* marteau *m*
hammock (*hæ*-meuk) *n* hamac *m*
hamper (*hæm*-peu) *n* panier d'osier
hand (hænd) *n* main *f*; **~ cream** crème pour les mains; **~ over** *remettre

handbag (*hænd*-bægh) *n* sac à main
handbook (*hænd*-bouk) *n* manuel *m*
handbrake (*hænd*-bréïk) *n* frein à main
handcuffs (*hænd*-kafs) *pl* menottes *fpl*
handful (*hænd*-foul) *n* poignée *f*
handicap (*hæn*-di-kæp) *n* handicap *m*; *v* handicaper
handicapped (*hæn*-di-kæpt) *adj* handicapé
handicraft (*hæn*-di-krâââft) *n* travail manuel; artisanat *m*
handkerchief (*hæng*-keu-tchif) *n* mouchoir *m*
handle (*hæn*-deul) *n* manche *m*, poignée *f*; *v* manipuler; traiter
hand-made (hænd-*mëïd*) *adj* fait à la main
handshake (*hænd*-chéïk) *n* poignée de main
handsome (*hæn*-seumm) *adj* beau
handwork (*hænd*-^{ou}eûk) *n* travail artisanal
handwriting (*hænd*-raï-tinng) *n* écriture *f*
handy (*hæn*-di) *adj* commode
***hang** (hæng) *v* suspendre; pendre
hanger (*hæng*-eu) *n* cintre *m*
hangover (*hæng*-ô^{ou}-veu) *n* gueule de bois
happen (*hæ*-peunn) *v* se *produire, arriver
happening (*hæ*-peu-ninng) *n* événement *m*
happiness (*hæ*-pi-neuss) *n* bonheur *m*
happy (*hæ*-pi) *adj* content, heureux
harbo(u)r (*hââ*-beu) *n* port *m*
hard (hââd) *adj* dur; difficile; **hardly** à peine
hardware (*hââd*-^{ou}è^{eu}) *n* quincaillerie *f*; ~ **store** quincaillerie *f*
hare (hè^{eu}) *n* lièvre *m*
harm (hââm) *n* mal *m*; tort *m*; *v* *faire du mal
harmful (*hââm*-feul) *adj* préjudiciable, nuisible
harmless (*hââm*-leuss) *adj* inoffensif
harmony (*hââ*-meu-ni) *n* harmonie *f*
harp (hââp) *n* harpe *f*
harpsichord (*hââp*-si-kood) *n* clavecin *m*
harsh (hââch) *adj* âpre; sévère; cruel
harvest (*hââ*-vist) *n* moisson *f*
has (hæz) *v* (pr have)
haste (héïst) *n* hâte *f*
hasten (*héï*-seunn) *v* se hâter
hasty (*héï*-sti) *adj* précipité
hat (hæt) *n* chapeau *m*; ~ **rack** porte-manteau *m*
hate (héït) *v* détester; *haïr; *n* haine *f*
hatred (*héï*-trid) *n* haine *f*
haughty (*hoo*-ti) *adj* hautain
haul (hool) *v* traîner
***have** (hæv) *v* *avoir; *faire; ~ **to** *devoir
hawk (hook) *n* faucon *m*
hay (héï) *n* foin *m*; ~ **fever** rhume des foins
hazard (*hæ*-zeud) *n* hasard *m*
haze (héïz) *n* brume *f*
hazelnut (*héï*-zeul-nat) *n* noisette *f*
hazy (*héï*-zi) *adj* brumeux; nébuleux
he (hii) *pron* il
head (hèd) *n* tête *f*; *v* diriger; ~ **of state** chef d'Etat; ~ **teacher** directeur d'école; ~ **waiter** maître d'hôtel
headache (*hè*-déïk) *n* mal de tête
heading (*hè*-dinng) *n* titre *m*
headlamp (*hèd*-læmp) *n* phare *m*
headland (*hèd*-leunnd) *n* promontoire *m*
headlight (*hèd*-laït) *n* phare *m*
headline (*hèd*-laïn) *n* manchette *f*
headmaster (hèd-*mââ*-steu) *n* directeur d'école

headquarters (hèd-*kouoo*-teuz) *pl* quartier général
head-strong (*hèd*-stronng) *adj* têtu
heal (hiil) *v* guérir
health (hèlθ) *n* santé *f*; ~ **centre** dispensaire *m*; ~ **certificate** certificat médical
healthy (*hèl*-θi) *adj* sain
heap (hiip) *n* amoncellement *m*, tas *m*
***hear** (hi^eu^) *v* entendre
hearing (*hieu*-rinng) *n* ouïe *f*
heart (hâât) *n* cœur *m*; **by** ~ par cœur; ~ **attack** crise cardiaque
heartburn (*hâât*-beûnn) *n* brûlures d'estomac
hearth (hââθ) *n* cheminée *f*
heartless (*hâât*-leuss) *adj* insensible
hearty (*hââ*-ti) *adj* cordial
heat (hiit) *n* chaleur *f*; *v* chauffer; **heating pad** coussin chauffant
heater (*hii*-teu) *n* appareil de chauffage; **immersion** ~ thermoplongeur *m*
heath (hiiθ) *n* lande *f*
heathen (*hii*-ðeunn) *n* païen *m*
heather (*hè*-ðeu) *n* bruyère *f*
heating (*hii*-tinng) *n* chauffage *m*
heaven (*hè*-veunn) *n* ciel *m*
heavy (*hè*-vi) *adj* lourd
Hebrew (*hii*-broû) *n* hébreu *m*
hedge (hèdj) *n* haie *f*
hedgehog (*hèdj*-hogh) *n* hérisson *m*
heel (hiil) *n* talon *m*
height (haït) *n* hauteur *f*; sommet *m*, apogée *m*
heir (hè^eu^) *n* héritier *m* (**to** de); ~ **apparent** héritier *m* présomptif
heir-at-law (*hèeu*-reut-loo) *n* héritier *m* légitime
heiress (*hèeu*-resse) *n* héritière *f*
helicopter (*hè*-li-kop-teu) *n* hélicoptère *m*
hell (hèl) *n* enfer *m*
hello! (hè-*lôou*) bonjour!
helm (hèlm) *n* barre *f*
helmet (*hèl*-mit) *n* casque *m*
help (hèlp) *v* aider; *n* aide *f*
helper (*hèl*-peu) *n* aide *m*/*f*
helpful (*hèlp*-feul) *adj* serviable
helping (*hèl*-pinng) *n* portion *f*
hem (hèm) *n* ourlet *m*
hemp (hèmp) *n* chanvre *m*
hen (hèn) *n* poule *f*
her (heû) *pron* la *art*/*pron*, lui; *adj* son
herb (heûb) *n* herbe *f*
herd (heûd) *n* troupeau *m*
here (hi^eu^) *adv* ici; ~ **you are** voilà
hereditary (hi-*rè*-di-teu-ri) *adj* héréditaire
hernia (*heû*-ni-eu) *n* hernie *f*
hero (*hieu*-rô^ou^) *n* (pl ~es) héros *m*
heron (*hè*-reunn) *n* héron *m*
herring (*hè*-rinng) *n* (pl ~, ~s) hareng *m*
herself (heû-*sèlf*) *pron* se; elle-même
hesitate (*hè*-zi-téït) *v* hésiter
heterosexual (hè-teu-reu-*sèk*-chou-eul) *adj* hétérosexuel
hiccup (*hi*-kap) *n* hoquet *m*
hide (haïd) *n* peau *f*
***hide** (haïd) *v* cacher; dissimuler
hideous (*hi*-di-euss) *adj* hideux
hierarchy (*haïeu*-rââ-ki) *n* hiérarchie *f*
high (haï) *adj* haut
highway (*haï*-^ou^éï) *n* route nationale; *nAm* autoroute *f*
hijack (*haï*-djæk) *v* détourner
hike (haïk) *v* faire des randonnées
hill (hil) *n* colline *f*
hillock (*hi*-leuk) *n* monticule *m*
hillside (*hil*-saïd) *n* coteau *m*
hilltop (*hil*-top) *n* sommet de colline
hilly (*hi*-li) *adj* accidenté
him (himm) *pron* le, lui
himself (himm-*sèlf*) *pron* se; lui-même
hinder (*hinn*-deu) *v* gêner
hinge (hinndj) *n* charnière *f*

hint (hinnt) *n* allusion *f*; signe *m*; *v* suggérer; faire allusion (**at** à)
hip (hip) *n* hanche *f*
hire (haï^{eu}) *v* louer; **for ~** à louer
hire purchase (haï^{eu}-*peû*-tcheuss) *n* achat à tempérament
his (hiz) *adj* son
historian (hi-*stoo*-ri-eunn) *n* historien *m*, -ne *f*
historic (hi-*sto*-rik) *adj* historique
historical (hi-*sto*-ri-keul) *adj* historique
history (*hi*-steu-ri) *n* histoire *f*
hit (hit) *n* succès *m*
***hit** (hit) *v* frapper; toucher
hitchhike (*hitch*-haïk) *v* *faire de l'auto-stop
hitchhiker (*hitch*-haï-keu) *n* auto-stoppeur *m*, -se *f*
hoarse (hooss) *adj* rauque, enroué
hobby (*ho*-bi) *n* hobby *m*, passetemps *m*
hockey (*ho*-ki) *n* hockey *m*
hoist (hoïst) *v* hisser
hold (hô^{ou}ld) *n* cale *f*
***hold** (hô^{ou}ld) *v* *tenir; garder; **~ on** s'accrocher; **~ up** *soutenir
hold-up (*hôoul*-dap) *n* attaque *f*
hole (hô^{ou}l) *n* trou *m*
holiday (*ho*-leu-di) *n* vacances; jour de fête; **~ camp** camp de vacances; **on ~** en vacances
Holland (*ho*-leunnd) Hollande *f*
hollow (*ho*-lô^{ou}) *adj* creux
holy (*hôou*-li) *adj* sacré
homage (*ho*-midj) *n* hommage *m*
home (hô^{ou}m) *n* maison *f*, foyer *m*, demeure *f*; *adv* chez soi; **at ~** à la maison
home-made (hô^{ou}m-*méïd*) *adj* fait à la maison
homesickness (*hôoum*-sik-neuss) *n* mal du pays
homosexual (hô^{ou}-meu-*sèk*-chou-eul) *adj* homosexuel
honest (*o*-nist) *adj* honnête; sincère
honesty (*o*-ni-sti) *n* honnêteté *f*
honey (*ha*-ni) *n* miel *m*
honeymoon (*ha*-ni-moûn) *n* lune de miel
honk (hanngk) *vAm* klaxonner
hono(u)r (*o*-neu) *n* honneur *m*; *v* honorer, rendre hommage
hono(u)rable (*o*-neu-reu-beul) *adj* honorable; honnête
hood (houd) *n* capuchon *m*; *nAm* capot *m*
hoof (hoûf) *n* sabot *m*
hook (houk) *n* crochet *m*
hoot (hoût) *v* klaxonner
hooter (*hoû*-teu) *n* klaxon *m*
hoover (*hoû*-veu) *v* passer l'aspirateur
hop¹ (hop) *v* sautiller; *n* saut *m*
hop² (hop) *n* houblon *m*
hope (hô^{ou}p) *n* espoir *m*; *v* espérer
hopeful (*hôoup*-feul) *adj* plein d'espoir
hopeless (*hôoup*-leuss) *adj* désespéré
horizon (heu-*raï*-zeunn) *n* horizon *m*
horizontal (ho-ri-*zonn*-teul) *adj* horizontal
horn (hoon) *n* corne *f*, cor *m*; klaxon *m*
horrible (*ho*-ri-beul) *adj* horrible; terrifiant, atroce, horrifiant
horror (*ho*-reu) *n* épouvante *f*, horreur *f*
horse (hooss) *n* cheval *m*
horseman (*hooss*-meunn) *n* (pl -men) cavalier *m*
horsepower (*hooss*-paou^{eu}) *n* chevalvapeur *m*
horserace (*hooss*-réïss) *n* course de chevaux
horseradish (*hooss*-ræ-dich) *n* raifort *m*
horseshoe (*hooss*-choû) *n* fer à cheval
horticulture (*hoo*-ti-kal-tcheu) *n*

horticulture *f*
hospitable (*ho*-spi-teu-beul) *adj* hospitalier
hospital (*ho*-spi-teul) *n* hôpital *m*
hospitality (ho-spi-*tæ*-leu-ti) *n* hospitalité *f*
host (hô^{ou}st) *n* hôte *m*
hostage (*ho*-stidj) *n* otage *m*
hostel (*ho*-steul) *n* auberge *f*
hostess (*hôou*-stiss) *n* hôtesse *f*
hostile (*ho*-staïl) *adj* hostile
hot (hot) *adj* chaud
hotel (hô^{ou}-*tèl*) *n* hôtel *m*
hot-tempered (hot-*tèm*-peud) *adj* coléreux
hour (aou^{eu}) *n* heure *f*
hourly (*aoueu*-li) *adj* toutes les heures
house (haouss) *n* maison *f*; habitation *f*; immeuble *m*; ~ **agent** agent immobilier; ~ **block** *Am* pâté de maisons; **public** ~ café *m*
houseboat (*haouss*-bô^{ou}t) *n* maisonbateau
household (*haouss*-hô^{ou}ld) *n* ménage *m*
housekeeper (*haouss*-kii-peu) *n* gouvernante *f*
housekeeping (*haouss*-kii-pinng) *n* travaux ménagers, ménage *m*
housemaid (*haouss*-méïd) *n* bonne *f*
housewife (*haouss*-^{ou}aïf) *n* ménagère *f*
housework (*haouss*-^{ou}eûk) *n* travaux ménagers
how (haou) *adv* comment; que; ~ **many** combien; ~ **much** combien
however (haou-*è*-veu) *conj* pourtant, cependant
hug (hagh) *v* *étreindre; *n* étreinte *f*
huge (hyoûdj) *adj* immense, énorme
hum (hamm) *v* fredonner
human (*hyoû*-meunn) *adj* humain; ~ **being** être humain
humanity (hyou-*mæ*-neu-ti) *n* humanité *f*
humble (*hamm*-beul) *adj* humble
humid (*hyoû*-mid) *adj* humide
humidity (hyou-*mi*-deu-ti) *n* humidité *f*
humorous (*hyoû*-meu-reuss) *adj* comique, drôle
humour (*hyoû*-meu) *n* humour *m*
hundred (*hann*-dreud) *n* cent
Hungarian (hanng-*ghèeu*-ri-eunn) *adj* hongrois; *n* Hongrois *m*
Hungary (*hanng*-gheu-ri) Hongrie *f*
hunger (*hanng*-gheu) *n* faim *f*
hungry (*hanng*-ghri) *adj* affamé
hunt (hannt) *v* chasser; *n* chasse *f*; ~ **for** chercher
hunter (*hann*-teu) *n* chasseur *m*
hurricane (*ha*-ri-keunn) *n* ouragan *m*; ~ **lamp** lampe-tempête *f*
hurry (*ha*-ri) *v* se dépêcher, se presser; *n* hâte *f*; **in a** ~ en vitesse
***hurt** (heût) *v* *faire mal, blesser; offenser
hurtful (*heût*-feul) *adj* nuisible
husband (*haz*-beunnd) *n* époux *m*, mari *m*
hut (hat) *n* hutte *f*
hydrogen (*haï*-dreu-djeunn) *n* hydrogène *m*
hygiene (*haï*-djiin) *n* hygiène *f*
hygienic (haï-*djii*-nik) *adj* hygiénique
hymn (himm) *n* hymne *m*
hyphen (*haï*-feunn) *n* trait d'union
hypocrisy (hi-*po*-kreu-si) *n* hypocrisie *f*
hypocrite (*hi*-peu-krit) *n* hypocrite *m*
hypocritical (hi-peu-*kri*-ti-keul) *adj* hypocrite, fourbe
hysterical (hi-*stè*-ri-keul) *adj* hystérique

I

I (aï) *pron* je
ice (aïss) *n* glace *f*; ~ **bag** sac à glace; ~ **cream** crème glacée, glace *f*
Iceland (*aïss*-leunnd) Islande *f*
Icelander (*aïss*-leunn-deu) *n* Islandais *m*
Icelandic (aïss-*læn*-dik) *adj* islandais
icon (*aï*-konn) *n* icône *f*
idea (aï-*dieu*) *n* idée *f*, pensée *f*, notion *f*, concept *m*
ideal (aï-*dieul*) *adj* idéal; *n* idéal *m*
identical (aï-*dèn*-ti-keul) *adj* identique
identification (aï-dèn-ti-fi-*kéï*-cheunn) *n* identification *f*
identify (aï-*dèn*-ti-faï) *v* identifier
identity (aï-*dèn*-teu-ti) *n* identité *f*; ~ **card** carte d'identité
idiot (*i*-di-eut) *n* idiot *m*
idiotic (i-di-*o*-tik) *adj* idiot
idle (*aï*-deul) *adj* oisif; futile
idol (*aï*-deul) *n* idole *f*
if (if) *conj* si
ignition (igh-*ni*-cheunn) *n* allumage *m*; ~ **coil** bobine d'allumage
ignorant (*igh*-neu-reunnt) *adj* ignorant
ignore (igh-*noo*) *v* ignorer
ill (il) *adj* malade; mauvais; méchant
illegal (i-*lii*-gheul) *adj* illégal
illegible (i-*lè*-djeu-beul) *adj* illisible
illiterate (i-*li*-teu-reut) *n* illettré *m*
illness (*il*-neuss) *n* maladie *f*
illuminate (i-*loû*-mi-néït) *v* illuminer
illumination (i-loû-mi-*néï*-cheunn) *n* illumination *f*
illusion (i-*loû*-jeunn) *n* illusion *f*
illustrate (*i*-leu-stréït) *v* illustrer
illustration (i-leu-*stréï*-cheunn) *n* illustration *f*
image (*i*-midj) *n* image *f*
imaginary (i-*mæ*-dji-neu-ri) *adj* imaginaire
imagination (i-mæ-dji-*néï*-cheunn) *n* imagination *f*
imagine (i-*mæ*-djinn) *v* imaginer; s'imaginer; se figurer
imitate (*i*-mi-téït) *v* imiter
imitation (i-mi-*téï*-cheunn) *n* imitation *f*
immediate (i-*mii*-dyeut) *adj* immédiat
immediately (i-*mii*-dyeut-li) *adv* surle-champ, tout de suite, immédiatement
immense (i-*mèns*) *adj* immense, énorme
immigrant (*i*-mi-ghreunnt) *n* immigrant *m*
immigrate (*i*-mi-ghréït) *v* immigrer
immigration (i-mi-*ghréï*-cheunn) *n* immigration *f*
immodest (i-*mo*-dist) *adj* immodeste
immunity (i-*myoû*-neu-ti) *n* immunité *f*
immunize (*i*-myou-naïz) *v* immuniser
impartial (imm-*pââ*-cheul) *adj* impartial
impassable (imm-*pââ*-seu-beul) *adj* impraticable
impatient (imm-*péï*-cheunnt) *adj* impatient
impede (imm-*piid*) *v* entraver
impediment (imm-*pè*-di-meunnt) *n* entrave *f*
imperfect (imm-*peû*-fikt) *adj* imparfait
imperial (imm-*pi*^eu-ri-eul) *adj* impérial
impersonal (imm-*peû*-seu-neul) *adj* impersonnel
impertinence (imm-*peû*-ti-neunns) *n* impertinence *f*
impertinent (imm-*peû*-ti-neunnt) *adj* insolent, effronté, impertinent
implement[1] (*imm*-pli-meunnt) *n*

instrument *m*, outil *m*
implement² (*imm*-pli-mènt) *v* réaliser
imply (imm-*plaï*) *v* impliquer; comporter
impolite (imm-peu-*laït*) *adj* impoli
import¹ (imm-*poot*) *v* importer
import² (*imm*-poot) *n* importation *f*; **~ duty** taxe d'importation
importance (imm-*poo*-teunns) *n* importance *f*
important (imm-*poo*-teunnt) *adj* important
importer (imm-*poo*-teu) *n* importateur *m*
imposing (imm-*pôou*-zinng) *adj* imposant
impossible (imm-*po*-seu-beul) *adj* impossible
impotence (*imm*-peu-teunns) *n* impotence *f*
impotent (*imm*-peu-teunnt) *adj* impotent
impress (imm-*prèss*) *v* *faire impression sur, impressionner
impression (imm-*prè*-cheunn) *n* impression *f*
impressive (imm-*prè*-siv) *adj* impressionnant
imprison (imm-*pri*-zeunn) *v* emprisonner
imprisonment (imm-*pri*-zeunn-meunnt) *n* emprisonnement *m*
improbable (imm-*pro*-beu-beul) *adj* improbable
improper (imm-*pro*-peu) *adj* impropre
improve (imm-*proûv*) *v* améliorer
improvement (imm-*proûv*-meunnt) *n* amélioration *f*
improvise (*imm*-preu-vaïz) *v* improviser
impudent (imm-pyou-deunnt) *adj* insolent
impulse (*imm*-pals) *n* impulsion *f*; stimulant *m*
impulsive (imm-*pal*-siv) *adj* impulsif
in (inn) *prep* en; dans, sur; *adv* dedans
inaccessible (i-næk-*sè*-seu-beul) *adj* inaccessible
inaccurate (i-*næ*-kyou-reut) *adj* incorrect
inadequate (i-*næ*-di-k^ou^eut) *adj* inadéquat
incapable (inng-*kéï*-peu-beul) *adj* incapable
incense (*inn*-sèns) *n* encens *m*
inch (inntch) *n* pouce *m*; pas *m*; **by inches** peu à peu, petit à petit; **within an ~ of** àdeux doigts de; **inch one's way** avancer petit à petit
incident (*inn*-si-deunnt) *n* incident *m*
incidental (inn-si-*dèn*-teul) *adj* fortuit
incite (inn-*saït*) *v* inciter
inclination (inng-kli-*néï*-cheunn) *n* penchant *m*
incline (inng-*klaïn*) *n* pente *f*
inclined (inng-*klaïnd*) *adj* disposé, enclin; ***be ~ to** *v* *avoir tendance
include (inng-*kloûd*) *v* *comprendre, *inclure
inclusive (inng-*kloû*-siv) *adj* compris
income (*inng*-keumm) *n* revenu *m*; **~ tax** impôt sur le revenu
incompetent (inng-*komm*-peu-teunnt) *adj* incompétent
incomplete (inn-keumm-*pliit*) *adj* incomplet
inconceivable (inng-keunn-*sii*-veu-beul) *adj* inconcevable
inconspicuous (inng-keunn-*spi*-kyou-euss) *adj* qui passe inaperçu; discret
inconvenience (inng-keunn-*vii*-nyeunns) *n* désagrément *m*, inconvénient *m*
inconvenient (inng-keunn-*vii*-nyeunnt) *adj* inopportun; gênant
incorrect (inng-keu-*rèkt*) *adj* incorrect

increase[1] (inng-*kriiss*) *v* augmenter; s'accumuler, *croître
increase[2] (*inng*-kriiss) *n* augmentation *f*; relèvement *m*
incredible (inng-*krè*-deu-beul) *adj* incroyable
incurable (inng-*kyoueu*-reu-beul) *adj* incurable
indecent (inn-*dii*-seunnt) *adj* indécent
indeed (inn-*diid*) *adv* en effet
indefinite (inn-*dè*-fi-nit) *adj* indéfini
indemnity (inn-*dèm*-neu-ti) *n* dédommagement *m*, indemnité *f*
independence (inn-di-*pèn*-deunns) *n* indépendance *f*
independent (inn-di-*pèn*-deunnt) *adj* indépendant; autonome
index (*inn*-dèks) *n* index *m*; ~ **finger** index *m*
India (*inn*-di-eu) Inde *f*
Indian (*inn*-di-eunn) *adj* indien; *n* Indien *m*
indicate (*inn*-di-kéït) *v* signaler, indiquer
indication (inn-di-*kéï*-cheunn) *n* signe *m*, indication *f*
indicator (*inn*-di-kéï-teu) *n* clignotant *m*
indifferent (inn-*di*-feu-reunnt) *adj* indifférent
indigestion (inn-di-*djèss*-tcheunn) *n* indigestion *f*
indignation (inn-digh-*néï*-cheunn) *n* indignation *f*
indirect (inn-di-*rèkt*) *adj* indirect
individual (inn-di-*vi*-djou-eul) *adj* particulier, individuel; *n* individu *m*
Indonesia (inn-deu-*nii*-zi-eu) Indonésie *f*
Indonesian (inn-deu-*nii*-zi-eunn) *adj* indonésien; *n* Indonésien *m*
indoor (*inn*-doo) *adj* intérieur
indoors (inn-*dooz*) *adv* à l'intérieur
indulge (inn-*daldj*) *v* céder
industrial (inn-*da*-stri-eul) *adj* industriel; ~ **area** zone industrielle
industrious (inn-*da*-stri-euss) *adj* industrieux
industry (*inn*-deu-stri) *n* industrie *f*
inedible (i-*nè*-di-beul) *adj* immangeable
inefficient (i-ni-*fi*-cheunnt) *adj* inefficace
inevitable (i-*nè*-vi-teu-beul) *adj* inévitable
inexpensive (i-nik-*spèn*-siv) *adj* bon marché
inexperienced (i-nik-*spieu*-ri-eunnst) *adj* inexpérimenté
infant (*inn*-feunnt) *n* nourrisson *m*
infantry (*inn*-feunn-tri) *n* infanterie *f*
infect (inn-*fèkt*) *v* infecter
infection (inn-*fèk*-cheunn) *n* infection *f*
infectious (inn-*fèk*-cheuss) *adj* infectieux
infer (inn-*feû*) *v* *déduire
inferior (inn-*fieu*-ri-eu) *adj* moindre, inférieur
infinite (*inn*-fi-neut) *adj* infini
infinitive (inn-*fi*-ni-tiv) *n* infinitif *m*
inflammable (inn-*flæ*-meu-beul) *adj* inflammable
inflammation (inn-fleu-*méï*-cheunn) *n* inflammation *f*
inflatable (inn-*fléï*-teu-beul) *adj* gonflable
inflate (inn-*fléït*) *v* gonfler
inflation (inn-*fléï*-cheunn) *n* inflation *f*
inflict (inn-*flikt*) *v* infliger (**on** à)
influence (*inn*-flou-eunns) *n* influence *f*; *v* influencer
influential (inn-flou-*èn*-cheul) *adj* influent
influenza (inn-flou-*èn*-zeu) *n* grippe *f*
inform (inn-*foom*) *v* informer; *mettre au courant, communiquer
informal (inn-*foo*-meul) *adj* sans

cérémonie
information (inn-feu-*méï*-cheunn) *n* information *f*; renseignement *m*, communication *f*; ~ **office** bureau des renseignements
infra-red (inn-freu-*rèd*) *adj* infrarouge
infrequent (inn-*frii*-k^{ou}eunnt) *adj* peu fréquent
ingredient (inng-*ghrii*-di-eunnt) *n* ingrédient *m*
inhabit (inn-*hæ*-bit) *v* habiter
inhabitable (inn-*hæ*-bi-teu-beul) *adj* habitable
inhabitant (inn-*hæ*-bi-teunnt) *n* habitant *m*
inhale (inn-*héïl*) *v* inhaler
inherit (inn-*hè*-rit) *v* hériter
inheritance (inn-*hè*-ri-teunns) *n* héritage *m*
inhibit (inn-*hi*-bit) *v* empêcher; inhiber
initial (i-*ni*-cheul) *adj* initial; *n* initiale *f*; *v* parapher
initiate (i-*ni*-chi-éït) *v* lancer, entreprendre; inaugurer; ~ **into** initier à
initiative (i-*ni*-cheu-tiv) *n* initiative *f*
inject (inn-*djèkt*) *v* injecter
injection (inn-*djèk*-cheunn) *n* injection *f*
injure (*inn*-djeu) *v* blesser; offenser
injury (*inn*-djeu-ri) *n* blessure *f*; lésion *f*
injustice (inn-*dja*-stiss) *n* injustice *f*
ink (inngk) *n* encre *f*
inlet (*inn*-lèt) *n* crique *f*
inn (inn) *n* auberge *f*
inner (*i*-neu) *adj* intérieur; ~ **tube** chambre à air
innocence (*i*-neu-seunns) *n* innocence *f*
innocent (*i*-neu-seunnt) *adj* innocent
inoculate (i-*no*-kyou-léït) *v* inoculer
inquire (inng-*kouaïeu*) *v* se renseigner, s'informer
inquiry (inng-*kouaïeu*-ri) *n* question *f*, enquête *f*; ~ **office** bureau de renseignements
inquisitive (inng-*koui*-zeu-tiv) *adj* curieux
insane (inn-*séïn*) *adj* fou
inscription (inn-*skrip*-cheunn) *n* inscription *f*
insect (*inn*-sèkt) *n* insecte *m*; ~ **repellent** insectifuge *m*
insecticide (inn-*sèk*-ti-saïd) *n* insecticide *m*
insensitive (inn-*sèn*-seu-tiv) *adj* insensible
insert (inn-*seût*) *v* insérer
inside (inn-*saïd*) *n* intérieur *m*; *adj* intérieur; *adv* à l'intérieur; dedans; *prep* dans, à l'intérieur de; ~ **out** à l'envers; **insides** ventre *m*
insight (*inn*-saït) *n* compréhension *f*
insignificant (inn-sigh-*ni*-fi-keunnt) *adj* insignifiant; sans importance; futile
insist (inn-*sist*) *v* insister; persister
insolence (*inn*-seu-leunns) *n* insolence *f*
insolent (*inn*-seu-leunnt) *adj* insolent
insomnia (inn-*somm*-ni-eu) *n* insomnie *f*
inspect (inn-*spèkt*) *v* inspecter
inspection (inn-*spèk*-cheunn) *n* inspection *f*; contrôle *m*
inspector (inn-*spèk*-teu) *n* inspecteur *m*, -trice *f*
inspire (inn-*spaïeu*) *v* inspirer
insta(l)l (inn-*stool*) *v* installer
installation (inn-steu-*léï*-cheunn) *n* installation *f*
instal(l)ment (inn-*stool*-meunnt) *n* versement partiel; **payment by instalments** paiement échelonné
instance (*inn*-steunns) *n* exemple *m*; cas *m*; **for** ~ par exemple

instant (*inn*-steunnt) *n* instant *m*
instantly (*inn*-steunnt-li) *adv* instantanément, tout de suite, immédiatement
instead of (inn-*stèd* ov) au lieu de
instinct (*inn*-stinngkt) *n* instinct *m*
institute (*inn*-sti-tyoût) *n* institut *m*; institution *f*; *v* instituer
institution (inn-sti-*tyoû*-cheunn) *n* institution *f*
instruct (inn-*strakt*) *v* *instruire
instruction (inn-*strak*-cheunn) *n* instruction *f*
instructive (inn-*strak*-tiv) *adj* instructif
instructor (inn-*strak*-teu) *n* instructeur *m*
instrument (*inn*-strou-meunnt) *n* instrument *m*; **musical ~** instrument de musique
insufficient (*inn*-seu-*fi*-cheunnt) *adj* insuffisant
insulate (*inn*-syou-léït) *v* isoler
insulation (inn-syou-*léï*-cheunn) *n* isolation *f*
insulator (*inn*-syou-léï-teu) *n* isolateur *m*
insult[1] (inn-*salt*) *v* insulter
insult[2] (*inn*-salt) *n* insulte *f*
insurance (inn-*choueu*-reunns) *n* assurance *f*; **~ policy** police d'assurance
insure (inn-*choueu*) *v* assurer
intact (inn-*tækt*) *adj* intact
integrate (*inn*-ti-ghréït) *v* (s')intégrer
intellect (*inn*-teu-lèkt) *n* intellect *m*, intelligence *f*
intellectual (inn-teu-*lèk*-tchou-eul) *adj* intellectuel
intelligence (inn-*tè*-li-djeunns) *n* intelligence *f*
intelligent (inn-*tè*-li-djeunnt) *adj* intelligent
intend (inn-*tènd*) *v* *avoir l'intention de
intense (inn-*tèns*) *adj* intense; vif
intensify (inn-*tèn*-si-faï) *v* (s')intensifier
intention (inn-*tèn*-cheunn) *n* intention *f*
intentional (inn-*tèn*-cheu-neul) *adj* intentionnel
intercourse (*inn*-teu-kooss) *n* rapports *mpl*
interest (*inn*-treust) *n* intérêt *m*; *v* intéresser
interesting (*inn*-treu-stinng) *adj* intéressant
interfere (inn-teu-*fieu*) *v* *intervenir; **~ with** se mêler de
interference (inn-teu-*fieu*-reunns) *n* ingérence *f*
interim (*inn*-teu-rimm) *n* intérim *m*
interior (inn-*tieu*-ri-eu) *n* intérieur *m*
interlude (*inn*-teu-loûd) *n* interlude *m*
intermediary (inn-teu-*mii*-dyeu-ri) *n* intermédiaire *m/f*
intermission (inn-teu-*mi*-cheunn) *n* entracte *m*
internal (inn-*teû*-neul) *adj* intérieur, interne
international (inn-teu-*næ*-cheu-neul) *adj* international
interpret (inn-*teû*-prit) *v* interpréter
interpreter (inn-*teû*-pri-teu) *n* interprète *m/f*
interrogate (inn-*tè*-reu-ghéït) *v* interroger
interrogation (inn-tè-reu-*ghéï*-cheunn) *n* interrogatoire *m*
interrogative (inn-teu-*ro*-gheu-tiv) *adj* interrogatif
interrupt (inn-teu-*rapt*) *v* *interrompre
interruption (inn-teu-*rap*-cheunn) *n* interruption *f*
intersection (inn-teu-*sèk*-cheunn) *n* intersection *f*

interval (*inn*-teu-veul) *n* entracte *m*; intervalle *m*
intervene (inn-teu-*viin*) *v* *intervenir
interview (*inn*-teu-vyoû) *n* entrevue *f*, interview *f*
intestine (inn-*tè*-stinn) *n* intestin *m*
intimate (*inn*-ti-meut) *adj* intime
into (*inn*-tou) *prep* dans
intolerable (inn-*to*-leu-reu-beul) *adj* intolérable
intoxicated (inn-*tok*-si-kéï-tid) *adj* ivre
intrigue (inn-*triigh*) *n* intrigue *f*
introduce (inn-treu-*dyoûss*) *v* présenter; *introduire
introduction (inn-treu-*dak*-cheunn) *n* présentation *f*; introduction *f*
invade (inn-*véïd*) *v* envahir
invalid[1] (*inn*-veu-liid) *n* infirme *m*; *adj* infirme
invalid[2] (inn-*vœ*-lid) *adj* nul
invasion (inn-*véï*-jeunn) *n* invasion *f*
invent (inn-*vènt*) *v* inventer
invention (inn-*vèn*-cheunn) *n* invention *f*
inventive (inn-*vèn*-tiv) *adj* inventif
inventor (inn-*vèn*-teu) *n* inventeur *m*
inventory (*inn*-veunn-tri) *n* inventaire *m*
invert (inn-*veût*) *v* intervertir
invest (inn-*vèst*) *v* investir; placer
investigate (inn-*vè*-sti-ghéït) *v* enquêter
investigation (inn-vè-sti-*ghéï*-cheunn) *n* investigation *f*
investment (inn-*vèst*-meunnt) *n* investissement *m*; placement *m*
investor (inn-*vè*-steu) *n* investisseur *m*
invisible (inn-*vi*-zeu-beul) *adj* invisible
invitation (inn-vi-*téï*-cheunn) *n* invitation *f*
invite (inn-*vaït*) *v* inviter
invoice (*inn*-voïss) *n* facture *f*
involve (inn-*volv*) *v* impliquer
inwards (*inn*-^{ou}eudz) *adv* vers l'intérieur
iodine (*aï*-eu-diin) *n* iode *m*
Iran (i-*râân*) Iran *m*
Iranian (i-*réï*-ni-eunn) *adj* iranien; *n* Iranien *m*
Iraq (i-*rââk*) Irak *m*
Iraqi (i-*rââ*-ki) *adj* irakien; *n* Irakien *m*
Ireland (*aïeu*-leunnd) Irlande *f*
Irish (*aïeu*-rich) *adj* irlandais
iron (*aï*-eunn) *n* fer *m*; fer à repasser; en fer; *v* repasser
ironical (aï-*ro*-ni-keul) *adj* ironique
irony (*aïeu*-reu-ni) *n* ironie *f*
irregular (i-*rè*-ghyou-leu) *adj* irrégulier
irreparable (i-*rè*-peu-reu-beul) *adj* irréparable
irrevocable (i-*rè*-veu-keu-beul) *adj* irrévocable
irritable (*i*-ri-teu-beul) *adj* irritable
irritate (*i*-ri-téït) *v* agacer, irriter
is (iz) *v* (pr be)
island (*aï*-leunnd) *n* île *f*
isolate (*aï*-seu-léït) *v* isoler
isolation (aï-seu-*léï*-cheunn) *n* isolement *m*; isolation *f*
Israel (*iz*-réïl) Israël *m*
Israeli (iz-*réï*-li) *adj* israélien; *n* Israélien *m*
issue (*i*-choû) *v* distribuer; *n* émission *f*, tirage *m*, édition *f*; question *f*, sujet *m*; issue *f*, résultat *m*, conclusion *f*, fin *f*
it (it) *pron* le
Italian (i-*tœl*-yeunn) *adj* italien; *n* Italien *m*
Italy (*i*-teu-li) Italie *f*
itch (itch) *n* démangeaison *f*; *v* démanger
item (*aï*-teumm) *n* article *m*; point *m*
its (its) *adj* son, sa; ses
itself (it-*sèlf*) lui-même, elle-même;

se, soi; **by ~** à part; tout seul; **in ~** en lui-même ; en soi, de soi; **of ~** tout seul; de lui-même, d'elle-même
itinerary (aï-*ti*-neu-reu-ri) *n* itinéraire *m*
ivory (*aï*-veu-ri) *n* ivoire *m*
ivy (*aï*-vi) *n* lierre *m*

J

jack (djæk) *n* cric *m*
jacket (*djæ*-kit) *n* veste *f*, veston *m*; jaquette *f*
jade (djéïd) *n* jade *m*
jail (djéïl) *n* prison *f*
jam (djæm) *n* confiture *f*; embouteillage *m*
janitor (*djæ*-ni-teu) *n* concierge *m*
January (*djæ*-nyou-eu-ri) janvier
Japan (djeu-*pæn*) Japon *m*
Japanese (djæ-peu-*niiz*) *adj* japonais; *n* Japonais *m*
jar (djââ) *n* jarre *f*
jaundice (*djoon*-diss) *n* jaunisse *f*
jaw (djoo) *n* mâchoire *f*
jealous (*djè*-leuss) *adj* jaloux
jealousy (*djè*-leu-si) *n* jalousie *f*
jeans (djiinz) *pl* blue-jean *m*
jelly (*djè*-li) *n* gelée *f*
jellyfish (*djè*-li-fich) *n* méduse *f*
jersey (*djeû*-zi) *n* jersey *m*; chandail *m*
jet (djèt) *n* jet *m*; avion à réaction
jetty (*djè*-ti) *n* jetée *f*
Jew (djoû) *n* juif *m*, juive *f*
jewel (*djoû*-eul) *n* bijou *m*
jewel(l)er (*djoû*-eu-leu) *n* bijoutier *m*
jewellery, *Am* **jewelry** (*djoû*-eul-ri) *n* bijoux; joaillerie *f*
Jewish (*djoû*-ich) *adj* juif
job (djob) *n* boulot *m*; emploi *m*, travail *m*
jobless (*djob*-lèss) *adj* sans travail
jockey (*djo*-ki) *n* jockey *m*
join (djoïn) *v* *joindre; s'affilier à, adhérer à; assembler, réunir
joint (djoïnt) *n* articulation *f* *adj* uni, conjoint
jointly (*djoïnt*-li) *adv* conjointement
joke (djô[ou]k) *n* blague *f*, plaisanterie *f*
jolly (*djo*-li) *adj* gai
Jordan (*djoo*-deunn) Jordanie *f*
Jordanian (djoo-*déï*-ni-eunn) *adj* jordanien; *n* Jordanien *m*
journal (*djeû*-neul) *n* périodique *m*
journalism (*djeû*-neu-li-zeumm) *n* journalisme *m*
journalist (*djeû*-neu-list) *n* journaliste *m/f*
journey (*djeû*-ni) *n* voyage *m*
joy (djoï) *n* plaisir *m*, joie *f*
joyful (*djoï*-feul) *adj* joyeux
jubilee (*djoû*-bi-lii) *n* anniversaire *m*
judge (djadj) *n* juge *m*; *v* juger; apprécier
judgment (*djadj*-meunnt) *n* jugement *m*
jug (djagh) *n* cruche *f*
Jugoslav (yoû-gheu-*slââv*) *adj* yougoslave; *n* Yougoslave *m*
Jugoslavia (yoû-gheu-*slââ*-vi-eu) Yougoslavie *f*
juice (djoûss) *n* jus *m*
juicy (*djoû*-si) *adj* juteux
July (djou-*laï*) juillet
jump (djammp) *v* sauter; *n* bond *m*, saut *m*
jumper (*djamm*-peu) *n* chandail *m*, pull *m*; *Am* robe à bretelles

junction (*djanngk*-cheunn) *n* carrefour *m*; jonction *f*
June (djoûn) juin
jungle (*djanng*-gheul) *n* jungle *f*
junior (*djoû*-nyeu) *adj* cadet
junk (djanngk) *n* rebut *m*
jury (*djoueu*-ri) *n* jury *m*
just (djast) *adj* légitime, juste; exact; *adv* à peine; juste
justice (*dja*-stiss) *n* droit *m*; justice *f*
justify (*dja*-sti-faï) *v* justifier
juvenile (*djoû*-veu-naïl) *adj* juvénile

K

kangaroo (kæng-gheu-*roû*) *n* kangourou *m*
keel (kiil) *n* quille *f*
keen (kiin) *adj* passionné; aigu
***keep** (kiip) *v* *tenir; garder; continuer; ~ **away from** se *tenir éloigné de; ~ **off** ne pas toucher; ~ **on** continuer; ~ **quiet** se *taire; ~ **up** persévérer; ~ **up with** *être à la hauteur de
kennel (*kè*-neul) *n* chenil *m*
Kenya (*kè*-nyeu) Kenya *m*
kerosene (*kè*-reu-siin) *n* pétrole *m*
kettle (*kè*-teul) *n* bouilloire *f*
key (kii) *n* clé *f*
keyboard (*kii*-bood) *n* clavier *m*
keyhole (*kii*-hô^{ou}l) *n* trou de la serrure
khaki (*kââ*-ki) *n* kaki *m*
kick (kik) *v* donner des coups de pied; *n* coup de pied
kickoff (ki-*kof*) *n* coup d'envoi
kid (kid) *n* enfant *m*, gosse *m*; chevreau *m*; *v* taquiner
kidney (*kid*-ni) *n* rein *m*
kill (kil) *v* tuer
kilogram (*ki*-leu-ghræm) *n* kilo *m*
kilometer *Am*, **kilometre** (*ki*-leu-mii-teu) *n* kilomètre *m*
kind (kaïnd) *adj* gentil, aimable; bon; *n* genre *m*
kindergarten (*kinn*-deu-ghââ-teunn) *n* école maternelle
king (kinng) *n* roi *m*
kingdom (*kinng*-deumm) *n* royaume *m*
kiosk (*kii*-osk) *n* kiosque *m*
kiss (kiss) *n* baiser *m*; *v* embrasser
kit (kit) *n* trousseau *m*
kitchen (*ki*-tchinn) *n* cuisine *f*; ~ **garden** jardin potager, ~ **towel** torchon *m*
knapsack (*næp*-sæk) *n* havresac *m*
knave (néïv) *n* valet *m*
knee (nii) *n* genou *m*
kneecap (*nii*-kæp) *n* rotule *f*
***kneel** (niil) *v* s'agenouiller
knew (nyoû) *v* (p know)
knife (naïf) *n* (pl knives) couteau *m*
knight (naït) *n* chevalier *m*
***knit** (nit) *v* tricoter
knob (nob) *n* bouton *m*
knock (nok) *v* frapper; *n* coup *m*; ~ **against** cogner contre; ~ **down** renverser
knot (not) *n* nœud *m*; *v* nouer
***know** (nô^{ou}) *v* *savoir, *connaître
knowledge (*no*-lidj) *n* connaissance *f*
knuckle (*na*-keul) *n* jointure *f*

L

label (*lêï*-beul) *n* étiquette *f*; *v* étiqueter
laboratory (leu-*bo*-reu-teu-ri) *n* laboratoire *m*
labo(u)r (*lêï*-beu) *n* travail *m*, labeur *m*; douleurs; *v* bûcher, peiner; **labor permit** *Am* permis de travail
labo(u)rer (*lêï*-beu-reu) *n* travailleur *m*, travailleuse *f*
labo(u)r-saving (*lêï*-beu-séï-vinng) *adj* qui économise du travail
labyrinth (*læ*-beu-rinnθ) *n* labyrinthe *m*
lace (léïss) *n* dentelle *f*; lacet *m*
lack (læk) *n* manque *m*; *v* manquer
lacquer (*læ*-keu) *n* vernis *m*
lad (læd) *n* garçon *m*
ladder (*læ*-deu) *n* échelle *f*
lady (*lêï*-di) *n* dame *f*; **ladies' room** toilettes pour dames
lagoon (leu-*ghoûn*) *n* lagune *f*
lake (léïk) *n* lac *m*
lamb (læm) *n* agneau *m*
lame (léïm) *adj* paralysé, boiteux
lamentable (*læ*-meunn-teu-beul) *adj* lamentable
lamp (læmp) *n* lampe *f*
lamppost (*læmp*-pô^{ou}st) *n* lampadaire *m*
lampshade (*læmp*-chéïd) *n* abat-jour *m*
land (lænd) *n* pays *m*, terre *f*; *v* atterrir; débarquer
landlady (*lænd*-léï-di) *n* logeuse *f*
landlord (*lænd*-lood) *n* propriétaire *m*; logeur *m*
landmark (*lænd*-mââk) *n* point de repère
landscape (*lænd*-skéïp) *n* paysage *m*
lane (léïn) *n* ruelle *f*, chemin *m*; voie *f*
language (*læng*-gh^{ou}idj) *n* langue *f*; **~ laboratory** laboratoire de langues
lantern (*læn*-teunn) *n* lanterne *f*
lap (læp) *n* pan *m*; tour *m* (de piste); *v* laper; envelopper (**in** de); clapoter; **~ of hono(u)r** tour *m* d'honneur; **in** (*or* **on**) **someone's ~** sur les genoux de quelqu'un
lapel (leu-*pèl*) *n* revers *m*
large (lââdj) *adj* vaste; spacieux
largely (*lââdj*-li) *adv* en grande partie
lark (lââk) *n* alouette *f*
laryngitis (læ-rinn-*djaï*-tiss) *n* laryngite *f*
last (lââst) *adj* dernier; précédent; *v* durer; **at ~** enfin; en fin de compte
lasting (*lââ*-stinng) *adj* durable
latchkey (*lætch*-kii) *n* clé de la maison
late (léït) *adj* tard; en retard
lately (*léït*-li) *adv* ces derniers temps, dernièrement, récemment
lather (*lââ*-ðeu) *n* écume *f*
Latin America (*læ*-tinn eu-*mè*-ri-keu) Amérique latine
Latin-American (læ-tinn-eu-*mè*-ri-keunn) *adj* sud-américain
latitude (*læ*-ti-tyoûd) *n* latitude *f*
laugh (lââf) *v* *rire; *n* rire *m*
laughter (*lââf*-teu) *n* rire *m*
launch (loontch) *v* lancer; *n* bateau à moteur
launching (*loon*-tchinng) *n* lancement *m*
launderette (loon-deu-*rèt*) *n* laverie automatique
laundry (*loon*-dri) *n* blanchisserie *f*; lessive *f*
lavatory (*læ*-veu-teu-ri) *n* cabinet *m*
lavish (*læ*-vich) *adj* prodigue
law (loo) *n* loi *f*; droit *m*; **~ court** tribunal *m*
lawful (*loo*-feul) *adj* légal
lawn (loon) *n* gazon *m*, pelouse *f*
lawsuit (*loo*-soût) *n* procès *m*

lawyer (*loo*-yeu) *n* avocat *m*; juriste *m*
laxative (*læk*-seu-tiv) *n* laxatif *m*
***lay** (léï) *v* placer, poser; ~ **bricks** maçonner
layer (léï^{eu}) *n* couche *f*
layman (*léï*-meunn) *n* profane *m*
lazy (*léï*-zi) *adj* paresseux
lead[1] (liid) *n* avance *f*; conduite *f*; laisse *f*
lead[2] (lèd) *n* plomb *m*
***lead** (liid) *v* diriger
leader (*lii*-deu) *n* leader *m*, dirigeant *m*
leadership (*lii*-deu-chip) *n* direction *f*
leading (*lii*-dinng) *adj* dominant, principal
leaf (liif) *n* (pl leaves) feuille *f*
league (liigh) *n* ligue *f*
leak (liik) *v* *fuir; *n* fuite *f*
leaky (*lii*-ki) *adj* ayant une fuite
lean (liin) *adj* maigre
***lean** (liin) *v* s'appuyer
leap (liip) *n* saut *m*
***leap** (liip) *v* bondir
leap year (*liip*-yi^{eu}) *n* année bissextile
***learn** (leûnn) *v* *apprendre
learner (*leû*-neu) *n* débutant *m*
lease (liiss) *n* location *f*; bail *m*; *v* donner en location, louer
leash (liich) *n* laisse *f*
least (liist) *adj* moindre; **at** ~ au moins
leather (*lè*-ðeu) *n* cuir *m*; en cuir
leave (liiv) *n* permission *f*
***leave** (liiv) *v* *partir, quitter; laisser; ~ **out** *omettre
Lebanese (lè-beu-*niiz*) *adj* libanais; *n* Libanais *m*
Lebanon (*lè*-beu-neunn) Liban *m*
lecture (*lèk*-tcheu) *n* cours *m*, conférence *f*
left[1] (lèft) *adj* gauche
left[2] (lèft) *v* (p, pp leave)
left-hand (*lèft*-hænd) *adj* à gauche, de gauche
left-handed (lèft-*hæn*-did) *adj* gaucher
leg (lègh) *n* pied *m*, jambe *f*
legacy (*lè*-gheu-si) *n* legs *m*
legal (*lii*-gheul) *adj* légitime, légal; juridique
legible (*lè*-dji-beul) *adj* lisible
legitimate (li-*dji*-ti-meut) *adj* légitime
leisure (*lè*-jeu) *n* loisir *m*; aise *f*
lemon (*lè*-meunn) *n* citron *m*
lemonade (lè-meu-*néïd*) *n* limonade *f*
***lend** (lènd) *v* prêter
length (lèngθ) *n* longueur *f*
lengthen (*lèng*-θeunn) *v* allonger
lengthways (*lèngθ*-^{ou}éïz) *adv* en long
lens (lènz) *n* lentille *f*; **telephoto** ~ télé-objectif *m*; **zoom** ~ zoom *m*
leprosy (*lè*-preu-si) *n* lèpre *f*
less (lèss) *adv* moins
lessen (*lè*-seunn) *v* diminuer
lesson (*lè*-seunn) *n* leçon *f*
***let** (lèt) *v* laisser; louer; ~ **down** *décevoir
letter (*lè*-teu) *n* lettre *f*; ~ **of credit** lettre de crédit; ~ **of recommendation** lettre de recommandation; ~ **opener** coupe-papier *m*
letterbox (*lè*-teu-boks) *n* boîte aux lettres
lettuce (*lè*-tiss) *n* laitue *f*
level (*lè*-veul) *adj* égal; plat, plan; *n* niveau *m*; *v* égaliser, niveler; ~ **crossing** passage à niveau
lever (*lii*-veu) *n* levier *m*
liability (laï-eu-*bi*-leu-ti) *n* responsabilité *f*
liable (*laï*-eu-beul) *adj* responsable; ~ **to** sujet à
liar (*laï*-eu) *n* menteur *m*, menteuse *f*
liberal (*li*-beu-reul) *adj* libéral; généreux, large
liberation (li-beu-*réï*-cheunn) *n* libération *f*

Liberia (laï-*bieu*-ri-eu) Libéria *m*
Liberian (laï-*bieu*-ri-eunn) *adj* libérien; *n* Libérien *m*
liberty (*li*-beu-ti) *n* liberté *f*
library (*laï*-breu-ri) *n* bibliothèque *f*
licence (*laï*-seunns) *n* licence *f*; permis *m*; **driving ~** permis de conduire
license (*laï*-seunns) *v* autoriser; *nAm* licence *f*; permis *m*; **driver's ~** permis de conduire; **~ number** numéro d'immatriculation; **~ plate** plaque d'immatriculation
lick (lik) *v* lécher
lid (lid) *n* couvercle *m*
lie (laï) *v* *mentir; *n* mensonge *m*
***lie** (laï) *v* *être couché; **~ down** se coucher
life (laïf) *n* (pl lives) vie *f*; **~ insurance** assurance-vie *f*
lifebelt (*laïf*-bèlt) *n* bouée de sauvetage
lifetime (*laïf*-taïm) *n* vie *f*
lift (lift) *v* soulever, lever; *n* ascenseur *m*
light (laït) *n* lumière *f*; *adj* léger; clair; **~ bulb** ampoule *f*
***light** (laït) *v* allumer
lighter (*laï*-teu) *n* briquet *m*
lighthouse (*laït*-haouss) *n* phare *m*
lighting (*laï*-tinng) *n* éclairage *m*
lightning (*laït*-ninng) *n* éclair *m*
like (laïk) *v* aimer; bien aimer; *adj* pareil; *conj* comme
likely (*laï*-kli) *adj* probable
like-minded (laïk-*maïn*-did) *adj* de même opinion
likewise (*laïk*-^{ou}aïz) *adv* de la même manière, également
lily (*li*-li) *n* lis *m*
limb (limm) *n* membre *m*
lime (laïm) *n* chaux *f*; tilleul *m*; limette *f*
limetree (*laïm*-trii) *n* tilleul *m*
limit (*li*-mit) *n* limite *f*; *v* limiter
limp (limmp) *v* boiter; *adj* flasque
line (laïn) *n* ligne *f*; trait *m*; fil *m*; rangée *f*; **stand in ~** *Am* *faire la queue
linen (*li*-ninn) *n* toile *f*; linge *m*
liner (*laï*-neu) *n* paquebot *m*
lining (*laï*-ninng) *n* doublure *f*
link (linngk) *v* relier; *n* lien *m*; maillon *m*
lion (*laï*-eunn) *n* lion *m*
lip (lip) *n* lèvre *f*
lipstick (*lip*-stik) *n* rouge à lèvres
liqueur (li-*kyoueu*) *n* liqueur *f*
liquid (*li*-k^{ou}id) *adj* liquide; *n* liquide *m*
liquor (*li*-keu) *n* spiritueux *mpl*; **~ store** magasin de vins et spiritueux
liquorice (*li*-keu-riss) *n* réglisse *f*
list (list) *n* liste *f*; *v* *inscrire
listen (*li*-seunn) *v* écouter
listener (*liss*-neu) *n* auditeur *m*
liter (*lii*-teu) *nAm* litre *m*
literary (*li*-treu-ri) *adj* littéraire
literature (*li*-treu-tcheu) *n* littérature *f*
litre (*lii*-teu) *n* litre *m*
litter (*li*-teu) *n* détritus *m*; immondices *fpl*; portée *f*
little (*li*-teul) *adj* petit; peu
live[1] (liv) *v* *vivre; habiter
live[2] (laïv) *adj* vivant
livelihood (*laïv*-li-houd) *n* subsistance *f*
lively (*laïv*-li) *adj* vif
liver (*li*-veu) *n* foie *m*
living (*li*-vinng) *adj* vivant, en vie; *n* vie *f*, gagne-pain *m*; **make** (*or* **earn**) **a ~** gagner sa vie (**by** en); **~ room** living *m*, (salle *f* de) séjour *m*; **~ space** espace *m* vital; **~ standard** niveau *m* de vie
lizard (*li*-zeud) *n* lézard *m*
load (lô^{ou}d) *n* chargement *m*; fardeau *m*; *v* charger
loaf (lô^{ou}f) *n* (pl loaves) miche *f*

loan (lô^{ou}n) *n* prêt *m*
lobby (*lo*-bi) *n* vestibule *m*
lobster (*lob*-steu) *n* homard *m*
local (*lôou*-keul) *adj* local; ~ **call** communication locale; ~ **train** train local
locality (lô^{ou}-*kæ*-leu-ti) *n* localité *f*
locate (lô^{ou}-*kéït*) *v* localiser
location (lô^{ou}-*kéï*-cheunn) *n* situation *f*
lock (lok) *v* fermer à clé; *n* serrure *f*; écluse *f*; ~ **up** enfermer
locker (lo-keu) *n* casier *m*
locomotive (lô^{ou}-keu-*môou*-tiv) *n* locomotive *f*
lodge (lodj) *v* loger; *n* pavillon de chasse
lodger (*lo*-djeu) *n* sous-locataire *m*
lodgings (*lo*-djinngz) *pl* logement *m*
log (logh) *n* bûche *f*
logic (*lo*-djik) *n* logique *f*
logical (*lo*-dji-keul) *adj* logique
lonely (*lôoun*-li) *adj* solitaire
long (lonng) *adj* long; ~ **for** désirer; **no longer** ne … plus
longing (*lonng*-inng) *n* envie *f*
longitude (*lonn*-dji-tyoûd) *n* longitude *f*
look (louk) *v* regarder; sembler, *avoir l'air; *n* coup d'œil, regard *m*; apparence *f*, aspect *m*; ~ **after** s'occuper de, *prendre soin de; ~ **at** regarder; ~ **for** chercher; ~ **out** *prendre garde, *faire attention; ~ **up** chercher
looking-glass (*lou*-kinng-ghlââss) *n* miroir *m*
loop (loûp) *n* boucle *f*
loose (loûss) *adj* lâche
loosen (*loû*-seunn) *v* desserrer
lord (lood) *n* lord *m*
lorry (*lo*-ri) *n* camion *m*
***lose** (loûz) *v* perdre
loser (*loû*-zeu) *n* perdant *m*, perdante *f*
loss (loss) *n* perte *f*
lost (lost) *adj* égaré; disparu; ~ **and found** objets trouvés; ~ **property office** bureau des objets trouvés
lot (lot) *n* sort *m*; tas *m*, quantité *f*
lotion (*lôou*-cheunn) *n* lotion *f*; **aftershave** ~ after-shave *m*
lottery (*lo*-teu-ri) *n* loterie *f*
loud (laoud) *adj* fort
loudspeaker (laoud-*spii*-keu) *n* haut-parleur *m*
lounge (laoundj) *n* foyer *m*
louse (laouss) *n* (pl lice) pou *m*
love (lav) *v* aimer; *n* amour *m*; **in** ~ amoureux; ~ **story** histoire d'amour
lovely (*lav*-li) *adj* délicieux, ravissant, beau
lover (*la*-veu) *n* amant *m*
low (lô^{ou}) *adj* bas; profond; déprimé; ~ **tide** marée basse
lower (*lôou*-eu) *v* baisser; amener; *adj* inférieur, bas
lowlands (*lôou*-leunndz) *pl* plaine *f*
loyal (*loï*-eul) *adj* loyal
lubricate (*loû*-bri-kéït) *v* huiler, lubrifier
lubrication (loû-bri-*kéï*-cheunn) *n* lubrification *f*; ~ **oil** lubrifiant *m*; ~ **system** système de lubrification
luck (lak) *n* chance *f*; hasard *m*; **bad** ~ malchance *f*
lucky (*la*-ki) *adj* chanceux; ~ **charm** porte-bonheur *m*
ludicrous (*loû*-di-kreuss) *adj* ridicule, grotesque
luggage (*la*-ghidj) *n* bagage *m*; **hand** ~ bagage à main; **left** ~ **office** consigne *f*; ~ **rack** porte-bagages *m*/filet à bagage; ~ **van** fourgon *m*
lukewarm (*loûk*-^{ou}oom) *adj* tiède
lumbago (lamm-*béï*-ghô^{ou}) *n* lumbago *m*
luminous (*loû*-mi-neuss) *adj*

lumineux
lump (lammp) *n* morceau *m*, grumeau *m*; bosse *f*; ~ **of sugar** morceau de sucre; ~ **sum** somme globale
lumpy (*lamm*-pi) *adj* grumeleux
lunacy (*loû*-neu-si) *n* folie *f*
lunatic (*loû*-neu-tik) *adj* fou; *n* aliéné mental
lunch (lanntch) *n* lunch *m*, déjeuner *m*
luncheon (*lann*-tcheunn) *n* déjeuner *m*
lung (lanng) *n* poumon *m*
luxurious (lagh-*joueu*-ri-euss) *adj* luxueux
luxury (*lak*-cheu-ri) *n* luxe *m*

M

machine (meu-*chiin*) *n* appareil *m*, machine *f*
machinery (meu-*chii*-neu-ri) *n* machinerie *f*; mécanisme *m*
mackerel (*mæ*-kreul) *n* (pl ~) maquereau *m*
mackintosh (*mæ*-kinn-toch) *n* imperméable *m*
mad (mæd) *adj* dément, insensé, fou; enragé
madam (*mæ*-deumm) *n* madame
madness (*mæd*-neuss) *n* démence *f*
magazine (mæ-gheu-*ziin*) *n* revue *f*
magic (*mæ*-djik) *n* magie *f*; *adj* magique
magician (meu-*dji*-cheunn) *n* prestidigitateur *m*
magistrate (*mæ*-dji-stréït) *n* magistrat *m*
magnetic (mægh-*nè*-tik) *adj* magnétique
magneto (mægh-*nii*-tô^{ou}) *n* (pl ~s) magnéto *f*
magnificent (mægh-*ni*-fi-seunnt) *adj* magnifique; grandiose, splendide
magnify (*mægh*-ni-faï) *v* grossir; **magnifying glass** *n* loupe *f*
magpie (*mægh*-paï) *n* pie *f*
maid (méïd) *n* bonne *f*
maiden name (*méï*-deunn néïm) nom de jeune fille
mail (méïl) *n* courrier *m*; *v* *mettre à la poste; ~ **order** *Am* mandat-poste *m*
mailbox (*méïl*-boks) *nAm* boîte aux lettres
main (méïn) *adj* principal; majeur; ~ **deck** pont principal; ~ **line** ligne principale; ~ **road** route principale; ~ **street** rue principale
mainland (*méïn*-leunnd) *n* terre ferme
mainly (*méïn*-li) *adv* principalement
mains (méïnz) *pl* secteur *m*
maintain (méïn-*téïn*) *v* *maintenir
maintenance (*méïn*-teu-neunns) *n* entretien *m*
maize (méïz) *n* maïs *m*
major (*méï*-djeu) *adj* grand; majeur
majority (meu-*djo*-reu-ti) *n* majorité *f*
***make** (méïk) *v* *faire, rendre; gagner; réussir; ~ **do with** se débrouiller avec; ~ **good** compenser; ~ **up** dresser
make-up (*méï*-kap) *n* maquillage *m*
malaria (meu-*lèeu*-ri-eu) *n* malaria *f*
Malay (meu-*léï*) *n* Malais *m*
Malaysia (meu-*léï*-zi-eu) Malaysia *m*
Malaysian (meu-*léï*-zi-eunn) *adj* malaisien
male (méïl) *adj* mâle
malicious (meu-*li*-cheuss) *adj* malveillant

malignant (meu-*ligh*-neunnt) *adj* malin
mallet (*mæ*-lit) *n* maillet *m*
malnutrition (mæl-nyou-*tri*-cheunn) *n* dénutrition *f*
mammal (*mæ*-meul) *n* mammifère *m*
man (mæn) *n* (pl men) homme *m*; **men's room** toilettes pour hommes
manage (*mæ*-nidj) *v* diriger; réussir
manageable (*mæ*-ni-djeu-beul) *adj* maniable
management (*mæ*-nidj-meunnt) *n* direction *f*; gestion *f*
manager (*mæ*-ni-djeu) *n* chef *m*, directeur *m*, -trice *f*
mandarin (*mæn*-deu-rinn) *n* mandarine *f*
mandate (*mæn*-déït) *n* mandat *m*
manger (*méïn*-djeu) *n* mangeoire *f*
manicure (*mæ*-ni-kyou^{eu}) *n* manucure *f*; *v* soigner les ongles
manipulate (meu-*ni*-pyou-léït) *v* manipuler ; manœuvrer
mankind (mæn-*kaïnd*) *n* humanité *f*
mannequin (*mæ*-neu-kinn) *n* mannequin *m*
manner (*mæ*-neu) *n* mode *m*, manière *f*; **manners** *pl* savoir-vivre *m*
manor house (*mæ*-neu-haouss) *n* manoir *m*
mansion (*mæn*-cheunn) *n* manoir *m*
manual (*mæ*-nyou-eul) *adj* manuel
manufacture (mæ-nyou-*fæk*-tcheu) *v* fabriquer
manufacturer (mæ-nyou-*fæk*-tcheu-reu) *n* fabricant *m*
manure (meu-*nyoueu*) *n* fumier *m*
manuscript (*mæ*-nyou-skript) *n* manuscrit *m*
many (*mè*-ni) *adj* beaucoup de
map (mæp) *n* carte *f*; plan *m*
maple (*méï*-peul) *n* érable *m*
marble (*mââ*-beul) *n* marbre *m*; bille *f*
March (mââtch) mars
march (mââtch) *v* marcher; *n* marche *f*
mare (mè^{eu}) *n* jument *f*
margarine (mââ-djeu-*riin*) *n* margarine *f*
margin (*mââ*-djinn) *n* marge *f*
maritime (*mæ*-ri-taïm) *adj* maritime
mark (mââk) *v* marquer; caractériser; *n* marque *f*; note *f*; cible *f*
market (*mââ*-kit) *n* marché *m*
marketplace (*mââ*-kit-pléïss) *n* place du marché
marmalade (*mââ*-meu-léïd) *n* marmelade *f*
marriage (*mæ*-ridj) *n* mariage *m*
married (*mæ*-rid) *adj* marié ; conjugal; **~ couple** ménage *m*
marrow (*mæ*-rô^{ou}) *n* moelle *f*
marry (*mæ*-ri) *v* épouser, se marier
marsh (mââch) *n* marais *m*
martyr (*mââ*-teu) *n* martyr *m*
marvel (*mââ*-veul) *n* merveille *f*; *v* s'émerveiller
marvel(l)ous (*mââ*-veu-leuss) *adj* merveilleux
mascara (mæ-*skââ*-reu) *n* cosmétique pour les cils
masculine (*mæ*-skyou-linn) *adj* masculin
mash (mæch) *v* écraser
mask (mââsk) *n* masque *m*
mass[1] (mæss) *n* messe *f*
mass[2] (mæss) *n* masse *f*; **~ production** production en série
massage (*mæ*-sââj) *n* massage *m*; *v* masser
masseur (mæ-*seû*) *n* masseur *m*
massive (*mæ*-siv) *adj* massif
mast (mââst) *n* mât *m*
master (*mââ*-steu) *n* maître *m*; patron *m*; professeur *m*, instituteur *m*; *v* maîtriser
masterpiece (*mââ*-steu-piiss) *n* chef-d'œuvre *m*
mat (mæt) *n* tapis *m*; *adj* mat

match (mætch) *n* allumette *f*; match *m*; *v* s'accorder avec
matchbox (*mætch*-boks) *n* boîte d'allumettes
material (meu-*tieu*-ri-eul) *n* matériel *m*; tissu *m*; *adj* matériel
mathematical (mæ-θeu-*mæ*-ti-keul) *adj* mathématique
mathematics (mæ-θeu-*mæ*-tiks) *n* mathématiques *fpl*
matrimony (*mæ*-tri-meu-ni) *n* mariage *m*
matter (*mæ*-teu) *n* matière *f*; affaire *f*, question *f*; *v* *avoir de l'importance; **as a ~ of fact** effectivement, en fait
matter-of-fact (mæ-teu-reuv-*fækt*) *adj* réaliste
mattress (*mæ*-treuss) *n* matelas *m*
mature (meu-*tyoueu*) *adj* mûr
maturity (meu-*tyoueu*-reu-ti) *n* maturité *f*
mausoleum (moo-seu-*lii*-eumm) *n* mausolée *m*
mauve (mô^{ou}v) *adj* mauve
May (méï) mai
***may** (méï) *v* *pouvoir
maybe (*méï*-bii) *adv* peut-être
mayor (mè^{eu}) *n* maire *m*
maze (méïz) *n* labyrinthe *m*
me (mii) *pron* moi; me
meadow (*mè*-dô^{ou}) *n* pré *m*
meal (miil) *n* repas *m*
mean (miin) *adj* mesquin; *n* moyenne *f*
***mean** (miin) *v* signifier; *vouloir dire
meaning (*mii*-ninng) *n* signification *f*
meaningless (*mii*-ninng-leuss) *adj* dénué de sens
means (miinz) *n* moyen *m*; **by no ~** aucunement, en aucun cas
in the meantime (inn ðeu *miin*-taïm) en attendant, entre-temps
meanwhile (*miin*-^{ou}aïl) *adv* entretemps
measles (*mii*-zeulz) *n* rougeole *f*
measure (*mè*-jeu) *v* mesurer; *n* mesure *f*
meat (miit) *n* viande *f*
mechanic (mi-*kæ*-nik) *n* monteur *m*, mécanicien *m*
mechanical (mi-*kæ*-ni-keul) *adj* mécanique
mechanism (*mè*-keu-ni-zeumm) *n* mécanisme *m*
medal (*mè*-deul) *n* médaille *f*
media (*mii*-di-eu)*n pl* medias *mpl*
mediaeval (mè-di-*ii*-veul) *adj* médiéval
mediate (*mii*-di-éït) *v* *servir d'intermédiaire
mediator (*mii*-di-éï-teu) *n* médiateur *m*
medical (*mè*-di-keul) *adj* médical
medicine (*mèd*-sinn) *n* médicament *m*; médecine *f*
medieval (mè-di-*ii*-veul) *adj* médiéval
meditate (*mè*-di-téït) *v* méditer
Mediterranean (mè-di-teu-*réï*-ni-eunn) Méditerranée *f*
medium (*mii*-di-eumm) *adj* moyen
***meet** (miit) *v* rencontrer
meeting (*mii*-tinng) *n* assemblée *f*, réunion *f*; rencontre *f*; **~ place** lieu de rencontre
melancholy (*mè*-leunng-keu-li) *n* mélancolie *f*
mellow (*mè*-lô^{ou}) *adj* moelleux
melodrama (*mè*-leu-drââ-meu) *n* mélodrame *m*
melody (*mè*-leu-di) *n* mélodie *f*
melon (*mè*-leunn) *n* melon *m*
melt (mèlt) *v* fondre
member (*mèm*-beu) *n* membre *m*; **Member of Parliament** député *m*
membership (*mèm*-beu-chip) *n* affiliation *f*
memo (*mè*-mô^{ou}) *n* (pl ~s) mémorandum *m*
memorable (*mè*-meu-reu-beul) *adj*

mémorable
memorial (meu-*moo*-ri-eul) *n* mémorial *m*
memorize (*mè*-meu-raïz) *v* *apprendre par cœur
memory (*mè*-meu-ri) *n* mémoire *f*; souvenir *m*
mend (mènd) *v* réparer
menstruation (mèn-strou-*éï*-cheunn) *n* menstruation *f*
mental (*mèn*-teul) *adj* mental
mention (*mèn*-cheunn) *v* mentionner; *n* mention *f*
menu (*mè*-nyoû) *n* carte *f*, menu *m*
merchandise (*meû*-tcheunn-daïz) *n* marchandise *f*
merchant (*meû*-tcheunnt) *n* commerçant *m*, marchand *m*
merciful (*meû*-si-feul) *adj* miséricordieux
mercury (*meû*-kyou-ri) *n* mercure *m*
mercy (*meû*-si) *n* miséricorde *f*, clémence *f*
mere (mi^eu^) *adj* pur
merely (*mieu*-li) *adv* seulement
merge (meûdj) *v* fusionner; amalgamer (**with, into** avec); se fondre (**with, into** dans); s'amalgamer
merger (*meû*-djeu) *n* fusion *f*
merit (*mè*-rit) *v* mériter; *n* mérite *m*
merry (*mè*-ri) *adj* joyeux
merry-go-round (*mè*-ri-ghô^ou^-raound) *n* chevaux de bois
mesh (mèch) *n* maille *f*
mess (mèss) *n* désordre *m*, gâchis *m*; ~ **up** gâcher
message (*mè*-sidj) *n* commission *f*, message *m*
messenger (*mè*-sinn-djeu) *n* messager *m*
metal (*mè*-teul) *n* métal *m*; métallique
meter (*mii*-teu) *n* compteur *m*
method (*mè*-θeud) *n* méthode *f*; ordre *m*
methodical (meu-*θo*-di-keul) *adj* méthodique
metre (*mii*-teu) *n* mètre *m*
metric (*mè*-trik) *adj* métrique
Mexican (*mèk*-si-keunn) *adj* mexicain; *n* Mexicain *m*
Mexico (*mèk*-si-kô^ou^) Mexique *m*
microphone (*maï*-kreu-fô^ou^n) *n* microphone *m*
microwave oven (*maï*-kreu-^ou^éïv *a*-veunn) *n* four à micro-ondes *m*
midday (*mid*-déï) *n* midi *m*
middle (*mi*-deul) *n* milieu *m*; *adj* du milieu; **Middle Ages** moyen-âge *m*; ~ **class** classe moyenne; **middle-class** *adj* bourgeois
midnight (*mid*-naït) *n* minuit
midsummer (*mid*-sa-meu) *n* milieu *m* de l'été; **in** ~ en plein été
midwife (*mid*-^ou^aïf) *n* (pl -wives) sagefemme *f*
might (maït) *n* puissance *f*
***might** (maït) *v* *pouvoir
mighty (*maï*-ti) *adj* puissant
mild (maïld) *adj* doux
mildew (*mil*-dyou) *n* moisissure *f*
mile (maïl) *n* mille *m*
mileage (*maï*-lidj) *n* nombre de milles
milepost (*maïl*-pô^ou^st) *n* poteau indicateur
milestone (*maïl*-stô^ou^n) *n* borne routière
milieu (*mii*-lyeû) *n* milieu *m*
military (*mi*-li-teu-ri) *adj* militaire; ~ **force** force armée
milk (milk) *n* lait *m*
milkman (*milk*-meunn) *n* (pl -men) laitier *m*
milkshake (*milk*-chéïk) *n* frappé *m*
milky (*mil*-ki) *adj* laiteux
mill (mil) *n* moulin *m*; usine *f*
miller (*mi*-leu) *n* meunier *m*
million (*mil*-yeunn) *n* million *m*

millionaire (mil-yeu-*nèeu*) *n* millionnaire *m/f*
mince (minns) *v* hacher
mind (maïnd) *n* esprit *m*; *v* prêter attention à
mine (maïn) *n* mine *f*
miner (*maï*-neu) *n* mineur *m*
mineral (*mi*-neu-reul) *n* minéral *m*; ~ **water** eau minérale
mingle (*minng*-gheul) *v* (se) mêler (**with** à); (se) mélanger (**with** avec)
miniature (*minn*-yeu-tcheu) *n* miniature *f*
minimum (*mi*-ni-meumm) *n* minimum *m*
mining (*maï*-ninng) *n* exploitation minière
minister (*mi*-ni-steu) *n* ministre *m*; pasteur *m*; **Prime Minister** premier ministre
ministry (*mi*-ni-stri) *n* ministère *m*
minor (*maï*-neu) *adj* petit, menu, mineur; *n* mineur *m*
minority (maï-*no*-reu-ti) *n* minorité *f*
mint (minnt) *n* menthe *f*
minus (*maï*-neuss) *prep* moins
minute[1] (*mi*-nit) *n* minute *f*; **minutes** compte rendu
minute[2] (maï-*nyoût*) *adj* minuscule
miracle (*mi*-reu-keul) *n* miracle *m*
miraculous (mi-*ræ*-kyou-leuss) *adj* miraculeux
mirror (*mi*-reu) *n* miroir *m*
misbehave (miss-bi-*héïv*) *v* se *conduire mal
miscarriage (miss-*kæ*-ridj) *n* fausse couche
miscellaneous (mi-seu-*léï*-ni-euss) *adj* divers
mischief (*miss*-tchif) *n* espièglerie *f*; mal *m*, dommage *m*, malice *f*
mischievous (*miss*-tchi-veuss) *adj* malicieux
miserable (*mi*-zeu-reu-beul) *adj* misérable, malheureux
misery (*mi*-zeu-ri) *n* détresse *f*, misère *f*
misfortune (miss-*foo*-tchèn) *n* infortune *f*, malheur *m*
mishap (*miss*-hæp) *n* mésaventure *f*; accident *m*
***mislay** (miss-*léï*) *v* égarer
misplaced (miss-*pléïst*) *adj* inopportun; mal placé
mispronounce (miss-preu-*naouns*) *v* mal prononcer
miss[1] (miss) mademoiselle, demoiselle *f*
miss[2] (miss) *v* manquer
missing (*mi*-sinng) *adj* manquant; ~ **person** disparu *m*
mist (mist) *n* brume *f*, brouillard *m*
mistake (mi-*stéïk*) *n* méprise *f*, faute *f*, erreur *f*
***mistake** (mi-*stéïk*) *v* confondre
mistaken (mi-*stéï*-keunn) *adj* erroné; ***be** ~ se tromper
mister (*mi*--steu) monsieur *m*
mistress (*mi*-streuss) *n* maîtresse de maison; patronne *f*, maîtresse *f*
mistrust (miss-*trast*) *v* se méfier de
misty (*mi*-sti) *adj* brumeux
***misunderstand** (mi-sann-deu-*stænd*) *v* mal *comprendre
misunderstanding (mi-sann-deu-*stæn*-dinng) *n* malentendu *m*
misuse (miss-*yoûss*) *n* abus *m*
mittens (*mi*-teunnz) *pl* moufles *fpl*
mix (miks) *v* mélanger, mêler; ~ **with** fréquenter
mixed (mikst) *adj* mêlé, mélangé
mixer (*mik*-seu) *n* mixeur *m*
mixture (*miks*-tcheu) *n* mélange *m*
moan (mô^{ou}n) *v* gémir
moat (mô^{ou}t) *n* douve *f*
mobile (*môou*-baïl) *adj* mobile; ~ **phone** (téléphone) portable; téléphone mobile

mock (mok) *v* se moquer de
mockery (*mo*-keu-ri) *n* moquerie *f*
model (*mo*-deul) *n* modèle *m*; mannequin *m*; *v* façonner, modeler
moderate (*mo*-deu-reut) *adj* modéré
modern (*mo*-deunn) *adj* moderne
modest (*mo*-dist) *adj* modeste
modesty (*mo*-di-sti) *n* modestie *f*
modify (*mo*-di-faï) *v* modifier
mohair (*môou*-hè^eu^) *n* mohair *m*
moist (moïst) *adj* mouillé, moite
moisten (*moï*-seunn) *v* humecter
moisture (*moïss*-tcheu) *n* humidité *f*; **moisturizing cream** crème hydratante
molar (*môou*-leu) *n* molaire *f*
moment (*môou*-meunnt) *n* instant *m*, moment *m*
momentary (*môou*-meunn-teu-ri) *adj* momentané
monarch (*mo*-neuk) *n* monarque *m*
monarchy (*mo*-neu-ki) *n* monarchie *f*
monastery (*mo*-neu-stri) *n* monastère *m*
Monday (*mann*-di) lundi *m*
monetary (*ma*-ni-teu-ri) *adj* monétaire; ~ **unit** unité monétaire
money (*ma*-ni) *n* argent *m*; ~ **exchange** bureau de change; ~ **order** mandat-poste *m*
monk (manngk) *n* moine *m*
monkey (*manng*-ki) *n* singe *m*
monologue (*mo*-no-logh) *n* monologue *m*
monopoly (meu-*no*-peu-li) *n* monopole *m*
monotonous (meu-*no*-teu-neuss) *adj* monotone
month (mannθ) *n* mois *m*
monthly (*mannθ*-li) *adj* mensuel; ~ **magazine** revue mensuelle
monument (*mo*-nyou-meunnt) *n* monument *m*
mood (moûd) *n* humeur *f*
moon (moûn) *n* lune *f*
moonlight (*moûn*-laït) *n* clair de lune
moor (mou^eu^) *n* bruyère *f*, lande *f*
moose (moûss) *n* (pl ~, ~s) élan *m*
moped (*môou*-pèd) *n* vélomoteur *m*
moral (*mo*-reul) *n* morale *f*; *adj* moral; **morals** mœurs *fpl*
morality (meu-*ræ*-leu-ti) *n* moralité *f*
more (moo) *adj* plus; **once** ~ une fois de plus
moreover (moo-*rôou*-veu) *adv* d'ailleurs, de plus
morning (*moo*-ninng) *n* matin *m*; ~ **paper** journal du matin
Moroccan (meu-*ro*-keunn) *adj* marocain; *n* Marocain *m*
Morocco (meu-*ro*-kô^ou^) Maroc *m*
morphia (*moo*-fi-eu) *n* morphine *f*
morphine (*moo*-fiin) *n* morphine *f*
morsel (*moo*-seul) *n* morceau *m*
mortal (*moo*-teul) *adj* fatal, mortel
mortgage (*moo*-ghidj) *n* hypothèque *f*
mosaic (meu-*zéï*-ik) *n* mosaïque *f*
mosque (mosk) *n* mosquée *f*
mosquito (meu-*skii*-tô^ou^) *n* (pl ~es) moustique *m*; ~ **net** moustiquaire *f*
moss (moss) *n* mousse *f*
most (mô^ou^st) *adj* le plus; **at** ~ au maximum, tout au plus; ~ **of all** surtout
mostly (*môoust*-li) *adv* le plus souvent
motel (mô^ou^-*tèl*) *n* motel *m*
moth (moθ) *n* mite *f*
mother (*ma*-ðeu) *n* mère *f*; ~ **tongue** langue maternelle; ~ **of pearl** nacre *f*
mother-in-law (*ma*-ðeu-rinn-loo) *n* (pl mothers-) belle-mère *f*
motion (*môou*-cheunn) *n* mouvement *m*
motivate (*môou*-ti-véït) *v* motiver
motive (*môou*-tiv) *n* motif *m*
motor (*môou*-teu) *n* moteur *m*; *v* voyager en auto; ~ **body** *Am* carrosserie *f*; **starter** ~ démarreur *m*

motorbike (*môou*-teu-baïk) *nAm* vélomoteur *m*
motorboat (*môou*-teu-bô^{ou}t) *n* canot automobile
motorcar (*môou*-teu-kââ) *n* automobile *f*
motorcycle (*môou*-teu-saï-keul) *n* motocyclette *f*
motorist (*môou*-teu-rist) *n* automobiliste *m*
motorway (*môou*-teu-^{ou}éï) *n* autoroute *f*
motto (*mo*-tô^{ou}) *n* (pl ~es, ~s) devise *f*
mouldy (*môoul*-di) *adj* moisi
mound (maound) *n* butte *f*
mount (maount) *v* monter; *n* mont *m*
mountain (*maoun*-tinn) *n* montagne *f*; ~ **pass** col *m*; ~ **range** chaîne de montagnes
mountaineering (maoun-ti-*nieu*-rinng) *n* alpinisme *m*
mountainous (*maoun*-ti-neuss) *adj* montagneux
mourning (*moo*-ninng) *n* deuil *m*
mouse (maouss) *n* (pl mice) souris *f*
moustache (meu-*stââch*) *n* moustache *f*
mouth (maouθ) *n* bouche *f*; gueule *f*; embouchure *f*
mouthwash (*maouθ*-^{ou}och) *n* eau dentifrice
movable (*moû*-veu-beul) *adj* mobile
move (moûv) *v* bouger; déplacer; se *mouvoir; déménager; *émouvoir; *n* tour *m*, pas *m*; déménagement *m*
movement (*moûv*-meunnt) *n* mouvement *m*
movie (*moû*-vi) *n* film *m*; **movies** *Am* cinéma *m*; ~ **theatre,** cinéma *m*
much (match) *adj* beaucoup de; *adv* beaucoup; **as** ~ autant
muck (mak) *n* gadoue *f*
mud (mad) *n* boue *f*
muddle (*ma*-deul) *n* fouillis *m*, pagaille *f*, confusion *f*; *v* embrouiller
muddy (*ma*-di) *adj* boueux
muffler (*maf*-leu) *nAm* silencieux *m*
mug (magh) *n* gobelet *m*, chope *f*
mule (myoûl) *n* mulet *m*, mule *f*
multiplication (mal-ti-pli-*kéï*-cheunn) *n* multiplication *f*
multiply (*mal*-ti-plaï) *v* multiplier
mumps (mammps) *n* oreillons *mpl*
municipal (myoû-*ni*-si-peul) *adj* municipal
municipality (myoû-ni-si-*pæ*-leu-ti) *n* municipalité *f*
murder (*meû*-deu) *n* assassinat *m*; *v* assassiner
murderer (*meû*-deu-reu) *n* meurtrier *m*, -ière *f*
muscle (*ma*-seul) *n* muscle *m*
muscular (*ma*-skyou-leu) *adj* musclé
museum (myoû-*zii*-eumm) *n* musée *m*
mushroom (*mach*-roûm) *n* champignon *m*
music (*myoû*-zik) *n* musique *f*; ~ **academy** conservatoire *m*; ~ **hall** music-hall *m*
musical (*myoû*-zi-keul) *adj* musical; *n* comédie musicale
musician (myoû-*zi*-cheunn) *n* musicien *m*, -ienne *f*
mussel (*ma*-seul) *n* moule *f*
***must** (mast) *v* *falloir
mustard (*ma*-steud) *n* moutarde *f*
mute (myoût) *adj* muet
mutiny (*myoû*-ti-ni) *n* mutinerie *f*
mutton (*ma*-teunn) *n* mouton *m*
mutual (*myoû*-tchou-eul) *adj* mutuel, réciproque
my (maï) *adj* mon
myself (maï-*sèlf*) *pron* me; moi-même
mysterious (mi-*stieu*-ri-euss) *adj* mystérieux
mystery (*mi*-steu-ri) *n* énigme *f*, mystère *m*
myth (miθ) *n* mythe *m*

N

nail (néïl) *n* ongle *m*; clou *m*; **~ file** lime à ongles; **~ polish** vernis à ongle; **~ scissors** ciseaux à ongles
nailbrush (*néïl*-brach) *n* brosse à ongles
naïve (nââ-*iiv*) *adj* naïf
naked (*néï*-kid) *adj* nu; dénudé
name (néïm) *n* nom *m*; *v* nommer; **in the ~ of** au nom de
namely (*néïm*-li) *adv* notamment
nap (næp) *n* somme *m*
napkin (*næp*-kinn) *n* serviette *f*
nappy (*næ*-pi) *n* couche *f*
narcosis (nââ-*kôou*-siss) *n* (pl -ses) narcose *f*
narcotic (nââ-*ko*-tik) *n* narcotique *m*
narrow (*næ*-rô^{ou}) *adj* serré, étroit
narrow-minded (næ-rô^{ou}-*maïn*-did) *adj* borné
nasty (*nââ*-sti) *adj* antipathique, désagréable; méchant
nation (*néï*-cheunn) *n* nation *f*; peuple *m*
national (*næ*-cheu-neul) *adj* national; de l'Etat; **~ anthem** hymne national; **~ dress** costume national; **~ park** parc national
nationality (næ-cheu-*næ*-leu-ti) *n* nationalité *f*
nationalize (*næ*-cheu-neu-laïz) *v* nationaliser
native (*néï*-tiv) *n* indigène *m*/*f*; *adj* indigène; **~ country** patrie *f*, pays natal; **~ language** langue maternelle
natural (*næ*-tcheu-reul) *adj* naturel; inné
naturally (*næ*-tcheu-reu-li) *adv* bien sûr, naturellement
nature (*néï*-tcheu) *n* nature *f*
naughty (*noo*-ti) *adj* polisson, méchant
nausea (*noo*-si-eu) *n* nausée *f*
naval (*néï*-veul) *adj* naval
navel (*néï*-veul) *n* nombril *m*
navigable (*næ*-vi-gheu-beul) *adj* navigable
navigate (*næ*-vi-ghéït) *v* naviguer
navigation (næ-vi-*ghéï*-cheunn) *n* navigation *f*
navy (*néï*-vi) *n* marine *f*
near (ni^{eu}) *prep* près de; *adj* proche, près
nearby (*nieu*-baï) *adj* proche
nearly (*nieu*-li) *adv* presque
neat (niit) *adj* soigné; pur
necessary (*nè*-seu-seu-ri) *adj* nécessaire
necessity (neu-*sè*-seu-ti) *n* nécessité *f*
neck (nèk) *n* cou *m*; **nape of the ~** nuque *f*
necklace (*nèk*-leuss) *n* collier *m*
necktie (*nèk*-taï) *n* cravate *f*
need (niid) *v* *falloir, *avoir besoin de; *n* besoin *m*; nécessité *f*; **~ to** *devoir
needle (*nii*-deul) *n* aiguille *f*
needlework (*nii*-deul-^{ou}eûk) *n* travail à l'aiguille
negative (*nè*-gheu-tiv) *adj* négatif; *n* négatif *m*
neglect (ni-*ghlèkt*) *v* négliger; *n* négligence *f*
neglectful (ni-*ghlèkt*-feul) *adj* négligent
negligee (*nè*-ghli-jéï) *n* négligé *m*
negotiate (ni-*ghôou*-chi-éït) *v* négocier
negotiation (ni-ghô^{ou}-chi-*éï*-cheunn) *n* négociation *f*
neighbour (*néï*-beu) *n* voisin *m*, -e *f*
neighbo(u)rhood (*néï*-beu-houd) *n* voisinage *m*
neighbo(u)ring (*néï*-beu-rinng) *adj* contigu, avoisinant
neither (*naï*-ðeu) *pron* ni l'un ni

l'autre; **neither … nor** ni … ni
neon (*nii*-onn) *n* néon *m*
nephew (*nè*-fyoû) *n* neveu *m*
nerve (neûv) *n* nerf *m*; audace *f*
nervous (*neû*-veuss) *adj* nerveux
nest (nèst) *n* nid *m*
net (nèt) *n* filet *m*; *adj* net
Netherlands (*nè*-ðeu-leunndz): **the ~** Pays-Bas *mpl*
network (*nèt*-^{ou}eûk) *n* réseau *m*
neuralgia (nyou^{eu}-*ræl*-djeu) *n* névralgie *f*
neurosis (nyou^{eu}-*rôou*-siss) *n* névrose *f*
neuter (*nyoû*-teu) *adj* neutre
neutral (*nyoû*-treul) *adj* neutre
never (*nè*-veu) *adv* ne … jamais
nevertheless (nè-veu-ðeu-*lèss*) *adv* néanmoins
new (nyoû) *adj* nouveau
news (nyoûz) *n* nouvelles, nouvelle *f*; actualités
newsagent (*nyoû*-zéï-djeunnt) *n* marchand de journaux
newspaper (*nyoûz*-péï-peu) *n* journal *m*
newsreel (*nyoûz*-riil) *n* actualités
newsstand (*nyoûz*-stænd) *n* kiosque à journaux
New Year (nyoû yi^{eu}) Nouvel An; **New Year's Eve** la Saint-Sylvestre
New Zealand (nyoû *zii*-leunnd) Nouvelle-Zélande *f*
next (nèkst) *adj* prochain, suivant; **~ to** à côté de
next-door (nèkst-*doo*) *adv* à côté
nice (naïss) *adj* gentil, joli, plaisant; bon; sympathique
nickel (*ni*-keul) *n* nickel *m*
nickname (*nik*-néïm) *n* surnom *m*
nicotine (*ni*-keu-tiin) *n* nicotine *f*
niece (niiss) *n* nièce *f*
Nigeria (naï-*djieu*-ri-eu) Nigeria *m*
Nigerian (naï-*djïeu*-ri-eunn) *adj* nigérien; *n* Nigérien *m*
night (naït) *n* nuit *f*; soir *m*; **by ~** de nuit; **~ cream** crème de nuit; **~ flight** vol de nuit; **~ rate** tarif de nuit; **~ train** train de nuit
nightclub (*naït*-klab) *n* boîte de nuit
nightdress (*naït*-drèss) *n* chemise de nuit
nightingale (*naï*-tinng-ghéïl) *n* rossignol *m*
nightly (*naït*-li) *adj* nocturne
nightmare (*naït*-mè^{eu}) *n* cauchemar *m*
nil (nil) rien
nine (naïn) *num* neuf
nineteen (naïn-*tiin*) *num* dix-neuf
nineteenth (naïn-*tiinθ*) *num* dix-neuvième
ninety (*naïn*-ti) *num* quatre-vingt-dix
ninth (naïnθ) *num* neuvième
no (nô^{ou}) non; *adj* aucun; **~ one** ne … personne
nobility (nô^{ou}-*bi*-leu-ti) *n* noblesse *f*
noble (*nôou*-beul) *adj* noble
nobody (*nôou*-bo-di) *pron* ne … personne
nod (nod) *n* inclination de la tête; *v* opiner de la tête
noise (noïz) *n* bruit *m*; fracas *m*, vacarme *m*
noisy (*noï*-zi) *adj* bruyant; sonore
nominate (*no*-mi-néït) *v* nommer
nomination (no-mi-*néï*-cheunn) *n* nomination *f*
none (nann) *pron* aucun
nonsense (*nonn*-seunns) *n* sottise *f*
non-smoker (*nonn*-smô^{ou}-keu) *n* non-fumeur *m*
noon (noûn) *n* midi *m*
nor (noo): **neither ~** ni; ne ... pas non plus; **nor do I** (ni) moi non plus
normal (*noo*-meul) *adj* normal
north (nooθ) *n* nord *m*; *adj* septentrional; **North Pole** pôle nord

north-east (nooθ-*iist*) *n* nord-est *m*
northerly (*noo*-ðeu-li) *adj* du nord
northern (*noo*-ðeunn) *adj* septentrional
north-west (nooθ-*ouèst*) *n* nord-ouest *m*
Norway (*noo*-^{ou}éï) Norvège *f*
Norwegian (noo-*ouii*-djeunn) *adj* norvégien; *n* Norvégien *m*
nose (nô^{ou}z) *n* nez *m*
nosebleed (*nôouz*-bliid) *n* saignement de nez
nostril (*no*-stril) *n* narine *f*
nosy (*nôou*-zi) *adj colloquial* curieux; indiscret
not (not) *adv* ne … pas
notary (*nôou*-teu-ri) *n* notaire *m*
note (nô^{ou}t) *n* note *f*; ton *m*; *v* noter; observer, constater
notebook (*nôout*-bouk) *n* carnet *m*
noted (*nôou*-tid) *adj* illustre
notepaper (*nôout*-péï-peu) *n* papier à lettres
nothing (*na*-θinng) *n* rien, ne … rien
notice (*nôou*-tiss) *v* observer, noter, remarquer; *n* avis *m*, nouvelle *f*; attention *f*
noticeable (*nôou*-ti-seu-beul) *adj* perceptible; remarquable
notify (*nôou*-ti-faï) *v* notifier; avertir
notion (*nôou*-cheunn) *n* notion *f*
notorious (nô^{ou}-*too*-ri-euss) *adj* notoire
nougat (*noû*-ghââ) *n* nougat *m*
nought (noot) *n* zéro *m*
noun (naoun) *n* nom *m*, substantif *m*
nourishing (*na*-ri-chinng) *adj* nourrissant
novel (*no*-veul) *n* roman *m*
November (nô^{ou}-*vèm*-beu) novembre
now (naou) *adv* maintenant; à l'heure actuelle; ~ **and then** de temps en temps
nowadays (*naou*-eu-déïz) *adv* actuellement
nowhere (*nôou*-^{ou}è^{eu}) *adv* nulle part
nozzle (*no*-zeul) *n* bec *m*
nuance (nyoû-*anss*) *n* nuance *f*
nuclear (*nyoû*-kli-eu) *adj* nucléaire; ~ **energy** énergie nucléaire
nucleus (*nyoû*-kli-euss) *n* noyau *m*
nude (nyoûd) *adj* nu; *n* nu *m*
nuisance (*nyoû*-seunns) *n* ennui *m*
numb (namm) *adj* engourdi
number (*namm*-beu) *n* numéro *m*; chiffre *m*, nombre *m*
numeral (*nyoû*-meu-reul) *n* nombre *m*
numerous (*nyoû*-meu-reuss) *adj* nombreux
nun (nann) *n* religieuse *f*
nunnery (*na*-neu-ri) *n* couvent *m*
nurse (neûss) *n* infirmière *f*; bonne d'enfants; *v* soigner; allaiter
nursery (*neû*-seu-ri) *n* chambre d'enfants; crèche *f*; pépinière *f*
nut (nat) *n* noix *f*; écrou *m*
nutcrackers (*nat*-kræ-keuz) *pl* cassenoix *m*
nutmeg (*nat*-mègh) *n* muscade *f*
nutritious (nyoû-*tri*-cheuss) *adj* nutritif
nutshell (*nat*-chèl) *n* coquille de noix
nylon (*naï*-lonn) *n* nylon *m*

O

oak (ô^{ou}k) *n* chêne *m*
oar (oo) *n* rame *f*
oasis (ô^{ou}-*éï*-siss) *n* (pl oases) oasis *f*
oath (ô^{ou}θ) *n* serment *m*
oats (ô^{ou}ts) *pl* avoine *f*
obedience (eu-*bii*-di-eunns) *n* obéissance *f*
obedient (eu-*bii*-di-eunnt) *adj* obéissant
obey (eu-*béï*) *v* obéir
object[1] (*ob*-djikt) *n* objet *m*; objectif *m*
object[2] (eub-*djèkt*) *v* objecter; **~ to** *faire objection à
objection (eub-*djèk*-cheunn) *n* objection *f*
objective (eub-*djèk*-tiv) *adj* objectif; *n* objectif *m*
obligatory (eu-*bli*-gheu-teu-ri) *adj* obligatoire
oblige (eu-*blaïdj*) *v* obliger; ***be obliged to** *être obligé de; *devoir
obliging (eu-*blaï*-djinng) *adj* obligeant
oblong (*ob*-lonng) *adj* oblong; *n* rectangle *m*
obscene (eub-*siin*) *adj* obscène
obscure (eub-*skyoueu*) *adj* vague, sombre, obscur
observation (ob-zeu-*véï*-cheunn) *n* observation *f*
observatory (eub-*zeû*-veu-tri) *n* observatoire *m*
observe (eub-*zeûv*) *v* observer
obsession (eub-*sè*-cheunn) *n* obsession *f*
obstacle (*ob*-steu-keul) *n* obstacle *m*
obstinate (*ob*-sti-neut) *adj* obstiné; opiniâtre
obtain (eub-*téïn*) *v* se procurer, *obtenir
obtainable (eub-*téï*-neu-beul) *adj* disponible
obvious (*ob*-vi-euss) *adj* évident
occasion (eu-*kéï*-jeunn) *n* occasion *f*
occasionally (eu-*kéï*-jeu-neu-li) *adv* de temps en temps
occupant (*o*-kyou-peunnt) *n* occupant *m*
occupation (o-kyou-*péï*-cheunn) *n* occupation *f*
occupy (*o*-kyou-paï) *v* occuper
occur (eu-*keû*) *v* se passer, se *produire, *survenir
occurrence (eu-*ka*-reunns) *n* événement *m*
ocean (*ôou*-cheunn) *n* océan *m*
October (ok-*tôou*-beu) octobre
octopus (*ok*-teu-peuss) *n* pieuvre *f*
oculist (*o*-kyou-list) *n* oculiste *m/f*
odd (od) *adj* bizarre; impair
odo(u)r (*ôou*-deu) *n* odeur *f*
of (ov, euv) *prep* de
off (of) *prep* de
offence (eu-*fèns*) *n* infraction *f*; offense *f*, outrage *m*
offend (eu-*fènd*) *v* blesser, offenser; outrager
offense (eu-*fèns*) *nAm* infraction *f*; offense *f*, outrage *m*
offensive (eu-*fèn*-siv) *adj* offensif; grossier; *n* offensive *f*
offer (*o*-feu) *v* *offrir; *n* offre *f*
office (*o*-fiss) *n* bureau *m*; fonction *f*; **~ hours** heures de bureau
officer (*o*-fi-seu) *n* officier *m*
official (eu-*fi*-cheul) *adj* officiel
off-licence (*of*-laï-seunns) *n* magasin de spiritueux
often (*o*-feunn) *adv* souvent
oil (oïl) *n* huile *f*, pétrole *m*; **fuel ~** mazout *m*; **~ filter** filtre à huile; **~ painting** peinture à l'huile; **~ pressure** pression d'huile; **~ refinery** raffinerie de pétrole; **~ well** gisement

de pétrole, puits de pétrole
oily (*oï*-li) *adj* huileux
ointment (*oïnt*-meunnt) *n* onguent *m*
okay! (ô^{ou}-*kéï*) d'accord!
old (ô^{ou}ld) *adj* vieux; **~ age** vieillesse *f*
old-fashioned (ô^{ou}ld-*fæ*-cheunnd) *adj* démodé
olive (*o*-liv) *n* olive *f*; **~ oil** huile d'olive
omelette (*omm*-leut) *n* omelette *f*
ominous (*o*-mi-neuss) *adj* sinistre
omit (eu-*mit*) *v* *omettre
omnipotent (omm-*ni*-peu-teunnt) *adj* omnipotent
on (onn) *prep* sur; à
once (^{ou}anns) *adv* une fois; **at ~** immédiatement, tout de suite; **for ~** pour un coup; **~ more** une fois de plus
oncoming (*onn*-ka-minng) *adj* venant en sens inverse; proche
one (^{ou}ann) *num* un; *pron* on
oneself (^{ou}ann-*sèlf*) *pron* soi-même
onion (*a*-nyeunn) *n* oignon *m*
only (*ôoun*-li) *adj* seul; *adv* rien que, seulement; *conj* cependant
onwards (*onn*-^{ou}eudz) *adv* en avant
open (*ôou*-peunn) *v* *ouvrir; *adj* ouvert; franc
opener (*ôou*-peu-neu) *n* ouvreur *m*
opening (*ôou*-peu-ninng) *n* ouverture *f*
opera (*o*-peu-reu) *n* opéra *m*; **~ house** opéra *m*
operate (*o*-peu-réït) *v* opérer, fonctionner
operation (o-peu-*réï*-cheunn) *n* fonctionnement *m*; opération *f*
operator (*o*-peu-réï-teu) *n* standardiste *m/f*
operetta (o-peu-*rè*-teu) *n* opérette *f*
opinion (eu-*pi*-nyeunn) *n* idée *f*, opinion *f*
opponent (eu-*pôou*-neunnt) *n* adversaire *m/f*
opportunity (o-peu-*tyoû*-neu-ti) *n* occasion *f*
oppose (eu-*pôouz*) *v* s'opposer
opposite (*o*-peu-zit) *prep* en face de; *adj* opposé, contraire
opposition (o-peu-*zi*-cheunn) *n* opposition *f*
oppress (eu-*prèss*) *v* oppresser, opprimer
optician (op-*ti*-cheunn) *n* opticien *m*, -ienne *f*
optimism (*op*-ti-mi-zeumm) *n* optimisme *m*
optimist (*op*-ti-mist) *n* optimiste *m/f*
optimistic (op-ti-*mi*-stik) *adj* optimiste
optional (*op*-cheu-neul) *adj* facultatif
or (oo) *conj* ou
oral (o*o*-reul) *adj* oral
orange (*o*-rinndj) *n* orange *f*; *adj* orange
orbit (*oo*-bit) *n* orbite *f*; *v* tourner autour de
orchard (*oo*-tcheud) *n* verger *m*
orchestra (*oo*-ki-streu) *n* orchestre *m*; **~ seat** *Am* fauteuil d'orchestre
order (*oo*-deu) *v* commander; *n* ordre *m*; commandement *m*; commande *f*; **~ form** bon de commande; **in ~** en règle; **in ~ to** afin de; **made to ~** fait sur commande; **out of ~** en dérangement; **postal ~** mandat-poste *m*
ordinary (*oo*-deunn-ri) *adj* commun, habituel
ore (oo) *n* minerai *m*
organ (*oo*-gheunn) *n* organe *m*; orgue *m*
organic (oo-*ghæ*-nik) *adj* organique
organization (oo-gheu-naï-*zéï*-cheunn) *n* organisation *f*
organize (*oo*-gheu-naïz) *v* organiser
Orient (*oo*-ri-eunnt) *n* Orient *m*
oriental (oo-ri-*èn*-teul) *adj* oriental

orientate (*oo*-ri-eunn-téït) *v* s'orienter
origin (*o*-ri-djinn) *n* origine *f*; descendance *f*, provenance *f*
original (eu-*ri*-dji-neul) *adj* authentique, original
originally (eu-*ri*-dji-neu-li) *adv* originairement
orlon (*oo*-lonn) *n* orlon *m*
ornament (*oo*-neu-meunnt) *n* ornement *m*
ornamental (oo-neu-*mèn*-teul) *adj* ornemental
orphan (*oo*-feunn) *n* orphelin *m*
orthodox (*oo*-θeu-doks) *adj* orthodoxe
ostrich (*o*-stritch) *n* autruche *f*
other (*a*-ðeu) *adj* autre
otherwise (*a*-ðeu-^{ou}aïz) *conj* sinon; *adv* autrement
***ought to** (oot) *devoir
ounce (aouns) *n* once *f*
our (aou^{eu}) *adj* notre
ours (aou^{eu}z) le (la) nôtre, les nôtres; à nous; **a ... of ~** un(e) de nos ...
ourselves (aou^{eu}-*sèlvz*) *pron* nous; nous-mêmes
out (aout) *adv* dehors, hors; **~ of** en dehors de, de
outbreak (*aout*-bréïk) *n* déchaînement *m*
outburst (*aout*-beûst) *n* explosion *f*, éruption *f*
outcome (*aout*-kamm) *n* résultat *m*
***outdo** (aout-*doû*) *v* surpasser
outdoors (aout-*dooz*) *adv* dehors
outer (*aou*-teu) *adj* extérieur
outfit (*aout*-fit) *n* équipement *m*
outline (*aout*-laïn) *n* contour *m*; *v* esquisser
outlook (*aout*-louk) *n* prévision *f*; point de vue
output (*aout*-pout) *n* production *f*
outrage (*aout*-réïdj) *n* outrage *m*
outside (aout-*saïd*) *adv* dehors; *prep* hors de; *n* extérieur *m*
outsize (*aout*-saïz) *n* hors série
outskirts (*aout*-skeûts) *pl* faubourg *m*
outstanding (aout-*stæn*-dinng) *adj* éminent
outward (*aout*-^{ou}eud) *adj* externe
outwards (*aout*-^{ou}eudz) *adv* vers l'extérieur
oval (*ôou*-veul) *adj* ovale
oven (*a*-veunn) *n* four *m*
over (*ôou*-veu) *prep* au-dessus de, pardessus; passé; *adv* au-dessus; *adj* fini; **~ there** là-bas
overall (*ôou*-veu-rool) *adj* total
overalls (*ôou*-veu-roolz) *pl* salopette *f*
overcast (*ôou*-veu-kââst) *adj* nuageux
overcoat (*ôou*-veu-kô^{ou}t) *n* pardessus *m*
***overcome** (ô^{ou}-veu-*kamm*) *v* *vaincre
overdo (ô^{ou}-veu-*doû*) *v* exagérer; prendre trop de ; excéder; trop cuire
overdraw (ô^{ou}-veu-*droo*) *v* exagérer; mettre à découvert
overdue (ô^{ou}-veu-*dyoû*) *adj* en retard; arriéré
overgrown (ô^{ou}-veu-*ghrôoun*) *adj* couvert de verdure
overhaul (ô^{ou}-veu-*hool*) *v* reviser
overhead (ô^{ou}-veu-*hèd*) *adv* en haut
overlook (ô^{ou}-veu-*louk*) *v* ignorer
overnight (ô^{ou}-veu-*naït*) *adv* de nuit
overseas (ô^{ou}-veu-*siiz*) *adj* d'outremer
oversight (*ôou*-veu-saït) *n* inadvertance *f*
***oversleep** (ô^{ou}-veu-*sliip*) *v* *dormir trop longtemps
overstrung (ô^{ou}-veu-*stranng*) *adj* à cordes croisées
***overtake** (ô^{ou}-veu-*téïk*) *v* dépasser; **no overtaking** défense de doubler
over-tired (ô^{ou}-veu-*taïeud*) *adj* épuisé
overture (*ôou*-veu-tcheu) *n* ouverture *f*

overweight (*ôou*-veu-^{ou}éït) *n* surcharge *f*
overwhelm (ô^{ou}-veu-*ouèlm*) *v* accabler; écraser
overwork (ô^{ou}-veu-*oueûk*) *v* se surmener
owe (ô^{ou}) *v* *devoir; **owing to** en raison de
owl (aoul) *n* hibou *m*
own (ô^{ou}n) *v* posséder; *adj* propre
owner (*ôou*-neu) *n* propriétaire *m/f*
ox (oks) *n* (pl oxen) bœuf *m*
oxygen (*ok*-si-djeunn) *n* oxygène *m*
oyster (*oï*-steu) *n* huître *f*
ozone (*ôou*-zô^{ou}n) *n* ozone *m*

P

pace (péïss) *n* allure *f*; pas *m*; rythme *m*
Pacific Ocean (peu-*si*-fik *ôou*-cheunn) Océan Pacifique
pacifism (*pæ*-si-fi-zeumm) *n* pacifisme *m*
pacifist (*pæ*-si-fist) *n* pacifiste *m*
pack (pæk) *v* emballer; **~ up** emballer
package (*pæ*-kidj) *n* colis *m*
packet (*pæ*-kit) *n* paquet *m*
packing (*pæ*-kinng) *n* emballage *m*
pact (pækt) *n* pacte *m*, contrat *m*
pad (pæd) *n* coussinet *m*; bloc-notes *m*
paddle (*pæ*-deul) *n* pagaie *f*
padlock (*pæd*-lok) *n* cadenas *m*
pagan (*péï*-gheunn) *adj* païen; *n* païen *m*
page (péïdj) *n* page *f*
pageboy (*péïdj*-boï) *n* page *m*
pail (péïl) *n* seau *m*
pain (péïn) *n* douleur *f*; **pains** peine *f*
painful (*péïn*-feul) *adj* douloureux
painkiller (*péïn*-ki-leu) *n* analgésique *m*
painless (*péïn*-leuss) *adj* sans douleur
paint (péïnt) *n* peinture *f*; *v* *peindre
paintbox (*péïnt*-boks) *n* boîte de couleurs
paintbrush (*péïnt*-brach) *n* pinceau *m*
painter (*péïn*-teu) *n* peintre *m*
painting (*péïn*-tinng) *n* peinture *f*
pair (pè^{eu}) *n* paire *f*
Pakistan (pââ-ki-*stâân*) Pakistan *m*
Pakistani (pââ-ki-*stââ*-ni) *adj* pakistanais; *n* Pakistanais *m*
pal (pæl) *n colloquial* copain *m*, copine *f*
palace (*pæ*-leuss) *n* palais *m*
pale (péïl) *adj* pâle
palm (pââm) *n* palme *f*; paume *f*; **~ (tree)** palmier *m*
palpitation (pæl-pi-*téï*-cheunn) *n* palpitation *f*
pan (pæn) *n* casserole *f*
pancake (*pæn*-kéïk) *n* crêpe *f*
pane (péïn) *n* carreau *m*
panel (*pæ*-neul) *n* panneau *m*
panic (*pæ*-nik) *n* panique *f*
pant (pænt) *v* haleter
panties (*pæn*-tiz) *pl* culotte *f*
pants (pænts) *pl* caleçon *m*; *plAm* pantalon *m*
pant suit (*pænt*-soût) *n* ensemble-pantalon
panty hose (*pæn*-ti-hô^{ou}z) *n* collants *mpl*
paper (*péï*-peu) *n* papier *m*; journal *m*; en papier; **carbon ~** papier carbone; **~ bag** sac en papier; **~ knife** coupe-papier *m*; **~ napkin** serviette de

papier; **typing ~** papier à machine; **wrapping ~** papier d'emballage
paperback (*péï*-peu-bæk) *n* livre de poche
parade (peu-*réïd*) *n* parade *f*
paradise (*pæ*-reu-daïs) *n* paradis *m*
paraffin (*pæ*-reu-finn) *n* pétrole *m*
paragraph (*pæ*-reu-ghrââf) *n* paragraphe *m*
parakeet (*pæ*-reu-kiit) *n* perruche *f*
parallel (*pæ*-reu-lèl) *adj* parallèle; *n* parallèle *m*
paralyse, *Am* **paralyze** (*pæ*-reu-laïz) *v* paralyser
parcel (*pââ*-seul) *n* colis *m*, paquet *m*
pardon (*pââ*-deunn) *n* pardon *m*; grâce *f*
parent (*pèeu*-reunnt) *n* père *m*, mère *f*; **parents** *pl* parents *pl*
parents-in-law (*pèeu*-reunnts-inn-loo) *pl* beaux-parents *mpl*
parish (*pæ*-rich) *n* paroisse *f*
park (pââk) *n* parc *m*; *v* se garer
parking (*pââ*-kinng) *n* stationnement *m*; **no ~** stationnement interdit; **~ fee** droit de stationnement; **~ light** feu de position; **~ lot** *Am* parking *m*; **~ meter** parcomètre *m*; **~ zone** zone de stationnement
parliament (*pââ*-leu-meunnt) *n* parlement *m*
parliamentary (pââ-leu-*mèn*-teu-ri) *adj* parlementaire
parrot (*pæ*-reut) *n* perroquet *m*
parsley (*pââ*-sli) *n* persil *m*
parson (*pââ*-seunn) *n* pasteur *m*
parsonage (*pââ*-seu-nidj) *n* presbytère *m*
part (pâât) *n* part *f*, partie *f*; morceau *m*; *v* séparer; **spare ~** pièce de rechange
partial (*pââ*-cheul) *adj* partiel; partial
participant (pââ-*ti*-si-peunnt) *n* participant *m*, -e *f*
participate (pââ-*ti*-si-péït) *v* participer
particular (peu-*ti*-kyou-leu) *adj* spécial, particulier; exigeant; **in ~** en particulier
parting (*pââ*-tinng) *n* adieu *m*; raie *f*
partition (pââ-*ti*-cheunn) *n* cloison *f*
partly (*pâât*-li) *adv* en partie, partiellement
partner (*pâât*-neu) *n* partenaire *m/f*; associé *m*
partridge (*pââ*-tridj) *n* perdrix *f*
party (*pââ*-ti) *n* parti *m*; surprise-partie *f*; groupe *m*
pass (pââss) *v* passer, dépasser; réussir; *vAm* doubler; **no passing** *Am* défense de doubler; **~ by** passer à côté; **~ through** traverser
passage (*pæ*-sidj) *n* passage *m*; traversée *f*
passenger (*pæ*-seunn-djeu) *n* passager *m*, passagère *f*; **~ car** *Am* wagon *m*; **~ train** train de voyageurs
passer-by (pââ-seu-*baï*) *n* passant *m*
passion (*pæ*-cheunn) *n* passion *f*; colère *f*
passionate (*pæ*-cheu-neut) *adj* passionné
passive (*pæ*-siv) *adj* passif
passport (*pââss*-poot) *n* passeport *m*; **~ control** contrôle des passeports; **~ photograph** photo d'identité
password (*pââss*-[ou]eûd) *n* mot de passe
past (pââst) *n* passé *m*; *adj* passé, dernier; *prep* le long de, au delà de
paste (péïst) *n* pâte *f*; *v* coller
pastime (*pââss*-taïm) *n* passe-temps *m*; distraction *f*
pastry (*péï*-stri) *n* pâtisserie *f*; **~ shop** pâtisserie *f*
pasture (*pââss*-tcheu) *n* pâture *f*
patch (pætch) *v* rapiécer; **~ up** réparer
patent (*péï*-teunnt) *n* brevet *m*
path (pââθ) *n* sentier *m*

patience (*péï*-cheunns) *n* patience *f*
patient (*péï*-cheunnt) *adj* patient; *n* patient *m*, -e *f*
patriot (*péï*-tri-eut) *n* patriote *m*
patrol (peu-*trôoul*) *n* patrouille *f*; *v* patrouiller; surveiller
pattern (*pæ*-teunn) *n* motif *m*, dessin *m*
pause (pooz) *n* pause *f*; *v* *faire une pause
pave (péïv) *v* paver
pavement (*péïv*-meunnt) *n* trottoir *m*; pavage *m*
pavilion (peu-*vil*-yeunn) *n* pavillon *m*
paw (poo) *n* patte *f*
pawn (poon) *v* donner en gage, *mettre en gage; *n* pion *m*
pay (péï) *n* salaire *m*, paye *f*
***pay** (péï) *v* payer; **~ attention to** *faire attention à; **~ cash** payer comptant; **~ desk** caisse *f*; **paying** rentable; **~ off** amortir
payee (péï-*ii*) *n* bénéficiaire *m/f*
payment (*péï*-meunnt) *n* paiement *m*
PC (pii-*sii*) *n* micro *m*; P.C. *m*
pea (pii) *n* pois *m*
peace (piiss) *n* paix *f*
peaceful (*piiss*-feul) *adj* paisible
peach (piitch) *n* pêche *f*
peacock (*pii*-kok) *n* paon *m*
peak (piik) *n* sommet *m*; apogée *m*; **~ hour** heure de pointe; **~ season** pleine saison
peanut (*pii*-nat) *n* cacahuète *f*
pear (pè^{eu}) *n* poire *f*
pearl (peûl) *n* perle *f*
peasant (*pè*-zeunnt) *n* paysan *m*
pebble (*pè*-beul) *n* galet *m*
peculiar (pi-*kyoûl*-yeu) *adj* spécial, particulier
peculiarity (pi-kyoû-li-*æ*-reu-ti) *n* particularité *f*
pedal (*pè*-deul) *n* pédale *f*
pedestrian (pi-*dè*-stri-eunn) *n* piéton *m*; **no pedestrians** interdit aux piétons; **~ crossing** passage clouté
peel (piil) *v* peler; *n* pelure *f*
peep (piip) *v* épier
peewit (*pii*-^{ou}it) *n* vanneau *m*
peg (pègh) *n* patère *f*
pelican (*pè*-li-keunn) *n* pélican *m*
pelvis (*pèl*-viss) *n* bassin *m*
pen (pèn) *n* plume *f*
penalty (*pè*-neul-ti) *n* amende *f*; peine *f*; **~ kick** penalty *m*
pencil (*pèn*-seul) *n* crayon *m*; **~ sharpener** taille-crayon *m*
pendant (*pèn*-deunnt) *n* pendentif *m*
penetrate (*pè*-ni-tréït) *v* pénétrer
penguin (*pèng*-gh^{ou}inn) *n* pingouin *m*
penicillin (pè-ni-*si*-linn) *n* pénicilline *f*
peninsula (peu-*ninn*-syou-leu) *n* péninsule *f*
penknife (*pèn*-naïf) *n* (pl -knives) canif *m*
penny (*pè*-ni) *n* (pl pence, pennies) penny *m*
pension¹ (*pan*-si-on) *n* pension *f*
pension² (*pèn*-cheunn) *n* pension *f*
Pentecost (*pèn*-ti-kost) *n* Pentecôte *f*
people (*pii*-peul) *pl* gens *mpl/fpl*; *n* peuple *m*
pepper (*pè*-peu) *n* poivre *m*
peppermint (*pè*-peu-minnt) *n* menthe *f*
perceive (peu-*siiv*) *v* *percevoir
percent (peu-*sènt*) *n* pour cent
percentage (peu-*sèn*-tidj) *n* pourcentage *m*
perceptible (peu-*sèp*-ti-beul) *adj* perceptible
perception (peu-*sèp*-cheunn) *n* perception *f*
perch (peûtch) (pl ~) perche *f*
percolator (*peû*-keu-léï-teu) *n* percolateur *m*
perfect (*peû*-fikt) *adj* parfait
perfection (peu-*fèk*-cheunn) *n*

perfection *f*
perform (peu-*foom*) *v* accomplir
performance (peu-*foo*-meunns) *n* performance *f*
perfume (*peû*-fyoûm) *n* parfum *m*
perhaps (peu-*hæps*) *adv* peut-être
peril (*pè*-ril) *n* péril *m*
perilous (*pè*-ri-leuss) *adj* périlleux
period (*pieu*-ri-eud) *n* époque *f*, période *f*; point *m*
periodical (pi^{eu}-ri-*o*-di-keul) *n* périodique *m*; *adj* périodique
perish (*pè*-rich) *v* périr
perishable (*pè*-ri-cheu-beul) *adj* périssable
perjury (*peû*-djeu-ri) *n* faux serment
permanent (*peû*-meu-neunnt) *adj* durable, permanent; stable, fixe; **~ press** pli permanent; **~ wave** permanente *f*
permission (peu-*mi*-cheunn) *n* permission *f*, autorisation *f*; permis *m*, licence *f*
permit¹ (peu-*mit*) *v* *permettre
permit² (*peû*-mit) *n* permis *m*
peroxide (peu-*rok*-saïd) *n* eau oxygénée
perpendicular (peû-peunn-*di*-kyou-leu) *adj* perpendiculaire
Persia (*peû*-cheu) Perse *f*
Persian (*peû*-cheunn) *adj* persan; *n* Persan *m*
person (*peû*-seunn) *n* personne *f*; **per ~** par personne
personal (*peû*-seu-neul) *adj* personnel
personality (peû-seu-*næ*-leu-ti) *n* personnalité *f*
personnel (peû-seu-*nèl*) *n* personnel *m*
perspective (peu-*spèk*-tiv) *n* perspective *f*
perspiration (peû-speu-*réï*-cheunn) *n* transpiration *f*, sueur *f*
perspire (peu-*spaïeu*) *v* transpirer, suer
persuade (peu-*souéïd*) *v* persuader; *convaincre
persuasion (peu-*souéï*-jeunn) *n* conviction *f*
pessimism (*pè*-si-mi-zeumm) *n* pessimisme *m*
pessimist (*pè*-si-mist) *n* pessimiste *m/f*
pessimistic (pè-si-*mi*-stik) *adj* pessimiste
pet (pèt) *n* animal familier; chouchou *m*
petal (*pè*-teul) *n* pétale *m*
petition (pi-*ti*-cheunn) *n* pétition *f*
petrol (*pè*-treul) *n* essence *f*; **~ pump** pompe à essence; **~ station** poste d'essence; **~ tank** réservoir d'essence
petroleum (pi-*trôou*-li-eumm) *n* pétrole *m*
petty (*pè*-ti) *adj* petit, futile, insignifiant; **~ cash** petite monnaie
pewter (*pyoû*-teu) *n* étain *m*
phantom (*fæn*-teumm) *n* fantôme *m*
pharmacist (*fââ*-meu-sist) *n* pharmacien *m*, pharmacienne *f*
pharmacology (fââ-meu-*ko*-leu-dji) *n* pharmacologie *f*
pharmacy (*fââ*-meu-si) *n* pharmacie *f*
phase (féïz) *n* phase *f*
pheasant (*fè*-zeunnt) *n* faisan *m*
Philippine (*fi*-li-païn) *adj* philippin
Philippines (*fi*-li-piinz) *pl* Philippines *fpl*
philosopher (fi-*lo*-seu-feu) *n* philosophe *m*
philosophy (fi-*lo*-seu-fi) *n* philosophie *f*
phone (fô^{ou}n) *n* téléphone *m*; *v* téléphoner
phonetic (feu-*nè*-tik) *adj* phonétique
photo (*fôou*-tô^{ou}) *n* (pl **~**s) photo *f*
photocopy (*fôou*-teu-ko-pi) *n*

photocopie *f*; *v* photocopier
photograph (*fôou*-teu-ghrââf) *n* photographie *f*; *v* photographier
photographer (feu-*to*-ghreu-feu) *n* photographe *m*
photography (feu-*to*-ghreu-fi) *n* photographie *f*
phrase (fréïz) *n* locution *f*; ~ **book** manuel de conversation
physical (*fi*-zi-keul) *adj* physique
physician (fi-*zi*-cheunn) *n* médecin *m*
physicist (*fi*-zi-sist) *n* physicien *m*
physics (*fi*-ziks) *n* physique *f*
pianist (*pii*-eu-nist) *n* pianiste *m*
piano (pi-*æ*-nô^ou^) *n* piano *m*; **grand** ~ piano à queue
pick (pik) *v* *cueillir; choisir; *n* choix *m*; ~ **up** ramasser; *aller chercher; **pick-up van** camionnette *f*
pickles (*pi*-keulz) *pl* conserves au vinaigre, marinades *fpl*
picnic (*pik*-nik) *n* pique-nique *m*; *v* pique-niquer
picture (*pik*-tcheu) *n* peinture *f*; illustration *f*; image *f*; ~ **postcard** carte postale, carte postale illustrée; **pictures** cinéma *m*
picturesque (pik-tcheu-*rèsk*) *adj* pittoresque
pie (paï) *n* pâté *m*; tourte *f*
piece (piiss) *n* morceau *m*, pièce *f*
pier (pi^eu^) *n* jetée *f*
pierce (pi^eu^ss) *v* percer
pig (pigh) *n* cochon *m*
pigeon (*pi*-djeunn) *n* pigeon *m*
pig-headed (pigh-*hè*-did) *adj* obstiné
piglet (*pigh*-leut) *n* cochon de lait
pigskin (*pigh*-skinn) *n* peau de porc
pike (païk) (pl ~) brochet *m*
pile (païl) *n* tas *m*; *v* entasser; **piles** *pl* hémorroïdes *fpl*
pilgrim (*pil*-ghrimm) *n* pèlerin *m*
pilgrimage (*pil*-ghri-midj) *n* pèlerinage *m*
pill (pil) *n* pilule *f*
pillar (*pi*-leu) *n* colonne *f*, pilier *m*
pillow (*pi*-lô^ou^) *n* oreiller *m*
pillowcase (*pi*-lô^ou^-kéïss) *n* taie d'oreiller
pilot (*paï*-leut) *n* pilote *m*
pimple (*pimm*-peul) *n* pustule *f*
pin (pinn) *n* épingle *f*; *v* épingler; **bobby** ~ *Am* pince à cheveux
pincers (*pinn*-seuz) *pl* tenailles *fpl*
pinch (pinntch) *v* pincer
pineapple (*paï*-næ-peul) *n* ananas *m*
ping-pong (*pinng*-ponng) *n* ping-pong *m*
pink (pinngk) *adj* rose
pint (païnt) *n* pinte *f*
pioneer (paï-eu-*nieu*) *n* pionnier *m*
pious (*paï*-euss) *adj* pieux
pip (pip) *n* pépin *m*
pipe (païp) *n* pipe *f*; tuyau *m*; ~ **cleaner** cure-pipe *m*; ~ **tobacco** tabac pour pipe
pipeline (*païp*-laïn) *n* pipe-line *m*
pirate (*païeu*-reut) *n* pirate *m*
pistol (*pi*-steul) *n* pistolet *m*
piston (*pi*-steunn) *n* piston *m*; ~ **ring** segment de piston
pit (pit) *n* fosse *f*; mine *f*
pitcher (*pi*-tcheu) *n* cruche *f*
pity (*pi*-ti) *n* pitié *f*; *v* *avoir pitié de; **what a pity!** dommage!
placard (*plæ*-kââd) *n* affiche *f*
place (pléïss) *n* place *f*; *v* poser, placer; ~ **of birth** lieu de naissance; ***take** ~ *avoir lieu
plague (pléïgh) *n* fléau *m*
plaice (pléïss) (pl ~) plie *f*
plain (pléïn) *adj* clair; ordinaire, simple; *n* plaine *f*
plan (plæn) *n* plan *m*; *v* planifier
plane (pléïn) *adj* plat; *n* avion *m*; ~ **crash** accident d'avion
planet (*plæ*-nit) *n* planète *f*
planetarium (plæ-ni-*tèeu*-ri-eumm) *n*

planétarium *m*
plank (plængk) *n* planche *f*
plant (plâânt) *n* plante *f*; usine *f*; *v* planter
plantation (plæn-*téï*-cheunn) *n* plantation *f*
plaster (*plââ*-steu) *n* plâtre *m*; sparadrap *m*
plastic (*plæ*-stik) *adj* plastique; *n* plastique *m*
plate (pléït) *n* assiette *f*; plaque *f*
plateau (*plæ*-tô^{ou}) *n* (pl ~x, ~s) plateau *m*
platform (*plæt*-foom) *n* quai *m*; **~ ticket** billet de quai
platinum (*plæ*-ti-neumm) *n* platine *m*
play (pléï) *v* jouer; *n* jeu *m*; pièce de théâtre; **one-act ~** pièce en un acte; **~ truant** *faire l'école buissonnière
player (pléï^{eu}) *n* joueur *m*, joueuse *f*
playground (*pléï*-ghraound) *n* terrain de jeux
playing card (*pléï*-inng-kââd) *n* carte de jeu
playwright (*pléï*-raït) *n* dramaturge *m*
plea (plii) *n* plaidoyer *m*
plead (pliid) *v* plaider
pleasant (*plè*-zeunnt) *adj* plaisant, sympathique, agréable
please (pliiz) s'il vous plaît; *v* *plaire; **pleased** content; **pleasing** agréable
pleasure (*plè*-jeu) *n* agrément *m*, divertissement *m*, plaisir *m*
plentiful (*plèn*-ti-feul) *adj* abondant
plenty (*plèn*-ti) *n* abondance *f*
pliers (plaï^{eu}z) *pl* pince *f*
plimsolls (*plimm*-seulz) *pl* chaussures de basket
plot (plot) *n* conspiration *f*, complot *m*; intrigue *f*; lopin *m*
plough (plaou) *n* charrue *f*; *v* labourer
plucky (*pla*-ki) *adj* courageux
plug (plagh) *n* fiche *f*; **~ in** brancher
plum (plamm) *n* prune *f*
plumber (*pla*-meu) *n* plombier *m*
plump (plammp) *adj* potelé
plural (*ploueu*-reul) *n* pluriel *m*
plus (plass) *prep* plus
pneumatic (nyoû-*mæ*-tik) *adj* pneumatique
pneumonia (nyoû-*môou*-ni-eu) *n* pneumonie *f*
poach (pô^{ou}tch) *v* braconner
pocket (*po*-kit) *n* poche *f*
pocketknife (*po*-kit-naïf) *n* (pl -knives) couteau de poche
poem (*pôou*-imm) *n* poème *m*
poet (*pôou*-it) *n* poète *m*
poetry (*pôou*-i-tri) *n* poésie *f*
point (poïnt) *n* point *m*; pointe *f*; *v* montrer du doigt; **~ of view** point de vue; **~ out** indiquer
pointed (*poïn*-tid) *adj* pointu
poison (*poï*-zeunn) *n* poison *m*; *v* empoisonner
poisonous (*poï*-zeu-neuss) *adj* vénéneux
Poland (*pôou*-leunnd) Pologne *f*
Pole (pô^{ou}l) *n* Polonais *m*
pole (pô^{ou}l) *n* poteau *m*
police (peu-*liiss*) *pl* police *f*; **~ station** commissariat de police
policeman (peu-*liiss*-meunn) *n* (pl -men) agent de police, policier *m*
policewoman (peu-*liiss*-^{ou}ou-meunn) *n* (pl-women) femme policier
policy (*po*-li-si) *n* politique *f*; police *f*
polio (*pôou*-li-ô^{ou}) *n* poliomyélite *f*
Polish (*pôou*-lich) *adj* polonais
polish (*po*-lich) *v* polir
polite (peu-*laït*) *adj* poli
political (peu-*li*-ti-keul) *adj* politique
politician (po-li-*ti*-cheunn) *n* politicien *m*, politicienne *f*
politics (*po*-li-tiks) *n* politique *f*
poll (pô^{ou}l) *n* vote *m* (par bulletins); scrutin *m*; *v* sonder l'opinion de; réunir; **(opinion) ~** sondage *m*

(d'opinion)
pollution (peu-*loû*-cheunn) *n* pollution *f*
pond (ponnd) *n* étang *m*
pony (*pôou*-ni) *n* poney *m*
pool (poûl) *n* flaque *f* d'eau; mare *f*
poor (pou^eu^) *adj* pauvre; indigent; piètre
pope (pô^ou^p) *n* pape *m*
pop music (pop *myoû*-zik) musique pop
poppy (*po*-pi) *n* coquelicot *m*; pavot *m*
popular (*po*-pyou-leu) *adj* populaire
population (po-pyou-*léï*-cheunn) *n* population *f*
populous (*po*-pyou-leuss) *adj* populeux
porcelain (*poo*-seu-linn) *n* porcelaine *f*
porcupine (*poo*-kyou-païn) *n* porc-épic *m*
pork (pook) *n* porc *m*
port (poot) *n* port *m*; bâbord *m*
portable (*poo*-teu-beul) *adj* portatif
porter (*poo*-teu) *n* porteur *m*; portier *m*
porthole (*poot*-hô^ou^l) *n* hublot *m*
portion (*poo*-cheunn) *n* portion *f*
portrait (*poo*-trit) *n* portrait *m*
Portugal (*poo*-tyou-gheul) Portugal *m*
Portuguese (poo-tyou-*ghiiz*) *adj* portugais; *n* Portugais *m*
posh (poch) *adj colloquial* chic, chouette
position (peu-*zi*-cheunn) *n* position *f*; situation *f*; attitude *f*
positive (*po*-zeu-tiv) *adj* positif; *n* positif *m*
possess (peu-*zèss*) *v* posséder; **possessed** *adj* possédé
possession (peu-*zè*-cheunn) *n* possession *f*; **possessions** biens *mpl*
possibility (po-seu-*bi*-leu-ti) *n* possibilité *f*
possible (*po*-seu-beul) *adj* possible; éventuel
post (pô^ou^st) *n* poteau *m*; poste *m*; poste *f*; *v* poster; **~ box** boîte *f* postale **~-office** bureau de poste
postage (*pôou*-stidj) *n* port *m*; **~ paid** port payé; **~ stamp** timbre-poste *m*
postcard (*pôoust*-kââd) *n* carte postale
poster (*pôou*-steu) *n* affiche *f*
poste restante (pô^ou^st rè-*stant*) poste restante
postman (*pôoust*-meunn) *n* (pl -men) facteur *m*
post-paid (pô^ou^st-*péïd*) *adj* port payé
postpone (peu-*spôoun*) *v* ajourner, *renvoyer à
pot (pot) *n* pot *m*
potato (peu-*téï*-tô^ou^) *n* (pl ~es) pomme de terre
pottery (*po*-teu-ri) *n* poterie *f*
pouch (paoutch) *n* pochette *f*
poulterer (*pôoul*-teu-reu) *n* marchand de volaille
poultry (*pôoul*-tri) *n* volaille *f*
pound (paound) *n* livre *f*
pour (poo) *v* verser
poverty (*po*-veu-ti) *n* pauvreté *f*
powder (*paou*-deu) *n* poudre *f*; **~ compact** poudrier *m*; **~ room** toilettes pour dames; **talc ~** talc *m*
power (paou^eu^) *n* force *f*, puissance *f*; énergie *f*; pouvoir *m*; **~ station** centrale *f*
powerful (*paoueu*-feul) *adj* puissant; fort
powerless (*paoueu*-leuss) *adj* impuissant
practical (*præk*-ti-keul) *adj* pratique
practically (*præk*-ti-kli) *adv* pratiquement
practice (*præk*-tiss) *n* pratique *f*
practise (*præk*-tiss) *v* pratiquer;

s'exercer
praise (préïz) *v* louer; *n* éloge *m*
pram (præm) *n* voiture d'enfant
prawn (proon) *n* crevette *f*, crevette rose
pray (préï) *v* prier
prayer (prè^eu^) *n* prière *f*
preach (priitch) *v* prêcher
precarious (pri-*kèeu*-ri-euss) *adj* précaire
precaution (pri-*koo*-cheunn) *n* précaution *f*
precede (pri-*siid*) *v* précéder
preceding (pri-*sii*-dinng) *adj* précédent
precious (*prè*-cheuss) *adj* précieux
precipice (*prè*-si-piss) *n* précipice *m*
precipitation (pri-si-pi-*téï*-cheunn) *n* précipitation *f*
precise (pri-*saïss*) *adj* précis, exact; méticuleux
predict (pri-*dikt*) *v* *prédire
prefer (pri-*feû*) *v* aimer mieux, préférer
preferable (*prè*-feu-reu-beul) *adj* préférable
preference (*prè*-feu-reunns) *n* préférence *f*
pregnant (*prègh*-neunnt) *adj* enceinte
prejudice (*prè*-djeu-diss) *n* préjugé *m*
preliminary (pri-*li*-mi-neu-ri) *adj* préliminaire
premature (*prè*-meu-tchou^eu^) *adj* prématuré
premier (*prèm*-i^eu^) *n* premier ministre
premises (*prè*-mi-siz) *pl* locaux *mpl*
premium (*prii*-mi-eumm) *n* prime *f*
prepaid (prii-*péïd*) *adj* payé d'avance
preparation (prè-peu-*réï*-cheunn) *n* préparation *f*
prepare (pri-*pèeu*) *v* préparer
prepared (pri-*pèeud*) *adj* prêt
preposition (prè-peu-*zi*-cheunn) *n* préposition *f*
prescribe (pri-*skraïb*) *v* *prescrire
prescription (pri-*skrip*-cheunn) *n* prescription *f*
presence (*prè*-zeunns) *n* présence *f*
present[1] (*prè*-zeunnt) *n* cadeau *m*; présent *m*; *adj* actuel; présent
present[2] (pri-*zènt*) *v* présenter
presently (*prè*-zeunnt-li) *adv* tout à l'heure
preservation (prè-zeu-*véï*-cheunn) *n* conservation *f*
preserve (pri-*zeûv*) *v* conserver; *mettre en conserve
president (*prè*-zi-deunnt) *n* président *m*, -e *f*
press (prèss) *n* presse *f*; *v* appuyer, presser; repasser; **~ conference** conférence de presse
pressing (*prè*-sinng) *adj* pressant, urgent
pressure (*prè*-cheu) *n* pression *f*; tension *f*; **atmospheric ~** pression atmosphérique
prestige (prè-*stiij*) *n* prestige *m*
presumable (pri-*zyoû*-meu-beul) *adj* probable
presume (pri-*zyoûm*) *v* présumer; prendre des libertés; se permettre (**to** de); **~ (up)on** abuser de
presumptuous (pri-*zammp*-cheuss) *adj* présomptueux
pretence (pri-*tèns*) *n* prétexte *m*
pretend (pri-*tènd*) *v* *feindre, prétendre
pretext (*prii*-tèkst) *n* prétexte *m*
pretty (*pri*-ti) *adj* beau, joli; *adv* assez, plutôt, passablement
prevent (pri-*vènt*) *v* empêcher; *prévenir
preventive (pri-*vèn*-tiv) *adj* préventif
preview (*prii*-vyoû) *n* avant-première *f*; aperçu *m*
previous (*prii*-vi-euss) *adj* précédent, antérieur, préalable

pre-war (prii-*ouoo*) *adj* d'avant-guerre
price (praïss) *v* fixer le prix; **~ list** prix courant *m*
priceless (*praïss*-leuss) *adj* inestimable
prick (prik) *v* piquer
pride (praïd) *n* orgueil *m*
priest (priist) *n* prêtre *m*
primary (*praï*-meu-ri) *adj* primaire; premier, primordial; élémentaire
prince (prinns) *n* prince *m*
princess (prinn-*sèss*) *n* princesse *f*
principal (*prinn*-seu-peul) *adj* principal; *n* proviseur *m*, directeur *m*
principle (*prinn*-seu-peul) *n* principe *m*
print (prinnt) *v* imprimer; *n* épreuve *f*; estampe *f*; **printed matter** imprimé *m*
printer (*prinn*-teu) *n* imprimeur *m*; imprimante *f*
prior (praï^{eu}) *adj* antérieur
priority (praï-*o*-reu-ti) *n* priorité *f*
prison (*pri*-zeunn) *n* prison *f*
prisoner (*pri*-zeu-neu) *n* détenu *m*, -e *f*, prisonnier *m*, prisonnière *f*; **~ of war** prisonnier de guerre
privacy (*praï*-veu-si) *n* intimité *f*, vie privée
private (*praï*-vit) *adj* particulier, privé; personnel
privilege (*pri*-vi-lidj) *n* privilège *m*
prize (praïz) *n* prix *m*; récompense *f*
probable (*pro*-beu-beul) *adj* vraisemblable, probable
probably (*pro*-beu-bli) *adv* probablement
problem (*pro*-bleumm) *n* problème *m*; question *f*
procedure (preu-*sii*-djeu) *n* procédure *f*
proceed (preu-*siid*) *v* procéder
process (*prôou*-sèss) *n* processus *m*, procédé *m*; procès *m*
procession (preu-*sè*-cheunn) *n* procession *f*, cortège *m*
proclaim (preu-*kléïm*) *v* proclamer
produce[1] (preu-*dyoûss*) *v* *produire
produce[2] (*prod*-yoûss) *n* produit *m*
producer (preu-*dyoû*-seu) *n* producteur *m*
product (*pro*-dakt) *n* produit *m*
production (preu-*dak*-cheunn) *n* production *f*
profession (preu-*fè*-cheunn) *n* métier *m*, profession *f*
professional (preu-*fè*-cheu-neul) *adj* professionnel
professor (preu-*fè*-seu) *n* professeur *m*
profit (*pro*-fit) *n* bénéfice *m*, profit *m*; avantage *m*; *v* profiter
profitable (*pro*-fi-teu-beul) *adj* profitable
profound (preu-*faound*) *adj* profond
programme (*prôou*-ghræm) *n* programme *m*
progress[1] (*prôou*-ghrèss) *n* progrès *m*
progress[2] (preu-*ghrèss*) *v* avancer
progressive (preu-*ghrè*-siv) *adj* progressif
prohibit (preu-*hi*-bit) *v* *interdire
prohibition (prô^{ou}-i-*bi*-cheunn) *n* interdiction *f*
prohibitive (preu-*hi*-bi-tiv) *adj* inabordable
project (*pro*-djèkt) *n* plan *m*, projet *m*
promenade (pro-meu-*nââd*) *n* promenade *f*
promise (*pro*-miss) *n* promesse *f*; *v* *promettre
promote (preu-*môout*) *v* *promouvoir
promotion (preu-*môou*-cheunn) *n* promotion *f*
prompt (prommpt) *adj* instantané, prompt
pronounce (preu-*naouns*) *v*

prononcer
pronunciation (preu-nann-si-*éï*-cheunn) *n* prononciation *f*
proof (proûf) *n* preuve *f*
propel (preu-*pèl*) *v* propulser
propeller (preu-*pè*-leu) *n* hélice *f*
proper (*pro*-peu) *adj* juste; convenable, pertinent, adéquat, approprié
property (*pro*-peu-ti) *n* propriété *f*
proportion (preu-*poo*-cheunn) *n* proportion *f*
proportional (preu-*poo*-cheu-neul) *adj* proportionnel
proposal (preu-*pôou*-zeul) *n* proposition *f*
propose (preu-*pôouz*) *v* proposer
proposition (pro-peu-*zi*-cheunn) *n* proposition *f*
proprietor (preu-*praï*-eu-teu) *n* propriétaire *m*/*f*
prospect (*pro*-spèkt) *n* perspective *f*
prospectus (preu-*spèk*-teuss) *n* prospectus *m*
prosperity (pro-*spè*-reu-ti) *n* prospérité *f*
prosperous (*pro*-speu-reuss) *adj* prospère
prostitute (*pro*-sti-tyoût) *n* prostituée *f*
protect (preu-*tèkt*) *v* protéger
protection (preu-*tèk*-cheunn) *n* protection *f*
protest[1] (*prôou*-tèst) *n* protestation *f*
protest[2] (preu-*tèst*) *v* protester
Protestant (*pro*-ti-steunnt) *adj* protestant
proud (praoud) *adj* fier; orgueilleux
prove (proûv) *v* démontrer, prouver; se révéler
proverb (*pro*-veûb) *n* proverbe *m*
provide (preu-*vaïd*) *v* fournir; **provided that** pourvu que
province (*pro*-vinns) *n* province *f*
provincial (preu-*vinn*-cheul) *adj* provincial
provisional (preu-*vi*-jeu-neul) *adj* provisoire
provisions (preu-*vi*-jeunnz) *pl* provision *f*
prune (proûn) *n* pruneau *m*
psychiatrist (saï-*kaï*-eu-trist) *n* psychiatre *m*
psychic (*saï*-kik) *adj* psychique
psychological (saï-ko-*lo*-dji-keul) *adj* psychologique
psychologist (saï-*ko*-leu-djist) *n* psychologue *m*
psychology (saï-*ko*-leu-dji) *n* psychologie *f*
pub (pab) *n* bistrot *m*
public (*pa*-blik) *adj* public; général; *n* public *m*; **~ garden** jardin public; **~ house** café *m*
publication (pa-bli-*kéï*-cheunn) *n* publication *f*
publicity (pa-*bli*-seu-ti) *n* publicité *f*
publish (*pa*-blich) *v* publier
publisher (*pa*-bli-cheu) *n* éditeur *m*, éditrice *f*
puddle (*pa*-deul) *n* flaque *f*
pull (poul) *v* tirer; **~ out** *partir; **~ up** s'arrêter
Pullman (*poul*-meunn) *n* voiture Pullman
pullover (*pou*-lô^{ou}-veu) *n* pull-over *m*
pulpit (*poul*-pit) *n* pupitre *m*, chaire *f*
pulse (pals) *n* pouls *m*
pump (pammp) *n* pompe *f*; *v* pomper
pun (pann) *n* jeu *m* de mots
punch (panntch) *v* donner des coups de poing; *n* coup de poing
punctual (*panngk*-tchou-eul) *adj* ponctuel
puncture (*panngk*-tcheu) *n* crevaison *f*
punctured (*panngk*-tcheud) *adj* crevé
punish (*pa*-nich) *v* punir

punishment (*pa*-nich-meunnt) *n* punition *f*
pupil (*pyoû*-peul) *n* élève *m/f*
puppet-show (*pa*-pit-chô^{ou}) *n* théâtre de marionnettes
purchase (*peû*-tcheuss) *v* acheter; *n* acquisition *f*, achat *m*; **~ price** prix d'achat
purchaser (*peû*-tcheu-seu) *n* acheteur *m*, acheteuse *f*
pure (pyou^{eu}) *adj* pur
purple (*peû*-peul) *adj* pourpre
purpose (*peû*-peuss) *n* intention *f*, but *m*; **on ~** intentionnel
purse (peûss) *n* bourse *f*, porte-monnaie *m*
pursue (peu-*syoû*) *v* *poursuivre; aspirer à
pus (pass) *n* pus *m*
push (pouch) *n* poussée *f*, coup *m*; *v* pousser
***put** (pout) *v* placer, poser, *mettre; **~ away** ranger; **~ off** ajourner; **~ on** *mettre; **~ out** *éteindre
puzzle (*pa*-zeul) *n* casse-tête *m*; énigme *f*; *v* embarrasser; **jigsaw ~** puzzle *m*
puzzling (*paz*-linng) *adj* embarrassant
pyjamas (peu-*djââ*-meuz) *pl* pyjama *m*

Q

quail (k^{ou}éïl) *n* (pl ~, ~s) caille *f*
quaint (k^{ou}éïnt) *adj* étrange; vieillot
qualification (k^{ou}o-li-fi-*kéï*-cheunn) *n* qualification *f*; réserve *f*, restriction *f*
qualified (*kouo*-li-faïd) *adj* qualifié; compétent
qualify (*kouo*-li-faï) *v* *être qualifié
quality (*kouo*-leu-ti) *n* qualité *f*; caractéristique *f*
quantity (*kouonn*-teu-ti) *n* quantité *f*; nombre *m*
quarantine (*kouo*-reunn-tiin) *n* quarantaine *f*
quarrel (*kouo*-reul) *v* se disputer; *n* querelle *f*
quarry (*kouo*-ri) *n* carrière *f*
quarter (*kouoo*-teu) *n* quart *m*; trimestre *m*; quartier *m*; **~ of an hour** quart d'heure
quarterly (*kouoo*-teu-li) *adj* trimestriel
quay (kii) *n* quai *m*
queen (k^{ou}iin) *n* reine *f*
queer (k^{ou}i^{eu}) *adj* étrange; drôle
query (*kouieu*-ri) *n* question *f*; *v* s'informer; *mettre en doute
question (*kouèss*-tcheunn) *n* question *f*; problème *m*; *v* interroger; *mettre en doute; **~ mark** point d'interrogation
queue (kyoû) *n* queue *f*; *v* *faire la queue
quick (k^{ou}ik) *adj* rapide
quick-tempered (k^{ou}ik-*tèm*-peud) *adj* irascible
quiet (*kouaï*-eut) *adj* paisible, calme, tranquille; *n* silence *m*, tranquillité *f*
quilt (k^{ou}ilt) *n* courtepointe *f*
quit (k^{ou}it) *v* cesser
quite (k^{ou}aït) *adv* entièrement, tout à fait; assez, plutôt
quiz (k^{ou}iz) *n* (pl ~zes) jeu concours
quota (*kouôou*-teu) *n* quote-part *f*
quotation (k^{ou}ô^{ou}-*téï*-cheunn) *n* citation *f*; **~ marks** guillemets *mpl*
quote (k^{ou}ô^{ou}t) *v* citer

R

rabbit (*ræ*-bit) *n* lapin *m*
rabies (*réï*-biz) *n* rage *f*
race (réïss) *n* course *f*
racecourse (*réïss*-kooss) *n* champ de courses, hippodrome *m*
racehorse (*réïss*-hooss) *n* cheval de course
racetrack (*réïss*-træk) *n* piste de courses
racial (*réï*-cheul) *adj* racial
racket (*ræ*-kit) *n* vacarme *m*; raquette *f*
radiator (*réï*-di-éï-teu) *n* radiateur *m*
radical (*ræ*-di-keul) *adj* radical
radio (*réï*-di-ô^{ou}) *n* radio *f*
radish (*ræ*-dich) *n* radis *m*
radius (*réï*-di-euss) *n* (pl radii) rayon *m*
raft (râââft) *n* radeau *m*
rag (rægh) *n* chiffon *m*
rage (réïdj) *n* fureur *f*, rage *f*; *v* rager, sévir
raid (réïd) *n* raid *m*
rail (réïl) *n* balustrade *f*, barre *f*
railing (*réï*-linng) *n* rampe *f*
railroad (*réïl*-rô^{ou}d) *nAm* voie ferrée, chemin de fer
railway (*réïl*-^{ou}éï) *n* chemin de fer, voie ferrée
rain (réïn) *n* pluie *f*; *v* *pleuvoir
rainbow (*réïn*-bô^{ou}) *n* arc-en-ciel *m*
raincoat (*réïn*-kô^{ou}t) *n* imperméable *m*
rainproof (*réïn*-proûf) *adj* imperméable
rainy (*réï*-ni) *adj* pluvieux
raise (réïz) *v* élever; relever; cultiver; *nAm* augmentation de salaire
raisin (*réï*-zeunn) *n* raisin sec
rake (réïk) *n* râteau *m*
rally (*ræ*-li) *n* rassemblement *m*
ramp (ræmp) *n* pente *f*
rancid (*ræn*-sid) *adj* rance
rang (ræng) *v* (p ring)
range (réïndj) *n* gamme *f*
rank (rængk) *n* grade *m*; rang *m*
ransom (*ræn*-seumm) *n* rançon *f*
rape (réïp) *v* violer
rapid (*ræ*-pid) *adj* rapide
rapids (*ræ*-pidz) *pl* rapide *m*
rare (rè^{eu}) *adj* rare
rarely (*rèeu*-li) *adv* rarement
rascal (*râââ*-skeul) *n* coquin *m*, fripon *m*
rash (ræch) *n* éruption *f*; *adj* imprudent, inconsidéré
raspberry (*râââz*-beu-ri) *n* framboise *f*
rat (ræt) *n* rat *m*
rate (réït) *n* tarif *m*; vitesse *f*; **at any ~** de toute façon, quoiqu'il en soit; **~ of exchange** cours du change
rather (*râââ*-ðeu) *adv* assez, passablement, plutôt
ration (*ræ*-cheunn) *n* ration *f*
rattan (ræ-*tæn*) *n* rotin *m*
raven (*réï*-veunn) *n* corbeau *m*
raw (roo) *adj* cru; **~ material** matière première
ray (réï) *n* rayon *m*
razor (*réï*-zeu) *n* rasoir *m*; **~ blade** lame de rasoir
reach (riitch) *v* *atteindre; *n* portée *f*
react (ri-*ækt*) *v* réagir
reaction (ri-*æk*-cheunn) *n* réaction *f*
***read** (riid) *v* *lire
reader (*rii*-deu) *n* lecteur *m*, lectrice *f*; maître *m* de conférences; livre *m* de lecture
reading (*rii*-dinng) *n* lecture *f*; **~ lamp** lampe de travail; **~ room** salle de lecture
ready (*rè*-di) *adj* prêt
ready-made (rè-di-*méïd*) *adj* de confection

real (ri^{eu}l) *adj* réel
reality (ri-*æ*-leu-ti) *n* réalité *f*
realizable (*rieu*-laï-zeu-beul) *adj* réalisable
realize (*rieu*-laïz) *v* se rendre compte; réaliser
really (*rieu*-li) *adv* vraiment, réellement; en réalité
rear (ri^{eu}) *n* arrière *m*; *v* élever; ~ **light** feu arrière
reason (*rii*-zeunn) *n* cause *f*, raison *f*; sens *m*; *v* raisonner
reasonable (*rii*-zeu-neu-beul) *adj* raisonnable; équitable
reassure (rii-eu-*choueu*) *v* rassurer
rebate (*rii*-béït) *n* réduction *f*, rabais *m*
rebellion (ri-*bèl*-yeunn) *n* révolte *f*, rébellion *f*
recall (ri-*kool*) *v* se rappeler; rappeler; révoquer
receipt (ri-*siit*) *n* reçu *m*; réception *f*
receive (ri-*siiv*) *v* *recevoir
receiver (ri-*sii*-veu) *n* combiné *m*
recent (*rii*-seunnt) *adj* récent
recently (*rii*-seunnt-li) *adv* l'autre jour, récemment
reception (ri-*sèp*-cheunn) *n* réception *f*; accueil *m*; ~ **office** réception *f*
receptionist (ri-*sèp*-cheu-nist) *n* hôtesse *f*
recipe (*rè*-si-pi) *n* recette *f*
recital (ri-*saï*-teul) *n* récital *m*
reckon (*rè*-keunn) *v* calculer; estimer; supposer
recognition (rè-keugh-*ni*-cheunn) *n* reconnaissance *f*
recognize (*rè*-keugh-naïz) *v* *reconnaître
recollect (rè-keu-*lèkt*) *v* se *souvenir
recommence (rii-keu-*mèns*) *v* recommencer
recommend (rè-keu-*mènd*) *v* recommander; conseiller
recommendation (rè-keu-mèn-*déï*-cheunn) *n* recommandation *f*
reconciliation (rè-keunn-si-li-*éï*-cheunn) *n* réconciliation *f*
record[1] (*rè*-kood) *n* disque *m*; record *m*; dossier *m*; **long-playing ~** microsillon *m*; **~ player** tourne-disque *m*
record[2] (ri-*kood*) *v* enregistrer
recorder (ri-*koo*-deu) *n* magnétophone *m*
recording (ri-*koo*-dinng) *n* enregistrement *m*
recover (ri-*ka*-veu) *v* récupérer; se *remettre, guérir
recovery (ri-*ka*-veu-ri) *n* guérison *f*
recreation (rè-kri-*éï*-cheunn) *n* récréation *f*; ~ **centre** centre de loisirs; ~ **ground** terrain de jeux
rectangle (*rèk*-tæng-gheul) *n* rectangle *m*
rectangular (rèk-*tæng*-ghyou-leu) *adj* rectangulaire
rector (*rèk*-teu) *n* pasteur *m*, recteur *m*
rectory (*rèk*-teu-ri) *n* presbytère *m*
red (rèd) *adj* rouge
redeem (ri-*diim*) *v* racheter, compenser
reduce (ri-*dyoûss*) *v* *réduire, diminuer
reduction (ri-*dak*-cheunn) *n* rabais *m*, réduction *f*
redundant (ri-*dann*-deunnt) *adj* superflu
reed (riid) *n* roseau *m*
reef (riif) *n* récif *m*
referee (rè-feu-*rii*) *n* arbitre *m*; *v* arbitrer; *v* être arbitre, faire fonction d'arbitre
reference (*rèf*-reunns) *n* référence *f*; rapport *m*; **with ~ to** relatif à
refer to (ri-*feû*) *renvoyer à
refill (*rii*-fil) *n* recharge *f*
refinery (ri-*faï*-neu-ri) *n* raffinerie *f*
reflect (ri-*flèkt*) *v* refléter

reflection (ri-*flèk*-cheunn) *n* reflet *m*
reflector (ri-*flèk*-teu) *n* réflecteur *m*
reformation (rè-feu-*méï*-cheunn) *n* réforme *f*
refresh (ri-*frèch*) *v* rafraîchir
refreshment (ri-*frèch*-meunnt) *n* rafraîchissement *m*
refrigerator (ri-*fri*-djeu-réï-teu) *n* frigidaire *m*, réfrigérateur *m*
refugee (rè-fyoû-*djii*) *n* réfugié *m*, réfugiée *f*
refund[1] (ri-*fannd*) *v* rendre, rembourser
refund[2] (*rii*-fannd) *n* remboursement *m*
refusal (ri-*fyoû*-zeul) *n* refus *m*
refuse[1] (ri-*fyoûz*) *v* refuser
refuse[2] (*rè*-fyoûss) *n* rebut *m*
regard (ri-*ghââd*) *v* considérer; *n* respect *m*; **as regards** quant à, concernant, en ce qui concerne
regarding (ri-*ghââ*-dinng) *prep* en ce qui concerne, concernant; à propos de
régime (réï-*jiim*) *n* régime *m*
region (*rii*-djeunn) *n* région *f*
regional (*rii*-djeu-neul) *adj* régional
register (*rè*-dji-steu) *v* s'*inscrire; recommander; **registered letter** lettre recommandée
registration (rè-dji-*stréï*-cheunn) *n* inscription *f*; **~ form** formulaire d'inscription; **~ number** numéro d'immatriculation; **~ plate** plaque d'immatriculation
regret (ri-*ghrèt*) *v* regretter; *n* regret *m*
regular (*rè*-ghyou-leu) *adj* régulier; ordinaire, normal
regulate (*rè*-ghyou-léït) *v* régler
regulation (rè-ghyou-*léï*-cheunn) *n* règlement *m*
rehabilitation (rii-heu-bi-li-*téï*-cheunn) *n* rééducation *f*
rehearsal (ri-*heû*-seul) *n* répétition *f*
rehearse (ri-*heûss*) *v* répéter
reign (réïn) *n* règne *m*; *v* régner
reimburse (rii-imm-*beûss*) *v* restituer, rembourser
reject (ri-*djèkt*) *v* refuser, rejeter
relate (ri-*léït*) *v* relater
related (ri-*léï*-tid) *adj* apparenté
relation (ri-*léï*-cheunn) *n* rapport *m*, relation *f*; parent *m*
relationship (ri-*léï*-cheunn-chip) *n* rapport *m*; parenté *f*
relative (*rè*-leu-tiv) *n* parent *m*; *adj* relatif
relax (ri-*læks*) *v* se détendre
relaxation (ri-læk-*séï*-cheunn) *n* détente *f*
reliable (ri-*laï*-eu-beul) *adj* digne de confiance
relic (*rè*-lik) *n* relique *f*
relief (ri-*liif*) *n* soulagement *m*; soutien *m*; relief *m*
relieve (ri-*liiv*) *v* soulager; relayer
religion (ri-*li*-djeunn) *n* religion *f*
religious (ri-*li*-djeuss) *adj* religieux
rely on (ri-*laï*) compter sur
remain (ri-*méïn*) *v* rester
remainder (ri-*méïn*-deu) *n* restant *m*, reste *m*
remaining (ri-*méï*-ninng) *adj* restant
remark (ri-*mââk*) *n* remarque *f*; *v* remarquer
remarkable (ri-*mââ*-keu-beul) *adj* remarquable
remedy (*rè*-meu-di) *n* remède *m*
remember (ri-*mèm*-beu) *v* se rappeler; *retenir
remembrance (ri-*mèm*-breunns) *n* souvenir *m*
remind (ri-*maïnd*) *v* rappeler
remit (ri-*mit*) *v* *remettre
remittance (ri-*mi*-teunns) *n* versement *m*
remnant (*rèm*-neunnt) *n* reste *m*, restant *m*

remote (ri-*môout*) *adj* éloigné, lointain
removal (ri-*moû*-veul) *n* déplacement *m*
remove (ri-*moûv*) *v* enlever
remunerate (ri-*myoû*-neu-réït) *v* rémunérer
remuneration (ri-myoû-neu-*réï*-cheunn) *n* rémunération *f*
renew (ri-*nyoû*) *v* renouveler
rent (rènt) *v* louer; *n* loyer *m*
repair (ri-*pèeu*) *v* réparer; *n* réparation *f*
reparation (rè-peu-*réï*-cheunn) *n* réparation *f*
***repay** (ri-*péï*) *v* rembourser
repayment (ri-*péï*-meunnt) *n* remboursement *m*
repeat (ri-*piit*) *v* répéter
repellent (ri-*pè*-leunnt) *adj* écœurant, répugnant
repentance (ri-*pèn*-teunns) *n* repentir *m*
repertory (*rè*-peu-teu-ri) *n* répertoire *m*
repetition (rè-peu-*ti*-cheunn) *n* répétition *f*
replace (ri-*pléïss*) *v* remplacer
reply (ri-*plaï*) *v* répondre; *n* réponse *f*; **in ~** en réponse
report (ri-*poot*) *v* relater; rapporter; se présenter; *n* compte rendu, rapport *m*
reporter (ri-*poo*-teu) *n* reporter *m*
represent (rè-pri-*zènt*) *v* représenter
representation (rè-pri-zèn-*téï*-cheunn) *n* représentation *f*
representative (rè-pri-*zèn*-teu-tiv) *adj* représentatif
reprimand (*rè*-pri-mâând) *v* réprimander
reproach (ri-*prôoutch*) *n* reproche *m*; *v* reprocher
reproduce (rii-preu-*dyoûss*) *v* *reproduire
reproduction (rii-preu-*dak*-cheunn) *n* reproduction *f*
reptile (*rèp*-taïl) *n* reptile *m*
republic (ri-*pa*-blik) *n* république *f*
republican (ri-*pa*-bli-keunn) *adj* républicain
repulsive (ri-*pal*-siv) *adj* repoussant
reputation (rè-pyou-*téï*-cheunn) *n* réputation *f*
request (ri-*kouèst*) *n* requête *f*; demande *f*; *v* *requérir
require (ri-*kouaïeu*) *v* exiger
requirement (ri-*kouaïeu*-meunnt) *n* exigence *f*
requisite (*rè*-k^{ou}i-zit) *adj* requis
rescue (*rè*-skyoû) *v* sauver; *n* sauvetage *m*
research (ri-*seûtch*) *n* recherche *f*
resemblance (ri-*zèm*-bleunns) *n* ressemblance *f*
resemble (ri-*zèm*-beul) *v* ressembler à
resent (ri-*zènt*) *v* s'offenser de, en *vouloir à
reservation (rè-zeu-*véï*-cheunn) *n* réservation *f*
reserve (ri-*zeûv*) *v* réserver; *retenir; *n* réserve *f*
reserved (ri-*zeûvd*) *adj* réservé
reservoir (*rè*-zeu-v^{ou}ââ) *n* réservoir *m*
reside (ri-*zaïd*) *v* résider
residence (*rè*-zi-deunns) *n* résidence *f*; **~ permit** permis de séjour
resident (*rè*-zi-deunnt) *n* résident *m*; *adj* domicilié; interne
resign (ri-*zaïn*) *v* démissionner
resignation (rè-zigh-*néï*-cheunn) *n* démission *f*
resin (*rè*-zinn) *n* résine *f*
resist (ri-*zist*) *v* résister
resistance (ri-*zi*-steunns) *n* résistance *f*
resolute (*rè*-zeu-loût) *adj* résolu, déterminé

respect (ri-*spèkt*) *n* respect *m*; estime *f*, considération *f*; *v* respecter
respectable (ri-*spèk*-teu-beul) *adj* honorable, respectable
respectful (ri-*spèkt*-feul) *adj* respectueux
respective (ri-*spèk*-tiv) *adj* respectif
respiration (rè-speu-*réï*-cheunn) *n* respiration *f*
respite (*rè*-spaït) *n* répit *m*
responsibility (ri-sponn-seu-*bi*-leu-ti) *n* responsabilité *f*
responsible (ri-*sponn*-seu-beul) *adj* responsable
rest (rèst) *n* repos *m*; reste *m*; *v* se reposer; **~ home** maison de repos; **~ room** toilettes
restaurant (*rè*-steu-ron) *n* restaurant *m*
restful (*rèst*-feul) *adj* reposant
restless (*rèst*-leuss) *adj* agité; inquiet
restrain (ri-*stréïn*) *v* *contenir, *retenir
restriction (ri-*strik*-cheunn) *n* restriction *f*
result (ri-*zalt*) *n* résultat *m*; effet *m*; *v* résulter
resume (ri-*zyoûm*) *v* *reprendre
résumé (*rè*-zyou-méï) *n* résumé *m*; *Am* curriculum vitae *m*; C.V. *m*
retail (*rii*-téïl) *v* détailler; **~ trade** commerce de détail
retailer (*rii*-téï-leu) *n* détaillant *m*, -e *f*
retina (*rè*-ti-neu) *n* rétine *f*
retired (ri-*taïeud*) *adj* retraité
return (ri-*teûnn*) *v* *revenir, retourner; *n* retour *m*; **~ flight** vol de retour; **~ journey** voyage de retour
reunite (rii-yoû-*naït*) *v* réunir
reveal (ri-*viil*) *v* révéler
revelation (rè-veu-*léï*-cheunn) *n* révélation *f*
revenge (ri-*vèndj*) *n* vengeance *f*
revenue (*rè*-veu-nyoû) *n* recettes, revenu *m*
reverse (ri-*veûss*) *n* contraire *m*; revers *m*; marche arrière; revirement *m*; *adj* inverse; *v* *faire marche arrière
review (ri-*vyoû*) *n* critique *f*; revue *f*
revise (ri-*vaïz*) *v* reviser
revision (ri-*vi*-jeunn) *n* révision *f*
revival (ri-*vaï*-veul) *n* reprise *f*
revolt (ri-*vôoult*) *v* se révolter; *n* rébellion *f*, révolte *f*
revolting (ri-*vôoul*-tinng) *adj* dégoûtant, révoltant, répugnant
revolution (rè-veu-*loû*-cheunn) *n* révolution *f*, rotation *f*
revolver (ri-*vol*-veu) *n* revolver *m*
revue (ri-*vyoû*) *n* revue *f*
reward (ri-*ouood*) *n* récompense *f*; *v* récompenser
rheumatism (*roû*-meu-ti-zeumm) *n* rhumatisme *m*
rhinoceros (raï-*no*-seu-reuss) *n* (pl **~**, **~**es) rhinocéros *m*
rhubarb (*roû*-bââb) *n* rhubarbe *f*
rhyme (raïm) *n* rime *f*
rhythm (*ri*-ðeumm) *n* rythme *m*
rib (rib) *n* côte *f*
ribbon (*ri*-beunn) *n* ruban *m*
rice (raïss) *n* riz *m*
rich (ritch) *adj* riche
riches (*ri*-tchiz) *pl* richesse *f*
rid (rid)*v* débarrasser (**of** de); **get ~ of** se débarrasser de
riddle (*ri*-deul) *n* énigme *f*
ride (raïd) *n* course *f*
***ride** (raïd) *v* aller; monter à cheval
rider (*raï*-deu) *n* cavalier *m*
ridge (ridj) *n* arête *f*
ridicule (*ri*-di-kyoûl) *v* ridiculiser
ridiculous (ri-*di*-kyou-leuss) *adj* ridicule
riding (*raï*-dinng) *n* équitation *f*; **~ school** manège *m*
rifle (*raï*-feul) *v* fusil *m*

right (raït) *n* droit *m*; *adj* correct, juste; droit; équitable; **all ~!** d'accord!; ***be ~** *avoir raison; **~ of way** priorité de passage
righteous (*raï*-tcheuss) *adj* juste
right-hand (*raït*-hænd) *adj* à droite, de droite
rightly (*raït*-li) *adv* justement
rim (rimm) *n* jante *f*; rebord *m*
ring (rinng) *n* bague *f*; cercle *m*; piste *f*
***ring** (rinng) *v* sonner; **~ up** téléphoner
rinse (rinns) *v* rincer; *n* rinçage *m*
riot (*raï*-eut) *n* émeute *f*
rip (rip) *v* déchirer
ripe (raïp) *adj* mûr
rise (raïz) *n* augmentation de salaire, augmentation *f*; élévation *f*; montée *f*; essor *m*
***rise** (raïz) *v* se lever; monter
rising (*raï*-zinng) *n* insurrection *f*
risk (risk) *n* risque *m*; danger *m*; *v* risquer
risky (*ri*-ski) *adj* dangereux, risqué
rival (*raï*-veul) *n* rival *m*, -e *f*; concurrent *m*, -e *f*; *v* rivaliser
rivalry (*raï*-veul-ri) *n* rivalité *f*; concurrence *f*
river (*ri*-veu) *n* fleuve *m*; **~ bank** rive *f*
riverside (*ri*-veu-saïd) *n* bord de la rivière
roach (rô^{ou}tch) *n* (pl ~) gardon *m*
road (rô^{ou}d) *n* rue *f*, route *f*; **~ fork** *n* bifurcation *f*; **~ map** carte routière; **~ system** réseau routier; **~ up** attention travaux
roadhouse (*rôoud*-haouss) *n* auberge *f*
roadside (*rôoud*-saïd) *n* bord de la route; **~ restaurant** auberge *f*
roadway (*rôoud*-^{ou}éï) *nAm* chaussée *f*
roam (rô^{ou}m) *v* vagabonder
roar (roo) *v* mugir, rugir; *n* rugissement *m*, grondement *m*
roast (rô^{ou}st) *v* griller, rôtir
rob (rob) *v* voler
robber (*ro*-beu) *n* voleur *m*
robbery (*ro*-beu-ri) *n* vol *m*
robe (rô^{ou}b) *n* robe *f*
robin (*ro*-binn) *n* rouge-gorge *m*
robust (rô^{ou}-*bast*) *adj* robuste
rock (rok) *n* rocher *m*; *v* balancer
rocket (*ro*-kit) *n* fusée *f*
rocky (*ro*-ki) *adj* rocheux
rod (rod) *n* barre *f*, tige *f*
roe (rô^{ou}) *n* œufs de poisson, laitance *f*
role, rôle (rô^{ou}l) *n* rôle *m*
roll (rô^{ou}l) *v* rouler; *n* rouleau *m*; petit pain
roller-skating (*rôou*-leu-skéï-tinng) *n* patinage à roulettes
Roman Catholic (*rôou*-meunn *kæ*-θeu-lik) catholique
romance (reu-*mæns*) *n* idylle *f*
romantic (reu-*mæn*-tik) *adj* romantique
roof (roûf) *n* toit *m*; **thatched ~** toit de chaume *m*
room (roûm) *n* pièce *f*, chambre *f*; espace *m*, place *f*; **~ and board** pension complète; **~ service** service d'étage; **~ temperature** température ambiante
roomy (*roû*-mi) *adj* spacieux
root (roût) *n* racine *f*
rope (rô^{ou}p) *n* corde *f*
rosary (*rôou*-zeu-ri) *n* rosaire *m*
rose (rô^{ou}z) *n* rose *f*; *adj* rose
rotten (*ro*-teunn) *adj* pourri
rouge (roûj) *n* rouge *m*
rough (raf) *adj* rugueux
roulette (roû-*lèt*) *n* roulette *f*
round (raound) *adj* rond; *prep* autour de; *n* reprise *f*; **~ trip** *Am* aller et retour
roundabout (*raoun*-deu-baout) *n* rond-point *m*
rounded (*raoun*-did) *adj* arrondi

route (roût) *n* route *f*
routine (roû-*tiin*) *n* routine *f*
row[1] (rô^{ou}) *n* rang *m*; *v* ramer
row[2] (raou) *n* querelle *f*
rowdy (*raou*-di) *adj* tapageur
rowing boat (*rôou*-inng-bô^{ou}t) *n* bateau à rames
royal (*roï*-eul) *adj* royal
rub (rab) *v* frotter
rubber (*ra*-beu) *n* caoutchouc *m*; gomme *f*; **~ band** élastique *m*
rubbish (*ra*-bich) *n* détritus *m*; radotage *m*, sottise *f*; **~ bin** poubelle *f*; **talk ~** baratiner
rucksack (*rak*-sæk) *n* sac à dos
rudder (*ra*-deu) *n* gouvernail *m*
rude (roûd) *adj* grossier
rug (ragh) *n* tapis *m*
ruin (*roû*-inn) *v* ruiner; *n* ruine *f*
rule (roûl) *n* règle *f*; régime *m*, gouvernement *m*, règne *m*; *v* régner, gouverner; **as a ~** généralement, en général
ruler (*roû*-leu) *n* monarque *m*, dirigeant *m*; règle *f*
Rumania (roû-*méï*-ni-eu) Roumanie *f*
Rumanian (roû-*méï*-ni-eunn) *adj* roumain; *n* Roumain *m*
rumo(u)r (*roû*-meu) *n* rumeur *f*
***run** (rann) *v* *courir; **~ into** rencontrer
runaway (*ra*-neu-^{ou}éï) *n* fugitif *m*
rung (rann) *v* (pp ring)
runner (*ra*-neu) *n* coureur *m*, coureuse *f*; patin *m*; coulisseau *m*
runway (*rann*-^{ou}éï) *n* piste de décollage
rural (*roueu*-reul) *adj* rural
ruse (roûz) *n* ruse *f*
rush (rach) *v* se presser; *n* jonc *m*; **~ hour** heure de pointe
Russia (*ra*-cheu) Russie *f*
Russian (*ra*-cheunn) *adj* russe; *n* Russe *m*
rust (rast) *n* rouille *f*
rustic (*ra*-stik) *adj* rustique
rusty (*ra*-sti) *adj* rouillé

S

sack (sæk) *n* sac *m*
sacred (*séï*-krid) *adj* sacré
sacrifice (*sæ*-kri-faïss) *n* sacrifice *m*; *v* sacrifier
sacrilege (*sæ*-kri-lidj) *n* sacrilège *m*
sad (sæd) *adj* triste; malheureux, affligé
saddle (*sæ*-deul) *n* selle *f*
sadness (*sæd*-neuss) *n* tristesse *f*
safe (séïf) *adj* sûr; *n* coffre-fort
safety (*séïf*-ti) *n* sécurité *f*; **~ belt** ceinture de sécurité; **~ pin** épingle de sûreté
sail (séïl) *v* naviguer; *n* voile *f*
sailing boat (*séï*-linng-bô^{ou}t) *n* bateau à voiles
sailor (*séï*-leu) *n* marin *m*
saint (séïnt) *n* saint *m*
salad (*sæ*-leud) *n* salade *f*; **~ oil** huile de table
salary (*sæ*-leu-ri) *n* paie *f*, salaire *m*
sale (séïl) *n* vente *f*; **clearance ~** soldes; **for ~** à vendre; **sales** soldes
saleable (*séï*-leu-beul) *adj* vendable
salesgirl (*séïlz*-gheûl) *n* vendeuse *f*
salesman (*séïlz*-meunn) *n* (pl -men) vendeur *m*
salmon (*sæ*-meunn) *n* (pl ~) saumon

m
salon (*sæ*-lon) *n* salon *m*
saloon (seu-*loûn*) *n* café *m*
salt (soolt) *n* sel *m*; ~ **cellar**, *Am* ~ **shaker** salière *f*
salty (*sool*-ti) *adj* salé
salute (seu-*loût*) *v* saluer
salve (sââv) *n* onguent *m*
same (séïm) *adj* même
sample (*sââm*-peul) *n* échantillon *m*
sanatorium (sæ-neu-*too*-ri-eumm) *n* (pl ~s, -ria) sanatorium *m*
sand (sænd) *n* sable *m*
sandal (*sæn*-deul) *n* sandale *f*
sandpaper (*sænd*-péï-peu) *n* papier de verre
sandwich (*sæn*-ᵒᵘidj) *n* sandwich *m*; tartine *f*
sandy (*sæn*-di) *adj* sableux
sanitary (*sæ*-ni-teu-ri) *adj* sanitaire; ~ **towel** (*Am* ~ **napkin**) serviette hygiénique
sardine (sââ-*diin*) *n* sardine *f*
satchel (*sæ*-tcheul) *n* cartable *m*
satellite (*sæ*-teu-laït) *n* satellite *m*
satin (*sæ*-tinn) *n* satin *m*
satisfaction (sæ-tiss-*fæk*-cheunn) *n* satisfaction *f*
satisfactory (sæ-tiss-*fæk*-teu-ri) *adj* satisfaisant
satisfy (*sæ*-tiss-faï) *v* *satisfaire
Saturday (*sæ*-teu-di) samedi *m*
sauce (sooss) *n* sauce *f*
saucepan (*sooss*-peunn) *n* poêle *f*
saucer (*soo*-seu) *n* soucoupe *f*
Saudi Arabia (saou-di-eu-*réï*-bi-eu) Arabie Séoudite
sauna (*soo*-neu) *n* sauna *m*
sausage (*so*-sidj) *n* saucisse *f*
savage (*sæ*-vidj) *adj* sauvage
save (séïv) *v* sauver; épargner
savings (*séï*-vinngz) *pl* économies; ~ **bank** caisse d'épargne
savio(u)r (*séï*-vyeu) *n* sauveur *m*
savo(u)ry (*séï*-veu-ri) *adj* savoureux; piquant
saw[1] (soo) *v* (p see)
saw[2] (soo) *n* scie *f*
sawmill (*soo*-mil) *n* scierie *f*
***say** (séï) *v* *dire
scaffolding (*skæ*-feul-dinng) *n* échafaudage *m*
scale (skéïl) *n* échelle *f*; gamme *f*; écaille *f*; **scales** *pl* balance *f*
scandal (*skæn*-deul) *n* scandale *m*
Scandinavia (skæn-di-*néï*-vi-eu) Scandinavie *f*
Scandinavian (skæn-di-*néï*-vi-eunn) *adj* scandinave; *n* Scandinave *m*
scapegoat (*skéïp*-ghôᵒᵘt) *n* bouc émissaire
scar (skââ) *n* cicatrice *f*
scarce (skeᵉᵘss) *adj* rare
scarcely (*skèeu*-sli) *adv* à peine
scarcity (*skèeu*-seu-ti) *n* pénurie *f*
scare (skèᵉᵘ) *v* effrayer; *n* panique *f*
scarf (skââf) *n* (pl ~s, scarves) écharpe *f*
scarlet (*skââ*-leut) *adj* écarlate
scary (*skèeu*-ri) *adj* inquiétant
scatter (*skæ*-teu) *v* disperser
scene (siin) *n* scène *f*
scenery (*sii*-neu-ri) *n* paysage *m*
scenic (*sii*-nik) *adj* pittoresque
scent (sènt) *n* parfum *m*
schedule (*chè*-dyoûl) *n* horaire *m*
scheme (skiim) *n* plan *m*; projet *m*
scholar (*sko*-leu) *n* érudit *m*; élève *m*/*f*
scholarship (*sko*-leu-chip) *n* bourse d'études
school (skoûl) *n* école *f*
schoolboy (*skoûl*-boï) *n* écolier *m*
schoolgirl (*skoûl*-gheûl) *n* écolière *f*
schoolmaster (*skoûl*-mââ-steu) *n* instituteur *m*, maître d'école
schoolteacher (*skoûl*-tii-tcheu) *n* instituteur *m*, institutrice *f*

science (*saï*-eunns) *n* science *f*
scientific (saï-eunn-*ti*-fik) *adj* scientifique
scientist (*saï*-eunn-tist) *n* savant *m*
scissors (*si*-zeuz) *pl* ciseaux *mpl*
scold (skô^{ou}ld) *v* gronder; insulter
scooter (*skoû*-teu) *n* scooter *m*; patinette *f*
score (skoo) *n* nombre de points; *v* marquer
scorn (skoon) *n* dédain *m*, mépris *m*; *v* mépriser
Scot (skot) *n* Ecossais *m*
Scotch (skotch) *adj* écossais; **scotch tape** ruban adhésif
Scotland (*skot*-leunnd) Ecosse *f*
Scottish (*sko*-tich) *adj* écossais
scout (skaout) *n* scout *m*
scrap (skræp) *n* morceau *m*
scrapbook (*skræp*-bouk) *n* album de collage
scrape (skréïp) *v* racler
scratch (skrætch) *v* érafler, gratter; *n* rayure *f*, égratignure *f*
scream (skriim) *v* hurler, crier; *n* cri *m*
screen (skriin) *n* écran *m*
screw (skroû) *n* vis *f*
screwdriver (*skroû*-draï-veu) *n* tournevis *m*
scrub (skrab) *v* frotter; *n* buisson *m*
sculptor (*skalp*-teu) *n* sculpteur *m*
sculpture (*skalp*-tcheu) *n* sculpture *f*
sea (sii) *n* mer *f*; **~ urchin** oursin *m*; **~ water** eau de mer
seabird (*sii*-beûd) *n* oiseau de mer
sea-coast (*sii*-kô^{ou}st) *n* littoral *m*
seafood (*sii*-foûd) *n* fruits *mpl* de mer
seagull (*sii*-ghal) *n* mouette *f*, goéland *m*
seal (siil) *n* sceau *m*; phoque *m*
seam (siim) *n* couture *f*
seaman (*sii*-meunn) *n* (pl -men) marin *m*
seamless (*siim*-leuss) *adj* sans couture
seaport (*sii*-poot) *n* port de mer
search (seûtch) *v* chercher; fouiller; *n* fouille *f*
searchlight (*seûtch*-laït) *n* projecteur *m*
seascape (*sii*-skéïp) *n* marine *f*
seashell (*sii*-chèl) *n* coquillage *m*
seashore (*sii*-choo) *n* bord de la mer
seasick (*sii*-sik) *adj* souffrant du mal de mer
seasickness (*sii*-sik-neuss) *n* mal de mer
seaside (*sii*-saïd) *n* bord de la mer; **~ resort** station balnéaire
season (*sii*-zeunn) *n* saison *f*; **high ~** pleine saison; **low ~** morte-saison *f*; **off ~** hors saison; **~ ticket** carte d'abonnement
seat (siit) *n* siège *m*; place *f*; **~ belt** ceinture de sécurité
second (*sè*-keunnd) *num* deuxième; *n* seconde *f*; instant *m*
secondary (*sè*-keunn-deu-ri) *adj* secondaire; **~ school** école secondaire
second-hand (sè-keunnd-*hænd*) *adj* d'occasion
secret (*sii*-kreut) *n* secret *m*; *adj* secret
secretary (*sè*-kreu-tri) *n* secrétaire *f*, secrétaire *m*
section (*sèk*-cheunn) *n* section *f*; case *f*, service *m*
secure (si-*kyoueu*) *adj* sûr; *v* s'assurer de
security (si-*kyoueu*-reu-ti) *n* sécurité *f*; caution *f*
sedative (*sè*-deu-tiv) *n* sédatif *m*
seduce (si-*dyoûss*) *v* *séduire
***see** (sii) *v* *voir; *comprendre, se rendre compte; **~ to** s'occuper de
seed (siid) *n* semence *f*
***seek** (siik) *v* chercher
seem (siim) *v* *paraître, sembler

seen (siin) *v* (pp see)
seesaw (*sii*-soo) *n* balançoire *f*
seize (siiz) *v* saisir
seldom (*sèl*-deumm) *adv* rarement
select (si-*lèkt*) *v* sélectionner, choisir; *adj* exquis, choisi
selection (si-*lèk*-cheunn) *n* choix *m*, sélection *f*
self (sèlf) (*pl* selves) **the ~** le moi
self-... (sèlf) *pref* de soi; auto-; automatique(ment)
self-centered *Am*, **self-centred** (sèlf-*sèn*-teud) *adj* égocentrique
self-employed (sèl-fimm-*ploïd*) *adj* indépendant
self-evident (sèl-*fè*-vi-deunnt) *adj* évident
self-government (sèlf-*gha*-veu-meunnt) *n* autonomie *f*
selfish (*sèl*-fich) *adj* égoïste
selfishness (*sèl*-fich-neuss) *n* égoïsme *m*
self-service (sèlf-*seû*-viss) *n* libre-service *m*
***sell** (sèl) *v* vendre
semblance (*sèm*-bleunns) *n* apparence *f*
semi- (*sè*-mi) semi-
semicircle (*sè*-mi-seû-keul) *n* demicercle *m*
semicolon (sè-mi-*kôou*-leunn) *n* point-virgule *m*
senate (*sè*-neut) *n* sénat *m*
senator (*sè*-neu-teu) *n* sénateur *m*
***send** (sènd) *v* expédier, *envoyer; **~ back** *renvoyer; **~ for** *faire venir; **~ off** expédier
sender (*sèn*-deu) *n* expéditeur *m*, expéditrice *f*
senile (*sii*-naïl) *adj* sénile
senior (*sii*-nyeu) *adj* aîné; plus âgé (**to** que); supérieur (**to** à); premier; **~ citizens** *pl* personnes *pl* âgées; **~ partner** associé *m* principal; aîné *m*, aîne *f*; le plus ancien *m*, la plus ancienne *f*; supérieur *m*, supérieure *f*
sensation (sèn-*séï*-cheunn) *n* sensation *f*
sensational (sèn-*séï*-cheu-neul) *adj* spectaculaire, sensationnel
sense (sèns) *n* sens *m*; bon sens, raison *f*; signification *f*; *v* *percevoir; **~ of honour** sens de l'honneur
senseless (*sèns*-leuss) *adj* insensé
sensible (*sèn*-seu-beul) *adj* raisonnable
sensitive (*sèn*-si-tiv) *adj* sensible
sentence (*sèn*-teunns) *n* phrase *f*; jugement *m*; *v* condamner
sentimental (sèn-ti-*mèn*-teul) *adj* sentimental
separate[1] (*sè*-peu-réït) *v* séparer
separate[2] (*sè*-peu-reut) *adj* distinct, séparé
separately (*sè*-peu-reut-li) *adv* à part
September (sèp-*tèm*-beu) septembre
septic (*sèp*-tik) *adj* septique; ***become ~** s'infecter
sequel (*sii*-k^{ou}eul) *n* suite *f*
sequence (*sii*-k^{ou}eunns) *n* succession *f*; série *f*
serene (seu-*riin*) *adj* serein; clair
serial (*sieu*-ri-eul) *n* feuilleton *m*
series (*sieu*-riiz) *n* (pl **~**) suite *f*, série *f*
serious (*sieu*-ri-euss) *adj* sérieux
seriousness (*sieu*-ri-euss-neuss) *n* sérieux *m*
sermon (*seû*-meunn) *n* sermon *m*
serum (*sieu*-reumm) *n* sérum *m*
servant (*seû*-veunnt) *n* domestique *m*
serve (seûv) *v* *servir
service (*seû*-viss) *n* service *m*; **~ charge** service *m*; **~ station** station-service *f*
serviette (seû-vi-*èt*) *n* serviette *f*
session (*sè*-cheunn) *n* séance *f*
set (sèt) *n* jeu *m*
***set** (sèt) *v* poser; **~ menu** menu fixe; **~**

out *partir
setting (*sè*-tinng) *n* cadre *m*; ~ **lotion** fixateur *m*
settle (*sè*-teul) *v* régler, arranger; ~ **down** s'établir
settlement (*sè*-teul-meunnt) *n* règlement *m*, arrangement *m*, accord *m*
seven (*sè*-veunn) *num* sept
seventeen (*sè*-veunn-*tiin*) *num* dixsept
seventeenth (*sè*-veunn-*tiin*θ) *num* dix-septième
seventh (*sè*-veunnθ) *num* septième
seventy (*sè*-veunn-ti) *num* soixantedix
several (*sè*-veu-reul) *adj* divers, plusieurs
severe (si-*vieu*) *adj* violent, sévère, grave
sew (sô^ou^) *v* *coudre
sewer (*soû*-eu) *n* égout *m*
sewing machine (*sôou*-inng-meu-chiin) *n* machine à coudre
sex (sèks) *n* sexe *m*
sexual (*sèk*-chou-eul) *adj* sexuel
sexuality sèk-chou-*æ*-leu-ti) *n* sexualité *f*
shade (chéïd) *n* ombre *f*; nuance *f*
shadow (*chæ*-dô^ou^) *n* ombre *f*
shady (*chéï*-di) *adj* ombragé
***shake** (chéïk) *v* secouer
***shall** (chæl) *v* *devoir
shallow (*chæ*-lô^ou^) *adj* peu profond
shame (chéïm) *n* honte *f*, déshonneur *m*; **shame!** quelle honte!
shampoo (chæm-*poû*) *n* shampooing *m*
shamrock (*chæm*-rok) *n* trèfle *m*
shape (chéïp) *n* forme *f*, *v* former
share (chè^eu^) *v* partager; *n* part *f*, action *f*
shark (chââk) *n* requin *m*
sharp (chââp) *adj* aigu
sharpen (*chââ*-peunn) *v* affiler, aiguiser
shave (chéïv) *v* se raser
shaver (*chéï*-veu) *n* rasoir électrique
shaving brush (*chéï*-vinng-brach) *n* blaireau *m*
shaving cream (*chéï*-vinng-kriim) *n* crème à raser
shaving soap (*chéï*-vinng-sô^ou^p) *n* savon à barbe
shawl (chool) *n* châle *m*
she (chii) *pron* elle
shed (chèd) *n* réduit *m*
***shed** (chèd) *v* verser; répandre
sheep (chiip) *n* (pl ~) mouton *m*
sheer (chi^eu^) *adj* absolu, pur
sheet (chiit) *n* drap *m*; feuille *f*, plaque *f*
shelf (chèlf) *n* (pl shelves) étagère *f*
shell (chèl) *n* coquille *f*
shellfish (*chèl*-fich) *n* crustacé *m*
shelter (*chèl*-teu) *n* abri *m*; *v* abriter
shepherd (*chè*-peud) *n* berger *m*
shift (chift) *n* équipe *f*
***shine** (chaïn) *v* briller; resplendir
ship (chip) *n* navire *m*; *v* expédier; **shipping line** compagnie de navigation
shipowner (*chi*-pô^ou^-neu) *n* armateur *m*
shipyard (*chip*-yââd) *n* chantier naval
shirt (cheût) *n* chemise *f*
shiver (*chi*-veu) *v* trembler, frissonner; *n* frisson *m*
shock (chok) *n* choc *m*; *v* choquer; ~ **absorber** amortisseur *m*
shocking (*cho*-kinng) *adj* choquant
shoe (choû) *n* chaussure *f*, **gym shoes** chaussures de gymnastique; ~ **polish** cirage *m*; ~ **shop** magasin de chaussures
shoelace (*choû*-léïss) *n* lacet *m*
shoemaker (*choû*-méï-keu) *n* cordonnier *m*

shook (chouk) *v* (p shake)
***shoot** (choût) *v* tirer
shop (chop) *n* boutique *f*; *v* *faire des achats; ~ **assistant** vendeur *m*, vendeuse *f*
shopping (*cho*-pinng) *n* achats *pl*; **go ~** *faire des achats; ~ **bag** sac à provisions; ~ **centre** centre commercial
shopkeeper (*chop*-kii-peu) *n* commerçant *m*, commerçante *f*
shopwindow (chop-*ouinn*-dôou) *n* vitrine *f*
shore (choo) *n* rive *f*, rivage *m*
short (choot) *adj* court; petit; ~ **circuit** court-circuit *m*
shortage (*choo*-tidj) *n* carence *f*, manque *m*
shorten (*choo*-teunn) *v* raccourcir
shortly (*choot*-li) *adv* sous peu, prochainement, bientôt
shorts (choots) *pl* short *m*; *plAm* caleçon *m*
short-sighted (choot-*saï*-tid) *adj* myope
shot (chot) *n* coup de feu; piqûre *f*; prise de vue
***should** (choud) *v* *devoir
shoulder (*chôoul*-deu) *n* épaule *f*
shout (chaout) *v* crier; *n* cri *m*
shovel (*cha*-veul) *n* pelle *f*
show (chôou) *n* représentation *f*, spectacle *m*; exposition *f*
***show** (chôou) *v* montrer; exposer; démontrer
showcase (*chôou*-kéïss) *n* vitrine *f*
shower (chaoueu) *n* douche *f*; averse *f*
showroom (*chôou*-roûm) *n* salle d'exposition
shriek (chriik) *v* pousser des cris; *n* cri aigu
shrimp (chrimmp) *n* crevette *f*
shrine (chraïn) *n* sanctuaire *m*
***shrink** (chrinngk) *v* rétrécir
shrinkproof (*chrinngk*-proûf) *adj* irrétrécissable
shrub (chrab) *n* arbuste *m*
shudder (*cha*-deu) *n* frisson *m*
shuffle (*cha*-feul) *v* *battre
***shut** (chat) *v* fermer; **shut** clos, fermé; ~ **in** enfermer
shutter (*cha*-teu) *n* persienne *f*, volet *m*
shy (chaï) *adj* farouche, timide
shyness (*chaï*-neuss) *n* timidité *f*
Siamese (saï-eu-*miiz*) *adj* siamois; *n* Siamois *m*
sick (sik) *adj* malade; ayant mal au cœur
sickness (*sik*-neuss) *n* maladie *f*; mal au cœur
side (saïd) *n* côté *m*; parti *m*; **onesided** *adj* unilatéral; ~ **street** rue transversale
sideburns (*saïd*-beûnnz) *pl* favoris
sidelight (*saïd*-laït) *n* lumière latérale
sidewalk (*saïd*-ouook) *nAm* trottoir *m*
sideways (*saïd*-ouéïz) *adv* de côté
siege (siidj) *n* siège *m*
sieve (siv) *n* passoire *f*; *v* tamiser
sift (sift) *v* tamiser
sight (saït) *n* vue *f*; spectacle *m*; curiosité *f*
sightseeing (*saït*-sii-inng) *n* visite *f* (de la ville)
sign (saïn) *n* marque *f*, signe *m*; geste *m*; *v* signer
signal (*sigh*-neul) *n* signal *m*; signe *m*; *v* signaler
signature (*sigh*-neu-tcheu) *n* signature *f*
significant (sigh-*ni*-fi-keunnt) *adj* significatif
signpost (*saïn*-pôoust) *n* poteau indicateur
silence (*saï*-leunns) *n* silence *m*; *v* *faire taire
silencer (*saï*-leunn-seu) *n* silencieux

m
silent (*saï*-leunnt) *adj* silencieux; ***be ~** se *taire
silk (silk) *n* soie *f*
silly (*si*-li) *adj* bête, sot
silver (*sil*-veu) *n* argent *m*; en argent
silversmith (*sil*-veu-smiθ) *n* orfèvre *m*
silverware (*sil*-veu-^{ou}è^{eu}) *n* argenterie *f*
similar (*si*-mi-leu) *adj* analogue, similaire
similarity (si-mi-*læ*-reu-ti) *n* similitude *f*
simple (*simm*-peul) *adj* ingénu, simple; ordinaire
simply (*simm*-pli) *adv* simplement
simulate (*si*-myou-léït) *v* simuler
simultaneous (si-meul-*téï*-ni-euss) *adj* simultané
sin (sinn) *n* péché *m*
since (sinns) *prep* depuis; *adv* depuis; *conj* depuis que; comme
sincere (sinn-*sieu*) *adj* sincère; **Yours sincerely** sincères salutations; veuillez agréer, chère Madame / cher Monsieur, l'expression de mes sentiments distingués
sinew (*si*-nyoû) *n* tendon *m*
***sing** (sinng) *v* chanter
singer (*sinng*-eu) *n* chanteur *m*, chanteuse *f*
single (*sinng*-gheul) *adj* seul; célibataire
singular (*sinng*-ghyou-leu) *n* singulier *m*; *adj* singulier
sinister (*si*-ni-steu) *adj* sinistre
sink (sinngk) *n* évier *m*
***sink** (sinngk) *v* s'enfoncer
sip (sip) *n* gorgée *f*
sir (seû) monsieur *m*
siren (*saïeu*-reunn) *n* sirène *f*
sister (*si*-steu) *n* sœur *f*
sister-in-law (*si*-steu-rinn-loo) *n* (pl sisters-) belle-sœur *f*
***sit** (sit) *v* *être assis; **~ down** s'*asseoir
site (saït) *n* site *m*
sitting room (*si*-tinng-roûm) *n* salon *m*
situated (*si*-tchou-éï-tid) *adj* situé
situation (si-tchou-*éï*-cheunn) *n* situation *f*
six (siks) *num* six
sixteen (siks-*tiin*) *num* seize
sixteenth (siks-*tiin*θ) *num* seizième
sixth (siksθ) *num* sixième
sixty (*siks*-ti) *num* soixante
size (saïz) *n* taille *f*, mesure *f*; dimension *f*, grandeur *f*; format *m*
skate (skéït) *v* patiner; *n* patin *m*
skating (*skéï*-tinng) *n* patinage *m*; **~ rink** patinoire *f*
sketch (skètch) *n* dessin *m*, esquisse *f*; *v* dessiner, esquisser
ski[1] (skii) *v* skier
ski[2] (skii) *n* (pl ~, ~s) ski *m*; **~ boots** chaussures de ski; **~ jump** saut à ski; **~ lift** téléski *m* **~ pants** pantalon de ski; **~ poles** *Am* bâtons de ski; **~ sticks** bâtons de ski
skid (skid) *v* déraper
skier (*skii*-eu) *n* skieur *m*, skieuse *f*
skiing (*skii*-inng) *n* ski *m*
skil(l)ful (*skil*-feul) *adj* habile, adroit
skill (skil) *n* habileté *f*
skilled (skild) *adj* habile; expert
skin (skinn) *n* peau *f*; **~ cream** crème de beauté
skip (skip) *v* sautiller; sauter
skirt (skeût) *n* jupe *f*
skull (skal) *n* crâne *m*
sky (skaï) *n* ciel *m*; air *m*
skyscraper (*skaï*-skréï-peu) *n* gratteciel *m*
slack (slæk) *adj* lâche; faible
slacks (slæks) *pl* pantalon *m*
slam (slæm) *v* claquer
slander (*slâân*-deu) *n* calomnie *f*

slang (slæng) *n* argot *m*
slant (slâânt) *v* s'incliner
slanting (*slâân*-tinng) *adj* oblique, en pente, incliné
slap (slæp) *v* *battre; *n* claque *f*
slate (sléït) *n* ardoise *f*
slave (sléïv) *n* esclave *m*
sledge (slèdj) *n* luge *f*, traîneau *m*
sleep (sliip) *n* sommeil *m*
***sleep** (sliip) *v* *dormir
sleeping bag (*slii*-pinng-bægh) *n* sac de couchage
sleeping car (*slii*-pinng-kââ) *n* wagonlit
sleeping pill (*slii*-pinng-pil) *n* somnifère *m*
sleepless (*sliip*-leuss) *adj* sans sommeil
sleepy (*slii*-pi) *adj* somnolent
sleeve (sliiv) *n* manche *f*; housse *f*
sleigh (sléï) *n* luge *f*, traîneau *m*
slender (*slèn*-deu) *adj* svelte
slice (slaïss) *n* tranche *f*
slide (slaïd) *n* glissade *f*; toboggan *m*; diapositive *f*
***slide** (slaïd) *v* glisser
slight (slaït) *adj* léger; faible
slim (slimm) *adj* mince; *v* maigrir
slip (slip) *v* déraper, glisser; s'échapper; *n* faux pas; combinaison *f*
slipper (*sli*-peu) *n* pantoufle *f*
slippery (*sli*-peu-ri) *adj* glissant
slope (slô^{ou}p) *n* versant *m*; *v* décliner
sloping (*slôou*-pinng) *adj* en pente
sloppy (*slo*-pi) *adj* négligé
slot (slot) *n* fente *f*; ~ **machine** appareil à jetons
slovenly (*sla*-veunn-li) *adj* mal soigné
slow (slô^{ou}) *adj* lent; ~ **down** ralentir; freiner
sluice (sloûss) *n* écluse *f*
slum (slamm) *n* bas quartier
slump (slammp) *n* baisse des prix
slush (slach) *n* boue *f*
sly (slaï) *adj* malin
smack (smæk) *v* donner une claque; *n* claque *f*
small (smool) *adj* petit; faible
smallpox (*smool*-poks) *n* variole *f*
smart (smâât) *adj* élégant; adroit, alerte
smash (smæch)*v* (se)briser, (se) fracasser; *n* fracas *m*; coup *m* (violent); collision *f*; ~ **hit** succès *m*
smell (smèl) *n* odeur *f*
***smell** (smèl) *v* *sentir; *sentir mauvais
smelly (*smè*-li) *adj* malodorant
smile (smaïl) *v* *sourire; *n* sourire *m*
smith (smiθ) *n* forgeron *m*
smog (smoog) *n* smog *m*
smoke (smô^{ou}k) *v* fumer; *n* fumée *f*; **no smoking** défense de fumer
smoker (*smôou*-keu) *n* fumeur *m*; compartiment fumeurs
smoking compartment (*smôou*-kinng-keumm-pâât-meunnt) *n* compartiment fumeurs
smooth (smoûð) *adj* uni, plat, lisse; doux
smuggle (*sma*-gheul) *v* passer en contrebande
snack (snæk) *n* casse-croûte *m*; ~ **bar** snack-bar *m*
snail (snéïl) *n* escargot *m*
snake (snéïk) *n* serpent *m*
snapshot (*snæp*-chot) *n* instantané *m*
sneakers (*snii*-keuz) *plAm* chaussures de gymnastique
sneeze (sniiz) *v* éternuer
snooty (*snoû*-ti) *adj* snob
snore (snoo) *v* ronfler
snorkel (*snoo*-keul) *n* tube de plongée
snout (snaout) *n* museau *m*
snow (snô^{ou}) *n* neige *f*; *v* neiger
snowstorm (*snôou*-stoom) *n* tempête de neige
snowy (*snôou*-i) *adj* neigeux

so (sô^{ou}) *conj* donc; *adv* ainsi; tellement, si; **and ~ on** et ainsi de suite; **~ far** jusqu'à présent; **~ that** de manière que, pour que, afin que
soak (sô^{ou}k) *v* tremper
soap (sô^{ou}p) *n* savon *m*; **~ powder** savon en poudre
sober (*sôou*-beu) *adj* sobre; sérieux, posé
so-called (*sôou-koold*) *adj* soi-disant
soccer (*so*-keu) *n* football *m*; **~ team** équipe *f*
social (*sôou*-cheul) *adj* social
socialism (*sôou*-cheu-li-zeumm) *n* socialisme *m*
socialist (*sôou*-cheu-list) *adj* socialiste; *n* socialiste *m*
society (seu-*saï*-eu-ti) *n* société *f*; association *f*; compagnie *f*
sock (sok) *n* chaussette *f*
socket (*so*-kit) *n* douille *f*
soda water (*sôou*-deu-^{ou}oo-teu) *n* eau de Seltz
sofa (*sôou*-feu) *n* canapé *m*
soft (soft) *adj* mou; **~ drink** boisson non alcoolisée
soften (*so*-feunn) *v* adoucir
software (*soft- ouèeu*) *n* logiciel *m*
soil (soïl) *n* sol *m*; terroir *m*, terre *f*
soiled (soïld) *adj* souillé
solar (*sôou*-leu) *adj* solaire; **~ cell** cellule *f* photovoltaïque; **~ eclipse** éclipse *f* du soleil; **~ plexus** plexus *m* solaire
sold (sô^{ou}ld) *v* (p, pp sell); **~ out** épuisé
soldier (*sôoul*-djeu) *n* soldat *m*
sole[1] (sô^{ou}l) *adj* unique
sole[2] (sô^{ou}l) *n* semelle *f*; sole *f*
solely (*sôoul*-li) *adv* exclusivement
solemn (*so*-leumm) *adj* solennel
solicitor (seu-*li*-si-teu) *n* avoué *m*, avocat *m*
solid (*so*-lid) *adj* robuste, solide; massif; *n* solide *m*
soluble (*so*-lyou-beul) *adj* soluble
solution (seu-*loû*-cheunn) *n* solution *f*
solve (solv) *v* *résoudre
somber *Am*, **somber** (*somm*-beu) *adj* sombre
some (samm) *adj* quelques; *pron* certains, quelques; un peu; **~ day** un jour ou l'autre; **~ more** encore un peu; **~ time** une fois
somebody (*samm*-beu-di) *pron* quelqu'un
somehow (*samm*-haou) *adv* d'une manière ou d'une autre
someone (*samm*-^{ou}ann) *pron* quelqu'un
something (*samm*-θinng) *pron* quelque chose
sometimes (*samm*-taïmz) *adv* parfois
somewhat (*samm*-^{ou}ot) *adv* quelque peu
somewhere (*samm*-^{ou}è^{eu}) *adv* quelque part
son (sann) *n* fils *m*
song (sonng) *n* chanson *f*
son-in-law (*sa*-ninn-loo) *n* (pl sons-) gendre *m*
soon (soûn) *adv* rapidement, sous peu, prochainement, bientôt; **as ~ as** dès que
sooner (*soû*-neu) *adv* plutôt
sore (soo) *adj* douloureux; *n* plaie *f*; **~ throat** mal de gorge
sorrow (*so*-rô^{ou}) *n* tristesse *f*, douleur *f*, chagrin *m*
sorry (*so*-ri) *adj* désolé; **sorry!** excusez-moi!, pardon!
sort (soot) *v* classer, ranger; *n* catégorie *f*, sorte *f*; **all sorts of** toutes sortes de
soul (sô^{ou}l) *n* âme *f*; esprit *m*
sound (saound) *n* son *m*; *v* sonner; *adj* solide
soundproof (*saound*-proûf) *adj*

insonorisé
soup (soûp) *n* soupe *f*
sour (saou^{eu}) *adj* aigre
source (sooss) *n* source *f*
south (saouθ) *n* sud *m*; **South Pole** pôle sud
South Africa (saouθ *æ*-fri-keu) Afrique du Sud
South America (saouθ eu-*mè*-ri-keu) Amérique du Sud
southeast (saouθ-*iist*) *n* sud-est *m*
southerly (*sa*-ðeu-li) *adj* méridional
southern (*sa*-ðeunn) *adj* méridional
southwest (saouθ-*ouèst*) *n* sud-ouest *m*
souvenir (*soû*-veu-ni^{eu}) *n* souvenir *m*
sovereign (*sov*-rinn) *n* souverain *m*
***sow** (sô^{ou}) *v* semer
spa (spââ) *n* station thermale
space (spéïss) *n* espace *m*; distance *f*, intervalle *m*; *v* espacer
spacious (*spéï*-cheuss) *adj* spacieux
spade (spéïd) *n* bêche *f*, pelle *f*
Spain (spéïn) Espagne *f*
Spanish (*spæ*-nich) *adj* espagnol
spanking (*spæng*-kinng) *n* fessée *f*
spanner (*spæ*-neu) *n* clé à écrous
spare (spè^{eu}) *adj* de réserve, disponible; *v* se passer de; **~ part** pièce détachée; **~ room** chambre d'ami; **~ time** temps libre; **~ tyre** (*Am* **tire**) pneu de rechange; **~ wheel** roue de secours
spark (spââk) *n* étincelle *f*
sparking plug (*spââ*-kinng-plagh) *n* bougie d'allumage
sparkle (*spââ*-keul) *v* briller
sparkling (*spââ*-klinng) *adj* scintillant; mousseux
sparrow (*spæ*-rô^{ou}) *n* moineau *m*
***speak** (spiik) *v* parler
speaker (*spii*-keu) *n* parleur *m*, parleuse *f*; haut-parleur *m*
spear (spi^{eu}) *n* lance *f*
special (*spè*-cheul) *adj* particulier, spécial; **~ delivery** exprès
specialist (*spè*-cheu-list) *n* spécialiste *m/f*
speciality (spè-chi-*æ*-leu-ti) *n* spécialité *f*
specialize (*spè*-cheu-laïz) *v* se spécialiser
specially (*spè*-cheu-li) *adv* particulièrement
species (*spii*-chiiz) *n* (pl ~) espèce *f*
specific (speu-*si*-fik) *adj* spécifique
speck (spèk) *n* tache *f*
spectacle (*spèk*-teu-keul) *n* spectacle *m*; **spectacles** lunettes *fpl*
spectator (spèk-*téï*-teu) *n* spectateur *m*, spectatrice *f*
speculate (*spè*-kyou-léït) *v* spéculer
speech (spiitch) *n* parole *f*; allocution *f*, discours *m*
speechless (*spiitch*-leuss) *adj* interloqué
speed (spiid) *n* vitesse *f*; rapidité *f*, hâte *f*; **cruising ~** vitesse de croisière; **~ limit** limite de vitesse, limitation de vitesse
***speed** (spiid) *v* foncer; rouler trop vite
speeding (*spii*-dinng) *n* excès de vitesse
speedometer (spii-*do*-mi-teu) *n* indicateur de vitesse
spell (spèl) *n* enchantement *m*
***spell** (spèl) *v* épeler
spelling (*spè*-linng) *n* orthographe *f*
***spend** (spènd) *v* dépenser; employer
sphere (sfi^{eu}) *n* sphère *f*
spice (spaïss) *n* épice *f*
spiced (spaïst) *adj* épicé
spicy (*spaï*-si) *adj* épicé
spider (*spaï*-deu) *n* araignée *f*; **spider's web** toile d'araignée
***spill** (spil) *v* répandre
***spin** (spinn) *v* filer; tourner

spinach (*spi*-nidj) *n* épinards *mpl*
spine (spaïn) *n* épine dorsale
spinster (*spinn*-steu) *n* vieille fille
spire (spaï^{eu}) *n* aiguille *f*
spirit (*spi*-rit) *n* esprit *m*; humeur *f*; **spirits** boissons alcoolisées, spiritueux *mpl*; moral *m*; **~ stove** réchaud à alcool
spiritual (*spi*-ri-tchou-eul) *adj* spirituel
spit (spit) *n* crachat *m*, salive *f*; broche *f*
***spit** (spit) *v* cracher
spite: in ~ of (inn spaït ov) en dépit de, malgré
spiteful (*spaït*-feul) *adj* malveillant
splash (splæch) *v* éclabousser
splendid (*splèn*-did) *adj* magnifique, splendide
splendo(u)r (*splèn*-deu) *n* splendeur *f*
splint (splinnt) *n* éclisse *f*
splinter (*splinn*-teu) *n* écharde *f*
***split** (split) *v* fendre
***spoil** (spoïl) *v* gâter
spoke[1] (spô^{ou}k) *v* (p speak)
spoke[2] (spô^{ou}k) *n* rayon *m*
sponge (spanndj) *n* éponge *f*
spook (spoûk) *n* spectre *m*, fantôme *m*
spool (spoûl) *n* bobine *f*
spoon (spoûn) *n* cuillère *f*
spoonful (*spoûn*-foul) *n* cuillerée *f*
sport (spoot) *n* sport *m*
sports car (*spoots*-kââ) *n* voiture de sport
sports jacket (*spoots*-djæ-kit) *n* veston sport
sportsman (*spoots*-meunn) *n* (pl -men) sportif *m*
sportswear (*spoots*-^{ou}è^{eu}) *n* vêtements de sport
spot (spot) *n* tache *f*; lieu *m*, endroit *m*
spotless (*spot*-leuss) *adj* immaculé
spotlight (*spot*-laït) *n* projecteur *m*
spotted (*spo*-tid) *adj* tacheté
spout (spaout) *n* jet *m*
sprain (sprëïn) *v* fouler; *n* foulure *f*
spray (spréï) *n* spray *m*, aérosol *m*; *v* vaporiser; arroser
***spread** (sprèd) *v* étendre
spring (sprinng) *n* printemps *m*; ressort *m*; source *f*
springtime (*sprinng*-taïm) *n* printemps *m*
sprouts (spraouts) **Brussels ~** *pl* choux de Bruxelles
spy (spaï) *n* espion *m*
square (sk^{ou}è^{eu}) *adj* carré; *n* carré *m*; square *m*, place *f*
squash (sk^{ou}och) *n* sirop *m*; *Am* courgette
squeeze (sk^{ou}iiz) *v* serrer; presser; extorquer (**from** à); **~ out** exprimer
squirrel (*sk^{ou}i*-reul) *n* écureuil *m*
squirt (sk^{ou}eût) *n* jet *m*
stable (*stéï*-beul) *adj* stable; *n* étable *f*
stack (stæk) *n* pile *f*
stadium (*stéï*-di-eumm) *n* stade *m*
staff (stââf) *n* personnel *m*
stage (stéïdj) *n* scène *f*, phase *f*, étape *f*
stain (stéïn) *v* tacher; *n* tache *f*; **stained glass** verre de couleur; **~ remover** détachant *m*
stainless (*stéïn*-leuss) *adj* immaculé; **~ steel** acier inoxydable
staircase (*stèeu*-kéïss) *n* escalier *m*
stairs (stè^{eu}z) *pl* escalier *m*
stale (stéïl) *adj* rassis
stall (stool) *n* étal *m*; **seat in the stalls** fauteuil d'orchestre
stamp (stæmp) *n* timbre *m*; *v* affranchir; piétiner; **~ machine** distributeur de timbres
stand (stænd) *n* stand *m*; tribune *f*
***stand** (stænd) *v* se *tenir debout
standard (*stæn*-deud) *n* norme *f*; standard; **~ of living** niveau de vie
stanza (*stæn*-zeu) *n* strophe *f*

staple (*stéï*-peul) *n* agrafe *f*
star (stââ) *n* étoile *f*
starboard (*stââ*-beud) *n* tribord *m*
stare (stè^eu^) *v* fixer
starling (*stââ*-linng) *n* étourneau *m*
start (stâât) *v* commencer; *n* début *m*
starting point (*stââ*-tinng-poïnt) *n* point de départ
state (stéït) *n* Etat *m*; état *m*; *v* déclarer; **the States** les Etats-Unis
statement (*stéït*-meunnt) *n* déclaration *f*
statesman (*stéïts*-meunn) *n* (pl -men) homme d'Etat
station (*stéï*-cheunn) *n* gare *f*; poste *m*
stationary (*stéï*-cheu-neu-ri) *adj* stationnaire
stationer's (*stéï*-cheu-neuz) *n* papeterie *f*
stationery (*stéï*-cheu-neu-ri) *n* papeterie *f*
statistics (steu-*ti*-stiks) *pl* statistique *f*
statue (*stæ*-tchoû) *n* statue *f*
stay (stéï) *v* rester; séjourner; *n* séjour *m*
steadfast (*stèd*-fââst) *adj* ferme
steady (*stè*-di) *adj* ferme
steak (stéïk) *n* bifteck *m*
***steal** (stiil) *v* voler
steam (stiim) *n* vapeur *f*
steamer (*stii*-meu) *n* bateau à vapeur
steel (stiil) *n* acier *m*
steep (stiip) *adj* abrupt, escarpé
steeple (*stii*-peul) *n* clocher *m*
steering column (*stieu*-rinng-koleumm) *n* colonne de direction
steering wheel (*stieu*-rinng-^ou^iil) *n* volant *m*
stem (stèm) *n* tige *f*
step (stèp) *n* pas *m*; marche *f*; *v* marcher
stepchild (*stèp*-tchaïld) *n* (pl -children) enfant d'un autre lit
stepfather (*stèp*-fââ-ðeu) *n* beau-père *m*
stepmother (*stèp*-ma-ðeu) *n* belle-mère *f*
stereo (*stè*-ri-ô^ou^) *n* stéréo *f*
sterile (*stè*-raïl) *adj* stérile
sterilize (*stè*-ri-laïz) *v* stériliser
stern (steûn) *adj* sévère
steward (*styoû*-eud) *n* steward *m*
stewardess (*styoû*-eu-dèss) *n* hôtesse de l'air
stick (stik) *n* bâton *m*
***stick** (stik) *v* coller
sticky (*sti*-ki) *adj* gluant
stiff (stif) *adj* raide
still (stil) *adv* encore; toutefois; *adj* tranquille
stimulant (*sti*-myou-leunnt) *n* stimulant *m*
stimulate (*sti*-myou-léït) *v* stimuler
sting (stinng) *n* piqûre *f*
***sting** (stinng) *v* piquer
stingy (*stinn*-dji) *adj* mesquin
***stink** (stinngk) *v* puer
stir (steû) *v* bouger; remuer
stitch (stitch) *n* point *m*, point de côté; suture *f*
stock (stok) *n* stock *m*; *v* *avoir en stock; **~ exchange** bourse des valeurs, bourse *f*; **~ market** marché des valeurs; **stocks and shares** actions
stocking (*sto*-kinng) *n* bas *m*
stole[1] (stô^ou^l) *v* (p steal)
stole[2] (stô^ou^l) *n* étole *f*
stomach (*sta*-meuk) *n* estomac *m*; **~ ache** mal au ventre, mal d'estomac
stone (stô^ou^n) *n* pierre *f*; pierre précieuse; noyau *m*; en pierre; **pumice ~** pierre ponce
stood (stoud) *v* (p, pp stand)
stop (stop) *v* arrêter; cesser; *n* arrêt *m*; **stop!** stop!
stopper (*sto*-peu) *n* bouchon *m*
storage (*stoo*-ridj) *n* emmagasinage *m*

store (stoo) *n* provision *f*; magasin *m*; *v* emmagasiner; ~ **house** magasin *m*
stor(e)y (*stoo*-ri) *n* étage *m*
stork (stook) *n* cigogne *f*
storm (stoom) *n* tempête *f*
stormy (*stoo*-mi) *adj* orageux
story (*stoo*-ri) *n* histoire *f*
stout (staout) *adj* gros, obèse, corpulent
stove (stô^ou^v) *n* fourneau *m*; cuisinière *f*
straight (stréït) *adj* droit; *adv* directement; ~ **ahead** tout droit; ~ **away** directement, tout de suite; ~ **on** tout droit
strain (stréïn) *n* effort *m*; tension *f*; *v* forcer
strainer (*stréï*-neu) *n* passoire *f*
strange (stréïndj) *adj* étrange; bizarre
stranger (*stréïn*-djeu) *n* étranger *m*; inconnu *m*
strangle (*stræng*-gheul) *v* étrangler
strap (stræp) *n* courroie *f*
straw (stroo) *n* paille *f*
strawberry (*stroo*-beu-ri) *n* fraise *f*
stream (striim) *n* ruisseau *m*; courant *m*; *v* couler
street (striit) *n* rue *f*
streetcar (*striit*-kââ) *nAm* tram *m*
strength (strèngθ) *n* vigueur *f*, force *f*
stress (strèss) *n* tension *f*; accent *m*; *v* souligner
stretch (strètch) *v* tendre; *n* section *f*
strict (strikt) *adj* sévère
strike (straïk) *n* grève *f*
***strike** (straïk) *v* frapper; *faire grève; amener
striking (*straï*-kinng) *adj* frappant, remarquable
string (strinng) *n* ficelle *f*; corde *f*
strip (strip) *n* bande *f*
stripe (straïp) *n* raie *f*
striped (straïpt) *adj* rayé
stroke (strô^ou^k) *n* attaque *f*
stroll (strô^ou^l) *v* flâner; *n* promenade *f*
strong (stronng) *adj* fort; puissant
stronghold (*stronng*-hô^ou^ld) *n* place forte
structure (*strak*-tcheu) *n* structure *f*
struggle (*stra*-gheul) *n* combat *m*, lutte *f*; *v* lutter
stub (stab) *n* souche *f*
stubborn (*sta*-beunn) *adj* têtu
student (*styoû*-deunnt) *n* étudiant *m*; étudiante *f*
study (*sta*-di) *v* étudier; *n* étude *f*; cabinet *m*
stuff (staf) *n* substance *f*; fatras *m*
stuffed (staft) *adj* farci
stuffing (*sta*-finng) *n* farce *f*
stuffy (*sta*-fi) *adj* mal aéré
stumble (*stamm*-beul) *v* trébucher
stung (stanng) *v* (p, pp sting)
stupid (*styoû*-pid) *adj* stupide
style (staïl) *n* style *m*
stylish (*staï*-lich) *adj* élégant; chic; à la mode
subject[1] (*sab*-djikt) *n* sujet *m*; ~ **to** sujet à
subject[2] (seub-*djèkt*) *v* *soumettre
submarine (sab-meu-*riin*) *n* sous-marin *m*
submit (seub-*mit*) *v* se *soumettre
subordinate (seu-*boo*-di-neut) *adj* subordonné; secondaire
subscriber (seub-*skraï*-beu) *n* abonné *m*
subscription (seub-*skrip*-cheunn) *n* abonnement *m*
subsequent (*sab*-si-k^ou^eunnt) *adj* postérieur
subsidy (*sab*-si-di) *n* subvention *f*
substance (*sab*-steunns) *n* substance *f*
substantial (seub-*stæn*-cheul) *adj* matériel; rêel; substantiel
substitute (*sab*-sti-tyoût) *v* substituer; *n* substitut *m*
subtitle (*sab*-taï-teul) *n* sous-titre *m*

subtle (*sa*-teul) *adj* subtil
subtract (seub-*trækt*) *v* *soustraire
suburb (*sa*-beûb) *n* banlieue *f*, faubourg *m*
suburban (seu-*beû*-beunn) *adj* suburbain
subway (*sab*-^{ou}éï) *nAm* métro *m*
succeed (seuk-*siid*) *v* réussir; succéder
success (seuk-*sèss*) *n* succès *m*
successful (seuk-*sèss*-feul) *adj* réussi
succumb (seu-*kamm*) *v* succomber
such (satch) *adj* tel; *adv* tellement; **~ as** tel que
suck (sak) *v* sucer
sudden (*sa*-deunn) *adj* soudain
suddenly (*sa*-deunn-li) *adv* soudain
suede (s^{ou}éïd) *n* daim *m*
suffer (*sa*-feu) *v* *souffrir; subir
suffering (*sa*-feu-rinng) *n* souffrance *f*
suffice (seu-*faïss*) *v* *suffire
sufficient (seu-*fi*-cheunnt) *adj* adéquat, suffisant
suffrage (*sa*-fridj) *n* droit de vote, suffrage *m*
sugar (*chou*-gheu) *n* sucre *m*
suggest (seu-*djèst*) *v* suggérer
suggestion (seu-*djèss*-tcheunn) *n* suggestion *f*
suicide (*soû*-i-saïd) *n* suicide *m*
suit (soût) *v* *convenir; adapter à; bien *aller; *n* complet *m*
suitable (*soû*-teu-beul) *adj* qui convient, approprié
suitcase (*soût*-kéïss) *n* valise *f*
suite (s^{ou}iit) *n* appartement *m*
sum (samm) *n* somme *f*
summary (*sa*-meu-ri) *n* sommaire *m*, résumé *m*
summer (*sa*-meu) *n* été *m*; **~ time** heure d'été
summit (*sa*-mit) *n* sommet *m*
sun (sann) *n* soleil *m*
sunbathe (*sann*-béïð) *v* *prendre un bain de soleil
sunburn (*sann*-beûnn) *n* coup de soleil
Sunday (*sann*-di) dimanche *m*
sunglasses (*sann*-ghlââ-siz) *pl* lunettes de soleil
sunlight (*sann*-laït) *n* lumière du soleil
sunny (*sa*-ni) *adj* ensoleillé
sunrise (*sann*-raïz) *n* lever du soleil
sunset (*sann*-sèt) *n* coucher du soleil
sunshade (*sann*-chéïd) *n* parasol *m*
sunshine (*sann*-chaïn) *n* soleil *m*
sunstroke (*sann*-strô^{ou}k) *n* insolation *f*
suntan oil (*sann*-tæn-oïl) huile solaire
super (*soû*-peu) *adj colloquial* super
superb (sou-*peûb*) *adj* grandiose, superbe
superficial (soû-peu-*fi*-cheul) *adj* superficiel
superfluous (sou-*peû*-flou-euss) *adj* superflu
superior (sou-*pieu*-ri-eu) *adj* supérieur, majeur
supermarket (*soû*-peu-mââ-kit) *n* supermarché *m*
superstition (soû-peu-*sti*-cheunn) *n* superstition *f*
supervise (*soû*-peu-vaïz) *v* superviser
supervision (soû-peu-*vi*-jeunn) *n* supervision *f*, surveillance *f*
supervisor (*soû*-peu-vaï-zeu) *n* surveillant *m*
supper (*sa*-peu) *n* souper *m*
supple (*sa*-peul) *adj* souple
supplement (*sa*-pli-meunnt) *n* supplément *m*
supply (seu-*plaï*) *n* fourniture *f*; stock *m*; offre *f*; *v* fournir
support (seu-*poot*) *v* supporter, *soutenir; *n* soutien *m*; **~ hose** bas élastiques
supporter (seu-*poo*-teu) *n* supporter *m*

suppose (seu-*pôouz*) *v* supposer; **supposing that** en admettant que
suppository (seu-*po*-zi-teu-ri) *n* suppositoire *m*
suppress (seu-*prèss*) *v* réprimer
surcharge (*seû*-tchââdj) *n* supplément *m*
sure (chou^{eu}) *adj* sûr
surely (*choueu*-li) *adv* sûrement
surface (*seû*-fiss) *n* surface *f*
surgeon (*seû*-djeunn) *n* chirurgien *m*; **veterinary ~** vétérinaire *m*
surgery (*seû*-djeu-ri) *n* opération *f*; cabinet de consultations
surname (*seû*-néïm) *n* nom de famille
surplus (*seû*-pleuss) *n* surplus *m*
surprise (seu-*praïz*) *n* surprise *f*; *v* *surprendre
surrender (seu-*rèn*-deu) *v* se rendre; *n* reddition *f*
surround (seu-*raound*) *v* entourer
surrounding (seu-*raoun*-dinng) *adj* environnant
surroundings (seu-*raoun*-dinngz) *pl* alentours *mpl*
survey (*seû*-véï) *n* résumé *m*
survival (seu-*vaï*-veul) *n* survie *f*
survive (seu-*vaïv*) *v* *survivre
suspect[1] (seu-*spèkt*) *v* soupçonner; suspecter
suspect[2] (*sa*-spèkt) *n* suspect *m*, -e *f*
suspend (seu-*spènd*) *v* suspendre
suspenders (seu-*spèn*-deuz) *plAm* bretelles *fpl*
suspension (seu-*spèn*-cheunn) *n* suspension *f*; **~bridge** pont suspendu
suspicion (seu-*spi*-cheunn) *n* soupçon *m*; soupçons *mpl*
suspicious (seu-*spi*-cheuss) *adj* suspect; soupçonneux, méfiant
sustain (seu-*stéïn*) *v* endurer
swallow (*souo*-lô^{ou}) *v* avaler; *n* hirondelle *f*
swam (s^{ou}æm) *v* (p swim)
swamp (s^{ou}ommp) *n* marais *m*
swan (s^{ou}onn) *n* cygne *m*
swap (s^{ou}op) *v* troquer
***swear** (s^{ou}è^{eu}) *v* jurer
sweat (s^{ou}èt) *n* sueur *f*; *v* suer
sweater (*souè*-teu) *n* chandail *m*
Swede (s^{ou}iid) *n* Suédois *m*
Sweden (*souii*-deunn) Suède *f*
Swedish (*souii*-dich) *adj* suédois
***sweep** (s^{ou}iip) *v* balayer
sweet (s^{ou}iit) *adj* sucré; gentil; *n* bonbon *m*; dessert *m*; **sweets** douceurs *fpl*, bonbons
sweeten (*souii*-teunn) *v* sucrer
sweetheart (*souiit*-hâât) *n* mon amour, chéri *m*
sweetshop (*souiit*-chop) *n* confiserie *f*
swell (s^{ou}èl) *adj* formidable
***swell** (s^{ou}èl) *v* enfler
swelling (*souè*-linng) *n* enflure *f*
swift (s^{ou}ift) *adj* rapide
***swim** (s^{ou}imm) *v* nager
swimmer (*soui*-meu) *n* nageur *m*, nageuse *f*
swimming (*soui*-minng) *n* natation *f*; **~ pool** piscine *f*
swimmingtrunks (*soui*-minng-tranngks) *n* caleçon de bain
swimsuit (*souimm*-soût) *n* maillot de bain
swindle (*souinn*-deul) *v* escroquer; *n* escroquerie *f*
swindler (*souinn*-dleu) *n* escroc *m*
swing (s^{ou}inng) *n* balançoire *f*
***swing** (s^{ou}inng) *v* balancer
Swiss (s^{ou}iss) *adj* suisse; *n* Suisse *m*
switch (s^{ou}itch) *n* commutateur *m*; *v* changer; **~ off** *éteindre; **~ on** allumer
switchboard (*souitch*-bood) *n* tableau de distribution
Switzerland (*souit*-seu-leunnd) Suisse *f*
sword (sood) *n* épée *f*

swum (s^{ou}amm) *v* (pp swim)
syllable (*si*-leu-beul) *n* syllabe *f*
symbol (*simm*-beul) *n* symbole *m*
sympathetic (simm-peu-*θè*-tik) *adj* compatissant, de sympathie
sympathy (*simm*-peu-θi) *n* sympathie *f*; compassion *f*
symphony (*simm*-feu-ni) *n* symphonie *f*
symptom (*simm*-teumm) *n* symptôme *m*
synagogue (*si*-neu-ghogh) *n* synagogue *f*
synonym (*si*-neu-nimm) *n* synonyme *m*
synthetic (sinn-*θè*-tik) *adj* synthétique
syphon (*saï*-feunn) *n* siphon *m*
Syria (*si*-ri-eu) Syrie *f*
Syrian (*si*-ri-eunn) *adj* syrien; *n* Syrien *m*
syringe (si-*rinndj*) *n* seringue *f*
syrup (*si*-reup) *n* sirop *m*
system (*si*-steumm) *n* système *m*; **decimal ~** système décimal
systematic (si-steu-*mæ*-tik) *adj* systématique

T

table (*téï*-beul) *n* table *f*; **~ of contents** table des matières; **~ tennis** ping-pong *m*
tablecloth (*téï*-beul-kloθ) *n* nappe *f*
tablespoon (*téï*-beul-spoûn) *n* cuillère *f*
tablet (*tæ*-blit) *n* tablette *f*
taboo (teu-*boû*) *n* tabou *m*
tactics (*tæk*-tiks) *pl* tactique *f*
tag (tægh) *n* étiquette *f*
tail (téïl) *n* queue *f*
taillight (*téïl*-laït) *n* feu arrière
tailor (*téï*-leu) *n* tailleur *m*
tailor-made (*téï*-leu-méïd) *adj* fait sur mesure
***take** (téïk) *v* *prendre; saisir; *conduire; **~ away** emporter; enlever; **~ off** décoller; **~ out** ôter; **~ over** *reprendre; **~ place** *avoir lieu; **~ up** occuper
take-off (*téï*-kof) *n* décollage *m*
tale (téïl) *n* conte *m*, récit *m*
talent (*tæ*-leunnt) *n* don *m*, talent *m*
talented (*tæ*-leunn-tid) *adj* doué
talk (took) *v* parler; *n* conversation *f*
talkative (*too*-keu-tiv) *adj* bavard
tall (tool) *adj* haut; grand
tame (téïm) *adj* domestiqué, apprivoisé; *v* apprivoiser
tampon (*tæm*-peunn) *n* tampon *m*
tangerine (tæn-djeu-*riin*) *n* mandarine *f*
tangible (*tæn*-dji-beul) *adj* tangible
tank (tængk) *n* réservoir *m*
tanker (*tæng*-keu) *n* bateau-citerne *m*
tanned (tænd) *adj* hâlé
tap (tæp) *n* robinet *m*; coup *m*; *v* frapper
tape (téïp) *n* bande *f*, ruban *m*; **adhesive ~** ruban adhésif; **~ recorder** magnétophone *m*
tar (tââ) *n* goudron *m*
target (*tââ*-ghit) *n* objectif *m*, cible *f*
tariff (*tæ*-rif) *n* taux *m*
task (tââsk) *n* tâche *f*
taste (téïst) *n* goût *m*; *v* *avoir goût de; goûter
tasteless (*téïst*-leuss) *adj* insipide

tasty (*téï*-sti) *adj* succulent, savoureux
taught (toot) *v* (p, pp teach)
tavern (*tæ*-veunn) *n* taverne *f*
tax (tæks) *n* impôt *m*; *v* imposer
tax-free (*tæks*-frii) *adj* exempt d'impôts
taxi (*tæk*-si) *n* taxi *m*; **~ driver** chauffeur de taxi; **~ rank** station de taxis; **~ stand** *Am* station de taxis
taximeter (*tæk*-si-mii-teu) *n* taximètre *m*
tea (tii) *n* thé *m*; **~ set** service à thé; **~ towel** torchon *m*
***teach** (tiitch) *v* *apprendre, enseigner
teacher (*tii*-tcheu) *n* professeur *m*, maître *m*; instituteur *m*, institutrice *f*, maître d'école
teachings (*tii*-tchinngz) *pl* enseignements
teacup (*tii*-kap) *n* tasse à thé
team (tiim) *n* équipe *f*
teapot (*tii*-pot) *n* théière *f*
tear[1] (ti^{eu}) *n* larme *f*
tear[2] (tè^{eu}) *n* déchirure *f*; ***tear** *v* déchirer
tear-jerker (*tieu*-djeû-keu) *n* mélo *m*
tease (tiiz) *v* taquiner
teashop (*tii*-chop) *n* pâtisserie-salon de thé
teaspoon (*tii*-spoûn) *n* cuillère à thé
teaspoonful (*tii*-spoûn-foul) *n* cuillerée à thé
technical (*tèk*-ni-keul) *adj* technique
technician (tèk-*ni*-cheunn) *n* technicien *m*
technique (tèk-*niik*) *n* technique *f*
technology (tèk-*no*-leu-dji) *n* technologie *f*
teenager (*tii*-néï-djeu) *n* adolescent *m*, -e *f*
teetotaller (tii-*tôou*-teu-leu) *n* antialcoolique *m*
telegram (*tè*-li-ghræm) *n* télégramme *m*
telephone (*tè*-li-fô^{ou}n) *n* téléphone *m*; **~ book** *Am* annuaire téléphonique; **~ booth** cabine téléphonique; **~ call** coup de téléphone, appel téléphonique; **~ directory** annuaire téléphonique, bottin *m*; **~ exchange** central téléphonique
television (*tè*-li-vi-jeunn) *n* télévision *f*; **~ set** télévision *f*; **cable ~** télévision par câble; **satellite ~** télévision par satellite
telex (*tè*-lèks) *n* télex *m*
***tell** (tèl) *v* *dire; raconter
telly (*tè*-li) *n colloquial* télé *f*
temper (*tèm*-peu) *n* colère *f*
temperature (*tèm*-preu-tcheu) *n* température *f*
tempest (*tèm*-pist) *n* tempête *f*
temple (*tèm*-peul) *n* temple *m*; tempe *f*
temporary (*tèm*-peu-reu-ri) *adj* provisoire, temporaire
tempt (tèmpt) *v* tenter
temptation (tèmp-*téï*-cheunn) *n* tentation *f*
ten (tèn) *num* dix
tenant (*tè*-neunnt) *n* locataire *m*
tend (tènd) *v* *avoir tendance; soigner; **~ to** tendre à
tendency (*tèn*-deunn-si) *n* inclination *f*, tendance *f*
tender (*tèn*-deu) *adj* tendre, délicat
tendon (*tèn*-deunn) *n* tendon *m*
tennis (*tè*-niss) *n* tennis *m*; **~ court** court de tennis; **~ shoes** chaussures de tennis
tense (tèns) *adj* tendu
tension (*tèn*-cheunn) *n* tension *f*
tent (tènt) *n* tente *f*
tenth (tènθ) *num* dixième
tepid (*tè*-pid) *adj* tiède
term (teûmm) *n* terme *m*; période *f*; condition *f*
terminal (*teû*-mi-neul) *n* terminus *m*

terrace (*tè*-reuss) *n* terrasse *f*
terrain (tè-*réïn*) *n* terrain *m*
terrible (*tè*-ri-beul) *adj* épouvantable, terrible
terrific (teu-*ri*-fik) *adj* formidable
terrify (*tè*-ri-faï) *v* terrifier
territory (*tè*-ri-teu-ri) *n* territoire *m*
terror (*tè*-reu) *n* terreur *f*
terrorism (*tè*-reu-ri-zeumm) *n* terrorisme *m*
terrorist (*tè*-reu-rist) *n* terroriste *m/f*
test (tèst) *n* test *m*, épreuve *f*; *v* essayer, éprouver
testify (*tè*-sti-faï) *v* témoigner
text (tèkst) *n* texte *m*
textbook (*tèks*-bouk) *n* manuel *m*
textile (*tèk*-staïl) *n* textile *m*
Thai (taï) *adj* thaïlandais; *n* Thaïlandais *m*
Thailand (*taï*-lænd) Thaïlande *f*
than (ðæn) *conj* que
thank (θængk) *v* remercier; ~ **you** merci
thankful (*θængk*-feul) *adj* reconnaissant
that (ðæt) *adj* ce; *pron* celui-là, cela; qui; *conj* que
thaw (θoo) *v* dégeler, fondre; *n* dégel *m*
the (ðeu, ði) *art* le *art*; **the … the** plus … plus
theater *Am*, **theatre** (*θieu*-teu) *n* théâtre *m*
theft (θèft) *n* vol *m*
their (ðè^eu^) *adj* leur
them (ðèm) *pron* les; leur
theme (θiim) *n* thème *m*, sujet *m*
themselves (ðeumm-*sèlvz*) *pron* se; eux-mêmes
then (ðèn) *adv* alors; ensuite, puis
theology (θi-*o*-leu-dji) *n* théologie *f*
theoretical (θi^eu^-*rè*-ti-keul) *adj* théorique
theory (*θieu*-ri) *n* théorie *f*
therapy (*θè*-reu-pi) *n* thérapie *f*
there (ðè^eu^) *adv* là
therefore (*ðèeu*-foo) *conj* donc
thermometer (θeu-*mo*-mi-teu) *n* thermomètre *m*
thermostat (*θeû*-meu-stæt) *n* thermostat *m*
these (ðiiz) *adj* ces
thesis (*θii*-siss) *n* (pl theses) thèse *f*
they (ðéï) *pron* ils
thick (θik) *adj* gros; épais
thicken (*θi*-keunn) *v* épaissir
thickness (*θik*-neuss) *n* épaisseur *f*
thief (θiif) *n* (pl thieves) voleur *m*, voleuse *f*
thigh (θaï) *n* cuisse *f*
thimble (*θimm*-beul) *n* dé *m*
thin (θinn) *adj* mince; maigre
thing (θinng) *n* chose *f*
***think** (θinngk) *v* penser; réfléchir; ~ **of** penser à; songer à; ~ **over** réfléchir à
third (θeûd) *num* troisième
thirst (θeûst) *n* soif *f*
thirsty (*θeû*-sti) *adj* assoiffé
thirteen (θeû-*tiin*) *num* treize
thirteenth (θeû-*tiinθ*) *num* treizième
thirtieth (*θeû*-ti-euθ) *num* trentième
thirty (*θeû*-ti) *num* trente
this (ðiss) *adj* ce; *pron* ceci
thistle (*θi*-seul) *n* chardon *m*
thorn (θoon) *n* épine *f*
thorough (*θa*-reu) *adj* minutieux, soigné
thoroughfare (*θa*-reu-fè^eu^) *n* route principale, artère *f*
those (ðô^ou^z) *adj* ces; *pron* ceux-là
though (ðô^ou^) *conj* bien que, encore que, quoique; *adv* pourtant
thought[1] (θoot) *v* (p, pp think)
thought[2] (θoot) *n* pensée *f*
thoughtful (*θoot*-feul) *adj* pensif; prévenant
thousand (*θaou*-zeunnd) *num* mille

thread (θrèd) *n* fil *m*; *v* enfiler
threadbare (*θrèd*-bè^{eu}) *adj* usé
threat (θrèt) *n* menace *f*
threaten (*θrè*-teunn) *v* menacer; **threatening** menaçant
three (θrii) *num* trois
three-quarter (θrii-*kouoo*-teu) *adj* trois quarts
threshold (*θrè*-chô^{ou}ld) *n* seuil *m*
threw (θroû) *v* (p throw)
thrifty (*θrif*-ti) *adj* parcimonieux
throat (θrô^{ou}t) *n* gorge *f*
throne (θrô^{ou}n) *n* trône *m*
through (θroû) *prep* à travers
throughout (θroû-*aout*) *adv* partout
throw (θrô^{ou}) *n* lancement *m*
***throw** (θrô^{ou}) *v* jeter, lancer
thrush (θrach) *n* grive *f*
thumb (θamm) *n* pouce *m*
thumbtack (*θamm*-tæk) *nAm* punaise *f*
thump (θammp) *v* marteler
thunder (*θann*-deu) *n* tonnerre *m*; *v* tonner
thunderstorm (*θann*-deu-stoom) *n* orage *m*
thundery (*θann*-deu-ri) *adj* orageux
Thursday (*θeûz*-di) jeudi *m*
thus (ðass) *adv* ainsi
thyme (taïm) *n* thym *m*
tick (tik) *n* coche *f*; **~ off** pointer
ticket (*ti*-kit) *n* billet *m*; contravention *f*; **~ collector** contrôleur *m*; **~ machine** distributeur de billets
tickle (*ti*-keul) *v* chatouiller
tide (taïd) *n* marée *f*; **high ~** marée haute; **low ~** marée basse
tidy (*taï*-di) *adj* ordonné; **~ up** ranger
tie (taï) *v* nouer, attacher; *n* cravate *f*
tiger (*taï*-gheu) *n* tigre *m*
tight (taït) *adj* serré; étroit, juste; *adv* fortement
tighten (*taï*-teunn) *v* serrer; resserrer; se resserrer
tights (taïts) *pl* collants *mpl*
tile (taïl) *n* carreau *m*; tuile *f*
till (til) *prep* jusqu'à; *conj* jusqu'à ce que
timber (*timm*-beu) *n* bois d'œuvre
time (taïm) *n* temps *m*; fois *f*; **all the ~** continuellement; **in ~** à temps; **~ of arrival** heure d'arrivée; **~ of departure** heure de départ
time-saving (*taïm*-séï-vinng) *adj* qui fait gagner du temps
timetable (*taïm*-téï-beul) *n* horaire *m*
timid (*ti*-mid) *adj* timide
timidity (ti-*mi*-deu-ti) *n* timidité *f*
tin (tinn) *n* étain *m*; boîte *f*; **~ opener** ouvreboîte *m*; **tinned food** conserves *fpl*
tinfoil (*tinn*-foïl) *n* papier d'étain
tiny (*taï*-ni) *adj* minuscule
tip (tip) *n* bout *m*; pourboire *m*
tire[1] (taï^{eu}) *n* pneu *m*; **~ pressure** pression des pneus
tire[2] (taï^{eu}) *v* fatiguer
tired (taï^{eu}d) *adj* fatigué; **~ of** las de
tiring (*taïeu*-rinng) *adj* fatigant
tissue (*ti*-choû) *n* tissu *m*; mouchoir de papier
title (*taï*-teul) *n* titre *m*
to (toû) *prep* jusque; à, pour, chez; afin de
toad (tô^{ou}d) *n* crapaud *m*
toadstool (*tôoud*-stoûl) *n* champignon *m*
toast (tô^{ou}st) *n* toast *m*
tobacco (teu-*bæ*-kô^{ou}) *n* (pl ~s) tabac *m*; **~ pouch** blague à tabac
tobacconist (teu-*bæ*-keu-nist) *n* débitant de tabac; **tobacconist's** bureau de tabac
today (teu-*déï*) *adv* aujourd'hui
toddler (*tod*-leu) *n* bambin *m*
toe (tô^{ou}) *n* orteil *m*
toffee (*to*-fi) *n* caramel *m*
together (teu-*ghè*-ðeu) *adv* ensemble

toilet (*toï*-leut) *n* toilettes *fpl*; ~ **case** nécessaire de toilette; ~ **paper** papier hygiénique
toiletry (*toï*-leu-tri) *n* articles de toilette
token (*tôou*-keunn) *n* signe *m*; jeton *m*
told (tô^{ou}ld) *v* (p, pp tell)
tolerable (*to*-leu-reu-beul) *adj* tolérable
toll (tô^{ou}l) *n* péage *m*
tomato (teu-*mââ*-tô^{ou}) *n* (pl ~es) tomate *f*
tomb (toûm) *n* tombe *f*
tombstone (*toûm*-stô^{ou}n) *n* pierre tombale
tomorrow (teu-*mo*-rô^{ou}) *adv* demain
ton (tann) *n* tonne *f*
tone (tô^{ou}n) *n* ton *m*; timbre *m*
tongs (tonngz) *pl* pince *f*
tongue (tanng) *n* langue *f*
tonic (*to*-nik) *n* tonique *m*
tonight (teu-*naït*) *adv* cette nuit, ce soir
tonsillitis (tonn-seu-*laï*-tiss) *n* amygdalite *f*
tonsils (*tonn*-seulz) *pl* amygdales *fpl*
too (toû) *adv* trop; aussi
took (touk) *v* (p take)
tool (toûl) *n* instrument *m*, outil *m*; ~ **kit** boîte à outils
toot (toût) *vAm* klaxonner
tooth (toûθ) *n* (pl teeth) dent *f*
toothache (*toû*-θéïk) *n* mal aux dents
toothbrush (*toûθ*-brach) *n* brosse à dents
toothpaste (*toûθ*-péïst) *n* pâte dentifrice
toothpick (*toûθ*-pik) *n* cure-dent *m*
toothpowder (*toûθ*-paou-deu) *n* poudre dentifrice
top (top) *n* sommet *m*; dessus *m*; couvercle *m*; supérieur; **on ~ of** au-dessus de; ~ **side** haut *m*
topic (*to*-pik) *n* sujet *m*
topical (*to*-pi-keul) *adj* actuel
torch (tootch) *n* torche *f*; lampe de poche
torment[1] (too-*mènt*) *v* tourmenter
torment[2] (*too*-mènt) *n* tourment *m*
torture (*too*-tcheu) *n* torture *f*; *v* torturer
toss (toss) *v* lancer
tot (tot) *n* bambin *m*
total (*tôou*-teul) *adj* total; complet, absolu; *n* total *m*
totalitarian (tô^{ou}-tæ-li-*tèeu*-ri-eunn) *adj* totalitaire
touch (tatch) *v* toucher; *n* contact *m*, attouchement *m*; toucher *m*
touching (*ta*-tchinng) *adj* touchant
tough (taf) *adj* coriace
tour (tou^{eu}) *n* excursion *f*
tourism (*toueu*-ri-zeumm) *n* tourisme *m*
tourist (*toueu*-rist) *n* touriste *m/f*; ~ **class** classe touriste; ~ **office** syndicat d'initiative
tournament (*toueu*-neu-meunnt) *n* tournoi *m*
tow (tô^{ou}) *v* remorquer
towards (teu-*ouoodz*) *prep* vers; envers
towel (taou^{eu}l) *n* serviette *f*
towel(l)ing (*taoueu*-linng) *n* tissu-éponge *m*
tower (taou^{eu}) *n* tour *f*
town (taoun) *n* ville *f*; ~ **centre** centre de la ville; ~ **hall** hôtel de ville
townspeople (*taounz*-pii-peul) *pl* citadins *mpl*
toxic (*tok*-sik) *adj* toxique
toy (toï) *n* jouet *m*
toyshop (*toï*-chop) *n* magasin de jouets
trace (tréïss) *n* trace *f*; *v* tracer, retracer
track (træk) *n* voie *f*; piste *f*
tractor (*træk*-teu) *n* tracteur *m*
trade (tréïd) *n* commerce *m*; métier *m*;

v *faire du commerce; ~ **union** syndicat *m*
trademark (*tréïd*-mââk) *n* marque de fabrique
trader (*tréï*-deu) *n* commerçant *m*, -e *f*
tradesman (*tréïdz*-meunn) *n* (pl -men) marchand *m*
tradition (treu-*di*-cheunn) *n* tradition *f*
traditional (treu-*di*-cheu-neul) *adj* traditionnel
traffic (*træ*-fik) *n* circulation *f*; ~ **jam** embouteillage *m*; ~ **light** feu de circulation
tragedy (*træ*-djeu-di) *n* tragédie *f*
tragic (*træ*-djik) *adj* tragique
trail (tréïl) *n* piste *f*, sentier *m*
trailer (*tréï*-leu) *n* remorque *f*; *nAm* caravane *f*
train (tréïn) *n* train *m*; *v* dresser, former; **slow** ~ omnibus *m*; **through** ~ train direct; ~ **ferry** ferry-boat *m*
trainee (tréï-*nii*) *n* apprenti *m*, e *f*; stagiaire *m,f*
trainer (*tréï*-neu) *n* entraîneur *m*, entraîneuse *f*; dresseur *m*, dresseuse *f*
training (*tréï*-ninng) *n* entraînement *m*
trait (tréït) *n* trait *m*
traitor (*tréï*-teu) *n* traître *m*
tram (træm) *n* tram *m*
tramp (træmp) *n* chemineau *m*, vagabond *m*; *v* vagabonder
tranquil (*træng*-k^{ou}il) *adj* tranquille
tranquillizer (*træng*-k^{ou}i-laï-zeu) *n* calmant *m*
transaction (træn-*zæk*-cheunn) *n* transaction *f*
transatlantic (træn-zeut-*læn*-tik) *adj* transatlantique
transfer (træns-*feû*) *v* transférer
transform (træns-*foom*) *v* transformer
transformer (træns-*foo*-meu) *n* transformateur *m*
transition (træn-*si*-cheunn) *n* transition *f*
translate (træns-*léït*) *v* *traduire
translation (træns-*léï*-cheunn) *n* traduction *f*
translator (træns-*léï*-teu) *n* traducteur *m*, traductrice *f*
transmission (trænz-*mi*-cheunn) *n* émission *f*
transmit (trænz-*mit*) *v* *émettre
transmitter (trænz-*mi*-teu) *n* émetteur *m*
transparent (træn-*spèeu*-reunnt) *adj* transparent
transport[1] (*træn*-spoot) *n* transport *m*
transport[2] (træn-*spoot*) *v* transporter
transportation (træn-spoo-*téï*-cheunn) *n* transport *m*
trap (træp) *n* piège *m*
trash (træch) *n* ordures *fpl*; ~ **can** *Am* boîte à ordures
travel (*træ*-veul) *v* voyager; ~ **agency** bureau de voyages; ~ **agent** agent de voyages; ~ **insurance** assurance voyages *f*; **travelling expenses** frais de voyage
travel(l)er (*træ*-veu-leu) *n* voyageur *m*, voyageuse *f*; **traveler's check** *Am*, **traveller's cheque** chèque de voyage
tray (tréï) *n* plateau *m*
treason (*trii*-zeunn) *n* trahison *f*
treasure (*trè*-jeu) *n* trésor *m*
treasury (*trè*-jeu-ri) *n* Trésor
treat (triit) *v* traiter
treatment (*triit*-meunnt) *n* traitement *m*
treaty (*trii*-ti) *n* traité *m*
tree (trii) *n* arbre *m*
tremble (*trèm*-beul) *v* frissonner, trembler; vibrer
tremendous (tri-*mèn*-deuss) *adj* énorme
trendy (*trèn*-di) *adj* à la (dernière) mode, dernier cri; dans le vent

trespass (*trèss*-peuss) *v* empiéter
trespasser (*trèss*-peu-seu) *n* intrus *m*
trial (traï^{eu}l) *n* procès *m*; essai *m*
triangle (*traï*-æng-gheul) *n* triangle *m*
triangular (traï-*æng*-ghyou-leu) *adj* triangulaire
tribe (traïb) *n* tribu *f*
tributary (*tri*-byou-teu-ri) *n* affluent *m*
tribute (*tri*-byoût) *n* hommage *m*
trick (trik) *n* truc *m*
trigger (*tri*-gheu) *n* gâchette *f*
trim (trimm) *v* tailler
trip (trip) *n* excursion *f*, voyage *m*
triumph (*traï*-eummf) *n* triomphe *m*; *v* triompher
triumphant (traï-*amm*-feunnt) *adj* triomphant
troops (troûps) *pl* troupes *fpl*
tropical (*tro*-pi-keul) *adj* tropical
tropics (*tro*-piks) *pl* tropiques *mpl*
trouble (*tra*-beul) *n* ennui *m*, peine *f*, dérangement *m*; *v* déranger
troublesome (*tra*-beul-seumm) *adj* gênant
trousers (*traou*-zeuz) *pl* pantalon *m*
trout (traout) *n* (pl ~) truite *f*
truck (trak) *nAm* camion *m*
true (troû) *adj* vrai; réel; loyal, fidèle
trumpet (*tramm*-pit) *n* trompette *f*
trunk (tranngk) *n* malle *f*; tronc *m*; *nAm* coffre *m*; **trunks** *pl* slip de bain
trunk-call (*tranngk*-kool) *n* appel interurbain
trust (trast) *v* *faire confiance; *n* confiance *f*
trustworthy (*trast*-^{ou}eû-ði) *adj* digne de confiance
truth (troûθ) *n* vérité *f*
truthful (*troûθ*-feul) *adj* véridique
try (traï) *v* essayer; tenter, s'efforcer; *n* tentative *f*; ~ **on** essayer
tube (tyoûb) *n* tuyau *m*, tube *m*
tuberculosis (tyoû-beû-kyou-*lôou*-siss) *n* tuberculose *f*
Tuesday (*tyoûz*-di) mardi *m*
tug (tagh) *v* remorquer; *n* remorqueur *m*; à-coup *m*
tuition (tyoû-*i*-cheunn) *n* enseignement *m*
tulip (*tyoû*-lip) *n* tulipe *f*
tumbler (*tamm*-bleu) *n* gobelet *m*
tumo(u)r (*tyoû*-meu) *n* tumeur *f*
tuna (*tyoû*-neu) *n* (pl ~, ~s) thon *m*
tune (tyoûn) *n* air *m*; *v* accorder
tuneful (*tyoûn*-feul) *adj* harmonieux
tunic (*tyoû*-nik) *n* tunique *f*
Tunisia (tyoû-*ni*-zi-eu) Tunisie *f*
Tunisian (tyoû-*ni*-zi-eunn) *adj* tunisien; *n* Tunisien *m*
tunnel (*ta*-neul) *n* tunnel *m*
turbine (*teû*-baïn) *n* turbine *f*
Turk (teûk) *n* Turc *m*
Turkey (*teû*-ki) Turquie *f*
turkey (*teû*-ki) *n* dinde *f*
Turkish (*teû*-kich) *adj* turc; ~ **bath** bain turc
turn (teûnn) *v* tourner; retourner, virer; *n* revirement *m*, tour *m*; tournant *m*; ~ **back** retourner; ~ **down** rejeter; ~ **into** changer en; ~ **off** fermer; ~ **on** allumer; *ouvrir; ~ **over** retourner; ~ **round** retourner; se retourner
turning (*teû*-ninng) *n* virage *m*; ~ **point** tournant *m*
turnover (*teû*-nô^{ou}-veu) *n* chiffre d'affaires; ~ **tax** impôt sur le chiffre d'affaires
turnpike (*teûnn*-païk) *nAm* route à péage
turpentine (*teû*-peunn-taïn) *n* térébenthine *f*
turtle (*teû*-teul) *n* tortue *f*
tutor (*tyoû*-teu) *n* tuteur *m*
tuxedo (tak-*sii*-dô^{ou}) *nAm* (pl ~s, ~es) smoking *m*
TV (tii-*vii*) *n* télévision *f*
tweed (t^{ou}iid) *n* tweed *m*

tweezers (*touii*-zeuz) *pl* pince *f*
twelfth (t^{ou}èlfθ) *num* douzième
twelve (t^{ou}èlv) *num* douze
twentieth (*touèn*-ti-euθ) *num* vingtième
twenty (*touèn*-ti) *num* vingt
twice (t^{ou}aïss) *adv* deux fois
twig (t^{ou}igh) *n* rameau *m*; branche *f*
twilight (*touaï*-laït) *n* crépuscule *m*
twine (t^{ou}aïn) *n* ficelle *f*
twins (t^{ou}innz) *pl* jumeaux *mpl*; **twin beds** lits jumeaux
twist (t^{ou}ist) *v* tordre; *n* torsion *f*
two (toû) *num* deux
two-piece (toû-*piiss*) *adj* deux-pièces *m*
type (taïp) *v* taper à la machine, dactylographier; *n* type *m*
typewriter (*taïp*-raï-teu) *n* machine à écrire
typhoid (*taï*-foïd) *n* typhoïde *f*
typical (*ti*-pi-keul) *adj* caractéristique, typique
typist (*taï*-pist) *n* dactylo *f*
tyre (taï^{eu}) *n* pneu *m*; **~ pressure** pression des pneus

U

ugly (*a*-ghli) *adj* laid
ulcer (*al*-seu) *n* ulcère *m*
ultimate (*al*-ti-meut) *adj* ultime
ultraviolet (al-treu-*vaïeu*-leut) *adj* ultra-violet
umbrella (amm-*brè-leu*) *n* parapluie *m*
umpire (*amm*-paï^{eu}) *n* arbitre *m*
unable (a-*néï*-beul) *adj* incapable
unacceptable (a-neuk-*sèp*-teu-beul) *adj* inacceptable
unaccountable (a-neu-*kaoun*-teu-beul) *adj* inexplicable
unaccustomed (a-neu-*ka*-steummd) *adj* inhabitué
unanimous (yoû-*næ*-ni-meuss) *adj* unanime
unanswered (a-*nâân*-seud) *adj* sans réponse
unauthorized (a-*noo*-θeu-raïzd) *adj* illicite
unavoidable (a-neu-*voï*-deu-beul) *adj* inévitable
unaware (a-neu-*ouèeu*) *adj* inconscient
unbearable (ann-*bèeu*-reu-beul) *adj* insupportable
unbreakable (ann-*bréï*-keu-beul) *adj* incassable
unbroken (ann-*brôou*-keunn) *adj* intact
unbutton (ann-*ba*-teunn) *v* déboutonner
uncertain (ann-*seû*-teunn) *adj* incertain
uncle (*anng*-keul) *n* oncle *m*
unclean (ann-*kliin*) *adj* malpropre
uncomfortable (ann-*kamm*-feu-teu-beul) *adj* inconfortable
uncommon (ann-*ko*-meunn) *adj* inhabituel, rare
unconditional (ann-keunn-*di*-cheu-neul) *adj* inconditionnel
unconscious (ann-*konn*-cheuss) *adj* inconscient
uncork (ann-*kook*) *v* déboucher
uncover (ann-*ka*-veu) *v* *découvrir
uncultivated (ann-*kal*-ti-véï-tid) *adj* inculte
under (*ann*-deu) *prep* en bas de, sous

undercurrent (*ann*-deu-ka-reunnt) *n* courant *m*
underestimate (ann-deu-*rè*-sti-méït) *v* sous-estimer
underground (*ann*-deu-ghraound) *adj* souterrain; *n* métro *m*
underline (ann-deu-*laïn*) *v* souligner
underneath (ann-deu-*niiθ*) *adv* dessous
underpants (*ann*-deu-pænts) *plAm* caleçon *m*
undershirt (*ann*-deu-cheût) *n* tricot de corps
***understand** (ann-deu-*stænd*) *v* *comprendre
understanding (ann-deu-*stæn*-dinng) *n* compréhension *f*
understatement (ann-deu-*stéït*-meunnt) *n* affirmation *f* qui reste au-dessous de la vérité; amoindrissement *m*
***undertake** (ann-deu-*téïk*) *v* *entreprendre
undertaking (ann-deu-*téï*-kinng) *n* entreprise *f*
underwater (*ann*-deu-ouoo-teu) *adj* sous-marin
underwear (*ann*-deu-ouèeu) *n* sous-vêtements *mpl*
undesirable (ann-di-*zaïeu*-reu-beul) *adj* indésirable
***undo** (ann-*doû*) *v* *défaire
undoubtedly (ann-*daou*-tid-li) *adv* sans aucun doute
undress (ann-*drèss*) *v* se déshabiller
unearned (a-*neûnnd*) *adj* immérité
uneasy (a-*nii*-zi) *adj* mal à l'aise
uneducated (a-*nè*-dyou-kéï-tid) *adj* ignorant
unemployed (a-nimm-*ploïd*) *adj* en chômage
unemployment (a-nimm-*ploï*-meunnt) *n* chômage *m*
unequal (a-*nii*-kouеul) *adj* inégal
uneven (a-*nii*-veunn) *adj* inégal, accidenté; irrégulier
unexpected (a-nik-*spèk*-tid) *adj* imprévu, inattendu
unfair (ann-*fèeu*) *adj* inéquitable, injuste
unfaithful (ann-*féïθ*-feul) *adj* infidèle
unfamiliar (ann-feu-*mil*-yeu) *adj* inconnu
unfasten (ann-*fââ*-seunn) *v* détacher
unfavo(u)rable (ann-*féï*-veu-reu-beul) *adj* défavorable
unfit (ann-*fit*) *adj* impropre
unfold (ann-*fôould*) *v* déplier
unfortunate (ann-*foo*-tcheu-neut) *adj* malheureux
unfortunately (ann-*foo*-tcheu-neut-li) *adv* hélas, malheureusement
unfriendly (ann-*frènd*-li) *adj* froid; hostile
ungrateful (ann-*ghréït*-feul) *adj* ingrat
unhappy (ann-*hæ*-pi) *adj* malheureux
unhealthy (ann-*hèl*-θi) *adj* malsain
unhurt (ann-*heût*) *adj* indemne
uniform (*yoû*-ni-foom) *n* uniforme *m*; *adj* uniforme
unimportant (a-nimm-*poo*-teunnt) *adj* insignifiant
uninhabitable (a-ninn-*hæ*-bi-teu-beul) *adj* inhabitable
uninhabited (a-ninn-*hæ*-bi-tid) *adj* inhabité
unintentional (a-ninn-*tèn*-cheu-neul) *adj* involontaire
union (*yoû*-nyeunn) *n* union *f*; ligue *f*
unique (yoû-*niik*) *adj* unique
unit (*yoû*-nit) *n* unité *f*
unite (yoû-*naït*) *v* unir
United States (yoû-*naï*-tid stéïts) Etats-Unis
unity (*yoû*-neu-ti) *n* unité *f*
universal (yoû-ni-*veû*-seul) *adj* général, universel
universe (*yoû*-ni-veûss) *n* univers *m*

university (yoû-ni-*veû*-seu-ti) *n* université *f*
unjust (ann-*djast*) *adj* injuste
unkind (ann-*kaïnd*) *adj* désagréable, peu aimable
unknown (ann-*nôoun*) *adj* inconnu
unlawful (ann-*loo*-feul) *adj* illicite
unleaded (ann-*lèd*-id) *adj* sans plomb
unlearn (ann-*leûnn*) *v* *désapprendre
unless (eunn-*lèss*) *conj* à moins que
unlike (ann-*laïk*) *adj* dissemblable, différent
unlikely (ann-*laï*-kli) *adj* improbable
unlimited (ann-*li*-mi-tid) *adj* illimité
unload (ann-*lôoud*) *v* décharger
unlock (ann-*lok*) *v* *ouvrir
unlucky (ann-*la*-ki) *adj* infortuné
unnecessary (ann-*nè*-seu-seu-ri) *adj* superflu
unoccupied (a-*no*-kyou-païd) *adj* vacant
unpack (ann-*pæk*) *v* déballer
unpleasant (ann-*plè*-zeunnt) *adj* ennuyeux, déplaisant; désagréable, antipathique
unpopular (ann-*po*-pyou-leu) *adj* peu aimé, impopulaire
unprotected (ann-preu-*tèk*-tid) *adj* non protégé
unqualified (ann-*kouo*-li-faïd) *adj* incompétent
unreal (ann-*rieul*) *adj* irréel
unreasonable (ann-*rii*-zeu-neu-beul) *adj* déraisonnable
unreliable (ann-ri-*laï*-eu-beul) *adj* douteux
unrest (ann-*rèst*) *n* agitation *f*; inquiétude *f*
unsafe (ann-*séïf*) *adj* dangereux
unsatisfactory (ann-sæ-tiss-*fæk*-teu-ri) *adj* insatisfaisant
unscrew (ann-*skroû*) *v* dévisser
unselfish (ann-*sèl*-fich) *adj* désintéressé
unskilled (ann-*skild*) *adj* non qualifié
unsound (ann-*saound*) *adj* malsain
unstable (ann-*stéï*-beul) *adj* instable
unsteady (ann-*stè*-di) *adj* branlant, instable
unsuccessful (ann-seuk-*sèss*-feul) *adj* infructueux
unsuitable (ann-*soû*-teu-beul) *adj* inadéquat
unsurpassed (ann-seu-*pââst*) *adj* sans pareil
untidy (ann-*taï*-di) *adj* désordonné
untie (ann-*taï*) *v* dénouer
until (eunn-*til*) *prep* jusqu'à
untrue (ann-*troû*) *adj* faux
untrustworthy (ann-*trast*-^{ou}eû-ði) *adj* sujet à caution
unusual (ann-*yoû*-jou-eul) *adj* inhabituel, insolite
unwell (ann-*ouèl*) *adj* indisposé
unwillingly (ann-*oui*-linng-li) *adv* à contrecœur
unwise (ann-*ouaïz*) *adj* imprudent
unwrap (ann-*ræp*) *v* déballer
up (ap) *adv* vers le haut, en haut
upholster (ap-*hôoul*-steu) *v* capitonner
upkeep (*ap*-kiip) *n* entretien *m*
uplands (*ap*-leunndz) *pl* hautes terres
upon (eu-*ponn*) *prep* sur
upper (*a*-peu) *adj* supérieur
upright (*ap*-raït) *adj* droit; *adv* droit
upset (ap-*sèt*) *v* déranger; *adj* bouleversé
upside-down (ap-saïd-*daoun*) *adv* sens dessus dessous
upstairs (ap-*stèeuz*) *adv* en haut
upstream (ap-*striim*) *adv* en amont
upwards (ap-^{ou}eudz) *adv* vers le haut
urban (*eû*-beunn) *adj* urbain
urge (eûdj) *v* exhorter; *n* impulsion *f*
urgency (*eû*-djeunn-si) *n* urgence *f*
urgent (*eû*-djeunnt) *adj* urgent
urine (*youeu*-rinn) *n* urine *f*

Uruguay (*youeu*-reu-gh^{ou}aï) Uruguay *m*
Uruguayan (you^{eu}-reu-*ghouaï*-eunn) *adj* uruguayen; *n* Uruguayen *m*
us (ass) *pron* nous
usable (*yoû*-zeu-beul) *adj* utilisable
usage (*yoû*-zidj) *n* usage *m*
use[1] (yoûz) *v* employer; ***be used to** *être habitué à; **~ up** user
use[2] (yoûss) *n* emploi *m*; utilité *f*; ***be of ~** *servir
useful (*yoûss*-feul) *adj* utile
useless (*yoûss*-leuss) *adj* inutile
user (*yoû*-zeu) *n* usager *m*
usher (*a*-cheu) *n* ouvreur *m*
usherette (a-cheu-*rèt*) *n* ouvreuse *f*
usual (*yoû*-jou-eul) *adj* ordinaire
usually (*yoû*-jou-eu-li) *adv* habituellement
utensil (yoû-*tèn*-seul) *n* outil *m*, ustensile *m*
utility (yoû-*ti*-leu-ti) *n* utilité *f*
utilize (*yoû*-ti-laïz) *v* utiliser
utmost (*at*-mô^{ou}st) *adj* extrême
utter (*a*-teu) *adj* complet, total; *v* *émettre

V

vacancy (*véï*-keunn-si) *n* vacance *f*
vacant (*véï*-keunnt) *adj* vacant
vacate (veu-*kéït*) *v* quitter
vacation (veu-*kéï*-cheunn) *n* congé *m*
vaccinate (*væk*-si-néït) *v* vacciner
vaccination (væk-si-*néï*-cheunn) *n* vaccination *f*
vacuum (*væ*-kyou-eumm) *n* vide *m*; *vAm* passer l'aspirateur; **~ cleaner** aspirateur *m*; **~ flask** thermos *m*
vague (véïgh) *adj* vague
vain (véïn) *adj* vaniteux; vain; **in ~** inutilement, en vain
valid (*væ*-lid) *adj* valable
valley (*væ*-li) *n* vallée *f*
valuable (*væ*-lyou-beul) *adj* de valeur, précieux; **valuables** *pl* objets de valeur
value (*væ*-lyoû) *n* valeur *f*; *v* estimer
valve (vælv) *n* soupape *f*
van (væn) *n* fourgon *m*
vanilla (veu-*ni*-leu) *n* vanille *f*
vanish (*væ*-nich) *v* *disparaître
vapo(u)r (*véï*-peu) *n* vapeur *f*
variable (*vèeu*-ri-eu-beul) *adj* variable
variation (vè^{eu}-ri-*éï*-cheunn) *n* variation *f*; changement *m*
varied (*vèeu*-rid) *adj* varié
variety (veu-*raï*-eu-ti) *n* variété *f*; **~ show** spectacle de variétés; **~ theatre** (*Am* **theater**) théâtre de variétés
various (*vèeu*-ri-euss) *adj* divers
varnish (*vââ*-nich) *n* laque *f*, vernis *m*; *v* vernir
vary (*vèeu*-ri) *v* varier; changer; différer
vase (vââz) *n* vase *m*
vaseline (*væ*-seu-liin) *n* vaseline *f*
vast (vââst) *adj* immense, vaste
vault (voolt) *n* voûte *f*; chambre forte
veal (viil) *n* veau *m*
vegetable (*vè*-djeu-teu-beul) *n* légume *m*; **~ merchant** marchand de légumes
vegetarian (vè-dji-*tèeu*-ri-eunn) *n* végétarien *m*, végétarienne *f*
vegetation (vè-dji-*téï*-cheunn) *n* végétation *f*
vehicle (*vii*-eu-keul) *n* véhicule *m*
veil (véïl) *n* voile *m*

vein (véïn) *n* veine *f*; **varicose ~** varice *f*
velvet (*vèl*-vit) *n* velours *m*
velveteen (vèl-vi-*tiin*) *n* velvet *m*
venerable (*vè*-neu-reu-beul) *adj* vénérable
venereal disease (vi-*nieu*-ri-eul di-*ziiz*) maladie vénérienne
Venezuela (vè-ni-*zouéï*-leu) Venezuela *m*
Venezuelan (vè-ni-*zouéï*-leunn) *adj* vénézuélien; *n* Vénézuélien *m*
ventilate (*vèn*-ti-léït) *v* ventiler; aérer
ventilation (vèn-ti-*léï*-cheunn) *n* ventilation *f*; aération *f*
ventilator (*vèn*-ti-léï-teu) *n* ventilateur *m*
venture (*vèn*-tcheu) *v* risquer
veranda (veu-*ræn*-deu) *n* véranda *f*
verb (veûb) *n* verbe *m*
verbal (*veû*-beul) *adj* verbal
verdict (*veû*-dikt) *n* sentence *f*, verdict *m*
verge (veûdj) *n* bord *m*
verify (*vè*-ri-faï) *v* vérifier
verse (veûss) *n* vers *m*
version (*veû*-cheunn) *n* version *f*
versus (*veû*-seuss) *prep* contre
vertical (*veû*-ti-keul) *adj* vertical
very (*vè*-ri) *adv* très; *adj* même, justement; tout
vessel (*vè*-seul) *n* vaisseau *m*; récipient *m*
vest (vèst) *n* chemise *f*; *nAm* gilet *m*
veterinary surgeon (*vè*-tri-neu-ri *seû*-djeunn) vétérinaire *m/f*
via (vaï^{eu}) *prep* via
vibrate (vaï-*bréït*) *v* vibrer
vibration (vaï-*bréï*-cheunn) *n* vibration *f*
vicar (*vi*-keu) *n* vicaire *m*
vice president (vaïss-*prè*-zi-deunnt) *n* vice-président *m*
vicinity (vi-*si*-neu-ti) *n* alentours *mpl*, voisinage *m*
vicious (*vi*-cheuss) *adj* vicieux
victim (*vik*-timm) *n* victime *f*; dupe *f*
victory (*vik*-teu-ri) *n* victoire *f*
video camera (*vi*-di-ô^{ou} *kæ*-meu-reu) *n* caméra vidéo *f*
video recorder (*vi*-di-ô^{ou} ri-*koo*-deu) *n* magnétoscope *m*
view (vyoû) *n* vue *f*; point de vue, opinion *f*; *v* contempler
viewfinder (*vyoû*-faïn-deu) *n* viseur *m*
vigilant (*vi*-dji-leunnt) *adj* vigilant
villa (*vi*-leu) *n* villa *f*
village (*vi*-lidj) *n* village *m*
vine (vaïn) *n* vigne *f*
vinegar (*vi*-ni-gheu) *n* vinaigre *m*
vineyard (*vinn*-yeud) *n* vignoble *m*
vintage (*vinn*-tidj) *n* vendange *f*
violation (vaï^{eu}-*léï*-cheunn) *n* violation *f*
violence (*vaïeu*-leunns) *n* violence *f*
violent (*vaïeu*-leunnt) *adj* violent
violet (*vaïeu*-leut) *n* violette *f*; *adj* violet
violin (vaï^{eu}-*linn*) *n* violon *m*
VIP (vii-aï-*pii*) *n* V.I.P. *m*
virgin (*veû*-djinn) *n* vierge *f*
virtue (*veû*-tchoû) *n* vertu *f*
visa (*vii*-zeu) *n* visa *m*
visibility (vi-zeu-*bi*-leu-ti) *n* visibilité *f*
visible (*vi*-zeu-beul) *adj* visible
vision (*vi*-jeunn) *n* vision *f*
visit (*vi*-zit) *v* visiter; *n* visite *f*; **visiting card** carte de visite; **visiting hours** heures de visite
visitor (*vi*-zi-teu) *n* visiteur *m*, -euse *f*, invité *m*, -e *f*
vital (*vaï*-teul) *adj* vital
vitamin (*vi*-teu-minn) *n* vitamine *f*
vivid (*vi*-vid) *adj* vif
vocabulary (veu-*kæ*-byou-leu-ri) *n* vocabulaire *m*
vocal (*vôou*-keul) *adj* vocal
vocalist (*vôou*-keu-list) *n* chanteur *m*

voice (voïss) *n* voix *f*
void (voïd) *adj* nul
volcano (vol-*kéï*-nô^{ou}) *n* (pl ~es, ~s) volcan *m*
volt (vô^{ou}lt) *n* volt *m*
voltage (*vôoul*-tidj) *n* voltage *m*
volume (*vo*-lyoum) *n* volume *m*; tome *m*
voluntary (*vo*-leunn-teu-ri) *adj* volontaire
volunteer (vo-leunn-*tieu*) *n* volontaire *m*
vomit (*vo*-mit) *v* vomir
vote (vô^{ou}t) *v* voter; *n* vote *m*
voter (*vôou*-teu) *n* votant *m*, votante *f*; électeur *m*, électrice *f*
voucher (*vaou*-tcheu) *n* reçu *m*, bon *m*
vow (vaou) *n* vœu *m*, serment *m*; *v* jurer
vowel (vaou^{eu}l) *n* voyelle *f*
voyage (*voï*-idj) *n* voyage *m*
vulgar (*val*-gheu) *adj* vulgaire, grossier
vulnerable (*val*-neu-reu-beul) *adj* vulnérable
vulture (*val*-tcheu) *n* vautour *m*

W

wade (^{ou}éïd) *v* patauger
wafer (*ouéï*-feu) *n* gaufrette *f*
waffle (*ouo*-feul) *n* gaufre *f*
wages (*ouéï*-djiz) *pl* gages *mpl*
wag(g)on (*ouæ*-gheunn) *n* wagon *m*
waist (^{ou}éïst) *n* taille *f*
waistcoat (*ouéïss*-kô^{ou}t) *n* gilet *m*
wait (^{ou}éït) *v* attendre; ~ **on** *servir
waiter (*ouéï*-teu) *n* garçon *m*
waiting (*ouéï*-tinng) *n* attente *f*; ~ **list** liste d'attente; ~ **room** salle d'attente
waitress (*ouéï*-triss) *n* serveuse *f*
***wake** (^{ou}éïk) *v* réveiller; ~ **up** s'éveiller, se réveiller
walk (^{ou}ook) *v* marcher; se promener; *n* promenade *f*; démarche *f*; **walking** à pied
walker (*ouoo*-keu) *n* promeneur *m*
walking stick (*ouoo*-kinng-stik) *n* canne *f*
wall (^{ou}ool) *n* mur *m*; cloison *f*
wallet (*ouo*-lit) *n* portefeuille *m*
wallpaper (*ouool*-péï-peu) *n* papier peint
walnut (*ouool*-nat) *n* noix *f*
waltz (^{ou}ools) *n* valse *f*
wander (*ouonn*-deu) *v* errer
want (^{ou}onnt) *v* *vouloir; désirer; *n* besoin *m*; carence *f*, manque *m*
war (^{ou}oo) *n* guerre *f*
warden (*ouoo*-deunn) *n* surveillant *m*, gardien *m*
wardrobe (*ouoo*-drô^{ou}b) *n* garde-robe *f*
warehouse (*ouèeu*-haouss) *n* magasin *m*, dépôt *m*
wares (^{ou}è^{eu}z) *pl* marchandise *f*
warm (^{ou}oom) *adj* chaud; *v* chauffer
warmth (^{ou}oomθ) *n* chaleur *f*
warn (^{ou}oon) *v* *prévenir, avertir
warning (*ouoo*-ninng) *n* avertissement *m*
wary (*ouèeu*-ri) *adj* prudent
was (^{ou}oz) *v* (p be)
wash (^{ou}och) *v* laver; ~ **and wear** sans repassage; ~ **up** *faire la vaisselle
washable (*ouo*-cheu-beul) *adj* lavable
washbasin (*ouoch*-béï-seunn) *n*

lavabo *m*
washing (*ouo*-chinng) *n* lavage *m*; lessive *f*; **~ machine** machine à laver; **~ powder** lessive
washroom (*ouoch*-roûm) *nAm* toilettes *fpl*
wasp (^{ou}osp) *n* guêpe *f*
waste (^{ou}éïst) *v* gaspiller; *n* gaspillage *m*; *adj* en friche
wasteful (*ouéïst*-feul) *adj* gaspilleur
wastepaper basket (^{ou}éïst-*péï*-peu-bââ-skit) *n* corbeille à papier
watch (^{ou}otch) *v* regarder, observer; surveiller; *n* montre *f*; **~ for** guetter; **~ out** *prendre garde
watchmaker (*ouotch*-méï-keu) *n* horloger *m*, horlogère *f*
watchstrap (*ouotch*-stræp) *n* bracelet pour montre
water (*ouoo*-teu) *n* eau *f*; **iced ~** eau glacée; **running ~** eau courante; **~ pump** pompe à eau; **~ ski** ski nautique; **~ softener** adoucisseur d'eau
watercolo(u)r (*ouoo*-teu-ka-leu) *n* couleur à l'eau; aquarelle *f*
watercress (*ouoo*-teu-krèss) *n* cresson *m*
waterfall (*ouoo*-teu-fool) *n* cascade *f*
watermelon (*ouoo*-teu-mè-leunn) *n* pastèque *f*
waterproof (*ouoo*-teu-proûf) *adj* imperméable
waterway (*ouoo*-teu-^{ou}éï) *n* voie d'eau
watt (^{ou}ot) *n* watt *m*
wave (^{ou}éïv) *n* ondulation *f*, vague *f*; *v* *faire signe
wavelength (*ouéïv*-lèngθ) *n* longueur d'onde
wavy (*ouéï*-vi) *adj* ondulé
wax (^{ou}æks) *n* cire *f*
waxworks (*ouæks*-^{ou}eûks) *pl* musée des figures de cire
way (^{ou}éï) *n* manière *f*, façon *f*; voie *f*; côté *m*, direction *f*; distance *f*; **by the ~** à propos; **one-way traffic** sens unique; **out of the ~** écarté; **the other ~ round** en sens inverse; **~ back** chemin du retour; **~ in** entrée *f*; **~ out** sortie *f*
wayside (*ouéï*-saïd) *n* bord de la route
we (^{ou}ii) *pron* nous
weak (^{ou}iik) *adj* faible; léger
weakness (*ouiik*-neuss) *n* faiblesse *f*
wealth (^{ou}èlθ) *n* richesse *f*
wealthy (*ouèl*-θi) *adj* riche
weapon (*ouè*-peunn) *n* arme *f*
***wear** (^{ou}è^{eu}) *v* porter; **~ out** user
weary (*ouieu*-ri) *adj* las, fatigué
weather (*ouè*-ðeu) *n* temps *m*; **~ forecast** bulletin météorologique
***weave** (^{ou}iiv) *v* tisser
wedding (*ouè*-dinng) *n* mariage *m*; **~ ring** alliance *f*
web (^{ou}èb) *n* tissu *m*; toile *f*; **the Web** le Web, la Toile
wedge (^{ou}èdj) *n* cale *f*
Wednesday (*ouènz*-di) mercredi *m*
weed (^{ou}iid) *n* mauvaise herbe
week (^{ou}iik) *n* semaine *f*
weekday (*ouiik*-déï) *n* jour de la semaine
weekly (*ouii*-kli) *adj* hebdomadaire
***weep** (^{ou}iip) *v* pleurer
weigh (^{ou}éï) *v* peser
weighing machine (*ouéï*-inng-meu-chiin) *n* bascule *f*
weight (^{ou}éït) *n* poids *m*
welcome (*ouèl*-keumm) *adj* bienvenu; *n* accueil *m*; *v* *accueillir
weld (^{ou}èld) *v* souder
welfare (*ouèl*-fè^{eu}) *n* bien-être *m*
well¹ (^{ou}èl) *adv* bien; *adj* sain; **as ~** également, aussi bien; **as ~ as** aussi bien que; **well!** bien!
well² (^{ou}èl) *n* source *f*, puits *m*
well-founded (^{ou}èl-*faoun*-did) *adj* bien fondé

well-known (*ouèl*-nô^{ou}n) *adj* connu
well-to-do (^{ou}èl-teu-*doû*) *adj* aisé
went (^{ou}ènt) *v* (p go)
were (^{ou}eû) *v* (p be)
west (^{ou}èst) *n* occident *m*, ouest *m*
westerly (*ouè*-steu-li) *adj* occidental
western (*ouè*-steunn) *adj* occidental
wet (^{ou}èt) *adj* mouillé; humide
whale (^{ou}éïl) *n* baleine *f*
wharf (^{ou}oof) *n* (pl ~s, wharves) quai *m*
what (^{ou}ot) *pron* quoi; ce que; ~ **for** pourquoi
whatever (^{ou}o-*tè*-veu) *pron* tout ce que
wheat (^{ou}iit) *n* blé *m*
wheel (^{ou}iil) *n* roue *f*
wheelbarrow (*ouiil*-bæ-rô^{ou}) *n* brouette *f*
wheelchair (*ouiil*-tchè^{eu}) *n* fauteuil roulant
when (^{ou}èn) *adv* quand; *conj* quand, lorsque
whenever (^{ou}è-*nè*-veu) *conj* n'importe quand
where (^{ou}è^{eu}) *adv* où; *conj* où
wherever (^{ou}è^{eu}-*rè*-veu) *conj* partout où
whether (*ouè*-ðeu) *conj* si; **whether … or** si … ou
which (^{ou}itch) *pron* quel; qui
whichever (^{ou}i-*tchè*-veu) *adj* n'importe quel
while (^{ou}aïl) *conj* tandis que; *n* moment *m*
whilst (^{ou}aïlst) *conj* tandis que
whim (^{ou}imm) *n* lubie *f*, caprice *m*
whip (^{ou}ip) *n* fouet *m*; *v* fouetter
whiskers (*oui*-skeuz) *pl* favoris
whisper (*oui*-speu) *v* chuchoter; *n* chuchotement *m*
whistle (*oui*-seul) *v* siffler; *n* sifflet *m*
white (^{ou}aït) *adj* blanc
whiting (*ouaï*-tinng) *n* (pl ~) merlan *m*
Whitsun (*ouit*-seunn) Pentecôte *f*
who (hoû) *pron* qui
whole (hô^{ou}l) *adj* complet, entier; intact; *n* ensemble *m*
wholesale (*hôoul*-séïl) *n* vente en gros; ~ **dealer** grossiste *m*
wholesome (*hôoul*-seumm) *adj* sain
wholly (*hôoul*-li) *adv* entièrement
whom (hoûm) *pron* à qui
whore (hoo) *n* putain *f*
whose (hoûz) *pron* dont; de qui
why (^{ou}aï) *adv* pourquoi
wicked (*oui*-kid) *adj* mauvais
wide (^{ou}aïd) *adj* vaste, large
widen (*ouaï*-deunn) *v* élargir
widow (*oui*-dô^{ou}) *n* veuve *f*
widower (*oui*-dô^{ou}-eu) *n* veuf *m*
width (^{ou}idθ) *n* largeur *f*
wife (^{ou}aïf) *n* (pl wives) épouse *f*, femme *f*
wig (^{ou}igh) *n* perruque *f*
wild (^{ou}aïld) *adj* sauvage; féroce
will (^{ou}il) *n* volonté *f*; testament *m*
***will** (^{ou}il) *v* *vouloir
willing (*oui*-linng) *adj* disposé
willingly (*oui*-linng-li) *adv* volontiers
willpower (*ouil*-paou^{eu}) *n* volonté *f*
***win** (^{ou}inn) *v* gagner
wind (^{ou}innd) *n* vent *m*
***wind** (^{ou}aïnd) *v* serpenter; enrouler; ~ **up** remonter
winding (*ouaïn*-dinng) *adj* serpentant
windmill (*ouinnd*-mil) *n* moulin à vent
window (*ouinn*-dô^{ou}) *n* fenêtre *f*
windowsill (*ouinn*-dô^{ou}-sil) *n* rebord de fenêtre
windscreen (*ouinnd*-skriin) *n* pare-brise *m*; ~ **wiper** essuie-glace *m*
windshield (*ouinnd*-chiild) *nAm* parebrise *m*; ~ **wiper** *Am* essuie-glace *m*
windy (*ouinn*-di) *adj* venteux
wine (^{ou}aïn) *n* vin *m*; ~ **cellar** cave *f*; ~ **list** carte des vins; ~ **merchant** négociant en vins

wine-waiter (*ouaïn-*^{ou}éï-teu) *n* sommelier *m*

wing (^{ou}inng) *n* aile *f*

winkle (*ouinng-*keul) *n* bigorneau *m*

winner (*oui-*neu) *n* vainqueur *m*

winning (*oui-*ninng) *adj* gagnant; **winnings** *pl* gains

winter (*ouinn-*teu) *n* hiver *m*; **~ sports** sports d'hiver

wipe (^{ou}aïp) *v* ôter, essuyer

wire (^{ou}aï^{eu}) *n* fil *m*; fil de fer

wireless (*ouaïeu-*leuss) *n* radio *f*

wisdom (*ouiz-*deumm) *n* sagesse *f*

wise (^{ou}aïz) *adj* sage

wish (^{ou}ich) *v* désirer, souhaiter; *n* désir *m*, souhait *m*

witch (^{ou}itch) *n* sorcière *f*

with (^{ou}ið) *prep* avec; chez; de

***withdraw** (^{ou}ið-*droo*) *v* retirer

within (^{ou}i-*ðinn*) *prep* dans; *adv* à l'intérieur

without (^{ou}i-*ðaout*) *prep* sans

witness (*ouit-*neuss) *n* témoin *m*

wit (^{ou}it) *n* esprit *m*; intelligence *f*

wits (^{ou}its) *pl* raison *f*

witty (*oui-*ti) *adj* spirituel

wolf (^{ou}oulf) *n* (pl wolves) loup *m*

woman (*ouou-*meunn) *n* (pl women) femme *f*

won (^{ou}ann) *v* (p, pp win)

wonder (*ouann-*deu) *n* miracle *m*; étonnement *m*; *v* se demander

wonderful (*ouann-*deu-feul) *adj* splendide, merveilleux; délicieux

wood (^{ou}oud) *n* bois *m*

wooded (*ouou-*did) *adj* boisé

wooden (*ouou-*deunn) *adj* en bois; **~ shoe** sabot *m*

woodland (*ououd-*leunnd) *n* pays boisé

wool (^{ou}oul) *n* laine *f*; **darning ~** laine à repriser

wool(l)en (*ouou-*leunn) *adj* en laine

word (^{ou}eûd) *n* mot *m*

wore (^{ou}oo) *v* (p wear)

work (^{ou}eûk) *n* travail *m*; activité *f*; *v* travailler; fonctionner; **working day** jour ouvrable; **~ of art** œuvre d'art; **~ permit** permis de travail

worker (*oueû-*keu) *n* ouvrier *m*, ouvrière *f*

working (*oueû-*kinng) *n* fonctionnement *m*

workman (*oueûk-*meunn) *n* (pl -men) ouvrier *m*

works (^{ou}eûks) *pl* usine *f*

workshop (*oueûk-*chop) *n* atelier *m*

world (^{ou}eûld) *n* monde *m*; **~ war** guerre mondiale

world-famous (^{ou}eûld-*féï-*meuss) *adj* de renommée mondiale

world-wide (*oueûld-*^{ou}aïd) *adj* mondial

worm (^{ou}eûmm) *n* ver *m*

worn (^{ou}oon) *adj* (pp wear) usé

worn-out (^{ou}oon-*aout*) *adj* usé

worried (*oua-*rid) *adj* soucieux

worry (*oua-*ri) *v* s'inquiéter; *n* souci *m*, inquiétude *f*

worse (^{ou}eûss) *adj* pire; *adv* pire

worship (*oueû-*chip) *v* adorer; *n* culte *m*

worst (^{ou}eûst) *adj* le plus mauvais; *adv* le pire

worth (^{ou}eûθ) *n* valeur *f*; ***be ~** *valoir; ***be worth-while** *valoir la peine

worthless (*oueûθ-*leuss) *adj* sans valeur

worthy of (*oueû-*ði euv) digne de

would (^{ou}oud) *v* (p will) *avoir l'habitude de

wound¹ (^{ou}oûnd) *n* blessure *f*; *v* offenser, blesser

wound² (^{ou}aound) *v* (p, pp wind)

wrap (ræp) *v* envelopper

wreck (rèk) *n* épave *f*; *v* *détruire

wrench (rèntch) *n* clé *f*; mouvement *m* violent de torsion; *v* tordre

wrinkle (*rinng*-keul) *n* ride *f*
wrist (rist) *n* poignet *m*
wristwatch (*rist*-^{ou}otch) *n* braceletmontre *m*
***write** (raït) *v* *écrire; **in writing** par écrit; **~ down** noter
writer (*raï*-teu) *n* écrivain *m*
writing pad (*raï*-tinng-pæd) *n* bloc-notes *m*
writing paper (*raï*-tinng-péï-peu) *n* papier à lettres
written (*ri*-teunn) *adj* (pp write) par écrit
wrong (ronng) *adj* impropre, incorrect; *n* tort *m*; *v* *faire tort à; ***be ~** *avoir tort
wrote (rô^{ou}t) *v* (p write)

X

Xmas (*kriss*-meuss) Noël
X-ray (*èks*-réï) *n* radiographie *f*; *v* radiographier

Y

yacht (yot) *n* yacht *m*; **~ club** yacht-club *m*
yachting (*yo*-tinng) *n* yachting *m*
yard (yââd) *n* cour *f*
yarn (yâân) *n* fil *m*
yawn (yoon) *v* bâiller
year (yi^{eu}) *n* année *f*
yearly (*yieu*-li) *adj* annuel
yeast (yiist) *n* levure *f*
yell (yèl) *v* hurler; *n* cri *m*
yellow (*yè*-lô^{ou}) *adj* jaune
yes (yèss) oui
yesterday (*yè*-steu-di) *adv* hier
yet (yèt) *adv* encore; *conj* pourtant, cependant
yield (yiild) *v* rendre; céder
yoke (yô^{ou}k) *n* joug *m*
yolk (yô^{ou}k) *n* jaune d'œuf
you (yoû) *pron* tu; te; vous
young (yanng) *adj* jeune
your (yoo) *adj* votre; ton; vos
yours (yooz) le tien, la tienne, les tiens, les tiennes; à toi; le (la) vôtre, les vôtres; à vous
yourself (yoo-*sèlf*) *pron* te; toi-même; vous-même
yourselves (yoo-*sèlvz*) *pron* vous; vous-mêmes
youth (yoûθ) *n* jeunesse *f*; **~ hostel** auberge de jeunesse

Z

zap (zæp) *colloquial v* zapper; agresser; assommer; détruire, filer (à toute allure); *n* vigueur *f*, énergie *f*, entrain *m*
zeal (ziil) *n* zèle *m*
zealous (*zè*-leuss) *adj* zélé
zebra (*zii*-breu) *n* zèbre *m*
zenith (*zè*-niθ) *n* zénith *m*; apogée *m*
zero (*zieu*-rô^{ou}) *n* (pl ~s) zéro *m*
zest (zèst) *n* entrain *m*
zinc (zinngk) *n* zinc *m*
zip (zip) *n* fermeture éclair; **~ code** *Am* code postal
zipper (*zi*-peu) *n* fermeture éclair
zodiac (*zôou*-di-æk) *n* zodiaque *m*
zone (zô^{ou}n) *n* zone *f*; région *f*
zoo (zoû) *n* (pl ~s) zoo *m*

Lexique gastronomique

Mets

almond amande
anchovy anchois
angel food cake gâteau aux blancs d'œufs
angels on horseback huîtres enrobées de lard, grillées et servies sur toast
appetizer amuse-gueule
apple pomme
~ **dumpling** sorte de chausson aux pommes
~ **sauce** compote de pommes
Arbroath smoky églefin fumé
artichoke artichaut
asparagus asperge
~ **tip** pointe d'asperge
assorted varié
avocado (pear) avocat
bacon lard à griller
~ **and eggs** œufs au lard
bagel petit pain en forme de couronne
baked au four
~ **Alaska** omelette norvégienne
~ **beans** haricots blancs dans une sauce tomate
~ **potato** pomme de terre en robe des champs cuite au four
Bakewell tart gâteau aux amandes et à la confiture
banana banane
~ **split** banane coupée en tranches, servie avec de la glace et des noix, arrosée de sirop ou de crème au chocolat
barbecue 1) hachis de bœuf dans une sauce relevée aux tomates, servi dans un petit pain 2) repas en plein air
~ **sauce** sauce aux tomates très relevée
barbecued grillé au charbon de bois
basil basilic
bass bar
bean haricot, fève
beef bœuf
~ **olive** paupiette de bœuf
beefburger bifteck haché, grillé et servi dans un petit pain
beet, beetroot betterave rouge
bilberry myrtille
bill addition
~ **of fare** carte des mets, menu
biscuit 1) petit gâteau sec, biscuit (GB) 2) biscuit sec (US)
black pudding boudin noir
blackberry mûre
blackcurrant cassis
bloater hareng saur
blood sausage boudin noir
blueberry myrtille
boiled bouilli
Bologna (sausage) sorte de mortadelle
boloney sorte de mortadelle
bone os
boned désossé
Boston baked beans haricots blancs au lard et à la mélasse dans une sauce tomate
Boston cream pie tourte à la crème en couches superposées, glacée au chocolat
brains cervelle
braised braisé
bramble pudding pudding aux mûres (souvent servi avec des pommes)
braunschweiger saucisson au foie fumé
bread pain
breaded pané
breakfast petit déjeuner

bream brème (poisson)
breast poitrine, blanc de volaille
brisket poitrine de bœuf
broad bean grosse fève
broth bouillon
brown Betty sorte de charlotte aux pommes et aux épices recouverte de chapelure
brunch repas qui tient lieu de petit déjeuner et de déjeuner
Brussels sprouts choux de Bruxelles
bubble and squeak sorte de galette de pommes de terre et choux, parfois accompagnés de morceaux de bœuf
bun 1) petit pain au lait avec des fruits secs 2) sorte de petit pain (US)
butter beurre
buttered beurré
cabbage chou
Caesar salad salade verte, ail, anchois, croûtons et fromage râpé
cake gâteau
cakes pâtisseries
calf veau
Canadian bacon carré de porc fumé, coupé en fines tranches
caper câpre
capercaillie, capercailzie grand coq de bruyère
carp carpe
carrot carotte
cashew noix de cajou
casserole en cocotte
catfish poisson-chat
catsup ketchup
cauliflower chou-fleur
celery céleri
cereal céréale, cornflakes
hot ~ porridge
check addition
Cheddar (cheese) fromage à pâte dure au goût légèrement acide
cheese fromage
~ board plateau de fromages
~ cake gâteau au fromage double crème
cheeseburger bifteck haché, grillé avec une tranche de fromage, servi dans un petit pain
chef's salad salade de jambon, poulet, œufs durs, tomates, laitue et fromage
cherry cerise
chestnut marron
chicken poulet
chicory 1) endive (GB) 2) (e)scarole, chicorée (US)
chili con carne hachis de bœuf aux haricots rouges et aux piments rouges
chili pepper piment rouge
chips 1) pommes frites (GB) 2) pommes chips (US)
chitt(er)lings tripes de porc
chive ciboulette
chocolate chocolat
choice premier choix
chop côtelette
~ suey émincé de porc ou de poulet, de riz et de légumes
chopped émincé, haché
chowder bisque
Christmas pudding cake anglais aux fruits secs, parfois flambé; très nourrissant et servi à Noël
chutney condiment indien épicé à saveur aigre-douce
cinnamon cannelle
clam palourde
club sandwich double sandwich au *bacon*, poulet, tomate, salade et mayonnaise
cobbler tourte aux fruits
cock-a-leekie soup crème de volaille et de poireaux
coconut noix de coco
cod cabillaud
Colchester oyster huître anglaise très

renommée
cold cuts/meat assiette anglaise, viandes froides
coleslaw salade de chou cru
cooked cuit
cookie biscuit
corn 1) blé (GB) 2) maïs (US)
~ **on the cob** épi de maïs
cornflakes flocons de maïs
cottage cheese fromage blanc égoutté
cottage pie hachis de viande aux oignons recouvert de purée de pommes de terre
course plat
cover charge prix du couvert
crab crabe
cracker biscuit salé, craquelin
cranberry canneberge
~ **sauce** sauce à la canneberge
crawfish, crayfish 1) écrevisse 2) langouste (GB) 3) langoustine (US)
cream 1) crème 2) velouté (potage) 3) crème (dessert)
~ **cheese** fromage double crème
~ **puff** chou à la crème
creamed potatoes pommes de terre coupées en dés dans une sauce béchamel
creole mets très relevé, préparé avec des tomates, des poivrons et des oignons, servi avec du riz blanc
cress cresson
crisps pommes chips
crumpet petite crêpe épaisse servie chaude et beurrée
cucumber concombre
Cumberland ham jambon fumé très réputé
Cumberland sauce sauce aigredouce; vin, jus d'orange, zeste de citron, épices et gelée de groseilles
cupcake petit gâteau
cured salé et parfois fumé
currant 1) raisin de Corinthe 2) groseille
curried au curry
custard crème anglaise, flan
cutlet sorte d'escalope, fine tranche de viande, côtelette
dab limande
Danish pastry pâtisserie ou gâteau riche en levure
date datte
Derby cheese fromage à pâte molle et au goût piquant, de couleur jaune pâle
devilled à la diable; assaisonnement très relevé
devil's food cake tourte au chocolat
devils on horseback pruneaux cuits dans du vin rouge et farcis d'amandes et d'anchois, enrobés de lard et grillés
Devonshire cream double crème, très épaisse
diced coupé en dés
diet food aliment diététique
dill aneth
dinner dîner, repas du soir
dish plat, assiette, mets
donut, doughnut beignet en forme d'anneau
double cream double crème, crème entière
Dover sole sole de Douvres, très réputée
dressing 1) sauce à salade 2) farce pour la volaille (US)
Dublin Bay prawn langoustine
duck canard
duckling caneton
dumpling boulette de pâte
Dutch apple pie tarte aux pommes saupoudrée de cassonade ou nappée de mélasse
eel anguille
egg œuf
boiled ~ à la coque

fried ~ au plat
hard-boiled ~ dur
poached ~ poché
scrambled ~ brouillé
soft-boiled ~ mollet
eggplant aubergine
endive 1) (e)scarole, chicorée (GB) 2) endive (US)
entrée 1) entrée (GB) 2) plat principal (US)
fennel fenouil
fig figue
fillet filet de viande ou de poisson
finnan haddock églefin fumé
fish poisson
~ **and chips** filets de poisson frits et pommes frites
~ **cake** galette de poisson et de pommes de terre
flan tarte
flapjack matefaim, crêpe épaisse
flounder flet, plie
forcemeat farce, hachis
fowl volaille
frankfurter saucisse de Francfort
French bean haricot vert
French bread baguette
French dressing 1) vinaigrette (GB) 2) sauce à salade crémeuse assaisonnée de ketchup (US)
French fries pommes frites
French toast croûte dorée
fresh frais
fried frit, grillé
fritter beignet
frogs' legs cuisses de grenouilles
frosting glaçage
fry friture
game gibier
gammon jambon fumé
garfish aiguille de mer
garlic ail
garnish garniture
gherkin cornichon
giblets abats, abattis
ginger gingembre
goose oie
~**berry** groseille à maquereau
grape raisin
~**fruit** pamplemousse
grated râpé
gravy jus de viande épaissi
grayling omble
green bean haricot vert
green pepper poivron vert
green salad laitue, salade verte
greens garniture de légumes verts
grilled grillé
grilse saumoneau
grouse petit coq de bruyère
gumbo 1) gombo (légume d'origine africaine) 2) plat créole à base d'*okra*, de viande, de poisson ou de fruits de mer et de légumes
haddock églefin
haggis panse de mouton farcie aux flocons d'avoine
hake colin
half moitié, demi
halibut flétan
ham jambon
~ **and eggs** œufs au jambon
hare lièvre
haricot bean haricot blanc
hash 1) émincé 2) hachis de bœuf recouvert de pommes de terre
hazelnut noisette
heart cœur
herb herbe aromatique
herring hareng
home-made fait maison
hominy grits bouillie de maïs, sorte de polenta
honey miel
~**dew melon** variété de melon très doux à la chair vert-jaune
horse-radish raifort
hot 1) chaud 2) épicé

~ **cross bun** brioche aux raisins (se mange pendant le Carême)
~ **dog** hot-dog, saucisse chaude dans un petit pain
huckleberry myrtille
hush puppy beignet de farine de maïs
ice-cream glace
iced glacé
icing glaçage
Idaho baked potato pomme de terre en robe des champs cuite au four
Irish stew ragoût de mouton aux oignons et aux pommes de terre
Italian dressing vinaigrette
jam confiture
jellied en gelée
Jell-O dessert à la gélatine
jelly gelée de fruits
Jerusalem artichoke topinambour
John Dory Saint-Pierre (poisson)
jugged hare civet de lièvre
juice jus
juniper berry baie de genièvre
junket lait caillé sucré
kale chou frisé
kedgeree miettes depoisson au riz, aux œufs et au beurre
kidney rognon
kipper hareng fumé
lamb agneau
Lancashire hot pot ragoût de côtelettes, de rognons d'agneau, de pommes de terre et d'oignons
larded lardé
lean maigre
leek poireau
leg gigot, cuisse
lemon citron
~ **sole** limande-sole
lentil lentille
lettuce laitue, salade verte
lima bean fève
lime lime, citron vert
liver foie
loaf pain, miche
lobster homard
loin filet, carré
Long Island duck canard de Long Island, très réputé
low-calorie pauvre en calories
lox saumon fumé
lunch déjeuner, repas de midi
macaroon macaron
mackerel maquereau
maize maïs
mandarin mandarine
maple syrup sirop d'érable
marinated mariné
marjoram marjolaine
marmalade confiture d'orange ou d'autres agrumes, marmelade
marrow moelle
~ **bone** os à moelle
marshmallow bonbon à la guimauve
marzipan pâte d'amandes
mashed potatoes purée de pommes de terre
meal repas
meat viande
~ **ball** boulette de viande
~ **loaf** rôti haché
medium (done) à point
melted fondu
Melton Mowbray pie croustade de viande
milk lait
mince hachis
~ **pie** tartelette aux fruits confits et aux épices
minced haché
~ **meat** viande hachée
mint menthe
mixed mélangé, panaché
~ **grill** assortiment de grillades
molasses mélasse
morel morille
mulberry mûre
mullet mulet

mulligatawny soup potage au poulet, très épicé, d'origine indienne
mushroom champignon
muskmelon sorte de melon
mussel moule
mustard moutarde
mutton mouton
noodle nouille
nut noix
oatmeal (porridge) porridge, bouillie d'avoine
oil huile
okra pousse de *gumbo* généralement utilisée pour lier les potages et les ragoûts
omelet omelette
onion oignon
ox tongue langue de bœuf
oyster huître
pancake crêpe
parsley persil
parsnip panais (racine comestible)
partridge perdrix
pastry pâtisserie
pasty pâté, chausson, rissole
pea petit pois
peach pêche
peanut cacahuète
~ butter beurre de cacahuètes
pear poire
pearl barley orge perlé
pepper poivre
peppermint menthe (poivrée)
perch perche
persimmon kaki
pheasant faisan
pickerel brocheton (poisson)
pickle 1) légume ou fruit au vinaigre 2) cornichon (US)
pickled en saumure, au vinaigre
pie tarte, recouverte le plus souvent d'une couche de pâte, farcie ou garnie de viande, de légumes, de fruits ou de crème anglaise
pig porc
pike brochet
pineapple ananas
plaice plie, carrelet
plain nature
plate plat, assiette
plum 1) prune 2) pruneau 3) raisin sec
~ pudding cake anglais aux fruits secs, parfois flambé; très nourrissant et servi à Noël
poached poché
popcorn grains de maïs éclatés
popover petit pain au lait
pork porc
porterhouse steak épaisse tranche de filet de bœuf
pot roast bœuf braisé aux légumes
potato pomme de terre
~ chips 1) pommes frites (GB) 2) pommes chips (US)
~ in its jacket pomme de terre en robe des champs
potted shrimps crevettes au beurre épicé (fondu et refroidi)
poultry volaille
prawn grosse crevette rose
prune pruneau
ptarmigan perdrix des neiges
pudding pudding (mou ou consistant) à base de farine, garni de viande, de poisson, de légumes ou de fruits
pumpernickel paim de seigle complet
pumpkin potiron, courge
quail caille
quince coing
rabbit lapin
radish radis
rainbow trout truite arc-en-ciel
raisin raisin sec
rare saignant
raspberry framboise
raw cru
red mullet rouget
red (sweet) pepper poivron rouge

redcurrant groseille rouge
relish condiment fait de légumes émincés au vinaigre
rhubarb rhubarbe
rib (of beef) côte (de bœuf)
rib-eye steak entrecôte
rice riz
rissole croquette de viande ou de poisson
river trout truite de rivière
roast(ed) rôti(e)
Rock Cornish hen variété de poulet de grain
roe œufs de poisson
roll petit pain
rollmop herring filet de hareng mariné au vin blanc, enroulé sur un cornichon
round steak quasi de bœuf
Rubens sandwich corned-beef sur toast, avec choucroute, emmenthal et sauce à salade, servi chaud
rumpsteak rumsteak
rusk biscotte
rye bread pain de seigle
saddle selle
saffron safran
sage sauge
salad salade
~ **bar** choix de salades
~ **cream** sauce à salade crémeuse, légèrement sucrée
~ **dressing** sauce pour salade
salmon saumon
~ **trout** truite saumonée
salt sel
salted salé
sauerkraut choucroute
sausage saucisse, saucisson
sauté(ed) sauté
scallop 1) peigne (coquille Saint-Jacques 2) escalope de veau
scone petit pain tendre à base de farine de blé ou d'orge
Scotch broth soupe à base d'agneau ou de bœuf et de légumes
Scotch woodcock toast avec œufs brouillés et beurre d'anchois
sea bass loup de mer
sea kale chou marin
seafood poissons et fruits de mer
(in) season (en) saison
seasoning assaisonnement
service charge montant à payer pour le service
service (not) included service (non) compris
set menu menu fixe
shad alose (sorte de sardine)
shallot échalote
shellfish crustacé
sherbet sorbet
shoulder épaule
shredded wheat croquettes de froment (servies au petit déjeuner)
shrimp crevette
silverside (of beef) gîte (de bœuf)
sirloin steak steak d'aloyau
skewer brochette
slice tranche
sliced coupé en tranches
sloppy Joe hachis de bœuf dans une sauce relevée aux tomates, servi dans un petit pain
smelt éperlan
smoked fumé
snack casse-croûte
soup potage, soupe
sour aigre
soused herring hareng au vinaigre et aux épices
spare rib côte de porc grillée
spice épice
spinach épinard
spiny lobster langouste
(on a) spit (à la) broche
sponge cake gâteau mousseline
sprat harenguet

squash courge
starter hors-d'œuvre
steak and kidney pie croustade de viande de bœuf et de rognons
steamed cuit à la vapeur
stew ragoût
Stilton (cheese) fromage anglais réputé (blanc ou à moisissures bleues)
strawberry fraise
string bean haricot vert
stuffed farci, fourré
stuffing farce
suck(l)ing pig cochon de lait
sugar sucre
sugarless sans sucre
sundae coupe de glace aux fruits, noix, crème Chantilly et parfois sirop
supper souper, léger repas du soir
swede rutabaga
sweet 1) doux 2) dessert
~ **corn** maïs jaune
~ **potato** patate douce
sweetbread ris de veau
Swiss cheese emmenthal
Swiss roll biscuit roulé à la confiture
Swiss steak tranche de bœuf braisée avec des légumes et des épices
T-bone steak morceau de contrefilet et de filet séparés par un os en forme de T
table d'hôte repas à prix fixe
tangerine mandarine
tarragon estragon
tart tarte (généralement aux fruits)
tenderloin filet (de viande)
Thousand Island dressing mayonnaise aux piments ou au ketchup, avec des poivrons, des olives et des œufs durs
thyme thym
toad-in-the-hole morceaux de viande ou de saucisse briochés
toasted grillé
~ **cheese** toast au fromage
tomato tomate
tongue langue
treacle mélasse
trifle sorte de charlotte russe à l'eau-de-vie avec amandes, confiture, crème Chantilly et crème anglaise
trout truite
truffle truffe
tuna, tunny thon
turkey dinde
turnip navet
turnover chausson
turtle tortue
underdone saignant
vanilla vanille
veal veau
~ **bird** paupiette de veau
vegetable légume
~ **marrow** courge
venison gros gibier
vichyssoise soupe froide aux poireaux, pommes de terre et crème
vinegar vinaigre
Virginia baked ham jambon cuit au four, piqué de clous de girofles, garni de tranches d'ananas, de cerises et glacé avec le jus des fruits
wafer gaufrette
waffle sorte de gaufre, chaude
walnut noix
water ice sorbet
watercress cresson de fontaine
watermelon pastèque
well-done bien cuit
Welsh rabbit/rarebit croûte au fromage
whelk buccin (mollusque)
whipped cream crème Chantilly
whitebait blanchaille
Wiener Schnitzel escalope viennoise
wine list carte des vins
woodcock bécasse
Worcestershire sauce condiment

liquide piquant, à base de vinaigre, de soja et d'ail
yoghurt yaourt
York ham jambon (fumé) d'York
Yorkshire pudding sorte de pâte à choux cuite et servie avec le rosbif
zucchini courgette
zwieback biscotte

Boissons

ale bière brune, légèrement sucrée, fermentée à haute température
bitter ~ brune, amère et plutôt lourde
brown ~ brune en bouteille, légèrement sucrée
light ~ blonde en bouteille
mild ~ brune à la pression, au goût prononcé
pale ~ blonde en bouteille
angostura essence aromatique amère ajoutée aux cocktails
applejack eau-de-vie de pomme
Athol Brose boisson écossaise composée de whisky, de miel, d'eau et parfois de flocons d'avoine
Bacardi cocktail cocktail au rhum avec du gin, du sirop de grenadine et du jus de lime (citron vert)
barley water boisson rafraîchissante à base d'orge et aromatisée de citron
barley wine bière brune très alcoolisée
beer bière
bottled ~ en bouteille
draft, draught ~ à la pression
bitters apéritifs et digestifs à base de racines, d'écorces ou d'herbes
black velvet champagne additionné de *stout* (accompagne souvent les huîtres)
bloody Mary vodka, jus de tomate et épices
bourbon whisky américain, à base de maïs
brandy 1) appellation générique désignant les eaux-de-vie de vin ou de fruit 2) cognac
~ Alexander mélange d'eau-de-vie, de crème de cacao et de crème fraîche
British wines vins «anglais» faits de raisins (ou de jus de raisin) importés en Grande-Bretagne
cherry brandy liqueur de cerise
chocolate chocolat
cider cidre
~ cup mélange de cidre, d'épices, de sucre et de glace
claret vin rouge de Bordeaux
cobbler *long drink* glacé à base de fruits, auquel on ajoute du vin ou une liqueur
coffee café
~ with cream crème
black ~ noir
caffeine-free ~ décaféiné
white ~ au lait
cordial liqueur
cream crème
cup boisson rafraîchissante composée de vin glacé, d'eau gazeuse, d'un spiritueux et décorée d'une tranche d'orange, de citron ou de concombre
daiquiri cocktail au rhum, au jus de lime et d'ananas
double double dose
Drambuie liqueur à base de whisky et de miel

dry martini 1) vermouth sec (GB) 2) cocktail au gin avec un peu de vermouth sec (US)
egg-nog boisson faite de rhum ou d'un autre alcool fort avec des jaunes d'œufs battus et du sucre
gin and it mélange de gin et de vermouth italien
gin-fizz gin avec jus de citron, sucre et soda
ginger ale boisson sans alcool, parfumée à l'essence de gingembre
ginger beer boisson légèrement alcoolisée, à base de gingembre et de sucre
grasshopper mélange de crème de menthe, de crème de cacao et de crème fraîche
Guinness (stout) bière brune légèrement sucrée, au goût très prononcé et à forte teneur en malt et houblon
half pint environ 3 décilitres
highball eau-de-vie ou whisky allongé d'eau gazeuse ou de *ginger ale*
iced glacé
Irish coffee café sucré, arrosé de whisky irlandais et nappé de crème Chantilly
Irish Mist liqueur irlandaise à base de whisky et de miel
Irish whiskey whisky irlandais, moins âpre que le *scotch*; outre l'orge, il contient du seigle, de l'avoine et du blé
juice jus
lager bière blonde légère, servie très fraîche
lemon squash citronnade
lemonade limonade
lime juice jus de lime (citron vert)
liquor spiritueux
long drink alcool allongé d'eau ou d'une boisson gazeuse, avec des glaçons
madeira madère
Manhattan whisky américain, vermouth et *angostura*
milk lait
~ shake frappé
mineral water eau minérale
mulled wine vin chaud aux épices
neat sans glace et sans eau, sec, pur
old-fashioned whisky, *angostura*, cerises au marasquin et sucre
on the rocks avec des glaçons
Ovaltine Ovomaltine
Pimm's cup(s) boisson alcoolisée mélangée à du jus de fruit ou du soda
~ No. 1 à base de gin
~ No. 2 à base de whisky
~ No. 3 à base de rhum
~ No. 4 à base d'eau-de-vie
pink champagne champagne rosé
pink lady mélange de blanc d'œuf, de Calvados, de jus de citron, de grenadine et de gin
pint environ 6 décilitres
port (wine) porto
porter bière brune et amère
quart 1,14 litre (US 0,95 litre)
root beer boisson gazeuse sucrée, aromatisée d'herbes et de racines
rum rhum
rye (whiskey) whisky de seigle, plus lourd et plus âpre que le *bourbon*
scotch (whisky) whisky écossais, généralement fait d'une combinaison de whisky d'orge et de whisky de blé
screwdriver vodka et jus d'orange
shandy *bitter ale* mélangée à une limonade ou une *ginger beer*
sherry xérès
short drink tout alcool non dilué
shot dose de spiritueux
sloe gin-fizz liqueur de prunelle avec soda et jus de citron
soda water eau de Seltz

soft drink boisson sans alcool
spirits spiritueux
stinger cognac et crème de menthe
stout bière brune fortement houblonnée et alcoolisée
straight alcool bu sec, pur
tea thé
toddy grog
Tom Collins gin, jus de citron, sucre, eau gazeuse
tonic (water) eau gazéifiée, aromatisée de quinine
water eau
whisky sour whisky, jus de citron, sucre et soda
wine vin
  dry ~ sec
  red ~ rouge
  sparkling ~ mousseux
  sweet ~ doux (de dessert) **white ~** blanc

Mini-grammaire anglaise

L'article

L'article défini (le, la, les) a une seule forme: *the*.

the room, the rooms	la chambre, les chambres

L'article indéfini (un, une, des) a deux formes: *a* s'emploie devant une consonne, *an* devant une voyelle ou un «h» muet.

a coat	un manteau
an umbrella	un parapluie
an hour	une heure

Some indique une quantité ou un nombre indéfini.

I'd like some water, please.	Je voudrais de l'eau, s.v.p.

Any s'emploie dans les phrases négatives et différents types d'interrogatives.

There isn't any soap.	Il n'y a pas de savon.
Do you have any stamps?	Avez-vous des timbres?

Le nom

Le pluriel de la plupart des noms se forme par l'addition de -(*e*)*s* au singulier.

cup – cups (tasse – tasses)	**dress – dresses** (robe – robes)

Note: Si un nom se termine par -*y* précédé d'une consonne, le pluriel se termine par -*ies*; si le -*y* est précédé d'une voyelle, il n'y a pas de changement.

lady – ladies (dame – dames)	**key – keys** (clef – clefs)

Quelques pluriels irréguliers:

man – men (homme – hommes)	**foot – feet** (pied – pieds)
woman – women (femme – femmes)	**tooth – teeth** (dent – dents)
child – children (enfant – enfants)	**mouse – mice** (souris – souris)

Le complément du nom (génitif)

1. Le possesseur est une personne: si le nom ne se termine pas par -*s*, on ajoute *'s*.

the boy's room	la chambre du garçon
the children's clothes	les vêtements des enfants

Si le nom se termine par *s*, on ajoute l'apostrophe (').

the boys' room	la chambre des garçons

2. Le possesseur n'est pas une personne: on utilise la préposition *of*:

the key of the door	la clef de la porte

L'adjectif

Les adjectifs se placent normalement avant le nom.

a large brown suitcase une grande valise brune

Il y a deux façons de former le comparatif et le superlatif des adjectifs:

1. Les adjectifs d'une syllabe et de nombreux adjectifs de deux syllabes prennent la terminaison *-(e)r* et *-(e)st.*

small (petit) **– smaller – smallest** pretty (joli) **– prettier – prettiest***

2. Les adjectifs de trois syllabes et plus, et certains de deux (en particulier ceux qui se terminent par *-ful* et *-less*) forment leurs comparatifs et superlatifs avec *more* et *most.*

expensive (cher) **– more expensive – most expensive**

Le pronom

		Sujet	Complément (dir./indir.)	Possessif 1	2
Singulier					
1re personne		**I**	**me**	**my**	**mine**
2e personne		**you**	**you**	**your**	**yours**
3e personne	(m)	**he**	**him**	**his**	**his**
	(f)	**she**	**her**	**her**	**hers**
	(n)	**it**	**it**	**its**	**–**
Pluriel					
1re personne		**we**	**us**	**our**	**ours**
2e personne		**you**	**you**	**your**	**yours**
3e personne		**they**	**them**	**their**	**their**

Note: L'anglais ignore le tutoiement. La forme *you* signifie donc «tu» et «vous».

Le cas complément s'emploie aussi après les prépositions.

Give it to me. Donnez-le-moi.

La forme 1 du possessif correspond à «mon», «ton», etc., la forme 2 à «le mien», «le tien», etc.

Where's my key? Où est ma clef? **That's not mine.** Ce n'est pas la mienne.

* L'«y» se change en «i» lorsqu'il est précédé d'une consonne.

Verbes auxiliaires

a. **to be** (être)

	Forme contractée	Négatif – formes contractées		
I am	**I'm**			**I'm not**
you are	**you're**	**you're not**	ou	**you aren't**
he is	**he's**	**he's not**		**he isn't**
she is	**she's**	**she's not**		**she isn't**
it is	**it's**	**it's not**		**it isn't**
we are	**we're**	**we're not**		**we aren't**
they are	**they're**	**they're not**		**they aren't**

Interrogatif: **Am I? Are you? Is he?** etc.

b. **to have** (avoir)

	Contraction		Contraction
I have	**I've**	**we have**	**we've**
you have	**you've**	**you have**	**you've**
he/she/it has	**he/she/it's**	**they have**	**they've**

Négation: **I have not (I haven't)**
Interrogation: **Have you? – Has he?**

c. **to do** (faire)

	Négatif contracté		Négatif contracté
I do	**I don't**	**we do**	**we don't**
you do	**you don't**	**you do**	**you don't**
he/she/it does	**he/she/it doesn't**	**they do**	**they don't**

Interrogation: **Do you? Does he/she/it?**

Autres verbes

L'infinitif est utilisé pour toutes les personnes du présent; on ajoute simplement -(*e*)*s* à la 3e personne du singulier.

	(to) love (aimer)	**(to) come** (venir)	**(to) go** (aller)
I	**love**	**come**	**go**
you	**love**	**come**	**go**
he/she/it	**loves**	**comes**	**goes**
we	**love**	**come**	**go**
they	**love**	**come**	**go**

La négation se forme au moyen de l'auxiliaire *do*/*does* + *not* + infinitif du verbe.

We do not (don't) like this hotel. Nous n'aimons pas cet hôtel.

L'interrogation se forme aussi avec l'auxiliaire *do* + sujet + infinitif.

Do you like her? L'aimez-vous?

Verbes irréguliers

L'imparfait et le participe passé des verbes réguliers se forment en ajoutant -*(e)d* à l'infinitif. La liste suivante vous donne les verbes irréguliers anglais. Les verbes composés ou précédés d'un préfixe se conjuguent comme les verbes principaux: p.ex. *withdraw* se conjugue comme *draw* et *mistake* comme *take*.

Infinitif	*Imparfait*	*Participe passé*	
arise	arose	arisen	*(se) lever*
awake	awoke	awoken	*(se) réveiller*
be	was	been	*être*
bear	bore	borne	*porter*
beat	beat	beaten	*battre*
become	became	become	*devenir*
begin	began	begun	*commencer*
bend	bent	bent	*plier*
bet	bet	bet	*parier*
bid	bade/bid	bidden/bid	*ordonner*
bind	bound	bound	*attacher*
bite	bit	bitten	*mordre*
bleed	bled	bled	*saigner*
blow	blew	blown	*souffler*
break	broke	broken	*briser*
breed	bred	bred	*élever*
bring	brought	brought	*apporter*
build	built	built	*bâtir*
burn	burnt/burned	burnt/burned	*brler*
burst	burst	burst	*éclater*
buy	bought	bought	*acheter*
can*	could	–	*pouvoir*
cast	cast	cast	*jeter*
catch	caught	caught	*attraper*
choose	chose	chosen	*choisir*
cling	clung	clung	*se cramponner*
clothe	clothed/clad	clothed/clad	*vêtir*
come	came	come	*venir*
cost	cost	cost	*coter*
creep	crept	crept	*ramper*
cut	cut	cut	*couper*
deal	dealt	dealt	*conclure (marché)*
dig	dug	dug	*creuser*
do (he does)	did	done	*faire*

* présent de l'indicatif

draw	drew	drawn	*dessiner*
dream	dreamt/dreamed	dreamt/dreamed	*rêver*
drink	drank	drunk	*boire*
drive	drove	driven	*conduire* (*auto*)
dwell	dwelt	dwelt	*habiter*
eat	ate	eaten	*manger*
fall	fell	fallen	*tomber*
feed	fed	fed	*nourrir*
feel	felt	felt	*ressentir*
fight	fought	fought	*combattre*
find	found	found	*trouver*
flee	fled	fled	*fuir*
fling	flung	flung	*lancer*
fly	flew	flown	*voler*
forsake	forsook	forsaken	*abandonner*
freeze	froze	frozen	*geler*
get	got	got	*obtenir*
give	gave	given	*donner*
go	went	gone	*aller*
grind	ground	ground	*moudre*
grow	grew	grown	*croître*
hang	hung	hung	*pendre*
have	had	had	*avoir*
hear	heard	heard	*entendre*
hew	hewed	hewed/hewn	*couper*
hide	hid	hidden	*cacher*
hit	hit	hit	*frapper*
hold	held	held	*tenir*
hurt	hurt	hurt	*blesser*
keep	kept	kept	*garder*
kneel	knelt	knelt	*s'agenouiller*
knit	knitted/knit	knitted/knit	*tricoter/unir*
know	knew	known	*savoir*
lay	laid	laid	*étendre, placer*
lead	led	led	*guider*
lean	leant/leaned	leant/leaned	*s'appuyer*
leap	leapt/leaped	leapt/leaped	*sauter*
learn	learnt/learned	learnt/learned	*apprendre*
leave	left	left	*quitter*
lend	lent	lent	*prêter*
let	let	let	*permettre*
lie	lay	lain	*être couché*
light	lit/lighted	lit/lighted	*allumer*
lose	lost	lost	*perdre*

make	made	made	*faire*
may*	might	–	*pouvoir*
mean	meant	meant	*signifier*
meet	met	met	*rencontrer*
mow	mowed	mowed/mown	*faucher*
must*	–	–	*falloir*
ought (to)*	–	–	*devoir*
pay	paid	paid	*payer*
put	put	put	*mettre*
read	read	read	*lire*
rid	rid	rid	*débarrasser*
ride	rode	ridden	*monter* (*à cheval*)
ring	rang	rung	*sonner*
rise	rose	risen	*se lever*
run	ran	run	*courir*
saw	sawed	sawn	*scier*
say	said	said	*dire*
see	saw	seen	*voir*
seek	sought	sought	*chercher*
sell	sold	sold	*vendre*
send	sent	sent	*envoyer*
set	set	set	*poser*
sew	sewed	sewed/sewn	*coudre*
shake	shook	shaken	*secouer*
shall*	should	–	*devoir*
shed	shed	shed	*verser*
shine	shone	shone	*briller*
shoot	shot	shot	*tirer*
show	showed	shown	*montrer*
shrink	shrank	shrunk	*rétrécir*
shut	shut	shut	*fermer*
sing	sang	sung	*chanter*
sink	sank	sunk	*couler*
sit	sat	sat	*s'asseoir*
sleep	slept	slept	*dormir*
slide	slid	slid	*glisser*
sling	slung	slung	*jeter*
slink	slunk	slunk	*s'esquiver*
slit	slit	slit	*fendre*
smell	smelled/smelt	smelled/smelt	*sentir* (*odeur*)
sow	sowed	sown/sowed	*semer*
speak	spoke	spoken	*parler*

* présent de l'indicatif

speed	sped/speeded	sped/speeded	*accélérer*
spell	spelt/spelled	spelt/spelled	*épeler*
spend	spent	spent	*dépenser*
spill	spilt/spilled	spilt/spilled	*renverser*
spin	spun	spun	*filer*
spit	spat	spat	*cracher*
split	split	split	*fendre, séparer*
spoil	spoilt/spoiled	spoilt/spoiled	*gâter*
spread	spread	spread	*répandre, enduire*
spring	sprang	sprung	*jaillir*
stand	stood	stood	*se tenir debout*
steal	stole	stolen	*dérober*
stick	stuck	stuck	*coller*
sting	stung	stung	*piquer*
stink	stank/stunk	stunk	*empester*
strew	strewed	strewed/strewn	*joncher*
stride	strode	stridden	*marcher à grands pas*
strike	struck	struck/stricken	*frapper*
string	strung	strung	*ficeler*
strive	strove	striven	*s'efforcer*
swear	swore	sworn	*jurer*
sweep	swept	swept	*balayer*
swell	swelled	swollen	*enfler*
swim	swam	swum	*nager*
swing	swung	swung	*se balancer*
take	took	taken	*prendre*
teach	taught	taught	*enseigner*
tear	tore	torn	*déchirer*
tell	told	told	*dire*
think	thought	thought	*penser*
throw	threw	thrown	*jeter*
thrust	thrust	thrust	*pousser*
tread	trod	trodden	*piétiner*
wake	woke/waked	woken/waked	*(se) réveiller*
wear	wore	worn	*porter (habit)*
weave	wove	woven	*tisser*
weep	wept	wept	*pleurer*
will*	would	–	*vouloir*
win	won	won	*gagner*
wind	wound	wound	*enrouler*
wring	wrung	wrung	*tordre*
write	wrote	written	*écrire*

* présent de l'indicatif

Abréviations anglaises

AA	*Automobile Association*	Automobile Club de Grande-Bretagne
AAA	*American Automobile Association*	Automobile Club des Etats-Unis
ABC	*American Broadcasting Company*	société privée de radiodiffusion et de télévision (US)
A.D.	*anno Domini*	apr. J.-C.
AIDS	*acquired immune deficiency syndrome*	SIDA
Am.	*America; American*	Amérique; américain
a.m.	*ante meridiem (before noon)*	du matin (de minuit à midi)
Amtrak	*American railroad corporation*	société privée des chemins de fer américains
AT & T	*American Telephone and Telegraph Company*	compagnie privée des téléphones et télégraphes (US)
Ave.	*avenue*	avenue
BBC	*British Broadcasting Corporation*	société britannique de radiodiffusion et de télévision
B.C.	*before Christ*	av. J.-C.
bldg.	*building*	immeuble
Blvd.	*boulevard*	boulevard
B.R.	*British Rail*	chemins de fer britanniques
Brit.	*Britain; British*	Grande-Bretagne; britannique
Bros.	*brothers*	frères
¢	*cent*	1/100 de dollar
Can.	*Canada; Canadian*	Canada; canadien
CBS	*Columbia Broadcasting System*	société privée de radiodiffusion et de télévision (US)
CID	*Criminal Investigation Department*	police judiciaire (GB)
CNN	*Cable News Network*	société privée de télévision
CNR	*Canadian National Railway*	société nationale des chemins de fer canadiens
c/o	*(in) care of*	p.a., aux bons soins de
Co.	*company*	compagnie
Corp.	*corporation*	type de société
CPR	*Canadian Pacific Railways*	société privée des chemins de fer canadiens
D.C.	*District of Columbia*	District de Columbia (Washington, D.C.)

DDS	*Doctor of Dental Science*	dentiste
dept.	*department*	département
e.g.	*for instance*	par exemple
Eng.	*England; English*	Angleterre; anglais
EU	*European Union*	UE
excl.	*excluding; exclusive*	non compris, exclu
ft.	*foot/feet*	pied/pieds (30,5 cm)
GB	*Great Britain*	Grande-Bretagne
H.E.	*His/Her Excellency; His Eminence*	Son Excellence; Son Eminence
H.H.	*His Holiness*	Sa Sainteté
H.M.	*His/Her Majesty*	Sa Mejesté
H.M.S.	*Her Majesty's ship*	bâtiment de la marine royale de Grande-Bretagne
hp	*horsepower*	chevaux-vapeur
i.e.	*that is to say*	c'est-à-dire
in.	*inch*	pouce (2,54 cm)
Inc.	*incorporated*	type de société anonyme américaine
incl.	*including, inclusive*	compris, inclus
£	*pound sterling*	livre sterling
L.A.	*Los Angeles*	Los Angeles
Ltd.	*limited*	type de société anonyme britannique
M.D.	*Doctor of Medicine*	médecin
M.P.	*Member of Parliament*	membre du Parlement britannique
mph	*miles per hour*	miles à l'heure
Mr	*Mister*	Monsieur
Mrs	*Missis*	Madame
Ms	*Missis/Miss*	Madame/Mademoiselle
nat.	*national*	national
NBC	*National Broadcasting Company*	société privée de radiodiffusion et de télévision (US)
No.	*number*	numéro
N.Y.C.	*New York City*	ville de New York
O.B.E.	*Officer (of the Order) of the British Empire*	Officier de l'Ordre de l'Empire britannique
p.	*page; penny/pence*	page; 1/100 de livre sterling
p.a.	*per annum*	par an, annuel
Ph.D.	*Doctor of Philosophy*	docteur en philosophie
p.m.	*post meridiem (after noon)*	de l'après-midi/du soir (de midi à minuit)
PO	*Post Office*	bureau de poste

P.T.O.	*please turn over*	tournez, s'il vous plaît
RAC	*Royal Automobile Club*	Automobile Club de Grande-Bretagne
RCMP	*Royal Canadian Mounted Police*	police royale montée canadienne
Rd.	*road*	route, rue
ref.	*reference*	voir, comparer
Rev.	*reverend*	pasteur dans l'Eglise anglicane
RFD	*rural free delivery*	distribution du courrier à la campagne
RR	*railroad*	chemin de fer
RSVP	*please reply*	répondez, s'il vous plaît
$	*dollar*	dollar
soc.	*society*	société
St.	*saint; street*	saint; rue
STD	*Subscriber Trunk Dialling*	téléphone automatique
UK	*United Kingdom*	Royaume-Uni
UN	*United Nations*	Nations Unies
UPS	*United Parcel Service*	service d'expédition de colis (US)
US	*United States*	Etats-Unis
USS	*United States Ship*	bâtiment de la marine de guerre américaine
VAT	*value added tax*	TVA
VIP	*very important person*	personne jouissant de privilèges particuliers
Xmas	*Christmas*	Noël
yd.	*yard*	yard (91,44 cm)
YMCA	*Young Men's Christian Association*	Union Chrétienne de Jeunes Gens
YWCA	*Young Women's Christian Association*	Union Chrétienne de Jeunes Filles
ZIP	*ZIP code*	code postal

Nombres

Nombres cardinaux

0	zero
1	one
2	two
3	three
4	four
5	five
6	six
7	seven
8	eight
9	nine
10	ten
11	eleven
12	twelve
13	thirteen
14	fourteen
15	fifteen
16	sixteen
17	seventeen
18	eighteen
19	nineteen
20	twenty
21	twenty-one
22	twenty-two
23	twenty-three
24	twenty-four
25	twenty-five
30	thirty
40	forty
50	fifty
60	sixty
70	seventy
80	eighty
90	ninety
100	a/one hundred
230	two hundred and thirty
500	five hundred
1,000	a/one thousand
10,000	ten thousand
100,000	a/one hundred thousand
1,000,000	a/one million

Nombres ordinaux

1st	first
2nd	second
3rd	third
4th	fourth
5th	fifth
6th	sixth
7th	seventh
8th	eighth
9th	ninth
10th	tenth
11th	eleventh
12th	twelfth
13th	thirteenth
14th	fourteenth
15th	fifteenth
16th	sixteenth
17th	seventeenth
18th	eighteenth
19th	nineteenth
20th	twentieth
21st	twenty-first
22nd	twenty-second
23rd	twenty-third
24th	twenty-fourth
25th	twenty-fifth
26th	twenty-sixth
27th	twenty-seventh
28th	twenty-eighth
29th	twenty-ninth
30th	thirtieth
40th	fortieth
50th	fiftieth
60th	sixtieth
70th	seventieth
80th	eightieth
90th	ninetieth
100th	hundredth
230th	two hundred and thirtieth
500th	five hundredth
1,000th	thousandth

L'heure

Les Britanniques et les Américains utilisent le système des douze heures. L'expression *a.m.* (*ante meridiem*) désigne les heures précédant midi, *p.m.* (*post meridiem*) celles de l'après-midi et du soir (jusqu'à minuit).
Toutefois, en Grande-Bretagne, les horaires sont progressivement libellés sur le modèle continental.

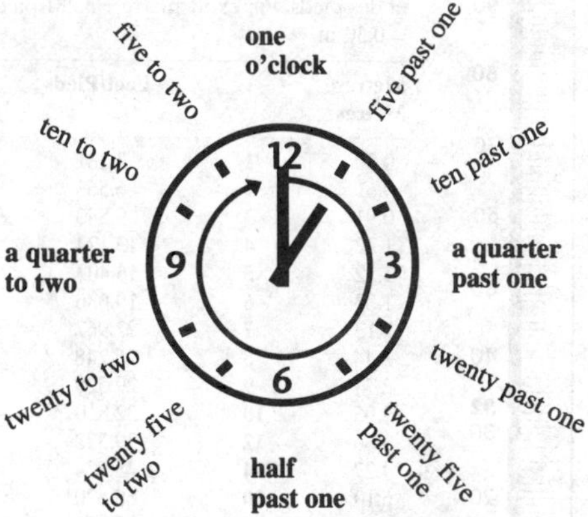

I'll come at seven a.m.	Je viendrai à 7 h. du matin.
I'll come at one p.m.	Je viendrai à 1 h. de l'après-midi.
I'll come at eight p.m.	Je viendrai à 8 h. du soir.

Les jours de la semaine

Sunday	dimanche	*Thursday*	jeudi
Monday	lundi	*Friday*	vendredi
Tuesday	mardi	*Saturday*	samedi
Wednesday	mercredi		

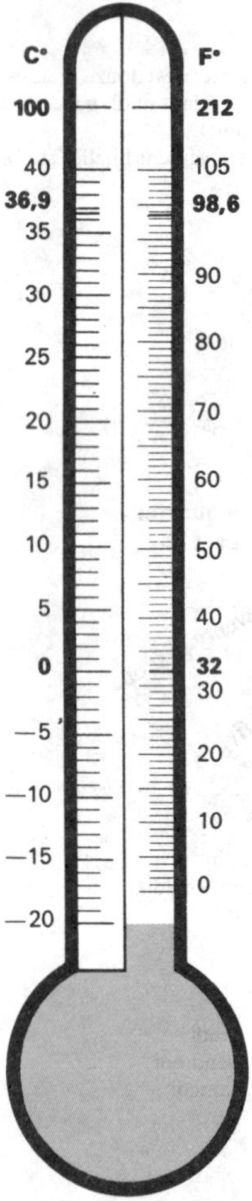

Conversion tables/ Tables de conversion

Metres and feet

The figure in the middle stands for both metres and feet, e.g. 1 metre = 3.281 ft. and 1 foot = 0.30 m.

Mètres et pieds

Le chiffre du milieu représente à la fois des mètres et des pieds. Par ex.: 1 mètre = 3,281 pieds et 1 pied = 0,30 m.

Metres/ Mètres		Feet/Pieds
0.30	**1**	3.281
0.61	**2**	6.563
0.91	**3**	9.843
1.22	**4**	13.124
1.52	**5**	16.403
1.83	**6**	19.686
2.13	**7**	22.967
2.44	**8**	26.248
2.74	**9**	29.529
3.05	**10**	32.810
3.66	**12**	39.372
4.27	**14**	45.934
6.10	**20**	65.620
7.62	**25**	82.023
15.24	**50**	164.046
22.86	**75**	246.069
30.48	**100**	328.092

Temperature

To convert Centigrade to Fahrenheit, multiply by 1.8 and add 32.
To convert Fahrenheit to Centigrade, subtract 32 from Fahrenheit and divide by 1.8.

Température

Pour convertir les degrés centigrades en degrés Fahrenheit, multipliez les premiers par 1,8 et ajoutez 32 au total obtenu.

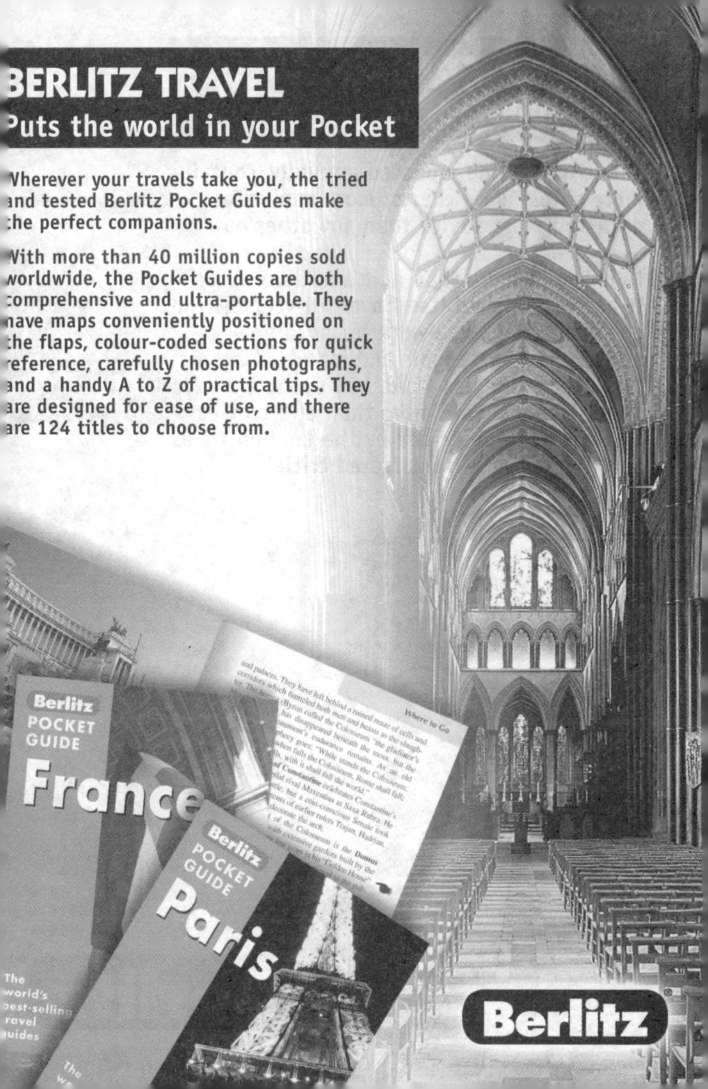
BERLITZ TRAVEL
Puts the world in your Pocket
Wherever your travels take you, the tried and tested Berlitz Pocket Guides make the perfect companions.
With more than 40 million copies sold worldwide, the Pocket Guides are both comprehensive and ultra-portable. They have maps conveniently positioned on the flaps, colour-coded sections for quick reference, carefully chosen photographs, and a handy A to Z of practical tips. They are designed for ease of use, and there are 124 titles to choose from.
Berlitz
POCKET
GUIDE
France
Where to Go
Berlitz
POCKET
GUIDE
Paris
Berlitz